SEXUALITY AND GERMAN FASCISM

SEXUALITY AND GERMAN FASCISM

Edited by

Dagmar Herzog

Berghahn Books

NEW YORK • OXFORD

Published in 2005 by
Berghahn Books

www.berghahnbooks.com

© 2005 Dagmar Herzog

Previously published as a special issue of the
Journal of the History of Sexuality, Vol. 11, Nos. 1 and 2

Library of Congress Cataloging-in-Publication Data

A C.I.P. catalogue record for this book is
available from the Library of Congress.

ISBN 1-57181-652-6 (alk. paper)
ISBN 1-57181-551-1 (pbk.: alk.paper)

British Library Cataloguing in Publication Data

A catalogue record for this book is available from
the British Library.

Permission to reprint from the University of Texas Press is gratefully acknowledged.

Printed in Canada on acid-free paper

CONTENTS

Hubris and Hypocrisy, Incitement and Disavowal: Sexuality and German Fascism

DAGMAR HERZOG

Michigan State University

WHAT IS THE relationship between sexual and other kinds of politics? Few cultures have posed this puzzle as urgently, or as disturbingly, as Nazi Germany. The answers are multiple and as yet unresolved; each emerging answer raises further questions. What exactly were Nazism's sexual politics? Were they repressive for everyone, or were some individuals and groups given sexual license while others were persecuted, tormented, and killed? How should we periodize transformations in the history of sexuality in Germany? How do we specify the continuities and ruptures that mark the transition from the Weimar era into the Third Reich, and how do we periodize changes that occurred in the course of both eras? How do we make sense of the evolution of postwar interpretations of Nazism's sexual politics? What do we make of the fact that scholars from the 1960s to the present have repeatedly diagnosed the "National Socialists' fear of sexuality" or assumed that the Third Reich was simply "sex-hostile," characterized by "rigid-bodily sexual norms of behavior" and "official German prudery," while in films and popular culture there has been a countervailing tendency to offer lurid and salacious anecdotes as a substitute for serious engagement with the complexities of life under German fascism?[1]

Another bundle of questions has to do with theoretical approaches. The topic of sexuality under Nazism exposes the poverty of our available conceptual languages and frameworks. Numerous scholars in the history of sexuality have turned away from the work of Sigmund Freud to that of

This is a revised version of the introduction to the special issue of the *Journal of the History of Sexuality* 11/1–2 (Jan.–Apr. 2002)

[1]Angela H. Mayer, "'Schwachsinn höheren Grades': Zur Verfolgung lesbischer Frauen in Österreich während der NS-Zeit," in *Nationalsozialistischer Terror gegen Homosexuelle: Verdrängt und ungesühnt* (Paderborn, 2002); Joachim Hohmann, *Sexualforschung und -aufklärung in der Weimarer Republik* (Berlin, 1985), 9; Christian de Nuys-Henkelmann, "'Wenn die rote Sonne abends im Meer versinkt ...': Die Sexualmoral der fünfziger Jahre," in *Sexualmoral und Zeitgeist im 19. und 20. Jahrhundert,* ed. Anja Bagel-Bohlan and Michael Salewski (Opladen, 1990), 109; Scott Spector, "Was the Third Reich Movie-Made? Interdisciplinarity and the Reframing of 'Ideology,'" *American Historical Review* 106/2 (April 2001), 472.

1

Michel Foucault, even as it is likely that we need both of them in order to understand and convey the distinctive qualities of life and death in a viciously savage but wildly popular dictatorship that was obsessed with issues of both reproduction and enjoyment. Yet the peculiar interpretive difficulties raised by the topic of sexuality under Nazism also make it valuable to revisit the work of such an intermittently neglected theorist of sex and power as Herbert Marcuse. All three thinkers struggled over how to put into words the coexistence of the seemingly contradictory; such Freudian terms as condensation, projection, splitting, transference, displacement, and disavowal are as indispensable as are Foucault's challenges to the repressive hypothesis and insistence on the mutual imbrication of power and knowledges. And few terms capture as well as Marcuse's famous "repressive desublimation" the regulatory components also of emancipatory injunctions. In addition, Marcuse was one of the first to try to articulate how Nazism's hubristic racism was inseparable from its attempts to reorganize sexual life, how central the politicization of the previously more private realm of sexuality was to the Nazis' political agenda, and how it was that sexual excitation could become a mechanism for social manipulation.

But there are many further interpretive dilemmas. It seems, for example, that we need to ask not only the increasingly more widely acknowledged—but still very pressing—questions of how categories of "race" and "class" cut across and complicate categories of gender and sexual orientation but also to explore such finer delineations of sexuality and related realms as arousal, inhibition, anxiety, satisfaction, attachment, repulsion, envy, longing, and ennui. We need to think as well about what insights queer theory can offer not only into male and female homosexuality but also into heterosexuality and a host of other emotions and practices. And we need to consider what it might mean to extend and adapt our still only tentative understanding of such phenomena as pornography, voyeurism, or exhibitionism—usually analyzed in the context of individual feelings and behaviors—to such an area of inquiry as the ideological work of a culture more generally.

Also challenging is the struggle to put our accounts of pleasure and horror under Nazism into some kind of relationship with each other. Sexuality in the Third Reich was, after all, also about the invasion and control and destruction of human beings. There was a "will to know" about the functioning of psyches and bodies that, over and over, crossed the border into violence, even as the resulting knowledges could appear as indistinguishable from the knowledges produced under liberal regimes. There was, also, manifestly, a will simply to destroy.

Recasting the terms of debate about sexuality in the Third Reich, this volume emphasizes not just the juxtapositions but also the recurrent interrelationships of stimulus and control, and of normality and exception-ality. Scholars of *Alltagsgeschichte* (daily life history) have long pointed out that developments within the so-called private sphere change according to rhythms that diverge substantially from those of high politics. The shapes of such daily life activities (like shopping or socializing with co-workers or childrearing) transform in response to events and pressures that may not always be clearly linked to what political regime happens to be in power. In some ways, sex fits the *Alltagsgeschichte* model, but in other ways—especially because Nazis ascribed tremendous importance to sex and strove to reshape sexual mores—it does not.

The Nazis, as they worked to consolidate power, sanctimoniously claimed to be restoring law and order and returning marriage and family life to their proper dignity. Many scholars have taken them at their word. No less an authority than George Mosse, in *Nationalism and Sexuality* (1985) and *The Image of Man* (1996), saw Nazis primarily as inheritors of a culture of bourgeois constraint rather than that culture's critics. Mosse described Nazism as intensely preoccupied with sexual propriety rather than liberation, and he argued at length that the ubiquitous nudes of the Third Reich were in actuality emptied of eroticism. Also the two more recent German-language studies claiming to offer a comprehensive overview of Nazism's sexual politics—Udo Pini's *Leibeskult und Liebeskitsch* (Cult of the Body and Love-Kitsch) and Stefan Maiwald and Gerd Mischler's *Sexualität unterm Hakenkreuz* (Sexuality under the Swastika)—reinforced the prevailing assumptions. Pini painted the picture of a world in which "eroticism as a sensibility was suppressed," bedrooms were "gloomy," and "feelings were as coordinated as the organizations."[2] In a similar spirit, Maiwald and Mischler's book announced succinctly that "The total state left no room in German beds for self-determined sex. The subjects of the NS-state had to forfeit their sexuality unconditionally to the regime."[3]

Studies such as these neglect the fact that the Nazis also used sexuality to consolidate their appeal—and that they did so in many different ways. It is useful here to remember Foucault's warning that repression is only one side of the history of sexuality; the other involves the positive play of power. We simply cannot understand why Nazism was attractive to so many people if we focus only on its sexually repressive aspects.

*

While there was no master plan for sexuality under Nazism and no coherent policy (but rather a cacophony of often competing injunctions), it is clear that over time a decisive trend against traditional mores emerged. Ultimately, the majority of the population did not experience the Third

[2]Udo Pini, *Leibeskult und Liebeskitsch: Erotik im Dritten Reich* (Munich, 1992), 9–11.
[3]Stefan Maiwald and Gerd Mischler, *Sexualität unterm Hakenkreuz: Manipulation und Vernichtung der Intimsphäre im NS-Staat* (Hamburg and Vienna, 1999), 57, 60.

Reich as a sexually conservative time, but rather one in which the general processes of liberalization of heterosexual mores which had been ongoing since the beginning of the twentieth century were perceived both as simply progressing further and as escalating under the combined effect of official Nazi encouragement and eventually the disruptive impact of labor mobilizations, population transfers, and total war. Although in countless instances, above all in its thorough racialization of sex and in its heightened homophobia, the Third Reich represented a brutal backlash against the progressivism of Weimar, Nazism brought with it not only a redefinition but also a perpetuation, expansion, and intensification of preexisting liberalizing trends. Indeed, one could potentially think of Nazi affirmations of sexual pleasure both within and outside of marriage also in the context of the broader modernization of consumer culture under Nazism—from the marketing of Coca Cola to the new travel opportunities afforded by the Strength through Joy (*Kraft durch Freude*) program.

The distinctive innovation of Nazi sexual politics was the attempt to harness popular liberalizing impulses and growing preoccupation with sex to a racist, elitist, and homophobic agenda. The goal was not so much to suppress sexuality. Rather the aim was to reinvent it as the privilege of non-disabled, heterosexual "Aryans" (all the while claiming to be "cleaning up" sexual morality in Germany and overcoming the "Jewish" legacy).

Especially in attending to the contradictory ways in which references to Jewishness were deployed in discussions of sex in the Third Reich, we can begin to develop a more differentiated picture of the reworking of mainstream sexual mores under Nazism. Whether antisemitism was deeply felt or simply strategically utilized, there is no question that it provided one of the premier sense-making systems in use in the Third Reich. Attempting to mobilize antisemitism for sexually conservative ends, for example, some Nazis argued that Jews undervalued spirituality and love and overvalued sensuality and physical contact.[4] Far from advocating a natural sexuality, Jews exhibited a "disgusting lechery."[5] Jews were working *"to strike the Nordic race at its most vulnerable point: sexual life."*[6]

Psychoanalysis and sexology became frequent antisemitic targets. Freud's Jewishness was emphasized, and he was accused of having a "dirty fan-

---

[4]E.g. see Alfred Zeplin, *Sexualpädagogik als Grundlage des Familienglücks und des Volkswohls* (Rostock, 1938), 31.

[5]Alfred Rosenberg, *Unmoral im Talmud* (Munich, 1943), 19. The book was originally published in 1933.

[6]"Die Rolle des Juden in der Medizin," *Deutsche Volksgesundheit aus Blut und Boden* (August/September 1933), reprinted in *"Hier geht das Leben auf eine sehr merkwürdige Weise weiter ..."*: *Zur Geschichte der Psychoanalyse in Deutschland,* ed. Karen Brecht et al. (Hamburg, 1985), 87.

tasy" and of inventing the idea of an id solely to keep the consciences of "Nordic" people from bothering them when they engaged in masturbation or extramarital relations.[7] As late as 1942, theologian Heinz Hunger (who in postwar West Germany would become a highly regarded specialist on youth sexuality) simultaneously insisted that there was "nothing original" about psychoanalysis—for to claim otherwise would be "to give too much honor to the un-productivity of the Jewish race"—and declared that "the whole of psychoanalysis is nothing other than the Jewish nation's rape of Western culture." Psychoanalysis, in Hunger's view, was "*Volk*-damaging" in its overemphasis on that which lay "below the navel."[8] The prominent Weimar-era physicians and sexologists Magnus Hirschfeld (leader of the campaign to decriminalize homosexuality) and Max Marcuse (the foremost expert on contraception)—both of them also strong advocates of consensual premarital heterosexual sex—became major objects of Nazi venom as well. As one Nazi-identified doctor put it, "the psychoanalysts are not yet the worst. Far more offensive is that which gathers around Magnus Hirschfeld, the director of the Institute for Sexual Science, and around Mr. Marcuse and Co. Here, one can be sure, there is a quite conscious effort to destroy the German soul."[9]

What was being denied in the constructions of Jews as the primary proponents of contraceptive use and as the main celebrants of sexual pleasure and of diversity and perversity in desire was that what these activists had offered was what also millions of non-Jewish Germans had fervently wanted. Indicative of such longings was that the birthrate in Germany had been declining in all classes since at least the turn of the twentieth century. Significantly, moreover, and despite the various monetary and other incentives proffered by the Nazis, nearly a third of all couples married in 1933 were still childless five years later, and a further quarter of them had only one child. And while the birthrate did rise in the first five or six years of the Third Reich, this was due not to a rise in the number of children per couple, but rather to a rise in the number of marriages. "All the efforts of the authorities to break the mold of the two-child couple failed."[10] While some contemporaries say that they never saw a condom during the Third Reich, others assert that in the Third Reich,

---

[7]Ibid.

[8]Heinz Hunger, "Jüdische Psychoanalyse und deutsche Seelsorge," in *Germanentum, Judentum und Christentum,* vol. 2, ed. Walter Grundmann (Leipzig, 1943), 314, 317, 332, 339. This volume was based on a conference held in 1942.

[9]Martin Staemmler, "Das Judentum in der Medizin," *Sächsisches Ärtzeblatt* 104 (1934), 210.

[10]Ute Frevert, *Women in German History: From Bourgeois Emancipation to Sexual Liberation* (Oxford, 1989), 232.

condoms were available in "abundance," in "vending machines on metro and railway platforms, in public toilets," and that the machines in public toilets also carried "tubes of Vaseline."[11] (It would not be until the 1950s that many of these "rickety old automats" were dismantled.)[12] Moreover, information about the rhythm method, just developed in the early 1930s, continued to be available during the Third Reich. And despite the much harsher penalties for abortions instituted by the Nazis, abortions were still avidly sought, and "for all the public pressure, the birthrate in the Third Reich did not ever equal the rates from the last years of the 'decadent' 1920s."[13] Meanwhile, it is crucial to register as well how significant a topic and goal sexual pleasure—for women as well as for men—had become in Germany in the early decades of the twentieth century. While assertions of the breadth and depth of sexual misery were prevalent, there was clearly also considerable hopefulness and expectation that this misery could be alleviated. And finally, both Weimar-era and Nazi-era documents indicate that premarital heterosexual sex was simply standard procedure for the majority of Germans; trends in this direction had begun already before World War I. One Protestant author, noting that "today birth control of some sort is nearly universal, also among Christians," observed in the late 1930s:

> Since with the use of protective means pregnancy does not have to be feared as it used to be, ['friendship' including bodily love] is widespread also in circles that before now hardly knew of it. It becomes a question also for those who live in a Christian environment. Why should sexual need in the long waiting period before marriage not be resolved in this way?[14]

As the Third Reich unfolded, the most striking aspect of sexual conservatives' writings was their dismay in the face of non-Jewish Germans' apparent disinterest in conforming to more constrictive mores. In a book published in 1938, for example, the Nazi-identified physician Ferdinand Hoffmann fumed that "approximately 72 million condoms are used in Germany each year." Premarital heterosexual intercourse was near-ubiquitous

---

[11]Report on conditions for foreign laborers in Nazi Germany prepared by the French Catholic Workers' Youth Movement, quoted in Pieter Lagrou, *The Legacy of Nazi Occupation: Patriotic Memory and National Recovery in Western Europe, 1945–1965* (Cambridge, UK, 2000), 145.

[12]See Gunter Schmidt, "Weshalb Sex alle (Un)schuld verloren hat," *taz-magazin*, 24–25 Apr. 1999, v.

[13]Claudia Koonz, *Mothers in the Fatherland: Women, the Family and Nazi Politics* (New York, 1987), 186.

[14]See Theodor Haug, "Die Sexuelle Frage in der Seelsorge," *Zeitwende* 15 (1938/39), 542, 609, 614.

in Nazi Germany, Hoffmann said. The idea that anyone should stay chaste until marriage "possesses absolutely no more validity." Perhaps five percent of brides were still virgins; many had already had numerous boyfriends. And even after marriage Germans did not often remain faithful to their spouses.[15]

Eager to persuade Germans of the value of more conservative mores, Hoffmann declared that "the demand for the full living-out of sexuality is a typical Jewish-liberalistic one, and the news should gradually have gotten around, that everything which on the Jewish side has become a battle cry, solely serves disintegrative and not constructive aims. The Jew has never talked us into something that could help us." The trouble was that although the populace had largely embraced Nazism in political terms, and Germans were appropriately antisemitic in most parts of their lives, they were evidently loathe to let go of their emancipated sexual habits. Trying to pin on Jews what he simultaneously admitted was a pandemic phenomenon, Hoffmann sought to reconcile his own contradictions by surmising that, due to the machinations of Jewish doctors, pop-song writers and filmmakers, individualism and materialism had come to "saturate the personality of the individual not only through to his economic interests, but through to his erotic deep structure [*erotische Tiefenschicht*]." As a result, numerous people believed that one could be a "good citizen of the Third Reich, if one is simply a good political soldier, and for the rest one can organize one's love-life ... in accordance with the previous liberalistic perspectives." Few things could be further from the truth, Hoffmann cautioned his readers. There was little doubt that sex remained the site at which it was "evidently the most difficult to be a good National Socialist."[16]

This was only the most elaborate exposition of the theory that "Jewishness" was deeply rooted also within non-Jewish Germans. Population policy expert Paul Danzer, for example, argued in 1936 that whether Jews "exploited our economy, whether they confused our legal life or encouraged social divisions, all that pales before the very most serious damage they have done to our *Volk*, the *poisoning of marital- and sex-morality*." And yet Danzer, too, like Hoffmann, worried openly that the German masses could not care less about cleaning up their sexual act. Despite the Nazis' political victory, men continued to see it as an "indispensable proof of their masculinity, to run after every skirt and in so doing notch up as many successes as possible.... And one cannot say that the female sex is

[15]Ferdinand Hoffmann, *Sittliche Entartung und Geburtenschwund* 2nd ed. (Munich, 1938), 13, 21, 24–25, 34.
[16]Ibid., 16, 30, 49, 50, 55.

much more narrow-minded."[17] Similarly, a NSDAP-affiliated physician vociferously lamented in 1937 how "we thoughtlessly repeat the Jewish or Jewish-influenced vulgarities concerning the relations of the two sexes.... It is astonishing how little our great National Socialist revolution has moved forward in this area!"[18] Sexually conservative Nazis—whether intentionally or not—reinforced the idea that what Jews supposedly represented also had undeniable appeal for vast numbers of non-Jewish Germans.

*

Meanwhile, the need for greater conservatism was not the sole message about sex promoted by Nazism. For there was also another strand of Nazi argumentation about sex, one which explicitly aimed at encouraging playful, pleasurable heterosexuality among those ideologically and "racially" approved by the regime. Importantly, however, this second strand of argumentation too was thoroughly saturated with antisemitism. For these pro-sex advocates, references to the supposed shamelessness and impropriety of "Jewish" versions of sexuality functioned preeminently as a technique of disavowal—a strategy to distract attention away from Nazism's own inducements to premarital and extramarital sexual activity.

Nazis were acutely aware that the regime was already in the mid-thirties developing a reputation for encouraging teenagers to engage in premarital intercourse, and they strove to manage the ensuing controversy—domestically and internationally—both by denying that they were doing any such thing *and* by avidly defending their own policy and practice. While in 1934 leaders in the Bund Deutscher Mädel (Federation of German Girls) still received a directive to encourage their young charges to have premarital love affairs under the rubric "top secret," by 1935 at the latest there was nothing particularly secret anymore about what went on in some (though surely not all) of the local BDM chapters.[19] In Dresden, for instance, Victor Klemperer noted the following in his diary in 1935: "Annemarie Köhler tells us in despair that the hospitals are overcrowded with fifteen-year-old girls, some pregnant, some with gonorrhea. The BDM. Her brother has vehemently refused to allow his daughter to join."[20] As

---

[17]Paul Danzer, "Die Haltung zum anderen Geschlecht als unentbehrliche Grundlage völkischen Aufbaus," in *Streiflichter ins Völkische: Ausgewählte Lesestücke für deutsche Menschen aus dem "Völkischen Willen"* (Berlin, 1936), 5–6.

[18]Knorr, "Eine noch nicht genügend beachtete weltanschauliche und bevölkerungspolitische Gefahr," *Ziel und Weg: Organ des Nationalsozialistischen Deutschen Ärztebundes* 7/22 (Nov. 1937), 570.

[19]See Michael Kater, "Die deutsche Elternschaft im nationalsozialistischen Erziehungssystem," *Vierteljahresschrift für Wirtschafts- und Sozialgeschichte* (1980), 489.

[20]Victor Klemperer, *I Will Bear Witness: A Diary of the Nazi Years 1933–1941*, trans. Martin Chalmers (New York, 1998), 137.

of 1937, the Social Democratic party in exile reported the news that in the Hitler Youth, "promiscuity is the concretely accepted situation."[21] In 1938, the American sociologist Clifford Kirkpatrick was at pains to present his major study on *Nazi Germany: Its Women and Family Life* as offering a more balanced portrait than the (by then already cliché) image of regime encouragement to "the conceiving of illegitimate children" and "polygamy."[22]

In the early 1940s, Herbert Marcuse, at that point working for the U.S. Office of Strategic Services, strove to articulate how the effectiveness of Nazi culture rested not least on its "abolition" of taboos, its "emancipation of sexual life" and its encouragement particularly of "extra-marital relations between the sexes." Pointing especially "to the deliberate herding of boys and girls in the training camps, to the license granted to the racial elite, to the facilitation of marriage and divorce, to the sanctioning of illegitimate children," Marcuse observed that "all this is, of course, in line with the population policy of the Reich." But he was quick to note as well that "the policy has still another aspect, which is far more hidden and touches the roots of National Socialist society." The aim, Marcuse surmised, was to tie individuals to the NSDAP by urging them to pursue pleasure: "The abolition of sexual taboos tends to make this realm of satisfaction an official political domain.... The individual recognizes his private satisfaction as a patriotic service to the regime, and he receives his reward for performing it."[23]

Although Marcuse indicated that the trends he was identifying were not in written documents but rather needed to be gleaned from an assessment of social dynamics, this is not the case. Already the mid-1930s—a few years into the Third Reich as the regime strove to strengthen its hold on the populace—saw an efflorescence of discussion of the acceptability of premarital and extramarital coitus. Nazi-endorsed authors openly espoused both.

In one widely discussed 1936 essay, for instance, the physician Walter Gmelin, reporting on his work evaluating couples' suitability for marriage, commented on the extant high incidence in Germany of premarital intercourse. Although Gmelin found that less than five percent of the women and men he had examined were virgins—indeed most had begun to have intercourse in their late teens and early twenties, approximately seven years before they married—Gmelin did not find this trend alarming. Premarital

[21] *Deutschland-Berichte der Sozialdemokratischen Partei Deutschlands (Sopade)* (Salzhausen and Frankfurt/ Main, 1980), report of Aug. 1937, 1070.

[22] Clifford Kirkpatrick, *Nazi Germany: Its Women and Family Life* (Indianapolis, 1938), 36.

[23] Herbert Marcuse, *Technology, War and Fascism: Collected Papers of Herbert Marcuse*, vol. 1, ed. Douglas Kellner (New York, 1998), 84–86, 90, 162–63.

sexual experience, he thought, was a good thing, a phenomenon to be read above all as "a healthy reaction against the social inhibitions and against morality-preachers." In fact, Gmelin interjected, those few who denied having had premarital experience "certainly did not display above-average hereditary resources [*Erbgut*]."[24]

Nazi-affiliated authors espoused their pro-sex vision especially in attacks on the Christian churches. As Hans Endres, a leading Nazi race theorist, told an audience of high-ranking Nazis and their guests in 1941, "We have been raised in criminal bigotry, because the Oriental Christian mentality has suppressed our healthy Germanic instincts in sexual matters. Our younger generations ... must become proud of their bodies and enjoy the natural pleasures of sex without being ashamed."[25] Already in 1936, the jurist Rudolf Bechert energetically defended extramarital affairs as well. In the context of explaining a proposed new law which would give illegitimate children the father's name and equal rights with legitimate children to financial support, Bechert ventured this:

> Nonmarital bonds are superior to marriages in many ways. It is not just life-experience that proves that nonmarital connections rooted in sexual love are an unchangeable fact, rather all of human culture teaches that they can represent the highest moral and aesthetic value. Without sexual love no poetry, no painting, indeed, no music! In all cultured nations concubinage is not criminalized, with churchy Italy ahead of all the rest.... Never can nonmarital sexual intercourse be prevented.

Indeed, Bechert concluded effusively: "Love is the only true religious experience in the world."[26]

Such a glorification of sex and emphatic rejection of Christian moralizing was even more evident in a 1937 book by the physician Carl Csallner. Csallner advocated a double standard: Premarital experience for men was fine, even useful, but female chastity before marriage was imperative; Csallner thought it unacceptable that a wife might have a comparative basis by which to judge her husband's love-making skills. But he certainly thought sexual intercourse deserved to be energetically defended against traditional religious scruples. Csallner opined that only "unnatural sancti-

---

[24]Excerpts from Gmelin's essay "Bevölkerungspolitik und Frühehe" (published in the *Deutsche Ärztezeitung*) reprinted in "Mütterheim Steinhöring," *Das Schwarze Korps* (hereafter *DSK*), 7 Jan. 1937, 13–14.

[25]Endres quoted in George W. Herald, "Sex is a Nazi weapon," *American Mercury* 54, no. 222 (June 1942), 661.

[26]Excerpt from Bechert's essay (published in *Deutsches Recht*), in "Mütterheim Steinhöring," 14.

moniousness" and "priestly cant" had turned the sexual drive, which was "wanted by nature and spontaneously presses toward activity," into something "base and mean ... a deadly sin." The sexual drive, in Csallner's view, was "great" and "holy."[27] The Nazi pedagogue Alfred Zeplin put his views yet more succinctly (as he unveiled his five-point plan for encouraging premarital heterosexual sex while discouraging masturbation and homosexuality). *"Sexual activity,"* Zeplin announced, *"is not sinful, it is sacred."*[28]

Whatever their variations in emphasis, the central notions advanced by these authors—about the unnaturalness of prudery or the transcendental qualities of human sexuality—were made generally available not least through the SS journal, *Das Schwarze Korps.* One of the most popular weeklies of the Third Reich—printed in hundreds of thousands of copies—and one enthusiastically endorsed by the regime, it was read far beyond SS circles (its circulation would be second only to the serious news weekly *Das Reich,* launched five years later). Through its entertaining style, acerbic humor, and self-reflexive argumentative techniques, *Das Schwarze Korps* advanced its recipe for national happiness and health. The cheerful tongue-in-cheek approach could not disguise the savagery of the paper's attacks on Jews, the handicapped, homosexuals, "asocial" criminals, and critics of the regime (all were recurrently thematized) but certainly it contributed mightily to the paper's morally disorienting effect.

Das Schwarze Korps brazenly mocked Christian efforts to defend the sanctity of marriage, and aligned itself with young people's impatience with traditional bourgeois mores. "Eager clerical 'moralists'" were accused of having "pathetic complexes" and "original sin" was presented as a "foreign" and "oriental" idea.[29] In no uncertain terms, the paper attacked "the denominational morality ... that sees in the body something to be despised, and wants to interpret what are natural processes as *sinful drives.*"[30] Although vociferously denying that it advocated "free love" (a notion it associated with the "Marxism" of the Weimar years), and recurrently insisting that Nazism was restoring marriage and family to their proper dignity (in opposition to what it described as "Jewish" attacks on the family), the paper repeatedly and openly defended both illegitimacy and nonreproductive premarital heterosexual intercourse.

Just as sexually conservative Nazi mores were expressed through antisemitism, so also were the Nazis' particular versions of sexually emancipatory ideas. Repeatedly, *Das Schwarze Korps'* strategy was to contrast the

---

[27]Carl H. Csallner, *Das Geschlechtsleben, seine Bedeutung für Individuum und Gemeinschaft* (Munich, 1937), 10.
[28]Zeplin, *Sexualpädagogik,* 12, 24.
[29]"Anstössig?," *DSK,* 16 Apr. 1936, 13.
[30]"... Unzucht in der Soldatenzeit," *DSK,* 5 March 1936, 6.

kind of "propaganda for nudism" evident during the Weimar era (or, as *Das Schwarze Korps* put it in 1935, during "the years of Jewish domination," when "the semitic manipulators" were busy working to undermine "every natural order, such as marriage and family") with the aims of National Socialism, which were to "represent the body in its natural shape" and to resist "that prudery... which has contributed to destroying the instinct for bodily nobility and its beauty in our *Volk*."[31] Along related lines, in 1938, in two full-page photo-spreads, *Das Schwarze Korps* showcased the "beautiful and pure" nudity advocated by Nazism—exemplified by pulchritudinous naked women luxuriating in sun, sand and sea—and juxtaposed this with the "shameless money-making" of the previous "cultural epoch" (illustrated by photos of titillatingly half-clothed and excessively made-up women from what look to be Weimar dance halls).[32] Not only the continual self-labeling as "pure" and "clean," then, but also the fiercely hyperbolic attacks on Jews, Marxists, and Weimar-era cultural arbiters for their purported advocacy of extramarital sex, pornography, and nakedness, served to distract attention from the Nazis' advocacy of those very same things. *Das Schwarze Korps,* in short, did precisely that which it said it was not doing. Incitement and disavowal were inseparable.

The effectiveness of Nazi manipulation of discourses of sexual morality was particularly evident at those moments when the regime managed to have things both ways at once: to present itself as the guardian of good taste and pristine morals and to titillate and pander to the pleasures of looking. A classic instance of this deliberate duality can be found in the women's journal *Frauenwarte* (Women's Watchtower), which in 1940 offered its own two-page photo-spread contrasting, on the one hand, images of women in bikinis and skimpy cabaret costumes with, on the other, more demurely clothed healthily athletic women as well as women wearing the traditional German dirndl. But unlike the photo-spread in *Das Schwarze Korps* two years earlier, in which the cabaret images had been taken from "the previous cultural epoch," i.e. Weimar, the *Frauenwarte* declared that all the images on its scantily clad side had been taken from pictures "that appeared in German illustrated periodicals in the last few weeks." Indeed, the journal pointed out that these images were being presented to the German *Volk* in "millions of copies." At the same time, and remarkably, the *Frauenwarte* labeled these images—as well as ones it claimed to have found in recent German film and theater productions—as "Jewish— all too Jewish." Striking a remonstrating pedagogical pose toward other Nazis, the *Frauenwarte* elaborated that

---

[31]"Ist das Nacktkultur? Herr Stapel entrüstet sich!," *DSK,* 24 April 1935, 12.
[32]"Schön und Rein," and "Geschäft ohne Scham," *DSK,* 20 Oct. 1938, 10 and 12.

The National Socialist idea is profoundly life-affirming. Nothing could lie further from it than prudery.... A beautiful girl is certainly not created to be a nun—however, and that is the difference between yesterday and today, also not to be a coquette! The shallow and frivolous degradation of the woman into an object of pleasure, the repulsive warping of a healthy, natural feeling for the body in the manner of a crass and undisguised sexual greed, this whole distorted, unhealthy atmosphere belongs exclusively to the chapter of Jewish disintegrative propaganda [*jüdische Zersetzungspropaganda*]! We will maintain a watchful eye so that such tendencies do not, under some falsified excuse, spread again among us.

On this somewhat surprising note—the idea that, seven years into the Third Reich, some (other) Nazis were behaving like Jews—the *Frauenwarte* concluded that the only explanation could be "how deeply the Jewish contamination has worked specifically in this area."[33] Once again, then, incitement and disavowal were inextricable. The purposely incoherent good cop-bad cop routine was evidently far more effective than any unified message could have been. In this way, multiple constituencies might be addressed at once. Sexual conservatives were never directly censored, but rather were both published *and* mocked. Overtly sexual images and pro-sex messages were both lauded *and* rhetorically chastised.

*

While the majority of Catholic and Protestant spokespeople initially welcomed the Nazi rise to power, within just two or three years Christian commentators found reasons to feel disillusionment over the Third Reich's sexual politics. One evangelical Christian missionary in Württemberg charged in 1935 that *"fleshly lust"* and a *"spirit of uncleanness"* were at work in the Third Reich and bemoaned the fact that although "at first we believed that morality would improve in the Third Reich—today *this hope* reveals itself *more and more as false*."[34] Catholic priest Matthias Laros in 1936 praised the Nazis for their dedication to race and *Volk* but also held Nazism responsible for exacerbating further the dissolution of sexual mores. The "era has succumbed to a horrifying barbarism and overstimulation of the sexual drive"; the "entirety of public and private life has today been gripped" by an "insane *overvaluation of the sensual-sexual*." The "false prophets" of a relaxed sexual morality were carrying their pernicious teachings "everywhere, into the smallest village." Laros singled out as especially abhorrent the new Nazi encouragement of coed sports at the workplace, in which

[33]"Sie Meinen: Apart und lustig," *Frauenwarte* 8/16 (Feb. 1940).
[34]Krupka's remarks in *Weg zum Ziel*, no. 18 (1935), quoted and discussed in "Pikanterien im Beichtstuhl," *DSK*, 26 June 1935, 5.

women and girls were obliged to "reveal their female secrets to a great extent": "All talk of naturalness and the beauty of the body cannot do away with the consequence, that on the male side an intensified sex drive results, and on the female side, if she has retained her true femininity, the most delicate bodily shame has been damaged and moral feeling deadened." Distancing himself from both Nazis and Jews (even as he reinforced the association of Jews with un-Christian sexual values), Laros declared that "the church, unconcerned by all semitic or antisemitic fashions of the day, holds fast to the ... Christian structure of marriage."[35]

Along related lines, when the Nazi party's Office for Racial Policy (*Rassenpolitisches Amt*) published a calendar with nude images, Catholic priests in Westphalia organized a campaign against its sale, arguing that the pictures were "piggish [*schweinig*]" and "indecent [*unanständig*]."[36] But Protestants too complained that the new Nazi paganism involved a "tendency towards nudism."[37] And in 1936, the Protestant pastor Stephan Vollert, in a letter to the editor of the main Nazi party newspaper, the *Völkischer Beobachter* (Racial Observer), chastised the journal for printing "obscene pictures" and demanded to know whether images of nude women were really proper objects for "German art."[38] Protestants also repeatedly expressed confusion about how best to respond to the quasi-spirituality of Nazism, with its "romantic idealistic" search for God in "the language of flowers and sounds or the wealth of our spiritual inwardness," and they scrambled to counter the Nazi charge that Christianity was a downbeat and depressing religion incompatible with the life-affirming message of Nazism.[39] Put on the defensive, they also rushed to prove that Christianity was not antisex. In this spirit, for instance, a Protestant author praised "the gift that God has given us in the powers of sex" and argued self-critically that "the isolating of sexual problems has brought much harm and cramped-up-ness into Christianity."[40]

As jurist Rudolf Bechert's comment that "love is the only true religious experience in the world" already suggests, sexual matters were utterly central to processes of secularization. In the early twentieth century, in the context of conflicting impulses towards secularization and searching for existential purposefulness, the yearning for romantic love—both its more immediate and its enduring joys—was already, and was becom-

---

[35]Matthias Laros, *Die Beziehungen der Geschlechter* (Cologne, 1936), 11–12, 15, 34, 70, 166–67.

[36]The story is reported in "Was ist schamloser?," *DSK*, 20. Jan. 1938, 8.

[37]Wilhelm Stapel, "'Neuheidentum,'" *Deutsches Volkstum*, April 1935, 293.

[38]The story is reported in "Anstössig?," 14.

[39]See the discussion in Adolf Köberle, "Unter den Studenten," in *Christus lebt!: Ein Buch von fruchtbarem Dienst in Lehre und Leben*, ed. Hans Dannenbaum (Berlin, 1939), 325–26.

[40]Haug, "Die sexuelle Frage in der Seelsorge," 542.

ing even more, invested with truly existential import. Hans von Hatting-berg, an acclaimed psychotherapist and medical doctor, put the point elo-quently in a book published in 1936: "After so much of faith has been destroyed, faith in love is for a growing number of people the only faith to which they still cling."[41] Secularization, in short, involved not just in-creasing numbers of people disaffiliating themselves from churches or rejecting church teachings; it was also very much about a reworking of languages and attitudes, a sort of compromise formation in which this-worldly matters were described as having divine significance.

It was in this context that Nazi-identified writers not only defended pre- and extramarital sex but also avidly celebrated marital passion. Many Germans remained uncomfortable with the most radical Nazi challenges to the institution of marriage, especially the open calls for infidelity and il-legitimacy.[42] But most would have been hard pressed to challenge the Nazi rhetoric of romance. After all, also according to contemporaries, this was an era in which "the erotic bases of marriage" were "pushed so much to the fore."[43] The deliberate sacralization of human love thus became a crucial aspect of National Socialism's reconfiguration of notions of moral-ity and furthering of ongoing processes of secularization. Without ques-tion, Nazism was concerned to advocate "racially" desirable matches and the production of numerous "healthy" children. But to read Nazis' paeans to the delights of love as simply tactical embellishment of what was actu-ally a narrowly reproduction-oriented agenda would be to miss the ways Nazi advice-givers inserted themselves into the most elemental desires for personal happiness—how much, in short, Nazism's appeal lay (in a Fou-caultian sense) in the positive rather than negative workings of power—even as the glorification of heterosexual romance provided the context for (and distracting counterpoint to) defenses of some of the most grotesque and violent aspects of Nazi politics.

On a quotidian level, by no means were all Germans eager to endorse the regime's emphasis on sexual incitement. Many parents felt keen dis-tress at the idea that their underage daughters should become illegitimate mothers, and many young women and men were repelled by the idea that they ought to become breeders for the Führer or have any sex outside of

[41]Hans von Hattingberg, *Über die Liebe: Eine Ärztliche Wegweisung* (Munich, 1936), 16.

[42]For a good example of open advocacy of infidelity (both intercourse and dalliance with-out the possibility of reproduction), see the instructions to civil servants about the accept-ability of affairs as long as the partner was racially suitable and the wife gave her permission, in Walter Menzel, "Ehebruch und ehewidriges Verhalten als Dienststrafvergehen," *Wirt-schaft und Recht* 9/6 (15 June 1942), 61–62 (this was a supplement to *Der deutsche Erzieher,* the official journal for schoolteachers).

[43]Frommolt, review of F. Kuenkel, *Charakter, Liebe und Ehe,* in *Zentralblatt für Gy-näkologie* 57, no. 22 (3 June 1933), 1326.

a longterm commitment. For many girls especially the concept of virginity until marriage remained a sincere and idealistic goal. Nor were many wives and girlfriends pleased with the Nazi encouragement of sexual infidelity among men as long as those men selected "racially appropriate" partners, and soldiers at the front were often rent with anxiety by the thought that their wives or sweethearts were cheating on them. The concerns of these constituencies may thus provide an important explanation for the regime's tendency to permit sexually conservative voices to coexist alongside more radical pronouncements. Indeed, the historian Gudrun Schwarz has expressed consternation at the contrast between the ease with which Nazis were able to make their anti-Jewish policies palatable to the populace and the difficulty they appear to have had convincing most Germans that marriage and marital fidelity were antiquated ideals.[44]

On the other hand, the combination of Nazi policies and the dynamics of total war did indisputably contribute to a loosening of sexual mores on the home front and the battle front. As one doctor phrased it in the aftermath of the war, precisely the cataclysmic intensity of the war years had caused a dramatic relaxation of mores: In "the most recent past," the mobilization of countless "young-blooded" bodies of both sexes, "the concentration of all forces into violence and highest achievement," and "finally the pressure of an uncertain personal and universal fate hanging over everything," led even the "previously satisfied or morally strict" to become uninhibited. "Everything we call 'love,'" he said, "came away badly." In his view, sex itself was reduced to a "primitive act," and whatever lack of quality the participants felt they simply "attempted to compensate for by the quantity of such encounters and adventures."[45]

Soldiers also availed themselves of local as well as Wehrmacht-sponsored brothels. As one soldier wrote after the war to his former fellows: "Dear war-comrades, have you forgotten so soon how in Smolensk, Odessa and Simferopol you went into the Russian houses? That in the retreat in the final years in the East Russian women had to come along with your battalion.... Do you still remember, how you stood in the long queues in the brothels of Paris and Le Havre, Lille and Besançon, Norway and Italy, in the Baltics and in Greece...?"[46] Another former soldier, an earnest Chris-

[44]Gudrun Schwarz, paper presented at conference on "Moral im Nationalsozialismus," Institut für Sozialforschung, Hamburg, 4 June 2002. See Harry Nutt, "Die Gewalt der Ehre: Moral im Nationalsozialismus—eine Hamburger Tagung," *Frankfurter Rundschau,* 11 July 2002.

[45]H. Schürmann, "Promiskuität—Zeichen der Zeit," *Liebe und Ehe* 3/9 (1951), 385.

[46]Letter to the editor of *Stern* quoted in Christoph Boyer and Hans Woller, "*'Hat die deutsche Frau versagt?': Die 'neue Freiheit' der Frauen in der Trümmerzeit 1945–1949," *Journal für Geschichte* 2 (1983), 36.

tian, remembered his acute discomfort as a teenager in the Wehrmacht at the pressure articulated by fellow soldiers that every young man must be sexually active: "'Every little Hans must have a little Sabine [*Jedem Hänschen sein Sabinchen*],' that was the motto. It was disgusting. The Nazis constantly insisted that sex before marriage or outside of marriage was morally acceptable, even necessary."[47] But others experienced the official encouragement as marvelous. One man, a young officer at the time, recorded in his memoirs the delight he and his comrades felt in the last months of the war when, stationed in a Western occupied nation, an auxiliary service contingent of twenty-one girls and young women arrived. The lieutenant-major made a speech before his assembled young charges. Gesturing toward the overwhelming sense of impending catastrophe (summarized in the then oft-repeated catchphrase "Enjoy the war—the peace will be awful"), he instructed that there should be neither petty fights nor jealousies, and insisted that precautions be taken against accidental pregnancy. Otherwise, he said: "Nothing may be noticed by the outside world. On the other hand, one may not forbid fucking.... Further: no sex in the normal sleep barracks (so that the goody-two-shoes will not be disturbed). But so that you can bang away, we have prepared an extra barrack with ten straw sacks, i.e. for ten couples!" As the memoir recorded, "These encouraging words let everyone hit the high point of exuberant euphoria."[48]

Women and girls in the Reich Labor Service also had ample opportunity for sexual encounters. One woman remembered the Reich Labor Service as having a "very sexual climate ... a thoroughly sexual climate." Females in the Reich Labor Service were deliberately brought together with young military men for coed "social evenings"; the expectation was clearly that romantic pairings would occur. If there was no one who appealed to a particular girl, it was "difficult to get out of there." Even after Germany's defeat at Stalingrad in 1943, the mood in the Third Reich was still one of "dancing and partying." The overall message young people received was that Nazis were in favor of premarital sex. It was not just that reproduction was desired; "in general, the Nazis were in favor of fun [*sie waren doch auch sonst für Spass*]."[49]

*

What is difficult to bring together into the same interpretive frame is the wealth of evidence for Nazism's breezily upbeat defense of heterosexual enjoyment with the terror and mass murder that were Nazism's most defin-

---

[47]Conversation with E. I., 1994.

[48]Memoirs of G. C.

[49]Conversation with R. W., 2004. For further discussion of the climate encouraging extramarital (sometimes also nonconsensual) sex in the Reich Labor Service, see Walter Brockman, "Illegitimacy in Germany," *Current History* 46/4 (July 1937) 67–69.

ing features and its raison d'être. The issue that requires emphasis here is that all the ugly aspects of Nazi sexual politics and other politics were not embedded in a broader antisexual attitude, as so many scholars have surmised, but, rather, coexisted with (however conventional and conformity-inducing) injunctions and encouragements to the majority of Germans to have pleasure.

The work of Dr. Johannes H. Schultz provides an instructive case in point. Schultz is, to this day, most famous for being the inventor in 1920 of "Autogenic Training," a system of self-hypnosis, relaxation and breathing techniques to enhance overall well-being that has been exceedingly popular in Germany and eventually found adherents the world over. But he was also a prolific writer on psychotherapy and author of the widely circulated regime-endorsed advice manual *Geschlecht-Liebe-Ehe* (Sex-Love-Marriage, 1940), in which he described intercourse as a "sacred" act and a lastingly loving marriage as "holy land."[50] Liberal antiguilt arguments were the hallmark of his texts, and he was especially noteworthy for his strong defenses of affectionate parenting and of child and adolescent masturbation and for his particular attention to women's pleasure. Schultz not only defended masturbation as "a necessary transitional phase of youthful life-searching" with no negative physical consequences whatsoever and raged against the "crippling in their love lives of quite numerous valuable people" by "punishment-threatening, cold-hearted," antimasturbation "tyrants." He also lamented the inadequate attention given to female sex education in all social strata. Declaring himself pleased that the worst suffering was over ("with profound gratitude every older physician will celebrate the fact that a ghost of his youth, the 'daughter of the upper bourgeoisie' with corset, hypocrisy, and lasciviousness, belongs to the past"), Schultz nonetheless worried that not enough women had overcome the damage of a repressive education and found their way through to the "vibrant humanness" they so richly deserved.[51]

In his advice manual, Schultz repeatedly emphasized the importance of orgasm for both women and men. He called his readers' attention to the sensitivity of the clitoris, encouraged gentle breast fondling, recommended stimulating the front wall of the vagina during intercourse, and celebrated the "most fiery physical passion," and the "shared diving-into the blisses of pure bodiliness, and finally the self-finding in the mystery of

[50]Johannes H. Schultz, *Geschlecht-Liebe-Ehe: Die Grundtatsachen des Liebes- und Geschlechtslebens in ihrer Bedeutung für Einzel- und Volksdasein* (Munich, 1940), 60, 77, 82, 113.

[51]Johannes H. Schultz, "Nervöse Sexualstörungen und ihre Behandlung in der allgemeinen Praxis," *Therapie der Gegenwart: Medizinisch-chirurgische Rundschau für praktische Ärzte* 78 (June 1937), 252–55.

highest union." Schultz also spelled out the diversity of possible experiences for men, distinguishing between quick and superficial orgasms and those, usually growing out of a longer love-making episode, which could lead to a "very intensive resolution," "extraordinarily profound destabilizations and shakings of the entire organism."[52]

Through both his deep-breathing techniques and his reassuring, affirmative sex advice (both of which bear some disconcerting similarities to techniques and advice advanced by the anti-Nazi, left-wing sex radical Wilhelm Reich), Schultz could fairly portray himself as a man not only committed to, but also succeeding in, enhancing heterosexuals' sex lives in various ways. But behind closed doors, Schultz choreographed torture. Many psychiatrists and psychologists in Germany in the 1990s still defended Schultz as "apolitical."[53] But during the Third Reich he not only endorsed the "extermination [*Vernichtung*]" of the handicapped, expressing the hope "that the institutions for idiots will soon in this sense be emptied."[54] He was also personally involved in making concrete decisions about which of those men accused of homosexuality would be set free and which would be sent to a concentration camp (and hence often also to death). Schultz theorized that there were two kinds of homosexuals: Some he considered "hereditarily ill" and therefore unredeemable; others he designated as "dear little brother [*liebes Brüderchen*]" types whom he thought could benefit from help. In Schultz's own words, a "thoughtful psychotherapist" like himself could transform such a man into a heterosexual. How did he arrive at a diagnosis in each individual's case? At the German Institute for Psychological Research and Psychotherapy, since 1936 under the direction of Mathias Heinrich Göring (cousin of Hermann Göring, one of the leading figures in the Nazi regime), Schultz and a commission of coworkers forced accused homosexuals to perform coitus with a female prostitute while the commission watched. Whoever performed heterosexually to their satisfaction under these conditions was set free; whoever did not, and hence had revealed his incurability, was sent on to a concentration camp.[55]

*

Taken together, the essays collected in this volume give ample evidence of the value *and* recalcitrance of sexuality as a focus of historical inquiry. Many of the essays testify to the inextricability of sexual repression

[52]Schultz, *Geschlecht-Liebe-Ehe*, 47, 74, 77, 82–83.
[53]See "Bluthaftes Verständnis," *Der Spiegel*, 27 June 1994, 183–86.
[54]J. H. Schultz's comments were printed in the *Zentralblatt für Psychotherapie*, no.12 (1940), quoted in Ulrich Schultz, "Autogenes Training und Gleichschaltung aller Sinne," *taz*, 20 June 1984.
[55]J. H. Schultz quoted in "Bluthaftes Verständnis," 185; and in U. Schultz, "Autogenes Training."

and sexual liberalization. As is suggested by the title of this introduction, with its deliberate borrowing and juxtaposition of terms taken from what are often considered to be incompatible interpretive paradigms (theological, secular-liberal, Foucaultian, and Freudian), the history of sexuality under and after Nazism does not fit into any easily available explanatory framework. The interpretive dilemmas raised by the empirical traces left behind by the Third Reich in both its ordinary and its grotesque manifestations, however, may also provide the beginnings of some answers to issues that trouble us now as we struggle to understand the significance of these defining events of the twentieth century from the perspective of an already traumatized start of a new millenium.

For example, did sexual detabooization further the social and political control of those not directly victimized by the Nazi regime? Or is it more accurate, and perhaps also more chilling, to think of some individuals more fully realizing themselves while others suffered profoundly? The apparent undecidability here may be precisely the point. Second, the destabilizing resemblances between knowledges sought after under liberal regimes, then and still now, and insights into bodies and psyches produced under conditions of horror and terror may also be exactly what we need to confront.[56] But third, and just as significant, the often surprising differences between conceptualizations of aspects of sexuality under Nazism from ways sexuality was thought about in the 1930s and 1940s United States may also offer us unexpected critical vantage points on sexual conflicts in our present.[57] Attending to the history of sexuality, then,

---

[56]For example, we are still lacking a comprehensive history of gynecology under Nazism, one which explores the double truth of, on the one hand, the hideous hubris and scientific uselessness of so many of the torturous so-called reproductive experiments conducted under Nazism (with due attention to those physicians who utilized the concentration and death camps to transfer their research focus from chicken, rabbits, and mice to humans) and, on the other, the disconcertingly protopostmodern successes achieved by German physicians in such areas as artificial vagina construction and the use of hormones to treat sexual dysfunction.

[57]For instance, one remarkably understudied aspect of Nazi attitudes about homosexuality is the conviction articulated that homosexuality was very much a possibility lurking within the majority of men, and even a phase that many men literally went through. This perspective, which could have been used for antihomophobic purposes, instead was—quite self-reflexively—deployed to fuel the regime's punitive homophobic radicalism. The very existence of this theoretical perspective, however, both calls attention to interesting beliefs about the fragility of heterosexuality and highlights the differences between cultural understandings in the United States and Germany in the same era. While scholars of the United States have emphasized that men in the 1930s and 1940s could engage in same-sex behavior without shaking their self-concept as heterosexuals, Germans stressed how hard it was for many men to develop desire for women and openly and self-consciously thematized the way Nazi single-sex organizations provided a worryingly conducive environment for homosexual relations and the development of homosexual self-concepts.

allows us not only to approach longstanding historiographical controversies over such matters as Germany's divergence from the West or Nazism's role in trajectories of modernization in new ways. It can also, we hope, point the way out of some of our current emotional and political impasses.

Sexuality and Nazism: The Doubly Unspeakable?

ELIZABETH D. HEINEMAN

University of Iowa

THE HISTORY OF SEXUALITY in Nazi Germany unites two subjects vulnerable to sensationalist coverage: sex and Nazism. Film scholars have observed a tendency to eroticize National Socialism in that medium, a phenomenon that reflects (and perhaps perpetuates) the dangerous allure of fascism.[1] Film, however, often claims to be fiction and always claims artistic license. Perhaps more startling is the persistent misrepresentation of sexuality under Nazism in outlets that allegedly produce nonfiction. In a recent front-page story, the *Los Angeles Times* characterized Lebensborn as a place where "11,000 children were born to women who mated with elite SS officers," although all serious investigations describe Lebensborn as a home for pregnant women who could demonstrate the racial acceptability of their offspring-to-be.[2] Popular perceptions of many historic episodes are stubbornly resistant to evidence, but it is worth asking whether there is something special about the combination of Nazism and sex.

I extend my heartfelt thanks to Dagmar Herzog for lengthy discussions on this topic. In many ways, this essay reflects a joint effort that emerged from those discussions. Doris Bergen, Sarah Hanley, Linda Kerber, and Johanna Schoen offered valuable comments on earlier versions of this essay; Almut Haboeck and Michael Hohenbrink provided research assistance. I thank also the Graduate School of the University of Iowa for its financial support of this project. So many individuals shared their works in progress, their thoughts about the state of the field, or additional references with me that it is impossible to list them all, so I will acknowledge here those whose works are not referenced in this article: Cindy Beal, Paul Betts, Anne Guldin, Maggie Heineman, Yvonne Huoy, Kathy Pence, Rosemarie Scullion, and Klaus Weinhauer. This essay encompasses only the English- and German-language literature.

[1] For well-known eroticized representations of Nazi Germany on film, see Liliana Cavani's *Night Porter* (1974) and Lina Wertmüller's *Seven Beauties* (1975). See also Susan Sonntag's statement on this point, "Fascinating Fascism," in *Under the Sign of Saturn* (New York, 1980).

[2] Carol J. Williams, "Breeding to Further the Reich," *Los Angeles Times,* 21 January 2000, A1, A14. On Lebensborn, see Catrine Clay and Michael Leapman, *Master Race: The Lebensborn Experiment in Nazi Germany* (London, 1995); Georg Lilienthal, *Der "Lebensborn e.V.": Ein Instrument nationalsozialistischer Rassenpolitik* (Stuttgart, 1985).

Journal of the History of Sexuality, Vol. 11, Nos. 1/2, January/April 2002
© 2002 by the University of Texas Press, P.O. Box 7819, Austin, TX 78713-7819

If words appear inadequate to describe either the excruciating violence of Nazism (Adorno's "to write poetry after Auschwitz is barbaric") or the sensory pleasures of sex (Barthes's "Bliss is unspeakable"), we might expect to be doubly frustrated as we struggle to conjure up the intersections of Nazism and sex.[3] Yet in the end, Adorno revised his claim that post-Holocaust poetry was impossible, and Barthes explored a language for sexual bliss.[4] Thus it is perhaps fitting that the last twenty-five years have seen remarkable advances in our understanding of sexuality under Nazism. Three major developments can account for this sea change. One is a growing interest in the scientific bases of Nazi racism, specifically, the science of eugenics. A second is the emergence of women's history. The third is the lowering of taboos about studying sexuality and, particularly, sexual minorities. As a result, some subfields within the history of sexuality in Nazi Germany are now well developed. We have detailed studies of the ways that Nazi racism shaped women's reproductive lives as well as good research on the persecution of homosexual men. One strength of this literature is its integration of the history of sexuality into the study of Nazi racial ideologies and practices. Another is its pursuit of larger issues of change and continuity. Historians of sexuality have carefully explored the balance between those aspects of Nazi policy and practice that were innovative and those that evolved from preexisting social mores and scientific ambitions.

Nevertheless, enormous gaps in the literature remain. One reason is the uneven nature of the sources. It is easier, for example, to formulate a research project on the persecution of homosexual men than on that of heterosexually "promiscuous" women. The former violated easily identified paragraphs of the criminal code (Paragraphs 175 and 175a) and, if sent to concentration camps, had their own label (the pink triangle). While a study of convictions under Paragraph 175 or of pink triangles hardly exhausts the history of gay men in Nazi Germany, it is an indispensable beginning and a relatively straightforward research task. There is no comparable, easily defined set of records on heterosexually "promiscuous" women (as distinct from those legally categorized as prostitutes), making it difficult for a researcher to identify and isolate women persecuted on the basis of "sexual promiscuity."

Even good sources, however, do not guarantee good research. A political climate, both inside and outside the academy, that considered sexuality trivial in comparison to other fields of study long made it difficult for scholars to get such research funded.[5] The relegation of certain themes to

---

[3]Theodor W. Adorno, *Prisms*, trans. Samuel and Sherry Weber (Cambridge, Mass., 1981); and Roland Barthes, *The Pleasure of the Text* (New York, 1975), 21.

[4]Theodor W. Adorno, *Negative Dialectics*, trans. E. B. Ashton (New York, 1973), 363.

[5]Rüdiger Lautmann, "Nichts für Ungut! Kommentierende Bemerkungen zur Forschungslage über den rosa Winkel im Konzentrationslager," in *Verfolgung von Homosexuellen im Nationalsozialismus* (Bremen, 1999), 104–11.

subfields of history, such as sexual violence against women to the subfield of women's history, has led scholars in other areas, such as the history of the Holocaust, to overlook evidence regarding sexuality.[6]

A related problem concerns the questions asked. We are in the habit of inquiring into groups persecuted by the Nazis, and we recognize the centrality of reproductive sex to the Nazis. But what about sex that was neither "deviant" nor primarily about reproduction? Although such matters are admittedly difficult to quantify, it is probably safe to say that most sexual activity in the Third Reich involved partners who were acceptable to the regime and whose immediate motivation was the desire for pleasure, not for a child. Did the experience of (or access to) sexual pleasure change during the Nazi regime? Did "ordinary Germans'" enthusiasm for the regime, their ability and willingness to perform certain functions, depend in part on their sexual contentedness? Did leaders of the regime, sensing a connection between sexual pleasure and popular support, work to foster an environment conducive to such pleasure?

Because it is difficult to research such questions, another major challenge to writing a history of sexuality in Nazi Germany concerns methodology. Professionally vulnerable, historians of women and historians of sexuality have understandably favored highly empiricist projects that permit reference to a seemingly unambiguous paper trail. This is particularly the case for those seeking careers in the German academy, whose greater conservatism has made it more risky not only to study gender and sexuality but also to employ methods loosely grouped under the rubric of "discursive analysis."[7] Even in the United States, Canada, and Britain, scholars sometimes fear that such methodologies might minimize the tangible reality of the immense human suffering caused by National Socialist Germany.[8]

Discursive analysis, however, entered investigations of the history of sexuality even before the 1978 publication of Michel Foucault's *History of Sexuality*.[9] Arguing against exaggerated fears of discursive analysis in

[6]Doris L. Bergen makes this point in "Gender and Genocide: Lessons from the Holocaust?" in *Men, Women, and War*, ed. Carol Rittner and Valerie Morgan (New York, forthcoming).

[7]Kathleen Canning emphasizes the "Atlantic divide" in the relationship between gender history and theoretical approaches in "German Particularities in Women's History/Gender History," *Journal of Women's History* 5, no. 1 (1993): 102–14. This essay cannot detail the distinctions between oft-confused terms such as postmodernism, poststructuralism, deconstruction, and discursive analysis; for useful overviews in the context of German historical writing, see Jane Caplan, "Postmodernism, Poststructuralism, and Deconstruction: Notes for Historians," *Central European History* 22, no. 3 (1989); David Crew, "Who's Afraid of Cultural Studies? Taking a 'Cultural Turn' in German History," in *A User's Guide to German Cultural Studies*, ed. Scott D. Denham, Irene Kacandes, and Jonathan Petropoulos (Ann Arbor, 1997), 45–62.

[8]On problems of representing the Holocaust more generally, see Dominick LaCapra, *Representing the Holocaust: History, Theory, Trauma* (Ithaca, 1994); Saul Friedländer, *Probing the Limits of Representation: Nazism and the "Final Solution"* (Cambridge, Mass., 1992).

[9]Michel Foucault, *The History of Sexuality*, 1st American ed. (New York, 1978). For lesser-known predecessors of the theoretical developments often associated with Foucault,

another context, Michael Geyer and Konrad Jarausch have noted that "complicating [the] presumed transparency" of texts can simply mean acknowledging the possibility that the "various layers" of our source materials allow "multiple readings."[10] But even such an approach is a step away from tallying up how many Germans were sterilized on the basis of which diagnosis or tracing the path of decrees regarding nonmarital children through the policy-making process—projects that have proved fruitful in their own right.[11] For many subjects related to sexuality, scholars must seek other types of evidence that require other methods of interpretation. In the absence of well-conceived analytic frameworks, attempts to explore such subjects as sexual pleasure and pain have often been dissatisfying at best, voyeuristic at worst.

Historians convinced that exploring sexual pain and pleasure might help us to understand Nazi Germany are uncomfortably aware that their work, taken out of context, might be utilized to sensationalize the grim subject of Nazi Germany. Yet questions about the relationship of sexual experience to Germans' (and other Europeans') encounter with Nazism and to the regime's successes and failures are important. Very recently, and very cautiously, historians have begun to voice them. The most exciting work on sexuality under Nazism may just be getting off the ground.

Was Nazism Seductive?

In an early foray into women's history, Richard Evans observed that "the most popular, the most widely repeated and (probably) the most generally accepted" explanation for women's support of Hitler was their "supposedly inherent irrationality." Probed a bit further, "irrationality" revealed itself as sexual desire. Evans pointedly observed that commentators who approached everything else Hitler said with skepticism had "taken Hitler's comments in his mob oratory [alone] at their face value, given them a Freudian twist, and presented them as a serious attempt to penetrate the secret of Hitler's appeal."[12] Women, in short, were "seduced" by Hitler.

To be fair, such reputable historians as Joachim Fest and Richard Grunberger—whom Evans named as offenders—did not simply "give"

as well as an introduction to their application in the context of sexuality studies, see Carole S. Vance, "Social Construction Theory: Problems in the History of Sexuality," in *Homosexuality, Which Homosexuality? International Conference on Gay and Lesbian Studies,* ed. Dennis Altman et al. (Amsterdam, 1989).

[10]Michael Geyer and Konrad Jarausch, "Great Men and Postmodern Ruptures: Overcoming the 'Belatedness' of German Historiography," *German Studies Review* 18, no. 2 (1995): 269, 255.

[11]Gisela Bock, *Zwangssterilisation im Nationalsozialismus: Studien zur Rassenpolitik und Frauenpolitik* (Opladen, 1986); Werner Schubert, "Der Entwurf eines Nichtehelichengesetzes vom Juli 1940 und seine Ablehnung durch Hitler," *Zeitschrift für das gesamte Familienrecht* 31 (1984): 1–10.

[12]Richard J. Evans, "German Women and the Triumph of Hitler," *Journal of Modern History* 48 (1976): 123–75, 125, 128. Ron Rosenbaum offers a witty account of historians'

Hitler's comments a Freudian twist. Rather, they drew on a Freudian language made available by social psychologists who had tried to explain the rise of fascism in psychoanalytic terms. Wilhelm Reich linked the rise of fascism to the repression of sexuality in a patriarchal and capitalist society; Erich Fromm and Max Horkheimer saw authoritarian-masochistic tendencies within the family as a breeding ground for fascism.[13] The Frankfurt School's influence helps to explain why even conservative historians considered a possible role for sexual desire in the rise of fascism, decades before women's history or the history of sexuality became fields of serious historical inquiry. The familiarity of West Germany's educated classes with the Frankfurt School and the revival of interest in that school among university students in the 1960s help to explain the broader popularity of analyses that linked repressed sexuality to fascism.[14] In many fields of history, the possibility that sexuality and politics were intricately linked was unthinkable until a few years ago, but this was not so in studies of Nazi Germany.

Evans's complaint was not that historians considered sexuality but, rather, that they applied different standards of evidence to different subjects. Sloppy reference to sexuality had become a cover for failure to research women's history. Thus blithe references to women's "irrationality," supported by a quick reference to the Frankfurt School, often stood side by side with excellent empirical research into other subjects. The inadequacy of such short cuts quickly became evident when serious research into women's history got under way. Evidence that Hitler turned women's knees (and brains) to jelly—much less that this was connected to political behavior—was meager. Annemarie Tröger needed only to point out that men had voted for Hitler in greater proportions than had women to discredit the thesis that erotic desire led women to "bring Hitler to power."[15]

Historians' selective recourse to a sexualized psychoanalytic framework to explain women's (but not men's) political behavior says a great deal

---

attempts at psychosexual explanations of Hitler's own madness (*Explaining Hitler: The Search for the Origins of His Evil*, 1st ed. [New York, 1998], 99–154). For an example of this genre, see Robert G. L. Waite, *The Psychopathic God: Adolf Hitler* (New York, 1977).

[13]Wilhelm Reich, *Massenpsychologie des Faschismus: Zur Sexualökonomie der politischen Reaktion und zur proletarischen Sexualpolitik* (Copenhagen, Prague, Zurich, 1933); Institut für Sozialforschung (Frankfurt am Main), *Studien über Autorität und Familie, Forschungsberichte aus dem Institut für Sozialforschung* (Paris, 1936); for an early American psychoanalytic approach, see Bertram Henry Schaffner, *Father Land: A Study of Authoritarianism in the German Family* (New York, 1948).

[14]Dagmar Herzog, "'Pleasure, Sex, and Politics Belong Together': Post-Holocaust Memory and the Sexual Revolution in West Germany," *Critical Inquiry* 24 (1998): 393–444.

[15]Annemarie Tröger, "Die Dolchstoßlegende der Linken," in *Mutterkreuz und Arbeitsbuch: Zur Geschichte der Frauen in der Weimarer Republik und im Nationalsozialismus*, ed. Frauengruppe Faschismusforschung (Frankfurt am Main, 1981). See the debate surrounding the work of Maria Macciocchi (*Jungfrauen, Mütter und ein Führer: Frauen im Faschismus* [Berlin, 1976]; and "Female Sexuality in Fascist Ideology," *Feminist Review* 1, no. 1 [1979]: 67–82); see also Jane Caplan, "Introduction to Female Sexuality in Fascist

about the status of women's history through the 1970s. It does not accurately reflect social psychologists' own efforts to explain Nazism's appeal. Members of the Frankfurt School described a "homosexual personality type" that was presumably male but that need not have been homosexually active. The supposed submissive/masochistic tendencies of this "type" made it vulnerable to fascism's seductive appeal. Andrew Hewitt exposes the lasting influence of this "homosexualization of fascism" by tracing such imagery beyond contemporary psychoanalytic treatments to such settings as postwar literature.[16] The homophobia inherent in a conflation of homosexual desire and fascism, Hewitt holds, is all too clear.

In *Male Fantasies*, literary scholar Klaus Theweleit adopted a psychoanalytic approach to describe neither men nor women "seduced" by Nazism but, rather, Freikorps men whose protofascist violence expressed their fear of castration by Red (Communist) women. Significantly, the men to whom fascism appealed were not, in Theweleit's telling, victims metaphorically "seduced" by Nazism; rather, they were perpetrators of very un-"metaphoric" violence. Furthermore, their pathology emerged not from homosexual desire but from misogyny. Men of the Freikorps feared the "disorder" that women created not only through their role in proletarian revolutionary movements but also through their indeterminate, fluid, messy bodies—that is, through their very womanliness. Men of the Freikorps battled "feminine" messiness in women by composing violent fantasies about the destruction of women; they battled "feminine" messiness in themselves by creating brutally "orderly" selves.[17]

Psychoanalytically influenced works have been criticized on grounds that range from the specific (can we conflate the Freikorps and the Nazis?) to the general (does psychoanalysis "overinflate" the sexual?).[18] Nevertheless, two important points must be made. First, the persistent search for social-psychological explanations for fascism has kept fascism's possible appeal to the erotic on the intellectual agenda and in the popular imagination. Even historians who reject psychoanalytic analyses must grapple with their influence. Second, such explanations have had relatively little impact

---

Ideology," *Feminist Review* 1, no. 1 (1979): 59–66; Eva Sternheim-Peters, "Brunst, Ekstase, Orgasmus: Männerphantasien zum Thema 'Hitler und die Frauen,'" *Psychologie Heute* 8 (1981): 36–41.

[16]Andrew Hewitt, *Political Inversions: Homosexuality, Fascism, and the Modernist Imaginary* (Stanford, Calif., 1996).

[17]Klaus Theweleit, *Male Fantasies*, 2 vols., trans. Stephen Conway, Erica Carter, and Chris Turner (Minneapolis, 1987, 1989). The Freikorps were rightist paramilitary units that came into being upon Germany's defeat in 1918. They battled the claims of new Eastern European states for formerly German territory, and they helped to put down worker uprisings in Germany as well as the short-lived Bavarian Communist government of 1919.

[18]Jessica Benjamin and Anson Rabinbach, "Foreword," in ibid., 2:xiv–xvii; Randall Halle, "Between Marxism and Psychoanalysis: Antifascism and Antihomosexuality in the Frankfurt School," *Journal of Homosexuality* 29 (1995): 295–317, 308.

on the historical literature. This is the case not just because historians have been "too conservative" to consider sexuality (except as it applies to women, in which case historians have often been "too sexist" to consider women in any other light) but also because of epistemological differences among disciplines. However thought-provoking the work of scholars like Reich, Fromm, and Theweleit, it does not rely on the type of evidence that historians typically require.

Historical examinations of popular culture and consumption may embed the erotic in a material context more convincing to historians.[19] However, as art historians Kathrin Hoffmann-Curtius and Silke Wenk warn, the deployment of cultural artifacts is not without its own dangers. The unexamined use of Nazi-era images of women, including female nudes, in media ranging from museum catalogs to news magazines can reveal problematic, sexualized strategies for achieving distance from Nazism.[20] Such presentations can make Nazi Germany an object of pornographic fascination, turn a feminized Germany into the victim of the "seducer" Hitler, or simply locate "sex" in women alone.

Since journalist Udo Pini's *Leibeskult und Liebeskitsch* (Cult of the body and love kitsch) is frequently cited by historians, it pays to examine it in Wenke's and Hoffmann-Kurtius's light. Pini draws attention to the erotic in hundreds of examples from everyday outlets such as dancing, fashion, and picture postcards. His collection of photographs is the centerpiece of the book, and it provides its own argument that the erotic had a firm place in Nazi-era culture. Yet the brief accompanying text too often equates "sex" with "women," who appear alternately as willing reproductive automatons and as lascivious counterparts of sexually hapless German men. Thus in Pini's telling, "some" young women (but evidently not men) chose spouses not for love (presumably the sole motivation for marriage before 1933) but according to the criteria established by the marriage loans. Lustful women had sex with foreign laborers because "this other male type aroused them with an erotic different from that of the conscientiously fantasyless German men." In military men's "fraternization" there is no hint of exploitation; instead, "Parisian girls loved the formal uniforms and the jealous glances of the *Blitzweiber*."[21]

More thoughtful consideration of the visual appears in works on fashion. Irene Guenther has described fashion as a site where three concerns

[19]A very useful introduction to these intersections is the edited collection by Victoria de Grazia and Ellen Furlough, *The Sex of Things: Gender and Consumption in Historical Perspective* (Berkeley, 1996).

[20]Kathrin Hoffmann-Curtius, "Feminisierung des Faschismus," in *Die Nacht hat zwölf Stunden*, ed. Claudia Keller (Berlin, 1996); Silke Wenk, "Hin-Weg Sehen," in *Erbeutete Sinne: Nachträge zur Berliner Ausstellung "Inszenierung der Macht,"* ed. Klaus Behnken and Frank Wagner (Berlin, 1988), 17–32.

[21]Udo Pini, *Leibeskult und Liebeskitsch: Erotik im Dritten Reich* (Munich, 1992), 219, 326, 353. *Blitzweiber* is a derogatory term for German female military auxiliaries.

intersected: racism, economic nationalism, and female eroticism.[22] A recent exhibition on fashion under National Socialism demonstrates that designers continued to cater to the elite's preference for haute couture—although they downplayed the French connection by calling it *Hauptmode*.[23] Fashion thus reached a compromise between popular ideals of female eroticism, on the one hand, and economic and racial nationalism, on the other.

A useful, larger framework for imagining the erotic in Nazi Germany emerges from Hans Dieter Schäfer's insistence that a more "normal," even "Americanized" popular culture coexisted with Nazified culture. Although gender and sex were not central to Schäfer's 1981 analysis, he revealed tantalizing tidbits about an erotic culture that survived Nazi pronouncements against "degeneracy," such as film magazines' defense of Marlene Dietrich's erotic appeal long after her denunciation by the regime.[24] Furthermore, while the regime claimed to battle "degenerate" sexuality, it also promised opportunities for a "healthy" sexuality—which, Schäfer claims, helps explain the regime's popularity. The German Labor Front (Reichsarbeitsdienst, RAD) offered cosmetics courses; Strength through Joy (Kraft durch Freude, KDF) hinted that travel might bring sexual adventure.[25] Schäfer's challenge to images of an utterly regimented culture that could not tolerate anything so individualistic as pleasure is crucial, yet his brief discussions of sexual experience are indicative of the early date of his work. What are we to make of the news that nine hundred girls from the League of German Girls (Bund deutscher Mädel, BDM) returned pregnant from the 1936 party rally? This statement is followed first by evidence of the sexual activity of presumably average East Prussian schoolgirls and then by information on sex within anti-Nazi youth cliques, leaving the reader to wonder about the interplay between political and sexual cultures. We can only conclude that, well, young people had sex.[26] If we are battling the crude belief that under the Nazis (or was it until 1968?) Germans were celibate until marriage, whereupon they had sex in order to make babies, then this may be a necessary statement. However, it might be time to investigate finer points.

Research into Nazi organizations—particularly those that created new sexual spaces—reveals in greater detail how the Nazis' provision of sexual

[22]Irene Guenther, "Nazi 'Chic'? German Politics and Women's Fashions, 1915-1945," *Fashion Theory: The Journal of Dress, Body, and Culture* 1 (1997): 29–58.

[23]Almut Junker, *Frankfurt Macht Mode 1933-1945* (Frankfurt am Main, 1999).

[24]Hans Dieter Schäfer, *Das gespaltene Bewusstsein: Über deutsche Kultur und Lebenswirklichkeit, 1933-1945* (Munich, 1981), 137. Other discussions of the regime's reconciliation of contrary cultural impulses include Philipp Gassert, *Amerika im Dritten Reich: Ideologie, Propaganda und Volksmeinung, 1933-1945* (Stuttgart, 1997); Jeffrey Herf, *Reactionary Modernism: Technology, Culture, and Politics in Weimar and the Third Reich* (Cambridge, 1984).

[25]Schäfer, 124. The German Labor Front was the party's labor organization; Strength through Joy offered recreational opportunities, including tourism, to workers.

[26]Ibid., 139.

opportunity might have made them appealing.[27] Robert Waite has noted
that the Hitler Youth (Hitler Jugend, HJ) gave young people an excuse to
be out after dark, while the RAD gave many young adults their first taste of
life away from their parents' homes and their first opportunity for unsuper-
vised contact with members of the other sex. Waite has also called attention
to wartime sexual activity in neighborhoods near military bases, Pieter
Lagrou notes French clerics' perception of a lively sexual culture in foreign
workers' barracks, while Ebba Drolshagen describes an occupied Western
Europe in which well-mannered German soldiers were attractive partners
for local women. Despite the greater brutality of the occupied Soviet Union,
Marlene Epp finds that ethnic German women there sometimes welcomed
German military men as partners. Birthe Kundrus observes that male conscription created a civilian space relatively free of husbands' supervision in
which military wives might have extramarital affairs.[28] Since all of these settings enabled sexual exploitation as well as consensual sex, all require a discussion of power even in consensual relationships in light of the intersecting
hierarchies of gender, "race," age, wealth, and political/military position.
Still, women as well as men, defeated as well as victorious people, and youths
as well as adults might have been attracted to opportunities for sex that the
unusual circumstances provided.[29]

Particularly in the case of youth, we should think carefully about what
we mean when we say "sexuality." In an effort to debunk images of the
BDM as a hotbed of promiscuity (an accusation that brought shame only to

[27]For a model historic study of sexualized spaces, see Judith R. Walkowitz, *City of Dreadful
Delight: Narratives of Sexual Danger in Late-Victorian London* (Chicago, 1992). For the
postwar period in Germany, Maria Hoehn's examination of military bases and camp followers in Rhineland-Palatinate and Jennifer Evans's research on sexual space in Berlin show the
mutual influence of postwar recovery and sexual geography: Maria Hoehn, *GIs and Fräuleins:
The German American Encounter in 1950s West Germany* (Chapel Hill, 2002); Jennifer
Evans, "Reconstruction Sites: Sexuality, Citizenship and the Limits of National Belonging
in Divided Berlin," Ph.D. diss., State University of New York at Binghamton, 2001.

[28]Robert G. Waite, "Teenage Sexuality in Nazi Germany," *Journal of the History of Sexu-
ality* 8, no. 3 (1998); Pieter Lagrou, *The Legacy of Nazi Occupation: Patriotic Memory and
National Recovery in Western Europe, 1945–1965* (New York, 2000), 144–56; Ebba D.
Drolshagen, *Nicht ungeschoren davonkommen: Das Schicksal der Frauen in den besetzten
Ländern, die Wehrmachtssoldaten liebten* (Hamburg, 1998); Birthe Kundrus, "Nur die halbe
Geschichte: Frauen im Umfeld der Wehrmacht zwischen 1939 und 1945," in *Hitlers
Wehrmacht: Mythos und Realität*, ed. Militärgeschichtliches Forschungsamt (Munich, 1999);
Marlene Epp, *Women without Men: Mennonite Refugees of the Second World War* (Toronto,
2000), 32–34. On romances in occupied Western Europe, see also Madeleine Bunting, *The
Model Occupation: The Channel Islands under German Rule, 1940–1945* (London, 1995).

[29]Studies of the postwar period, in which rape and "hunger prostitution" coexisted with
some German women's excitement at the prospect of romance with occupation soldiers,
make the same point: Sibylle Meyer and Eva Schulze, *Wie wir das alles geschafft haben:
Alleinstehende Frauen berichten über ihr Leben nach 1945* (Munich, 1984); Elizabeth D.
Heineman, "The Hour of the Woman: Memories of Germany's 'Crisis Years' and West
German National Identity," *American Historical Review* 101, no. 2 (1996): 354–95.

the girls, not to their male partners), scholars such as Claudia Koonz have noted that BDM girls, by and large, subscribed to conservative sexual mores. They disapproved, for example, of nonmarital pregnancy, despite the regime's claim that it valued all racially approved births.[30] In focusing on the frequency of premarital sex or the acceptability of nonmarital pregnancy, however, we may be looking in the wrong places. Adult definitions of sexual activity may be inappropriate for adolescents; late-twentieth-century standards for age of first intercourse may not apply to the 1930s. Rejection of nonmarital pregnancy—even a rejection of intercourse for teenagers—need not mean that HJ boys, BDM girls, and RAD recruits of both sexes did not enjoy the erotic opportunities presented by their service. A setting for petting and kissing might have been quite enough to make fourteen-year-old boys and girls look forward to mixed-sex activities with the HJ, and youth who loudly denounced premarital sex at sixteen might well have engaged in it at twenty.[31] We should also be careful not to minimize the dangers of sexual abuse that could accompany the loss of parental protection even if, in an adolescent setting, abuse did not always include heterosexual intercourse.[32] This is not to deny the considerable evidence of nonmarital, adolescent intercourse—it is simply to plead for greater consideration of nonpenetrative sexuality, particularly among adolescents.

If we accept that sexual opportunity as well as sexual repression characterized Nazi Germany, then what is the relationship between the two? Originally published in 1972, Hans Bleuel's *Das saubere Reich* (The clean Reich) rejected monolithic images of sexuality in Nazi Germany, whether of a repressive or a libertine nature. Yet Bleuel stumbled over the difficult task of reconciling Nazism's evident contradictions. Following totalitarian interpretations of Nazism, Bleuel presented neopagan rituals and orders regarding the imperative to breed as evidence of sexual experience under Nazism, suggesting a rejection of bourgeois sexual morality, which, presumably, was connected to other Nazi horrors. In the end, however, he concluded that Germans' adherence to a narrow sexual morality made

[30]Claudia Koonz, *Mothers in the Fatherland: Women, the Family, and Nazi Politics* (New York, 1987), 399. For accounts that emphasize the BDM as a site of heterosexual activity, see Gerhard Rempel, *Hitler's Children: The Hitler Youth and the SS* (Chapel Hill, 1989), esp. 51, 87; Martin Klaus, *Mädchenerziehung zur Zeit der faschistischen Herrschaft in Deutschland: Der Bund deutscher Mädel,* 1st ed. (Frankfurt am Main, 1983), 270–72. In such accounts, male heterosexual activity among the HJ appears unproblematic (it is rarely mentioned at all); only homosexuality in the HJ is problematic.

[31]Memoirists' accounts of the HJ/BDM as a setting for adolescent romance include Renate Finckh, *Mit uns zieht die neue Zeit* (Baden-Baden, 1979); Margarete Hannsmann, *Der helle Tag bricht an: Ein Kind wird Nazi* (Hamburg, 1982).

[32]See, for example, Jost Hermand's harrowing account of "strong boys'" use of sexual practices ranging from mutual masturbation to rape to enforce hierarchies in HJ evacuation camps: Jost Hermand and Margot Bettauer Dembo, *A Hitler Youth in Poland: The Nazis' Program for Evacuating Children during World War II* (Evanston, 1997).

them susceptible to Nazism's promise to restore a wholesome Germany and that postwar societies, unless they shook off restrictive sexual norms, might face renewed danger.[33]

Rather than allow National Socialism's apparent inconsistencies to become our own, Dagmar Herzog has suggested that we consider their interrelationships.[34] Constant reminders that some types of sex by some types of people were unacceptable let members of "superior" groups know that different rules applied to them. A rhetoric of selective natalism gave racially acceptable Germans permission to enjoy the sex that, incidentally, might lead to pregnancy. In his "sociological semantic analysis" of Nazi Germany, Torsten Reters too has grappled with evidently contradictory messages regarding sexuality. He holds, however, that Nazi-era cultural production was neither incoherent nor hypocritical but offered a vocabulary of options, from *Jede Nacht ein neues Glück* (Every night a new happiness) to *Es wird einmal ein Wunder gescheh'n* (One day a miracle [true love] will occur), to name two popular Nazi-era films. While the regime was neither "prosex" nor "antisex," the overall message was not that "anything goes." Rather, it was a coherent whole that simultaneously rejected Victorian prudery and the "degenerate" sexuality associated with Weimar in favor of a "clean" but distinctly sexual life.[35]

Ideally, work on such subjects as consumption, culture, Nazi organizations, and the ways that the regime encouraged the racially privileged in their sexual lives will allow even those who have misgivings about psychoanalytic frameworks to consider how Nazism appealed to erotic desires. We need not subscribe to a notion of society-wide neurosis to imagine that Germans might have fantasized about sexual adventure while on a stint with the Labor Service, hoped that stylish clothing would enhance their erotic appeal, or felt their sexual desire reaffirmed since the regime valued their potential offspring. Nazism's appeal to the erotic lay not just in the "aestheticization of politics," to use Walter Benjamin's phrase, but also in the ways the regime addressed leisure, entertainment, work, and consumption. If we focus on such subjects, however, we find that those who felt this appeal become more "normal" and their desire more familiar than if we crudely apply social psychological diagnoses such

[33]Hans Peter Bleuel, *Das saubere Reich: Theorie und Praxis des sittlichen Lebens im Dritten Reich* (Bern, Munich, Vienna, 1972). A more recent overview, which includes useful information but remains superficial, is Stefan Maiwald and Gerd Mischler, *Sexualität unter dem Hakenkreuz: Manipulation und Vernichtung der Intimsphäre im NS-Staat* (Hamburg, 1999).

[34]Dagmar Herzog, "Sexuelle Revolution und Vergangenheitsbewältigung," *Zeitschrift für Sexualforschung* 13, no. 2 (2000): 87–103, esp. 96. See also Dagmar Herzog, "Desperately Seeking Normality: Sex and Marriage in the Wake of War," in *Life after Death: Violence, Normality, and the Construction of Postwar Europe*, ed. Richard Bessel and Dirk Schumann (New York, forthcoming).

[35]Torsten Reters, *Liebe, Ehe und Partnerwahl zur Zeit des Nationalsozialismus: Eine soziologische Semantikanalyse* (Dortmund, 1997).

as "submissive homoerotic masochism" to an entire population. What we learn from examining the intersections of erotic desire and political responsibility can help us understand the appeal of Nazism and might have application outside the Nazi context.

Same-Sex Desire: Persecution, Homoeroticism, and the Männerbund

Although systematic examination of homosexuality in Nazi Germany awaited the post-Stonewall era, the silence in prior decades was less deafening than one might expect. Raids on gay organizations were headline news during the Nazi years, and men with pink triangles were visible in concentration camps. Accordingly, accounts by eyewitnesses often mentioned the persecution of gay men. In his 1938 book on women in Nazi Germany, American sociologist Clifford Kirkpatrick noted the closing of homophile organizations and the tightening of antihomosexual legislation.[36] In his 1946 analysis of the concentration camp system, survivor Eugen Kogon discussed gay men's disadvantageous position in the social hierarchy of prisoners, their brutal treatment at the hands of the SS, medical experimentation on gay men, rape, and the exchange of homosexual sex for food.[37]

Contemporary accounts, however, did not focus only on persecution. Unsurprisingly, early opponents of Nazism discovered a certain utility in linking Nazis to homosexuality. Despite the leftist parties' official support for the decriminalization of homosexual acts, for example, Socialists and Communists exploited Storm Troop (Sturmabteilung, SA) leader Ernst Röhm's homosexuality in efforts to defame the National Socialists.[38] The temptation to bait the Nazis with simultaneous accusations of homosexuality and homophobia was too great to resist, and a single author could at once disparage homosexuals and denounce the Nazi persecution of them.[39]

However indicative of contemporaries' mixed attitudes toward homosexuality, this discourse constituted something other than silence. It

[36]Clifford Kirkpatrick, *Nazi Germany: Its Women and Family Life* (New York, 1938), 104, 265.

[37]Eugen Kogon, *The Theory and Practice of Hell* (New York, 1968), 42, 48, 153, 171, 258–59. Originally published as Eugen Kogon, *Der SS-Staat: Das System der deutschen Konzentrationslager* (Munich, 1946). Page numbers throughout refer to the English-language edition.

[38]Manfred Herzer, "Communists, Social Democrats, and the Homosexual Movement in the Weimar Republic," in *Gay Men and the Sexual History of the Political Left*, ed. Gert Hekma, Harry Oosterhuis, and James D. Steakley (Binghamton, 1995), 197–226; see also Alexander Zinn, *Die soziale Konstruktion des homosexuellen Nationalsozialisten: Zu Genese- und Etablierung eines Stereotyps* (Frankfurt am Main, 1997); Friedrich Koch, *Sexuelle Denunziation: Die Sexualität in der politischen Auseinandersetzung* (Frankfurt am Main, 1986).

[39]The former was the case with a physician's 1951 account of "sexual problems in the SS": M. Brustmann, "Sexuelle Probleme in der SS," cited in Herzog, "Desperately Seeking Normality." Kogon, generally sympathetic to the plight of gay men in the camps, described

expressed the impression that Nazism and homosexuality were in some way linked. As recent research has made clear, the claim that this link included both homophobia and homoeroticism did not just reflect contemporary critics' inconsistent attitudes toward homosexuality. It reflected, at least in part, the Nazi movement's own ambiguous relationship to the subject.

It is appropriate, however, to speak of "silence" in one regard. Until the late 1970s we had almost no testimony from acknowledged gay men or lesbians.[40] Robert Moeller has evoked the homophobic postwar environment that discouraged those who had been persecuted from coming forward: their crime under the Nazis was still a crime.[41] By the time the political climate had changed, survivors had died, become infirm, or were too wary to give testimony. The handful of existing testimonies of gay survivors is invaluable, but compared to the roughly fifty thousand memoirs (published and unpublished) of Jewish survivors reported by the Israeli Holocaust memorial, Yad Vashem, it is scanty evidence indeed.

The emergence of a gay liberation movement in the 1970s provided the setting for the publication of the first memoir of a survivor, the first systematic scholarly treatment, and activists' efforts to document the persecution of homosexuals.[42] Although the earliest efforts aimed mainly to record the persecution of gay men (whose sexual activities, unlike those of lesbians, were criminalized), comparative questions were inevitable. Were gay men, like Jews, persecuted simply for being who they were, and did they suffer a similar fate in concentration camps? The outrage that this suggestion provoked revealed a problematic perception that a comparison to gay men was an insult to Jewish victims. In light of this outrage, it is crucial to note that gay-sympathetic scholarship now argues, with a single

---

homosexual inmates as including "large numbers of criminals and especially blackmailers" and explained that they might enter "sordid relationships" to improve their chances of survival (42). Survivors' memoirs often reveal that authors' homophobia survived the transition from civilian to camp life intact; see, for example, Olga Lengyel, *Five Chimneys: The Story of Auschwitz* (New York, 1983), 197–99.

[40]Erik Jensen, this volume.

[41]Robert G. Moeller, "'The Homosexual Man Is a "Man," the Homosexual Woman Is a "Woman"': Sex, Society, and the Law in Postwar West Germany," *Journal of the History of Sexuality* 4, no. 3 (1994): 395–429. See also Hans-Georg Stuemke, "Vom unausgeglichenen Geschlechtshaushalt: Zur Verfolgung Homosexueller," in *Verachtet—Verfolgt—Vernichtet: Zu den "vergessenen" Opfern des NS-Regimes*, ed. Projektgruppe für die vergessenen Opfer des NS-Regimes (Hamburg, 1988), 46–63, esp. 63. An additional source problem is the disappearance of the records of the SS's Office for the Fight against Homosexuality and Abortion.

[42]For early survivors' memoirs, see Heinz Heger, *The Men with the Pink Triangle* (Boston, 1980); also the writings of the gay refugee Richard Plant, *The Pink Triangle: The Nazi War against Homosexuals* (New York, 1986). For early academic work, see Rüdiger Lautmann, Winfried Grikschat, and Egbert Schmidt, "Der rosa Winkel in den nationalsozialistischen Konzentrationslagern," in *Seminar: Gesellschaft und Homosexualität*, ed. Rüdiger Lautmann (Frankfurt am Main, 1977); Rüdiger Lautmann, "Eine Sexualität am sozialen Rande: Die Schwulen. Damals—Alltag im Nationalsozialismus," in *Der Zwang zur Tugend:*

voice, that the persecution of gay men was different, both in kind and in scale, from that of the Jews.[43]

The distinctions lay at the heart of Nazi racism. The Nazis sought to eliminate Jews from all of Europe; they endeavored to eliminate homosexuality only from Germany, since homosexuals' threat to "the race" applied only to "Aryans." The Nazis' effort to eliminate homosexuality, even in Germany, did not require the physical extermination of all men who performed homosexual acts. Nazi leaders believed that most homosexuality was not hereditary but learned and thus that many acting homosexuals could be "reeducated," albeit in settings (prisons, concentration camps) that in fact were often deadly. In contrast, they thought that people of Jewish ancestry who did not practice Judaism—who were even baptized— were still Jews: there could be no "reeducation." Even in the case of men whom the regime considered "real" homosexuals, as Geoffrey Giles has documented, the regime hoped that castration could provide a "correction."[44] The experience and effects of castration or internment were horrible, often deadly, but the logic behind the Nazis' responses to homosexuality was different from that behind their treatment of Jews.

Finally, key figures in the Nazi hierarchy, notably Hitler, were simply less obsessed with homosexuals than with Jews. This meant that homosexuality might be punished harshly, mildly, or not at all, depending on the social and political placement of the accused. Thus not only was Ernst Röhm's homosexuality tolerated until he became politically inconvenient, but, as Burkhard Jellonnek notes, solid social standing provided protection against police crackdowns on street prostitution and sex in public places, both the province of the young and the poor.[45] Claudia Schoppmann has revealed that hunting down lesbians was less important than protecting from wrongful suspicion wholesome "Aryan" maidens who expressed conventional female intimacies. For this reason, among others, proposals to criminalize female homosexual acts were rejected. Lesbians suffered less from persecution unique to themselves than from the regime's larger vision for women, which hit unwed women particularly hard since it included intense pressure to marry and discrimination against women in the workplace.[46]

Die gesellschaftliche Kontrolle der Sexualitäten, ed. Rüdiger Lautmann (Frankfurt am Main, 1984), 156–80. Activists' work includes the collection from the Berlin Museum, *Eldorado: Homosexuelle Frauen und Männer in Berlin, 1850–1950: Geschichte, Alltag und Kultur* (Berlin, 1984).

[43]The same was not necessarily true of gay activists; see Jensen, this volume. For a good summary of the arguments, see Günter Grau, "Introduction," in *Hidden Holocaust? Gay and Lesbian Persecution in Germany 1933–45*, ed. Günter Grau (New York, 1995).

[44]Geoffrey J. Giles, "'The Most Unkindest Cut of All': Castration, Homosexuality, and Nazi Justice," *Journal of Contemporary History* 27 (1992): 41–61.

[45]Burkhard Jellonnek, *Homosexuelle unter dem Hakenkreuz: Die Verfolgung von Homosexuellen im Dritten Reich* (Paderborn, 1990).

[46]Claudia Schoppmann, *Nationalsozialistische Sexualpolitik und weibliche Homosexualität* (Pfaffenweiler, 1991); summarized in English in Claudia Schoppmann, "National Socialist

The use of different frameworks for understanding the persecution of gay men and Jews has enabled scholars to move beyond the "concentration camp paradigm." But this paradigm has not been the only handicap confronted by scholars studying the persecution of homosexuals under Nazism. As both Rüdiger Lautmann and Günter Grau have noted, much work on the persecution of gay men has simply reiterated the *fact* of persecution, describing the "macropolitical actions" of the Nazis, on the one hand, and offering chronologies and statistical summaries of the persecution in various localities, on the other.[47]

As valuable as this detail is, recent and ongoing studies demonstrate a greater range of gay male experience than such accounts suggest. Jellonnek's analysis of regional variations in the persecution of gay men demonstrates, at the local level, the differences between anti-Semitic and antigay persecution. The Nazi regime sought Jews everywhere—in major cities, in small towns, in the countryside. By contrast, its efforts against homosexuals were more aggressive in urban areas with well-developed gay subcultures than in small town and rural settings.[48] John Fout's ongoing work on gay men in Nazi Germany emphasizes the variety of sites, beyond the concentration camps, that were significant in the persecution. Tens of thousands of men convicted of homosexuality in civilian courts were sent to prison, where a majority either completed their sentences or perished without setting foot in a concentration camp. Those convicted by the military judicial system were either executed or given punitive assignments in "cannon fodder" units. Homosexual men categorized as mentally ill were sent to mental hospitals, where they were sometimes "euthanized."[49] Andreas Pretzel and Gabrielle Roßbach's anthology on Berlin includes chapters that detail the methods of collecting evidence

---

Policies towards Female Homosexuality," in *Gender Relations in German History: Power, Agency, and Experience from the Sixteenth to the Twentieth Century*, ed. Lynn Abrams and Elizabeth Harvey (Durham, 1997). In 1938, when Austria was incorporated into the Reich, its laws criminalizing female homosexual acts remained valid for that territory. In this context, women were prosecuted under a Nazified system of justice for lesbian sexual acts. See Claudia Schoppmann, *Verbotene Verhältnisse: Frauenliebe 1938–1945*, 1st ed. (Berlin, 1999). Despite the great value of Schoppmann's work, it is unfortunate that the study of lesbians in Nazi Germany remains a one-woman show. See also Claudia Schoppmann's oral histories (*Days of Masquerade: Life Stories of Lesbians during the Third Reich*, trans. Allyson Brown [New York, 1996]).

[47]Lautmann, "Nichts für Ungut!"; see also Günter Grau's review of several recent books in *Zeitschrift für Sexualforschung* 13 (2000): 263–71.

[48]Jellonnek. On the special dangers of the big city, see Andreas Pretzel and Vera Kruber, "Jeder 100. Berliner: Statistiken zur Strafverfolgung Homosexueller in Berlin," in *Wegen der zu erwartenden hohen Strafe: Homosexuellenverfolgung in Berlin 1933–1945*, ed. Andreas Pretzel and Gabrielle Roßbach (Berlin, 2000), 169–85.

[49]John Fout, "Background Presentation," paper delivered at USHMM colloquium, April 2000.

and obtaining confessions and the distinct roles of the criminal police, the Gestapo, and the Special Courts (Sondergerichte).[50] Even within concentration camps, gay men's experience varied by preinternment community and date of imprisonment.[51]

Unlike earlier overviews of the persecution of gay men, these more detailed studies force us to confront the permeable border between victimization and complicity. As Manfred Herzer points out, the majority of homosexuals, "due to their extremely effective disguise, among other things, belonged to the willing subjects and beneficiaries of the Nazi state just like other German men and women."[52] Pretzel and Roßbach reveal that gay men, particularly prostitutes, denounced their sexual contacts to the police, enabling further arrests.[53] Men who were prosecuted upon their outing might previously have persecuted others from their positions in organizations such as the Hitler Youth and the SS.[54] Although many gay men in the SA were killed in the Röhm Purge of June 1934, the fact remains that Ernst Röhm and his friends enthusiastically pummeled Jews and political opponents in service to the Nazi cause. Fout notes that 70 percent of the men sentenced under Paragraphs 175 and 175a served their sentences, were released, and were then drafted into the Wehrmacht, where they aided Germany's domination of Europe.[55]

Military draftees and voluntary SA recruits can hardly be compared. Yet the fact that gay men, as men, participated in such organizations as the Wehrmacht and the SA draws our attention to a question that alternately concerned and titillated earlier commentators on the Nazi regime. What was the relationship between all-male organizations, hypermasculine militarism, homoeroticism, homosexuality, and Nazism?[56]

---

[50]Andreas Pretzel, "Erst dadurch wird eine wirksame Bekämpfung ermöglicht: Polizeiliche Ermittlungen," in Pretzel and Roßbach, eds., 43–73; Gabrielle Roßbach, "Sie sahen das Zwecklose ihres Leugnens ein: Verhöre bei Gestapo und Kripo," in ibid., 74–98; see also Frank Sparing, *". . . wegen Vergehen nach Section 175 verhaftet": Die Verfolgung der Düsseldorfer Homosexuellen während des Nationalsozialismus* (Düsseldorf, 1997).

[51]Joachim Müller, "'Wohl dem,'" Andreas Sternweiler, ". . . wegen dringenden Verdachts," and Andreas Sternweiler, "Nachteiliges über ihn," all in Joachim Müller and Andreas Sternweiler, *Homosexuelle Männer im KZ Sachsenhausen* (Berlin, 2000).

[52]Manfred Herzer, "Das dritte Geschlecht und das Dritte Reich," *Siegessäule* 2, no. 5 (May 1985): 31, quoted in Jensen, this volume.

[53]Pretzel, "Erst dadurch," 62; Roßbach, 81.

[54]Andreas Pretzel, "Ich wünsche meinem schlimmsten Feind nicht, daß er das durchmacht, was ich da durchgemacht habe: Vorfälle im Konzentrationslager Sachsenhausen vor Gericht in Berlin," in Pretzel and Roßbach, eds., 119–68, esp. 127, 140–47; Brade, "Was einmaliges im Lager," in Müller and Sternweiler.

[55]Fout.

[56]A recent biography of Hitler has attracted considerable criticism for the author's slippage from evidence that the young Hitler inhabited a homosocial, even homoerotically charged environment to the claim that Hitler was probably homosexual. See Lothar Machtan, *The Hidden Hitler*, trans. John Brownjohn (New York, 2001).

In a series of works spanning more than three decades, George L. Mosse explored precisely this relationship.[57] According to Mosse, in the late eighteenth century the European bourgeoisie began to articulate an ideal masculinity that united intellectual strength, moral virtue, and physical beauty. It projected the antithesis of these qualities onto various "others": women as well as working-class, Jewish, and homosexual men. The Männerbund, which translates imperfectly as "male collective," united men of disciplined mind and body who, undistracted by women, transformed their deep bonds with each other and their leader into a powerful creative force. Prior to the First World War, sympathetic theorists of the Männerbund declared this productive male bond to be homoerotic in nature, although true men of the Männerbund bore no similarity to the dandified homosexuals of negative stereotype.[58] After the First World War, the ideology of the Männerbund reached its peak in fascism—the ultimate anti-Socialist, anti-Semitic, homophobic, misogynist ideology. But in the masculinity of the interwar period, especially as practiced in fascism, a powerful tension existed between the homoerotic bonds of the Männerbund and the vilification of the homosexual, whose "otherness" was necessary for positive definitions of masculinity.

Mosse's overall framework was powerful, but it awaited testing and refinement. While Mosse described sweeping transformations in ideologies of masculinity in the modern period, subsequent research has explored the Männerbund in greater detail and in more limited settings. In this context, Eve Sedgwick's effort to theorize the relationship between homosociality and homoeroticism has proven significant, even if the object of her focus, late-eighteenth- and early-nineteenth-century Anglo-American literature, initially appears remote from Nazi Germany. Sedgwick cites feminist analyses that establish "an intelligible continuum of aims, emotions, and valuations link[ing] lesbianism with other forms of women's attention to women: the bond of mother and daughter, for instance, the bond of sister and sister, women's friendship, 'networking,' and the active struggles of feminism."[59] Although Sedgwick does not say so, Nazi authorities would have recognized this continuum. After all, it was their belief that female friendship and lesbianism might easily be confused that prompted them to reject proposals to criminalize lesbian acts, even as the fear that feminism and lesbianism were linked had been an argument in

---

[57]George L. Mosse, *The Crisis of German Ideology: Intellectual Origins of the Third Reich*, 1st ed. (New York, 1964); George L. Mosse, *Nationalism and Sexuality: Respectability and Abnormal Sexuality in Modern Europe*, 1st ed. (New York, 1985); George L. Mosse, *The Image of Man: The Creation of Modern Masculinity* (New York, 1996).

[58]Hans Blüher, *Die deutsche Wandervogelbewegung als erotisches Phänomen* (Berlin, 1914); Hans Blüher, *Die Rolle der Erotik in der männlichen Gesellschaft* (Jena, 1917). See also Mosse, *The Crisis of German Ideology*, 204–17.

[59]Eve Kosofsky Sedgwick, *Between Men: English Literature and Male Homosocial Desire* (New York, 1985), 2.

favor of criminalization.[60] Sedgwick asks: If we accept this continuum for women, why, in the case of men, do we assume a radical break between homosexuality and male bonding—a break so radical that scholars often consider homophobia to be a *necessary* element of male homosociality? Adopting the notion of "homosocial desire," Sedgwick instead posits a continuum between male homosociality and male homosexuality.

It was precisely this continuum, Eleanor Hancock asserts, that made the case of SA chief Ernst Röhm so explosive. Röhm, according to Hancock, found his masculinity, homosexuality, devotion to the Nazi movement, and membership in the Männerbund perfectly compatible. His differences with other Nazi leaders over the acceptability of homosexuality addressed a basic conflict about whether sexuality was a public or a private matter. The significance Nazis attributed to race and reproduction has led some historians to conclude that they did not recognize a "private" sphere of sexuality. Yet high-ranking Nazis accepted nonprocreative affairs and low birth rates among their ranks, and Hitler was not alone in considering Röhm's homosexuality irrelevant as long as he was effective. Still, Röhm's homosexuality "broke the distinctions established between homosexual desire and homosocial male bonding" and thus elicited a violent response among many within the party's upper ranks. For men who found deep meaning in the homosocial element of Nazism, Hancock suggests, Röhm's blurring of boundaries was intolerable.[61]

Geoffrey Giles, too, argues that concerns about homosexuality were not simply an ex post facto explanation for the Röhm Purge, intended to deflect attention from the "true" reason for the action: the need to ease the army's concerns about the power of the SA. Does this mean we should see fears of homosexuality rather than institutional competition as the "real" reason for the purge? Giles does not propose that we replace one explanation with another; rather, we should see the Röhm Purge as having been designed to serve multiple functions. The purge would reassure the army that the SA would be kept in check. The leadership also intended the purge to mollify an important group of allies: cultural conservatives, who were as troubled by the SA's rowdiness as they were by Berlin's gay nightlife. Likewise linking concerns about sexuality to the purge, Todd Ettelson emphasizes different styles of Männerbunde. The SA's brand of Männerbund, whose raucous brutality and open homosexuality displayed contempt for "feminized bourgeois morals," was useful in the Nazis' efforts to sow disorder in the Weimar Republic and to gain power. This style of masculinity, however, became a liability when the Nazis had to govern a state. Once in power, the Nazis required a more disciplined form of Männerbund, such as that of the armed

[60]Schoppmann, *Nationalsozialistische Sexualpolitik*.
[61]Eleanor Hancock, "'Only the Real, the True, the Masculine Held Its Value': Ernst Röhm, Masculinity, and Male Homosexuality," *Journal of the History of Sexuality* 8, no. 4 (1998): 640.

forces and the SS. Thus, confirming the army's position and addressing the place of homosexuality in the Männerbund were linked.[62]

According to Nicolaus Sombart, Germany was unusual in the extent to which ideologies of the Männerbund permeated political life, which may help explain why Sedgwick's homosocial locus is in literature, while Hancock's, Giles's, and Ettelson's are in the SA.[63] Peter von Rönn and Harry Oosterhuis also hold that the tension between homosociality and homosexuality was central to the life of the Nazi state. In his work on Nazi-era psychiatry, Rönn proposes that in the mid-1930s, when the authority and work of policing bodies such as the Gestapo and the SS expanded, the practical importance of the Männerbund increased. In this context, the fight against homosexuality became too important to be left to medicine; consequently, to justify taking control of the battle against them, SS chief Heinrich Himmler declared homosexuals to be a political threat rather than a medical problem.[64] Oosterhuis has noted that Nazi ideologues openly declared their ambition to create a state based on the Männerbund theorized at the turn of the century, though they were fully (albeit uncomfortably) aware that the Männerbund had been theorized as homoerotic. Thus, when Himmler began his harsh persecution of homosexual men, he was not just battling homosexual individuals who incidentally had found their way into such institutions as the SS or into such larger collectives as the German *Volk*. Rather, in Oosterhuis's formulation, he feared that "the National Socialist men's *state* threatened to destroy itself because organizations like the SS and the Hitler Youth could become hothouses for homosexuality" (emphasis added).[65] In this context, Gudrun Schwarz's claim that SS wives were not peripheral to an organization conceived as utterly male but, rather, that SS couples were understood as the cell of elite

[62]Geoffrey J. Giles, "The Institutionalization of Homosexual Panic in the Third Reich," in *Social Outsiders in the Third Reich*, ed. Robert Gellately and Nathan Stoltzfus (Princeton, 2000), 233–55; Todd Ettelson, "Old Warriors and New SA Men: Masculinity in 'The Night of the Long Knives,'" paper presented at the conference "Gender, Power, Religion: Forces in Cultural History," German Historical Institute, Washington, D.C., 2001.

[63]Nicolaus Sombart, "Männerbund und politische Kultur in Deutschland," in *Männergeschichte, Geschlechtergeschichte: Männlichkeit im Wandel der Moderne*, ed. Thomas Kühne (Frankfurt am Main, 1996), 136–54. Sombart's assertion, however, is not based on a thorough comparative exploration of political cultures; historians of other states may take issue with Sombart's claim that women's minimal role in public life in turn-of-the-century Germany was exceptional. In Bernd Widdig, *Männerbünde und Massen: Zur Krise männlicher Identität in der Literatur der Moderne* (Opladen, 1992), debates about the Männerbund in Wilhelmine and Weimar Germany are intimately linked to debates about the form of state and political power.

[64]Peter von Rönn, "Politische und psychiatrische Homosexualitätskonstruktion," *Zeitschrift für Sexualforschung* 11, nos. 2–3 (1998): 99–129, 220–60.

[65]Harry Oosterhuis, "Male Bonding and the Persecution of Homosexual Men in Nazi Germany," *Amsterdams Sociologisch Tijdschrift* 17, no. 4 (1991): 27–45, esp. 37.

"Aryan" society could help to bridge the current yawning chasm between studies of the Männerbund and women's history.[66]

And what of the lived experience—as opposed to the ideology—of male homosexuality and the Männerbund? John Fout, who has researched thousands of interrogations of men accused of homosexual behavior, believes that suspects' testimony may represent "the largest source of autobiographical statements from men who had sex with other men to be found in the modern world."[67] Aside from their obvious value in researching the Nazi persecution, these records constitute an incomparable source for reconstructing the lives of men who engaged in same-sex behavior—and not only for the Nazi years, since suspects often described decades of sexual experience. Particularly in the case of groups whose same-sex experience is otherwise poorly documented, Nazi-generated records might recast the narrative of modern gay history more generally. Fout discovers, for instance, that sexual practices of rural men differed significantly from those of urban men.[68]

Thomas Kühne turns our attention back to men's organizations. In his work on masculinity and the Wehrmacht, Kühne challenges not the claim that homosociality excludes homosexuality (as Sedgwick does) but, rather, the claim that masculinity as practiced in the Wehrmacht excluded femininity. According to Kühne, men of the Wehrmacht simultaneously valorized "hard" masculinity in battle and "soft" feminine tenderness to one's comrades. Interestingly, Kühne characterizes the latter as "maternal masculinity"—caring for one's comrade as a mother would—rather than as an erotic bond.[69] Kühne's claim that the mother-son bond was a model for warmth between men is a useful reminder of the significance of loving relationships between men and women who were not sexually involved (or interested).[70] Indeed, Kühne's analysis might be seen as a challenge not only to the privileging of the heterosexual couple but also to queer studies' privileging of sexuality.

[66]Gudrun Schwarz, *Eine Frau an seiner Seite: Ehefrauen in der "SS-Sippengemeinschaft"* (Hamburg, 1997).

[67]John C. Fout, "The Nazi Demonization of the Homosexual in World War II," paper presented at the conference "Departures: New Feminist Perspectives on the Holocaust," University of Minnesota, April 2001.

[68]John C. Fout, "Homosexuality in Rural Hesse and Saxony in the Nazi Era," manuscript, 2001.

[69]Thomas Kühne, "'. . . aus diesem Krieg werden nicht nur harte Männer heimkehren': Kriegskameradschaft und Männlichkeit im 20. Jahrhundert," in Kühne, ed., 174–92; see also Thomas Kühne, "Zwischen Männerbund und Volksgemeinschaft: Hitlers Soldaten und der Mythos der Kameradschaft," *Archiv für Sozialgeschichte* 38 (1998): 165–89.

[70]See also my discussion of this point in Elizabeth D. Heineman, "Whose Mothers? Generational Difference, War, and the Nazi Cult of Motherhood," *Journal of Women's History* 12, no. 4 (2001): 139–63.

If homoeroticism is marginal to Kühne's analysis of masculinity, however, heteroeroticism as an element of male camaraderie is also curiously absent. Although he describes the "masculine/hard" bonding devices of "sarcastic language and excessive alcohol use,"[71] Kühne does not inquire into heterosexually marked (and often exploitative) practices that frequently accompany such rituals of male bonding: bragging about heterosexual conquests, sharing pornography, setting out as a group to seek women for sex. Rather, he finds a tender heteroeroticism (for example, bonds with wives back home) to be in tension with the tender homosocial bonds of the Männerbund.

Perhaps Kühne's ongoing work will address these points. In the meantime, in theorizing homosocial bonds in a gendered manner, Kühne has taken a step few students of Männerbünde in Nazi Germany (outside the gay history "ghetto") have been willing to take.[72] In recent years, we have seen important studies of the internal dynamics of such groups as the Wehrmacht and the order police, which massacred Jews in occupied Poland.[73] While it is possible that the sources examined by the authors of these studies offer little information about homosexuality per se, it is impossible to miss the fact that the Wehrmacht, order police, and countless other organizations were Männerbünde. Nearly a century has passed since the publication of works that theorized a homoerotic element to the Männerbund and nearly forty years since Mosse's elaboration of the role of the Männerbund in fascism. It is now time that more historians of the male organizations so critical to the functioning of the Nazi state address masculinity and sexuality in a systematic manner.

RACE AND REPRODUCTION: WHAT'S SEX GOT TO DO WITH IT?

In his history of the movement for homosexual rights, Magnus Hirschfeld described the place of sexuality in German medical training of the 1890s:

> Venereal disease was talked about, to be sure. . . . Professors did speak about normal and abnormal births, described in anatomy the final structure and in evolutionary biology the developing structure of sexual organs . . . [but] their functions, to say nothing of sexual feelings and needs, went entirely unmentioned. . . . Such a thing as normal sex drive (that is, desires and acts) was officially nonexistent, and

[71]Thomas Kühne, "Kameradschaft—'Das Beste im Leben des Mannes,'" *Geschichte und Gesellschaft* 22 (1996). Kühne notes in passing homoerotic overtones in some soldiers' diaries and letters.

[72]On this point, see also Ann Taylor Allen, "The Holocaust and the Modernization of Gender: A Historiographical Essay," *Central European History* 30, no. 3 (1997): 349–64.

[73]Particularly important for English-language readers are Omer Bartov, *Hitler's Army: Soldiers, Nazis, and War in the Third Reich* (New York, 1991); Christopher R. Browning, *Ordinary Men: Reserve Police Battalion 101 and the Final Solution in Poland* (New York, 1992).

concerning drive disturbances, which went by the name of "perversities," people only whispered strange and horrible things.[74]

Hirschfeld's observations raise a point pertinent to the history of sexuality, not just nineteenth-century medical education. Is a history of reproduction, reproductive politics, or venereal disease a history of sexuality? Because the "racial state" implemented such radical eugenic policies, this question comes to the fore in the case of Nazi Germany.

Some of our best work in Nazi-era women's history concerns reproductive policies such as compulsory sterilization, selective abortion, screening for marriage, and marriage loans. Yet curiously, like Hirschfeld's professors, the authors of these works discuss reproduction while making little mention of the sexual desires and experiences that make conception possible in the first place. The point is not that such works are unsatisfying. In studying racialized reproductive politics, scholars like Gisela Bock and Gabriele Czarnowski have helped unravel one of the most significant aspects of racial policy under the Nazi regime: the relationship between racial ideology, population policy, and reproductive experience. The point is that histories of reproduction that omit any discussion of sexual desire or sexual experience throw into especially sharp relief the absence of crucial elements of sexuality from our discussions.

As Gisela Bock observed in an early essay, attempts to control reproduction ranged from incentives to marriage and childbearing for the racially and eugenically "fit" to disincentives, roadblocks, and compulsory sterilization for those whose offspring the regime considered undesirable. Efforts to control the composition of the population extended further to "euthanasia" and genocide.[75] By describing this continuum, Bock rejected a sharp division between studies of those privileged and those despised by the regime, and she insisted that race and sex were intertwined all along the continuum. This framework has profoundly shaped the field.

For Bock, the denial of reproductive autonomy made women, as a group, victims of Nazism. The denial of birth control and abortion turned childbearing and rearing into "compulsory labor" for "desirable" women and made sterilization the fate of "undesirables." In the context of debates about women's status in the Nazi regime, Bock's work has proven highly controversial. Rather than revisit these debates, which have been

---

[74]Quoted in James D. Steakley, "Per Scientiam Ad Justitiam: Magnus Hirschfeld and the Sexual Politics of Innate Homosexuality," in *Science and Homosexualities*, ed. Vernon A. Rosario (New York, 1997), 133–54, 135–36.

[75]Gisela Bock, "Racism and Sexism in Nazi Germany: Motherhood, Compulsory Sterilization, and the State," in *When Biology Became Destiny: Women in Weimar and Nazi Germany*, ed. Renate Bridenthal, Atina Grossmann, and Marion A. Kaplan (New York, 1984), 271–96.

well analyzed elsewhere, I will focus here on the implications of her work for a history of sexuality in Nazi Germany.[76]

In Bock's work, sexual activity per se entered the discussion when it served as a diagnostic marker. A girl's or woman's errant sexual behavior could earn her the label "asocial" or a medical diagnosis of "feebleminded," making her a candidate for sterilization. Czarnowski noted a similar phenomenon in rejections of applications to marry, and Irmgard Weyrauther found that inappropriate sexual deportment could result in the denial of a Mother's Cross to otherwise qualified women.[77] In short, "sexually promiscuous" women faced penalties in the Nazi state. The regime not only denied them medals and restricted their reproduction; it also institutionalized them, imprisoned them, and sent them to concentration camps. We will return to the subject of sexually errant women as targets of the regime later. First, however, it is important to note the limitations as well as the contributions of this research.

In emphasizing that the goal of a "perfect Aryan race" made it necessary to prevent "imperfect" Aryans from reproducing, such analyses link "sex" and "race." However, they accept the division between "races" ("Aryan," Jewish, Slavic, etc.) as a priori. Indeed, in the Reich proper, such documents as birth certificates and baptismal papers generally established "racial" membership, and evaluations of sexual behavior assumed independent knowledge of the subject's racial classification. But in broadening her investigation to occupied Europe, where the task of identifying "ethnic Germans" was complicated by such factors as linguistic difference and an absence of satisfactory documentation, Doris Bergen has discovered a more complex relationship between racial designation and sexual deportment. A woman's application to be recognized as an "ethnic German" might stand or fall on the German authorities' evaluation of her sexual history (just as men's or women's applications might stand or fall on other nonbiological criteria, such as work habits). It is not clear how often such evaluations came into play, but Bergen's observations could require that we revise our assumptions regarding the independence of Nazi notions of "race."[78]

[76]Atina Grossmann, "Feminist Debates about Women and National Socialism," *Gender and History* 3 (1991): 350–58; Adelheid von Saldern, "Victims or Perpetrators? Controversies about the Role of Women in the Nazi State," in *Nazism and German Society 1933–1945*, ed. David Crew (London, 1994), 141–65. Bock has recently devoted greater attention to female perpetrators; see Gisela Bock, "Ordinary Women in Nazi Germany: Perpetrators, Victims, Followers, and Bystanders," in *Women in the Holocaust,* ed. Dalia Ofer and Lenore J. Weitzman (New Haven, 1998), 85–100.

[77]Bock, *Zwangssterilisation*, 389–410; Gabriele Czarnowski, *Das kontrollierte Paar: Ehe- und Sexualpolitik im Nationalsozialismus*(Weinheim, 1991), esp. 205–9; Irmgard Weyrather, *Muttertag und Mutterkreuz: Der Kult um die "deutsche Mutter" im Nationalsozialismus* (Frankfurt am Main, 1993).

[78]Doris L. Bergen, "Sex, Blood, and Vulnerability: Women Outsiders in German-Occupied Europe," in Gellately and Stoltzfus, eds. Similarly, Polish men's applications for

Even for those classified a priori as "Aryans," the limitations of common analyses become clear when we inquire into the significance of sex for other categories of eugenically defined "outsiders." In Bock's analysis, "promiscuity" is simply one marker of outsider status, unique only in its greater application to women, with sterilization just one of many possible penalties. Yet other groups targeted for sterilization and denied marriage licenses, such as epileptics, became pregnant or sired children only by having sex. The fact that they were presumably sexually active (or would be upon marriage), not the mere fact of their epilepsy, made it necessary to sterilize them or deny them permission to marry.

The fact that Nazi eugenicists appear to have thought in purely reproductive terms helps explain why historians have written a "sexless" history of reproductive politics under Nazism. We have taken our cues from our sources. If we broaden our vision beyond the years 1933–45, however, we find that this "sexless" discussion of reproduction is not a given; rather, it needs to be explained. In her work on birth control and abortion, Atina Grossmann has observed that some Weimar-era reformers explicitly linked sexual pleasure with reproductive health, considering both in the context of class justice.[79] Working-class lovers met furtively in borrowed rooms or hidden stairwells, fearing intruders and rushing their encounters, while bourgeois lovers conducted their sexual affairs in comfort and privacy. Denied contraceptives and abortion, sexual intercourse brought as much fear as pleasure to working-class women. If impulsive pleasure resulted in unwanted pregnancy, the proletariat was disproportionately vulnerable to poverty and to maternal and infant death.

Because proponents of such class analyses were silenced after 1933, Grossmann too represents a Nazi-era bureaucracy that was obsessed with reproduction but uninterested in sexual pleasure. Nevertheless, her work suggests useful questions about the role of sexual pleasure in reproductive politics after 1933. Did Nazi-era eugenicists react only against Weimar-era language regarding pleasure, or did they appropriate and transform it? For example, might they have discovered a "right to pleasure" for "Aryans," whose enjoyment of sex had been assaulted by fears of what Hitler

---

"Aryanization" (that is, bureaucratic reclassification from "Slavic" to "Aryan" racial membership) upon discovery of their wartime relationships with German women depended in part on details of the sexual story. If the woman was married or a prostitute, the application was denied and the man usually executed or sent to a concentration camp; if she was single and pregnant, he might be "Aryanized" in order to enable marriage and a legitimate birth. See Elizabeth D. Heineman, *What Difference Does a Husband Make? Women and Marital Status in Nazi and Postwar Germany* (Berkeley, 1999), 58–59.

[79] Atina Grossmann, *Reforming Sex: The German Movement for Birth Control and Abortion Reform, 1920–1950* (New York, 1995). Although her book includes the Nazi and immediate postwar period, the discussion summarized here applies to the Weimar period (see esp. ix–x, 116–30). See also Randall Halle's discussion of Herbert Marcuse on this point.

termed the "Jewish disease"—syphilis?[80] What was the experience of the impoverished masses for whom increased access to contraceptives and abortion, Weimar-era reformers hoped, would bring greater pleasure? Did the crackdown on abortion and contraceptives mean greater sexual misery? Did the booming economy and the expansion of social programs for those who qualified make sex without contraceptives more pleasurable, since unplanned pregnancy less often meant poverty?

Considering how much we know about sterilization and abortion, it is surprising how poorly informed we are about contraceptive use in Nazi Germany. Historians frequently refer to directives that limited the advertisement and distribution of contraceptives and note that the use of contraceptives *other than condoms* was criminalized in 1941. But condoms constitute a pretty big loophole, and their use needs further research. Vending machines selling condoms could be found in hotels and public toilets at least as early as 1927, and they remained there after 1933 despite new regulations regarding the packaging and advertising of condoms and new restrictions on who was licensed to sell them.[81] During the war, military men by the millions were provisioned with condoms.

To be sure, health authorities intended condoms to be used to prevent the spread of STDs, not as contraceptives.[82] Because of their association with STDs and prostitution, many potential users considered condoms unsavory. Furthermore, condom use was a male, not a female, prerogative. However, just because health authorities endorsed condoms only for STD prevention does not mean that the German public was unaware of their contraceptive applications. Just because women were dependent on men's cooperation does not mean that men never agreed to use condoms for contraceptive purposes—or, for that matter, that men never *initiated* such use. While condoms may be of secondary interest in the history of women's struggle to control their own fertility, they are important in the history of contraceptive practice among cooperating couples.

Annette Timm has argued that we must look beyond the Nazis' public declarations on race and reproductive health to consider the unspoken ways that authorities may have been concerned with sexual pleasure. Although the documentary trail indicates that it was a fear of sterility and congenital syphilis that led the regime to construct brothels for military men, Timm

[80]Adolf Hitler, *Mein Kampf*, trans. Ralph Manheim (Boston, 1943), 253.

[81]Nazi-era illustrated magazines, prohibited from advertising contraceptives, instead carried advertisements for catalogs of "hygienic rubber articles," an easily recognized euphemism for condoms and pessaries. See Elizabeth Heineman, "Sexual Consumer Culture in the Miracle Years," paper presented at the conference "The Miracle Years Revisited," Oxford, Mississippi, April 2002. On condom automats in foreign laborers' barracks, see Lagrou, 145; on teenagers' access to condoms, see Waite, "Teenage Sexuality."

[82]Annette F. Timm, "The Politics of Fertility: Bevölkerungspolitik and Health Care in Berlin, 1919–1972," Ph.D. diss., University of Chicago, 1999, 115–17, 408–10.

notes that the spread of STDs in the general population during the war elicited little public-health activity. This has led her to conclude that military brothels may have served another, more important, function: to improve men's military performance by providing heterosexual outlets.[83] In a sense, Timm's thesis is a logical extension of the analyses of brothels in concentration camps, which can *only* be understood as an incentive for male inmates, since their reproductive health was a decidedly low priority for the authorities.[84] In declaring that the regime's noisy concern with reproductive health may not be the whole story, however, Timm illuminates a methodological challenge. Assumptions about men's "need" for heterosexual outlets may have been so widely held that Nazi policymakers found it unnecessary to discuss the matter explicitly. If this is the case, historians must consider indirect evidence as well as what appears directly in the mountains of documents.

In the case of "race defilement," we may be closer to integrating discussions of Nazi racial policy with our historical subjects' experiences of sexual intimacy. There are two reasons for this. First, in their attempts to humanize relationships that the regime saw as purely racial contacts and persecuted viciously, scholars have frequently presented accounts of individuals. These stories rarely include details of the subjects' sex lives per se, but they embed the presumed sexual activity in a genuinely human experience.[85] Second, records of investigations of "race defilement" include detailed accounts of sexual events. These records offer information about how, when, and what kind of sex figured into relationships. They also say much about the authorities' obsession with sexual practice.

The literature on "race defilement" between Germans and either foreign slave-laborers or prisoners of war has focused on the intersecting gender, racial, and political concerns that made both partners vulnerable

---

[83]See Timm, this volume; also Annette F. Timm, "The Ambivalent Outsider: Prostitution, Promiscuity, and VD Control in Nazi Berlin," in Gellately and Stoltzfus, eds.; for a more limited but useful discussion, see Franz Seidler, *Prostitution, Homosexualität, Selbstverstümmelung: Probleme der deutschen Sanitätsführing 1939–1945* (Neckargemünd, 1977), 135–36. See also Insa Meinen, "Wehrmacht und Prostitution: Zur Reglementierung der Geschlechterbeziehungen durch die deutsche Militärverwaltung im besetzten Frankreich 1940–1944," *1999: Zeitschrift für Sozialgeschichte des 20. und 21. Jahrhunderts* 14, no. 2 (1999): 35–55.

[84]Kogon; for more recent discussions, see Christa Paul, *Zwangsprostitution: Staatlich errichtete Bordelle im Nationalsozialismus* (Berlin, 1994); Christa Schulz, "Weibliche Häftlinge aus Ravensbrück in Bordellen der Männerkonzentrationslager," in *Frauen in Konzentrationslagern: Bergen-Belsen, Ravensbrück*, ed. Claus Füllberg-Stolberg et al. (Bremen, 1994), 135–46; Ulrich Bauche et al., eds., *Arbeit und Vernichtung: Das Konzentrationslager Neuengamme, 1938–1945* (Hamburg, 1991), 225–30.

[85]Marion A. Kaplan, *Between Dignity and Despair: Jewish Life in Nazi Germany* (New York, 1998), esp. 74–93; Robert Gellately, *The Gestapo and German Society: Enforcing Racial Policy 1933–1945* (Oxford, 1990); Raul Hilberg, *Perpetrators Victims Bystanders: The Jewish Catastrophe, 1933–1945* (New York, 1992), 131–38.

upon exposure.[86] This, however, begins the story at the end of the relationship and tells us nothing about the interplay of sex, love, and power within the relationship itself. As prisoners or slaves, were foreign men deferential to their German female partners, or did deep-seated habits of male dominance and female subordination characterize such couples' intimate interactions? Did sexual intimacy confuse the hierarchies that presumably defined nonsexual relationships between German women and foreign men? The intersection of power and intimacy in "German-Jewish" relationships has been better articulated.[87] In mixed marriages, the non-Jewish partner could exercise the privilege of a quick divorce, leaving the Jewish partner alone vulnerable, but those who failed to divorce were themselves subject to harassment. As Marion Kaplan reveals, the result was an astonishing variety of human experiences, such as that of the "Aryan" husband whose refusal to divorce cost him his medical practice but who in deference to the new order informed his wife that they could no longer have sex.[88]

We might expect concerns about reproduction to have been central in the regime's treatment of race defilement. Yet, as recent work demonstrates, sex in this context, as in the context of eugenics, had "a life of its own" that extended beyond any connection to conception. In interpreting the Nuremberg Laws, Saul Friedländer notes, the Supreme Court instructed the police and courts to consider heterosexual activities that served "to satisfy the sex drive of at least one of the partners," even if sterility or nonpenetrative activity ruled out any danger of conception.[89] In her analysis of legal proceedings against accused race defilers, Patricia Szobar has found that the police's and courts' obsession with the details of heterosexual practice went far beyond what was necessary to secure a conviction and stood completely apart from concerns about reproduction. Rather, the proceedings were part of a "discursive struggle to define the nature of erotic experience within the aegis of the law." Given the state's efforts to

---

[86]See, for example, Bernd Boll, "'. . . das gesunde Volksempfinden auf das Gröbste verletzt': Die Offenburger Strafjustiz und der 'verbotene Umgang mit Kriegsgefangenen' während des 2. Weltkriegs," *Die Ortenau*, no. 71 (1991): 645–78; Heineman, *What Difference*, 56–59; Gerd Steffens, "Die praktische Widerlegung des Rassismus: Verbotene Liebe und ihre Verfolgung," in *"Ich war immer gut zu meiner Russin": Zur Struktur und Praxis des Zwangsarbeitssystems im Zweiten Weltkrieg in der Region Südhessen*, ed. Fred Dorn and Klaus Heuer (Pfaffenweiler, 1991), 185–200; Kundrus, this volume.

[87]Cases involving a German man and a foreign woman were less often prosecuted and thus have received less study. See, however, Jill R. Stephenson, "Triangle: Foreign Workers, German Civilians, and the Nazi Regime: War and Society in Württemberg, 1939–1945," *German Studies Review* 15, no. 2 (1992): 339–59.

[88]Kaplan, 90.

[89]Judgment quoted in Saul Friedländer, *Nazi Germany and the Jews* (New York, 1997), 159; see also Hermann Graml, "Die Behandlung der an Fällen von sogenannter Rassenschande beteiligten 'deutschblutigen' Personen," *Gutachten des Instituts für Zeitgeschichte* 1 (1958): 72–76.

label nonprocreative sex as deviant, the result was ironic if not surprising to anyone familiar with Foucault's analysis of the Victorians. Legal discourse, according to Szobar, "served to expand the realm of the sexual by attributing sexual meaning to even the most casual social interaction," such as a Jewish man's glance at an "Aryan" woman across the street.[90] At the same time, the records are full of incidents that were nonpenetrative yet undisputedly sexual by most Western definitions, since they resulted in orgasm: partners masturbated in each other's presence, masturbated each other, and performed oral sex.

A careful scholar's response should be to wonder not only at the Nazis' ability to find sex in nonsexual encounters but also at our own tendency to examine noncommercial, heterosexual acts only in the context of reproduction. We must not only remember that other kinds of sex exist but also resist treating them as marginal (as "foreplay" or as the sexual play of immature partners, automatically less significant than the "real thing"). Even allowing for the possibility of forced, false confessions, the court records make clear that penetration was not always central to Germans' erotic experience, perhaps because other practices were pleasurable, perhaps because they were good contraceptive strategy. Furthermore, the drive to protect German "blood *and* honor"—racial purity but also more nebulous standards of propriety—reveals that the Nazis were not *solely* concerned with reproduction. If, as historians, we consider noncommercial heterosexual activity only in its capacity for conception, we do more than just miss an important element of human experience in Nazi Germany. We also overlook an aspect of sexuality that deeply concerned the authorities.

HETEROSEXUALLY ERRANT WOMEN, SOCIAL CONTROL, AND MODERNIZATION

Research on heterosexually nonconformist women, ranging from prostitutes to women who had sexual relationships with forced laborers during the war, paints a grim picture of the costs of deviating from the regime's sexual standards. This very range, however, raises interesting questions about the ways the Nazis' identification of outsiders linked sexuality to other criteria such as race, class, and medical or psychiatric condition. Existing research suggests that the link between sexuality and gender, at least, was clear: the gender was female. For women, nonmarital sex was a primary marker of "asociability" or "feeblemindedness." For men, it was not. In his study of "asocials," Klaus Scherer prints the succinct words of Wolfgang Knorr, physician and expert on "asocials": "Men and women of equal hereditary basis reveal their inadequacy for social life in different ways. The wife or sexual partner corresponding to a criminal or work-shy

---

[90]See Szobar, this volume.

man is the prostitute or, later, slattern."[91] Errant male sexuality was essentially synonymous with criminal sexuality: nonmarital sexual violence, sex with children, and homosexual forays.[92]

Recognizing that heterosexually nonconformist women faced significant pressures prior to 1933, scholars have inquired into questions of change and continuity. To what extent did the Nazis' treatment of heterosexually errant women represent an expansion of previously existing trends toward control in the name of modern science and reform, and to what extent did the Nazi era signal something new? The Nazis did not invent the double standard by which women's nonmarital sex was brutally condemned while men's was considered regrettable but unavoidable. Rather, they inherited it from the nineteenth-century bourgeoisie, which had articulated the ideology of "separate spheres," including distinct sexual expectations for men and women. Michael Burleigh has discovered horrifying consequences of popular acceptance of this ideology in cases of Germans who had women of their families institutionalized because of "moral deficiency" and declined to remove their relatives even when they learned that inmates of the same institutions were being "euthanized."[93]

Burleigh's larger concern, however, is not the sexual double standard but, rather, the role of modern science and the welfare state in creating an environment that made euthanasia possible—indeed, that welcomed it as a solution to social strains. He thus engages historians such as Detlev Peukert, who find in modern science and the modern welfare state the roots of Nazism.[94] Medical professionals lobbied for a law enabling mandatory sterilization prior to 1933; Weimar-era social workers demanded legislation that would permit them to limit "asocials'" freedom of movement.[95] Women perceived as promiscuous and prostitutes were among those whose behavior such measures were intended to correct or isolate, as Gaby Zürn illustrates in her treatment of Hamburg prostitutes.[96] Social

[91]Quoted in Klaus Scherer, *"Asozial" im Dritten Reich: Die vergessenen Verfolgten* (Münster, 1990), 15.

[92]For brief discussions of male sexual crimes, see Michael Burleigh, *Death and Deliverance: "Euthanasia" in Germany 1900–1945* (New York, 1994), 184–86; Patrick Wagner, *Volksgemeinschaft ohne Verbrecher: Konzeptionen und Praxis der Kriminalpolizei in der Zeit der Weimarer Republik und des Nationalsozialismus* (Hamburg, 1996).

[93]Burleigh, 68–69.

[94]Detlev J. K. Peukert, "The Genesis of the 'Final Solution' from the Spirit of Science," in *Reevaluating the Third Reich*, ed. Thomas Childers and Jane Caplan (New York, 1993), 234–52. Burleigh, however, also emphasizes the "medieval" conditions that prevailed in psychiatric institutions and the nonindustrialized killing of the post-1941 euthanasia program (see esp. 238–66).

[95]Bock, *Zwangssterilisation*; see also the edited collections *Der Griff nach der Bevölkerung: Aktualität und Kontinuität nazistischer Bevölkerungspolitik*, ed. Heidrun Kaupen-Haas (Nördlingen, 1986); *Soziale Arbeit und Faschismus: Volkspflege und Pädagogik im Nationalsozialismus*, ed. Hans-Uwe Otto and Heinz Sünker (Bielefeld, 1986).

[96]Gaby Zürn, "'A ist Prostituiertentyp': Zur Ausgrenzung und Vernichtung von Prostituierten und moralisch nicht-angepaßten Frauen im Nationalsozialistischen Hamburg," in Projektgruppe für die vergessenen Opfer des NS-Regimes, ed., 128–51.

workers and medical professionals, frustrated by their lack of progress in the Great Depression and with only the weak Weimar state to support them, welcomed the Nazi state's support of their efforts. The path from social control to sterilization, euthanasia, and genocide was, in a horrifying way, logical.

Although they do not use the term "cumulative radicalization," studies of the institutional structures of oppression that emphasize interactions among psychiatry, medicine, social work, academic scientists, the police, and the judiciary suggest a process parallel to the "cumulative radicalization" that, according to functionalists, helps to explain the Holocaust.[97] As members of varying professions tried to expand their authority, the police and judiciary identified certain individuals as criminal, physicians gave them medical diagnoses and psychiatrists psychiatric diagnoses, and social workers pointed to "asocial" behaviors. Each office might also, however, expand its territory by working with other offices, and new administrative guidelines encouraged cooperation in the interests of efficiency. The simultaneous cooperation and competition among these offices drew sexually errant women into an ever-tightening web. All offices had an interest in expanding the interpretive framework for individuals' missteps; none had an interest in questioning the seriousness of errant behaviors.[98]

Many historians have noted the importance of professional ambition in medical professionals' decisions to work with the euthanasia program.[99] The theme of careerism is less well developed in the literature on sexuality, but careerism as a motivation for physicians researching methods of sterilization or "cures" for homosexuals deserves further study. Peter von Rönn has examined Hans Bürger-Prinz, who built a successful career by pathologizing homosexuals in ways convenient to the regime. Historians might similarly consider the ways professionals' attention to heterosexually "promiscuous" women could simultaneously advance their careers and provide ammunition for the regime's persecution of the sexually errant.[100]

[97]A useful summary of debates between "functionalists" and "intentionalists" can be found in Ian Kershaw, *The Nazi Dictatorship: Problems and Perspectives of Interpretation,* 4th ed. (New York, 2000), 69–133.

[98]Scherer, 40–41; Christiane Rothmaler, "Die 'Volksgemeinschaft' wird ausgehorcht und 'wichtiges Material der Zukunft' zusammengetragen," in Projektgruppe für die vergessenen Opfer des NS-Regimes, ed., 109–17, esp. 109–10; Bock, *Zwangssterilisation,* 182–209; similarly, Wagner notes the overlapping competencies of the Kripo and Gestapo in pursuing "race defilement" (251).

[99]Claudia Koonz, "Ethical Dilemmas and Nazi Eugenics: Single-Issue Dissent in Religious Contexts," in *Resistance against the Third Reich, 1933–1990,* ed. Michael Geyer and John W. Boyer (Chicago, 1994), 15–38; Otto and Sünker, eds.; Gitta Sereny, *Into That Darkness: An Examination of Conscience* (New York, 1983); Henry Friedlander, *The Origins of Nazi Genocide: From Euthanasia to the Final Solution* (Chapel Hill, 1995); Robert Proctor, *Racial Hygiene: Medicine under the Nazis* (Cambridge, Mass., 1988).

[100]Rönn. On the postwar impact of these professionals, see Sophinette Becker, "Bemerkungen zur Debatte über Bürger-Prinz," *Zeitschrift für Sexualforschung* 4, no. 3

While recognizing that the drive for social control in the name of modern science predated 1933, historians have recently argued for a more refined consideration of change and continuity over that date. Grossmann insists that, despite the eugenic nature of Weimar-era population programs, only a sharp break in 1933 could transform the programs to the Nazi racist vision.[101] Birthe Kundrus notes that while some professional groups were centrally committed to "modern" precepts of racial hygiene, others retained other reference points, such as the family social work tradition.[102] I have argued that change versus continuity depended in part on the targets of efforts to control heterosexually errant women and the institutions called upon to control them.[103] Girls and women who offended common bourgeois standards of female sexual behavior ("promiscuous" women, prostitutes) had been the focus of official attention and social ostracism well before 1933, and the Nazi government inherited institutions and personnel accustomed to working with this population. Adulterous wives of military men—also a central concern for Kundrus—appeared as a "special problem" during war, and although adultery was also unacceptable in peacetime, the apparent mass phenomenon of wartime adultery required that the state develop new ways of dealing with such women, balancing "public" interests with the interests of the women's husbands.[104] Finally, those who violated Nazi strictures against "interracial" sex confronted a novel legal structure and apparatus of enforcement in Nazi Germany. While the first two groups ("promiscuous" women and adulterous war wives) were strictly female, this last group included men "of German blood" as well as male "non-Aryan" lovers of German women.

Recent research demonstrates tensions between change and continuity even for women who had long been ostracized because of their sexual behavior: prostitutes. With the reintroduction of regimented prostitution in 1933, local police could prosecute women suspected of practicing prostitution without a license and establish conditions (such as restrictions on movement) that limited the liberties of licensed prostitutes.[105] Significantly,

(1991): 265–70; Ernst Klee, *Was sie taten, was sie wurden: Ärzte, Juristen und andere Beteiligte am Kranken- oder Judenmord* (Frankfurt am Main, 1986).

[101]Grossmann, *Reforming Sex.*

[102]Birthe Kundrus, "Frauen und Nationalsozialismus," *Archiv für Sozialgeschichte* 36 (1996): 481–99.

[103]Heineman, *What Difference.*

[104]Birthe Kundrus, "Die Unmoral deutscher Soldatenfrauen: Diskurs, Alltagsverhalten und Ahndungspraxis 1939–1945," in *Zwischen Karriere und Verfolgung: Handlungsspielräume von Frauen im Nationalsozialistischen Deutschland,* ed. Kirsten Heinsohn (Frankfurt am Main, 1997), 96–110; Birthe Kundrus, *Kriegerfrauen: Familienpolitik und Geschlechtsverhältnisse im Ersten und Zweiten Weltkrieg* (Hamburg, 1995).

[105]In addition to Zürn, see Gisela Bock, "'Keine Arbeitskräfte in diesem Sinne': Prostituierte im Nazi-Staat," in *"Wir sind Frauen wie andere auch!" Prostituierte und ihre Kämpfe,* ed. Pieke Biermann (Reinbek, 1980); Sabine Haustein, "Zur Geschichte von

however, the 1933 measure reversed a 1927 law that had banned the registration and regimentation of prostitution in the name of modern reform. Physicians and social reformers, including feminists, had argued for medical control of STDs rather than police control of prostitutes. The rational methods of modern science triumphed over the moralistic, judgmental practices of the nineteenth century, which had blamed a particular group of women for the spread of disease and, unsurprisingly, failed to control it.[106] The 1927 law, however, was not free of restrictive features, such as mandatory STD checks for those "strongly suspected" of carrying disease—a provision that, as Gaby Zürn emphasizes, resulted in the de facto continued surveillance of prostitutes. Furthermore, with health and social welfare agencies, not the police, now responsible for work with prostitutes, medical professionals and social workers performed punitive functions formerly reserved for the police—assigning prostitutes to workhouses for "reeducation," for example.[107] Observing these consequences of the 1927 law, Bock offered a classic "continuity" argument in an early essay: Weimar-era "reform" helped to pave the way for the Nazis' treatment of "asocials."[108]

New work challenges this emphasis on continuity on two counts. Julia Roos has found the liberating features of the 1927 law to have been more significant than heretofore acknowledged. Police continued to harass prostitutes, but prostitutes were now political subjects who could protest this harassment—indeed, who organized against it. The redefinition of licensed prostitutes as women with deficient civil liberties in 1933 thus marked a profound reversal of Weimar liberalism.[109] Drawing attention to questions of change and continuity within the Nazi period, Annette Timm has traced a shift in the uses of licensed prostitution, from a peacetime focus on public health and the control of "asocials," to wartime efforts to maximize men's fighting capacity by offering sexual opportunities.[110]

Timm's and Roos's research reopens questions about the relationship between modern science, social welfare, and Nazism. If modern science, social welfare, and Nazism enjoyed such affinity in so many other spheres of

---

Prostituierten in Leipzig in der NS-Zeit," in *Frauenalltag in Leipzig: Weibliche Lebenszusammenhänge im 19. und 20. Jahrhundert*, ed. Susanne Schuetz (Weimar, 1997); Margot D. Kreuzer, *Prostitution: Eine sozialgeschichtliche Untersuchung in Frankfurt a.M.: Von der Syphilis bis AIDS* (Stuttgart, 1988).

[106]Elisabeth Meyer-Renschhausen, *Weibliche Kultur und soziale Arbeit: Eine Geschichte der Frauenbewegung am Beispiel Bremens 1810–1927* (Cologne, 1989); Nancy Ruth Reagin, *A German Women's Movement: Class and Gender in Hanover, 1880–1933* (Chapel Hill, 1995); Timm, "The Politics of Fertility."

[107]Zürn.

[108]Bock, "'Keine Arbeitskräfte in diesem Sinne.'"

[109]See Roos, this volume; also Julia Roos, "Prostitutes, Civil Society, and the State in Weimar Germany," in *Paradoxes of Civil Society: New Perspectives on Modern German and British History*, ed. Frank Trentmann (New York, 2000), 263–81.

[110]Timm, "The Ambivalent Outsider."

action, might this affinity have had unique limits in the sphere of sexuality? If deregimentation was a triumph for modern science and social welfare, did the Nazis *reject* modern science and social welfare in reintroducing regimentation? Or did they *redirect* the object of "modern" methods of state control, sacrificing public health writ large in order better to rationalize the sexual lives of military and laboring men?

Rather than a woman's exchange of sex for a client's money or goods, we might see this as an exchange in which the state—not the woman—offered sex in exchange for men's labor and loyalty. This analysis can apply not only to military brothels but also to brothels for concentration camp inmates and for foreign laborers. The fact that the prostitute becomes nearly invisible in this scenario testifies to her unfree condition: even less than registered prostitutes in more "normal" times, these women could not opt out of the exchange or bargain for its terms. Men and the state could: the state could withhold access to brothels, and men could choose not to visit them.

Understanding this as an exchange between state and men may help us to recognize the grotesque inappropriateness of the word "prostitution" in this context. Christa Paul calls it "forced prostitution" in order to establish a parallel with other types of forced labor during the Nazi period, Christa Schikorra simply calls it "forced labor," and the collective authors of *Sittengeschichte des Zweiten Weltkrieges* bluntly call it "rape."[111] To be sure, women sometimes volunteered for work in the brothels, calculating that brothel work was preferable to death by starvation and overwork in the concentration camps or to hunger and deprivation in occupied Europe. But in civilian settings, women also sometimes decide to submit to rape, favoring it over death or a severe beating. The nature of the exchange in the Nazi setting—between state and man—might require a new analytical framework for understanding the identity and activity of the rapist. Was it the man, who performed the sexual act knowing of the woman's unfree condition and who had the option not to visit the brothel? Or was it the state, which denied the woman free will to choose whether, when, or with whom to have sex and which established violent conditions for the sexual act? Understanding this type of prostitution as an exchange between men and the state is a profound insight into the "rationalized" uses of male sexuality—and its costs to women.

SEX AND THE HOLOCAUST

What does it mean to explore sexuality in connection with genocide? There is always a danger that sexual images, rather than helping us understand genocide, might serve a pornographic function of simultaneously disgusting

[111]Paul; Christa Schikorra, "Prostitution weiblicher KZ-Häftlinge als Zwangsarbeit," *Dachauer Hefte* 16 (2000): 112–24; Magnus Hirschfeld, Andreas Gaspar, and F. Aquila, eds., *Sittengeschichte des Zweiten Weltkrieges* (Hanau, 1968), 341.

and fascinating the reader, making genocide, in a perverse way, appealing. Omer Bartov has described how even Israeli youth—the literal and figurative children of the survivors—were titillated and not just sobered by images of sexual sadism in the camps.[112] Furthermore, survivors' testimony about sexual shame raises difficult questions about common methods of representing the Holocaust in illustrated books and in the classroom. If appearing naked before members of a shooting squad humiliated the victims, do we demean them yet further if we include in our publications, course materials, and museum exhibits photographs of naked Jews at the killing fields, photographs whose making marked a further moment of dehumanization?[113]

Problematic modes of representation and reception, however, should not be confused with serious attempts to understand the intersections of sexuality and genocide. The earliest postwar publications on the concentration camps discussed such subjects as the brothels, Kapos who demanded homosexual sex, and moments of sexual humiliation for women such as appearing nude before guards; we know these phenomena existed, and we cannot wish them away. We can only decide whether to investigate them as carefully as we investigate other aspects of the "concentration camp universe." Failure to investigate evidence that appears time and time again is, in an academic sense, bad scholarship. In a moral sense, it disregards the imperatives both to commemorate past victims and to prevent future atrocities. If we shy away from confronting the impact of sexual torture on a victim of the Nazi genocide, we have diminished that victim's sufferings. If we shy away from exposing the ways that sex enables people to commit genocide, and if future regimes successfully use sex to motivate their killers, we bear some small part of the responsibility for having willfully refused to learn everything we can from the best-documented genocide in history.

This portion of the essay will examine sex and the Holocaust from two perspectives: the victims' and the perpetrators'. We cannot review the vast genre of survivors' memoirs, but because scholars rely so heavily on it in their discussions of sexuality in the camps, it is worth noting some of the themes that emerge.[114] Women memoirists recall their sexual humiliation upon being shaved and appearing nude before SS guards. They describe mixed feelings about ceasing to menstruate: they feared becoming infertile, but they also feared that visible menstrual flow could result in torture or

[112]Omer Bartov, "Kitsch and Sadism in Ka-Tzetnik's Other Planet: Israeli Youth Imagine the Holocaust," *Jewish Social Studies* 3, no. 2 (1997): 42–76.

[113]Sybil Milton, "The Camera as Weapon: Documentary Photography and the Holocaust," *Simon Wiesenthal Center Annual* 1 (1984): 45–68; Marianne Hirsch, "Surviving Images: Holocaust Photographs and the Work of Postmemory," in *Visual Culture and the Holocaust*, ed. Barbie Zelizer (New Brunswick, 2001), 244 n. 232.

[114]Edited collections and teaching materials most often draw on memoir literature to articulate sexual themes of victims of the Holocaust; most usefully, see Carol Ann Rittner and John K. Roth, eds., *Different Voices: Women and the Holocaust*, 1st ed. (New York, 1993).

selection for the gas chambers. They note the grim situation of pregnant women. They describe camp brothels, lesbian relationships between inmates (though never their own), and exchanges of sex for food or protection (again, not their own). The fact that sexuality is so often connected to sheer survival (sex could be exchanged for food; pregnancy or menstruation could mean death) should alert us to the importance of the subject.[115]

Accounts of inmates who had lesbian relationships or exchanged sex for food reflect complicated attitudes toward such activities.[116] While acknowledging that these women suffered enormously and feared for their lives, memoirists often express disgust at their actions. Such sexual activities would have warranted condemnation outside the concentration camp, and traditional standards of morality did not disappear when prisoners entered the camp gates.

Historians, like memoirists, display mixed attitudes about discussing female sexuality. Even those researching women often seem more comfortable integrating motherhood than sex into their accounts. Frequently, they let reports of sexual activity stand without further analysis: while no historian can be faulted for citing a primary source, the danger of making inappropriate commentary appears too great to risk.[117] For some historians, it is only the victims' and survivors' insistence upon recording sexual stories that legitimizes the effort.[118]

The literature about the camp brothels reveals this ambivalence. Both Christa Paul and Christa Schikorra note that memoirists who were not brothel inmates often dwell on the fact that such inmates were rarely forced into brothels and that many had been prostitutes or "asocials" before their internment. Speculation about inmates' willingness to perform their duties otherwise arises only in reference to those who, in the eyes of other prisoners, were complicit with the SS administration—such as Kapos.[119] In fact, in a life-threatening environment that offered only varieties of compulsion, some inmates were literally forced into the brothels. Others accepted the assignment with the hope that it would offer greater chances

[115]Among the many that explicitly discuss sexuality are Lengyel; Fania Fénelon and Marcelle Routier, *Playing for Time* (New York, 1977). Oral and unpublished written testimonies of survivors are also an important source for sexuality and sexual abuse; see, for example, Felicja Karay, "Women in the Forced-Labor Camps," in Ofer and Weitzman, eds., 285–309.

[116]See Hester Baer and Elizabeth R. Baer's treatment of this problem in their introduction to and annotations of Nanda Herbermann, Hester Baer, and Elizabeth Roberts Baer, *The Blessed Abyss: Inmate #6582 in Ravensbrück Concentration Camp for Women* (Detroit, 2000). The same is true of interview subjects; see Joan Ringelheim, "Women and the Holocaust: A Reconsideration of Research," in Rittner and Roth, eds., 373-418.

[117]For example, Ruth Bondy, "Women in Theresienstadt and the Family Camp in Birkenau," in Ofer and Weitzman, eds., 310–26.

[118]Dalia Ofer, "Gender Issues in Diaries and Testimonies of the Ghetto: The Case of Warsaw," in ibid., 143–67, esp. 162–63.

[119]Paul, 38; Schikorra.

of survival than the alternatives.[120] In making assignments, camp administrators sometimes sought prisoners who had worked as prostitutes before incarceration, but such women were not the only inmates of the brothels, and it would be abhorrent to assume that former prostitutes found work in a camp brothel a "good fit." In any case, unlike Kapos, brothel inmates did not exercise power over other inmates.

What do we know about the experiences of brothel inmates? We know that conditions in the brothels were better than those in much of the rest of the camp. Brothel inmates had more food and shorter working hours than other inmates; they had furnished rooms, clean clothes, and access to washing facilities. Former brothel inmates sometimes report on displays of humanity by their prisoner-visitors, displays that ranged from bringing gifts (to women who had to provide sex anyway) to providing relief from overwork, either by declining sex or by arranging that prisoners under their authority in the camp hierarchy not demand sex. In the end, of course, camp administrators broke such promises as release from imprisonment after six months' brothel service, and the women returned to their former posts physically degraded, sick, and sometimes subject to medical experimentation. The advantages of brothel work did not overcome the generally deadly environment, but a decision to accept brothel work could buy an inmate just enough time to survive the war.

For scholars examining sites outside the brothels, the role of sex in preserving life has been an equally difficult theme. In an innovative essay published in *Signs* in 1985 and revised for John Roth and Carol Ritter's 1993 collection, *Different Voices*, philosopher and oral historian Joan Ringelheim openly explored her complicated relationship to this subject. Ringelheim's interviewees told many stories about their sexual lives during the Holocaust. After drafting material that emphasized the role of female support networks in women's survival, Ringelheim became concerned that the resulting work verged on "valorizing [the] oppression" in which these stories of strength emerged at the expense of a full reckoning with the ultimate fate of death that awaited most of Europe's Jews. Turning to the statistical record, Ringelheim found that women were more vulnerable than men to deportation from the ghettos to the death camps—a death sentence against which women's friendships were powerless.[121] Ringelheim thus faced a classic quandary. If, in the end, only death matters, then everything else becomes trivial.[122] Yet focusing on the statistical record eliminated the route through which stories of the texture of life—and not just the fact of death—emerged. As the work of Ringelheim and others

---

[120]See also Schulz.

[121]Ringelheim, "Women and the Holocaust." On women's greater vulnerability to deportation, see also Hilberg, 126–30.

[122]On this point, see also Judith Tydor Baumel, *Double Jeopardy: Gender and the Holocaust* (London, 1998), 26.

demonstrates, however, the texture of life and the fact of death cannot be fully separated, and sex was sometimes crucial to the connection.

As uncomfortable as it may be, we should consider how sex marked power within victim communities and not just the ways that it marked the German authorities' power over their victims. Jewish female survivors, for example, describe Jewish men's exploitation of powerful positions in the ghettos to reward women who made themselves sexually available and withhold life-saving favors from those who did not.[123] We should also consider how sex might have served as an affirmation of life or a source of strength and comfort. Discussions of concentration camps typically proceed from the assumption that life was sex-segregated, but there were exceptions: the Terezin "model camp," the "family camps" in Auschwitz for Gypsies and deportees from Terezin.[124] The ghettos, of course, were a heterosocial environment.[125] Marion Kaplan has documented the ways sexual relationships with non-Jewish Germans both secured protection and expressed love for Jewish Germans in hiding; Nechama Tec has noted that sex could be both exploitative and life-affirming in partisan bands.[126] As Ringelheim's self-criticism indicates, however, analyses of any aspect of life—sexual or otherwise—in the ghettos, camps, or hiding places must integrate the overwhelming presence of death and must grapple with the awesome power that German authorities had over all people marked for annihilation.

Since female witnesses so often refer to pregnancy, menstruation, and sexual humiliation, references to sexuality have helped to argue the need to discuss the uniquely female experiences of the Holocaust. The point is well made, but we should be careful: raising sexuality solely for this purpose can reinforce the equation of women with sex. Women's sexuality did not create uniquely female experiences because sexuality was uniquely female but, rather, because men's sexuality shaped different experiences.

Male inmates did not need to worry about menstruation or pregnancy. They did, however, have to worry about guards and Kapos who demanded sex; they exchanged sex for food and food for sex; they visited the brothels. In addition to reports by memoirists, we now have the scholarship of

[123]Ofer; Ringelheim, "Women and the Holocaust"; Bondy.

[124]The rare writings on these sexually integrated camps have little or nothing to say about inmates' sexual lives. On the Gypsy camp in Auschwitz, see Guenter Lewy, *The Nazi Persecution of the Gypsies* (New York, 2000), 152–66; on the Terezin family camp in Auschwitz, see Nili Keren, "The Family Camp," in *Anatomy of the Auschwitz Death Camp*, ed. Yisrael Gutman and Michael Berenbaum (Bloomington, 1994); Bondy.

[125]In addition to works on the ghettos cited elsewhere in this essay, see Raul Hilberg's brief mention of sex in the ghettos in Hilberg, 127.

[126]Kaplan, esp. 208, 220, 261 n. 215. See also Ofer, 148–54; on sexual exploitation of hidden Jews, see Joan Ringelheim, "The Split between Gender and the Holocaust," in Ofer and Weitzman, eds., 340–50, esp. 342–43; Nechama Tec, "Women among the Forest Partisans," in ibid., 223–33.

historians such as Andreas Pretzel and Joachim Müller on homosexual activity—consensual and exploitative—in camps.[127] We do not have equivalent work on men's brothel visits or exchanges of food for sex, but our knowledge of these phenomena (via consideration of the "sexually marked" women whose sex involved exchange) raises important questions. After all, if brothel inmates were better fed, clothed, and housed than other women, it was not because the camp administration wanted to treat them nicely. Conditions in the brothels were good because clean, well-fed women in private rooms provided greater sexual pleasure for the men who visited them.

Despite postwar assertions that hunger and overwork caused male prisoners to lose their sexual appetites, camp administrators evidently knew otherwise when they calculated that passes to brothels would motivate inmates to good work and obedience.[128] Men who worked well enough to obtain this privilege and who chose to keep it rather than barter it away were surely a select group among inmates. If sexual desire and competence were characteristics of what Wolfgang Sofsky terms the "prisoner aristocracy," however, we might want to investigate the meanings and uses of sex in men's struggle for survival.[129] Perhaps sex was not just a perquisite for the "prominents," in the ways Sofsky describes; perhaps instead, as Paul hypothesizes, demonstrated sexual vitality and not just the ability to gain a pass to the brothel helped to establish hierarchies among male prisoners.[130] If camp administrators believed potential participants in resistance activity were sexually alive enough for the offer of a brothel pass to be useful in corrupting them, then this suggests another way that male sexual virility may have intersected with camp social structures and even possibilities of resistance.

We can comfortably say that SS men who demanded sex from brothel inmates added sexual abuse to their long list of crimes. Did male inmates who visited the brothels also victimize their sexual partners? Men who obtained brothel passes evidently had a choice about whether or not to require sex; brothel inmates recall visitors who declined it. However, inmate visitors may have feared that they risked punishment if they did not perform: a peephole in the door made brothel visits a spectacle for guards. Camp authorities thus extended the general atmosphere of danger into the brothels. For this reason, although some inmate visitors may

[127]Plant; Heger; Pretzel, "Ich wünsche"; Joachim Müller, "'Wie die Bewegung, so die Verpflegung': Die Strafkompanie Schuläufer," in Müller and Sternweiler, 181–89.

[128]Camp administrations also used the brothels in efforts to corrupt political prisoners and to "test" their "reeducation" of homosexuals. See Paul, 23–28; Kogon; Schulz. For a claim that male prisoners lost their sexual appetites, see H. L. Lennard, "Sex in the Concentration Camps," *Sexology* 18, no. 3 (1950): 176–79.

[129]Wolfgang Sofsky, *Die Ordnung des Terrors: Das Konzentrationslager*, 3rd ed. (Frankfurt am Main, 1993), 145–52.

[130]Paul, 81–82.

have been unkind or even violent to brothel inmates (we simply do not know), historians have proceeded from the assumption that the male inmates were not fundamentally responsible for the sexual exploitation of (and, often, injury to) the women.

While the vast majority of male inmates never visited a brothel, we should not assume that sexuality ceased to be important to them. Surely many men engaged in sex (heterosexual, homosexual, or—most likely—solitary) without material exchange, recalled earlier sexual encounters, experienced inopportune erections, felt sexual desire that found no outlet, faced humiliation as guards examined circumcised penises, feared lost virility, and worried about their sexual futures after liberation.[131] Michael Zimmermann has noted that when camp authorities required inmates to undress, they forced Roma (Gypsy) men to violate their own sexual taboos against being seen naked by their wives and children.[132] Even losing interest in sex because of starvation or apathy did not erase sexuality from the picture. Rather, it became an event in a man's sexual history, significant enough to attract comment by many memoirists. Oral historians have demonstrated that it is possible to ask female survivors tactfully about their sexual experiences, eliciting evidence that has escaped the written record while respecting the wishes of survivors who prefer not to discuss such matters. As we approach the passing of the last survivors, oral historians interviewing men as well as women should keep in mind that survivors' memories may carry rare evidence of how sexuality created opportunities for material and emotional support and how it contributed to victims' fears and pain.

When we turn our attention from the victims to the perpetrators, we encounter two major questions. Did sex help perpetrators to kill? If so, what kind and with whom? Citing the prohibition against race defilement, many have assumed that the Germans' crimes in the occupied East did not include widespread rape.[133] Although such a claim reiterates the depths of Nazi racism, it inadvertently supports a positive image of the German forces as disciplined and professional.[134]

A prohibition against race defilement from above did not guarantee restraint below. Birgit Beck cites wartime documents estimating that 50 to 80 percent of the SS and police forces stationed in Eastern Europe would be in

[131]Vera Laska discusses noncommercial and nonpenetrative heterosexual and homosexual sex as well as masturbation in commonsense, if brief, language. See Vera Laska, *Women in the Resistance and in the Holocaust: The Voices of Eyewitnesses* (Westport, 1983), 22–25.

[132]Michael Zimmermann, *Rassenutopie und Genozid: Die nationalsozialistische "Lösung der Zigeunerfrage"* (Hamburg, 1996), 173–74.

[133]Laska, 26. Ringelheim discusses her colleagues' assumptions that there was no rape in Ringelheim, "The Split."

[134]Recent scholarship has challenged this "clean" image of the Wehrmacht without, however, integrating sexual crimes into a revised history. Hannes Heer and Klaus Naumann, eds., *Vernichtungskrieg: Verbrechen der Wehrmacht 1941–1944* (Hamburg, 1995); Bartov, *Hitler's Army*. Although she does not adequately explore the different contexts and functions of rape

trouble if racial laws were strictly applied to them, and Doris Bergen finds plentiful evidence from National Socialist sources for sexual violence against "non-Aryan" women.[135] However, much of the existing literature has come from scholars interested in the general phenomenon of rape in wartime, which raises challenging questions about the particular versus the universal.[136] By bringing to light something the Germans did *not* do in the Second World War, however, the Balkan wars in the 1990s have demonstrated that sexual violence in the context of war and genocide has varied uses. While the Serbs used rape to achieve deracination in their genocidal project against Bosnian Muslims, we have no evidence of such a strategy in the genocide of the Second World War.[137] Bergen has thus argued for an understanding of sexual violence that takes into account the distinctive aspects of the Nazi racial vision and genocidal project. Although sexual violence against Slavic women could be "a form of torture, mockery, and humiliation," Germans might also seek sexual pleasure in forced relations with Slavs since taboos against sex with Slavs were more permeable than taboos against sex with Jews or Gypsies. In the case of Jews and Gypsies, Bergen suggests, sexual violence was part of the project of complete annihilation.[138] By utterly degrading its victims, sexual violence dehumanized them and allowed perpetrators to overcome deeply internalized taboos against murdering innocent, defenseless *humans* who posed no identifiable threat.

Promoting the fantasy of a "Jewish threat" was another strategy for overcoming qualms that "ordinary Germans" might otherwise have had about annihilating Jews. In this context, claims that Jews constituted a sexual danger—for example, propaganda representing Jewish men as leering seducers of Aryan maidens—could help make "ordinary Germans" less concerned about the passage of anti-Jewish legislation or the disappearance of Jewish neighbors. Could sexual defamation have enabled men to kill? Omer Bartov hypothesizes that commanders' claims that Russian

---

by Germans and Soviets in the Second World War, Helke Sander does challenge the image of a German force too disciplined to rape in her film *BeFreier und Befreite* and the companion book: Helke Sander and Barbara Johr, eds., *BeFreier und Befreite: Krieg, Vergewaltigungen, Kinder* (Munich, 1992).

[135]Birgit Beck, "Vergewaltigung von Frauen als Kriegsstrategie im Zweiten Weltkrieg?" in *Gewalt im Krieg: Ausübung, Erfahrung und Verweigerung von Gewalt in Kriegen des 20. Jahrhunderts,* ed. Andreas Gestrich, *Jahrbuch für historische Friedensforschung; 4. Jahrg.* (Münster, 1996), 34–50; Bergen, "Gender and Genocide."

[136]Ruth Seifert, "The Second Front: The Logic of Sexual Violence in Wars," in *Violence and Its Alternatives,* ed. Manfred B. Steger and Nancy S. Lind (New York, 1999), 145–53, 151; Susan Brownmiller, *Against Our Will: Men, Women, and Rape* (New York, 1975).

[137]On Bosnia, see Alexandra Stiglmayer, ed., *Mass Rape: The War against Women in Bosnia-Herzegovina* (Lincoln, 1994).

[138]Bergen, "Gender and Genocide." For an attempt to distinguish between genocidal projects that do and do not require complete physical annihilation, see Yehuda Bauer, *Rethinking the Holocaust* (New Haven, 2001).

women were both infected with STDs and largely of Jewish origin may have helped soldiers overcome traditional scruples against killing women and children in the battle against alleged "partisans" in the East.[139] Since Ingrid Schmidt-Harzbach's pioneering work, scholars have noted that Nazi depictions of Soviet rapists were intended to spur Germans to continue fighting when all was lost, although these scholars have not ventured claims about the effectiveness of this propaganda.[140]

As Bergen notes, the concept of dehumanization is familiar to scholars of genocide. Yet, curiously, Holocaust scholars who employ the concept have resisted the notion that sexual violence might have been part of the process. Instead, assuming a priori dehumanization, they have typically held that, since Jews as subhumans were unthinkable as sexual partners, they were unlikely targets of rape. Such assertions assume that Germans accepted propagandists' insistence that Jews were unthinkable as sexual partners. Moreover, these claims demonstrate an innocence of analyses of rape that distinguish sex as a tool of violence and domination from sex as an expression of sexual desire.[141] The same is true of accounts that explain the supposedly low level of sexual violence by noting the poor physical condition of Jewish women in the ghettos and camps.[142]

This latter argument also overlooks an important site of the Holocaust: the killing fields, where shooting squads massacred 1.5 million Jews driven directly from their villages. Since such Jews were not much worse fed than their non-Jewish neighbors, were not shaven, and wore ordinary clothing, they could have been objects of sexual desire in a conventional sense. If we think about all of occupied Europe and not just the well-demarcated ghettos and camps as the site of the genocide, we can recognize a far broader range of possibilities for sexual violence.

Finally, should we consider sex between members of the ruling "race" to have been relevant for the genocide? In *Hitler's Willing Executioners*, Daniel Goldhagen noted that the world of the camp guards was a heterosocial and heterosexually active one. He then offered his readers a vivid but purely imagined scenario of a German couple recounting the thrill of beating Jews as they caught their breath after sex.[143] In these pages,

[139]Bartov, *Hitler's Army*, 93–94.

[140]Ingrid Schmidt-Harzbach, "Eine Woche im April: Berlin 1945: Vergewaltigung als Massenschicksal," 1984, repr. in Sander and Johr, eds. An examination of rapes by the victorious allies, like other topics relating to the aftermath of the war, is beyond the scope of this essay; see, however, Atina Grossmann, "A Question of Silence: The Rape of German Women by Occupation Soldiers," *October*, no. 72 (1995): 43–63; Norman M. Naimark, *The Russians in Germany: A History of the Soviet Zone of Occupation, 1945–1949* (Cambridge, Mass., 1995), 69–140; Heineman, "The Hour of the Woman."

[141]For a reiteration of this analysis in the context of wartime rape, see Ruth Seifert, "War and Rape: A Preliminary Analysis," in Stiglmayer, ed., esp. 55–56.

[142]Laska, 26.

[143]Daniel Jonah Goldhagen, *Hitler's Willing Executioners: Ordinary Germans and the Holocaust* (New York, 1996), 338–39.

Goldhagen illuminated both the potential utility and the potential dangers of considering sexuality in the context of perpetratorship. If the outraged reader is supposed to ask, "How *could* they discuss their beatings of Jews right after having sex? That's *sick!*" (and my anecdotal evidence from lay readers suggests that this is precisely the response elicited), then the only answer can be that we have no evidence to support this scenario. Goldhagen's less speculative passages, by contrast, simply declare, reasonably, that if sexual affairs contributed to camaraderie and power struggles among camp staff, then we should consider this fact when we examine the camps' functioning.

There has been no systematic treatment of female German perpetrators in the concentration camp system. Our fleeting images of them focus disproportionately on a handful of women who linked brutality with flamboyant sexuality.[144] Such cases have been more often recounted than analyzed, and attempts to analyze them have employed hopelessly crude psychological frameworks, such as a physician's diagnosis of Ilse Koch in 1951: "the multiplicity of her loves is explained by a thirst for vengeance because of her resentment at not having been born a man."[145] More systematic examination, giving due space to less lurid cases, might help us better to understand the world of the camps for female perpetrators. Yet we still lack the basic information on nonsexual matters needed to interpret the interplay of sexuality and other aspects of female staff members' lives.[146] How often did female guards actively seek their posts, and how often were they assigned? In addition to professional opportunity, did guard duty represent a chance for sexual contacts for young women anxious to escape their parents' authority? Did taboo-breaking sexual pleasure enhance women's ability to employ taboo-breaking violence (or vice versa)? Did the isolated setting, the absolute authority of the camp administration, and the secretive nature of camp life make female guards sexually vulnerable to SS men? Did romances with male staff make women anxious

---

[144]See, for example, the frequent evocation of the sexual excesses of Ilse Koch, the wife of the commandant of Buchenwald, and the sadomasochism of Irma Griese, a famously brutal guard. For an example from the scholarly literature, see Kogon, 124, 232; from a best-selling novelist, Hans Habe, *Off Limits: A Novel of Occupied Germany* (London, 1956); from memoirists, Lengyel, and Fénelon and Routier. For analyses of this phenomenon, see Susanna Heschel, "Feminist Theory and the Perpetrators," paper presented at the conference "Lessons and Legacies," Chicago, 2000; Alexandra Przyrembel, "Transfixed by an Image: Ilse Koch, the 'Kommandeuse of Buchenwald,'" *German History* 19, no. 3 (2001): 369–99.

[145]Marc Lanval, "Ilse Koch—Sex Terrorist," *Sexology* 19, no. 1 (1951): 30–36, 33.

[146]See, however, the three case studies in Claudia Taake, *Angeklagt: SS-Frauen vor Gericht* (Oldenburg, 1998). Gudrun Schwarz is working on the first systematic study of SS women. The first volume, *Eine Frau an seiner Seite*, concerns wives of SS men. Preliminary published results of her research on female camp guards do not address sexuality. See Gudrun Schwarz, "SS-Aufseherinnen in nationalsozialistischen Konzentrationslagern (1933–1945)," *Dachauer Hefte* 10, no. 10 (1994): 32–49.

to please at the workplace in order to avoid transfer? Did prisoners ultimately pay for any exploitation female guards may have suffered at the
hands of male staff? How did the imperative to breed intersect with the
imperative to do one's job?

Many of the above questions apply to men as well, but since men did
almost all of the actual killing, the question becomes especially pertinent.
Did sex help them to kill? In *Mothers in the Fatherland*, Claudia Koonz has
argued that German women's maintenance of a comfortable "domestic
sphere" enabled men to commit atrocities. By returning to the homes and
families that women maintained, men could recuperate from their grisly
work and assure themselves that they were decent men.[147] Gudrun Schwarz
extends Koonz's thesis into the explicitly sexual realm. Sexual access to
their wives at the camps, it appears, cured some hesitant SS men of their
inability to function, and a wife's death could limit a man's effectiveness by
triggering undisciplined sexual relationships with "non-Aryan" women.
Discomfort with their duties, however (not all men were "well suited" to
camp duty), could also produce impotence.[148] Aware of the importance of
sexual contentedness, the SS leadership planned opportunities for nonresi-
dent wives or long-term mistresses to provide sexual comfort to its men.
While the internal reports Schwarz cites on the sexual lives of SS men in the
camps do not appear to discuss the scenario Goldhagen describes (sexual
relationships between men and women on the camp staff), elsewhere
Schwarz has described SS couples who met at work and later married.[149]

In *Ordinary Men*, Christopher Browning has carefully described the
ways alcohol first helped men of the shooting squads commit atrocities,
then dulled memories of the shootings, making it possible to work another day.[150] Could sex also have served to release tension—a release necessary to the continuing functioning of the genocide? If we wish to propose
a link between sex and the performance of nonsexual atrocities, we would
do well to broaden our consideration of sexual activities. Men may well
have sought sexual release in the brothels, in consensual or forcible contact with indigenous women, with German women (including their wives)
in occupied Europe, or during their periods of leave. Still, for many men
at the front lines of the genocide, contact with women was the exception
rather than the rule. If sex served as an outlet for tensions produced by the
job of killing, it might very often have been in the form of masturbation
or mutual masturbation—both common enough in barracks life of any
kind, with no necessary connection to atrocities.[151]

[147]Koonz, *Mothers in the Fatherland*.

[148]Schwarz, *Eine Frau an seiner Seite*, 109, 120, 128–30, 161–68.

[149]Gudrun Schwarz, "Frauen in der SS: Sippenverband und Frauenkorps," in Heinsohn,
ed., 223–44, 227.

[150]Browning.

[151]See, for example, Waite, "Teenage Sexuality," 458, 461; Hermand and Dembo, passim;
Giles, "The Institutionalization of Homosexual Panic"; for popular references to ubiquitous

To write about sexuality and the Holocaust is an intimidating task—and a weighty responsibility. While the use of eroticized images of Nazism in popular culture (whether Hollywood films or pornography) may appear problematic and even deeply offensive, we gain more if we demonstrate the benefits of a nonexploitative approach than if we simply object. The work discussed here shows that discussions of sexuality in connection with the Holocaust can be serious, responsible, and illuminating.

CONCLUSIONS

Historians of sexuality can be proud of the impact their work has had on our understanding of the Nazi era. Standard histories of that period now consider the National Socialist efforts to control reproduction as well as persecute homosexuals and such "asocials" as "promiscuous" women. These subjects are also mentioned in college and university classrooms, though in practice they are often bracketed off as women's or gay history. Scholars and teachers who read carefully, however, can learn from the existing literature that the persecution of sexual minorities and the efforts to control reproduction were not marginal but central to National Socialist racial theory and practice.

While other sexual themes are less frequently included in the general literature on Nazi Germany, newer research links sexuality to many of the burning questions about National Socialism. One question concerns everyday life and popular support for the regime. What aspects of "ordinary Germans'" experience help to explain their support for National Socialism? While historians of sexuality would hardly diminish the importance of such phenomena as the economic recovery of the mid-1930s, their research suggests another part of an answer. The perception or reality of erotic opportunities that were not tainted by the stigma of "degeneracy" or the misery of the Weimar years may have appealed to those Germans not targeted for persecution. A second question concerns perpetrators of the Holocaust. Did sex help the killers to kill, either by helping them to dehumanize their victims or by offering opportunities to release tension that might otherwise have interfered with killing operations? A third concerns the victims. What role did sex play in enabling survivors to survive, and what role did it play in the downward spiral of victims who did not?

Although this essay has focused on sexuality under the Nazi regime, it should be clear that many of the questions and findings are more broadly relevant. Indeed, investigations into these matters in the context of National Socialism have stretched the common boundaries of sexuality studies. How should we define heterosexual acts, and how inevitably are such acts tied to reproduction? Scholars of Nazi Germany have discovered that

---

masturbation in the U.S. military context, see Joan Smith, *Misogynies: Reflections on Myths and Malice*, 1st American ed. (New York, 1991), 141–56.

nonpenetrative practices were important even in settings where the connection between sex and reproduction should have been most central: in noncommercial relationships between adult partners of different sexes in a state obsessed with eugenics. Where do sex and violence intersect? The Holocaust reveals that sexual violence may not be the whole story, that nonviolent sex may have enabled nonsexual violence. What happens to sex and violence when we add commerce to the picture? Research into Nazi-era brothels challenges our use of the model of "prostitution" (which forefronts exchange) to describe acts that might better be described as "rape" (which forefronts violence) without forgetting that it was the commercial, not the coercive, description that shaped contemporaries' interpretation of the "prostitutes'" activities. How should we understand the relationship between gender, sexuality, and state power? The delicate distinctions between male comradeship, male homoeroticism, and male homosexuality in Nazi Germany may help us to understand other political structures.

The works discussed here mark only a beginning; we still have much to learn. Yet historians of National Socialism are using old sources to answer new questions, discovering (and, in the case of oral history, creating) new sources, and becoming methodologically and theoretically bolder than they have been in the past. In the next few years we should not be surprised if histories of sexuality in Nazi Germany bring dramatic new insights into the functioning of National Socialism and the uses of human sexuality.

Backlash against Prostitutes' Rights: Origins and Dynamics of Nazi Prostitution Policies

JULIA ROOS

University of Minnesota, Twin Cities

IN *MEIN KAMPF,* Adolf Hitler attacked prostitution as a major cause of Germany's decline. The "prostitution of love," he claimed, was responsible for the "terrible poisoning of the health of the national body" through syphilis. "Even if its results were not this frightful plague, it would nevertheless be profoundly injurious to man, since the moral devastations which accompany this degeneracy suffice to destroy a people slowly but surely." According to Hitler, many of Germany's troubles could be blamed on "this Jewification of our spiritual life and mammonization of our mating instinct" that threatened to annihilate future generations of healthy Germans.[1] Hitler's tirades about the moral and racial dangers of venal sex suggested that, once in power, the Nazis would show little tolerance for the persistence of "vice." Paradoxically, however, state-regulated prostitution increased dramatically under Nazism. Especially during wartime, the regulated brothel became a key institution of Nazi sexual policy. How can we make sense of this tension?

As this essay intends to show, to gain a fuller understanding of Nazi attitudes toward prostitution, it is vital to analyze them in the context of Weimar conflicts over prostitution reform. Recent studies on the history of prostitution in the Third Reich tend to neglect pre-1933 developments.[2]

For their helpful comments and criticisms, I would like to thank the anonymous referee for the *Journal of the History of Sexuality* as well as Dagmar Herzog, Fritz Ringer, and Bill Scheuerman.

[1]See Adolf Hitler, *Mein Kampf,* trans. Ralph Manheim (Boston, 1971), 246–47.

[2]See especially Christa Schikorra, "Prostitution weiblicher KZ-Häftlinge als Zwangsarbeit: Zur Situation 'asozialer' Häftlinge im Frauen-KZ Ravensbrück," *Dachauer Hefte* 16, no. 16 (November 2000): 112–24; Gaby Zürn, "'Von der Herbertstraße nach Auschwitz,'" in *Opfer und Täterinnen: Frauenbiographien des Nationalsozialismus,* ed. Angelika Ebbinghaus (Frankfurt am Main, 1996), 124–36; Christa Paul, *Zwangsprostitution: Staatlich errichtete Bordelle im Nationalsozialismus* (Berlin, 1994); and Gisela Bock, "'Keine Arbeitskräfte in

If historians mention the topic of Weimar prostitution policy at all, it is primarily to emphasize basic continuities in this area after the Nazi take-over. Thus, Gisela Bock has argued that Weimar prostitution reforms paved the way for the sexual and economic exploitation of prostitutes under National Socialism.[3] However, the notion of unbroken continuities between Weimar and Nazi attitudes toward venal sex is problematic for several reasons. The exclusive focus on continuity tends to obscure important differences between the two periods. Far from representing a mere prelude to the brutal persecution of prostitutes after 1933, the nationwide abolition of state-regulated prostitution in 1927 led to significant improvements in prostitutes' civil and legal status. To acknowledge these (albeit limited) gains in prostitutes' rights is key for the analysis of the impact that concerns about "immorality" had on the crisis of the Weimar Republic and the rise of Nazism.[4]

The more liberal aspects of Weimar prostitution reforms triggered a powerful right-wing backlash. In the eyes of religious conservatives, the state's perceived failure to enforce "moral order" and cleanse the streets of prostitutes profoundly discredited Weimar democracy. Among large segments of the police, the loss of authority to control and punish streetwalkers similarly bred resentment against the democratic government. The Nazis were keenly aware of the propagandistic value of the issue of prostitution. Nazi attacks on the 1927 prostitution reform as yet another expression of Weimar's "materialism" and "moral decay" aimed to widen the party's appeal among the religious Right and conservative officials. During the early 1930s, the Nazis' successful attempt to portray themselves as guardians of conventional morality intent on eliminating "vice" was key to winning them the approval and collaboration of many conservatives. We can only account fully for this dynamic, however, if we recognize some of the positive achievements of Weimar prostitution reforms. The abolition of state-regulated prostitution was one of the major successes of the 1920s movement for sexual reform, which failed to achieve other goals such as the decriminalization of abortion and homosexuality. This is why Weimar prostitution reforms became a central target of Nazi propaganda.

---

diesem Sinne': Prostituierte im Nazi-Staat," in *"Wir sind Frauen wie andere auch!" Prostituierte und ihre Kämpfe*, ed. Pieke Biermann (Reinbek bei Hamburg, 1980), 70–106.

[3]See Bock, "'Keine Arbeitskräfte in diesem Sinne,'" 86; for a similar argument, see Patrick Wagner, *Volksgemeinschaft ohne Verbrecher: Konzeptionen und Praxis der Kriminalpolizei in der Zeit der Weimarer Republik und des Nationalsozialismus* (Hamburg, 1996), 367.

[4]For a discussion of the destructive effects of the "moral" agenda on Weimar democracy, see Richard Bessel, *Germany after the First World War* (Oxford, 1993), chap. 8. On the backlash against Weimar sexual reform, see Atina Grossmann, *Reforming Sex: The German Movement for Birth Control and Abortion Reform, 1920–1950* (New York, 1995), chaps. 5 and 6; and Cornelie Usborne, *The Politics of the Body in Weimar Germany: Women's Reproductive Rights and Duties* (Ann Arbor, 1992), esp. chap. 2.

Moreover, the emphasis on unbroken continuities in the history of prostitution after 1933 tends to obscure the special nature of Nazi prostitution policy. Nazi prostitution policies aimed to reverse key Weimar achievements—most importantly, the abolition of state-regulated prostitution. At first sight, the Nazis' endorsement of police-controlled prostitution might appear as a revival of older repressive attitudes toward venal sex. But under the mask of conventional authoritarian police practices for the control of "vice," Nazi prostitution policies increasingly served radically different ends. Although the police had previously justified the institution of the regulated brothel as the most effective means to protect respectable society from prostitutes, this concern increasingly became secondary under the Nazis.

The first part of this essay focuses on the backlash against Weimar prostitution reforms during the late 1920s and early 1930s. This backlash, I argue, had a decisive impact on the course of Nazi prostitution policy. The second part of the essay analyzes the different stages in Nazi attitudes toward prostitution, with a special emphasis on the early years of the regime. The initial stage, which lasted from 1933 to mid-1934, is characterized by the Nazis' effort to appeal to conservative concerns about "immorality" and to present themselves as defenders of established notions of sexual propriety. During this phase, important representatives of the Nazi leadership sided with the opponents of police-controlled brothels. However, to the extent that the regime consolidated its power and became more and more independent of religious conservatives, National Socialist Party leaders and administrators pushed openly for state-regulated prostitution. The period between 1934 and 1939 was marked by the triumph of the institution of the regulated brothel and by an increasingly brutal suppression of streetwalkers. The rise of Heinrich Himmler and the SS and the declining power of the Catholic and Protestant churches during these years decisively tipped the balance in favor of police-controlled prostitution. As preparations for war intensified, the military also lobbied for the establishment of regulated brothels. After 1939, the Nazis finally abandoned all efforts to accommodate the religious Right and launched a massive campaign to set up brothels throughout the Reich. It was during this third, radicalized phase that Nazi prostitution policy truly came into its own and most clearly revealed its unique features.

I.

In 1927 the Law for Combating Venereal Diseases (Reichsgesetz zur Bekämpfung der Geschlechtskrankheiten) abolished state-regulated prostitution (*Reglementierung*, or "regulationism").[5] Until 1927, prostitution in general had been illegal in Germany. However, cities with *Reglementierung*

---

[5]See *Reichsgesetzblatt*, part 1, February 22, 1927, 61–63. On the history of the anti-VD law, see Usborne, 109–12; see also Paul Weindling, *Health, Race and German Politics between National Unification and Nazism, 1870–1945* (Cambridge, 1993), esp. 357–59.

tolerated registered prostitutes.[6] State-regulated prostitution subjected prostitutes to compulsory medical exams for sexually transmitted diseases as well as to numerous other restrictions on their personal freedom. Thus, regulated prostitutes were banned from major public areas, could only reside in lodgings approved by the police, and had to obtain permission if they wanted to travel. A special section of the police, the morals police (Sittenpolizei), was responsible for the supervision of prostitution. Registered prostitutes' exceptional legal status marked them as social pariahs.[7] Women arrested for street soliciting and registered by the police generally had no recourse to the courts. The legal principle of due process did not apply to prostitutes.

In the Weimar Republic, popular support for state-regulated prostitution quickly waned for several reasons. Most important, regulationism's moral double standard became increasingly untenable after the introduction of woman suffrage in 1919. Feminists had long criticized the misogynistic rationale for regulated prostitution, which imposed repressive controls on prostitutes yet condoned men's use of commercial sex.[8] Winning the vote greatly increased feminists' leverage in their fight against regulationism. Other factors contributed to the downfall of *Reglementierung*. Social Democrats and liberals objected that the extensive arbitrary powers of the morals police were incompatible with the new democratic constitution. After the war, principled opponents of state-regulated prostitution, the "abolitionists," increasingly focused on the system's failure to stem the rise in sexually transmitted diseases (STDs).[9] Abolitionists pointed out that unlicensed streetwalkers, who according to some estimates outnumbered registered prostitutes by a ratio of 10:1, were not subject to controls for STDs. Moreover, sexual promiscuity had increased to such an extent that professional prostitutes had ceased to represent the major source of venereal infections. To encourage all streetwalkers infected with STDs to seek medical treatment, abolitionists demanded that prostitution be decriminalized.[10]

[6]See Richard J. Evans, "Prostitution, State, and Society in Imperial Germany," *Past & Present*, no. 70 (February 1976): 106–29; Regina Schulte, *Sperrbezirke: Tugendhaftigkeit und Prostitution in der bürgerlichen Welt* (Hamburg, 1994), esp. chap. 4; and Lynn Abrams, "Prostitutes in Imperial Germany, 1870–1918: Working Girls or Social Outcasts?" in *The German Underworld: Deviants and Outcasts in German History*, ed. Richard J. Evans (London, 1988), 189–209.

[7]See the detailed discussion of the legal aspects of regulated prostitution in Jill Harsin, *Policing Prostitution in Nineteenth-Century Paris* (Princeton, 1985), chap. 2. See also Abraham Flexner, *Prostitution in Europe* (Montclair, 1969 [originally 1914]), esp. 136–37.

[8]See Anna Pappritz, "Das Reichsgesetz zur Bekämpfung der Geschlechtskrankheiten vom Standpunkt der Frau," *Mitteilungen der deutschen Gesellschaft zur Bekämpfung der Geschlechtskrankheiten* 25 (1927): 133, emphasis in the original; see also Anna Pappritz, "Die abolitionistische Föderation," in *Einführung in das Studium der Prostitutionsfrage*, ed. A. Pappritz (Leipzig, 1919), 220–60.

[9]See Max Quarck, *Gegen Prostitution und Geschlechtskrankheiten* (Berlin, 1921), 20.

[10]See, for instance, Curt Geyer and Julius Moses, *Gesetz zur Bekämpfung der Geschlechtskrankheiten nebst Erläuterungen und Kommentar* (Berlin, 1927), 15–16.

Widespread fears about the "racial poisons" of STDs led to the passage of the 1927 Law for Combating Venereal Diseases (anti-VD law).[11] To curb venereal infections, the anti-VD law promised financial support to uninsured patients and criminalized people who knowingly spread STDs. In many ways, the 1927 law marked a victory for the abolitionists. The law decriminalized prostitution in general, abolished the morals police, and outlawed regulated brothels. These were major achievements from the perspective of prostitutes' rights. However, to secure passage of the reform, Social Democrats and liberals were forced to make important concessions to the moral Right, who opposed a consistent decriminalization of prostitution. Clause 16/4 of the anti-VD law, dubbed by critics the "church-tower paragraph" (*Kirchturmparagraph*), made street soliciting illegal in areas adjacent to churches and schools as well as in towns with a population smaller than 15,000.[12] Abolitionists immediately pointed out that the church-tower paragraph potentially could lead to a resurgence of regulated prostitution.[13] Andreas Knack and Max Quarck, two of the Social Democratic Party's major experts on public health, warned that the repeal of *Reglementierung* would "cause *considerable opposition* among the organs of the administration" and called on socialists to be vigilant.[14] As subsequent developments showed, their concerns about a possible backlash against the more liberal aspects of the 1927 prostitution reform were to prove prescient.

Opposition from within the State: The Police

When the Prussian minister of welfare asked police presidents in February 1921 to comment on recent demands to abolish state-regulated prostitution, the responses were overwhelmingly negative.[15] Most officials rejected the proposal as unrealistic and dangerous. Many would have agreed with the Berlin police, who accused abolitionists of manipulating the issue of prostitution reform for "women's rights [*frauenrechtlerisch*] and general political agitation."[16] Erfurt's chief of police predicted that in the event of a repeal of regulated prostitution, "street whores will shoot up from the

[11]See "Entwurf eines Gesetzes zur Bekämpfung der Geschlechtskrankheiten," in *Verhandlungen des deutschen Reichstages*, vol. 401 (Berlin, 1925), doc. no. 975. For a critical discussion of Weimar debates about STDs, see Usborne, esp. 110; and Bessel, 233–39.

[12]See Paragraph 16, section 4 of the anti-VD law.

[13]See Marie Elisabeth Lüders, "Befreiung von Krankheit und Lüge," *Die Frau* 34 (1927): 302–5.

[14]See Andreas V. Knack and Max Quarck, *Das Reichsgesetz zur Bekämpfung der Geschlechtskrankheiten und seine praktische Durchführung*, ed. Hauptausschuß der Arbeiterwohlfahrt (Berlin, 1928), 23, emphasis in the original.

[15]See the extensive correspondence in Geheimes Staatsarchiv preussischer Kulturbesitz Berlin (GStA-PK) I. HA Rep. 76 VIII B/3822.

[16]See the report of Berlin's chief of police of April 20, 1921, in ibid., 16.

ground like mushrooms."[17] Like many of his colleagues, he claimed that without *Reglementierung*, the police would be unable to protect respectable citizens and to control crime associated with commercial sex. The police president of Hanover warned that the decriminalization of prostitution would lead to an explosion of STDs. In times of intense "sittliche Verflachung" [moral shallowness], the police fulfilled a vital function as protector of public morality.[18] Misogynistic views often underpinned the defense of regulationism. In 1926 Stuttgart's chief of police complained that "women's organizations of all kinds [are] blinded by the slogan 'Against the moral double standard.'" In contrast to feminists, he believed that "against the woman who has sunken to the level of the whore and who is much more dangerous to the public than the dissolute [*liederlich*] man, special preventive measures are necessary."[19]

To the dismay of proregulationists, the 1927 prostitution reform limited the police's ability to impose special controls on prostitutes. Regulations that banned streetwalkers from certain areas (*Strichverbot*) or that restricted them to special streets or houses (*Kasernierung*) were no longer permitted. According to the revised version of Clause 361/6 of the penal code, the police could intervene against prostitutes if the latter solicited publicly "in einer Sitte und Anstand verletzenden oder andere belästigenden Weise" [in a manner that violates morals and decency or harasses others].[20] This rather vague formulation led to substantial discrepancies in jurisprudence.[21] One of the most contentious legal issues was the question of whether it sufficed that a streetwalker's behavior objectively was suited to offend morality (*Gefährdungsdelikt*) or whether proof was needed that members of the public had actually been offended or harassed (*Verletzungsdelikt*). Where courts interpreted Clause 361/6 in the narrow sense of the *Verletzungsdelikt*, arrests of prostitutes declined sharply, since citizens generally avoided filing charges or giving testimony in such cases. In the summer and fall of 1928, the Saxon State Supreme Court (Sächsisches Oberlandesgericht) overruled numerous convictions of Leipzig streetwalkers for violations of Clause 361/6. The justices argued that a prostitute's solicitation of passersby, even if conducted in a conspicuous, sexually explicit manner—"nach Dirnenart" [in the manner of hookers]—in itself did not constitute a criminal offense. Rather, additional evidence was necessary to demonstrate that public morals had indeed been violated. As a result of the ruling, convictions of Leipzig prostitutes on

[17]See ibid., 81.

[18]See ibid., 95.

[19]See Bundesarchiv Berlin (BArch) R 1501/11890, 71–72.

[20]This clause of the criminal code was identical with Paragraph 16/3 of the anti-VD law.

[21]See Leopold Schäfer, "Prostitution und Rechtsprechung," *Mitteilungen der deutschen Gesellschaft zur Bekämpfung der Geschlechtskrankheiten* 27 (1929): 412–31; see also Dorothea Karsten, "Prostitution und Straßenbild: Neue gesetzliche Bestimmungen?" *Freie Wohlfahrts-pflege* 7 (1932): 310–15.

the basis of Clause 361/6 sank from 227 in 1928 to 11 in 1930.[22] The verdict caused great frustration among the Saxon police, who complained that it tied their hands in the fight against prostitution.

Police officials in other states faced similar problems. In the fall of 1931, amidst growing public pressure to cleanse the streets of prostitution, Munich's police felt humiliated by local judges who often acquitted streetwalkers. As one police report noted, "It happens frequently during public trials that the judges ridicule the officers with their remarks and questions and then acquit the prostitutes or hand down minor sentences. . . . During one such trial, a judge remarked that he preferred four other cases to a single one that had to do with matters concerning the morals police since in this area, there existed no legal basis whatsoever."[23] The decriminalization of prostitution led to a broad backlash among the police. Throughout Germany, police officials argued that the 1927 anti-VD law deprived them of the requisite means for suppressing street solicitations. In 1928 Magdeburg's police president reported a sharp rise in casual prostitution "since the deterrent of the morals police is absent, and the bad example is contagious." Public prostitution, he claimed, had become far more conspicuous after 1927 because the police lacked authority to intervene against the growing "shamelessness and excesses" of streetwalkers.[24] Similarly, the Prussian district president (*Regierungspräsident*) in Düsseldorf reported that "all police chiefs in my district . . . have observed a substantial increase in street soliciting since passage of the new [anti-VD] law. . . . Without doubt, the abolition of the morals police is a main cause for the growth in prostitution."[25] In 1931 the police presidents of major Prussian cities, including Cologne, Essen, and Dortmund, demanded a revision of Clause 361/6 of the penal code to outlaw all forms of street soliciting.[26]

A key to this reaction against liberal prostitution reforms was the political mobilization of prostitutes. The decriminalization of prostitution energized streetwalkers to resist attacks on their civil and economic rights. Thus, Leipzig prostitutes founded an association that employed legal counsel to defend its members against the police. In March 1931 the Saxon Ministry of Labor and Welfare (Sächsisches Arbeits- und Wohlfahrtsministerium) reported that a "large number of Leipzig prostitutes have submitted a petition to the city magistrate and the chief of police, in which

---

[22]See "Sachverständigenkonferenz über das Straßenbild nach dem Inkrafttreten des RGBG," *Mitteilungen der deutschen Gesellschaft zur Bekämpfung der Geschlechtskrankheiten* 29 (1931): 80–81.

[23]See the report of November 3, 1931, in Bayerisches Hauptstaatsarchiv München (BayHStAM), M-Inn/72644.

[24]See GStA-PK I. HA Rep. 76 VIII B/3831, 222.

[25]See the report of December 5, 1928, in ibid., 356.

[26]See the list of police presidents' proposals for the revision of Clause 361/6 of the penal code in GStA-PK I. HA Rep. 84a/869, 175.

they protest against unduly repressive measures on the side of the police. They argue that they have the right to pursue their business like any other tradesperson since they pay taxes and would become dependent on social welfare if the severe controls continued."[27] In the city-state of Bremen, prostitutes challenged what they considered illegal forms of police repression. According to the Bremen health office, streetwalkers there had founded "a kind of protective association which represents the supposed rights of its members . . . through a certain lawyer."[28] After July 1932 the Bremen police arrested streetwalkers on the basis of the Law for the Temporary Arrest and Detention of Persons (Gesetz betreffend das einstweilige Vorführen und Festhalten von Personen), which allowed the police to detain individuals for a period of up to twenty-four hours if this appeared necessary to protect the person's own or the public's safety. Prostitutes opposed this practice as incompatible with the decriminalization of prostitution and sued the police for false imprisonment and grievous bodily harm.[29] Bremen police officials were exasperated by the conflict, especially since negotiations with the court had cast doubt on the legality of the police measure.[30]

Despite its flaws, the 1927 anti-VD law introduced important improvements in prostitutes' status. The general decriminalization of prostitution enabled streetwalkers more effectively to challenge police violations of their personal liberties. From the perspective of police officials, these gains in prostitutes' rights threatened to undermine their own authority and jeopardize public order. However, under democratic conditions an open return to regulationism faced sizable obstacles. As we will see, their frustration over the detrimental impacts of the 1927 prostitution reform led many police officials to abandon Weimar democracy and endorse the resurgence of an authoritarian state that granted them greatly extended powers to control "vice."

Popular Opposition: The "Moral" Right

Growing public protests against the perceived rise in street soliciting put additional pressure on the police. A year after implementation of the 1927 anti-VD law, the Council of German Cities (Deutscher Städtetag) conducted a survey among local health offices.[31] One important question focused on public reactions to the reform. Of the twenty-four cities included in the

---

[27]See the report to the Reich Ministry of the Interior of March 17, 1931, in GStA-PK I. HA Rep. 84a/869, 163.

[28]See the health office's report of January 1932 in Staatsarchiv Bremen (StAB) 4,130/1-R.I.1.-17.

[29]See the legal brief of September 29, 1932, in StAB 4,130/1-R.I.1.-24.

[30]See the report of a meeting at the Bremen health office on August 28, 1928, in StAB 4,130/1-R.I.1.-24.

[31]See *Die Bekämpfung der Geschlechtskrankheiten in deutschen Städten*, Schriftenreihe des deutschen Städtetages, vol. 8, ed. Otto Schweers and Franz Memelsdorff (Berlin, 1930).

survey, only three (Hamburg, Berlin, and Stettin) reported generally positive responses from the population. In a range of cities, the perceived rise
in prostitution mobilized citizens against the anti-VD law. This was true
especially of the overwhelmingly Catholic cities of Munich, Nuremberg,
Augsburg, Cologne, and Münster.[32] In subsequent years, religious conservatives organized a vocal movement against the more liberal elements
of the 1927 prostitution reform. While Catholic politicians and associations often spearheaded initiatives to impose tougher controls on prostitutes, Protestants supported such efforts as well. In April 1930 the Reichstag
Bevölkerungspolitischer Ausschuß (Committee on Population Policy)
passed a resolution that called for the strict suppression of street soliciting
and of lodging houses (*Absteigequartiere*) used by prostitutes to meet their
clients. Author of the motion was Reinhard Mumm, the Lutheran pastor
and leader of the conservative Christian-Social People's Service (Christlich-
Sozialer Volksdienst).[33] The resolution reflected demands communicated
to Mumm by leading representatives of Lutheran churches and morality
associations.[34]

Major centers of conservative reaction against the 1927 reform were
Catholic-dominated cities in the Prussian Rhine Province. Cologne, a Center Party stronghold where Konrad Adenauer was mayor (*Oberbürgermeister*), was at the forefront of efforts to reintroduce harsher penalties
for street soliciting.[35] During the early 1930s the Catholic morality association, Volkswartbund, coordinated the local campaign against the anti-
VD law.[36] The Bund organized public protests and petitions and pressured
Cologne's chief of police to implement more punitive measures against
prostitutes. In April 1932 the Working Group of Cologne Catholics
(Arbeitsgemeinschaft Kölner Katholiken) alerted Reich chancellor Heinrich

---

[32]See ibid., 103.

[33]On Mumm, see Kurt Nowak, *Evangelische Kirche und Weimarer Republik: Zum
politischen Weg des deutschen Protestantismus zwischen 1918 und 1932* (Weimar, 1988), 36–
37, 142–45; see also Peter Fritzsche, *Rehearsals for Fascism: Populism and Political Mobilization in Weimar Germany* (New York, 1990), esp. 50–51.

[34]See BArch 90 Mn (N 2203 [estate of Reinhard Mumm]), no. 531, esp. 33–37.

[35]The Center Party was founded in 1870–71 to represent the political and religious
interests of Germany's sizable Catholic minority. It gained widespread support among Catholics during the *Kulturkampf* of the 1870s, when Reich chancellor Bismarck implemented a
range of anticlerical laws that aimed to curb the influence of the Catholic Church. During
the Weimar period, the Center Party and its Bavarian counterpart, the Bayerische Volkspartei,
predominated in Catholic areas. Of all the Weimar parties, the Center maintained the most
stable electorate. On the history of the Center Party, see David Blackbourn, "Catholics and
Politics in Imperial Germany: The Centre Party and Its Constituency," in David Blackbourn,
Populists and Patricians: Essays in Modern German History (London, 1987), 188–214. On
Catholic support for the Center Party in the Weimar Republic, see Jürgen Falter, *Hitlers
Wähler* (Munich, 1991), esp. 169–75.

[36]See "Sitzung des Volkswartbundes in Köln am 25. Januar 1933," in Archiv des
deutschen Caritasverbandes (ADCV), Sozialdienst katholischer Frauen (SKF), 319.4 D01/
05e, Fasz. 1.

Brüning to the dramatic proliferation of commercial sex.[37] "Growing poverty and the resulting moral degeneration of whole strata of the population have produced such an increase in prostitutes that prostitution has become a veritable plague [*Volksplage*]. . . . Responsibility for this terrible situation largely lies with the Law for Combating Venereal Diseases." The petition called for an emergency decree authorizing the police to suppress any form of street solicitation. Similar conservative grass-roots movements against the 1927 reform emerged in Essen, Krefeld, and Dortmund.[38] Catholic politicians increasingly pushed for a general criminalization of prostitution. In June 1932 the National Women's Caucus of the Center Party (Reichsfrauenbeirat der deutschen Zentrumspartei) appealed to the Reich Minister of the Interior to outlaw street soliciting.[39] On July 9, 1932, the Prussian State Council, the representative body of the Prussian provinces, supported a motion to criminalize public prostitution that had been submitted by Konrad Adenauer and the other members of the Center Party delegation.[40]

Less than two weeks later, conservative critics of Weimar prostitution reforms could be hopeful that a policy shift toward more repressive measures was imminent. The *Preußenschlag* (Papen Putsch) against Prussia's Social Democratic government brought to power prominent opponents of the 1927 reform. Historians have pointed out that Papen justified the coup with charges "that the Prussian government was unable to maintain law and order."[41] They focus especially on Papen's criticism that Social Democrats were "soft on Communism." Unfortunately, most existing scholarship tends to neglect the significance of the backlash against the liberalization of sexual mores for understanding the political origins of the *Preußenschlag*. For religious conservatives, the Prussian regime's perceived failure to combat "immorality" effectively was a major reason to support Papen's coup. Franz Bracht, a Center Party politician and federal commissioner for Prussia

[37]See the petition of April 19, 1932, in BArch R 1501/26315, 16–18. See also "Gegen die öffentliche Unsittlichkeit," *Kölnische Volkszeitung*, April 19, 1932.

[38]See the petition to Brüning by the Altstädtischer Verein Essen of November 22, 1931, in BArch R 1501/27217/8, 55; on the movement against the 1927 reform in Dortmund, see "Wann folgt Dortmund?" *Tremonia*, December 29, 1932; on Krefeld, see the minutes of a meeting of the Krefeld Alliance for the Protection of Spiritual Welfare (Krefelder Hilfsbündnis für geistige Wohlfahrtspflege) on October 25, 1932, in Archiv des Katholischen deutschen Frauenbundes (AKDF), Morality Commission 1-27-6.

[39]See "Bekämpfung der Geschlechtskrankheiten," *Mitteilungen des Reichsfrauenbeirats der deutschen Zentrumspartei* 7 (1932): 194–95; see also "Der Widerstand gegen das Gesetz zur Bekämpfung der Geschlechtskrankheiten," *Der Abolitionist* 31 (1932): 67–69.

[40]For the debate in the Prussian state council, see GStA-PK I. HA Rep. 169 D IX E/6, 155–59; see also Dorothea Karsten, "Zur Frage der Bekämpfung der Prostitution," *Soziale Praxis* 41 (1932): 1277–86.

[41]See Dietrich Orlow, *Weimar Prussia, 1925–1933: The Illusion of Strength* (Pittsburgh, 1991), 228; see also Gotthard Jasper, *Die gescheiterte Zähmung: Wege zur Machtergreifung Hitlers, 1930–1934* (Frankfurt am Main, 1986), 93–104.

after July 20, 1932, swiftly implemented several decrees aimed at restoring public morality. On August 8 Bracht outlawed nude bathing; on August 19 he forbade nudity and other "indecent performances" in theaters.[42] As former mayor of Essen, Bracht brought with him to the capital his chief of police, Kurt Melcher.[43] Melcher, who became Berlin's new police president, was one of the most prominent critics of the 1927 anti-VD law.[44]

For religious conservatives, Bracht's appointment was an important victory. An article in *Volkswart*, the organ of Cologne's Volkswartbund, stressed that the path was now clear for a more rigorous repression of prostitution in Prussia.[45] Bracht did not disappoint such expectations. The federal commissioner installed a new chief of police in Cologne, Walter Lingens, who in December 1932 outlawed street soliciting.[46] During subsequent weeks, the police presidents of Neuss, Münster, and Dortmund followed Lingens's example. But the religious Right was somewhat divided about the question of how best to combat prostitution. Protestants supported demands for a revision of Clause 361/6 of the penal code to increase the police's authority to intervene against streetwalkers. Unlike many Catholics, though, representatives of Lutheran churches and women's associations opposed total criminalization of prostitution for fear that this would pave the way for the return of regulated brothels.[47] In October 1932 Paula Müller-Otfried, a Reichstag delegate for the conservative German-National People's Party and president of the German-Lutheran Women's Federation (Deutsch-Evangelischer Frauenbund, or DEF), commended Bracht on his measures "against the degenerative developments in public life."[48] Müller-Otfried admitted that the anti-VD law offered no adequate legal means to curb street soliciting but warned that the complete criminalization of prostitution would revive *Reglementierung*. "A

[42]See "Die neuen preußischen Verordnungen gegen sittliche Entartung," *Volkswart: Monatsschrift zur Bekämpfung der öffentlichen Unsittlichkeit*, no. 1 (1932): esp. 149.

[43]See Hsi-Huey Liang, *The Berlin Police Force in the Weimar Republic* (Berkeley, 1970), esp. 153–54.

[44]See Kurt Melcher, "Grundsätzliches zur Behandlung der Prostitution im Geschlechtskrankengesetz," *Die Polizei* 29 (1932): 381–83.

[45]See "Die neuen preußischen Verordnungen gegen sittliche Entartung," *Volkswart*, no. 1 (1932): esp. 150–51.

[46]See the minutes of a meeting of the Volkswartbund in ADCV, SKF 319. 4 D 01/05 e, Fasz. 1; see also "Köln in Front: Zur Wahrung der öffentlichen Sittlichkeit," *Tremonia*, December 29, 1932. On Lingens, see Adolf Klein, *Köln im Dritten Reich: Stadtgeschichte der Jahre 1933–1945* (Cologne, 1983), 49.

[47]See Hermine Bäcker, "Änderung des Reichsgesetzes zur Bekämpfung der Geschlechtskrankheiten durch Notverordnung?" *Die Rundschau: Mitteilungsblatt der Inneren Mission* 27 (1932): 272–74; see also "Eingaben der Vereinigung evangelischer Frauenverbände Deutschlands zum RGBG," *Aufgaben und Ziele: Monatsblatt der Vereinigung evangelischer Frauenverbände Deutschlands* 12 (1932): 70–71.

[48]See Müller-Otfried's letter to federal commissioner Franz Bracht of October 8, 1932, in Archiv des diakonischen Werks (ADW), Central-Ausschuß der inneren Mission (CA), Gf/St no. 291.

return to the old system of regulationism . . . would cause great concern among women and the wider public." Bracht's own draft of a revision of Clause 361/6 strove to mediate between the diverging Catholic and Lutheran positions. While the federal commissioner's proposal made all forms of public solicitation "suited to harass individuals or the public" punishable, it stopped short of outright criminalization of prostitution.[49]

The Papen Putsch fulfilled key conservative demands for a tougher stance on "immorality" and a reversal of the more liberal aspects of Weimar prostitution reforms. This greatly strengthened the moral Right's support for the semi-authoritarian presidential regime of the early 1930s, which was based on rule by emergency decree and tended to minimize meaningful participation by parliament. The Nazis were keenly aware of the propagandistic potential of the issue of prostitution and used the backlash against the 1927 reform to advance their own political agenda.

Nazi Attacks on Weimar Prostitution Reforms

In *Mein Kampf*, Hitler focused on the failure of the Weimar government to prevent the German people's "pollution" through STDs.

> The struggle against syphilis and the prostitution which prepares the way for it is one of the most gigantic tasks of humanity, gigantic because we are facing, not the solution of a single question, but the elimination of a large number of evils which bring about this plague as a resultant manifestation. For in this case the sickening of the body is only the consequence of a sickening of the moral, social, and racial instincts. . . . But how did they try to deal with this plague in old Germany? Viewed calmly, the answer is really dismal.[50]

Neither the medical supervision of prostitutes nor the introduction of "a 'protective' paragraph according to which anyone who was not entirely healthy or cured must avoid sexual intercourse under penalty of law" had succeeded in eradicating venereal disease.[51] According to Hitler, Weimar politicians had failed because their measures against prostitution and STDs merely addressed the symptoms, not the roots, of Germany's deep moral and racial crisis. As Hitler stressed, "Anyone who wants to attack prostitution must first of all help to eliminate its spiritual basis. He must clear away the filth of the moral plague of big-city 'civilization.'"[52] Hitler supported

[49]See Bracht's proposals for a revision of Clause 361/6 of September 29, 1932, in GStA-PK I. HA Rep. 84A/869, 247a–b.

[50]See Hitler, 255–56.

[51]See ibid., 256. Since *Mein Kampf* was published two years prior to passage of the 1927 anti-VD law, this reference to antivenereal legislation probably pertains to the Decree for Combating Venereal Diseases of December 11, 1918, which criminalized knowingly infecting others with STDs.

[52]See ibid., 254–55.

demands raised by the religious Right that "indecent" literature, art, and entertainments be banned; he also argued that the regeneration of the German nation required that "defective people be prevented from propagating equally defective offspring."

Key, however, to averting Germany's national and racial "extinction" through the "plague" of venereal diseases was the destruction of those who allegedly had conspired to pollute the German people. The Nazis accused Jews and "Marxists" of being the primary beneficiaries of prostitution and the spread of STDs. Hitler stressed that his observation of Jewish procurers in Vienna had converted him to anti-Semitism. "When thus for the first time I recognized the Jew as the cold-hearted, shameless, and calculating director of this revolting vice traffic in the scum of the big city, a cold shudder ran down my back."[53] The Nazi press was filled with propaganda about the alleged Jewish-controlled "white slave trade" in Christian women. Such articles frequently blamed the Weimar state and its staunchest supporter, Social Democracy, for complicity in Jewish "sex crimes." *Der Angriff*, a weekly edited by Joseph Goebbels in Berlin, attacked deputy police president Bernhard Weiß, a Jew and a Democrat, for protecting Jewish "slave traffickers" (*Mädchenhändler*) from criminal prosecution.[54] In another issue, the paper accused the SPD coalition government of Berlin of supporting the establishment of licensed brothels to "increase the profits of Jewish businessmen."[55] The pornographic weekly *Der Stürmer* claimed that Jewish and socialist sex reformers aimed to contaminate Germany's youth with venereal diseases.[56] Nazi propaganda about prostitution and STDs fused anti-Semitism with conservative fears about "moral decay" and "sexual Bolshevism." By stressing Weimar's alleged "immorality," the Nazis strove to undermine popular support for the democratic regime. The backlash against the 1927 prostitution reform offered them an ideal opportunity to apply this strategy.

Two days before implementation of the anti-VD law, *Völkischer Beobachter*, the official organ of the Nazi Party, ran a front-page article attacking the reform.[57] Contrary to its professed aim, the article claimed, the law would produce a great increase in venereal diseases because it

---

[53]See ibid., 59–60. On Jewish feminists' efforts to combat anti-Semitic propaganda about alleged Jewish control of the traffic in women, see Marion Kaplan, *The Jewish Feminist Movement in Germany: The Campaigns of the jüdischer Frauenbund, 1904–1938* (Westport, 1979), esp. 113–17.

[54]See "'Es gibt keinen Mädchenhandel,'" *Der Angriff*, August 13, 1928; and "Menschenhändler am Werk," *Der Angriff*, October 22, 1928. On Goebbels's campaign against Weiß, see Liang, 153, 160–61.

[55]See "Bordelle für die Innenstadt," *Der Angriff*, January 2, 1928.

[56]See, for instance, "Kamaradschaftsehe und freie Liebe," *Der Stürmer* 6, no. 49 (December 1928); and "Geschlechtskranke Kinder," *Der Stürmer* 7, no. 9 (February 1929).

[57]See "Der Sieg der Prostitution über die 'deutsche' Demokratie: Das volkszerstörende Gesetz zur 'Bekämpfung' der Geschlechtskrankheiten als Wegbereiter der Prostituierung und Verseuchung der ganzen Nation," *Völkischer Beobachter*, September 29, 1927.

elevated prostitution to the status of a respectable profession. Responsible for this were the Jews and Social Democrats, who had pushed for the decriminalization of prostitution to undermine the moral and racial foundations of the family. Under the banners of democracy and equal rights for women, the anti-VD law jeopardized the health of the German people. "Respectable houses are rendered breeding grounds for immorality while procurers, pimps, and whores rejoice that their time has come. The golden age has commenced! This is how Marxism perceives of the solution to the prostitution problem." Another article in *Völkischer Beobachter* praised the old system of state-regulated prostitution. "The tight organization of the morals police is better suited to protect the health of the people than the proclamation of 'free love' through this [anti-VD] law."[58]

At the local level as well, the Nazis joined conservative movements against the 1927 prostitution reform. In a speech before Munich's parliament in October 1927, Karl Fiehler, the Nazi city councilor and future major of that city, attacked Social Democrats who had "stripped prostitution of its dishonorable character." Fiehler's verbal assaults focused especially on Julius Moses, the Social Democratic spokesman on health and a Jew, whom Fiehler blamed for the rise in commercial sex and STDs.[59] In Bremen, National Socialists mobilized citizens against the decriminalization of prostitution. In a series of articles published during the fall of 1931, the *Bremer Nationalsozialistische Zeitung* called on the government to cleanse the streets of "vice."[60] The spread of street soliciting, the paper proclaimed, was a crime against Germany's youth, "the most precious possession of our nation." In their campaign against the 1927 reform, the Nazis claimed broad support among Bremen officials and citizens' associations.

II.

Prostitution, the "Moral" Agenda, and the Establishment of Nazi Rule

During the months following Adolf Hitler's appointment as Reich chancellor on January 30, 1933, the Nazis continued to present themselves as guardians of conventional sexual morality. This strategy aimed to strengthen support for National Socialism among religious conservatives. Hitler was especially concerned to overcome the Catholic episcopate's opposition. In January 1931 Cardinal Adolf Bertram of Breslau, the head of the Fulda

[58]See "Nochmals das Gesetz zur Bekämpfung der Geschlechtskrankheiten," *Völkischer Beobachter*, December 27, 1927.

[59]See "Sitzung des Stadtrates am 11. Oktober 1927," *Münchener Gemeinde-Zeitung*, supplement no. 83, October 19, 1927.

[60]See "Wir verlangen: Restlose Bereinigung der Bahnhofstr. und der angrenzenden Straßenzüge," parts 2–4, *Bremer Nationalsozialistische Zeitung*, September 11, 1931, September 12, 1931, and September 15, 1931.

Bishops Conference, had condemned Nazi racial ideologies as incompatible with Christianity. As a result, Catholic clergy often admonished their parishioners not to join the Nazi Party or to vote for the NSDAP.[61] To expand their power in the spring of 1933, the Nazis urgently needed conservative Catholics' support. In particular, they had to secure the Center Party's approval of the Enabling Act (Ermächtigungsgesetz) of March 24, 1933, which granted the government sweeping dictatorial powers.[62] The "moral" agenda played a crucial role in winning Hitler the support of the religious Right. In his speech before the Reichstag on March 23, Hitler assured conservatives of the Nazis' commitment to the defense of Christian values.

> By its decision to carry out the political and moral cleansing of our public life, the government is creating and securing the conditions for a really deep and inner religious life. . . . The national government sees in both Christian denominations the most important factor for the maintenance of our society. It will observe the agreements drawn up between the Churches and the provinces. . . . And it will be concerned for the sincere cooperation between church and state. The struggle against the materialistic ideology and for the erection of a true people's community serves as much the interests of the German nation as of our Christian faith.[63]

The next day, the Reichstag passed the Enabling Act with the support of the Center Party delegates. Shortly thereafter, the Catholic bishops revoked their condemnation of Nazi "paganism."[64] Catholic as well as Lutheran conservatives were hopeful that the Nazis would stamp out "sexual Bolshevism" and reverse Germany's perceived "moral decay."

The Nazis consciously cultivated their image as purifiers of public morality. They focused especially on the fight against prostitution, since this was a key concern of the religious Right. As federal commissioner for the Prussian Ministry of the Interior, Hermann Göring issued a series of decrees against "public immorality."[65] On February 22, 1933, Göring announced that preparations were under way for a revision of Clause 361/6

---

[61]See J. S. Conway, *The Nazi Persecution of the Churches, 1933–45* (London, 1968), 6–7. Nazism's electoral gains among Catholics trailed far behind those among Protestants, who on the average voted twice as often for the NSDAP between 1930 and 1933. See Falter, 169–93.

[62]On the Center Party's support for the Enabling Law, see Jasper, 135–37; and Ellen Lovell Evans, *The German Center Party, 1870–1933* (Carbondale, 1981), esp. 384–86.

[63]See Hitler's speech on government policy before the Reichstag on March 23, 1933, quoted in Conway, 20; for the complete text of the speech, see *Dokumente der deutschen Politik und Geschichte von 1848 bis zur Gegenwart*, ed. Johannes Hohlfeld (Berlin and Munich, n.d.), 4:29–36.

[64]See Conway, 21–23; Evans, *The German Center Party*, 387.

[65]See "Maßnahmen der preußischen Regierung zur Bekämpfung der öffentlichen Unsittlichkeit," *Volkswart: Monatsschrift zur Pflege der Volkssittlichkeit* 26 (1933): 54–56;

of the penal code that would grant the police greater authority to combat public prostitution. In the meantime, the police were to make "full use" of existing legal provisions against street soliciting. The decree of February 22 expressly forbade special police regulations for the control of prostitutes, a measure that would have alienated conservative opponents of regulationism. On February 23 Göring issued another decree that demanded the strict suppression of *Absteigequartiere*.

In May 1933 the Nazis effectively outlawed street soliciting. The revised Clause 361/6 criminalized any form of public solicitation pursued "in a conspicuous manner or in a manner suited to harass individuals or the public."[66] Parallel to these new legal restrictions on prostitution, the police engaged in massive raids on streetwalkers. Though no comprehensive figures exist, it has been estimated that "thousands, even more likely tens of thousands" of prostitutes were arrested during the spring and summer of 1933.[67] In Hamburg the police arrested 3,201 women suspected of prostitution between March and August 1933; of these, 814 were taken into preventive detention (*Schutzhaft*), and 274 were subjected to compulsory medical treatment for STDs.[68] In a single nightly raid in June 1933, the Düsseldorf police, reinforced by local SS units, arrested 156 women and 35 men accused of street soliciting.[69] The dubious legal basis for these mass arrests was provided by the Emergency Decree for the Protection of People and State of February 28, 1933, which suspended civil liberties.

Religious conservatives welcomed the Nazis' measures against prostitution. Adolf Sellmann, head of the Protestant West German Morality Association (Westdeutscher Sittlichkeitsverein), praised Hitler for "saving" Germany from the "moral decay" of Weimar: "It was a great and wonderful day for us when our leader and Reich chancellor Adolf Hitler took charge of the government on January 30, 1933. At one blow, everything changed in Germany. All trash and filth disappeared from the public. Once again, the streets of our cities were clean. Prostitution, which previously had been able to spread in our big cities as well as in many smaller towns, was scared away. . . . Suddenly, everything we had hoped

---

see also Adolf Sellmann, *50 Jahre Kampf für Volkssittlichkeit und Volkskraft: Die Geschichte des westdeutschen Sittlichkeitsvereins von seinen Anfängen bis heute, 1885–1935* (Schwelm, 1935), 108–9.

[66]The revision of Clause 361/6 was included in the Law for the Alteration of Criminal Provisions (Gesetz zur Abänderung strafrechtlicher Vorschriften) of May 26, 1933. See *Reichsgesetzblatt*, part 1, May 29, 1933. See also Leopold Schäfer, "Neue Gesetzgebung und Rechtsprechung zur Prostitutionsfrage," *Deutsche Zeitschrift für Wohlfahrtspflege* 9 (1933): 157–65.

[67]See Bock, "'Keine Arbeitskräfte in diesem Sinne,'" 83.

[68]See "Der Kampf gegen die Prostitution," *Hamburger Fremdenblatt*, September 8, 1933.

[69]See "Aus der Arbeit der Sittenpolizei," *Volkswart* 26 (1933): 125.

and wished for had come true."[70] Similarly, the Catholic Volkswartbund rejoiced at the *frischer Zug* [vigorous attitude] of the new regime toward "vice." An article published in *Volkswart* in the summer of 1933 favorably compared the Nazis' suppression of prostitution and other forms of "indecency" with the "laxity" of the Weimar state. "How grateful we all are in the Volkswartbund about the new government's level-headed yet firm approach toward filth wherever it is visible. . . . Therefore: *Siegheil!*"[71] And the new rulers indeed proved responsive to the demands of the religious Right. On March 16, 1933, leaders of Lutheran and Catholic morality associations met with representatives of the Prussian Ministry of the Interior and the police to discuss proposals for a more effective fight against "immorality." With evident delight, the Volkswartbund noted that at the meeting, Prussian officials emphasized "the need for cooperation between the government and the local branches of the individual morality associations."[72] During the spring and summer of 1933, the Nazis convinced the religious Right of their genuine determination to defend traditional Christian ideals of sexual purity. This was a key precondition for the extension and stabilization of Nazi power during this vital period.

Against the Moraltuerei: *Regulationism after 1934*

In the fall of 1933 conservatives witnessed with alarm a growing movement among police officials to reintroduce regulated brothels. The city of Essen spearheaded the revival of *Reglementierung*. In October 1933 the journal *Die Polizei* published the new regulations for the control of prostitutes issued by Essen's chief of police.[73] The author of the article, Dr. G. Müller, critically observed that the abolition of the morals police through the 1927 Law for Combating Venereal Diseases had led to a dramatic increase in prostitution. The anti-VD law had failed, Müller argued, because it combined beneficial measures against the spread of STDs with "the 'emancipation' of the prostitute, a demand of eastern Marxism and of a feminist movement contaminated by Marxist ideas."[74] The Essen regulations openly disregarded Paragraph 17 of the anti-VD law, which forbade the police to confine prostitutes to special streets or blocks (*Kasernierung*). In Essen registered prostitutes were banned from public areas and restricted to certain houses. Müller stressed that the anti-VD law's provisions concerning prostitution were no longer binding, since they represented "the formal law of a regime whose ethos has become entirely incomprehensible and

---

[70]See Sellmann, 107.

[71]See "Der frische Zug im neuen Staat," *Volkswart* 26 (1933): 170–71.

[72]See the circular of the Volkswartbund of March 24, 1933, in ADCV, SKF 319.4 D01/ 05e, Fasz. 1.

[73]See G. Müller, "Zur Kasernierung der Dirnen in Essen," *Die Polizei* 30 (1933): 440–43.

[74]See ibid., 440.

alien to us today."[75] Instead, Essen officials based their measures on the Emergency Decree of February 28, 1933. During the fall and winter of 1933, a range of other cities, including Hamburg, Altona, and Bremen, followed suit and introduced new systems of police-controlled prostitution.[76]

A memorandum on National Socialist criminal law by the Prussian minister of justice published in the fall of 1933 mobilized conservative opponents of state-regulated prostitution into action.[77] The Prussian minister proposed the legalization of regulated brothels. Shortly after publication of the memorandum, the welfare organization of the Lutheran Church, Inner Mission (Innere Mission), approached Reich bishop Ludwig Müller to present Hitler with a petition against the reintroduction of police-controlled prostitution. The petition, submitted to Hitler in late November or early December 1933, emphasized the detrimental impacts of regulationism.[78] "A new *Reglementierung* or *Kasernierung* would greatly endanger the goal of the National Socialist state to enforce the health of the people, racial purity, and the moral education of the population." Regulated brothels, the petition stressed, failed to prevent the spread of STDs since only a small minority of prostitutes were subjected to these controls. Instead, brothel districts represented a dangerous source of moral and physical "pollution," confused popular conceptions of decency, and undermined the family. To drive home their message to the Reich chancellor, the petitioners used arguments derived from Nazi racial ideology. "Moreover, *Reglementierung* [is] an institution alien (*artfremd*) to the Germanic peoples of the Nordic race. [Through its introduction] Germany would once again assume an exceptional status among these peoples." The Catholic welfare organization, Caritas, similarly condemned efforts to return to state-regulated prostitution. Regulationism, a Caritas memo stressed, "damages the reputation of the state and ruins the moral beliefs of the people."[79] Because it signified state sanction of extramarital sexuality, *Reglementierung* incited people to engage in "vice" and destroyed the family. Caritas urged that only a total criminalization of street soliciting provided a viable protection of public morality.

---

[75]See ibid., 441.

[76]On Altona, see the report of the district president in Schleswig of November 30, 1933, in BArch R 1501/27217/8, 157–58; on Bremen, see the police report of March 17, 1941, in StAB 4, 130/1-R.I.1.-14; for a copy of the Hamburg police regulations of November 1933, see Landesarchiv Berlin (LAB), B Rep. 235 (Helene Lange Archiv), microfilm no. 3395.

[77]The memorandum is discussed in Hermann Wagner, "Kirche und Staat," *Christliche Volkswacht* (November/December 1933): 163–68.

[78]See the circular by the Central Committee of the Inner Mission of December 4, 1933, in Archiv des diakonischen Werkes der evangelischen Kirche Deutschlands (ADW), Central Ausschuß (CA), Gf/St/287.

[79]See "Stellung des deutschen Caritasverbandes zur Frage der staatlichen Reglementierung der Prostitution," ca. 1934, in ADCV, SKF 319.4 D01/05e, Fasz. 1.

The authoritarian abolitionism of the religious Right received support from other sides as well. One of the major critics of the pro-regulationist movement among the police was Bodo Spiethoff, whom the Nazis had installed as the new president of the German Society for Combating Venereal Diseases (Deutsche Gesellschaft zur Bekämpfung der Geschlechtskrankheiten, or DGBG). In a report of January 1934, the head of the DGBG sharply criticized the situation in Cologne and Essen where the police restricted licensed prostitutes to special streets.[80] Spiethoff argued that *Kasernierung* failed to achieve its professed aims, the protection of public health and public order. In Cologne, 150 prostitutes lived in tolerated brothels. However, 1,600 women suspected of prostitution and subject to regular medical controls through the health office lived in various neighborhoods throughout the city. This meant that *Kasernierung* was utterly ineffective in shielding respectable citizens from the "pollutive" impact of streetwalkers. To the contrary, the licensed brothels exacerbated the moral and physical dangers of prostitution since they were centers for the proliferation of "sexual perversions." Spiethoff demanded the strict suppression of street soliciting and the extension of regular medical controls for STDs to include all female persons "who engage in frequent promiscuity." Violations of these controls should be severely penalized with extended prison and workhouse sentences. "The state cannot recognize . . . the right to extramarital sexual relations if it does not want to undermine the foundations of the family."

The police reacted with hostility to such criticisms. Cologne's police president Walter Lingens, whose appointment conservative Catholics had welcomed so enthusiastically in 1932, sharply rejected the DGBG's position. Lingens took exception to the independent "inspection" of Cologne brothels by representatives of the anti-VD society and demanded that the police be given "free rein in the fight against the insufferable whoredom."[81] In an article published in *Westdeutscher Beobachter* during March 1935, Lingens defended Cologne's system of *Kasernierung*, which allowed the police to intervene "vigorously" against nonlicensed streetwalkers. "Decisive for the police's actions is not narrow moralism [*Moraltuerei*] but the maintenance of public order."[82] Even after the revision of Clause 361/6 of the penal code, police officials continued to complain about the lack of effective means to combat prostitution. The "privileged" status the 1927 anti-VD law had conferred on prostitutes was no longer acceptable. Throughout

[80]See Bodo Spiethoff, "Zur Regelung der Prostitutionsfrage," January 29, 1934, in BArch R 15.01/26314, 93–103. See also Bodo Spiethoff, "Der Kampf gegen die Gefahren der Prostitution," *Die Rheinprovinz* 12, no. 12 (December 1936): 853–62.

[81]See the letter by Lingens of January 17, 1934, in BArch R 15.01/27217/8, 174.

[82]See Walter Lingens, "Wie bekämpfen wir das Dirnenunwesen?" *Westdeutscher Beobachter*, March 21, 1935, reprinted in *Der Dienst: Zeitschrift des deutsch-evangelischen Vereins zur Förderung der Sittlichkeit und der Rettungsarbeit* 49 (July/September 1935): 2–4.

Germany, police presidents defied the law's provisions against *Kasernierung* and established licensed brothels.[83]

Despite Reich Bishop Müller's intervention, no evidence exists that Hitler supported the conservative opponents of regulationism. However, another member of the Nazi leadership, Reich Minister of the Interior Wilhelm Frick, took the side of the abolitionists. In a decree of July 12, 1934, Frick criticized the reintroduction of regulated brothels.[84] The decree stressed "that according to Paragraph 17 of the Law for Combating Venereal Diseases, . . . the *Kasernierung* of prostitution is illegal." The police were ordered to abide by the law. However, religious conservatives soon learned that Frick's announcement had little impact on prostitution policy at the local level. In Hamburg the Lutheran Volkswachtbund published Frick's decree in its organ, *Mitteilungen für die Freunde der Mitternachtsmission Hamburg*, and criticized the establishment of regulated brothels by the police. On September 6, 1934, the paper's editor, Helene Sillem, received "a very serious warning" from the secret police (Geheime Staatspolizei, or Gestapo) that "not only would the paper be confiscated, but the entire work of the Volkswachtbund would be terminated if any issues of the paper ever again contained such a critique of the Hamburg administration."[85]

Conflicts over regulationism persisted for a while after 1934. Ultimately, however, religious conservatives could not halt the rise of the regulated brothel. A major reason for the triumph of *Reglementierung* was the declining power of the churches during the second half of the 1930s. The Nazis stepped up their repression of Catholic associations and clergy after the Saar plebiscite in January 1935; in March 1935 there were mass arrests of members of the Lutheran Confessing Church who opposed a Reich church dominated by the Nazi state.[86] As early as July 1933 the Prussian government had prepared a revision of the 1927 anti-VD law that reintroduced the morals police and legalized regulated brothels.[87] But such plans were not made public to avoid alienating the religious Right. Only when the regime became independent of the support of religious conservatives did Nazi leaders push openly for regulationism.[88] At the same time that

[83]See Rohne, "Dirne und polizeiliche Praxis," *Reichsverwaltungsblatt*, no. 56 (1935): 769–72.

[84]See BArch R 15.01/27217/8, 251.

[85]See Sillem's letter of November 9, 1934, in ibid., 278.

[86]J. S. Conway has argued that during 1936 and 1937, "the ideological campaign against the Churches was to reach its zenith" (141).

[87]See "Entwurf eines Gesetzes zur Bekämpfung der Geschlechtskrankheiten" of July 19, 1933, in GStA-PK, I. HA Rep. 84A/869, 272–75.

[88]Of course, another key precondition for the resurgence of police-controlled prostitution after 1933 was the demise of an independent women's movement and the defeat of those Nazi women who envisioned a racial community where "Aryan" men and women shared the same rights and privileges. See Claudia Koonz, *Mothers in the Fatherland: Women, the Family, and Nazi Politics* (New York, 1987), esp. chaps. 5 and 6.

the political influence of the Christian churches deteriorated, the police gained power. During the late 1920s and early 1930s, the police had closed ranks with the moral Right in efforts to reverse the more liberal aspects of the 1927 prostitution reform. Unlike religious conservatives, however, police officials believed that state-regulated prostitution represented an indispensable tool for controlling prostitutes and their criminal associates. The rise of Heinrich Himmler and the SS played a key role in the emergence of Nazi-era regulationism. Under Himmler, who was appointed chief of the German police in June 1936, the police became increasingly autonomous vis-à-vis the other branches of the administration.[89] Himmler was one of the most fanatic proponents of regulated brothels and a major driving force behind the massive expansion of police-controlled prostitution during the Second World War.

The Nazis' support for regulationism also reflected the demands of the military. As preparations for war intensified during the second half of the 1930s, the Wehrmacht insisted on regulated prostitution to control the spread of STDs among the troops and to strengthen military morale. In February 1936 the Deutscher Gemeindetag, the organization of German municipalities, met in Hamburg and discussed the details of a projected correctional custody law. One topic was the inclusion of prostitutes in the provisions of the law. During the debate, a Hanover official pointed out that "in our province, there exist numerous military training camps. The military command has declared that the establishment of brothels is an urgent necessity. . . . Therefore we have to be more lenient in the control [*Erfassung*] of prostitutes."[90] The vital importance of regulated prostitution for Germany's military goals ultimately overruled concerns about the need to eradicate "vice."

The Radicalization of Nazi Prostitution Policies during the Second World War

Immediately after the beginning of war, the government issued several decrees for the control of prostitution and STDs. On September 9, 1939, the Reich Ministry of the Interior ordered the strict supervision of prostitutes through the police "to protect members of the Wehrmacht and the civilian

---

[89]See Hans Buchheim, "Die SS—Das Herrschaftsinstrument," *Anatomie des SS-Staates*, vol. 1 (Munich, 1989), esp. 50–59. On the rise of Himmler and the SS, see also Franz Neumann, *Behemoth: Struktur und Praxis des Nationalsozialismus, 1933–1944* (Frankfurt am Main, 1984 [originally published in English, 1942]), 572–81.

[90]See the minutes of the meeting of the Gemeindetag's committee on social welfare on February 27, 1936, in BArch R36/1827, quoted in Detlev Peukert, *Grenzen der Sozialdisziplinierung: Aufstieg und Krise der deutschen Jugendfürsorge von 1878 bis 1932* (Cologne, 1986), 281. See also Paul, 12; Annette Timm, "The Ambivalent Outsider: Prostitution, Promiscuity, and VD Control in Nazi Berlin," in *Social Outsiders in Nazi Germany*, ed. Robert Gellately and Nathan Stoltzfus (Princeton, 2001), 195.

population against the dangers emanating from prostitution, especially in relation to health."[91] The decree called for the suppression of street soliciting and for the establishment of licensed brothels: "Where special houses for prostitutes do not exist, the police have to [establish] them in the appropriate neighborhoods." The brothels had to comply with Nazi racial policies. At least officially, Jewish prostitutes were entirely banned.[92] In cities with a considerable contingent of foreigners, certain brothels had to house non-German prostitutes to protect "racial purity." New regulations, clearly directed against sadomasochism, outlawed certain sexual toys and instruments.[93] The decree authorized the police to impose curfews and numerous other restrictions on streetwalkers. Women who violated these regulations could be taken into "preventive detention" (*Vorbeugungshaft*), which generally meant internment in a concentration camp.[94]

A subsequent decree of September 18, 1939, greatly extended the scope of medical supervision of women suspected of prostitution. It called on the police and the health offices to organize special "social welfare patrols" (*Fürsorgestreifen*) for the surveillance of people who engaged in "frequent promiscuity" (*häufig wechselnder Geschlechtsverkehr*, or hwG), a term that referred primarily to women accused of prostitution. "HwG persons" infected with a venereal disease were subject to compulsory medical treatment and hospitalization. The decree stipulated that "persons who resist or disregard the orders of the health office can be taken into protective detention on account of their antisocial behavior." The decrees of September 1939 marked the radicalization of Nazi prostitution policies. Despite the continued illegality of *Kasernierung*, the regime now openly promoted the massive proliferation of police-controlled brothels.[95] The parallel brutal repression of unlicensed streetwalkers served to buttress

---

[91] *Erlaßsammlung vorbeugende Verbrechensbekämpfung*, Schriftenreihe des Reichskriminalpolizeiamtes Berlin, no. 15 (Berlin, 1941), 144–45. (Page numbers indicated in the text refer to the copy of the *Erlaßsammlung* in the possession of the Institut für Zeitgeschichte in Munich.) The decree of September 9, 1939, initially pertained only to those areas within the German Reich affected by military operations (*Operationsgebiet des Heeres*). On March 16, 1940, the decree was extended to include the entire Reich territory. See ibid., 173.

[92] In reality, Jewish women were often forced to work in military brothels. See Paul, 104–5; see also Franz Seidler, *Prostitution-Homosexualität-Selbstverstümmelung: Probleme der deutschen Sanitätsführung, 1939–1945* (Neckargemünd, 1977), 181–82.

[93] The decree of September 9, 1939, forbade prostitutes to manufacture, own, or distribute instruments "that can be used for sadistic or masochistic purposes."

[94] On the growing importance of preventive detention in the persecution of "antisocials," see Martin Broszat, "Nationalsozialistische Konzentrationslager, 1933–1945," in *Anatomie des SS-Staates*, vol. 2 (Munich, 1989), esp. 66–67. See also Wolfgang Ayaß, *"Asoziale" im Nationalsozialismus* (Stuttgart, 1995), chap. 6.

[95] Only in November of 1940 was Paragraph 17 of the anti-VD law, which outlawed *Kasernierung*, formally repealed. See Ayaß, 192.

the monopoly of the regulated brothel as the only legitimate form of prostitution.[96] The severe penalties for "hwG" persons who violated the health offices' regulations for the control of STDs effectively undermined sociohygienic criticisms of *Reglementierung*. Opponents of state-regulated prostitution like Bodo Spiethoff of the anti-VD society argued that the system failed to curb the spread of STDs because it only controlled the small minority of licensed prostitutes, while so-called clandestine streetwalkers continued to spread venereal infections. But under the conditions of an increasingly ruthless dictatorship that confined "unruly" streetwalkers to concentration camps, this argument lost much of its power. After 1939 it seemed more and more feasible that unlicensed prostitution would be eradicated in the near future.

In their efforts to make the regulated brothel the exclusive site of prostitution, Nazi leaders completely disregarded conventional moral concerns. They were also unresponsive to the objections of city officials who argued that the establishment of new brothels would greatly exacerbate the housing shortage. The example of Würzburg illustrates the single-mindedness with which the Nazis and the police pursued their goal. At a meeting in November 1936, leading Würzburg officials and politicians had decided that regulated brothels were "neither useful nor successful in the containment of venereal diseases." This position conflicted with the decree of September 9, 1939, which made the establishment of brothels compulsory for cities that lacked them. On May 30, 1940, the chief of the Bavarian police reprimanded Würzburg's mayor for the city's refusal to open a licensed brothel.[97] In his response, the mayor emphasized his general support for the measure but objected that he faced great difficulties. "An apartment building rented to a number of tenants cannot be vacated in light of the well-established housing shortage in Würzburg." He suggested instead the use of a house "currently serving as a shelter for Jews. . . . Under no circumstances must the general housing market be affected."[98]

However, when the house was designated officially as the future site of Würzburg's regulated brothel, neighbors mobilized public protests. In a letter to the Nazi Welfare Organization for War Victims (Nationalsozialistische Kriegsopferversorgung) of March 1942, one neighbor complained that the buildings adjacent to the prospective brothel housed "eight families, four of whose sons thus far have sacrificed their young hopeful lives on the altar of the fatherland, three others have been wounded seriously. . . .

---

[96]For a detailed discussion of how policies against so-called antisocials affected prostitutes, see ibid., 184–96; Zürn; Gisela Bock, *Zwangssterilisation im Nationalsozialismus: Studien zur Rassenpolitik und zur Frauenpolitik* (Opladen, 1986), esp. 401–10, 417–19.

[97]See the letter of Würzburg's mayor to the chief of the Bavarian police of May 21, 1940, as well as the police chief's response of May 30, 1940, in BayHStAM, M-Inn/72645.

[98]See ibid., as well as the mayor's letter of May 31, 1940.

We cannot believe that the Führer . . . would give his approval that the holiest feelings of the parents of fallen soldiers are violated . . . this way."[99] The Catholic bishop of Würzburg supported the protests against the brothel: "The preservation of the people's *moral* health is equally important and as necessary as the preservation of its *physical* health. . . . From the beginning, the Third Reich has fought the excesses of pornography [*Nacktkultur*] and brothels."[100] But times had changed. In a report to the head of the SS (Reichsführer SS, RFSS), Heinrich Himmler, the Bavarian chief of police pointed out "that the opposition to the establishment of a brothel originates mainly in church-affiliated circles." This clearly discredited the Würzburg protesters. The letter emphasized that the city urgently needed a public brothel since large military contingents were stationed there.[101] On August 16, 1942, Himmler authorized the opening of the Würzburg brothel.[102]

For the Reichsführer SS and other Nazi leaders, the need to provide German men with a "safe" sexual outlet was paramount, superseding concerns about "immorality." In fact, Himmler resented the churches' "moralistic" stance on extramarital sex, which he believed was conducive to the spread of male homosexual relations. In a speech before SS commanders (Gruppenführer) during February 1937, the RFSS defended the use of female prostitution as a weapon in the fight against male homosexuality.

> You see, it is possible to regulate all kinds of things by means of the state and through police measures. One can organize the question of female prostitution [*Dirnenfrage*], which by comparison with this question [of male homosexuality] in principle is completely harmless, in a way that is acceptable for a civilized people [*Kulturvolk*]. In this area, we will be generous beyond bounds. One cannot prevent the entire youth from drifting toward homosexuality if at the same time one blocks all the alternatives. That is madness. After all, every barred opportunity to get together with girls in the big cities—even if it is for money—will motivate a large contingent to join the other side.[103]

Himmler's toleration of female prostitution was not, as George Mosse suggested, "in direct conflict with the official policy of the Third Reich."[104]

[99]See BArch NS 19/1598, 2.

[100]See the bishop's letter of November 22, 1940, in BayHStAM, M-Inn/72645, emphasis in the original.

[101]See BArch NS 19/1598, 8.

[102]See ibid., 12.

[103]See Himmler's speech before SS commanders on February 18, 1937, reprinted in excerpts in Heinrich Himmler, *Geheimreden 1933 bis 1945 und andere Ansprachen*, ed. Bradley F. Smith and Agnes F. Peterson (Ludwigsburg, 1974), 93–104, 98.

[104]George L. Mosse, *Nationalism and Sexuality: Middle-Class Morality and Sexual Norms in Modern Europe* (Madison, 1985), 167.

By the time the Reichsführer SS gave his speech, *Reglementierung* was firmly established in many of Germany's major cities. As the example of Würzburg showed, after the onset of war even cities initially opposed to the establishment of regulated brothels had to fall in line. In wartime Nazi Germany, the regulated brothel became a thriving state institution under the special care and protection of the police.

The attitude of Munich's police was typical. In the summer of 1940, the Munich police converted a former hotel into a brothel "for more distinguished tastes [*bessere Ansprüche*]."[105] The brothel was officially run by a madam with a long experience "of renting her rooms to prostitutes," yet the police fixed the rates at no more than fifteen Reichmarks per customer. The prostitutes were subject to regular medical controls for STDs through the health office. Munich's police also planned to establish a second "public house" that would cater specifically to a working-class clientele. This brothel, a police report stressed, aimed to provide a sexual outlet for "the less affluent workers and soldiers" and had to comply with the standards of excellence typical of public services in the Third Reich. "It must not be a brothel of the old style in a decayed, filthy . . . building. With this house . . . something has to be offered to the ordinary worker and soldier . . . which compares well indeed with all the other institutions which the new time has created for him." How much the Munich police considered the regulated brothel an exemplary state institution is reflected in their inquiry with the Reich minister of the interior "whether the raising of the flag during general occasions should be tolerated at the public houses?"

Regulated brothels fulfilled a key function in upholding Nazi racial policies. This becomes especially apparent in the case of the brothels for foreign and forced laborers (*fremdvölkische Arbeiter*) established after 1940. The Nazis' solution to Germany's acute wartime labor shortage was the massive deployment of mostly forced foreign workers and prisoners of war (POWs).[106] By mid-1940 approximately 700,000 forcefully conscripted Poles worked in Germany. In the course of the war, the number of foreign workers within the German Reich increased dramatically. Ulrich Herbert has estimated that by the end of the war "there were . . . some seven million foreigners laboring for the Germans inside the Reich." Of the civilian foreign workers, roughly one third were women.[107] Nazi authorities were especially concerned about the danger of "miscegenation," the so-called crimes of intercourse (*Geschlechtsverkehr-Verbrechen*) between foreign workers and German women. Poles and Russians, who occupied the lowest ranks within the Nazi racial hierarchy of foreign workers, were punished with death if

[105]See the report by the Munich police to the Reich Minister of the Interior of June 29, 1940, in BayHStAM, M-Inn/72645.

[106]See Ulrich Herbert, *A History of Foreign Labor in Germany, 1880–1980* (Ann Arbor, 1990), chap. 4; see also Ulrich Herbert, *Hitler's Foreign Workers: Enforced Foreign Labor in Germany under the Third Reich* (Cambridge, 1997).

[107]See Herbert, *History of Foreign Labor,* 152–53.

they engaged in sexual relations with German women. German women who had sexual contacts with Polish workers were sent to prison or to a concentration camp in addition to humiliating public shaming.[108]

Despite these harsh penalties, incidents of "forbidden contact" between German women and foreign workers remained numerous. To preserve the "purity of the German blood," Hitler himself ordered the establishment of special brothels for foreign workers in December 1940.[109] The first brothel for *fremdvölkische Arbeiter* was opened at the Hermann Göring Works in Linz.[110] The Linz operation served as a model for other cities throughout the Reich. A report of the Gauleitung Oberdonau of December 21, 1940, stated that "the labor force of the Reichswerke Hermann Göring in Linz is comprised to a substantial part of Czechs, Slovaks, Bulgarians, and Italians. To combat recurrent unwelcome contacts between foreign workers and German women, the *Gauleitung* . . . decided to establish a brothel." The police were responsible for the recruitment and supervision of the foreign prostitutes working in the brothel. As the report about Linz stressed, the prostitutes belonged to the same nationality as the workers who had access to the brothel. "It is to be strictly enforced that no Germans go to the houses staffed with foreign girls, and that no foreign workers get into the German houses already existing in the city." Similarly, a circular of January 16, 1941, issued by Reinhardt Heydrich, the chief of the Security Service (Sicherheitsdienst, or SD), emphasized that "the houses cannot be staffed with German prostitutes [*Prostituierte deutschen Volkstums*] but only with foreign prostitutes and gypsies."[111] In Bremen foreign prostitutes were handed guidelines that expressly forbade them to engage in sexual relations with German men. The prostitutes were not allowed to solicit outside the brothel and needed a special pass to leave the brothel barracks. Any violation of the regulations could lead to internment in a concentration camp.[112]

By 1939 at the latest, Nazi prostitution policies diverged in important ways from previous systems of regulationism. Conventionally, state-regulated prostitution aimed to protect "respectable" society against moral "pollution" by prostitutes. The Nazis also strove to eradicate street soliciting and to confine prostitutes to tightly supervised brothels. However, their primary motivation was not concern about the suppression of "immorality." For the first time, a German government made the establishment of supervised brothels compulsory for all cities and issued standardized regulations for the operation of "public houses." What was new about the Nazi system of *Reglementierung* was the attempt to use the state in this direct

---

[108]See Herbert, *Hitler's Foreign Workers*, esp. 75, 131–33.
[109]See Paul, 117–18; Herbert, *Hitler's Foreign Workers*, esp. 130–31.
[110]See the circular of Hitler's deputy, Rudolf Hess, of December 7, 1940, in StAB 4,130/1-R.I.3.-9, vol. 1.
[111]See Heydrich's circular of January 16, 1941, in ibid.
[112]See "Merkblatt für ausländische Prostituierte," in ibid., vol. 2.

way to create a certain form of human sexuality. Nazi brothels aimed to maintain the physical fitness and morale of "Aryan" men.[113] At the same time, the persecution of prostitutes intensified greatly. Previously, prostitutes who violated police orders were punished with fines or short prison and workhouse sentences. In the Third Reich, such violations frequently led to streetwalkers' internment in a concentration camp. The brutality of the suppression of prostitutes in Nazi Germany marks an important break with older forms of state-regulated prostitution. Another key difference is the racialization of Nazi regulationism. As the campaign to establish special brothels for foreign workers shows, regulated prostitution played a crucial role in upholding racist hierarchies between Germans and nationalities the Nazis considered "racially inferior."

CONCLUSION

In *The Origins of Totalitarianism*, Hannah Arendt argued that the key function of the Nazi concentration camps was to eradicate human individuality.

> The concentration and extermination camps of totalitarian regimes serve as the laboratories in which the fundamental belief of totalitarianism that everything is possible is being verified. . . . Total domination, which strives to organize the infinite plurality and differentiation of human beings as if all of humanity were just one individual, is possible only if each and every person can be reduced to a never-changing identity of reactions, so that each of these bundles of reactions can be exchanged at random for any other. . . . The camps are meant not only to exterminate people and degrade human beings, but also serve the ghastly experiment of eliminating . . . spontaneity itself as an expression of human behavior and of transforming the human personality into a mere thing, into something that even animals are not; for Pavlov's dog, which . . . was trained to eat not when it was hungry but when a bell rang, was a perverted animal.[114]

According to Arendt, total domination required the transformation of human beings into lifeless "bundles of reactions." This dynamic had serious implications for sexuality. The history of prostitution in Nazi Germany during the Second World War provides preliminary evidence that the Nazis radically tried to alter sexual behavior. Thus, regulated brothels for "Aryan" men were supposed to eradicate homosexual and sadomasochistic "perversions" and instead foster a concept of (male) sexuality as mechanical physical need. The misogynistic rationale of Nazi sexual policies reduced prostitutes to the status of instruments for the satisfaction of this need.

---

[113]On this point, see also Timm, this volume.

[114]See Hannah Arendt, *The Origins of Totalitarianism* (New York, 1973), 437–38.

The concentration camp brothels came closest to representing a labo-
ratory where human sexuality was transformed into a mere animal function devoid of spontaneity, individuality, and eroticism. In March 1942
Himmler first issued orders that "industrious" prisoners in concentration
camps should be rewarded with a visit to the brothel.[115] After an inspection of Buchenwald during March 1943, the RFSS criticized the lack of a
brothel within the confines of the camp. Like special monetary payments
and rations in cigarettes, sex was a key incentive to stimulate productivity
among the prisoners. "This whole issue is not particularly pretty, but it is
natural, and if I can use nature as an incentive for higher performance,
then I think we have to take advantage of this incentive."[116] By the summer of 1944, brothels had been opened in eight major concentration camps,
including Auschwitz, Buchenwald, Sachsenhausen, and Dachau.[117] Sex in
these brothels indeed reduced intercourse to a mere animal function. As
one woman forced to work in the camp brothel at Buchenwald told historian Christa Paul, "It was nothing personal, one felt like a robot. They did
not take notice of us; we were the lowest of the low. We were only good
for this. No conversation or small talk, not even the weather was on the
agenda. Everything was so mechanical and indifferent. . . . They finished
their business and left."[118]

Of course, traditional regulationism had always entailed the degradation of prostitutes. But by hinting at the dystopian possibility of a perfectly mechanized system of sexuality organized according to misogynistic
and racist ideas, Nazi prostitution shed the traditional confines of earlier
forms of regulationism.

[115]See Paul, 23.
[116]See Himmler's letter to Oswald Pohl of March 5, 1943, in *Reichsführer! Briefe an
und von Himmler*, ed. Helmut Heiber (Stuttgart, 1968), 194–96.
[117]See Paul, 23–26.
[118]See ibid., 107.

Homophobic Propaganda and the Denunciation of Same-Sex-Desiring Men under National Socialism

STEFAN MICHELER

University of Hamburg

> Because after all it had been made explicitly clear to us that we must do
> away with such things.
>> Testimony of Else K. to the criminal police, July 10, 1934

IN 1935, UNDER THE GUISE of wide-ranging legal reforms, the National Socialist regime in Germany stiffened the provisions of Paragraph 175 and introduced a new subclause (Paragraph 175a) that laid the legal groundwork for increasingly radical measures against homosexual behavior. Such behavior became subject to harsh persecution, as many thousands of men were sentenced to prison terms or penal servitude, incarcerated in psychiatric institutions, and castrated or murdered in concentration camps.

The radicalization of the Nazi regime's persecution of male homosexual behavior took effect at different rates across the various regions of the German Reich. In Prussia the homosexual movement was dealt a crippling blow as early as 1933, when the government banned the *Freundschaftblätter* (friendship bulletins) that had been published in Berlin for same-sex-desiring men and women and disbanded the Berlin-based homosexual organizations. This had the effect of undermining the communication network that was essential to the organizational efforts of associations of same-sex-desiring persons across Germany.[1] In that same year, in urban areas of Prussia, many pubs frequented by same-sex-desiring persons were shut down. In

---

[1] Little is known regarding the dissolution of the federations. On this topic, see Stefan Micheler, "Kampf, Kontakt, Kultur: Die Freundschaftsverbände gleichgeschlechtlich begehrender Männer und Frauen in der Weimarer Republik in Norddeutschland. Ein Werkstattbericht," in *Querschnitt—Gender Studies: Ein interdisziplinärer Blick nicht nur auf Homosexualität*, ed. Paul M. Hahlbohm and Till Hurlin (Kiel, 2001), 42–81.

Hamburg, on the other hand, similar pubs remained in business until the summer of 1936. However, by 1936 at the latest, a harsh and comprehensive policy of persecution had taken hold across the German Reich. Its aim was to eliminate homosexuality from the public sphere. Bars and public lavatories in a number of cities were raided by the police. Police permission for cross-dressing in women's clothing was withdrawn, and transvestites and male prostitutes were subjected to internment in concentration camps.

The National Socialist regime's professed goal was to eradicate homosexual behavior and not the "homosexual" per se, although the end result was often the same.[2] Like other minorities, "homosexuals," who were deemed degenerate and unhealthy, could not be assimilated into the Aryan German ideal.[3] "Alien to the species," they were excluded from the *Volksgemeinschaft* (*Volk* community) and exposed to slander and persecution. Homosexual behavior was regarded as inconsistent with National Socialist population policies on several grounds. Men who engaged in it were unlikely to fulfill their duty to reproduce and were thus "population policy zeros"; such men might pass on to their offspring a "constitutional predisposition to homosexuality";[4] and such men were the antithesis of the National Socialist masculine ideal, which linked manliness to physical and mental strength, heroism, and a capacity for self-sacrifice—an ideal that achieved its apotheosis in the figure of the soldier. Unlike this ideal figure, "homosexual" men were soft, effeminate, and unable to exert the control over physical urges that was necessary to uphold civil society.[5]

These ascriptions were not new but had their basis in traditional stereotypes that date back to late-nineteenth-century constructions of the

[2]Burkhard Jellonnek first developed this thesis in his dissertation, "Homosexuelle unter dem Hakenkreuz: Die Verfolgung von Homosexuellen im Dritten Reich" (Paderborn, 1990), 327. See also Harry Oosterhuis, "Reinheit und Verfolgung: Männerbünde, Homosexualität und Politik in Deutschland (1900–1945)," *Österreichische Zeitschrift für Geschichte* 5, no. 3 (1994): 388–409, and the nearly identical English version of this essay, "Medicine, Male Bonding and Homosexuality in Nazi Germany," *Journal of Contemporary History* 32 (1997): 187–205. However, the empirical basis for these arguments was established as early as 1977 by scholars who refuted the notion of a "homocaust," an idea that had been awarded wide currency by German gay groups in the early 1970s. See Rüdiger Lautmann, Winfried Grikschat, and Egbert Schmidt, "Der rosa Winkel in den nationalsozialistischen Konzentrationslagern," in *Seminar: Gesellschaft und Homosexualität: Mit Beiträgen v. Hanno Beth u.a.*, ed. Rüdiger Lautmann (Frankfurt am Main, 1977), 325–65.

[3]Since many of the same-sex-desiring and -acting men I describe in my study would not have used the term "homosexual" to describe themselves, I enclose it in quotation marks. The term was based on a late-nineteenth-century construction of the "homosexual personality," and it would be ahistorical and incorrect to describe all same-sex-desiring men from earlier and later periods simply as "homosexual." In my sources, when the term "homosexual" is used, this generally refers to "homosexual men."

[4]My research on Hamburg criminal justice files demonstrates that many same-sex-desiring men were married and had children. These men did not ordinarily identify as "homosexuals."

[5]To date there have been few studies of masculinity under the National Socialist regime. The groundbreaking theoretical works on the topic remain the studies by George Mosse

"homosexual personality." However, while many same-sex-desiring men in Wilhelmine and Weimar Germany had developed and articulated a variety of models of subjectivity and identity that survived into the Nazi era, the stereotype of the "homosexual" as "effeminate and degenerate," "depraved," and "corrupt" became the unifying view of the "homosexual personality" and a focus for homophobic hostility.[6] So too did another common stereotype, that of the "seducer" and "corrupter" of youth (*Jugendverführer* and *Jugendverderber*), a uniquely dangerous figure who lured "normal" young men into depravity and thus spread the "epidemic" of homosexuality.[7] In addition, after the overthrow of Ernst Röhm and his associates within the Sturmabteilung (SA) and the attendant rise of Heinrich Himmler and the Schutzstaffel (SS) in 1934, the rumor that "homosexual cliques" planned to seize power took hold, giving "homosexuals" another identity as "enemies of the state."[8] Indeed, as Rüdiger Lautmann, Winfried Grikschat, and Egbert Schmidt have pointed out, in helping to marginalize the sexual within the movement's masculine fraternal order, homophobia played a key role in stabilizing the National Socialist regime.[9]

All in all, the Nazi regime was characterized by contradictory attitudes toward homosexuality. Such contradictions became particularly evident in the medical profession's "search for the roots" of homosexuality and the attendant search for a "homosexual cure." Conflicts were also evident in the struggle between the police and legal apparatus over jurisdiction over the prosecution of "homosexuals."[10]

---

and Klaus Theweleit. In my opinion, however, Theweleit's analysis must be regarded as at least somewhat homophobic, since he assumes that homosexuality had a "structural importance" in "the functioning and maintenance of the National Socialist system of rule" and fails to distinguish adequately between ideas linked with masculinist associations and homosexual behaviors. See George L. Mosse, *Nationalism and Sexuality: Respectability and Abnormal Sexuality in Modern Europe* (New York, 1985); Mosse, *The Image of Man: The Creation of Modern Masculinity* (New York, 1996); and Klaus Theweleit, *Männerphantasien*, 2 vols. (Reinbek, 1977).

[6]The designation of a particular behavior as "masculine" or "unmanly" has little to do with any universal gender order but varies among individuals, societies, and cultures. As the Hamburg criminal justice records demonstrate, the designations of behavior varied widely even under National Socialism. In some instances, it was deemed "particularly masculine" or "manly" to make a complete confession; in other instances, the same behavior was interpreted by policemen, prosecutors, and judges as a "female desire for gossip."

[7]On the stereotype of the "corruptor of youth," see Jürgen Müller, "Ausgrenzung der Homosexuellen aus der Volksgemeinschaft: Homosexuellenverfolgung im Nationalsozialismus am Beispiel der Stadt Köln" (thesis, Universität-Gesamthochschule Duisburg, 2001), 165–70.

[8]Peter von Rönn, "Politische und psychiatrische Homosexualitätskonstruktion im NS-Staat. Teil I: Die politische Genese des Homosexuellen als Staatsfeind," *Zeitschrift für Sexualforschung* 11 (1998): 99–129; and von Rönn, "Teil II: Die soziale Genese der Homosexualität als defizitäre Heterosexualität," *Zeitschrift für Sexualforschung* 11 (1998): 220–60.

[9]Lautmann, Grikschat, and Schmidt, 359.

In their persecution of same-sex-desiring individuals, the National Socialist regime relied upon a tradition of homophobia that was deeply rooted
in German society and both preceded and outlived Nazi rule. Homosexual activities between men or women were incompatible with traditional notions of morality and respectability and with the gender ideology
of a patriarchal, heteronormative bourgeois society. In its persecution of
homosexuality, therefore, the Nazi regime was able to "depict itself as
the bastion of bourgeois respectability."[11] As was the case in the regime's
euthanasia, forced sterilization, and castration programs and in the persecution and murder of Jews, the policies and ideas enacted by the Nazi
regime were a radical extension of measures that had already been proposed prior to 1933.

Despite the recent increase in the number of studies relating to the
persecution of same-sex-desiring men and women under National Socialism, the topic remains marginal to much historical work on the Nazi era,
particularly when compared to historical studies of other categories of
victims. How did representations of homosexuality in public discourse
change between the era of the Weimar Republic and that of National Socialism? What role did homosexuality play in daily discourse? What role
did stereotypes play in the functioning of homophobic propaganda?[12] How
significant was the practice of denunciation in the persecution of same-
sex-desiring men?[13] Although historical scholarship in the field has touched
upon these questions, the interrelationships of these issues have yet to be
considered in a systematic fashion. This essay proposes to remedy this gap
in historical scholarship.

This study will focus on evidence from Hamburg, which, as a seaport
and the second largest city in the Reich, was reputed to be a "homosexual
stronghold." For my analysis of public discourse, I shall consider three

---

[10]See von Rönn, "Teil II."

[11]Frank Sparing, ". . . wegen Vergehen nach §175 verhaftet": Die Verfolgung der Düsseldorfer
Homosexuellen während des Nationalsozialismus (Düsseldorf, 1997), 54. See also Mosse,
Nationalism and Sexuality, 157–58, 164–65.

[12]By the terms "homophobia" and "homophobic," I do not intend to connote "fear" in
the medical or psychological sense of the term but, rather, "hostility" and "rejection" in a
social and political sense.

The important studies of the press and propaganda under National Socialism are Oron J.
Hale, The Captive Press in the Third Reich (Princeton, 1964); Zbynek A. B. Zeman, Nazi
Propaganda (London, 1964); Joseph Wulf, Presse und Funk im Dritten Reich: Eine
Dokumentation (Gütersloh, 1964); Jürgen Hagemann, Die Presselenkung im Dritten Reich
(Bonn, 1970); Ian Kershaw, Popular Opinion and Political Dissent: Bavaria, 1933–1945 (Ox-
ford, 1985); and Norbert Frei and Johannes Schmitz, Journalismus im Dritten Reich, 3rd ed.
(Munich, 1999). In these studies, the problem of "homophobia" is barely discussed.

[13]The past few decades have witnessed an increase in the number of publications on the
historical significance of denunciation. Two address the subject comparatively: Sheila
Fitzpatrick and Robert Gellately, eds., Accusatory Practices: Denunciation in Modern European History, 1789–1989 (Chicago, 1997); Günter Jerouschek, Inge Marßolek, and Hedwig

Hamburg newspapers, including the *Hamburger Fremdenblatt,* one of the largest German newspapers, with a wide readership both within Germany and abroad.[14] I shall also examine contemporary reference works, the Sopade's *Deutschland-Berichte* (the reports on the German Reich by the executive board of the Sozialdemokratische Partei Deutschlands [SPD] in exile, which were based on reports provided by informants within Germany), and reports issued by the Reich's Sicherheitshauptamt (Central Security Office). Finally, to examine the phenomenon of denunciation, I shall draw upon the Hamburg criminal justice records, sources that offer a rich base of evidence for the larger history of National Socialist persecution as well as important evidence for social history, the history of everyday life, and the history of mentalities. My goal is to develop a more nuanced and refined chronology of the evolution of homophobic propaganda and its dissemination, to specify more precisely the stereotypes that were mobilized against those classed as "homosexual," and to investigate the relationships between regime propaganda and denunciations at the grass roots. To the extent that future comparative research qualifies my study, any differences are likely to be the result of regional variations in the application of administrative measures rather than in mentality.

THE TRANSFORMATION OF PUBLIC DISCOURSE ON HOMOSEXUALITY FROM THE WEIMAR REPUBLIC TO THE NAZI STATE

Popular representations of homosexuality varied widely in the Weimar Republic. This is true within broad public discourse as well as in the specialized, professional discourses of law, criminology, medicine, and sexology. In addition, same-sex-desiring men and women contributed their own knowledge and perspective to the other discourses on homosexuality.

The variety of attitudes toward homosexuality is evident in contemporary encyclopedia articles on the topic, in which depictions of homosexuality range from harsh portrayals of pathology and moral condemnation to toleration tinged with pity. (Although they professed to include female homosexuality, these reference essays implicitly focus on theories and concepts relevant to male homosexuality.) The fifteenth edition of the *Große Brockhaus* (published between 1928 and 1935), for example, refers to

---

Röckelein, eds., *Denunziationen: Historische, juristische und psychologische Aspekte* (Tübingen, 1997). Others consider the problem specifically under National Socialism: Robert Gellately, *The Gestapo and German Society: Enforcing Racial Policy, 1933–1945* (Oxford, 1990); Gisela Diewald-Kerkmann, *Politische Denunziation im NS-Regime oder die kleine Macht der "Volksgenossen"* (Bonn, 1995); and Eric A. Johnson, *Nazi Terror: The Gestapo, Jews, and Ordinary Germans* (London, 2000).

[14]Hale, 2, 6. As a point of comparison, I shall also examine selected articles from newspapers published in other cities. I wish to thank Bettina Ramm of Hamburg for her assistance in analyzing the newspapers.

"individuals who suffer from homosexuality" and depicts the condition as abnormal and wholly pathological. The fourth edition of the *Große Herder* (published between 1931 and 1935) states: "[Homosexuality] is contrary to nature since it is inconsistent with the natural purpose of sexual intercourse." This work also notes that sexual relations between men are prohibited by law (with Austrian law extending the prohibition to relations between women) and comments on the planned reform of the German penal code. In contrast, the seventh edition of *Meyers Lexikon* (published between 1924 and 1930) expresses considerable empathy for homosexuals. It refers to "persons who often possess great intellectual and moral capacity" and "often experience severe emotional suffering" as a consequence of the social ostracism of "homosexuals." The entry in *Meyers* cites as references the *Jahrbücher für sexuelle Zwischenstufen* (Yearbook for the intermediate stages of sexuality); the Bund für Menschenrecht (BfM, or Alliance for Human Rights), an organization with a large membership of same-sex-desiring individuals; and the BfM's publication, the *Blätter für Menschenrecht* (Journal of human rights). A separate lexical entry discusses the Wissenschaftlich-humanitäre Komitee (Scientific Humanitarian Committee), the first homosexual rights organization, founded in 1897, while the supplemental volumes contain entries on transvestites and Magnus Hirschfeld, a leading sexologist and leader of the Wissenschaftlich-humanitäre Komitee. However, even the *Meyers Lexikon* cannot be said to display a uniformly positive image of homosexuality as it, too, proffers "therapeutic advice." Not a single reference article regards homosexuality as a "normal" phenomenon. All of them discuss whether homosexuality was a hereditary or an acquired trait and whether a "cure" or "remedy" for it might yet be found. Finally, all the articles link male homosexuality with "effeminacy" of mind and body, thus lending further support to the claim that it was a condition "contrary to nature."[15]

The 1924 press accounts of the investigation and trial in Hanover of the serial sex-murderer Fritz Haarmann contain a similar spectrum of representations of male homosexuality, ranging from moral condemnation to pity, and even include isolated instances of acceptance.[16] The investigation during the summer of 1924 and the ensuing trial in December were the

[15]"Homosexualität," in *Der Große Brockhaus: Handbuch des Wissens in zwanzig Bänden*, 15th rev. ed., vol. 8 (Leipzig, 1931); "Homosexualität," in *Der Große Herder: Nachschlagewerk für Wissen und Leben*, 4th rev. ed., vol. 6 (Freiburg/Breisgau, 1933); "Homosexualität," in *Meyers Lexikon*, 7th rev. ed., vol. 5 (Leipzig, 1926); "Wissenschaftliches humanitäres Komitee," in *Meyers Lexikon*, 7th rev. ed., vol. 12 (Leipzig, 1930); "Hirschfeld, Magnus," in *Meyers Lexikon*, 7th rev. ed., vol. 14 (Leipzig, 1933); "Transvestiten," in *Meyers Lexikon*, 7th rev. ed., vol. 15 (Leipzig, 1933).

[16]The shop assistant Fritz Haarmann (1879–1935) murdered between twenty-four and twenty-seven young men (age thirteen to twenty-one) during sexual intercourse, then dismembered their corpses and threw the bodies into the Leine. Haarmann was convicted of twenty-four counts of murder in December 1924 and executed in April 1925.

subject of extensive coverage in the Hamburg press as well as in other local and national newspapers. In many instances, the press reports display contradictory attitudes toward homosexuality, sometimes within a single newspaper. Some accounts, for example, depict "homosexuals" as "very peaceable and charming individuals," noting that Haarmann was the first "homosexual sadist" murderer known to criminal history.[17] The chief criminal inspector of Berlin, Dr. Koop, who assisted with the investigation, commented on the case in a similar manner: "Many are blaming homosexuals for these deeds. But homosexuals have as much and as little to do with this case as heterosexuals do with the Großmann mass murders."[18] Other accounts of the case, however, draw a connection between "sex killings" and homosexuality and use the case as a pretext to vilify homosexuality and the sexual permissiveness of the Weimar Republic. The conservative *Hamburger Nachrichten* refers to ten same-sex-desiring men arrested by the Hanover police as Haarmann's "homosexually inclined comrades," implicitly depicting them as accomplices in Haarmann's deeds.[19] A final press summary of the trial employs particularly hostile and extravagant language:

> When several months ago the vile deeds of this beast in human form became known, when bones and skulls were fished out of the Leine, the populace was seized with horror. Many wondered, aghast, how it was possible that this monster, this ravager of morality and budding youth, could exercise his rage amongst our nation's youth unnoticed for so long. The only possible explanation is the barbarity that has taken hold since the revolution, the licentiousness that Marxism has promoted throughout our schools, in the arts, and in our civic life.

The existence of the "bestial Haarmann" served as a warning to reject the "licentiousness and the degeneration of morals, the shameful propagandizing, and the wicked raging of Germans against Germans."[20]

The broad range of political and social attitudes toward homosexuality in the Weimar Republic stands out in the critical reviews of Richard Oswald's and Magnus Hirschfeld's educational film *Anders als die*

---

[17]"Der Fall Haarmann," *Hamburger Anzeiger*, July 17, 1924, 2.

[18]"Der Fall des Massenmörders Haarmann: Drahtmeldung unserer Berliner Schriftleitung," *Hamburger Nachrichten*, July 20, 1924, morning ed., 2. In 1921 the butcher Georg Karl Großmann murdered up to twenty prostitutes in his Berlin apartment following sexual activities. Großmann dismembered the bodies and sold them as pork. Großmann was arrested in August 1921 and convicted of only three murders, since evidence was lacking for the rest. He was executed in 1931.

[19]"Provinz Hannover: Ein siebenfacher Lustmörder," *Hamburger Nachrichten*, July 3, 1924, morning ed., 3.

[20]"Das Todesurteil gegen Haarmann und Grans," *Hamburger Nachrichten*, December 19, 1924, morning ed., 3.

Anderen—§ 175 (Different from the others—§ 175) and of other films, plays, and books.[21] For both audience and critics, male and female homosexuality was a topic of interest within cinema, theater, literature, and the arts—a visible, if controversial, matter of public discourse. The majority of artistic and literary representations depicted homosexuality as "unnatural"; the rare positive representations were usually penned by same-sex-desiring persons themselves.

Although the 1920s were not as golden, liberal, or tolerant as has often been assumed, many heretofore marginal social groups, including same-sex-desiring men and women, were able to find a niche in the Weimar Republic and occupy positions of public influence. The sexologist Magnus Hirschfeld was highly renowned and able to publicize his views and those of the Wissenschaftlich-humanitäre Komitee in the leftist and liberal press.[22] Although the conservative press vilified and denounced Hirschfeld's research, even this negative reportage helped publicize his research and political goals.

While the *Freundschaftsverbände* (friendship federations) of same-sex-desiring individuals received no mention in the popular press, their publications succeeded in drumming up "homophilic" publicity. Approximately twenty periodicals for same-sex-desiring men and women appeared between 1919 and 1933. According to their own sales figures, some of these were mass publications with a circulation of over 100,000. Occasionally, they sold out immediately upon publication. These periodicals were subject to censorship throughout the Weimar Republic, and some were placed on the index of banned books, but despite these repressive measures, most were published regularly, without interruption.[23]

[21]The film was reviewed in at least four newspapers in Hamburg alone. The reviewer in the *Hamburger Fremdenblatt*, which was associated with the German Democratic Party (Deutsche Demokratische Partei, or DDP), lauded the film's objectivity and sensitivity. See "Theater, Kunst und Wissenschaft: Besprechung von 'Anders als die anderen,'" *Hamburger Fremdenblatt*, August 20, 1919, evening ed., 8. See also the review by "L. B." in the *Neue Hamburger Zeitung*, August 18, 1919; the review by "C. Wgr." in the *Hamburger Volkszeitung*, August 18, 1919; and the review by "k." in the *Generalanzeiger für Hamburg-Altona*, August 19, 1919.

[22]Articles by the Wissenschaftliches humanitäres Komitee were published in the *Arbeiter-Illustrierte-Zeitung*, a paper affiliated with the KPD. See Richard Linsert, "Magnus Hirschfeld's Lebenswerk: Zum 60. Geburtstag des Forschers," *Arbeiter-Illustrierte-Zeitung*, no. 21 (1928): 13; "Schmerzlust: Von Sanitätsrat Dr. Magnus Hirschfeld und Richard Linsert. Mit Aufnahmen aus einem Berliner Salon für 'Individuelle Körperpflege,'" *Arbeiter-Illustrierte-Zeitung*, no. 43 (1928): 4–5. I wish to thank Jens Schmidt of Hamburg for bringing this article to my attention. Schmidt examined the topic of masculinity in weekly magazines published over a span of several years under the Weimar Republic. See Jens Schmidt, *"Sich hart machen, wenn es gilt": Männlichkeitskonzepte in Illustrierten der Weimarer Republik* (Münster, 2000), 81.

[23]See Micheler, "Kampf, Kontakt, Kultur"; and Klaus Petersen, *Zensur in der Weimarer Republik* (Stuttgart, 1995).

The ascension of Adolf Hitler to the office of chancellor of the Reich and the seizure of the German government by the National Socialist coalition cabinet spelled the end to all positive representations of homosexuality and the death of the emancipatory movement of same-sex-desiring men and women in the German Reich. These developments appear in the professional discourses of law and medicine as well as in the popular media.

This transformation can be documented in *Meyers Lexikon*. In the seventh edition, published during the Weimar Republic, the entry on "homosexuality" largely reflects the views of the Wissenschaftlich-humanitäre Komitee. But the eighth edition, published since 1936, denounces Magnus Hirschfeld as an "infamous 'sex researcher'" and "Jew." The Nazi-era *Meyers Lexikon* drew upon a law dissertation submitted in 1937 by the SS leader Rudolf Klare. This homophobic dissertation, which examined the legality of homosexual behavior, is the foundation for the encyclopedia article and is cited as a suggestion for further reading. According to the lexical entry, the majority of "homosexual" men "preferred boys and youths," and homosexuality resulted from seduction. "Homosexuality must be regarded as a threat to the *Volk* community, since homosexuals exhibit a tendency to form cliques, seduce the young, and, above all, undermine the natural will to life by propagating an aversion to marriage and the family." Despite its ostensible function as a neutral manual of reference, this article debated the political question of whether homosexuality should be subject to harsh punishment. With "lesbian love" more common than believed, the article continued, "the question arises whether in the future this should also be subjected to punishment."[24] It appears that National Socialist Party officials and the state exerted direct influence over the content of some encyclopedia articles.[25] While it is impossible to determine whether the *Meyers* entry on homosexuality was subjected to such interference, the entry displays such striking similarities to Rudolf Klare's views that it is certainly plausible that he authored it himself.

If the theme of male-male desire emerged in literature and the arts under National Socialism, it was implicit and desexualized—expressed as camaraderie, male friendship, and hero worship within the works of nationalistic authors.[26]

[24]"Hirschfeld, Magnus," in *Meyers Lexikon*, 8th rev. ed., vol. 5 (Leipzig, 1938); Rudolf Klare, *Homosexualität und Strafrecht* (Hamburg, 1937); and "Homosexualität," in *Meyers Lexikon*, 8th rev. ed., vol. 5 (Leipzig, 1938).

[25]For example, the *Meyers Lexikon* entry on "Jews" was criticized and debated by both the Parteiamtlichen Prüfungskommission zum Schutze des NS-Schrifttums (Official Party Board of Examiners for the Protection of National Socialist Publications) as well as the Reich Central Security Office until finally a member of the SS Security Office, Dr. Six, was commissioned with writing a section of the article. See Bundesarchiv Berlin: R58/984 RSHA, 213–15, directive dated May 2, 1938, regarding the *Meyers Lexikon* article on "Jews."

[26]Christian Klein, *Schreiben im Schatten: Homoerotische Literatur im Nationalsozialismus* (Hamburg, 2000). I find Klein's methodology and his choice of terminology ("gays") to

Under the Weimar Republic, occasional positive depictions of homosexuality had appeared in the essay section of newspapers, in science reportage, and in the coverage of the Haarmann case. But after the spring of 1933, when the Hamburg press was "coordinated" (*gleichgeschaltet*) with Nazi policy, either forcibly or voluntarily, such positive depictions disappeared.[27] Newspaper coverage thereafter referred to same-sex-desiring men only as criminals and did not mention female homosexuality.

In 1933, the Hamburg newspapers reported on the "Battle against Trash and Smut" and the "Battle against Public Immorality" waged by the police of Hamburg and Berlin. These campaigns entailed a ban on erotic literature, a crackdown on prostitution outside of brothels, and the closing of Berlin pubs, including many "homosexual bars." Most of the reports, particularly those in the *Hamburger Fremdenblatt*, were objective in tone, although a few did contain derogatory depictions. Most were brief local news bulletins on such topics as illegal abortion and sexual acts with children, including acts between adult men and boys. Some covered the many judicial directives on forced castration issued by the Reich Supreme Court as well as local courts in Hamburg and other cities. Newspapers occasionally enjoined the population to protect children against "fiendish strangers." According to articles written in 1933 and 1934 on criminality in Hamburg, the overall number of crimes declined under the new government, but the number of sexual offenses increased, a fact accounted for by the intensity with which such offenses were investigated and prosecuted.[28] During those years, the Hamburg papers were not yet subject to direct interference, as the Ministry of Propaganda was still formulating its position and had yet to issue concrete orders.[29] But thereafter, the Hamburg press depicted homosexuality as a crime and a perversion and promoted the bourgeois, "child-

---

be questionable. To date there has been no research on the representation of female homosexuality in literature and the arts in the Nazi era.

[27]Regarding the *Gleichschaltung* of the *Hamburger Anzeiger,* see Wulf, 32; on that of the *Hamburger Fremdenblatt,* see Hale, 210–11. Jürgen Fromme has argued that the *Hamburger Fremdenblatt,* once the largest paper in northwest Germany as well as one of the largest liberal newspapers in Germany, had already adopted a nationalistic perspective in the closing years of the Weimar Republic but continued to remain free of the direct, personal influence of National Socialists even after 1933. See Jürgen Fromme, *Zwischen Anpassung und Bewahrung: Das Hamburger Fremdenblatt im Übergang von der Weimarer Republik zum "Dritten Reich." Eine politisch-historische Analyse* (Hamburg, 1981). However, my analysis of the *Fremdenblatt* from 1933 to 1936 demonstrates that the process of *Gleichschaltung* was completed by April 1933.

[28]See "Die Kriminalität geht zurück," *Hamburger Fremdenblatt,* August 30, 1933, evening ed., 3; "Die Kriminalität und Verbrechensbekämpfung in Hamburg," *Hamburger Fremdenblatt,* November 13, 1934, evening ed., 6.

[29]Frei and Schmitz have argued that the National Socialist regime was never able to exert complete control over the press. By the same token, however, no newspaper was able to remain entirely free of National Socialist influence. See Frei and Schmitz, 96.

rich" marriage, the lifestyle officially favored by the National Socialist regime. As early as 1934, pronatalist population policies that aimed at dramatically increasing the birth rate of "Aryan children" found their expression in press accounts that debated the role and duties of "mothers, marriages, and family," extolled the virtues of "young, happy couples," and promoted "early marriage and child-rich families."[30]

HOMOPHOBIC PROPAGANDA UNDER NATIONAL SOCIALISM

In the Third Reich, press accounts reinforced an image of the "homosexual" as criminal and sustained the regime's homophobic propaganda. The press exploited at least three events for this purpose: the assassination of the SA leader Ernst Röhm in 1934, the trials of sex murderers August Seefeld and Otto Krepp in 1936, and the second wave of prosecutions of Catholic clergymen for sexual offenses in 1937. In the "Röhm Purge" and the "sex offender trials," homosexuality was deployed to justify political goals and actions. In the cases of supposedly "homosexual" sex offenders and sex murderers, the extensive coverage was designed to demonstrate the regime's resolve in prosecuting "immorality" and "crime" and to underscore its claim to "bourgeois respectability."[31]

The assassination of Ernst Röhm on June 30, 1934, is generally regarded as a turning point in the National Socialist regime's treatment of homosexuality. Following his nomination as chief of staff of the SA in 1931, Ernst Röhm was denounced as a "homosexual" by the opposition Social Democratic press. His homosexuality also made him a controversial figure within the Nazi Party, which advocated harsh prosecution of homosexuality.[32] However, Hitler defended Röhm against attacks both within the party and

---

[30]"Die Ehe im neuen Staat: Schutz der Mutter," *Hamburger Fremdenblatt*, April 17, 1934, morning ed., 2; "Warum sie einmal 'ja' gesagt haben: Junge Ehepaare erklären die Gründe, die zur Ehe führen—Es gibt auch noch Romantik," *Hamburger Fremdenblatt*, October 25, 1934, morning ed., 8; "Jung-Hamburg heiratet," *Hamburger Fremdenblatt*, November 1, 1934, evening ed., 5. The image of the family as "germ cell" can also be found in "Eröffnung der HJ-Ausstellung," *Hamburger Fremdenblatt*, October 22, 1934, morning ed., 5; "Förderung von Frühehe und Kinderreichtum," *Hamburger Nachrichten*, June 6, 1937, morning ed., 2.

[31]Mosse, *Nationalism and Sexuality*, 157–58, 164–65.

[32]See Hans-Georg Stümke and Rudi Finkler, *Rosa Winkel, Rosa Listen: Homosexuelle und "Gesundes Volksempfinden" von Auschwitz bis heute* (Reinbek, 1981), 119–45; Jellonnek, "Homosexuelle unter dem Hakenkreuz," 57–79; Alexander Zinn, "'Die Bewegung der Homosexuellen': Die soziale Konstruktion des homosexuellen Nationalsozialisten im antifaschistischen Exil," in *Die Linke und das Laster: Schwule Emanzipation und linke Vorurteile*, ed. Detlef Grumbach (Hamburg, 1995), 38–84; Zinn, *Die soziale Konstruktion des homosexuellen Nationalsozialisten: Zur Genese und Etablierung eines Stereotyps* (Frankfurt am Main, 1997); Friedrich Koch, *Sexuelle Denunziation: Die Sexualität in der politischen Auseinandersetzung*, rev. ed. (Hamburg, 1995), 21–25.

in public, declaring the private life of SA leaders to be their own affair.[33] Röhm was held in high political esteem by the Nazi Party, as he was believed to be the only person capable of transforming the SA into an organization that could assist in the Nazis' "seizure of power." In 1934, however, Röhm was deposed and assassinated. These events followed a decision made by Hitler and the party leadership to back the Reichswehr in its ongoing conflict with the SA regarding which organization would serve as the army of the "new Germany." Hitler also exploited the purge to consolidate his own power and insure his status as the sole Führer. In addition to Röhm, many innocent bystanders as well as a number of other SA leaders and supposedly conservative, reactionary, or monarchist competitors were assassinated, including the former Reich chancellor Kurt von Schleicher.

According to Nazi propaganda, the assassinations were a preemptive measure to subvert a coup planned by Schleicher and Röhm, who were said to be in the employ of a foreign power—an accusation that quite obviously had no basis in reality. In order to justify the purge and to disguise its true motives, the regime exploited homophobia. On the day of the assassination, June 30, 1934, the National Socialist Party's press office issued a report that, according to Max Domarus, was written by Hitler himself. Reprinted in numerous newspapers, the report claimed that there had been an attempt to drive a wedge between the SA and the party and between the SA and the state:

> We are uncovering more and more evidence to support our suspicion that this plot can be attributed to a clique of like-minded conspirators. . . . Our chief of staff, Röhm, in whom our Führer has placed such extraordinary trust, did nothing to oppose these actions; indeed, he undoubtedly supported them. His widely known unfortunate predisposition over time resulted in so unbearable a strain and a burden that Röhm, a leader of our movement and the chief of the SA, became torn by a profound crisis of conscience.[34]

Thus the report blamed Röhm's supposed disloyalty upon his "unfortunate predisposition" and surmised that a "homosexual clique" had formed to subvert the state, a supposition that was often exploited later to justify the persecution of same-sex-desiring men. In his Reichstag address of July 13, 1934, Hitler reiterated his professed belief that a "small group of individuals joined by a common predisposition" had engaged in plans for treason and the overthrow of the government. As evidence for existence of a

[33]Adolf Hitler, Directive No. 1 of February 3, 1931, reprinted in Heinrich Bennecke, *Hitler und die SA* (Munich, 1962), 253; also reprinted in Koch, 253. *Völkischer Beobachter*, April 8, 1932, reprinted in Max Domarus, *Hitler: Reden und Proklamationen 1932–1945. Kommentiert von einem deutschen Zeitgenossen. Teil I: Triumph 1932–1938*, 4th ed. (Leonberg, 1988), 102.

[34]*Erklärung der Reichspressestelle der NSDAP*, June 30, 1934, reprinted in Domarus, 398–99.

"clique," Hitler claimed that Röhm had promoted SA men "simply because they belonged to the circle of those afflicted with this particular predisposition."[35] The full text of this speech was reprinted in newspapers and publicized in radio broadcasts.

According to a statement released by the Reich press office on June 30, 1934, "some SA leaders were accompanied by catamites. One SA leader was surprised in a most revolting situation and was arrested." However, a supposed "eyewitness account" issued by the press agencies later that day states only that the SA leader of Silesia, Edmund Heines, was arrested with an eighteen year old in his bed. The reports are focused on the purported "traitors" and their "plot" and "plans for high treason," while the indignation over the "shameless appearance" of the "loathsome scene" receives only fleeting mention.[36] On the same day, Hitler issued a twelve-point directive to the new SA chief of staff, Viktor Lutze, stating in point seven:

> I expect all SA leaders to help the SA maintain and reinforce its standing as a pure and untainted organization. I want every mother to be able to send her son to the SA, the party, and the HJ [Hitler Youth] without fearing that he might there be debased in his manners or morals. For this reason, I want all SA leaders to be strict in ensuring that any offenses against §175 result in the immediate expulsion of the accused from the SA and party. SA men should be leaders, not ludicrous apes.[37]

The propaganda surrounding the affair deploys many metaphors of order and cleanliness, such as the claim that Hitler had cleaned up a "pigsty." But contrary to the historical accounts offered by Max Domarus, Hans-Georg Stümke, Rudi Finkler, and Friedrich Koch, homosexuality was only one among a number of accusations made by the regime. The central accusation was high treason, supplemented by accusations of homosexuality and luxurious living. The party newspapers proffered a similar version of the purge.[38] What remains unclear is whether the party press office deliberately or accidentally introduced the homophobic slant in its accounts of the purge. Given the inconsistency and confusion in the depictions of homosexuality and the real or alleged homosexual activities of those arrested and murdered, it seems unlikely that the homophobia that permeated these accounts was premeditated. Whether the press statements were prepared in advance of the actual purge and, if so, by whom remains

[35]Adolf Hitler, *Reichstagsrede*, July 13, 1934, reprinted in ibid., 410–24.
[36]*"Augenzeugenbericht" zu den Verhaftungen der SA-Führer*, June 30, 1934, reprinted in ibid., 399–400.
[37]"Tagesbefehl an Chef des Stabes, Viktor Lutze," June 30, 1934, reprinted in ibid., 401.
[38]See, for example, "Hitler reißt den Meuterern die Achselstücke von den Schultern. Mit eiserner Entschlossenheit das Treiben der Verschwörer beendet. Der Luxus wird ausgerottet," *Der Angriff: Die nationalsozialistische Abendzeitung*, June 30, 1934, 1. I wish to thank Jakob Michelsen of Hamburg for this reference.

an open question. The private diary of the Reich Minister of Propaganda, Joseph Goebbels, makes no mention of any plan to exploit Röhm's assassination for purposes of homophobic propaganda, in spite of the fact that an entry dated June 29, 1934, makes it clear that Goebbels, though not involved in planning the assassinations, was informed of the purge, approved of it, and took part in its implementation.[39] It was not until later, in the years following the purge, that the party leadership and other influential members of the regime began to promote the idea that homosexuality had played a role in the murders of the SA leadership.[40]

The Reich Press Agency accounts appeared on the radio and in newspapers, reached a wide audience, and became a topic of gossip and speculation for weeks. Placards of Hitler's "daily directives" were posted on advertising pillars throughout the Reich, where they remained for several days as a visible reminder of events.[41] The reports of the exiled SPD suggest the success of this propaganda campaign, as the population began to adopt the metaphors of order and cleanliness advanced by the regime. In taking "vigorous action," Hitler had garnered prestige and approval.[42] Even old SPD functionaries were said to have forgotten that their party had condemned Röhm for homosexuality in 1931.[43] The reports confirm that the German public's speculation and indignation remained focused on the homosexuality and the lavish lifestyle of the murdered leaders and that the real reason for the purge—to eliminate political competition and neutralize the SA—did not become apparent for many months.[44] Although they do not mention the accusations of "homosexuality," the Sopade reports make it clear that this was a useful propaganda issue. Nonetheless, the Hamburg trial of a man accused of violating the sedition law (*Heimtücke-Gesetz*) demonstrates that some Germans saw through the propaganda surrounding the Röhm case. In this 1937 case, the master locksmith Paul Carmohn was overheard saying in a pub that the SPD had long accused Röhm of being a "bum fucker" but that Hitler had not turned against Röhm until the SA leader became a political threat. This was proof that Hitler was nothing but a "giant scoundrel."[45] As Eugen Lenz, a Hamburg lawyer repeatedly convicted for homosexual

[39] *Die Tagebücher von Joseph Goebbels: Sämtliche Fragmente. Band 2: 1931–1936*, ed. Elke Fröhlich (Munich, 1987).

[40] See, for example, a speech by the minister of propaganda, Joseph Goebbels, reprinted as "Deutschlands Antwort," *Hamburger Nachrichten*, May 29, 1937, evening ed., 1; "Abrechnung: Dr. Goebbels spricht," *Hamburger Nachrichten*, May 29, 1937, evening ed., 2–3. See also Stümke and Finker, 206.

[41] For a photo of an advertising column, see *Hamburger Anzeiger*, July 5, 1934, 1.

[42] *Deutschland-Berichte der Sozialdemokratischen Partei Deutschlands (Sopade) 1934–1940*, vol. 1 (1934) (Frankfurt am Main, 1980), 198–99, 297, 298, 309, 310.

[43] Ibid., 210.

[44] Ibid., 761.

[45] Staatsarchiv Hamburg 213-11, Staatsanwaltschaft Landgericht—Strafsachen, repository number 1027/38. All subsequent repository numbers (Rep.), unless stated otherwise, refer to this holding.

activities under the Nazi regime, explained in 1946, the Röhm assassination was politically motivated. Hitler had protected Röhm for many years, although he was well aware of the accusations of homosexuality.[46]

The Röhm Putsch signaled that the Nazi regime would no longer tolerate homosexuality within its ranks. In the months that followed, further waves of purges took place within the SA and the Nazi ranks. By these means, the Nazi Party was able to put an end to the contradictory situation in which it had found itself—of condemning homosexual behavior while simultaneously permitting a top position to be occupied by a "homosexual." At the same time, the putsch demonstrated that homosexuality would no longer be tolerated elsewhere in the Reich.

In its portrayal of the Röhm putsch, the press deployed a kind of symbolic politics but did not precipitate the persecution of "homosexuals" across the Reich, as scholars have often assumed.[47] In the aftermath of the Röhm affair, most persecutory measures were directed against members of the Nazi Party and affiliated organizations. The legal groundwork for widespread persecution of other men who engaged in homosexual activities was not laid until the general reform of the penal code in 1935. No attempt was made to establish a list or registry of "homosexuals." The Reichszentrale zur Bekämpfung der Homosexualität und der Abtreibung (Central Reich Agency for Combating Homosexuality and Abortion), established in 1936, required only members of certain groups to register with its office: members of the party and affiliated organizations, Wehrmacht soldiers, Jews, clergy and members of religious orders, and those individuals who had occupied important social positions prior to 1933. In practice, however, many local police officials passed on the names of "ordinary homosexuals" to the Reichszentrale.[48]

A general persecution of "homosexuals" began in different locations at different times. While certain categories of persons, such as male prostitutes and transvestites, were subject to prosecution across the Reich as early as 1933 and existing laws were enforced in Prussia at that time, no systematic persecution of "homosexuals" began in Hamburg until the summer of 1936.[49] As Peter von Rönn has documented in detail, the introduction of such persecution was closely linked to the rise of Heinrich Himmler. The official SS weekly, *Das schwarze Korps,* which after its initial publication in February 1935 became the second largest newspaper in the

[46]Text dictated by Dr. Eugen Lenz on December 10, 1946, at the public prosecutor's office during the reopening of his case. Rep. 3007/40.

[47]See, for example, Jellonnek, "Homosexuelle unter dem Hakenkreuz," 329.

[48]Müller, 79.

[49]Röhm was not able to protect "homosexuals" prior to his assassination, a notion that has occasionally been advanced by scholars. He did not intervene during the February 1933 banning of the friendship bulletins, the destruction of Magnus Hirschfeld's Institute for Sexual Science in Berlin in May 1933, or the closing of numerous "homosexual bars" in

Reich, was instrumental in propagating the crucial myth of "homosexual cliques."[50] In 1937, the paper published a series of articles characterizing (male) "homosexuals" as "enemies of the state" who tended to form cliques, seduce the young, and threaten to feminize the *Männerstaat* and calling for the enactment of more drastic measures.[51] The belief that homosexuals were "enemies of the state" was thereupon propagated by the daily press. The *Hamburger Nachrichten*, for example, referred to and based its accounts on the series of articles published in *Das schwarze Korps*.[52] By means of these articles, which were probably influenced by the Reichszentrale zur Bekämpfung der Homosexualität und der Abtreibung, the Gestapo and the SS staked their claim to authority in the "battle against homosexuality" in opposition to the claims of the courts.[53] As Peter von Rönn has emphasized, "The propaganda directed against homosexuals as enemies of the state, which began in early 1937, was accompanied by the organizational and ideological consolidation of Himmler's empire of power."[54]

Press coverage of the jury trials of two accused murderers, Adolf Seefeld and Otto Krepp, was also tainted by homophobia. Reporters covering Adolf Seefeld's trial and execution in 1936 linked the themes of homosexuality

---

Berlin. The idea that Röhm intervened to protect "homosexual" men is founded on a mistaken belief in a homogeneous and unified identity among same-sex-desiring men. As Eleanor Hancock's research has demonstrated, Röhm's conception of homosexuality, which was based on an image of male homosexual virility, existed in stark contradiction to Magnus Hirschfeld's image of the homosexual as a "third sex" and had little in common with the concepts of homosexuality advocated by the Alliance for Human Rights. Although Röhm was a member of the Alliance, he did not intercede on its behalf. At most, he could have provided protection only to those "homosexuals" in his own cohort. See Eleanor Hancock, "'Only the Real, the True, the Masculine Held Its Value': Ernst Röhm, Masculinity, and Male Homosexuality," *Journal of the History of Sexuality* 8, no. 4 (1998): 616–41.

[50]At the end of 1935, *Das schwarze Korps* had a circulation of 200,000 copies. By mid-1937, this had increased to a circulation of 500,000. In 1944, with a circulation of 750,000, it was the second-largest German newspaper, following *Das Reich. Das schwarze Korps* was an example of "yellow journalism" that promoted anti-Semitism and took part in the campaign against the Catholic Church. See Frei and Schmitz, 102.

[51]Von Rönn, "Teil I," 115–20. An article published in *Das schwarze Korps* in the summer of 1936 did not yet include "homosexuals" in its listing of "enemies of the state." See "Wer ist ein Staatsfeind?" in *Das schwarze Korps, Zeitung der Schutzstaffel der NSDAP. Organ der Reichsführung der SS*, August 27, 1936, 1. This image of the enemy was not formulated or expanded upon until the Gestapo Sonderkommando "special campaigns" against "homosexuals" began in various cities in the summer of 1936 and was not propagated until after the successful campaigns and the founding of the Central Reich Agency. Among the campaigns that have already been the subject of historical investigation are the Hamburg campaign conducted by the Prussian Gestapo's Sonderkommando Nord in August and September 1936 (which I also examine in detail below) and the Gestapo Sonderkommando campaign in the Rhineland from the summer of 1936 until April 1937. See Sparing, 85–87.

[52]"Staatsfeinde," *Hamburger Nachrichten*, March 5, 1937.

[53]Von Rönn, "Teil I," 102–5, 115–20.

[54]Ibid., 103.

and sexually motivated murder in ways that echo the accounts of Fritz Haarmann's trial in 1924. Seefeld, an itinerant watchmaker and "tramp," had, over the course of many years in northeastern Germany, sexually assaulted at least thirty boys age four to eleven, poisoned them with a narcotic, and buried their bodies in wooded areas. On the basis of circumstantial evidence and the credible testimony of witnesses, Seefeld was convicted of twelve counts of murder and sentenced to death. Shortly before his execution, he was alleged to have confessed to additional murders. From the trial's inception on January 21, 1936, to the reading of the verdict on February 22, newspapers across the Reich published extensive accounts on a near daily basis. The *Hamburger Fremdenblatt*, the *Hamburger Anzeiger*, and the *Hamburger Nachrichten* reported the death sentence and the execution on their front pages and with oversize headlines. The *Hamburger Fremdenblatt* sent its own reporter to the trial and occasionally reprinted accounts from the Deutsches Nachrichtenbüro (German Press Agency). The press accounts stress repeatedly that the case demonstrated the soundness of National Socialist lawmaking. Seefeld, it was claimed, would have been "neutralized" much earlier if only forced castration and preventive detention had been available to law enforcement before the Nazi era.[55] The press urged that "German youth" be protected from such "beasts"[56] and reprinted prosecuting attorney Beusch's homophobic final address: "One gets the feeling that the devil himself was wandering through our German provinces in the person of the accused. Seefeld is evil personified. The defendant corrupted more than 100 boys. He alone is to blame for his victims' degeneration, since for them this was their first sexual experience. When pursued to their natural end, perverse tendencies often result in murder."[57]

Rather than commenting critically on these assertions, the newspaper reporters lent further support to such claims. In its account of the death sentence and execution, the *Hamburger Nachrichten* argued that the crimes had been facilitated by the "humanitarian liberal-Marxist past." Other

[55]See, for example, "Vor dem Schwurgericht Schwerin. Zwölf Knabenmorde sollen aufgeklärt werden. Bericht des Sonderberichterstatters," *Hamburger Fremdenblatt*, January 21, 1936, evening ed., 6; "Die ersten Zeugen im Prozeß Seefeld. Der Angeklagte erscheint in Zivilkleidung—Erörterung der Familienverhältnisse. Bericht des Sonderberichterstatters," *Hamburger Fremdenblatt*, January 30, 1936, evening ed., 6; and "Seefelds Ankläger spricht. Die Kette des Schuldbeweise Bericht von Kp.," *Hamburger Fremdenblatt*, February 20, 1936, evening ed., 6. Regarding the significance of the Seefeld case, see Patrick Wagner, *Volksgemeinschaft ohne Verbrecher: Konzeptionen und Praxis der Kriminalpolizei in der Zeit der Weimarer Republik und des Nationalsozialismus* (Hamburg, 1996), 231–32.

[56]"Der Seefeld-Prozeß: Die zwei Knabenmorde bei Neuruppin. Bericht des dn.," *Hamburger Fremdenblatt*, February 9, 1936, morning ed., 6; "Die Lehren aus dem Seefeld-Prozeß. Die Notwendigkeit gründlicher Verhandlung. Bericht des dn.," *Hamburger Fremdenblatt*, February 14, 1936, evening ed., 6.

[57]"Seefelds Ankläger spricht. Die Kette der Schuldbeweise Bericht von Kp.," *Hamburger Fremdenblatt*, February 20, 1936, evening ed., 6.

accounts mention "atonement" and "satisfaction" over the demise of the "beast in human form."[58]

A year earlier, a Hamburg murder case had been the subject of homophobic propaganda in the local press. In March 1935, during or after sexual activities in his apartment, twenty-two-year-old barber Otto Krepp murdered a forty-seven-year-old sailor with a hammer. The police, the public prosecutor, the court, and the press termed the incident a case of murder in the course of robbery, although Krepp himself claimed to have acted in a state of "sexual frenzy." One indication that the crime was not premeditated is the fact that the corpse remained hidden for months in a suitcase under Krepp's cellar steps, the odor of decay finally leading to its discovery in June 1935.[59] The *Hamburger Nachrichten*'s accounts of the discovery of the corpse and Krepp's investigation and trial are reasonably objective, sticking closely to the official Altona police press statements. However, the stories in the *Hamburger Fremdenblatt* and the *Hamburger Anzeiger* are quite homophobic. Even before the investigators had determined whether Otto Krepp, his subtenant, or his friends had anything to do with the murder, the *Hamburger Fremdenblatt* stated that Krepp "seems without a doubt to be involved in the murder. . . . This basement apartment was one of the most disreputable sites of moral aberration, where men of all ages consorted in the most shameful manner day and night. The police placed the apartment under observation some time ago and in fact had already carried out a raid on the apartment in order to put an end to the suspicious goings-on among Otto Krepp's circle of acquaintances."[60]

The newspaper account implies that Krepp's friends and acquaintances were possible accomplices to the crime. According to the *Hamburger Anzeiger*, Krepp's apartment was a "strange nest to which the homosexual acquaintances of its tenant flocked." The article continues: "Although there is not yet concrete evidence to link the discovery of the body to this apartment and its tenant, the apartment is strongly reminiscent of other dens of iniquity in which similar crimes have taken place in recent criminal history."[61] A later article in the *Fremdenblatt* counters an accusation that the

---

[58]"Das Urteil von Schwerin," *Hamburger Nachrichten*, February 22, 1936, evening ed., 1; "Das Ende des Knabenmörders," *Hamburger Nachrichten*, May 23, 1936, evening ed., 1.

[59]Krepp's investigation, trial, and execution were documented at length. The majority of the files are located in Landesarchiv Schleswig-Holstein, Section 352 Altona, Staatsanwaltschaft beim Landgericht Altona, 7102–9. For a voyeuristic and homophobic depiction of the case, see Helmut Ebeling, "Ein Koffer unter der Kellertreppe und eine Leiche darin," in *Schwarze Chronik einer Weltstadt: Hamburger Kriminalgeschichte 1919 bis 1945*, ed. Helmut Ebeling (Hamburg, 1980), 361–88.

[60]"Die Männer-Leiche im Koffer. Grauenhafter Fund in einem Keller," *Hamburger Fremdenblatt*, June 13, 1935, evening ed., 5.

[61]"Neue furchtbare Bluttat in Altona aufgedeckt! Entsetzlicher Leichenfund in einem Keller am Brunnenhof," *Hamburger Anzeiger*, June 13, 1935, supplement, 2.

police should have taken action against Krepp long before this incident occurred: "On the contrary, the police are aware of the actions of nearly all of the morally abnormal men in this city and intervene ruthlessly and without mercy whenever possible." The article then enjoins the population to cooperate with the Altona police and to inform the authorities of the names of the owners, employees, and guests of pubs "often frequented by homosexuals."[62]

The "immorality trials" of Catholic priests in April and May 1937 mark the peak of homophobic propaganda in the media during the Nazi era. Numerous priests and members of religious orders were accused of having had "unnatural sexual relations" or of having lured children and youth into sexual acts. The National Socialist regime exploited these trials to damage the reputation of the Catholic Church in hopes of undermining its influence in youth groups and in schools, particularly in predominantly Catholic regions with large numbers of parochial schools. Some trials also involved charges of seduction and rape of adult women and of offenses against the currency regulations.[63] A few trials of Franciscan friars occurred as early as 1936 but received at most cursory coverage in predominantly Protestant regions.[64] Soon thereafter, the regime issued a directive ordering that individual trials be delayed until they could be clustered at a more auspicious moment. It would be easier to exploit the trials for purposes of propaganda, if one could depict the "offenses against morality" as a massive problem within the Catholic Church.[65] In the spring of 1937, the moment seemed ripe, and numerous cases involving Catholic priests were brought to trial. Over the course of eight weeks between April and June, the daily and party newspapers and radio devoted extensive, front-page coverage to the trials. The more sensationalist headlines trumpeted talk of a "quagmire" and the "heart of an epidemic" in the monasteries, proclaiming evidence of "moral degeneracy," "spiritual criminals," and "corrupters of youth clad in cassocks." Other headlines announced "Bottomless Depravity in the Monastery." In contrast to ordinary judicial procedure, in these sex trials the public

[62]"Der Mord am Brunnenhof. Raubmord an einem Hamburger Seemann—Aufklärung trotz verwischter Spuren," *Hamburger Fremdenblatt*, June 19, 1935, evening ed., 5.

[63]For a discussion of the sex trials, see Hans Günter Hockerts, *Die Sittlichkeitsprozesse gegen katholische Ordensangehörige und Priester 1936/1937. Eine Studie zum nationalsozialistischen Kirchenkampf* (Mainz, 1971); Stümke and Finkler, 201–11; and Detlev Müller and Jürgen Müller, "'Dienstags gesündigt, mittwochs gebeichtet': Die Sittlichkeitsprozesse gegen die Katholische Kirche in den Jahren 1936/1937," in *"Verführte" Männer: Das Leben der Kölner Homosexuellen im Dritten Reich,* ed. Cornelia Limpricht, Jürgen Müller, and Nina Oxenius (Cologne, 1991), 76–81.

[64]A rare account of a Koblenz trial can be found in "Der Sittlichkeitsprozeß gegen die Franziskanerbrüder. Bruder Angelicus auf der Anklagebank," *Hamburger Nachrichten,* June 16, 1936, evening ed., 6.

[65]Directive of the Reich Ministry of Justice, reprinted in Harry Wilde, *Das Schicksal der Verfemten: Die Verfolgung der Homosexuellen im "Dritten Reich" und ihre Stellung in der heutigen Gesellschaft* (Tübingen, 1969), 203.

was often permitted to view the proceedings. Thus the press was able to report extensively on the "perverse activities" of the "devils clad in cassocks" whose "faces were contorted with greed" as they "reveled" in "unnatural fornication."[66] The coverage focused on the seduction of children and youth, the exploitation of relationships of dependence, and the abuse of rank and office. The press ignored cases where investigations were dropped or trials resulted in acquittals due to lack of evidence or ill-founded accusations.[67] Pamphlets documenting the alleged crimes were distributed in Catholic regions. One of these brochures, titled "You shall know them by their deeds!" contained a summary of Nazi newspaper accounts of trials of Catholic clergy, focusing mainly on accusations of sexual offenses. The pamphlet, which cost 65 pfennig, had a print run of 100,000.[68] To accompany the trials, a number of party organizations, including the SA and the Hitler Youth, organized "informational" campaigns aimed at their own members, as well as public campaigns against the supposed "moral corruption" of Catholic priests.[69] Although the Catholic Church defended itself against the accusations, it declined to offer protection to any clerics who were convicted of homosexual activities.

As the Sopade reports demonstrate, the population in both Catholic and Protestant regions of the Reich recognized the trials as anti-Church propaganda, which meant that they had the opposite of the intended effect. However, some Sopade correspondents noted that under the influence of the propaganda, many children and youth avoided Catholic clerics or subjected priests to public verbal abuse.[70] Regardless of whether the reports of the moral failings of clerics were believed, it is apparent that the association of homosexuality with crime and seduction was a stereotype that few were willing to question.

Although large-scale persecution of same-sex-desiring men began in Hamburg in July 1936, the press did not pick up the story of the Gestapo's *Sonderaktion* (special campaign) until the end of August. In all likelihood, the investigating authorities had initially elected to delay informing the press in order to avoid warning potential targets of the new measures. Soon,

---

[66]See, for example, "'Seelenhirte' als Seelenverbrecher. Furchtbare Sittlichkeitsverbrechen vor dem Landgericht in Trier," *Hamburger Nachrichten*, May 8, 1937, 2nd supplement, 1; Beilage, 1.

[67]The Sopade reports make specific mention of the case of the former member of the Bavarian parliament, Präses Waltherbach, who was held in custody for six months during investigation. Although they gave the investigation extensive and hostile coverage, the newspapers failed to report that the charges against Waltherbach were eventually dropped.See *Deutschland-Berichte der Sozialdemokratischen Partei Deutschlands (Sopade) 1934–1940*, vol. 2 (1936) (Frankfurt am Main, 1980), 915.

[68]*Deutschland-Berichte der Sozialdemokratischen Partei Deutschlands (Sopade) 1934–1940*, vol. 3 (1937) (Frankfurt am Main, 1980), 412.

[69]Sopade, 2 (1936), 921; Sopade, 3 (1937), 509.

[70]See, for example, Sopade, 2 (1936), 921; Sopade, 3 (1937), 1182.

however, they judged it important that the public be informed of the success of the campaign, which had been carried out during the Berlin Summer Olympics by a special unit of the Reich criminal police headquarters under the direction of Criminal Police Commissioner Gerhard Günther Kanthack.[71] The articles characterize same-sex-desiring men as dangerous criminals and are replete with talk of a "battle against homosexuals," a "crackdown on moral degeneracy," a "cleanup campaign," "epidemics," and "a settling of scores with homosexuality."[72] Two lengthy articles that appeared in both the *Hamburger Fremdenblatt* and the *Hamburger Anzeiger*, most likely based on the same source, employ metaphors of order, cleanliness, and health and homophobic stereotypes of degeneracy, seduction of youth, and criminality. According to the *Fremdenblatt*, the decline in moral standards in Weimar Germany had led to increased homosexuality, forcing the National Socialist government to take vigorous action beginning in the summer of 1934. However, neither the current campaign nor the strengthening of Paragraph 175 had resulted in a "total eradication of this moral degeneracy" that "constitutes a grave threat to German youth." Only the "vigorous crackdown" by the Gestapo Sonderkommando had succeeded in "rapidly purging Berlin and other cities of homosexual excesses and thus prevent it from speading."[73] The *Hamburger Anzeiger*, in turn, stated that homosexuality was "unhealthy" and a "symptom of degeneracy" that manifested itself in "overbred peoples":

> At best it turns men into effeminate, furtive seekers of pleasure. It erodes their moral fiber and character, it destroys their righteous male honor, and in many cases, unfortunately, it leads to crime. The most hardened criminals often are recruited from homosexual circles. The new Germany has no use for criminals and weaklings, perverts and

---

[71]On May 22, 1935, Gerhard Günther Kanthack was appointed divisional head within the Reich Gestapo department on homosexuals. See Andreas Pretzel and Gabriele Roßbach, *"Wegen der zu erwartenden hohen Strafe . . .": Homosexuellenverfolgung in Berlin 1933–1945,* ed. Kulturring in Berlin e.V. (Berlin, 2000), 334; Wagner, 248–50; and Stefan Micheler, "'. . . eben homosexuell, wie andere Leute heterosexuell': Der Fall Heinrich Erich Starke," in *Verfolgung Homosexueller im Nationalsozialismus: Beiträge zur Geschichte der nationalsozialistischen Verfolgung in Norddeutschland,* vol. 5, ed. KZ-Gedenkstätte Neuengamme (Bremen, 1999), 77–92.

[72]"Gegen die Sittenentartung. Strafprozesse im Bereiche des § 175," *Hamburger Fremdenblatt*, August 26, 1936, evening ed., 5; "Der Durchgriff gegen Sittenentartung," *Hamburger Fremdenblatt*, August 29, 1936, evening ed., 5; "Säuberungsaktion in Hamburg. Massenverhaftungen von Homosexuellen," *Hamburger Nachrichten*, August 26, 1936, 2; "Der Kampf gegen die Homosexuellen," *Hamburger Nachrichten*, August 30, 1936, 6. See also "Es wird durchgegriffen . . . im Kampf gegen die Homosexualität," *Hamburger Anzeiger*, August 26, 1936, 1; "Die Abrechnung mit der Homosexualität," *Hamburger Anzeiger*, August 30, 1936, 1.

[73]"Gegen die Sittenentartung. Strafprozesse im Bereiche des § 175," *Hamburger Fremdenblatt*, August 26, 1936, evening ed., 5.

inverts, but requires instead straightforward and sincere manly souls, and so we must combat homosexuality with the means available to us—education, observation, the law, the police, and the courts.

The article concludes by noting that such "homosexual filth" needed to be eliminated in a "clean sweep."[74] Employing a similar tone and nearly the same wording, the *Essener National-Zeitung*, which Hermann Göring had adopted as his mouthpiece, reported on the campaign conducted by the Gestapo Sonderkommando in Hamburg.[75] Although the newspapers had previously only publicized violations of Paragraph 176, which involved sexual activities with minors, now the police and court sections of Hamburg local newspapers began to include coverage of arrests and trials of same-sex-desiring men under Paragraph 175, often mentioning the defendants by name.

Nearly all Germans came into contact with Nazi homophobic propaganda. Many read the daily newspapers, and most subscribed or were compelled to subscribe to one of the Nazi Party or party-affiliated papers.[76] A few of the newspapers were even posted in public display boxes. Many Nazi organizations, including the Hitler Youth, the SA, the Reichsarbeitsdienst (Reich Labor Service), and the Wehrmacht, disseminated "educational information" on the "dangers of homosexuality."[77] In addition, the relatively new media of the radio had a large audience.

It is difficult to measure directly the impact that these years of National Socialist homophobic propaganda had on the German population. No opinion polls on attitudes toward homosexuality exist for the Weimar or the National Socialist eras, nor do the Sopade reports or the SD's *Lageberichte* (the "status reports" issued by the Sicherheitsdienst of the SS) mention the antihomosexuality campaigns or the persecution of same-sex-desiring men.[78] Although the effect of Nazi propaganda can-

---

[74]"Es wird durchgegriffen . . . im Kampf gegen die Homosexualität," *Hamburger Anzeiger*, August 26, 1936, 1.

[75]See a reprint of the *Essener National-Zeitung* article dated August 28, 1936, in Hans-Georg Stümke, "Vom 'unausgeglichenen Geschlechtshaushalt.' Zur Verfolgung Homosexueller," in *Verachtet, verfolgt, vernichtet: Zu den "vergessenen" Opfern des NS-Regime*, ed. Projektgruppe für die vergessenen Opfer des NS-Regimes, 2nd rev. ed. (Hamburg, 1988), 47–63, 57.

[76]Frei and Schmitz, 97.

[77]Günter Grau discusses several Nazi-era sources that support these conclusions, such as the *Sonderrichtlinien: Die Bekämpfung gleichgeschlechtlicher Verfehlungen im Rahmen der Jugenderziehung*, ed. Reichsjugendführung (Berlin), June 1, 1943. Part of the *Sonderrichtlinien* are reprinted in Günter Grau, *Homosexualität in der NS-Zeit: Dokumente einer Diskriminierung und Verfolgung* (Frankfurt am Main, 1993), 294–99.

On an informational session on homosexuality at the Reich Labor Service following the arrest of a male prostitute, see Rep. 8393/36. On the Hitler Youth sessions, see Rep. 7391/36. See also Ramm, 90; Andreas Pretzel, "'Als Homosexueller in Erscheinung getreten': Anzeigen und Denunziationen," in Pretzel and Roßbach, 18–42, 31.

[78]Heinz Boberach, ed., *Meldungen aus dem Reich 1938–1945: Die geheimen Lageberichte des Sicherheitsdienstes der SS* (Herrsching, 1984).

not be measured precisely, it is reasonable to infer that such propaganda was effective to the extent to which it was founded on existing stereotypes.[79] Homophobic portrayals of homosexuals as criminals, "enemies of the state," and "corrupters of youth" were widespread, and their truth was seldom questioned, particularly given the dearth of other, more positive public images.

The homophobic propaganda certainly fueled a hostile atmosphere that encouraged the acceptance of persecutory measures. The press appealed to the German population to preserve "German youth" from the lures of "seducers," and leading Nazi functionaries urged the population to report the names of criminals and anyone "detrimental to the *Volk*," including those who undeservedly held positions of status in the party, state, or society. These press and party appeals laid the groundwork for the cooperation of the German population in the persecution of same-sex-desiring men. Although "being homosexual" was not against the law, the National Socialist propaganda implied that the mere "inclination" was itself a crime. Branding such men as criminals made them vulnerable to denunciation, and "*Volk* comrades" were encouraged by the regime to be vigilant in carrying out their duty to denounce the "homosexual."[80]

RUMOR, DENUNCIATION, AND PERSECUTION

In addition to the propaganda disseminated in Nazi organizations and the popular media, rumors about same-sex-desiring men, spread in daily conversations, abounded throughout the Reich. The files of the Hamburg district court document numerous instances of gossip about "homosexuals" circulating in neighborhoods, at the workplace, on board ships, and within party organizations, the Hitler Youth, the SA, Nazi training camps (*Kameradschaftslagern*), and even the police.[81] Gossip about "homosexuals" seems to have been a popular pastime in many communities—urban and rural, densely populated as well as sparsely settled.[82] Such rumors display three important traits: they arose quickly whenever a man failed to

---

[79]Regarding the difficulty of "measuring" the success of propaganda, see Ian Kershaw, "How Effective Was Nazi Propaganda?" in *Nazi Propaganda: The Power and the Limitations,* ed. David Welch (London, 1983), 180–205.

[80]See Pretzel, 22; and Burkhard Jellonnek, "Staatspolizeiliche Fahndungs- und Ermittlungsmethoden gegen Homosexuelle: Regionale Differenzen und Gemeinsamkeiten," in *Die Gestapo: Mythos und Realität,* ed. Gerhard Paul and Michael Mallmann (Darmstadt, 1995), 343–56.

[81]For gossip among acquaintances, see Rep. 7573/37, 8451/38, 9828/38; in the workplace, Rep. 1224/37, 6001/38, 2298/42; on ships, Rep. 7435/37, 9942/38, 10531/39; within Nazi organizations, Rep. 2524/35, 2111/37, 7907/37, 56/38, 38/46, Al 5955; and within the police, Rep. 6376/37.

[82]For suggestions of gossip in various districts and towns, see Rep. 5885/39, 7523/38, 373/37, 3101/37, 2111/37, 10814/39, 1090/38, 10960/39, 424/38, and 7272/41.

conform to the prevailing masculine ideal, they spread over long distances, and they were replete with homophobic stereotypes.[83] In 1934, for example, neighborhood youth spread rumors about the homosexuality of a thirty-one-year-old dentist, Friedrich Schlappkohl, but while everyone claimed Schlappkohl's homosexuality was widely known, no one could provide the police with concrete evidence.[84] In the mid-1930s rumors circulated in the Hamburg police department about an attorney, the friend of a police officer, who was conspicuously "soft and girlish in behavior, with a veiled gaze and an always deliberately quiet manner of speech." In 1936 rumors spread among the population of Bergedorf regarding the "homosexual disposition" of a local physician, Rudolf Brachmann. He was reputed to have allowed a nineteen-year-old orphan to live in his home in order "to satisfy his homosexual urges," to have approached and used "other boys" as "tools for his homosexual desires," and to have taken advantage of his position as physician to satisfy his lust. In December 1936, in the Jenfeld district, the sixty-one-year-old master harness maker Wilhelm Warnke was considered to be "a crank and a slovenly and flabby fellow" who "molested children," an accusation wholly without foundation. In August 1937 businessman Detert Iderhoff, an "important citizen" of the North Sea island of Norderney, was denounced to the Hamburg police for "having the reputation of being homosexually inclined." Because of his effeminate manner and appearance, the inhabitants of Norderney referred to him as the "little girl." Early in 1938, the rumor began to circulate in the district of St. George that the young man residing at 6 Koppel Street was a "homosexual" who "lived in a separate room and entertained one young man after another there at all hours of the day and night."[85]

Such rumors were almost impossible to escape. Hermann Scheibel, a forty-four-year-old tax inspector and party member who demanded that a local grocer retract his accusation that Scheibel was a "homosexual," was denounced soon after sending copies of the retraction to several people. Adolf Großkopf, a thirty-year-old party member, entered into a sham marriage in hopes of countering rumors of his homosexuality, but to no avail.[86]

While the physician Rudolf Brachmann could report that rumors of his homosexuality had prompted many same-sex-desiring men to visit his offices, often in search of advice, most men found that such rumors threatened their economic survival. The barber Otto Krepp was forced to close

[83]Epithets such as "queers," "poofters," and "bum fuckers" were the order of the day. See Rep. 2524/35, 3674/35, 1138/36; Rep. 1138/36, 2909/36; and Rep. 2524/35, 1090/38, respectively.

[84]I have used pseudonyms for all private individuals who were born after January 1, 1911, for whom no date of death is known. All individuals for whom no date of birth or death is known have also been cited under pseudonyms. In abbreviations of surnames, I have changed the first letter of all surnames in the interest of anonymity.

[85]Rep. 1138/36, 6376/37, 2111/37, 373/37, 9831/38, 467/39.

[86]Rep. L189/35, 9180/36.

his business when his customers abandoned the shop, and the dentist Werner J. had to relocate his practice to another neighborhood and apply for an injunction to halt the rumormongers' "character assassination."[87]

Rumors led to denunciations as well as disgrace. Since few relevant records exist for the Weimar period, it is difficult to compare the denunciations of same-sex-desiring men under National Socialism with earlier practices. Most police records for the Weimar era have been destroyed, and the few remaining court records reveal little about what triggered an investigation. Of approximately sixty Weimar-era court files from Hamburg and Altona that I have examined, six relate to denunciations for same-sex sexual activities. In each of these cases, the denouncer witnessed the activities in question, which took place in parks, public lavatories, and lodging houses. Since the number of investigations of same-sex-desiring men under National Socialism was significantly higher than under the Weimar Republic, and since only a small number of these cases were initiated by police investigative efforts, it follows that the number of denunciations must have increased.

To date, over 180 denunciations of same-sex-desiring men by private individuals have been documented for Hamburg under the Nazi regime. Although the records contain numerous cases of denunciations made anonymously or by strangers, the majority came from men and women who were acquainted with those whom they denounced. The denouncers included men and women of every age and class[88]—neighbors, landlords and tenants, employees and coworkers, restaurant and hotel staff, and even family members.[89]

---

[87] Rep. 2111/37. "Das Verbrechen am Brunnenhof. War Krepp mit seinem Opfer allein? Beitrag von p.," *Hamburger Anzeiger*, June 12, 1936, 1. See Rep. 7218/39.

[88] Burkhard Jellonnek has argued that a disproportionately high number of women were among the denouncers of same-sex-desiring men; however, Frank Sparing, examining the same Düsseldorf records, has contested Jellonnek's claim and methods (see Jellonnek, "Staatspolizeiliche Fahndungs- und Ermittlungsmethoden," 350; Sparing, 128). Gisela Diewald-Kerkmann, who believes that the notion that women predominated among denouncers under National Socialism is a cliché that remains unproven, suggests that men predominated ("Politische Denunziation—eine 'weibliche Domäne'? Der Anteil von Männern und Frauen unter Denunzianten und ihren Opfern," *1999* 11, no. 2 [1996]: 14; see also Katrin Dördelmann, "Denunziationen im Nationalsozialismus. Geschlechtsspezifische Aspekte," in Jerouschek, Marßolek, and Röckelein, eds., 157–67). According to Robert Gellately and Peter Hüttenberger, political denunciations typically were directed against members of the same social class as the accuser, a finding borne out in my random sample of Hamburg sedition cases. Although members of other social classes were among those denounced in Hamburg (particularly academics, physicians, and work supervisors), the majority of denunciations were directed against members of the same social class (see Gellately, *The Gestapo and German Society*, 125; Peter Hüttenberger, "Heimtückefälle vor dem Sondergericht München 1933–1939," in *Bayern in der NS-Zeit*, ed. Martin Broszat, Elke Fröhlich, and Anton Grossmann, vol. 4 [Munich, 1981], 435–526, 517).

[89] For denunciations by neigbors, see Rep. 3185/35, 5688/36, 7394/36, 196/37, 424/38, 1029/38, 1033/38, 1090/38, 10251/38, 467/39, 6355/41; for those by landlords,

Since the police rarely inquired about or recorded an accuser's motives, such information is available in only a few of the cases where same-sex-desiring men and women in Hamburg were denounced. While some denouncers were probably moved by a personal consideration such as profit or revenge, they were unlikely to admit this to the authorities.[90] Many who may have barely known their victims either believed that "homosexuals" were a danger to society or sought to maintain or gain status and power by participating in some of the National Socialists' campaigns. The records do provide ample evidence of homophobia, for many denunciations make reference to "effeminacy," "enemies of the state," "child molesters," "corruptors of youth," and "perversion." In their December 1937 denunciation of the thirty-one-year-old porter Ernst-Heinrich Hinze, his former supervisor and former coworker remarked that Hinze was "a bad person" and "not a real man."[91] Several denouncers made reference to press announcements urging the German population to join in informing on "homosexual" men. When one of these, Elisabeth Cohrs, denounced her neighbor in 1938, she stated: "I read in the newspaper that we should not go easy on such individuals but that the police should pursue them without mercy, so I decided it was my duty to report this situation."[92]

Some denouncers, like the two mothers who reported their adolescent sons in hopes of "protecting" them from further contact with men, may not have realized the consequences of their acts, but most must have understood.[93] Like those who denounced political offenses, the denouncers of "homosexuals" had personal grudges or a desire to maintain or share in

---

see Rep. 3549/38, 724/39, 5353/41, 7101/41; for those by tenants, see Rep. 8842/37, 3454/38, 5327/39.

[90]A denouncer's personal motives are sometimes alleged by the accused in his defense. See, for example, attorney Erich Wandschneider's letter to the Hamburg prosecutor, dated July 30, 1934 (Rep. L189/35), which claims that "the origin of the accusations was the psychosis that resulted from the Röhm affair and the irresponsible statements of individuals who were avenging their anger and bitterness toward the accused in a biased and personal manner." The accused had stopped purchasing his groceries from the shop since the food there was so often already spoiled, a fact that he had mentioned to other customers. Other motives can be inferred from their context. In September 1936, sixty-seven-year-old pensioner Hermann Köster denounced his wife and stepson in order to obtain evidence supporting his application for divorce. According to Köster, his wife tolerated, even promoted, his stepson's homosexual relationships and had helped convert their apartment into a flophouse (Rep. 8689/38).

[91]Rep. 2632/38.

[92]Testimony by Elisabeth Cohrs to the criminal police, Department K 24, on April 27, 1938 (Rep. 467/39). For other cases, see testimony by Else N. to the criminal police, Department F 31, on July 10, 1934 (Rep. L189/35), Rep. 124/37, and Rep. 709/39.

[93]In both cases, the fifteen-year-old boys were convicted of prostitution. Egon V. admitted to the court that he loved men and received a prison sentence of two years (Rep. 1821/38). Richard N., termed "a rent boy of the foulest sort," also received a sentence of two years. His mother's application for a pardon was later denied (Rep. 3533/42). For similar cases in Berlin, see Pretzel, 25.

the regime's power.[94] Those who did not sympathize with the regime and its aims would have been unlikely to cooperate with it.[95]

While certain behaviors, such as visiting public gathering places, heightened the risk of denunciation and arrest, all same-sex-desiring men were vulnerable to denunciation—even those who led quiet lives. Gustav Pannier, a twenty-eight-year-old office clerk, was denounced by Rudolf Arnold, a janitor, who had observed that Pannier often visited a neighborhood lavatory in the evening hours. On August 17, 1938, Arnold followed Pannier to another public lavatory and then brought him—presumably by force—to the police station. Nineteen-year-old waiter Börge F. was denounced by his landlords, who read some of his correspondence, including a number of love letters. Shop assistant Rudolf G. and decorator's apprentice Alfred P. were denounced by P.'s building superintendent, who noted that G. brought flowers when he came to visit. The superintendent peeked through the keyhole of P.'s door, observed the two men engaged in sexual acts, locked the door, and notified the police.[96]

Hotel guests were also vulnerable. Between 1935 and 1937 the staff of the Concordia lodging house, located near the Reeperbahn, contacted the police on at least seventeen occasions to inform on men suspected of engaging in same-sex sexual activities. On most of these occasions, the staff had spied upon their victims for quite some time. Although the files are silent on the issue, it is certainly possible that the staff were pressured by the police to act as informers, for the Concordia lodging house had been named as a notorious "homosexual" haven in need of more stringent surveillance during an October 1934 meeting between the Hamburg youth welfare department and the head of the Hamburg vice squad. It doubtless took some time before rumors began to circulate that the staff of the Concordia were involved in many denunciations.[97]

Some hotels found alternative ways to comply with the regime's dictates, as the story of Erich P. demonstrates. Several times in the early 1940s,

---

[94]See, for example, Günter Jerouschek, Inge Marßolek, and Hedwig Röckelein, "Denunziation—ein interdisziplinäres Forschungsfeld," in Jerouschek, Marßolek, and Röckelein, eds., 9–25, esp. 17; Gellately, *The Gestapo and German Society*, 136; Gisela Diewald-Kerkmann, "Denunziantentum und Gestapo. Die freiwilligen 'Helfer' aus der Bevölkerung," in Gerhard and Mallmann, 285–305, esp. 302; and Gisela Diewald-Kerkmann, "Politische Denunziationen im NS-Regime. Die kleine Macht der 'Volksgenossen,'" in Jerouschek, Marßolek, and Röckelein, eds., 146–56, 150.

[95]Jellonnek has argued that "the Nazi leadership and the population were in complete agreement on the importance of persecuting homosexuals," which is demonstrated by the fact that only a "narrow segment of intellectuals and politicians" under the Weimar Republic had supported the plan to repeal some of the legal discrimination against homosexual acts (see Jellonek, "Staatspolizeiliche Fahndungs- und Ermittlungsmethoden," 350). This argument is certainly plausible though impossible to prove.

[96]Rep. 9210/37; Rep. 5353/41; Rep. 1724/36.

[97]On the Concordia lodging house denunciations, see Ramm, 91; Rep. 1149/37, 10599/38, 3383/38, 5034/36, 2399/38, 6622/38, 741/38; Rep. 9286/36, 1876/36, 2882/

while stationed in occupied Brussels, P. spent the night in a hotel with a male friend. On the third occasion, the receptionist told him, "The Gestapo has informed us that we may no longer provide you with a room."[98] On this occasion, the hotel staff chose to warn their guest rather than denounce him.

Workplace denunciations were typically directed against adult men who entered into relationships with underage male apprentices or coworkers, even when both consented to the relationship.[99] Family denunciations were made for reasons that are not always clear. In February 1937, thirty-two-year-old lathe operator Alfred Beckmann and forty-five-year-old bicycle fitter Wilhelm Wilck, who had a relationship of long standing and had for a time lived together, were denounced by Wilck's brother.[100] In July 1937, sixteen-year-old errand boy Karl-Heinz Dellin died after a suicide attempt, mistakenly believing his love for another man was unrequited. In the days that followed, his mother brought to the police a telegram and several letters addressed to her son that included the names of many of his same-sex-desiring friends.[101]

Most of those denounced for homosexuality were men, but some were women, even though sexual contacts between women were not punishable under German law. In addition to being marginalized in the workforce, they could be prosecuted for "asocial" criminal offenses.[102] Ellen E., a twenty-year-old sales representative, and Paul-Reimer I., a painter, lived as tenants with the family of a dentist. The couple pretended to be engaged and planned a "sham marriage" in hopes of keeping their same-sex desires a secret. But in 1941 an anonymous letter of denunciation was sent to the criminal police, stating: "You should conduct a raid . . . on E.'s love nest. This is the residence of a 'mannish woman' who often invites her 'own

---

36, 1595/38; Rep. 324/38, 1048/38, 1060/38; and *Niederschrift über die am 5.10.1934 im Jugendamt Hamburg statgefundene Besprechung über Fragen der Zusammenarbeit zwischen Hitler-Jugend u. Jugendamt,* Staatsarchiv Hamburg, 354–55, Jugendbehörde I, 232e: Einsetzung und Tätigkeit des HJ-Streifendienstes der NSV Jugendhilfe 1934–1941. This text is reprinted by both Grau and Stümke, who unfortunately fail to provide a citation for the original source (see Grau, 70–74; Hans-Georg Stümke, "Die Verfolgung der Homosexuellen in Hamburg," in *Heilen und Vernichten im Mustergau Hamburg: Bevölkerungs- und Gesundheitspolitik im Dritten Reich,* ed. Angelika Ebbinghaus, Heidrun Kaupen-Haas, and Karl Heinz Roth [Hamburg, 1984], 80–84, esp. 83–84).

[98]Unpublished interview of Erich P. conducted by the Arbeitskreis schwule Geschichte Hamburg on July 22, 1992.

[99]See, for example, Rep. 7942/37, 323/38, 456/38, 2033/38, 7893/38, 8011/38, 8938/38, 7192/41, 2298/42, 3496/44. It seems unlikely that relationships or sexual advances involving adult men with underage female apprentices would have resulted in similar moral indignation.

[100]See, for example, Rep. 4036/37, 2752/38.

[101]Rep. 584/38.

[102]Regarding the persecution of same-sex-desiring women, see Claudia Schoppmann, "Zur Situation lesbischer Frauen in der NS-Zeit," in Grau, 35–42. See also Claudia

kind,' sometimes more than just one, into her lodgings. In times like these, we clearly should not tolerate such § 175 activities (à la Röhm). Since there are children living in the house, immediate action must be taken. Obviously, it is inadvisable for our youth to observe such activities." Paul-Reimer I. was sentenced to eight months in prison and was enjoined by the prosecutor and the court to have himself castrated, which he did. The fate of Ellen E. remains unknown.[103]

Some denunciations, of course, were false, but establishing the accused's innocence could be difficult, as the following case illustrates. In 1937 a Hamburg professor of public law, Rudolf Laun, and his wife spent their summer vacation on the North Sea island of Sylt, where their son, who was in the Reich Labor Service, was stationed. Before going to work, the son occasionally met his parents on the beach, where they breakfasted together and then bathed. On a few occasions, Laun's wife did not join her husband and son, and on one of these Laun was observed giving his son "a brief kiss on departure" before carrying out his morning exercise routine. On August 7, Laun learned that the criminal police had "passed on the following information" to the Reich Labor Service:

> On several mornings, some Westerland residents observed a young worker meet an elderly man at wicker beach chair No. 1435 at roughly 7 A.M., apparently for the purpose of engaging in unnatural sexual practices. They were observed bathing together and sitting on the canopied beach chair. At the end of the encounter, the older man gave the young laborer some money and kissed him upon departure. Following the laborer's departure, the older man satisfied himself sexually while carrying out a gymnastics routine.

Laun immediately filed slander charges with the local police, where he discovered that several persons had been spying on him and his son for a number of days. The Sylt police had even placed the beach under observation on a morning when the son had not visited. On August 12 Laun wrote to the Flensburg prosecutor, arguing that the denunciation was clearly a product of deliberate malice, since the nature of his meetings with his son must have been obvious to anyone. "Two men bathing in the sea together and sitting on beach chairs is nothing out of the ordinary." Nor was it

---

Schoppmann, *Nationalsozialistische Sexualpolitik und weibliche Homosexualität*, 2nd rev. ed. (Pfaffenweiler, 1997); and Claudia Schoppmann, *Verbotene Verhältnisse: Frauenliebe 1938–1945* (Berlin, 1999). Regarding the stigma of the "antisocial" label, see Schoppmann, *Nationalsozialistische Sexualpolitik*, 260–61.

[103]Anonymous letter to the criminal police dated April 28, 1941, Rep. 6776/41. For other cases see Rep. 465/38, 2448/42, 2336/43, and 7979/38. Collective fantasies about the supposed lesbian sexuality of nuns and nurses affiliated with religious orders lent credibility to the accusation of lesbian sexuality. It is impossible to tell from the records whether these accusations were deemed plausible, thus forcing these women to attempt to refute their accusers.

strange for someone to do exercises on the beach. The accusation that he had masturbated on the beach in full public view was grotesque. In any case, no one would have been able to see what it was that he had handed to his son. It was pure chance that he had decided to extend his holiday; had he already departed, it would have been very difficult for his son to prove the truth. "On the contrary, had we chosen that very morning to depart, this would have been taken as an indication of our guilt. . . . My son, though completely innocent . . . might well have become the victim of a terrible, unjust conviction." The denunciation could have driven his son to ruin and damaged his own reputation as a scholar. The fact that the Sylt police refused to divulge the name of the denouncers and that the Flensburg prosecutor's office abandoned the investigation of Laun as "unfounded" supports Laun's assessment of events. Had the case involved two men other than father and son or men who were not members of the higher social classes, the outcome might have been far different.[104] Among those convicted of homosexual activities in Hamburg, it is likely that some were victims of false denunciations who had been unable to convince the court of that fact. In some cases, they may even have confessed to the accusation under the pressure of interrogation and trial.[105]

While one cannot demonstrate that homophobia increased among the German population in the 1930s, the Nazi regime certainly promoted an atmosphere that encouraged many to act upon their prejudices by publicizing its revisions to the penal code, encouraging denunciation, and aggressively pursuing investigations of homosexuals. Thus, the masseur Stanislaus Kasperski and the unemployed tax accountant Albert Küssow, who had met in 1921, were able to live together in an apartment as a couple for eleven years without interference until 1937, when they were denounced.[106]

Though one cannot correlate the frequency of denunciation with the intensity of homophobic propaganda, a number of the denunciations made during periods when the media were reporting extensively on "homosexual criminals" show a clear link to the press accounts. During the 1934 Röhm affair, for example, the rumors that began to circulate about the homosexuality of a Nazi Party member prompted his denunciation to the police. Shortly following the news accounts of the Krepp murder and supposed intrigues, one neighbor denounced a thirty-two-year-old tailor for using his apartment as a "flophouse for rent boys," and another informed on a twenty-two-year-old for "homosexual intrigues," even though both

[104]Staatsarchiv Hamburg: 241-2, Justizverwaltung, Personalakten A 3210, Rudolf Laun. I wish to thank Thomas Mohr of Hamburg for his assistance.
    [105]Regarding false denunciation in Berlin, see Pretzel, 28–29. In addition to the cases noted above, other instances of false accusations revolved around unrequited love, envy when another soldier was granted leave from the front, or attempts to wrest custody of a child from a spouse (see Rep. 4536/40, 5310/41, 6512/41).
    [106]Rep. 1033/38.

neighbors had been aware of the situations for quite some time. In a third case, the denouncers made explicit mention of the Seefeld child murders.[107] Although the National Socialist regime generally encouraged denunciation, on occasion it tried to check the flood of denunciations in the realization that the multitude of false ones were overburdening the investigative apparatus. Adolescents were notable for their enthusiasm in denouncing offenses.[108] In 1934 the Hamburg Hitler Youth organization insisted on participating in the campaign against "homosexuals" and organized patrols to uncover "homosexuals" and rent boys across the city. A number of the Hitler Youth offered themselves as "decoys" or "bait," pretending to offer sexual services in order to entrap men. Within a few weeks, however, the Hamburg police called a halt to the "impudent" investigative techniques of these "amateur criminologists."[109] After Röhm's assassination, newspapers published repeated appeals to the population in an effort to stem the tide of informers. However, as Martin Broszat has noted, such appeals led to a wave of further denunciations. The regime's messages on denunciation were thus ambivalent and sometimes contradictory.[110]

As rumors invited denunciations, denunciations prompted investigations and prosecutions. Contrary to what earlier historians have assumed, recent research using the repositories of Gestapo and police records from Berlin and Hamburg, the two largest cities in Germany, demonstrates that "active" investigation methods such as surveillance and raids were not the basis for most arrests of same-sex-desiring men. In Hamburg, the percentage of cases originating from such methods was twenty-two in 1936, when the Berlin Gestapo Sonderkommando was active there, twelve in 1937, and eight in 1938. For the entire twelve-year period of Nazi rule,

[107]Rep. L189/35, 2782/36, 3185/35, 6693/36. Regarding homosexual stereotyping of Nazi leaders, see Zinn, "'Die Bewegung der Homosexuellen'"; Zinn, *Die soziale Konstruktion des homosexuellen Nationalsozialisten*; Jörn Meve, *"Homosexuelle Nazis": Ein Stereotyp in Literatur und Politik des Exils* (Hamburg, 1990). For cases of sexual denunciation, see Bernward Dörner, *"Heimtücke": Das Gesetz als Waffe: Kontrolle, Abschreckung und Verfolgung in Deutschland 1933–1945* (Paderborn, 1998), 189–91. For cases from Hamburg, see Rep. 2055/35, 2581/35, 5113/37, 1556/38, 127/39, 1335/40, 559/43. For cases from Düsseldorf, see Johnson, 297–98.

[108]Gellately, *The Gestapo and German Society*, 156. Denunciations by the Hitler Youth prompted a significant number of investigations.

[109] See Rep. L735/34, 2729/35, 3333/35, 3476/35, 4984/35, 1138/36, 8809/38, 6514/37, 2492/45, 38/46; Staatsarchiv Hamburg: 354-5, Jugendbehörde I, 232e: Einsetzung und Tätigkeit des HJ-Streifendienstes der NSV Jugendhilfe 1934–1941. Regarding the debate on the Hitler Youth patrol at the central train station, see Ramm, 27–28.

[110]"Chef des Stabes Lutze warnt die Denunzianten," *Hamburger Fremdenblatt*, July 19, 1934, morning ed., 1; "Rudolf Heß gegen die Denunzianten," *Hamburger Fremdenblatt*, July 24, 1934, morning ed., 1, and evening ed., 2; "Gegen Gerüchtemacher und anonyme Denunzianten," *Hamburger Fremdenblatt*, July 31, 1934, evening ed., 2; Gellately, *The Gestapo and German Society*, 138–39; Martin Broszat, "Politische Denunziationen in der NS-Zeit: Aus Forschungserfahrungen im Staatsarchiv München," *Archivalische Zeitschrift* 73 (1977): 221–38, 223.

an average of only 14 percent of the cases in Hamburg were derived from police initiatives. As was the case with political offenses, the state apparatus was only effective in its pursuit of male same-sex behaviors because neighbors, coworkers, and even family members were willing to denounce.[111] My examination of the surviving records of the Hamburg district court for the years 1936 and 1937 indicates that more than one fourth of all the lower court trials involving Paragraphs 175 and 175a violations were the result of third-party denunciations.[112] If one includes the denunciations by adult men who had been approached for sexual favors, that figure rises to 32.9 percent for 1936 and 31.7 percent for 1937. Analysis of a portion of 1938 cases bears out these statistics, as do random samples from the remaining years of Nazi rule, which show that approximately 30 percent of all lower court cases from 1933 to 1945 resulted from denunciations.[113]

Regarding the discussion among Nazi elites whether denunciation should be encouraged or banned, see Diewald-Kerkmann, "Denunziantentum und Gestapo," 285–305; Diewald-Kerkmann, "Politische Denunziation—eine 'weibliche Domäne'?" 11–35; Diewald-Kerkmann, "Politische Denunziationen im NS-Regime," 146–56; Gellately, *The Gestapo and German Society*, 139.

[111]Robert Gellately, "The Gestapo and German Society: Political Denunciation in the Gestapo Case Files," *Journal of Modern History* 60, no. 4 (1988): 654–94. Regarding the importance of denunciation to the regime, see Diewald-Kerkmann, "Denunziantentum und Gestapo," 289–90; Gellately, *The Gestapo and German Society,* 129–30, 135–36. Johnson also emphasizes the importance of denunciation but argues that Gellately and Diewald-Kerkmann attribute too much responsibility to the denouncers and too little to the Nazi apparatus of persecution (433–34). I disagree with Johnson's critique. The importance of denunciation to the apparatus of persecution was detailed by Martin Broszat as early as 1977 ("Politische Denunziationen").

[112]Staatsarchiv Hamburg: 213–11, Staatsanwaltschaft Landgericht—Strafsachen. Between 1986 and 1996, authorized by the Hamburg state archive, the legal staff destroyed most of the records of the Hamburg public prosecutor's office dating from the National Socialist era. These records were a crucial repository of information regarding the investigative methods of the Hamburg police as well as the workings of the public prosecutor and court system. Although the records for the years from 1938 onward had been preserved in near entirety, today less than 20 percent of the records survive. Since there were no statistical criteria employed in selecting which records should be preserved, the surviving records cannot be taken as representative. Following international protest, the destruction of records relating to violations of Paragraph 175 was halted by the senator of justice in 1996. The judicial records dating from the years prior to 1937 had already been culled by the National Socialists when the courts were consolidated in the newly established greater Hamburg region. Regarding the destruction of these records, see Stefan Micheler, "'Verfahren nach § 175 übertrafen in ihrer Häufigkeit die Verfahren gegen andere Verfolgte erheblich'— daher wurden sie vernichtet. Zum Umgang des Hamburger Staatsarchivs mit NS-Justizakten," in *Verfolgung Homosexueller im Nationalsozialismus: Beiträge zur Geschichte der nationalsozialistischen Verfolgung in Norddeutschland*, vol. 5, ed. KZ-Gedenkstätte Neuengamme (Bremen, 1999), 112–21.

[113]Due to the destruction of records by the Hamburg state archives and the errors made by the archive in selecting from the existing records, these figures should not be regarded as definitive. Nonetheless, some obvious trends are apparent. Since the original grounds for

Data from many other areas confirm the importance of denunciations. The court records from Altona, which was incorporated into greater Hamburg in 1937, show that nearly 42 percent of the investigations conducted between 1933 and 1937 resulted from denunciations. According to Andreas Pretzel, 38 percent of approximately three hundred cases in Berlin resulted from denunciations by a third party and 11 percent from denunciations by those approached for sexual favors. While Frank Sparing's research on Düsseldorf and Jürgen Müller's on Cologne have yielded a lower percentage of denunciations, this might be accounted for by the fact that only a fragment of the original case records for these cities survived the war. Although no statistics have been compiled for the city of Munich, Stephan Heiss has surmised that the active cooperation of the population was key in that city as well.[114]

The majority of same-sex-desiring men who were investigated came to official attention after a sexual partner or an acquaintance revealed their names under the pressure of interrogation. Many men who were interrogated submitted a sort of "wholesale confession," naming all of their previous sexual partners and engaging in great self-reproach for their sexual desires. Few could withstand interrogation and refuse to

---

investigation played no role in the later choice of which records to destroy and which to preserve, I believe my statistical analysis to be legitimate. I examined all 130 surviving files for convictions dated 1936. In 82 cases, or 63 percent, what triggered the investigation is apparent from the record. For the year 1937, I examined all 183 surviving records and was able to make a clear determination in 145 records, or 78 percent. For convictions dating to 1938, Moritz Terfloth and I examined 232 of the 500 surviving case files. In almost all the records (99 percent), the reason for investigation is apparent. The analysis of the files from the years 1933–35 is still in progress. For the years 1933–45, evidence has survived for 1,828 trials of violations of Paragraphs 175 and 175a. Of these cases, I have examined 646 files, while Moritz Terfloth has analyzed an additional 115 cases. Our summary statistic is based on our analysis of these 761 cases, which represents 42 percent of the surviving case records. The Hamburg state archive is not able to provide information regarding the original number of cases that were tried during the Nazi years.

[114]Landesarchiv Schleswig-Holstein, Section 352 Altona, Staatsanwaltschaft beim Landgericht Altona.

Pretzel grouped government agencies and businesses under one heading (22), but I have chosen to list denunciations from the workplace under the heading of "personal denunciations." It is thus likely that the percentage of denunciations from private individuals in Berlin will exceed 50 percent.

In his study of Cologne cases, Jürgen Müller argued for a lower estimate for the percentage initiated following denunciation. However, the surviving records for Cologne are too fragmentary to permit Müller to undertake an empirical quantification ("Die Kölner Kriminalpolizei zwischen Verbrechensaufklärung und 'vorbeugender Verbrechensbekämpfung,'" in *Polizei und schwule Subkulturen* [*Comparativ* 9, no. 1], ed. Stephan Heiss and Wolfgang Schmale [Leipzig, 1999], 25–47).

In 1990, Burkhard Jellonnek conducted comparative research on this question, examining one urban region (Düsseldorf), one midsize town (Würzburg), and one rural area (Pfalz). In Düsseldorf, 15 percent of cases followed from denunciations; in Würzburg, 9 percent; in

provide the names of their former sexual partners.[115] Thus, the focus of the police investigative apparatus was on interrogating men who had already been arrested. Consequently, each denunciation led to the arrest and conviction of not just the man accused but many others. Nearly half of all Hamburg convictions thus ultimately were the result of denunciation.[116]

Unlike those made during the Weimar Republic, denunciations made under National Socialism often led to prosecutions. The Weimar police and courts had required concrete evidence of sexual acts akin to "natural," heterosexual intercourse, which most denouncers would have been unable to provide. Until 1936 the Hamburg vice squad focused mainly on the

---

Neustadt/Pfalz, 11 percent ("Homosexuelle unter dem Hakenkreuz," 193–99, 236–42, 282–93, 330). His assumption, most likely correct, is that the Gestapo engaged in active investigation only in urban areas and relied in rural regions on denunciations and on pressuring those whom they had arrested into providing the names of additional "homosexuals." It was, of course, more difficult for police to pursue "active" investigations in rural areas since there were no meeting places for same-sex-desiring men.

According to Frank Sparing, Jellonnek mistakenly included a portion of the records from the Düsseldorf regional high court district, which extended considerably beyond the boundaries of the city itself. Only a fraction of these high court cases would have issued directly from the city of Düsseldorf. When Sparing examined the same records analyzed by Jellonnek, he arrived at different figures (10, 12, 15, 104).

Moreover, Jellonnek's analysis does not reflect that the criminal police, not the Gestapo, were responsible for most prosecutions of homosexual men. He also overlooked the fact that a high proportion of the Gestapo's investigative efforts took place within the framework of a *Sonderaktion* (special campaign). The more likely conclusion is that presumably no such campaigns were conducted in small towns and rural regions. On the whole, Jellonnek's results must be approached with caution, since he based his analysis on a restricted number of sources and, in the case of Düsseldorf, made errors in the regional distribution of cases.

In his own study of Düsseldorf, Frank Sparing also arrived at a lower estimate for cases initiated following denunciation. However, he based his analysis on only 360 Gestapo case files, since the Kripo files could no longer be located, even though they had been examined for a commemorative history of the Düsseldorf police in 1983 (11).

Stephan Heiss's argument is based on an analysis of surviving police case records, but unfortunately he did not provide any information about the number or completeness of the records he analyzed ("München: Polizei und schwule Subkulturen 1919–1944," in Heiss and Schmale, eds., 61–79).

In his important study of Frankfurt am Main, Dieter Schiefelbein did not consider the issue of cases triggered by denunciation ("Zur Verfolgung von Homosexuellen in Frankfurt am Main," in *Verfolgung und Widerstand in Hessen 1933–1945*, ed. Renate Knigge-Tesche and Axel Ulrich [Frankfurt am Main, 1996], 404–14).

[115]Heinrich Erich Starke, a traveling salesman from Hamburg, and Hans-Georg S., a resident of Düsseldorf, were among the very few men who resisted the pressure of interrogation and refused to provide names. Regarding Starke, see Micheler, "eben homosexuell"; regarding S., see Jürgen Müller, "Die alltägliche Angst: Denunziationen als Instrument zur Ausschaltung Missliebiger," in Limpricht, Müller, and Oxenius, eds., 96–103, esp. 100.

[116]This figure is a reasonable estimate, since statistical analysis of the grounds of investigation is no longer possible due to gaps in the preservation of records.

[117]Micheler, "eben homosexuell," 78.

investigation of male prostitutes and blackmailers.[117] In September of that year a denouncer complained to the Gestapo that he had repeatedly brought his accusation to the attention of the criminal police but had been ignored.[118] Starting in the summer of 1936, the police (until the summer of 1937 the Gestapo, and from the summer of 1937 until 1945 the Kripo) investigated all accusations, regardless of the motive of the denouncer or the plausibility of the accusation, for under the Nazis, the mere suspicion that a person might be "homosexual" sufficed to trigger an investigation. The mere fact that a man had been called a "homosexual" justified the questioning of acquaintances, coworkers, and neighbors. In most instances, the accused were summoned to appear before the police, where they were interrogated and often taken into "protective custody."[119]

An analysis of the denunciations of same-sex-desiring men in Hamburg refutes Eric Johnson's recent thesis that popular denunciations either did not prompt official investigations or resulted in only minor sentences.[120] The denunciations of same-sex-desiring men had serious consequences for the accused: Heinrich Erich Starke was murdered in the Neuengamme concentration camp; Alfred Beckmann died while a resident of the Meseritz-Obrawalde psychiatric hospital in Brandenburg, where he had been incarcerated by order of the court. Following their lengthy imprisonment, Eugen Lenz and Gustav Pannier were forced to undergo "voluntary castration" in order to secure release from the concentration camp. Other victims cited in this study "merely" received lengthy prison sentences. But because the court records ordinarily do not mention later forced castration or subsequent confinement to a concentration camp, it is reasonable to assume that many victims were subjected to punishment beyond what is officially documented. Many of those convicted of a Paragraph 175 violation lost not only their jobs, homes, and friends but also their health and even their lives.

Same-sex-desiring men under National Socialism thus lived in a climate of fear. All aspects of their daily lives were affected by persecution. The friendship federations were banned, bars were shut down or subjected to police surveillance, lavatories and parks were observed for evidence of "homosexual" assignations, magazines for same-sex-desiring men and women were banned. The fear of blackmail was ever present, as was the fear of denunciation. It became impossible for same-sex-desiring men to feel secure even in their own homes or among friends and colleagues. Those who were arrested and convicted often found themselves abandoned by their friends. Others were forced to keep their desires hidden. They withdrew from the homosexual subculture and abandoned friendships with other

[118]Rep. 8689/38.

[119]See Gellately, *The Gestapo and German Society*, 165.

[120]Johnson's argument, which addresses Jews, is contradicted by the research of both Robert Gellately and Gisela Diewald-Kirkmann and seems implausible given the evidence that Johnson himself cites in his work (484).

same-sex-desiring men in fear of coming to the attention of the state. This climate of fear led to withdrawal, to increasing loneliness, to suicide. For young men who discovered that they had same-sex desires, it was virtually impossible to develop a positive sexual identity. In addition to the homophobia expressed in the media and popular opinion, they were confronted with the homophobic propaganda campaigns of the Hitler Youth. The plight of these young men, who had never experienced the comparatively liberal atmosphere of the Weimar Republic, was particularly tragic.[121]

Although the National Socialist regime, defeated in war, came to an end in 1945, its legal code and police and court apparatus were taken over by the Federal Republic, along with the medical theories on the genesis of homosexuality that the Nazis had developed and articulated so effectively. Homophobic stereotypes have further determined German society's views on homosexuality, and social discrimination affected the handling of homosexuals until the 1960s. While the state no longer prescribed death or mutilation for "homosexuals," it continued to inflict considerable psychological damage.

Translated by Patricia Szobar

---

[121]Under National Socialism a few individuals did demonstrate solidarity with same-sex-desiring men. Some refused to cooperate with investigating authorities or provided false and misleading information to protect accused men. Others maintained personal contact and association with convicted men, and some employers went out of their way to rehire those convicted upon release.

Telling Sexual Stories in the Nazi Courts of Law: Race Defilement in Germany, 1933 to 1945

PATRICIA SZOBAR

Rutgers University

IN THE NINETEENTH-CENTURY imagination, miscegenation with "non-European" races, particularly Jews and blacks, who were deemed figures of pathological and deviant sexuality, was posited as a key source of the physical degeneration of the "European" individual, race, and nation. By the 1920s in Germany, even some progressive adherents of the new theories of eugenics had adopted similar notions, arguing that miscegenation led to a form of "species alienation" that caused the individual and nation to lose "life force" and biological fertility. Such concerns about intermarriage and miscegenation were to become a central ideological obsession among National Socialists, who even before the demise of the Weimar Republic began to issue calls for measures to prevent the sexual contamination of Aryan women and the birth of "mixed race" offspring. Indeed, fulminations against "race defilement" and the sullying of "Aryan maidens" featured prominently in Hitler's tract, *Mein Kampf,* and numerous other Nazi ideologists joined him in demanding an end to the mingling of races.[1] Thus, in their 1931

For helpful comments on early drafts, I thank the members of the Women's History and European History seminars at Rutgers University and the members of the Berlin Program for Advanced German and European Studies seminar at the Freie Universität Berlin. I especially wish also to thank the anonymous reviewer and Elizabeth Heineman for suggestions on the latest version and Omer Bartov, Dagmar Herzog, and Ralph Scott for their continued support. In accordance with German privacy laws, the names of all individuals cited in this article are pseudonyms except where otherwise noted.
    [1]Adolf Hitler, *Mein Kampf,* combined ed. (Munich, 1940) and also, for example, Alfred Rosenberg, *Der Mythos des zwanzigsten Jahrhunderts,* 2nd ed. (Munich, 1932). On the general European background to ideas of race, miscegenation, and national decline, see Sander Gilman, *Difference and Pathology: Stereotypes of Sexuality, Race, and Madness* (Ithaca, 1985); and Daniel Pick, *The Faces of Degeneration: A European Disorder, c. 1848–1918* (Cambridge, 1989). The specific National Socialist ideological constellations are discussed in Jeremy Noakes, "Nazism and Eugenics: The Background to the Nazi Sterilization Law

annual convention, the organization of National Socialist physicians called
for a prohibition on marriage between Jews and non-Jews. Once in power,
Nazi Party members immediately began to appeal to the new regime to
enact legislation criminalizing relations between "German" women and
Jews, suggesting that "attempted contact should be punished by stripping
the woman of her German citizenship and turning her over to the work
camp, and by sterilization in cases of actual physical contact. The German
Volk will survive only if it immediately undertakes measures to remain
racially pure in spirit and body."[2]

Two years later, at the 1935 Nuremberg party rally, the regime announced legislation that forbade "mixed marriages" and extramarital relationships between "full Jews" and persons of "German or related blood."
Formally titled the Law for the Protection of German Blood and Honor,
the Nuremberg Laws were immediately heralded as a fundamental pre-
cept of the new Germany. Prison sentences under the law ranged from
one day to fifteen years, although in the law's official formulation only
men were liable for prosecution. (Women, both Aryan and Jewish, were
not liable for criminal prosecution and could be charged only as witnesses
in race-defilement proceedings.) Over the course of the next decade, several thousand Germans were tried for violations of the Nuremberg Laws.[3]

---

of 14 July 1933," in *Ideas into Politics*, ed. R. J. Bullen, H. Pogge von Strandmann, and A.
B. Polonsky (London, 1984), 75–94; and Robert Proctor, *Racial Hygiene: Medicine under
the Nazis* (Cambridge, Mass., 1988).

[2]While I am aware of the problems associated with using National Socialist terminology
such as the term *Aryan*, to avoid cumbersome constructions I do not enclose these terms in
quotation marks. This should by no means be taken to imply that I accept the validity of
Nazi racial categorizations. Indeed, as I argue in the course of this essay, the race-defilement investigations and trials were one of the key sites in which racial identities were constructed and contested under the new regime. Moreover, a sizeable minority of those
individuals who were regarded as Jews under Nazi racial laws did not consider themselves
Jewish, further complicating any reading of Nazi racial groupings as transparent and self-
evident categories. For a discussion of the passage of the Nuremberg Laws, see Lothar
Gruchmann, "'Blutschutzgesetz' und Justiz: Zur Entstehung und Auswirkung des
nürnberger Gesetzes vom 15 September 1935," in *Vierteljahrheft für Zeitgeschichte* 31
(1983): 418–42, 425. See also Michael Ley, *"Zum Schutze des deutschen Blutes": "Rassen-
schande"-Gesetze im Nationalsozialismus* (Bodenheim b. Mainz, 1997); Otto Dov Kulka,
"Die nürnberger Rassegesetze und die deutsche Bevölkerung im Lichte geheimer NS-Lage-
und Stimmungsberichte," *Vierteljahreshefte für Zeitgeschichte* 32 (1984): 582–624; Uwe
Dietrich Adam, "An Overall Plan for Anti-Jewish Legislation in the Third Reich," *Yad
Vashem Studies* 11 (1976): 33–55; and Cornelia Essner, "Die Alchemie der
Rassengesetzgebung," *Jahrbuch für Antisemitismus Forschung* 4 (1995): 201–25. For a
general discussion of anti-Jewish legislation in the Third Reich, see Bruno Blau, *Das
Ausnahmerecht für Juden in Deutschland* (Düsseldorf, 1965); and also Kai Henning and
Josef Kestler, *Die Rechtsstellung der Juden in Staatsrecht und Staatsrechtslehre im Dritten
Reich* (Heidelberg, 1985).

[3]According to the *Statistisches Jahrbuch für das deutsche Reich*, 1,911 cases of race defilement were prosecuted between 1935 and 1940. The peak years for race-defilement trials
were 1937 and 1938, but trials continued at declining rates through the end of the war. See

For every individual brought to trial for the crime of race defilement (*Rassenschande*), scores of others were investigated but not charged. As both a racial and sexual crime, race defilement loomed large in the ideological and popular imagination over the remaining ten years of the Nazi regime. Sexuality, the site where private and public realms of politics, · morality, and social order converged, in turn became a critical arena for the deployment of the regime's racial ideology and a focus of particularly intense regulation and control.

In the past several decades, an influential stream of scholarship has laid claim to the notion that the Nazi era cannot be understood purely as an aberration in modern history but needs to be interpreted within the framework of a larger German and European trajectory. However, this has not been the case for the historiography of law in National Socialist Germany, which remains largely wedded to traditional methodological and theoretical approaches. Though scholars have pointed to elements of continuity with law in Wilhelmine and Weimar Germany, and a few have made glancing comparisons to the legal systems of other authoritarian or totalitarian regimes, the law under National Socialism is typically regarded as having constituted a complete break from modern legal norms and standards.[4] Given the undeniable brutality of the law under National Socialism and its enthusiastic embrace of a racially driven framework for judicial decisions, it is not surprising that historians have tended to regard Nazi law solely as a coercive mechanism, an instrument of state authority, political repression, and terror.[5] No longer the handmaiden of

---

Statistisches Jahrbuch für das deutsche Reich, vol. 577 (Berlin, 1942). Both men and women could be charged for violating the other paragraphs of the Nuremberg Laws, which forbade the employment of Aryan women under the age of forty-five in Jewish households and outlawed the flying of the Reich flag by Jews. In practice, a small number of women charged as witnesses in race-defilement cases also faced criminal prosecution, mainly for "aiding and abetting" or perjury. In German, the term *Zeuge* (or *Zeugin*, in its feminine form) is used to refer to the female partners of men accused of race defilement as well as the wide array of other individuals who were questioned and called to testify over the course of a race-defilement investigation or trial. When necessary for clarity, I distinguish between the two categories by adding the descriptors "female witness" or "outside witness."

[4]The Nazi era has thus been variously analyzed as an exemplar of fascism or totalitarianism, as both a rejection and as the apotheosis of modernity, as the inheritor of nineteenth-century biological racism, and as the precursor to social institutions and practices of the welfare state. For two general introductions to the historical interpretation of National Socialist Germany, see Thomas Childers and Jane Caplan, eds., *Reevaluating the Third Reich* (New York, 1993) and Ian Kershaw, *The Nazi Dictatorship: Problems and Perspectives of Interpretation*, 3rd ed. (London, 1993). That Nazi law has been regarded wholly as an aberration in the history of modern Western nations is true in spite of the fact that, for instance, Nazi Germany is not the only country to have enacted racial discrimination into its legal fabric; a possible comparison to the Nuremberg Laws, for example, might be the former antimiscegenation laws enacted in a number of states in the United States.

[5]Hinrich Rüping, "Strafrechtspflege und politische Justiz im Umbruch vom liberalen Rechtsstaat zum NS-Regime," in *1933–fünfzig Jahre danach: Die nationalsozialistichen Machtergreifung in historischer Perspektive*, ed. Josef Becker (Munich, 1983), 153–68;

justice, law under National Socialism is rightly seen as a tool of an exterminatory racism, imperialist expansionism, and the subjugation of groups deemed marginal, defective, or oppositional.

Particularly striking in the field of National Socialist legal historiography is the fact that legal scholars and historians have been slow to apply the insights of critical legal theorists and other thinkers associated with what has been termed the "linguistic turn." Such critical legal and post-Foucaultian theories—though they do not constitute a unified set of interpretive practices—elsewhere have yielded a rich framework of insights and approaches for historical scholarship. Among the most significant points of theoretical departure has been an expansion in the understanding of the disciplinary functionality of law. While traditional instrumentalist conceptions regard law as "a tool, a weapon, which authorities try to use (with or without success) to mold or influence behavior," more recently scholars have also located within law a constitutive function in shaping "meanings and self-understandings."[6] In its constitutive function, the law works to enforce and legitimize a range of social hierarchies. Thus the law has been shown to have a key regulatory role in the larger arena of gender and sexuality, including issues of marriage, reproduction, sexual access and behavior, and men's and women's place in the family, workplace, and community. Likewise, as legal theorists such as Ian Haney López have demonstrated, law operates in a complex fashion to encourage the social production of race by functioning both as a method of coercion and a kind of "taxonomical practice" that helps to organize society into races that seem natural and biologically real. In participating in the establishment and enforcement of social categories such as gender and race, law has been theorized to function as a "system of knowledge" as well as a "system of rules," an insight that as yet remains to be applied to the history of law in Nazi Germany.[7]

Matthew Lippmann, "Law, Lawyers, and Legality in the Third Reich: The Perversion of Principle and Professionalism," in *Temple International and Comparative Law Journal* 11, no. 2 (1997): 199–308, 199. For other useful introductions to law under National Socialism, see Bernhard Diestelkamp and Michael Stolleis, *Justizalltag im Dritten Reich* (Frankfurt am Main, 1998); Diemut Majer, *Grundlagen des nationalsozialistischen Rechtsystems* (Stuttgart, 1987); Ralf Dreier and Wolfgang Sellert, eds., *Recht und Justiz im Dritten Reich* (Frankfurt am Main, 1989); and Lothar Gruchmann, *Justiz im Dritten Reich: Anpassung und Unterwerfung in der Ära Gürtner* (Munich, 1988). For literature in English, see also Ingo Müller, *Hitler's Justice: The Courts of the Third Reich* (Cambridge, Mass., 1991).

[6]Laurence M. Friedman, "Review of Austin Sarat and Thomas R. Kearns, eds., 'Law in Everyday Life,'" in *Law and History Review* 13, no. 2 (1995): 427–28, 428.

[7]See Ian F. Haney López, *White by Law: The Legal Construction of Race* (New York, 1996); Carol Smart, *Feminism and the Power of Law* (London, 1989), 6. For a demonstration of the usefulness of gender and legal theory to historical analysis, see the contributions in the volume *Women-in-Law: Explorations in Law, Family, and Sexuality*, ed. Julia Brophy and Carol Smart (London, 1985), 50–70; see also Gerald Turkel, "Michel Foucault: Law, Power, Knowledge," *Journal of Law and Society* 17, no. 2 (1990): 170–93, for a useful account of the influences and congruities between Foucaultian and critical legal theories.

This essay is an introduction to the phenomenon of race defilement in National Socialist Germany. In it I shall begin with an outline of the more immediate effects of the Nuremberg Laws and their enforcement. Next, I shall consider some of the social implications of policing interracial sexuality. Finally, moving to the level of discursive constructions and effects, I shall consider some of the ways that the trials served to fashion complex and productive discourses on sexuality that were inflected by images and categories of race. In working through culturally prevailing notions of sexuality and gender, legal discourse in turn enabled the formation of racial identity and the enforcement of racial policy. Thus, even in Nazi Germany, the law had a constitutive function as well as a coercive and instrumental one. Law was not simply a thing apart, an abstract body of statutes and rulings imposed by the judiciary to regulate behavior through punishment. Rather, law under National Socialism was also a set of institutions, practices, and actors that participated and interacted with what Friedman has termed the "battery of normative ideas and habits" of everyday life and as such was instrumental both in mobilizing consent and helping to construct modes of self-perception and subjectivity.[8] Although the race-defilement trials enforced only one law among hundreds and commented on only one category of offender (men and women in "mixed" relationships), what was said about these issues constructed a set of social proscriptions and norms that had both ideological and practical significance for the German population as a whole.[9]

THE NUREMBERG LAWS AND THE FATE OF INDIVIDUALS

Even before the passage of the Nuremberg Laws in September 1935, many mixed couples had grown weary of the condemnation and harassment they faced on a near daily basis. Particularly in smaller towns, where mixed couples lacked the protective camouflage of urban anonymity, the records contain many remarks that indicate that mixed relationships sparked "a great deal of unrest" in the community. In the Rheinland town of Emmerich, for example, community "uproar" forced one mixed couple

---

[8]Friedman, 428. My methodology thus implicitly argues for the explanatory potential of discursive analysis in illuminating everyday politics and social experience even under conditions of extremity, including National Socialist Germany. For a discussion of the explanatory potential and moral adequacy of discursive and linguistic interpretative methodologies, particularly in relation to National Socialist Germany and the Holocaust, see the contributions by leading historians in the special issue of *Central European History* 22, nos. 3–4 (1989), as well as the contributions in *Probing the Limits of Representation: Nazism and the Final Solution*, ed. Saul Friedländer (Cambridge, Mass., 1982).

[9]Until recently, the race-defilement investigations and trials have received comparatively little sustained scholarly attention. Most scholars who have mentioned the race-defilement trials have done so in passing as an example of the political persecution of German Jews, one stage of many in the regime's larger project of isolating Jews from the mainstream of German society in preparation for eventual deportation and annihilation. Race-defilement investigations and trials have also received mention in studies of Nazi anti-Semitic legislation and the

to stop appearing at the riverfront together in their "bathing costumes."[10] In Ramscheid, another mixed couple tried twice to marry in the year preceding the issuance of the Nuremberg Laws. On both occasions, their banns were torn down, delaying their marriage. After his girlfriend bore his child, the Jewish man was taken into protective custody, ostensibly because community outrage was so intense that he needed to be removed for his own protection. Though Ramscheid officials exaggerated the extent of "community outrage" as a pretext for his arrest, the couple clearly was the subject of considerable scandal, as evinced by a neighbor's comment that "even the children were whispering all sorts of things about their concubinage." Countless similar incidents of harassment of mixed couples were orchestrated by the Storm Troopers (Sturm Abteilung, SA) during the first years of Nazi rule. In one typical incident in 1933, a crowd of "twenty to thirty persons," headed by local SA members, cornered two Jewish men and their girlfriends on the street. The young women were slapped and shoved about, resulting in "scrapes and bruises." The two Jewish men were paraded about town while being forced to carry signs announcing their "crime." The regime in turn played up such incidents as part of their justification for introducing new laws governing interracial relationships, arguing that they would render such "spontaneous" outbursts superfluous.[11] As rumors of a forthcoming "legal solution" to the problem of interracial relationships circulated in the summer of 1935, many couples became increasingly wary about appearing together in public or acknowledging their relationship.

While community disapproval of mixed relationships was often intense, the situation for mixed couples became far more fraught with danger once the Nuremberg Laws were enacted in September 1935. Arrests for race defilement began immediately, and the first cases were brought to court within weeks of the issuance of the new blood purity laws. Under the strain of community disapproval, social and economic discrimination, and finally legal sanction, many mixed couples did in fact end their relationships. In some instances, it was clearly the Aryan partner who decided that

---

"nazification" of the German legal system. See, for example, Sarah Gordon, *Hitler, Germans and the "Jewish Question"* (Princeton, 1984), 171–80, 218–45; Raul Hilberg, *The Destruction of European Jews* (New York, 1985), 27–38; Müller, 90–119; and Hans Robinsohn, *Justiz als politische Verfolgung: Die Rechtsprechung in "Rassenschandefällen" beim Landgericht Hamburg* (Stuttgart, 1977). More recent studies have begun to consider race defilement as a phenomenon in its own right, illustrative of larger processes of cultural and social enforcement in Nazi Germany. See Saul Friedländer, *Nazi Germany and the Jews: Volume I. The Years of Persecution, 1933–1939* (New York, 1997); and Robert Gellately, *The Gestapo and German Society: Enforcing Racial Policy, 1933–1945* (Oxford, 1990).

[10]Staatsarchiv Düsseldorf, Aussenstelle Kalkum (StAD/K) 7/900.

[11]StAD/K 89/114; Hessisches Hauptstaatsarchiv (HHStA) 483/5008. For an informative discussion of the Nazi practice of protective custody (*Schutzhaft*), see Bundesminister der Justiz, ed., *Im Namen des deutsches Volkes: Justiz und Nationalsozialismus* (Cologne, 1989).

the relationship had become a burden. Thus, for instance, one Aryan man, denounced on suspicion of race defilement, insisted that he had long before ended his relationship, stating, "We used to insult and berate each other about our differing racial backgrounds and descent. Over time, we became estranged from one another." Another Aryan woman, interviewed in 1937, stated that her relationship with her Jewish boyfriend had undergone a "marked cooling off" following the promulgation of the Nuremberg Laws. Recognizing the "futility" of their relationship, she elected to end their affair "in order to spare myself further trouble and inconvenience." Other couples appear to have come to a mutual conclusion that their relationship was too dangerous to continue. A number of couples reported deciding to end their relationship after reading newspaper accounts, while another couple told of having heard the Nuremberg Laws announced on the radio, whereupon they agreed, "This is the end of our friendship."[12]

The passage of the Nuremberg Laws also affected the behavior of couples who elected to continue their relationships in secret despite the fear of legal sanction. Some mixed couples appear to have ended the sexual side of their relationship or found substitutes for intercourse while still maintaining their romantic attachment. Since convictions often hinged on whether the date of the last sexual intercourse took place before or after the issuance of the Nuremberg Laws, quite a few couples under investigation for race defilement attempted to argue that they had ended the sexual side of their relationship upon hearing of the new blood purity laws. In other instances, the couple continued their relationship but claimed to have altered their sexual practices to substitute other forms of gratification for coitus. However, couples' claims to have abandoned their sexual relationship upon the issuance of the Nuremberg Laws were only rarely a successful defense against charges of race defilement.

On the whole, the Nuremberg Laws had a less immediate effect on the behavior of mixed couples than might be supposed given the very real danger of arrest and imprisonment. Usually the Nuremberg Laws dealt the final blow only to relationships that had been fairly casual from the start. A surprising number of couples of longer standing, whose relationships had overnight become criminal offenses, continued to see one another in secret.

---

[12]Staatsarchiv München (StAM), Staatsanwaltschaft (StAnw) 4529; HHStA 461/16145; HHStA 461/16133. Many Nazi officials were also in favor of extending the principle of racial separation to married couples as well, though efforts to relax divorce law were fraught with difficulty, as the regime was concerned to maintain the appearance of upholding the sanctity of the family. On 6 July 1938, however, the regime enacted a new marriage law that facilitated divorce under certain circumstances, including racial and other "irreconcilable" differences. A few disaffected Aryan spouses subsequently sued for divorce on the basis of their new-found "racial consciousness." See Hans Wrobel, "Die Anfechtung der Rassenmischehe: Diskriminierung und Entrechtung der Juden, 1933 bis 1945," in *Der Unrechtsstaat: Recht und Justiz im Nationalsozialismus*, ed. Redaktion Kritische Justiz (Baden-Baden, 1984), 99 ff.

Even couples who were interrogated by the Gestapo but released for lack of evidence often continued their relationship despite their brush with the Nazi police apparatus. Despite their realization that they were undergoing a significant risk, many mixed couples employed considerable subterfuge to meet, often arranging liaisons under the cover of darkness or outdoors on the outskirts of town. Other couples met in secret at the homes of friends or tried to disguise their identity to avoid denunciation and discovery. A few attempted to leave the country to marry, which was also a crime under the Nuremberg Laws. Other couples, particularly those with a "half-Jewish" partner, submitted applications for special permission to marry (Antrag für Beseitigung des Ehehindernis). Permission to marry was granted only rarely; many such couples, having thus come to the attention of the authorities, were subsequently charged with race defilement.[13] Many found their lives shattered when the Nuremberg Laws suddenly criminalized a relationship of very long standing. One couple, for example, had cohabited in a "relationship akin to marriage" for more than fifteen years, only to find themselves investigated for race defilement.[14] Indeed, Nazi police and legal officials often distinguished such long-standing and devoted relationships, noting in the official record that the relationship was no fly-by-night encounter but a "true love affair." Such seeming sympathy, however, had little effect on the ultimate conviction, though in some instances it may have served as a mitigating factor in sentencing, at least during the early years of the laws' enforcement.

Even among couples who ended their relationship upon the promulgation of the Nuremberg Laws, it was not always the Aryan partner who decided the risk was too great. At times, Jewish men elected to end the relationship out of a well-justified fear of punishment. In one such case, the decision to separate was clearly made at the cost of great anguish: "In the period that followed, he attempted to end the relationship with Miss Bernhard, who was very much in love with the defendant. . . . The result of their many discussions was that, at the defendant's urgent request, Bernhard agreed with a heavy heart to end the relationship. In the following period, Bernhard repeatedly attempted to reestablish contact, but the defendant continued to rebuff her efforts." According to the police, despite repeated interrogations the woman continued to deny the existence of a relationship out of love for the defendant. Finally, when threatened under oath at the judicial interrogation, she admitted their affair. Another Jewish man told interrogators that he had been dissuaded from ending his relationship by his girlfriend, who "promised that she would sooner allow

---

[13]Landesarchiv Berlin (LAB) 58/4005/1643. Going abroad for the express purpose of marrying in contravention of blood purity laws was a criminal act under the regulations governing the enforcement of the Nuremberg Laws. See, for example, StAD/K 17/22. For examples of couples who filed an Application for Special Permission to Marry, only to be subsequently charged with race defilement, see StAD/K 2/101 and 2/102.

[14]StAD/K 29/119.

her tongue to be torn from her mouth than make a confession." Yet another Jewish man tried to end his relationship following his release from a one-year sentence for race defilement, but his girlfriend could not bear to let him go. Tragically, the couple was caught a second time. Though the woman had steadfastly denied the relationship, following repeated interrogations she finally confessed, sobbing, "It was I who pressured Friedrich into sexual relations. . . . It was our hour of weakness, and we are both to blame." The police interrogator then noted in the record: "the female witness is full of self-reproach . . . she says that she will take her own life if the Jew is again sent to the penitentiary." As a repeat offender, her lover received a particularly high sentence of five years. Had she not admitted that she was the "driving force" behind the relationship, the court noted, the sentence would have been even higher.[15] With such threats of discovery and punishment, even when couples continued to see one another in secret, their relationships became fearful and guilt-ridden, torn by conflicting impulses of self-preservation and love.

The passage of the Nuremberg Laws was thus a tragic blow for many mixed couples. For many, the Nuremberg Laws dashed hopes of marriage. An investigation for race defilement, even in instances where no charges were filed, brought with it a great deal of unwelcome official attention and, for Jews, often presaged later investigation and official harassment for any number of supposed offenses against the Jewish regulations. For the Jewish partner, an arrest for race defilement could, and often did, result in death. Sentences for convicted Jewish race defilers in the earliest weeks of the enforcement of the blood purity laws generally ranged from three months to a year of jail. Soon, however, under official direction from the Ministry of Justice, sentences for Jewish men became increasingly severe, ranging from a year to four years or more of penal servitude (*Zuchthaus*). Conditions in penitentiaries were extremely harsh, and more than a few prisoners died while incarcerated. Jewish men released after serving their sentences often found their health ruined, their fortunes lost, and their families torn apart. In addition, while incarcerated, Jewish men were unable to take advantage of opportunities to leave Germany; indeed, the records are replete with instances of Jewish families pleading with the authorities for the release of their incarcerated sons, brothers, and husbands so that they might emigrate abroad. Though women could not be charged with and sentenced for race defilement, Jewish women typically were held in protective custody during the entire investigation and often for months after the trial as well. By 1937, Reinhard Heydrich, head of the Security Service (Sicherheitsdienst, SD) began to argue in party meetings and in written directives that protective custody should be considered for all Jewish women involved in race-defilement cases and for Jewish men who had served their sentences. By the early

[15]StAM StAnw 18037; StAD/K 10/181; LAB 58/4005/1714.

1940s, it had become official policy to turn Jewish women charged as witnesses in race-defilement cases and Jewish men who had served sentences for race defilement directly over to the secret state police (Geheime Staatspolizei, Gestapo). Jewish men who were convicted of race defilement and subsequently transferred to camps such as Sachsenhausen there faced special forms of torture and death. Following the start of deportations, many Jewish men and women were transported directly to the ghettos and death camps in the East after serving their term in protective custody or prison.[16] By contrast, Aryan men who were convicted of race defilement generally received shorter punishments and were more likely to be sentenced to jail time rather than penal servitude. Yet upon release, Aryan men often found themselves virtual outcasts, officially stripped of their rights of citizenship ("bürgerliche Ehrenrechte") and unable to find employment.[17] Aryan women charged as witnesses often spent weeks or months in protective custody; many lost their jobs, their reputation and standing in the community, and the custody of their children.

POLICING INTERRACIAL SEXUALITY

By most accounts, the majority of Germans accepted the promulgation of the Nuremberg Laws as a welcome stabilizing measure, a regulation that would end "wild" outbursts of anti-Semitism. Indeed, had it not been for the complicity and even cooperation of large segments of the German population, as the historian Robert Gellately has pointed out, it would have been impossible to enforce laws that infringed upon the most intimate realms of private life. Only the fact that many Germans readily provided authorities with evidence of other Germans' friendships and intimate associations with Jews made it possible for the criminal police and Gestapo to persecute racial offenders on such a grand scale.[18] Race-defilement records testify to the eagerness of denouncers who carefully monitored the comings and goings

[16]In Sachsenhausen in 1940, Jewish race defilers were tortured and killed by suffocation in a broom closet and by being hosed with cold water. See Raul Hilberg, *Perpetrators, Victims, Bystanders: The Jewish Catastrophe, 1933–1945* (New York, 1992). See also Bundesarchiv Potsdam (BAP) R22/1143, p. 221.

[17]For a statistical analysis of sentencing patterns that contrasts the treatment of Aryan and Jewish race defilers in Hamburg, Cologne, and Frankfurt am Main, see Robinsohn, 78 ff.

[18]On the reaction of the German population to the promulgation of the Nuremberg Laws, see Otto Dov Kulka, "Die nürnberger Rassegesetze und die deutsche Bevölkerung im Lichte geheimer NS-Lage- und Stimmungsberichte," *Vierteljahreshefte für Zeitgeschichte* 32 (1984): 582–624. According to Robert Gellately's statistical analysis of denunciations in Würzburg, 54 percent of race-defilement cases investigated by the Gestapo were initiated by a denunciation from the population (162). For a theoretical and comparative discussion of the phenomenon of denunciation, see also Gellately's "Denunciations in Twentieth-Century Germany: Aspects of Self-Policing in the Third Reich and the German Democratic Republic," *Journal of Modern History* 68 (December 1996): 931–67. The issue of female denouncers is discussed by Rita Wolters, *Verrat für die Volksgemeinschaft: Denunziantinnen im Dritten Reich* (Pfaffenweiler, 1996).

of their neighbors, acquaintances, and workplace colleagues, paying keen attention to evidence such as the apparent degree of intimacy connoted by forms of greeting, the time of day or duration of a visit, and a myriad of other seemingly suggestive details. Even the most fleeting of encounters could serve as the basis for suspicions of race defilement. Such suspicions were sometimes pursued to extreme lengths, as in one 1937 case in which a man went so far as to hire a detective to spy on his brother-in-law, whom he subsequently denounced to the Gestapo.[19] The police, in turn, cooperated by investigating any rumors of race defilement brought to their attention, thereby providing a venue for snoops to voice their suspicions and giving denouncers a legitimacy that they would not have had as simple neighborhood gossips.

Investigative records thus support Gellately's conclusion that the majority of race-defilement cases were initiated by a denunciation rather than through the Gestapo's own investigative efforts. However, what is also apparent is that in some instances friends, neighbors, and coworkers were aware of forbidden relationships yet failed to inform the authorities. In this, the phenomenon of denunciation in race-defilement investigations also lends support to Eric Johnson's caveat that the system of Nazi terror was able to function effectively even with only a fraction of the German population actively participating in denunciation.[20] In a 1940 case, for example, a neighbor questioned by the police admitted to long-standing knowledge of an instance of race defilement. In this as in similar cases, the woman was not officially rebuked for her failure to bring the relationship to official attention. Indeed, quite often the police reports note that an affair was "general knowledge" in the neighborhood and workplace of the accused. Hans Kosterlitz, a Jewish man who successfully eluded official investigation for race defilement, similarly recounted in a later interview that many of his colleagues had known of his relationship with an Aryan coworker but had pretended to be unaware of the affair. Though Kosterlitz trusted his colleagues not to inform on him, his knowledge of the consequences of discovery led him to the brink of "nervous collapse." Thus, despite a general atmosphere of suspicion and a widespread propensity to denounce, at times individuals who suspected an interracial affair preferred to allow their knowledge to remain ambiguous and unverbalized. In a few instances, friends and family members provided active support to mixed couples, as in the case of one woman who made her apartment available to her brother for liaisons with his Jewish girlfriend.[21] Yet however unspoken, when knowledge of

[19]HHStA 461/16145.

[20]Eric A. Johnson, *Nazi Terror: The Gestapo, Jews, and Ordinary Germans* (New York, 2000), 362–63.

[21]LAB 58/4005/1722; Hans Kosterlitz, "Das Ende einer Beziehung," in *Sie dürfen nicht mehr deutsch sein: Jüdischer Alltag in Selbszeugnissen, 1933–1938*, ed. Margarete Limberg and Hubert Rübsaat (Frankfurt am Main, 1990), 164–66. (The name Hans Kosterlitz is

an affair was widespread, it became increasingly likely that someone would choose to inform the authorities. A single denunciation then sufficed to initiate the investigative process. When confronted by a police investigator at their door, even those who had previously remained silent usually admitted knowledge of the affair.

Scholarship on denunciation has also paid a great deal of attention to explaining the motivation of denouncers, distinguishing between those who denounced for "affective" reasons such as adherence to Nazi ideology and those who brought accusations to official attention for "instrumental" reasons such as avenging personal resentments and grievances. Historians such as John Conolly, who has examined how the trope of the *Volk* community served to undergird a wide spectrum of denunciations and letters of appeal, have also begun the process of a more discursive analysis of the phenomenon of denunciation, an analysis that takes into account not only motivation but also modes of perception and legitimation.[22] In the case of race defilement, what remains particularly striking is the gendered dimension of the phenomenon of denunciation. Although it was ultimately the Aryan or Jewish man who was charged, for example, in many instances the target of the denunciation was the woman rather than the man. Thus, one denouncer, in an anonymous postcard addressed to the Gestapo, fulminated about the "offensive indecency" of many "bitches" and "whores," especially "that little so-and-so, Miss Lange," who consorted with Jewish men yet believed her "deceit" and "repulsive lies" would be overlooked. Another denouncer went so far as to write anonymous letters directly to an Aryan woman, threatening her, "We are going to keep on watching you, and we won't allow anyone to fall prey to your dirty tricks. . . . You are and will always be the biggest tramp we know, and we will warn everyone about you."[23] Particularly in the case of extramarital relationships, the target of the denunciation was most often the adulterous woman. Married Aryan women suspected of having affairs were regularly denounced, and community outrage tended to be particularly intense when the woman was the wife of a Wehrmacht soldier, as in the case of a Jewish man who was given an exceptionally harsh sentence of seven years for his affair with a married woman whose husband was on the eastern front.[24] Particularly in light of the fact that women could not be charged with race defilement, it is striking that so many of the denunciations were directed against the female partner. In the most vituperative denunciations, which typically fulminated against

---

not a pseudonym.) For another case in which colleagues claim to have warned an Aryan woman to discontinue her affair without actually denouncing her, see HHStA 461/16900.

[22] John Conolly, "The Uses of Volksgemeinschaft: Letters to the NSDAP Kreisleitung Eisenach, 1939–1940," *Journal of Modern History* 68 (December 1996): 899–930.

[23] HHStA 461/15666; StAD 58/15207.

[24] LAB 58/4005/1544; LAB 58/4005/1704. For two other cases where married women were denounced for their adulterous affairs, see HHStA 461/16145 and StAM StAnw 3530.

the "betrayers of the *Volk*" and "the Jew's fancy women," such misogynistic language clearly drew upon existing cultural images of the sexually loose woman, now colored by the additional accusation of racial as well as sexual infidelity. In the case of adulterous relationships, the community was particularly likely to denounce on behalf of the cuckolded Aryan husband whose property and sexual rights were being violated by the affair. By contrast, a masculine and racial privilege appears to have exempted Aryan men from the most intrusive community scrutiny. Cultural notions of female sexuality, it seems, were particularly effective in functioning as a mode via which intense community surveillance and "self-policing" of interracial sexuality could be enacted.

Because an entire community was responsible for maintaining sexual standards, the scope of the investigations was broad. Prior to race-defilement arrests it was not uncommon for formal statements to be taken from as many as a dozen people, with investigators questioning friends, neighbors, coworkers, and family members for evidence of an "intimate relationship." In addition, at trials the net could be cast even wider when it came time to call for outside witnesses. In one case, a man called to testify before the court submitted a written complaint to his local prosecuting attorney, stating: "Yesterday I received a summons to appear as a witness in the criminal proceedings against Mr. Haacke for race defilement. I have never even heard of this person, Haacke, and I certainly know nothing relevant to the matter at hand." In yet another investigation, the police noted that the arrest had "resulted in the gathering of a crowd of about 60 persons."[25] Moreover, far more individuals were investigated for race defilement than were later actually charged with the crime. Even in those investigations ultimately deemed to be without basis, the broad scope of investigations meant that an accusation of race defilement became an event of public drama and scandal.

The presence of an audience in the courtroom in turn served to lend further publicity to the trials. Race-defilement proceedings were usually open to the public, though often the audience was cleared from the courtroom on the grounds of endangerment of public morals ("Gefährdung der Sittlichkeit"). Yet even when the audience was cleared from the courtroom, as in one Munich trial, all of the outside witnesses and the press were allowed to remain. For the reading of the verdict, which repeated many of the more intimate details of the relationship, the full audience was allowed to return.[26] Indeed, some Nazi officials attempted to quash the press publicity surrounding the trials. Despite their efforts, local officials continued to worry that the public commotion was having a dangerously "exciting"

[25]StAD/K 92/31; LAB 58/4005/1543. For two other examples of cases where large numbers of people were interviewed and called to testify, see StAM 6430 and LAB 58/4005/1656.

[26]StAM StAnw I/18162.

effect on schoolboys, who avidly followed accounts of trials in newspapers and the luridly sensationalist *Der Stürmer*. As a form of sexual spectacle, the race-defilement trials thus became all the more effective in inciting a form of community surveillance based on the sexual policing of women and Jews.

DISCOURSES ON RACE AND GENDER

In the process that Raul Hilberg terms "definition by decree," the Reich Citizenship Law, passed in conjunction with the new blood-purity laws, attempted to define who was a Jew and what constituted "German or related blood." A "full Jew" was a person with at least three grandparents who "adhered to the Jewish religion." *Mischlinge* of the First Degree were individuals with one Jewish parent, while *Mischlinge* of the Second Degree had one Jewish grandparent. The legal definition of the Aryan remained largely a negative one, characterized only by the absence of "Jewish blood." As numerous scholars have noted, this definition of Jewishness ultimately rested on the confessional allegiance of the grandparents, making a mockery of Nazi claims that Jewishness was a biological category unrelated to religion.[27] Consequently, past scholarship has often branded National Socialist definitions of Jewishness as irrevocably "absurd" and illogical, devoid of any explanatory meaning. The often contradictory and ambiguous enforcement of the Nuremberg Laws, in turn, is explained as the product of a haphazard, confused, and inconsistent legal bureaucracy.[28] Yet the regime's attempts to invest the process of racial classification with an aura of scientific and legal objectivity might be more meaningfully interpreted. The fact that definitions of Aryan and Jew remained unstable and contested in judicial practice instead may serve as evidence of a struggle over the social meaning of race, a struggle in which conceptions of gender and sexuality played a critical role.

To convict a person on a race-defilement charge, the courts needed first to determine the racial classification of both partners. Although members of the Nazi paramilitary organization (the SS) and party members had earlier been required to present proof of racial purity, quite a few individuals charged with race defilement first obtained their "certificate of racial descent" at the instigation of the court. Routine investigation into

[27] *Mischlinge* of both the First and Second Degree were exempt from prosecution under the blood purity laws—with the notable exception of those *Mischlinge* of the First Degree who were formal members of the Jewish religious community and thus classed as "Jewish equivalents" (*Geltungsjuden*). The new law stripped Jews (and single women) of their citizenship, making them instead subjects of the German Reich. For a discussion of the Reich Citizenship Law, see Hilberg, *The Destruction of European Jews*, esp. chap. 2; Müller, 98–99; and Proctor, 131 ff.

[28] See, for example, Ley, who also categorically rejects the notion that the Nuremberg Laws and the race-defilement trials had anything to say about Aryan racial constructions. Indeed, he argues that though Aryan men were also punished for race defilement, the Nuremberg Laws were "Jewish laws" in the medieval Christian tradition and as such were "only directed against Jews" (80).

birth and marriage registers, church and synagogue records, and tax rolls sufficed to determine to the courts' satisfaction the racial classification of the majority of Germans. In a surprisingly large number of cases, however, the court encountered problems assigning racial classifications. As the distinction between a Jew and a "half-Jew" was critical to a race-defilement proceeding, the prosecution often hinged on the racial classification of one parent. In practice, most cases of doubtful racial classification arose when the paternity of the accused or of the female witness came into question. Normally a child born out of wedlock to an Aryan woman was regarded as Aryan under the law, providing no reason existed to suspect an "incursion of foreign blood."[29] However, assigning the racial status to children born out of wedlock to Jewish mothers often proved more problematic in judicial practice.

One particularly difficult case was the 1937 trial of the Jewish architect Horst Berge. Although Berge confessed to an affair with an Aryan woman, the Wiesbaden court was thrown into confusion: Berge's mother claimed that her son's biological father was not her Jewish husband but an Aryan man, now long dead. When a racial anthropological examination conducted with the assistance of Dr. Mengele proved inconclusive, the court turned to the testimony of neighborhood gossips, who confided that Berge's true parentage had long been a topic of local speculation. On the basis of this testimony, the court concluded that Berge was indeed a half-Jew and acquitted him. However, the court noted, if Berge believed himself to be Jewish, it might nonetheless become necessary to convict him of "attempted race defilement," a charge as yet without precedent in Nazi judicial practice. Clearly unsettled by the implication that an individual's subjective racial identification might conflict with his or her "objective" racial categorization, the Wiesbaden court concluded that Berge had certainly been aware—if only "inwardly"—of his "mixed" parentage from childhood. Though legal discourse had called into being the concept of subjective racial identification, in most other instances the courts dismissed defendants' claims that their subjective racial identification conflicted with the "objective facts of racial descent." In such cases, the courts often attempted to find clues in the defendants' stories that would prove they had, in fact, known subjectively all along that they were full Jews—though some might have partially repressed that knowledge.[30]

---

[29]See Josef Wulf, *Die Nürnberger Gesetze* (Berlin-Grunewald, 1960), 20. The Certificate of Racial Descent (Abstammungsnachweis) is discussed also by Eric Ehrenreich in "The Institutionalization of Racism: From Pre-Nazi Genealogy to the Reich Genealogical Authority," manuscript, 2001.

[30]HHStA 461/16669. Documents from this case are also reprinted in Ernst Noam and Wolf-Arno Kropat, eds., *Juden vor Gericht, 1933–1945* (Wiesbaden, 1986), 139–50. In my discussion of this case, I use the same pseudonym adopted by Noam and Kropat (Horst Berge). See also LAB 58/1533.

When official documentation was inadequate, it was not uncommon for police and judicial investigators to consult neighbors, friends, and family to help establish the racial classification of the defendant and witnesses to the courts' satisfaction. Often this "common knowledge" of an individual's racial descent was based on the flimsiest of gossip and conjecture. When questioned by judicial investigators, for example, a clearly aggrieved step-father stated: "If I am asked whether I know anything about the descent of [my adoptive daughter] Natalie's biological father, then I can with certainty declare that he must have been a Jew. Where my wife is living at the moment, I can't say." Neighbors likewise confirmed that they believed Natalie Wittstock's natural father to have been Jewish, though they could offer no concrete evidence to support their assumption.[31] In other race-defilement trials, family members were compelled to appear before the court to testify to their knowledge of the racial descent of the accused.

In addition to drawing the German population into the process of creating and assigning racial classifications, legal discourse served to instruct the population on the finer details of race relations in the new Germany. Though Nazi racial thinking held that Jewishness was not only a matter of descent but an essential aspect of physiognomy, many defendants and female witnesses argued that they had not been able to recognize their partner as Jewish. Repeatedly when questioned, Aryan defendants argued that their partner didn't "look Jewish" or "make the impression of being Jewish or of mixed race." In one case, the defendant admitted that he had become suspicious when he heard the name "Rosenbaum," but as the woman didn't "appear at all Jewish," he had been prepared to believe she was a *Mischling*. Both police and court officials took it upon themselves to instruct the German population on the methods of racial identification. In a number of trials, the court lectured the accused on ways to distinguish an Aryan from a Jew. One judge instructed a defendant on the clues to a woman's "non-Aryan" descent: "Some possible hints would be a woman's Jewish appearance, the fact that she has Jewish acquaintances or entertains other relations toward Jews, or that she uses Jewish expressions or displays other characteristically Jewish traits." In another trial, the court referred to a photograph of the female witness and noted, "She has a typically Jewish appearance," although another judge conceded that the "uneducated" might have difficulty making such fine distinctions: "The witness . . . has blue eyes and blond hair. These features obscure her Jewish racial characteristics so strongly that a lay person will have difficulty recognizing her as Jewish."[32] By these means, the enforcement of the intermarriage and blood purity laws helped to create a new institutional apparatus and system of knowledge to investigate, record, adjudicate, and educate on the question of race.

[31]LAB 58/1543.
[32]LAB 58/1544; verdict reprinted in Robinsohn, 38, 91.

The daily enforcement of the Nuremberg Laws by the police and the courts also produced images of race inflected by notions of gender. In legal representations of Jewish masculinity and femininity, racially stereotyped characterizations at least partially obscured the markers of gender. Jewish men were portrayed as deviant by definition; they were called the "seducers of maidens" who displayed "unbridled appetites," "unnatural inclinations," and "perverse desires." Jewish male sexuality was represented as animalistic and base yet possessed of a calculated, "shameless and criminal" desire to defile the Aryan woman. Here legal discourse echoed longstanding myths that branded Jewish men as pimps, pornographers, and "white slave traders" whose sole desire was to sexually exploit "German women" and spread syphilis and other sexual diseases through the population in a plot to undermine the Aryan race. Jewish employers, in particular, were repeatedly accused of wishing to molest any Aryan girl or woman under their employ, which served to buttress the rationale for prohibiting the employment of Aryan domestic help in Jewish households. Another common theme expressed in the investigative records was that the Jewish man had "concealed his Jewish identity" and made false promises of marriage in order to make the Aryan woman amenable to seduction. Time and again, the courts heaped abuse on Jewish men, who "in typical Jewish fashion" tried to exploit Aryan women "for their own sexual gratification." Such sexual hysteria, in turn, was extremely effective in fomenting anti-Semitic discrimination and widespread public and police harassment of Jewish men. In Berlin, for example, hysteria surrounding the supposed pornographic exploitation of "German women" by Jews was exploited to drive Jewish gynecologists out of professional practice, while elsewhere Jewish medical students were prohibited from conducting gynecological examinations on Aryan female patients. Thus, as Robert Jay Lipton has suggested, a form of "sexual anti-Semitism" was potently added to existing economic and political persecution as an effective means to stigmatize and socially marginalize Jewish men.[33]

Jewish women were characterized in similar fashion as promiscuous, morally corrupt, and sexually predatory and were often accused of concealing their Jewish identity from the hapless Aryan man. A 1937 verdict described the Jewish woman summoned as a witness in a race-defilement

[33]Robert Jay Lipton, *The Nazi Doctors: Medical Killing and the Psychology of Genocide* (New York, 1986), 10. Regarding the persecution of Jewish gynecologists and medical students, see Friedländer, 159–61, and Michael Burleigh and Wolfgang Wipperman, *The Racial State: Germany, 1933–1945* (Cambridge, 1991), 78. Borrowing from the title of Klaus Theweleit's study, Friedländer terms the prurience and explicitness of sexual anti-Semitism a projection of National Socialist "male fantasies." In a highly intentionalist line of argument, James Glass further suggests that a particularly German "culturewide phobia against touching Jewish flesh" directly accounts for not only the Nuremberg Laws and their enforcement but for the Holocaust itself. See *Life Unworthy of Life: Racial Phobia and Mass Murder in Nazi Germany* (New York, 1997), xiii, 50–55.

case in typically derogatory terms: "The witness is a sexually predatory, morally depraved Jewess. With her unrestrained sexual drives and her brazen behavior she held the two accused men in thrall." Another court commented on the Jewish woman's "exceptional tenacity" in seduction.[34] Curiously, however, legal discourse devoted less attention to interrogating Jewish femininity and female sexuality than might be supposed, given the seeming likelihood that Jewish women would figure centrally as exotic, liminal creatures within the fascistic sexual imagination.[35] Nonetheless, in depicting Jewish women as sexually aggressive and corrupt, legal rhetoric effectively denied them the esteem rhetorically accorded Aryan femininity. Both Jewish men and women were depicted as sexual predators intent on spreading disease and degeneracy throughout the population, thus rhetorically legitimizing their exclusion from the body politic.

Representations of Jewish women as sexually dominating rested uneasily alongside images of a powerful and aggressive Aryan masculinity. On the one hand, judicial rhetoric depicted Aryan masculinity as naturally dominant and oriented toward sexual gratification, characterizing Aryan men's relationships with Jewish women as understandable, though unfortunate, lapses in judgment. Yet at the same time, sexual relations with a "Jewess" were regarded as a uniquely dishonorable act, a besmirching of the honor of the *Volk* that violated the most fundamental duty of the citizen of "German blood." As such, the act of race defilement constituted a moment of crisis in the representation of Aryan masculinity. To mitigate the image of the sexually errant and undisciplined Aryan man, legal discourse often attempted to highlight potentially extenuating or mitigating circumstances. It was often suggested that the Aryan man had been seduced, a circumstance that served partially to excuse the sexual lapse while at the same time problematizing the image of Aryan male dominance and self-control. Time and again, magistrates characterized Aryan male defendants as "weak willed," "in need of leadership," and "highly susceptible to outside influence." Other judicial verdicts suggested diminished capacity even in cases where the defendant had been found legally responsible for his acts. Often the courts described the Aryan defendant as "not particularly intelligent," "mentally backward," or possessed of a "moderate grade mental deficiency," which served to explain his diminished capacity and inability to exercise sexual restraint.[36] Aryan masculinity within legal

[34]Verdict quoted in Robinsohn, 67; see also HHStA 461/16892.

[35]This silence about the Jewish female body and sexuality is replicated in the scholarly literature. Burleigh and Wipperman, for example, devote little attention to Jewish women in their section on the "purification" of Jewish influence from the body of the nation (77–112). Likewise, Sander Gilman's studies of discourses of Jewish sexuality focus on representations of Jewish men and masculinity (see *Difference and Pathology*, and Sander Gilman, *The Jew's Body* [New York, 1991]).

[36]See, for example, HHStA 461/16143; HHStA 461/16677; HHStA 461/17795; HHStA 461/16679. Aryan masculinity remains as yet to be explained fully in the historical

discourse thus remained an unstable ideal, not least because many Aryan men brought before the courts on charges of race defilement had clearly failed to uphold its standards.

The case of Mr. Knopp, an Aryan man whose Jewish wife was accused of conducting an affair with a family friend, illustrates the courts' response to men who most flagrantly violated the masculine Aryan ideal. When questioned, Knopp admitted knowledge of his wife's affair but said that he felt it was not his place to object to his wife's extramarital liaison since he had for years suffered from nervous disorders and impotence. Their marriage was a happy one, Knopp asserted, if companionate rather than sexual in nature. The court lavished contempt upon Knopp for his failure to uphold the standards of Aryan masculinity, stating in its verdict: "If he is impotent, his impotence does not have only a physical basis, but is a result of psychological defect. He is limp, womanish, and lacking in energy. . . . He reads Schopenhauer and plays chess, but isn't good for much else. This kind of man is completely irrelevant to the *Volk* community. . . . He is a wretched, weak-willed, listless human being." In short, the court concluded, "He is useless as a man." Clearly, such an egregious violation of the standards of Aryan masculinity demanded an exceptional judicial response. Although Knopp initially appeared only as a witness in his wife's trial, the court convicted him of "procuring" and "aiding and abetting."[37]

Even though women could only be summoned as witnesses in race-defilement proceedings, they were far from minor players in the trials. The Aryan women summoned to testify before the courts were subject to severe scrutiny and judgment. As the primary bearers of racial honor and the biological key to racial purity, the figure of the Aryan woman became the representational and physical ground upon which the struggle for racial purity was carried out. In this, judicial rhetoric echoed official Nazi ideology, which placed much of the blame for the perceived moral decay of the Weimar Republic on the figure of the sexually aggressive, independent "New Woman."[38] In linking women's sexual honor, racial purity, and the fate of the nation, legal discourse in turn enhanced cultural tensions inherent in the role and status of Aryan women. Thus, though legal rhetoric often pointed to the Aryan woman's sexual inexperience as the cause of her seduction, Aryan women were simultaneously depicted as saturated with sexuality and always potentially available and corruptible. The court's characterization of one Aryan woman called as a witness is typical: "She is a fairly frivolous girl who has been ruined by these perverted relations and

---

scholarship. In Burleigh and Wippermann's insightful and pathbreaking chapter on men in the Third Reich, for example, class ultimately largely stands for and subsumes Aryan masculinity per se (267–302).

[37]Verdict reprinted in Robinsohn, 69.

[38]For an analysis of the extent to which the "New Woman" of Weimar and Nazi rhetoric existed in reality, see Atina Grossmann, "*Girlkultur* or Thoroughly Rationalized Female?" in *Women in Culture and Politics*, ed. Judith Friedlander et al. (Bloomington, 1986).

is now in danger of becoming a harlot."[39] Often the verdicts implicitly expressed puzzlement that the Aryan woman, though of "full blood," offered no resistance to the seduction. Commenting on one female witness, a verdict remarked, "From the very beginning, Miss Friese put up no resistance to the accused. She is descended from four grandparents all of German blood, and by birth she is a national of the German Reich [*Reichsangehörige*]." Friese's lack of resistance was cited in turn as a mitigating factor in her Jewish lover's sentencing. In the notorious 1942 trial of Leo Katzenberger, the court similarly alluded to the witness Irene Seiler's sexual availability, suggesting that in having accepted small gifts from Katzenberger, she had entered into a "relation of dependence" and made herself "amenable" to him. The court rebuked Seiler for her "undisciplined manner," her "stubbornness," and her lack of "repentance," while outside witnesses supplemented these metaphors of dangerous independence by commenting disapprovingly on Seiler's "liking for cigarettes."[40]

The courts repeatedly invoked the needs and expectations of the *Volk* community when chastising Aryan women for their sexual transgressions. Even though the actual number of cases had been declining since 1939, in part because so many German Jews had emigrated, police and legal personnel worried that incidents of race defilement were on the rise due to wartime conditions and the absence of husbands and fathers at the front. This perception had practical implications in the daily enforcement of the law, as judges rebuked Aryan women severely for taking advantage of the "lack of supervision" they enjoyed when men were not home to "maintain order" while giving exceptionally harsh sentences to Jewish men who had "taken advantage of wartime conditions."[41] According to legal rhetoric, the innately pure and honorable Aryan girl, left to her own devices, was all too likely to become a fallen woman. Legal discourse thus fashioned an image of Aryan femininity that drew on shifting and fluid cultural stereotypes of femininity and female sexuality to explain the behavior of the sexually errant Aryan woman. While functioning as a method of explanation, legal discourse in turn also served the dual purpose of regulation and control.

What has emerged as a relative consensus within the historiographical debate is that the National Socialist prescriptive image of the Mother of the *Volk* cloaked the reality that women, like men, were divided into two

---

[39]Verdict quoted in Robinsohn, 62.

[40]StAM StAnw 18081; United States National Archives (USNA) RG238/NG154. On the Katzenberger trial, see also the journalistic recreation by Christiane Kohl, *Der Jude und das Mädchen: Eine verbotene Freundschaft in Nazideutschland* (Hamburg, 1997). The names of Leo Katzenberger and Irene Seiler are not pseudonyms.

[41]One Jewish defendant was sentenced to death as a "dangerous habitual criminal" for having an affair with a woman whose husband was serving at the front; see LAB 58/4005/1710. Concern about the sexual infidelity of women whose husbands had been called to the front reached the highest official level. See, for example, BAP R22/1085, pp. 5–7, 36.

broad categories: first, the healthy and racially pure Aryan; second, the racially "other"—Jews and Gypsies, the hereditarily "inferior" (*minderwertig*), and the "asocial." The overarching ideological imperative for the racially valuable woman was to serve the nation, primarily in her reproductive but also in her productive capacity.[42] In reducing the role of racially valuable women's sexuality to that of fertility, Annette Timm argues, Nazi discourse contributed to the desexualization of "ordinary" women. By contrast, outsiders—in this case, prostitutes and "asocials"—were oversexualized, and their sexuality and behavior were subjected to intense surveillance. Other scholars such as Stefan Maiwald and Gerd Mischler have characterized the Nazi era similarly as a time of prudery, when love and individual desire were to be subordinated to the needs of the *Volk*, to increasing the population of healthy Aryans.[43] Despite the social and sexual conservatism of the majority of Nazi officials, however, German society was not entirely desexualized, nor was the ordinary Aryan woman figured simply as an asexual being. Though the exclusion of women from prosecution under the Nuremberg Laws was in part justified by the notion that it was the male partner who was sexually active while the female was weak and sexually passive, a simultaneous ideological construction figured all women as hypersexual, governed by emotions and eminently corruptible. In this, the National Socialist ideology on women drew upon prevailing modern discursive constructions wherein women figured as a fundamentally "problematic and unruly body" whose sexuality, if not constantly regulated, would disrupt the social and moral order.[44] Despite their

---

[42]Although the notion of a "racial state" has rightly been criticized by Atina Grossmann for ignoring the immense differences between those labeled as racially inferior and particularly for eliding the specificity of Nazi anti-Semitism, it nonetheless has been useful for focusing attention on the underlying biopolitical logic of the Nazi regime. For helpful overviews of the historiography of women in Nazi Germany, see Atina Grossmann, "Feminist Debates about Women and National Socialism," *Gender & History* 3 (1991): 350–58; Eve Rosenhaft, "Inside the Third Reich: What Is the Women's Story?" *Radical History Review* 43 (1989): 72–87; and Adelheid von Saldern, "Victims or Perpetrators? Controversies about the Role of Women in the Nazi State," in *Nazism and German Society*, ed. David F. Crew (London, 1994), 141–65.

[43]Annette F. Timm, "The Ambivalent Outsider: Prostitution, Promiscuity, and VD Control in Nazi Berlin," in *Social Outsiders in Nazi Germany*, ed. Robert Gellately and Nathan Stoltzfus (Princeton, 2001), 192–211; and Stefan Maiwald and Gerd Mischler, *Sexualität unter dem Hakenkreuz: Manipulation und Vernichtung der Intimsphäre im NS-Staat* (Hamburg, 1999). Arguments for sexual self-determination and enjoyment for its own sake flourished only briefly in Germany during the Weimar years, as documented in Atina Grossmann's study, *Reforming Sex: The German Movement for Birth Control and Abortion Reform, 1920–1950* (Oxford, 1995).

[44]Carol Smart, "Introduction," in *Regulating Womanhood: Historical Essays on Marriage, Motherhood, and Sexuality* (New York, 1992), 8. For a useful survey of the way in which the paradox of the simultaneously asexual and hypersexualized female has functioned since the Victorian era, see Carolyn J. Dean, *Sexuality and Modern Western Culture* (New York, 1996).

supposed innate purity and honor, Aryan women could not be completely relied upon to devote their energies to producing healthy and racially pure offspring for the *Volk*. Indeed, the National Socialist regime devoted significant personnel and resources to the racial education of girls and women. This intense focus on the proper sexual and racial comportment of girls and women was double-edged, since the image of the young Aryan maiden—sturdy, blond-plaited, uniform-clad, pure of heart and body—remained ever discursively twinned to her negative image—the wan and wispy maiden of the *Stürmer* caricature, defiled and lured into depravity by the treacherous wiles of the lecherous Jewish man. Moreover, at the highest level of the party bureaucracy, there was official recognition that the rhetoric of female sexual propriety did not correspond to reality. The idealized image of the naturally pure and good Aryan maiden and mother of the *Volk*, often invoked in National Socialist discourse, thus was inherently unstable, symptomatic of substantial ideological and cultural anxiety. Such anxieties served in turn to sanction a level of surveillance that was directed not only against "outsiders" but against "insiders" as well.[45]

STRATEGIES OF DEFENSE

Defendants' and witnesses' attempts at self-defense are equally revealing about the manner in which the German population absorbed racial ideology through the prism of cultural assumptions about gender and sexuality. Many defendants, for example, claim to have misunderstood the finer aspects of the Nuremberg Laws, which was certainly plausible given the complexity of the laws and their implementation. One common misunderstanding involved defendants and witnesses who took the formal title of the Nuremberg Laws—the Law for the Protection of German Blood and Honor—too literally. In a number of cases, for example, defendants and witnesses took the notion of "protection of German blood" more literally than intended. In a letter to the prosecuting attorney, one defendant

[45]See, for example, the "Tätigkeitsberichte der Gau- und Kreisamtsleitungen" of the Office of Racial Policy (Rassenpolitisches Amt) in StAM, NSDAP 145. Within the Justice Ministry, officials were preoccupied with the problem of the proliferation of adultery among war wives and the particularly troubling statistics regarding relations of German women with POWs and foreign workers. Officials remarked that the "sexual hardship" (*Geschlechtsnot*) women faced while their husbands were away at the front also fueled the wave of adultery among war wives. See, for example, BAP R55/1442; BAP R55/1443; and BAP R22/845. There were also practical, evidentiary reasons for exempting women from prosecution for race defilement. See, for example, Herbert Gräml, "Die Behandlung der an Fällen von sogenannter Rassenschande beteiligten 'deutschblütigen' Personen," in *Gutachten des Instituts für Zeitgeschichte* (Munich, 1958), 1:72–76. On the immense bureaucracy and recording apparatus that monitored the morals and behavior of the German population in an attempt to distinguish between the worthy and unworthy, see Lisa Pine, *Nazi Family Policy* (New York, 1997); and Elizabeth D. Heineman, *What Difference Does a Husband Make? Women and Marital Status in Nazi and Postwar Germany* (Berkeley, 1999).

pointedly remarked that his Jewish girlfriend "had been sterilized in May 1939, so there was *no* danger that relations with her could result in off-spring." In this and similar cases, however, the courts refused to consider as a mitigating factor the fact that one or both of the partners in a mixed relationship had been medically certified as sterile.[46] Other defendants told investigators that they had not realized that sexual intercourse with prosti-tutes fell under the scope of the Nuremberg Laws, an assumption that was widespread in the larger community. Even the courts implied that prosti-tutes had forfeited their racial honor and their right to protection from race defilement. In one case, the court convicted a Jewish man who had a long-standing arrangement with an Aryan prostitute. However, in assessing his sentence, the court considered as a mitigating factor that the defendant had "already been punished by having contracted syphilis from the witness . . . who, in any case, cannot herself be counted among the more valuable mem-bers of the German *Volk*."[47] Many defendants and their attorneys and fami-lies echoed such assumptions about prostitutes' lack of honor and attempted to defend themselves by arguing that they had been lured into sexual rela-tions by the superior wiles of the professional. As one defense lawyer wrote in a letter to the court, it was well known that such "female personages" were highly practiced at "approaching men and luring them into inter-course." Similarly, another Jewish man explained in self-defense, "I did not seek an acquaintance there with a woman of ill repute; rather, the opposite is true. As in all such cases, it is the woman who wishes to make the acquain-tance of the man."[48] With such arguments, defendants and their attorneys hoped to shift the majority of blame for the sexual encounter to the woman while attempting to win judicial sympathy by appealing to male solidarity and knowledge of the world.

Other men, both Aryan and Jewish, attempted to excuse their behavior by claiming that they had been inebriated, an explanation for misbehavior seldom employed by women in race-defilement cases. Aryan and Jewish men also blamed their actions on "foolishness," invoking the cultural script of the male youth led astray by dint of folly rather than calculated mis-deed. Often, Aryan men claimed to have been unaware that their partner was Jewish until after their first sexual encounter. Young Aryan men also occasionally succeeded in winning judicial sympathy by claiming seduc-tion. As one Aryan defendant argued, "In my defense, however, I wish to state that I was seduced by Miss Jakob. . . . Miss Jakob very cleverly was able to beguile me with her words, saying that I was an attractive man, and that she was fond of me. I then succumbed to her lures." The police

[46]LAB 58/4005/1543, emphasis in original. See also, for example, LAB 58/4005/1520.

[47]LAB 58/4005/3000. See also LAB 58/4005/1618; LAB 58/4005/1544.

[48]LAB 58/4005/1686; LAB 58/4005/1533. Race-defilement records testify to a fair amount of casual prostitution and relationships that subsisted on gifts and help with the rent.

investigator agreed: "The accused was completely at the mercy of the
Jewess's seductive wiles. . . . The Jewess behaved like a whore and is mainly
to blame for events." Though the Aryan man was convicted, his seduction
was regarded as a mitigating factor in sentencing. For Jewish men, claims
of seduction rarely encountered a sympathetic judicial hearing. In a typical case, the courts reacted to a Jew's claim of seduction with derision,
characterizing it as a "prime example of Talmudic effrontery. . . . He claims
not to have been the seducer; rather, it was Miss Schmidt." Another Gestapo officer, in an equally scornful aside in an interrogation record, commented, "Isenberg is trying to place the entire blame for the sexual activities
on Mrs. Glade. He claims never to have instigated the sexual intercourse;
rather, it was always Mrs. Glade. In typical Jewish fashion, Isenberg refuses to take any responsibility for his errors."[49]

Women, even though they could only be called as witnesses, were far
from passive bystanders in the trials. Over the course of a race-defilement
investigation and trial, a complex pattern of negotiation and accommoda-
tion often developed among Aryan and Jewish women and police and
court officials. Such negotiations often assumed a gendered form as women
colluded with stereotypical images of masculinity and femininity to deflect
police and judicial interrogations and rationalize their behavior. Several
verdicts suggest that Aryan women occasionally utilized the courts' representations of injured innocence, as in the statement given by one young
Aryan woman: "I am convinced today that he took advantage of my innocence and my purity in the crudest possible way, and that his only desire
was sexual gratification. His sexual perversity has left me psychologically
damaged."[50] Both Aryan and Jewish women supported claims of innocence by invoking images of domestic virtue. When witnesses attempted
to question Irene Seiler's propriety by claiming she had been seen on several occasions waving to Katzenberger "through one of the back windows
of her flat," Seiler countered this accusation of public visibility by invoking an image of domestic propriety, claiming she only stood before the
window when performing household chores such as dishwashing.[51] Other
women testified that their only contact with the accused man took place
in the course of normal household duties, such as shopping and entertaining their husband's business partners. Thus, it seems, both Aryan and
Jewish women called as witnesses in race-defilement trials often tried to
manipulate popular assumptions about gender and sexuality in their own
defense. Quite understandably, the central concern of both women and
men called to testify before the police and courts in such cases was to
deflect the accusation of race defilement and avoid unofficial sanction and
official punishment whenever possible. Imbedded in their statements of

[49]StAD/K 8/38, 8/39; StAD/K 29/72; StAD/K 29/115.
[50]Verdict reprinted in Robinsohn, 109.
[51]USNA RG238/NG154.

self-defense are both deliberate and unconscious discursive strategies of negotiation that drew on available images and scripts of masculinity, femininity, and sexuality. In employing cultural images and norms in self-defense, female witnesses and male defendants hoped to achieve popular and official sympathy and lenient treatment before the police and courts.

RULES OF EVIDENCE

One of the investigator's central tasks was compiling and reconstructing the evidence for the illegal sexual relationship. Over the course of an investigation, defendants and witnesses were interrogated repeatedly until they offered a sufficiently detailed and convincing account of the alleged sexual encounter. Interrogators questioned defendants and female witnesses about the most precise and intimate facts, probing for information on the maneuvers of seduction, the couple's state of arousal, where and how they touched, what clothing they wore and what they removed, the positions of their bodies, and whether "gratification" was achieved. Investigators were careful to document all trysts and encounters as precisely as possible. A Munich Gestapo report was typical in its exquisite attention to detail, describing at length how the couple drove through the city streets "for quite a long time" before stopping the car in front of a local landmark to consummate their relationship. Subsequent encounters were again documented with the utmost precision, naming times, dates, and locations in detail.[52]

Many of the facts elicited with such vigor in the course of interrogations appear irrelevant to the assessment of guilt and to the sentencing process. For example, during the course of interrogations, investigators routinely inquired whether intercourse had taken place "with protection" or "without protection," a detail that never served as a mitigating or exacerbating factor in sentencing despite the avowed intent of the Nuremberg Laws to "prevent the birth of mixed race offspring." Investigators also routinely pursued the possibility that the woman had received gifts or money from her lover. Again, however, even women who replied in the affirmative faced no formal legal charge, though presumably the implication of casual prostitution carried with it an added social stigma. Other sexual details were of greater practical significance to the investigation. For example, a key focus of police and judicial interrogation was the sexual history of the female witness. Jewish women were subjected to particularly harsh interrogation when they denied having other relations with Aryan men. In one interrogation record, it is apparent that the "half-Jewish" woman was placed under significant duress: "I wish to state under oath that I had no other intimate relationships with men following my

---

[52]See, for example, StAM Landratsämter (LRA) 30755; StAD/K 169/31; StAD/K 8/ 38, 8/39; StAM StAnw 15031. Quote from StAM 8154.

affair with Nicklas. Even after being advised about the consequences of perjury, I continue to insist on the truth of my claim." In another case, a young Aryan woman who admitted to engaging in "petting" with her Jewish boyfriend was subjected to relentless questioning about her prior sexual history in an attempt to belie her claim of chastity and so uphold the race-defilement charge. Jewish men who denied having relationships with other Aryan women were also questioned aggressively in an attempt to uncover further instances of race defilement.[53]

Police and judicial interrogations also devoted a great deal of attention to whether intercourse had taken place "in a normal fashion" or whether what were termed "perversions" were involved. Investigators asked specific and direct questions about any sexual acts outside of "normal" coitus. When the couple did engage in "perversions," the investigative and court records described the acts in explicit detail. Many investigation records reveal the fact that oral sex and forms of masturbation were the object of intense police and judicial interest and scrutiny. Investigative and judicial records also commented extensively on any aspects of the case that pointed to the couple's deviant sexuality. In one case, for example, the court remarked that the witness's "red Russian boots"—among other things—had "incited the defendant's lust." Investigators went so far as to ask specific questions regarding acts that failed to take place. One interrogator noted, for example, that the accused had "tried two or three times to engage in oral intercourse with her. . . . Whether on this occasion Miss Geyer took the defendant's member in her hand and stroked it could not be determined."[54]

In filling in gaps in the narrative of a sexual liaison and assessing the evidence for race defilement, investigators constantly appealed to the "life experience" of observant neighbors to determine the facts of a case. One case, for example, rested on the testimony of a neighbor whose presumption of a sexual relationship was based on the fact that the Jewish defendant had a key to the woman's apartment. Another case rested on the testimony of a subletter who told judicial investigators that she was certain that the witness and the defendant had a sexual relationship; when the defendant came to visit, the couple locked the bedroom door, whereupon she heard the "rhythmic squeaks" of the bedsprings "until the door was opened fifteen minutes later."[55] Police officials also searched homes for physical clues of a sexual relationship such as intimate articles of clothing or "prophylactics," and outside witnesses were encouraged to recount telltale physical signs of sexual activity, such as mussed or stained sheets, details that were recounted with precision in the records of the case.[56]

To rebut defendants' "unbelievable" stories, the prosecutors also invoked "life experience" and "worldly understanding," announcing their

[53]LAB 58/4005/1544; StAM StAnw 15809. See also LAB 58/4005/1572.
[54]HHStA 461/KLs 1.37; StAM StAnw 18081.
[55]LAB 58/4005/1544; LAB 58/4005/1656.
[56]See, for example, StAM 6430; StAD/K 7/900.

skepticism with such routine phrases as "The defendant's statement of self-defense and the witness's testimony are implausible and will be refuted." Couples who claimed to have ended their relationship upon hearing of the Nuremberg Laws were subjected to particularly rigorous interrogation. One couple, for example, claimed to have ended their love affair in 1933, though they continued to see each other nearly every day. Commenting on the plausibility of their account, the court remarked, "There is no apparent reason why the relationship, which lasted many years, should have come to an end in 1933. The defendant's explanation that he had grown old cannot be taken seriously."[57] Contradictions and gaps in testimony were often resolved by similar appeals to "worldly experience." In the trial of a Jewish shopkeeper, for example, the court commented on the original testimony, stating, "This account seems implausible, or at the very least incomplete. Our experience indicates that a girl won't allow herself to be used sexually in this way unless previous intimacies have taken place—even if . . . she has consumed two glasses of wine." "To this day," the judge declared, the female witness "refuses to tell the whole truth." Because of her refusal to endorse the court's version of the sexual encounter, the woman was convicted of aiding and abetting.[58]

Writing to a local attorney in charge of a race-defilement case, a head prosecutor instructed his subordinate on the necessary standards of evidence:

> The results of the investigation are quite meager. In particular, what is missing is a more precise description of how the two persons in question met, how their relationship developed, and finally, how it came about that they engaged in sexual intercourse. . . . It would also have been advisable to inquire more precisely into the nature of the observations made by Ingrid Link that enabled us to conclude that the accused had sexual intercourse with Elisabeth Eckert from April 1935 until 1936.[59]

Such relentless attention to detail on the part of Gestapo and judicial interrogators can partially be accounted for by a standard of proof that necessitated painstaking documentation of the crime. For one, repeated acts of race defilement were deemed evidence of "criminal intent," and a "continued offense" required harsher punishment than a one-time misdeed. Police interrogations also elicited details that potentially had a bearing on the sentencing, including such mitigating factors as the defendant's inebriation or the female witness's aggressive seduction or "lack of honor." Moreover, sexual details elicited during an initial interrogation could in turn be used as leverage in subsequent interrogations of reluctant defendants and witnesses.

[57]StAD/K 7/900.
[58]HHStA 461/KLs 7.38.
[59]StAD/K 10/175.

Quite often, police officials moved between interrogation rooms, using details elicited from one of the partners to pressure additional information or a confession from the other. However, the sheer repetition of sexual details elicited during the course of an investigation is striking and cannot entirely be accounted for by the practical exigencies of the legal process. Sexual details that appear in the police investigative records were repeated in court records before the investigating magistrate and again in summary form for the final verdict. Written reports were similarly lavish in repeating sexual detail, and the bureaucratic enforcement apparatus generated a seemingly unceasing flow of descriptively explicit reports to higher courts, to the Reich Ministry of Justice, to local health authorities (Gesundheitsämter), to the Office of Racial Policy (Rassenpolitisches Amt), and to a myriad of other social welfare, educational, medical, psychological, and military agencies and officials. In their "will to knowledge" and obsessive attention to sexual detail, police and judicial interrogators thus displayed a desire to document that went beyond the requirements of legal proof. Moreover, in fashioning a narrative of the sexual encounter, legal discourse surrounding the trials became highly sexualized. This reiteration of sexual detail throughout the levels of prosecution and enforcement in turn created its own dynamic and constellation of effects.

TELLING SEXUAL STORIES

Legal rhetoric enforced a normative definition of sexuality that was both racist and sexually conservative in its implications, condemning as "perverse" all sexuality not designed to produce racially pure offspring within the bonds of marriage. Paradoxically, however, over time legal discourse served to expand the realm of the sexual by attributing sexual meaning to even the most casual social interaction. Although the first decree governing the implementation of the Nuremberg Laws stated that only sexual intercourse was punishable under the law, in practice local courts gradually began to expand the definition of sexual intercourse in their rulings. This practice was ultimately ratified by a decision of the Supreme Court (Reichsgericht), which asserted that any behavior that could serve to "gratify the desires of at least one of the partners" was sexual and fell under the scope of the racial purity laws.[60] Though local courts welcomed

[60]Martin Tarrab-Maslaton, *Rechtliche Strukturen der Diskriminierung der Juden im Dritten Reich* (Berlin, 1993), 84. For other accounts of the actions of the Supreme Court (Reichsgericht) in race-defilement cases, see Müller, 100–105; Rolf Lengemann, "Höchstrichterliche Strafgerichtsbarkeit unter der Herrschaft des Nationalsozialismus," Ph.D. diss., Marburg, 1974; Friedrich Karl Kaul, *Geschichte des Reichsgerichts*, vol. 4 (Glashütten, 1971); Uwe Diederichsen, "Nationalsozialistische Ideologie in der Rechtsprechung des Reichsgerichts zum Ehe- und Familienrecht" in *Recht und Justiz im Dritten Reich*, ed. Ralf Dreier and Wolfgang Sellert (Frankfurt am Main, 1989), 241–72; Hans Wullenweber, *Sondergerichte im Dritten Reich: Vergessene Verbrechen der Justiz* (Frankfurt am Main, 1990), 198–202.

the high court decision as a precedent-setting advance, in practice the need to determine whether an act was designed to achieve sexual "gratification" resulted in considerable confusion.

Using the high court decision as precedent, local police officials began to investigate with remarkable thoroughness whether the "sexual desires" of one or both partners had in fact been gratified. One near-verbatim transcript of an interrogation gives an unusual glimpse of the methods of police persuasion. After recording background information, the police official opened the interrogation by instructing the Aryan woman on the legal definition of the sexual act: "What constitutes criminal sexual intercourse is not only normal intercourse between the man and the woman but also all other manual actions that are intended to lead to sexual arousal or gratification or which do result in gratification. (The term is further explained to the female witness.) . . . When you leave the building, you should have the liberating feeling that you have told the truth and that nothing can happen to you." Alternating veiled threats with the reassuring metaphor of the confessional, the police interrogator successfully elicited all the necessary details of the woman's sexual history and her one-night liaison with a Jewish traveling salesman. In other instances when defendants confessed to sexual intercourse, interrogators probed for physical evidence to document male "gratification." Both male defendants and female witnesses were thus routinely asked to report whether the man had ejaculated. In the case of women, however, "gratification" was more difficult to document by physical means. For example, when pressured by an interrogator, one Jewish man admitted: "I also tried to satisfy Miss Liedl's sexual desire using my hand. However, I can't say with certainty if my efforts in this respect met with success." In other cases, interrogators relied on the woman's own reports of gratification or lack thereof. After repeated questioning, one Jewish woman maintained, "As far as I can recall, the last time I obtained sexual satisfaction from Ludwig was three years ago." Dissatisfied with the woman's denials, the interrogators questioned her Aryan boyfriend, who was forced to concur: "Though I achieved sexual satisfaction by these means, Mrs. Grünbaum did not."[61] Though legal discourse explicitly acknowledged the reality of female orgasm, simple participation ultimately substituted for more specific evidence of "gratification." Over time, such interrogative practices began to assume a dynamic of their own, as police and judicial investigators probed for evidence of gratification even in instances where no sexual intercourse or "substitute actions" had taken place. Thus, for instance, when an Aryan woman admitted that she often exchanged a casual embrace with a male Jewish friend, she was subjected to rigorous questioning. After lengthy denials, the woman reluctantly admitted that it was possible that their "sexual organs" had indeed touched through their clothing during an embrace.

[61]StAD/K 29/70, parentheses in original; StAD/K 29/48; StAD/K 29/117.

Finally, following exhaustive interrogation, she admitted, "I really can't be sure whether Siegfried might not have obtained sexual pleasure of some sort from our contact."[62]

In the absence of evidence of gratification, police and legal officials next turned to searching for evidence of sexual desire. In the resulting narrative, the construction of the erotic experience required that the "actions that were intended to initiate sexual intercourse" be delineated in graphic detail. Thus, for example, interrogators elicited precise information about one defendant's maneuvers of seduction: "He was possessed of a keen desire for sexual intercourse with her. In order to make her amenable to the act, on one or two occasions, when he was alone with her in the bathroom, he pulled her toward him, touched her breasts through her clothing, and kissed her." In another case, the interrogator noted in an aside on the record, "By these means, he hoped to awaken carnal appetites in the girl and make her amenable to coitus."[63] Such interrogative practices paved the way for the more radical local courts to expand even further the definition of criminal sexual intercourse. In some instances, courts used evidence of sexual desire or attempts at seduction to convict Jewish men of "attempted" race defilement. Other courts asserted that race defilement could take place without any attempts at seduction or physical contact at all. In 1939, for example, a Jewish man was convicted of race defilement for glancing at a young Aryan girl across the street. The court ruled that, although the man had no physical or verbal contact with the girl, his glance "had a clearly erotic basis."[64]

One 1938 case tried in the Berlin courts is particularly illustrative of the discursive struggle to define the nature of erotic experience within the aegis of the law. In May of that year, Leo Wallach, a Jewish salesman, was arrested and charged with repeated violations of the blood purity law. The objective circumstances of his case were not in dispute, as Wallach readily admitted to being a habitual visitor at the establishment of Mrs. Ziegler, who advertised her place of business under the guise of a massage institute. During an early visit, Wallach took a liking to a young woman, Miss Diamand. As he chatted with her in an upstairs room, he observed her make repeated small adjustments to the lapels of her dressing gown. At this point, Wallach suggested that she disrobe and, in the words of the prosecutor, "walk back and forth, bending and turning her body, in the manner he requested." Over the following months, this procedure was repeated on four or five occasions. In a few instances, Miss Diamand disrobed entirely, while on other occasions she modeled various undergarments—including twelve camisoles, by the prosecutor's count. On the last occasion, Wallach and Diamand were discovered during a routine police patrol.

[62] StAD/K 92/121.
[63] StAM StAnw 18081; StAM StAnw 15809.
[64] HHStA 461/KMs 51.39.

Leo Wallach's legal counsel mounted an energetic defense. Wallach's actions, the defense counsel argued, had not displayed that quality necessary to establishing the act of intercourse, namely, that there be "contact between" the two parties. Wallach had "stood there quietly, neither touching her nor touching his own body in any fashion." Such "one-sided offenses of a sexual nature" did not meet the legal definition of intercourse and in fact had been explicitly excluded as such by the Supreme Court. This, the defense counsel suggested, was to prevent actions such as attending a revue or cabaret from falling under the purview of the Nuremberg Laws. Furthermore, Wallach's only motivation was one of aesthetic appreciation for the unclothed female form. The prosecutor emphatically rejected the defense arguments. First, "contact between" the two partners was unnecessary to establish the act of intercourse. Nor were Wallach's actions a mere one-sided offense, as the presence of Miss Diamand's body and her behavior had acted in a contributory fashion. Moreover, Wallach had not remained content with the mere act of looking but had in fact been an active partner who aimed at obtaining sexual satisfaction. Thus "intercourse" had in fact taken place "between" the two partners.

Though not entirely persuaded of the artistic nature of Leo Wallach's interest, the court could find no evidence that he had engaged in sexual activity, noting: "Coitus is always sexual intercourse, but the reverse is not necessarily the case. The performance of indecent acts may constitute sexual intercourse, but not every indecent act is sexual intercourse." While Wallach's behavior was certainly intended to procure erotic stimulation, it was "commonly understood" that the mere sight of the nude female body was insufficient to obtain actual gratification. The court did wonder whether Wallach might have achieved gratification on the occasion of his first visit, when he kept his hand in his right pants pocket. However, the court noted, "He carries himself to the left." Moreover, Miss Diamand insisted that she had on no occasion observed any physical evidence of arousal and, as the court remarked, "she must be considered something of an expert in such matters." In a scathing rebuttal, the prosecutor challenged the magistrate's assessment. "Had the court consulted a specialist, it would have been forced to acknowledge that its belief in the objective impossibility of obtaining sexual satisfaction by such means is medically insupportable—quite apart from the fact that it is a contravention of all principles of logic to invoke a 'common understanding' with reference to sexual perversions." The findings of medical science, the prosecutor concluded, would undoubtedly determine this to be an instance of "one of the so-called psychic onanism-related manifestations." Though the prosecutor requested a sentence of three years' penal servitude, Wallach was acquitted on grounds of insufficient evidence. While the prosecutor's appeal was pending, Leo Wallach "absconded," leaving notice of his departure for the United States.[65]

---

[65]LAB 58/4005/1695, emphasis in original.

CONCLUSION

Before 1933, the majority of German Jews considered themselves as much German as Jewish. Yet within the space of a few years, Jews had become outcasts on the margins of German society. Much of this isolation was accomplished by way of legislation, as over the course of the 1930s the Nazi regime enacted hundreds of anti-Jewish laws, from early measures that excluded Jews from the civil service to later decrees that forbade them to own pets or radios. But it was the Nuremberg Laws that arguably penetrated most deeply into the private and intimate spheres of social and family relations, fatefully separating Jewish from non-Jewish Germans. Unlike many other anti-Semitic laws, whose discriminatory effects were experienced with near exclusivity by the Jewish population, the blood purity laws drew Jews and non-Jews alike into the enforcement process. As historians such as Marion Kaplan have noted, the mere existence of the Nuremberg Laws sufficed to intimidate Jews and to cause many Germans to withdraw from Jewish friends and from family members in "mixed" relationships and marriages.[66] Thus the Nuremberg Laws heightened a process of internal conformity and behavioral adjustment to accord with National Socialist norms. Moreover, though the actual number of convictions remained relatively small (perhaps three thousand over the course of ten years), far more individuals were investigated than were charged. Each investigation and trial in turn had a rippling effect across entire communities, as neighbors, friends, and coworkers were interrogated and drawn into the spectacle of enforcement.

National Socialist discourse and practice surrounding sexuality was a complex and often contradictory linking of the health of the nation, racial purity, and the virtues and duties of men and women in the new Germany. Though the avowed aim of the Nuremberg Laws was to quash all interracial sexuality, legal discourse paradoxically narrated the proliferation of illegal and "deviant" sexual encounters. In eliciting a level of descriptive and explicit detail well in excess of what was necessary from the standpoint of legal proof, investigators turned the trials into a dramatic reenactment of deviance. Indeed, the excessive zeal with which police and judicial investigators questioned women about details of their sexual encounters evoked concern at the highest official levels. In August 1942 the Reich Ministry of Justice issued a directive stating that official questioning of female witnesses should be aimed only at determining whether a sexual encounter had taken place. More explicit inquiries about the nature ("Art und Weise") of the sexual encounter should not be pursued; to persist in such inquiries "would raise the question of a peculiar 'inner or mental attitude'" on the part of the interrogator.[67] Paradoxically, in recounting

[66]Marion Kaplan, *Between Dignity and Despair: Jewish Life in Nazi Germany* (New York, 1998), 46, 78–81.
[67]BAP R22/845.

and reiterating sexually explicit testimony, legal rhetoric suggested the rampant sexualization of daily life. Such sexualization, by authorizing voyeurism and prurient fantasies, in turn enabled the co-opting of citizens into a network of sexualized surveillance and self-policing. Given the very short lifetime of the Third Reich, such modes of enforcement could only function successfully by resting upon older, existing patterns of explanation and control, most prominently, the sexual monitoring of women and of racial "others." In critical ways, therefore, Nazi discourses and practices of racial enforcement demonstrate lines of continuity for a regime that is often regarded as the very antithesis of a democratic society.

Fascism and the Female Form:
Performance Art in the Third Reich

TERRI J. GORDON

Barnard College, Columbia University

NAZI GERMANY IS generally understood to have been a sexually repressive society, and in fundamental social and political ways, it *was* repressive. The National Socialist Party intervened in the private space of the body to an extent never before experienced and in hitherto unprecedented ways. The state instituted a politics of the body that rendered the individual body a public site whose purpose was to further the larger social organism. In the drive toward the establishment of a pure, thriving *Volk*, the National Socialist regime conducted a dual campaign, a pronatalist campaign encouraging "healthy" Aryan women to bear and rear children and an antinatalist policy aimed at preventing the reproduction of "undesirable" elements (Jews, Poles, Africans, and the mentally disabled, among others). Whereas pronatalist policies operated through incentives, such as government subsidies, child allowances, tax rebates, and medals for childbearing, antinatalist measures were carried out through repressive laws, including compulsory sterilization of the genetically "inferior," forced abortions, and marriage prohibitions.[1] The body became a social site onto

This essay is part of a larger study on projections of femininity in the Third Reich. Research on the cabaret under the Third Reich and *Ausdruckstanz* comes from the following sources: the Staatsbibliothek, the Zentrum für Berlin-Studien at the Zentral- und Landesbibliothek Berlin, the Landesarchiv, the Akademie der Künste, and the Kunstbibliothek. I am grateful to the reference librarians at the Film Department of the Bundesarchiv and the Stiftung deutsche Kinemathek (SDK) (now the Film Museum Berlin, Deutsche Kinemathek) for their assistance in my research into the staged revue and the revue film. I would like to express my appreciation to Dagmar Herzog for her close attention to this essay in its various stages and for her invaluable suggestions. I am also grateful for the careful reading of two referees, whose insightful comments allowed me both to sharpen and extend my arguments. All translations are mine unless otherwise noted.

    [1]Gisela Bock, "Equality and Difference in National Socialist Racism," in *Feminism and History*, ed. Joan Wallach Scott (New York, 1996), 268–81. The law of compulsory

which political ideals were mapped. The notion of the healthy body as a microcosm for the healthy state was reiterated in the images of the "sacred wife and mother" in officially sanctioned art and promoted in a vast propaganda campaign enjoining women to lend their bodies to the movement to maintain the vitality of the race.

Yet despite the radical political intervention into domestic life, sexual iconography persisted in Nazi Germany in ways highly reminiscent of that of the Weimar period. Another face of sexuality was visible in the Third Reich, one that was reflected in the cult of the body that marked much of the performance art of the period. Both the cabaret revue and *Ausdruckstanz* (expressionist dance) flourished in the Nazi period. These two forms of dance signal two distinct areas in which nudity and female eroticism were employed in Nazi culture: the revue in the realm of mass culture, *Ausdruckstanz* in the realm of the avant-garde. Both forms were culturally continuous with the Weimar period, against whose "decadent" and "degenerate" norms Nazi Germany continually positioned itself. In the Nazi period, the Hiller Girls provided the German counterpart to the British Tiller Girls, the fashionable dance troupe whose highly synchronized movements set the tone for popular entertainment in the Weimar period. Touted in the press as the "New Woman," the Tiller Girl was heralded by many as an icon of modern sexuality, the new, independent woman whose control over her body and her life reflected the liberated norms of the Roaring Twenties. Expressionist dance, the deeply subjective, avant-garde dance form developed by the schools of Rudolf von Laban, Mary Wigman, Jutta Klamt, Berthe Trümpy, and others in the Weimar period, was integral to state-sponsored events in the Nazi period, including the German Dance Congresses (Tanzfestspiele) held in Berlin in 1934 and 1935 and the opening night ceremonies of the 1936 Olympic Games. On an aesthetic level, the prevalence of both the cabaret revue and expressionist dance under the Nazi regime is surprising. Why was the revue, the prototypical expression of modernity, appropriated by the regime? On the other hand, why did expressionist dance continue to prosper under the Third Reich while expressionist art was cast out, castigated as degenerate in the *Entartete Kunst Ausstellung* (Degenerate art exhibition) in Munich in 1937? And why did Rudolf von Laban and Mary Wigman fall out of favor with the regime despite their aesthetic endeavors to further a National Socialist ideology?

---

sterilization that was instituted in 1933 resulted in the sterilization of almost all Afro-Germans in 1937 and about 200,000 other German women by 1945 (275). As Bock points out, the sterilization law was based on psychiatric, not ethnic, conditions, but it was applied in large part to "inferior" groups such as Jews, Gypsies, and Afro-Germans. For a larger discussion of eugenics policies and sterilization measures in the Third Reich, see Gisela Bock, *Zwangssterilisation im Nationalsozialismus* (Opladen, 1986).

This essay advances the thesis that the cultural liberation of sexuality in performance art in the Third Reich served in a number of cases to fortify the otherwise restrictive sexual politics of the state. The redeployment of sexuality in Nazi Germany often had domestic and political resonance, reinforcing the role of woman as "natural" wife and mother and rechanneling female sexuality into the service of the state. As opposed to anti-Semitic propaganda, whose aim was to induce aversion and separation, projections of femininity in the Third Reich fostered desire. This essay examines the complexity of the issue of desire in the Third Reich, exploring the extent to which a discourse of inclusion in the social body provided the necessary complement to a discourse of exclusion from it. It examines the extent to which the successful deployment of a Nazi ideology was driven as much by seduction as by separation, by the projection of female iconography in positive identificatory images and individually overwhelming spatial patterns.[2] In drawing on but also reworking Weimar norms, some of the performance art in the period performed a twofold operation whereby it simultaneously met audience expectations and desires and redirected them into the interests of the larger *Gemeinschaft* (community).

This thesis builds upon an observation made by Herbert Marcuse in his writings of the 1940s. According to Marcuse, sexuality in the Third Reich was marked not by repression but rather by liberation, by a liberation from the Christian precepts of chastity, monogamy, and the sanctity of the

[2]While a substantial amount of work has been done on the aestheticization of politics under National Socialism, very little of it pertains to the representation of women. The armored fascist male body has been a considerable object of study, from Klaus Theweleit's two-volume *Male Fantasies* (Minneapolis, 1987–1989) to Susan Sontag's "Fascinating Fascism," in *Under the Sign of Saturn* (New York, 1980; originally published in the *New York Review of Books*, February 6, 1975) to more recent work by Peter Reichel, George Mosse, and Harold Segel. The exploration of the female body constitutes a relatively new area of interest. Two important historical works treat the dance phenomenon in the Nazi period: Hedwig Müller and Patricia Stöckemann, eds., " . . . jeder Mensch ist ein Tänzer": Ausdruckstanz in Deutschland zwischen 1900 and 1945 (Gießen, 1993), a catalog of the expressionist dance exhibition "Weltenfriede—Jugendglück" (World peace—youthful joy) held at the Akademie der Künste in Berlin from May 2 through June 13, 1993; and Lilian Karina and Marion Kant, *Tanz unterm Hakenkreuz: Eine Dokumentation* (Berlin, 1996), an archival study of Nazi dance policy. Particularly important is Susan Manning's *Ecstasy and the Demon* (Berkeley, 1993), a study of feminism and nationalism in Mary Wigman's work. Furthermore, only recently has criticism begun to approach the specific concern of mass entertainment in relationship to mass politics. In 1979 the SDK hosted a revue film retrospective, out of which the work *Wir tanzen um die Welt: Deutsche Revuefilme 1933–1945*, ed. Helga Belach (Munich and Vienna, 1979), a collection of articles on the German revue film in the Nazi period, was compiled. Karsten Witte's work on the German revue provides an essential foundation for my study of the staged revue and the revue film. Also important are a number of more recent works, notably, Eric Rentschler's invaluable study of Nazi cinema, *The Ministry of Illusion: Nazi Cinema and Its Afterlife* (Cambridge, Mass., 1996); Linda Schulte-Sasse's critical examination of entertainment film in the Nazi period, *Entertaining the Third Reich: Illusions of Wholeness in Nazi Cinema* (Durham, 1996); and Peter Jelavich's essential study of the cabaret in Weimar and the Third Reich, *Berlin Cabaret* (Cambridge, Mass., 1993).

home that have informed so much of Western morality: "The Third Reich has done away with discrimination against illegitimate mothers and children, it has encouraged extra-marital relations between the sexes, introduced a new cult of nudity in art and entertainment, and dissolved the protective and educational functions of the family."[3] Marcuse argues that the abolition of taboos in the Third Reich led paradoxically to a "greater repression of liberty" in that it coordinated the private and political sphere, integrating private functions into political life and deepening individual allegiances to the political system. "The *abolition of highly sanctioned taboos* is one of the most daring enterprises of National Socialism in the field of mass domination," Marcuse writes. "For, paradoxical as it may seem, the liberty or license implied in this abolition serves to intensify the 'Gleichschaltung' of individuals into the National Socialist system."[4] Marcuse designates three factors that effectively counteracted the "abolition of taboos" under National Socialism:

1. The emancipation of sexual behavior was bound up with the eugenics policies of the Third Reich, which connected released sexual desires to an external state end.

2. The political intervention in sexual life destroyed the emancipatory potential of the private sphere, which no longer served as a locus of privacy and protest.

3. The exclusive nature of Third Reich sexual privilege fostered antagonistic sentiments of racism and biological superiority.

This essay takes up what Marcuse has called the "new cult of nudity in art and entertainment," examining the question of *Gleichschaltung* (coordination) of the sexual and the social in the realm of performance art. In the larger context of a discussion of the staged revue and revue film, the *Körperkultur* (body culture) movement as it developed from the early nineteenth century, and the expressionist dance movements of Laban and Wigman, I will focus specifically on two films, the 1939 German revue film, *Wir tanzen um die Welt* (We're dancing around the world), and Leni Riefenstahl's two-part documentary of the 1936 Olympic Games in Berlin. In exploring the aesthetic significance of dance in the Nazi period, this study aims to further our understanding of the complicated relationship between sexuality and sexual politics.

FROM TROUPES TO TROOPS: FASCIST APPROPRIATION OF THE FEMALE REVUE

In the winter of 1933, German dramatist and National Socialist Hanns Johst made a visit to the Folies-Bergère in Paris. The holiday show featured the

[3]Herbert Marcuse, "State and Individual under National Socialism," in *Technology, War and Fascism: Collected Papers of Herbert Marcuse*, vol. 1, ed. Douglas Kellner (London, 1998), 84. I am grateful to Dagmar Herzog for drawing my attention to this connection.
[4]Ibid., 84.

leading French music-hall artist, Mistinguett, and a giant Christmas tree lit
up by the luminous bodies of twenty naked women. In the show,
Mistinguett wants to clothe the living candles but finds that her wallet is
empty. At a signal, the orchestra intones a mass, and a prayer is sent to the
heavens. The prayer is answered, thanks are offered, and an English waltz
sweeps the entire group off to the latest fashion studio. In *Maske und
Gesicht: Reise eines Nationalsozialisten von Deutschland nach Deutschland*,
Johst draws our attention to three central elements of the theatrical display:
the sounds of "unleashed jazz" opening the act, the "stark naked virgins"
adorning the tree, and the unholy mixture of the secular and the sacred.
Johst is appalled at the depths to which the "foreign industry in eroticism"
has sunk. "If we staged the same tastelessness and infamy against the sacred
rites of the church in Germany," he writes, "the whole world would gnash
their teeth and clack their typewriters in indignation and offer up psalms
against heathenism."[5]

Hanns Johst's verdict is emblematic of a National Socialist stance. As a
cultural paradigm, the cabaret revue stood for all that National Socialism
eschewed: modernity, mass culture, and French and American decadence.
Associated with "Nigger-jazz" music and Jewish capitalist interests, the
Weimar revue was considered a form of pseudoculture that reflected the
overall degeneration of the modern metropolis.[6] For Propaganda Minister
Joseph Goebbels, Berlin in the Weimar period was a "Babylon of Sin," a
den of iniquity whose throbbing nightlife bore the imprint of foreign
hands.[7] In an article entitled "Rund um die Gedächtniskirche" that appeared in *Der Angriff* in January 1928, Goebbels describes the "spirit of
the asphalt democracy" as "the eternal repetition of corruption and decay,

[5]Hanns Johst, *Maske und Gesicht: Reise eine Nationalsozialisten von Deutschland nach
Deutschland* (Munich, 1935), 181–82. I am indebted to Karsten Witte for this example.
For a discussion of the revue film under the Third Reich, see Karsten Witte, "Gehemmte
Schaulust: Momente des deutschen Revuefilms," in Belach, ed., 7–52, translated as "Visual
Pleasure Inhibited: Aspects of the German Revue Film," *New German Critique* 24–25
(fall/winter 1981–82): 238–63.

[6]National Socialist critics attributed "foreign" dances, such as the fox-trot and the Charleston, to blacks and Jews. The theater world was seen to lie largely in Jewish hands, domi-
nated by a vast network of Jewish impresarios, producers, and critics. In Nazi discourse,
jazz was linked via America to Jews. Epithets in articles in the press at the time include
"Jazzproduktion—Judendomäne" and "Der Jazz als Kampfmittel des Judentums und des
Amerikanismus" (Max Merz, *Die Bewegung*, December 6, 1938, in Karina and Kant, 50;
Carl Hannemann, "Der Jazz als Kampfmittel des Judentums und des Amerikanismus,"
Musik in Jugend und Volk [1943], in Joseph Wulf, *Musik im Dritten Reich: Eine
Dokumentation* [Frankfurt am Main, 1983], 392). See Michael H. Kater's *Different Drum-
mers: Jazz in the Culture of Nazi Germany* (New York, 1992) for an excellent discussion of
the fate of jazz under the Third Reich. Kater argues that jazz continued to exist and at times
to flourish in Nazi Germany for a variety of reasons, including competition with British
broadcasts and the desire to maintain normalcy in a state of war.

[7]Elke Fröhlich, ed., *Die Tagebücher von Joseph Goebbels: Sämtliche Fragmente* (Munich,
1987), 1:144, quoted in Kater, 23.

of failing ingenuity and genuine creative power, of inner emptiness and despair, with the patina of a Zeitgeist sunk to the level of the most repulsive pseudoculture."[8] Berlin West, a metropolitan mixture of pan-Europeanism, bolshevism, and jazz, which Goebbels attributes to the "Israelites," has rendered the German people alien and superfluous. *Zivilisation* has replaced *Kultur*. Judea has conquered Rome. "This is not the true Berlin," Goebbels laments.[9]

Yet, following the Nazi purification of the arts in 1933, the "Girls" remained an important staple of Berlin's entertainment industry, performing for civilians in the city's major music halls and for German soldiers stationed abroad.[10] In the 1930s three variety theaters, the Wintergarten, the Scala, and the Plaza, regularly showcased revues, and the German revue film, which borrowed heavily in style and content from Busby Berkeley musicals, became a genre in itself. Under the direction of Rolf Hiller, the German Hiller Girls became a national icon: "It is Germany's best and most famous Girl troupe. What the Tiller-Girls are for America [*sic*], the Hiller-Girls are for Germany: our most spirited and most thoroughbred Girl troupe."[11]

This appropriation of the "decadent" dance by the far Right is surprising. The erotic images deployed on stage stand in sharp counterpoint to the natural, healthy body espoused under the Third Reich. The female iconography in the eight *Great German Art Exhibitions* held at the House of German Art in Munich from 1937 to 1944 presented a monotonous variation on the theme of the sacred wife and mother.[12] Frequently depicted were neoclassical nudes in allegorical poses by Ivo Saliger and

---

[8]Joseph Goebbels, "Rund um die Gedächtniskirche," *Der Angriff*, January 23, 1928, translation in *The Weimar Republic Sourcebook*, ed. Anton Kaes, Martin Jay, and Edward Dimendberg (Berkeley, 1994), 561.

[9]Ibid.

[10]Under the direction of Robert Ley, the Kraft durch Freude (Strength through Joy, or KdF) division of the Deutsche Arbeitsfront organized entertainment events (theater, cabaret, variety shows, and the like) and Wehrmacht tours. In November 1940 the Hiller Girls went on a month-long KdF *Wehrmachtstournee* to occupied Belgium and northern France. According to Maria Milde's memoirs, the motto of the tour was "Die Wachtparade kommt" (The *Wachtparade* is coming). See Maria Milde, *Berlin glienicker Brücke* (Berlin, 1978), 41. For a larger discussion of the revue under National Socialism, see Jelavich, "Cabaret under National Socialism," in *Berlin Cabaret*, 228–57.

[11]Press release from 1938 (source unspecified) in Milde, 17. The "national" character of the Scala Girls, "Europas Elitetrupp" (Europe's elite troupe), was also emphasized in the press and publicity of the period, as is evident in the program notes to the October 1934 Scala-Festspiel: "The fairy tale that only English or American Girls can form good troupes will finally be buried this month. In four weeks, the inventive director Anthony Nelle has made the Elite Troupe of Europe out of German girls" (7).

[12]For a discussion of the "Great German Art Exhibitions," see Peter Adam, *Art of the Third Reich* (New York, 1992), 92–119. As Claudia Koonz has pointed out, Nazism was understood by its own proponents to be an "entirely male event" (*Mothers in the Fatherland: Women, the Family and Nazi Politics* [New York, 1987], 56). In the ideology of a

Friedrich Wilhelm Kalb and neorealist paintings of the nurturing mother
with child by pastoral artists such as Franz Eichhorst, Alfred Kitzig, and
Fritz Mackensen. Nudity in the Third Reich was to be "schön und rein"
(beautiful and pure), as the headline in an article entitled "Für echte und
edle Nacktheit" (For authentic and noble nudity) reads. The piece, which
appeared in October 1938 in the SS organ *Das Schwarze Korps*, features a
photographic series of nude women bathing and hiking in nature.[13] As
Peter Jelavich points out, the appropriation of the revue under National
Socialism points to a contradiction and hypocrisy in Nazi rhetoric, which
some on the far Right did not hesitate to protest.[14] In 1936, for example,
a storm trooper registered outrage at the display of three half-naked dancers at the Stella-Palast in Berlin: "One feels that one has been sent back to
the worst times of the Weimar era. National Socialism has not fought its
battles so that today, in the seventh year of the Third Reich, German people
are offered such Semitic–oriental–erotic veil–games as diversion."[15]

What accounts for the prevalence of these "Semitic–oriental–erotic veil–
games" in cinematic and theatrical productions under the Third Reich?
This question rejoins the larger issue of the significance of entertainment
film in the Nazi period. Under the aegis of Ufa (Universum-Film
Aktiengesellschaft), the "deutsche Bildimperium" (German empire of
images), the Nazi period was the "golden age of German cinema," producing over one thousand feature films.[16] In a diary entry dated March 1,
1942, Goebbels noted that entertainment was of particular political value
due to its capacity to promote "unsichtbare Propaganda" (invisible propaganda): "Even entertainment can be politically of special value, because

---

world structured according to a natural order, women were considered a support for the
male soldier at home, biologically reproductive machines upholding the race and regime in
the separate, private sphere of a female *Lebensraum*. See Koonz, "Nazi Women and Their
'Freedom Movement,'" in ibid., 53–90. The notion of the sacred German wife and mother
was a recurrent theme in Hitler's written and public discourse. In a speech to the National
Socialist Women's Congress in 1935, for example, Hitler declared, "The woman has her
own battlefield. With every child she brings to the world, she fights her battle for the
nation. The man stands up for the *Volk*, exactly as the woman stands up for the family"
(*Völkischer Beobachter*, September 15, 1935, quoted in translation in Adam, 140).

[13] See Jelavich, 253.

[14] Ibid., 251.

[15] Harmut Reichenbach to *Reichskulturkammer*, June 26, 1939, quoted in translation in
ibid., 253. See also ibid., 228-57, for a fuller discussion of responses from the far Right to
the persistence of *Girlkultur* during the Nazi period.

[16] Rentschler, *The Ministry of Illusion*, 2–4. Rentschler refers to the nostalgia of Ufa stars
of the epoch who "appear on talk shows to reminisce about the 'golden age of German
cinema'" (4). See Rentschler's study of Nazi cinema for an in-depth analysis of the importance of mass culture and entertainment to the politics of the Third Reich. For full-length
studies of Ufa, see Hans Borgelt, *Die UFA—Ein Traum: Hundert Jahre deutscher Film*
(Berlin, 1993), and Klaus Kreimeier, *The Ufa Story: A History of Germany's Greatest Film
Company 1918–1945*, trans. Robert and Rita Kimber (New York, 1996).

the moment a person is conscious of propaganda, propaganda becomes ineffective. However, as soon as propaganda as a tendency, as a characteristic, as an attitude, remains in the background and becomes apparent through human beings, then propaganda becomes effective in every respect."[17] Outside of any manifest political import, entertainment was useful in and of itself as a powerful tool for distraction, particularly in the war years. In a speech made in March 1942, Goebbels claimed that "auch die gute Laune ist kriegswichtig" [good spirits are also important to the war effort].[18] In a speech entitled "Der Film als Erzieher" (Film as educator), made on the occasion of the opening of the Filmarbeit der HJ (Cinema of the Hitler Youth) in October 1941, Goebbels announced that "we should not fail to appreciate the fact that film, as the greatest and most profound form of mass art there is, also serves as a medium of entertainment. But in this time, in which the entire nation is burdened with such heavy weights and worries, entertainment also takes on particular political value."[19]

On a formal level, the aesthetic of the revue lends itself to political appropriation. A troupe, which dance critic André Levinson calls "a caterpillar with thirty-two feet," performs as a geometrical unit.[20] In the press of the Weimar period, the collective ethos of the popular dance troupes gave rise to visions of the assembly line and the military corps.[21] Products of a thriving "Girl" industry, the girls performed in kaleidoscopic patterns that reflected the regularity and replication characteristic of mass production. In "Girls und Krise" (Girls and crisis), a review of the performance of the Alfred Jackson Girls at the Scala in 1931, Siegfried Kracauer compared the revue as a whole to the "ideal of the machine," a "girl contraption" comprised of indivisible and indistinguishable parts.[22] For German critic Alfred Polgar, the collective corps of the revue evoked not the movements of the machine but "the magic of militarism": "the obedience to invisible but ineluctable orders, the marvelous 'drill,' the submersion of the individual into the group, the concentration of bodies

[17]Institut für Zeitgeschichte, Munich, *Goebbels Tagebuch* (unpublished sections), entry for March 1, 1942, quoted in translation in David Welch, *Propaganda and the German Cinema: 1933–1945* (Oxford, 1983), 45.

[18]Goebbels, "Der treue Helfer," speech dated March 1, 1942: "Good spirits are also important to the war effort. Keeping spirits high, especially when we have particularly heavy burdens to bear, is necessary to the successful command of the war effort on the front and at home." In Joseph Goebbels, *Das eherne Herz: Reden und Aufsätze aus den Jahren 1941/42* (Munich, 1943), 233.

[19]Goebbels, "Der Film als Erzieher," in ibid., 38.

[20]André Levinson, "The Girls," trans. Ralph Roeder, in *André Levinson on Dance*, ed. Joan Acocella and Lynn Garafola (Hanover, 1991), 91, from *Theatre Arts Monthly* (August 1928).

[21]For a discussion of machine and military metaphors in the Weimar press, see Jelavich, "Girls and Crisis," in *Berlin Cabaret*, 175–86.

[22]Siegfried Kracauer, "Girls und Krise," *Frankfurter Zeitung*, May 26, 1931, translation in Kaes, 565.

into a single collective 'body.'"[23] The girls themselves often assumed the form of the images they evoked, appearing on stage as automatons, factory parts, conveyor belts, wooden dolls, and uniformed soldiers. Due to the absolute synchronicity of their gestures and the highly mechanical nature of their movements, the dancers deployed notions of order, discipline, and control.

The reactionary potential of such an aesthetic is most clearly expressed in the works of L.-F. Céline, whose passion for cabaret dancers is reflected in his entire oeuvre as well as in his raw writing style, a style that formally emulates the art of the dance.[24] In his works published in the early 1930s such as *Voyage au bout de la nuit* (1932), *L'Eglise* (1933), and *Progrès* (1932), Céline saw the Anglo-Saxon cabaret dancer as a model of biological strength and hygiene. The American dancer in *Progrès*, for example, fulfills the promise of a new world order based on health and harmony. In a *maison de rendez-vous*, she reveals the strong, rhythmic lines of her contoured body, giving rise to a vision of "the day in which women will be dressed only in muscle . . . and music."[25] In his correspondence in the 1930s, Céline wrote: "This stay in England was an enchantment. What a cult of physical beauty! What marvelous music halls! What legs! What out-of-this-world entertainers! Ah! How one feels boring, insipid and tired next to these muscular comics. Life is there, nowhere else, alas!"[26] In a piece that appeared in *Theatre Arts Monthly* in 1928, André Levinson took a more critical stance on this serialized cult of beauty, viewing the girls as a sign of the supremacy bestowed upon the biological and mechanical in the modern age. "They are pure symbol, the living image of our life, which substitutes for the glamour of the mind and the quest of the sublime the worship of biological forces and mechanical forces," Levinson wrote. "That is the lesson we should take to heart, as we watch—like the Romans of the Decadence—the parade of these 'sturdy, blonde Barbarians.'"[27]

[23]Alfred Polgar, "Girls," in *Auswahl: Prosa aus vier Jahrzehnten* (Reinbek, 1968), 186–87, quoted in translation in Detlev J. K. Peukert, *The Weimar Republic*, trans. Richard Deveson (New York, 1987), 180.

[24]"I only want to work for dancers," Céline declares in his reactionary political pamphlet, *Bagatelles pour un massacre* (1937). "Everything for the dance! Nothing but the dance!" (L.-F. Céline, *Bagatelles pour un massacre* [Paris: Denoël, 1937], 12). At the opening of *Bagatelles*, Céline reveals to his Jewish interlocuter, Léo Gutman, his "despotic desire," his "devastating passion" for dancers: "I recently opened up to a buddy of mine, Léo Gutman, a good old physician like me, only better, about this more and more persistent, pronounced, virulent, what am I saying, absolutely despotic desire that has come over me for dancers. . . . I confessed everything about my devastating passion" (12).

[25]Céline, *Progrès*, in *Oeuvres*, vol. 9 (Paris, 1981), 276.

[26]Quoted in André Derval, "'Je suis tout à la danse,'" *Magazine littéraire* 292 (October 1991): 52.

[27]Levinson, "The Girls," 94.

It is the esprit de corps at the heart of the aesthetic that, I suggest, allowed for the fascist appropriation of the revue. In their projection of uniform images of health and harmony, the dance troupes generated an illusion of wholeness, which, as Linda Schulte-Sasse has persuasively argued, was integral to cinematic productions in the Third Reich. According to Schulte-Sasse, Nazi spectacle was both "creative and camouflaging," fulfilling the function of renewing communal sensations, "of incessantly reinforcing an imaginary collective identity via rituals sustaining the illusion of social harmony."[28] The performances of the German Hiller Girls constituted a *rappel à l'ordre*, an aesthetic that is most clearly manifested in the opening sequence of *Es leuchten die Sterne* (The stars are shining) (Tobis 1937–38), in which a starry-eyed young hopeful finds herself transported into a royal performance in the genre of the baroque court ballet. To the sounds of a march, long lines of soldier-girls in matching uniforms march up and down a sweeping staircase, forming rhythmic patterns of vertical and diagonal lines and performing court-martial exercises with their swords. Already the disciplined body of the British Tiller girls had left a strong impression on Hitler, who described these "Aryan dancers" as the "fantastic Tiller Girls."[29]

As Karsten Witte points out, the geometric ordering of space in the revue provided a ready forum for the manifestation of military spirit, mediating both a fear of chaos and a fear of decadence.[30] "By 1939, the Girls had already joined the gigantic process of getting into uniform . . . ," Witte states, "turning troupes into troops from which the soldiers of art were supposed to sally forth."[31] In their formal composition, the troupes provided an aesthetic vehicle for political propaganda, often appearing on stage in full military attire. In a 1937 performance at the Wintergarten featuring the Hiller Girls, the show opened with a parade march in front of the Brandenburg Gate. The 1940 program of the Scala, whose insignia is an iconographic imprint of saluting soldiers, shows the Scala girls executing a Prussian military march under a waving red banner.[32] A 1939 poster features a shot of the Hiller girls outfitted in military uniform and fully armed, above which a caption reads: "Das Hiller-Ballet: Deutschlands beste Girltruppe: Ein Körper-, Ein Rhythmus-, Ein Schlag-!" [The Hiller-Ballet: Germany's best Girl troupe: one body-, one rhythm-, one beat-!].[33] Troupes become troops,[34] and the revue takes on its original meaning as military parade. Hiller Girl Maria Milde disavowed any political import, claiming in

[28]Schulte-Sasse, 28.
[29]Henry Picker, *Hitlers Tischgespräche im Führerhauptquartier, 1941–42*, 2nd ed. (Stuttgart, 1965), 209, quoted in part in Jelavich, 253.
[30]Witte, "Visual Pleasure Inhibited," 244.
[31]Ibid., 242.
[32]See Jelavich, 254–55.
[33]Reprinted in Müller and Stöckemann, 137.
[34]I owe this terminology to Karsten Witte.

her memoires, "Wir wollen uns mit Kunst beschäftigen, nicht mit Politik" [We want to deal with art, not politics].[35]

Wir tanzen um die Welt (Karl Anton), a revue film produced by state-controlled Tobis in 1939, exemplifies the military ethos characteristic of the staged revue in the Nazi period. The film, characterized by Gerd Albrecht in his *Nationalsozialistische Filmpolitik* as an "H" (*heitere*) film, a "light" or "cheerful" film, centers around the eighteen Jenny Hill girls, a dance troupe that conquers the world. Making a clear allusion to the Hiller Girls, the film provides a cinematographic rendition of the trials and tribulations of "Germany's best Girl troupe." *Wir tanzen um die Welt* premiered on December 22, 1939, in Düsseldorf and opened on January 19, 1940, in the Ufa-Palast am Zoo in Berlin, accompanied by a full press and advertising campaign. The film grossed over 1.6 million RM in its run in Germany, ranking it among the most popular of the light entertainment films of the 1939 season.[36] Evaluated twice by NS film censors in December 1939, the film was rated as "künstlerisch wertvoll" (artistically worthwhile).

The film opens in the Jenny Hill dance studio to the sound of the ticking of a metronome, whose rhythmic beat is picked up in a montage of initial shots. Like the British Tiller Girls, whose "machinelike precision" served as a "regulating metronome," the German Jenny Hill girls perform with clocklike precision, the beat of the metronome resounding in the martial movements of their dance.[37] Outfitted in metallic Roman gladiator costumes and feathered helmets, the girls perform a singular military march on the stages of Europe's capital cities, from Paris to Bucharest to Stockholm to Rome (fig. 1). Set against a backdrop of Olympic torches perched on Roman pillars, the dance sequence recasts antiquity in a modern mode. The curtain opens to a backlit stage. Like figures in a shadow show, the girls

---

[35]Milde, 92. Revue film star Marika Rökk makes a similar claim, claiming to be "unpolitical, through and through": "I made my career in Germany during the time of National Socialism. That was bitterly thrown back at me after the war. For three of my most vital years, I was forbidden to work [*Berufsverbot*] and people were allowed to call me a 'spy,' to spit at me, to show me to the door. What was I paying for? . . . I liked, loved, and admired Germany, and I couldn't judge the regime, I was totally unpolitical then, and am totally unpolitical now. I always concentrated on my career. Obviously, as an Ufa star, I stood on the sunny side of life in Nazi Germany, while Jacoby had to contend with all sorts of difficulties. . . . I am unpolitical. Through and through. I never vote, never joined a party. . . . When I received my first invitation to a reception at the 'Führer's,' I thought, above all: What should I wear? I was twenty-six years old" (*Herz mit Paprika: Erinnerungen* [Munich, 1988], 132–33).

[36]Of the twenty-four films that Gerd Albrecht classifies as "H" films in the 1939 season, *Wir tanzen um die Welt* ranks in the top 20 percent in box office returns. See Albrecht, *Nationalsozialistische Filmpolitik* (Stuttgart, 1969), 410–11. For a synopsis of the film, see Karsten Witte, "Revue als montierte Handlung," in Belach, ed., 222–23.

[37]On the Haller Revue, "Wann und Wo" (1927), Weimar critic Adam Kuckhoff refers to the "machine-like precision of the Tiller Girls [that] seems like a regulating metronome" [die maschinenhafte Präzision der Tillergirls (die) wie das regelnde Metronom erscheint] ("Größe und Niedergang der Revue," *Die Volksbühne* 3, no. 1 [April 1928]: 6).

Figure 1. *Wir tanzen um die Welt* (Tobis, 1939): the German Jenny Hill girls performing a military march. Photo courtesy of the Film Museum Berlin, Deutsche Kinemathek.

march in silhouette to the top of the steps, at which point the lights go up, the Olympic torches burst into flame, and the dancers swing their batons in the air with a flourish. In groups of two, they march dramatically down the steps, forming a military V formation and performing a synchronized dance and tap routine. As the performance comes to a climactic finale, the music reaches a crescendo, and the troupe sweeps triumphantly down the steps in a final military march. The whole of the sequence is filmed with sharp camera angles, visible cuts, and a high depth of field that add a dimension of magnitude, power, and space to the visual iconography.

In *Wir tanzem um die Welt*, troupe is an extended metaphor for troop. The legs of the girls, which Kracauer compared to the hands of the factory worker, now figure as a metaphor for the arms of war. The caption of a publicity piece of the time reads: "36 Beine erobern die Welt" [36 legs conquer the world].[38] The troupe, whose motto is "to be young and victorious," is organized according to militaristic, hierarchical principles, with Jenny Hill (Lucie Höflich) as the general, Norma (Charlotte Thiele) as the lieutenant, and Eva (Irene von Meyendorff) as the second-in-command. Under the guiding hand of Norma, the "iron-willed" blond "captain-girl,"

[38]Publicity matter reproduced in *Wir tanzen um die Welt* program (SDK Schriftgut Archiv).

the girls develop a deep sense of discipline and order. An article in the press extols, "Hard work, camaraderie, discipline and readiness to assume responsibility—herein lies the secret to the Girls' success in all of the major variety theaters of the world."[39] The troupe prevails heroically in the face of a series of sinister sabotage attempts by Jonny Hester, the fast-talking, cigar-smoking New York agent who represents "Jewish" capitalist interests. Even a fire that destroys their dressing rooms and costumes cannot prevent them from taking the stage in the last performance on their tour, a feat that the emcee calls "ein Musterbeispiel von Beherrschung und Disziplin" [a model of control and discipline].[40] The final victory of the troupe marks an international triumph, as is indicated by the closing image of a rotating globe, upon which images of a ship, a train, and a plane are superimposed.

On the surface, *Wir tanzen um die Welt* appears to follow in the tradition of the nonintegrated, escapist entertainment film in the genre of the Busby Berkeley musical. The film contains elements of classic Hollywood light entertainment fare: a clear demarcation between good and evil (the pure Jenny Hill Girls versus the three "bad boys" of the corrupt entertainment industry), a transparent plot (Jonny Hester's attempt to destroy the troupe through the decoy of handsome Harvey Swington), a linear narrative development (a series of sabotage attempts that increase in seriousness as the film progresses), passion and romance, and a moralistic happy ending (the troupe prevails, Norma and Harvey are united, Harvey is reformed and repentant). Like the nonintegrated musical, dance numbers are interspersed (here in ever briefer sequences) throughout the story in the "real" setting of a stage. But on a more profound level, *Wir tanzen um die Welt* acts in a decidedly "unrevue" way. Karsten Witte suggests that the German revue reverses the hierarchy of spectacle over plot that prevails in American musicals, a thesis that is borne out by *Wir tanzen um die Welt*. "It is not at all a question of a revue film!" claimed composer-writer Willi Kollo in an interview. "Dance in this film is only background. The subject matter of the story is the life of a world-famous girl troupe, how, behind the scenes of the glittering music halls, so to speak, it furthers its inexorable fate through every single Girl and through the community!"[41] In an article entitled "The Soul of the Girls," critic H. W. Fürth deplored the "triumph of the body over the soul" evident in the militarized erotic of the revue but also emphasized the

[39] Publicity notice in "*Wir tanzen um die Welt* Reklame-Ratschläge" (SDK Schriftgut Archiv).

[40] *Wir tanzen um die Welt*, screenplay by Willi Kollo and Felix von Eckardt, archived at the SDK. It is to the discipline at the heart of the organization that Jenny Hill appeals in the moment of crisis: "Costumes and coiffures don't matter, only discipline. Our slogan states: Be young and victorious! So girls . . ." The program note from the October 1934 Scala-Festspiele echoes the sentiment of the emcee: "Our 24 Scala-Girls: . . . A model of discipline and community spirit, . . . never has there been a girl troupe that displayed so much rhythmic precision and at the same time so much grace" (7).

[41] V. Wlemer, "Synkopen, Skalen, Step, Esprit," in "*Wir tanzen um die Welt* Informations-Unterlagen" (n.d.), publicity material from Bundesarchiv, Film Abteilung.

film's "deeper" import. "When you see them on the stage, when they, moved by a single, taut rhythm, goose-stepping and tapping in a hard staccato, perform their art, they blend into an anonymous whole, into a singular, giant ornamental figure. But the deeper appeal of this show lies precisely in the fact that living, blooming, sensitive Girl-bodies are hiding behind this masquerade, and that their hearts beat just as quick and strong as the hearts of all girls and women."[42]

The deeper meaning of the film lies not in the romantic life of the girls but, rather, in the communal ethos that binds them together, the end of which remains unnamed. Articles in the press of the period repeatedly refer to the *Gemeinschaftsgeist* (communal spirit) of the group and its *Gemeinschaftsschicksal* (communal fate). As opposed to the thematic divide between socially realistic narratives and escapist numbers that often mark Busby Berkeley musicals, here narrative and numbers cohere.[43] Here we find none of the spectacular flights of fancy that are the hallmark of the American musical, none of the sweeping transformations in space and time that are typical of the genre. Unlike the Busby Berkeley–styled films of the 1930s and 1940s, such as the Depression-era classics *Footlight Parade* (1933) and *Gold Diggers of 1933* (1933) or the World War I musical *For Me and My Gal* (1942), whose magical dance sequences provide a utopian elsewhere to a grim social reality, the stirring martial dance in *Wir tanzen um die Welt* formally reinforces the plotline. With the film's emphasis on the communal good, the collective dance sequences themselves take on deeper meaning as a physical expression of the spirit of the troupe. This vision of community for community's sake allows the film to differentiate the German revue from its American counterpart. Here, the National Socialist–oriented vision of the Weimar revue as a decadent Jewish phenomenon serving capitalist interests is projected onto the American entertainment industry, while the "German" troupe stands outside of the system in which it operates. A publicity notice emphasizes the stark divide between the values of the principled troupe and the "evil machinations" of their American rivals: "Berlin—Copenhagen—Rotterdam—Bucharest—Paris—Rome—Lisbon—Oslo—Vienna—Stockholm—these are the cities of their triumph, but also the scenes of their worries, their plight and their struggle: through the most evil machinations of their American rivals and their unscrupulous agents, the girls will be put in grave danger. But the lowest schemes of the enemy founder against the formidable strength of will of the principled leader [*Führerin*] of this troupe, Norma, and the unity of

[42]H. W. Fürth, "Die Seele der Girls," in ibid.

[43]For a discussion of the "utopian sensibility" in American musicals and the relationship between narrative and number that structures them, see Richard Dyer, "Entertainment and Utopia," in *Genre: The Musical*, ed. Rick Altman (London, 1981), 175–89. For a further discussion of the modes in the musical, see Martin Sutton, "Patterns of Meaning in the Musical," in ibid., 190–96.

the Girls."[44] In his famous 1927 essay, Kracauer called the mass ornament an "end in itself," a self-contained system that reflects the closed economy of the larger capitalist system.[45] *Wir tanzen um die Welt* effects a shift in the end of the revue from capitalist consumption toward a greater good. The primordial principle of the troupe is the troupe itself. Participation in the organization is guided solely by principle, not pecuniary or personal gain. Sylvia, Julika, and Margrit, the three performers who leave the troupe to pursue independent careers, are considered deserters. "We belong together," Norma berates them. "There is no such thing as autonomy. Get that through your heads."[46] In sharp contrast to the purity of the world of the Jenny Hill ballet, the "deserters" end up as prostitutes in the quintessential space of capitalist corruption, an exotic strip joint, where they perform half-naked in Oriental attire.

In its culture of physical and spiritual collectivity, the world of the Jenny Hill Girls resembles that of the Bund deutscher Mädel (League of German Girls, or BDM), the female equivalent of the Hitler Youth. In 1939 there were over 1.5 million girls registered in the BDM.[47] An organization for girls between the ages of fourteen and twenty-one, the BDM, whose activities included nature walks, sporting events, social services, and political rallies, provided training in body and mind.[48] Like the members of the Hitler Youth, the girls in the BDM received instruction in National Socialist ideology, learning at a tender age to direct their personal interests into service of the state. "The oath that the girls swear when they are initiated on the eve of Hitler's birthday includes the clause of self-sacrifice," writes Gregor Ziemer in *Education for Death*. "From the minute they don the BDM uniforms, elaborate with emblems, letters, triangles, and swastikas, one thought governs their lives; a mature thought, nourished by biological eagerness and restlessness: What can we do, what can we learn, how can we live to prepare ourselves for our great mission—to be the mothers of Hitler's future soldiers?"[49]

[44]Publicity notice in "*Wir tanzen um die Welt* Reklame–Ratschläge."

[45]Siegfried Kracauer, "The Mass Ornament," *New German Critique* 5 (spring 1975): 68–69.

[46]*Wir tanzem um die Welt*, screenplay. In "Revue als montierte Handlung," Karsten Witte points to the militaristic aspect of deserting that informs the troupe's notion of unity: "To take on another engagement means 'to desert'" (in Belach, ed., 222).

[47]Koonz, 196. For an historical analysis of the Bund deutscher Mädel, see Dagmar Reese, *Straff, aber nicht stramm—Herb, aber nicht derb* (Weinheim and Basel, 1989).

[48]See Gregor Ziemer, *Education for Death: The Making of the Nazi* (New York, 1941), 123–44. Ziemer describes a typical day at a camp north of Berlin where a group of girls resided during their *Land Jahr*: "The girls got up at six o'clock, had outdoor calisthenics, prepared their own meals, had an hour of instruction in BDM ideology daily. They carried a heavy program of sports. Often they were sent out into the neighborhood to help the peasant women with their housework or their field work. In the evenings they sang, listened to more lectures on the duties of women in the Third Reich" (127).

[49]Ibid., 123. As Claudia Koonz points out, while boys in the Third Reich were taught to act, girls were taught to *be*. Whereas the Hitler Youth educated its members to fight in

Like the Bund deutscher Mädel, the Jenny Hill dance school ingrained ideals of discipline, camaraderie, leadership, and service for a higher cause. An indissoluble unit, the Jenny Hill Girls danced, ate, and traveled together, dressing in uniform and often speaking in chorus. Like the members of the BDM, the girls were initiated into the life of the group at a very young age, as the refrain of the theme song indicates:

> Dance with us, be young
> Sing with us, be young
> Laugh with us, be young . . .
> Dance with us, victor
> Sing with us, victor
> Laugh with us, victor
> Such is the motto of our troupe
> And we're dancing, dancing,
> dancing across the entire world.[50]

As in the BDM, communal physical activities provided the means to achieve a more profound sense of unity and camaraderie. "What is at stake in my school is not that the children learn to dance but, rather, that they learn to bond with one another at an early age and to become real comrades," says Jenny Hill in the opening scene of the film.[51] With the emphasis placed on communal service and self-sacrifice in the aim of a greater good, *Wir tanzen um die Welt* transformed the paradigm of the revue. Through a redeployment of the popular aesthetic that characterized the Roaring Twenties, the film manages simultaneously to renounce the "decadence" of the Weimar period and to promote a more reactionary vision in its place. This subtle operation, by which the film disavows the very aesthetic that it deploys, allows it to both meet audience expectations and reconstitute them. In this reorientation of the end of the revue from entertainment *for* the masses to an indoctrination *into* the mass, the Jenny Hill ballet school fulfills the dictate of Nazi education programs, whose aim was "to redirect students' values away from 'decadent' Weimar individualism and toward Nazi self-sacrifice."[52] In the most dramatic scene of the film (a close-up of Eva's luminous face superimposed over the movements of the dance troupe), the tragic figure dies, the sound of the troupe's theme song a final music to her ears. In the others, her *Geist* will live on, as the embodied soul of the surrogate family-troupe.[53]

---

service of the state (according to the motto "Live Faithfully, Fight Bravely, and Die Laughing!"), the BDM prepared its girls "for a lifetime membership in the second sex" (196).

[50] *Wir tanzen um die Welt*, screenplay.

[51] Ibid.

[52] Koonz, 201.

[53] According to an article in the press from January 1940, Irene von Meyendorff's performance as Eva makes the most powerful and lasting impression of the film: "Irene von

In its lightly veiled promotion of youthful self-sacrifice, *Wir tanzen um die Welt* serves a function similar to that of *Hitlerjunge Quex* (Hitler Youth Quex) (Hans Steinhoff, 1933), a German propaganda film that premiered in Munich in September 1933. Subtitled *Ein Film vom Opfergeist der deutschen Jugend* (A film on the sacrificial spirit of German youth), the film narrates the story of Heini Völker, a fifteen-year-old boy who breaks away from the violent disorder of his proletariat surroundings to join the Hitler Youth, eventually becoming a martyr for the cause. The distinction between the decadence of the Communist Party and the purity of the National Socialist movement is drawn most sharply in the summer solstice sequence, in which Heini escapes a rowdy, proletarian gathering in a smoke-filled tavern to stumble upon an open-air Hitler Youth celebration in the woods. As we move from proletarian disorder to the wholeness of nature, the music sweeps us up into the film's elevating refrain, "Unsere Fahne flattert uns voran" [Our flag waves before us]. In a ceremonial gathering, the Hitler Youth stand four square around the mythical emblem of a large bonfire. As the flag with a swastika waves in the wind, the leader makes a rousing speech to youth and Germany. In the morning, the call of the bugle heralds a sun-dappled day to be filled with a series of communal activities, from bathing in the lake to marching on the sandy beach. At this moment, Heini is seduced into the party for which he will give his life.

While *Wir tanzen um die Welt* contains no overt political symbolism, the film promotes the same vision of order and sacrifice to the whole as *Hitlerjunge Quex*, fulfilling Goebbel's call for "invisible propaganda." Both films center around a cult of youth. Like the Hitler Youth, the Jenny Hill girls are incorporated at a very young age into the group, which stands as a substitute for the biological family. As Eric Rentschler writes, "National Socialism sought to organize the will of youth, to enlist it in a historical mission. . . . The NSDAP institutionalized Oedipal revolt, directing the young against 'the parental home, church, school, and other outdated forms and role models. In its youth organizations it assumed the central role in the rebellion of sons against their fathers.'"[54] In both films, the display of order in the whole provides a counterpoint to the chaos and corruption of countermovements (Communism and the International in *Hitlerjunge Quex*, capitalism and decadence in *Wir tanzen um die Welt*). Like Heini, who dies in the service of the Third Reich, Eva sacrifices herself for the

Meyendorff, as the guardian angel [*guter Geist*] of the troupe, as a comrade, who, for the sake of the troupe, overworks her weak heart and thereby dies, makes a powerful impression and undertakes dramatically what is the most difficult and at the same time most successful performance" (Albert Schneider, *Licht Bild Bühne*, January 20, 1940).

[54]Rentschler, *The Ministry of Illusion*, 58. Incorporated quote from Axel Eggebrecht, "Rückblicke ins Dritte Reich," *Nordwestdeutsche Hefte* 1, no. 1 (1946): 8. For a detailed analysis of the film, see Rentschler, "Emotional Engineering: *Hitler Youth Quex* (1933)," in *The Ministry of Illusion*, 53–69.

cause. As Heini's death dissolves into a montage of waving swastikas and huge crowds of Nazis marching in cross-cut formations in ever-swelling numbers, Eva's death is intercut with a triumphant performance of the troupe under the watchful eyes of mother-figure Jenny Hill. In both cases, the sacrificial death enables the life of the organization, filled as it were with the spirit and soul of the martyred youth.

If the revue mediates a fear of chaos, this chaos takes on the particular form of female sexuality. In his analysis of the aesthetic composition of the revue film, Karsten Witte claims that the German revue film contains more frequent cuts than its American counterpart, severing the flow of physical movement. Visual pleasure, then, never stands still: "The inhibition of visual pleasure must lie at a deeper level than in the fear of decadence which pervaded the consciously National Socialist body. This fear of decay was a physical fear of flowing into dissipation. That is why the fragmented dancers are so hastily reassembled by the cutting technique, as if it had to be ashamed of every jump, every excursion into daydreaming, in short: of the dancing conquest of erotic fantasy."[55] The fear of decay is also mediated in the formal aesthetic of the revue itself. In *Male Fantasies*, a two-volume study of the diaries and writings of Freikorps members, many of whom became SA officers and functionaries in the Third Reich, Klaus Theweleit understands fascism in gendered terms. The obsession with swamps and floods in the diaries, with overflows and excesses, with all that exceeds and threatens to break down borders, reveals a deep-seated fear of dissolution, a fear arising from the pre-Oedipal struggle for existence itself. Woman in the (fascist) male unconscious is a "nameless force that seeks to engulf," a tidal wave, a deluge, an overwhelming force against which the soldier-male must armor himself.[56] In the case of the revue in the Nazi period, the excesses associated with female sexuality are harnessed and directed into the service of the state. The feminine is deployed in a particularly masculine form as a singular, ordered, disciplined body fully inscribed in the nation's ego boundaries. To this end, a description by Captain Heydebreck of his troops in retreat in Belgium in November 1918 is of interest: "The demeanor of the troops was exemplary. . . . In Prussian goose-step, they marched past me through the square in front of the city hall. They halted and stood firm there, a rock amid the surge of the gaping masses."[57] The military troop, then, was a unit, a boulder, a stronghold against which the surging masses could not make headway. In rendering the swelling tide a stronghold, the girl troupe served a curious function of deploying female sexuality in order to contain it.

The use of the revue in the Nazi period provides a particularly interesting lens through which we may assess the significance of the cultural material of

[55]Witte, "Visual Pleasure Inhibited," 257.
[56]Barbara Ehrenreich, foreword, in Theweleit, 1:xv.
[57]Quoted in ibid., 1:49.

the Third Reich. The popularity of the staged revue and the revue film under National Socialism brings out the ambiguous nature of many of the cinematic and theatrical products of the Third Reich, an ambiguity that recent film critics stress and that highlights the regime's complicated relationship to modernism and mass culture. In its continued deployment of the controlled sexuality of the revue, Nazi culture perpetuates a heterosexual norm integral to the larger patriarchal culture in which it is embedded. The Propaganda Ministry's embrace of this prototypically modern and machinelike form provides a cultural instance of what Jeffrey Herf has called reactionary modernism, the incorporation of modern technology into the romantic and irrational vitalism of German nationalism.[58] In its visible similarity to cultural products in the preceding period and political products in its own time, the revue in the Nazi period stood at a particular crossroads between mass culture and mass politics. As a larger field of investigation, two points of comparison are of interest here: a diachronic comparison of the revue in the Nazi and Weimar periods and a synchronic comparison of the German entertainment revue and the military revue proper. While an in-depth comparison is beyond the scope of this study, a few preliminary remarks may be of interest here.

The elements of collectivity and order that lend the revue to political appropriation are characteristic not only of the genre in the Nazi period but also of the staged revue in American and European capitals in the interwar period (and the American musical in the 1930s and 1940s).[59] What, then, distinguishes the German revue in the Nazi period from its cultural predecessors? According to Kracauer, the Weimar revue lacked the political meaning and import that he attributes to the mass ornamental patterns of Nazi spectacle. The "living constellations" of girls are for Kracauer self-referential units that provide no greater military meaning due to their lack of patriotic content and effect.[60] For André Levinson,

---

[58]See Jeffrey Herf, *Reactionary Modernism: Technology, Culture, and Politics in Weimar and the Third Reich* (Cambridge, 1984).

[59]Germany was not the only nation to make use of the revue for propaganda purposes in the period of World War II. We can find many examples of dance sequences in American musicals of the 1930s and 1940s, for example, that are designed to arouse patriotic sentiment, such as the famous Busby Berkeley *Shanghai Lil* number in *Footlight Parade* (1933), in which chorus lines of male soldiers and Chinese women draw panels designing the American flag and president, or uniformed Judy Garland's stirring song and dance numbers for the American troupes in Paris in *For Me and My Gal* (1942). While a few revue films, such as *Die große Liebe* (1942), with Zarah Leander, treat the situation of war on a narrative level, this kind of explicit propaganda is generally lacking in the German counterpart.

[60]In "The Mass Ornament," Kracauer writes, "Nor do the living constellations in the stadiums have the meaning of military demonstrations. No matter how orderly the latter appeared, that order was considered a means to an end; the parade march evolved out of patriotic feelings and in turn aroused them in soldiers and loyal subjects. The constellations of Girls, however, have no meaning outside of themselves, and the masses are not a moral unit like a company of soldiers" (68).

on the other hand, the staged revue was a form of military propaganda, a parade march "where desirable and delicate beings evoke in a martial manner military glories of days gone by."[61] Referring to a performance of the Jackson Girls in Berlin, Levinson wrote, "The other day, when the Jackson Girls, helmeted and be-plumed, descended the great staircase of the German Reichstag, hands on hips, in a goose-step, were they not alluding to the pomp of the vanished Empire, to the solemn splendor of its *Wachtparade?*"[62] If for Levinson the Weimar revue harked back to the German Empire, the revue under the Third Reich pointed forward to the dream of a greater Germany. As I have suggested in a longer study of the girl troupes that emerged in the wake of World War I, it is likely that the synchronized troupes suggested a fantasy of restoration, a restoration of the individual and social body, one that would be particularly appealing to a nation emasculated by military defeat.[63] However, direct patriotic effects were limited as the great majority of girl troupes playing in Weimar Germany, including the Tiller Girls, the Empire Girls or Lawrence Tiller Girls, the Jackson Girls, and the Hoffman Girls, were international performers trained in the United States and Great Britain and exported to European capitals for consumption. What is particular to the Nazi period is its explicit nationalization and instrumentalization of the genre. The visual display of the female form in ornamental patterns in the Weimar period was imbued with political content in the Nazi era, finding its ultimately hypertrophic form in fascist mass spectacles. The Propaganda Ministry capitalized on the latent political content of the staged revue, drawing on the collectivity, discipline, order, and control inherent in the form and redirecting it into the interests of the larger community. By supporting the production of a national girl troupe and the development of the genre of the revue film, the National Socialist regime offered the German public a homegrown counterpart to American mass cultural productions. Similar to its vision of a cinematic "dream machine" that would rival Hollywood studios and lower the need for foreign imports, the Propaganda Ministry fulfilled the public's apparent wants in the context of its own national borders, in the hopes of rendering Germany a self-sufficient and self-sustaining cultural unit.[64]

In the context of Nazi Germany, such an effort was of course fraught with contradiction. If a coordination (*Gleichschaltung*) of the sexual and the social is what was ultimately at stake in the appropriation of *Girlkultur*

---

[61]Andre Levinson, "Revues à grand spectacle," *L'Art Vivant*, January 15, 1928, 63.

[62]Levinson, "The Girls," 91.

[63]See Terri J. Gordon, "*Girls Girls Girls:* Re-Membering the Body," in *Rhine Crossings*, ed. Peter Schulman and Aminia Brueggemann (New York, forthcoming).

[64]As Patrice Petro indicates, the German film industry had captured its home market by the late 1930s and had finally achieved a "national cinema." See Petro, "Nazi Cinema at the Intersection of the Classical and the Popular," *New German Critique* 74 (spring/summer 1998): 48. See also Rentschler, *Ministry of Illusion*, 1–24.

by the Third Reich, as I am suggesting, then the Cultural Ministry ran the double risk of diminishing entertainment value and trivializing politics. The particularities in the German revue film that Karsten Witte has so aptly analyzed—its accentuation of melodramatic meaning over spectacle, its emphasis on psychic over physical energy, its sharp and frequent cuts, its vertically oriented visual field, and the explicit militarization of the genre of the staged revue—all combine to produce sexuality in a straitjacket, to release but simultaneously restrain desire, to "inhibit" and inhabit visual pleasure. Of course, desire can never be wholly contained. While the African American dancers associated with the "primitive" and the "exotic" in the Weimar period (forcibly) disappeared from the stage, erotic elements still prevailed in staged and film performances in the Nazi period. The most fashionable popular performers of the day were the Hungarian Marika Rökk, the Swedish Zarah Leander, and self-styled "exotic" Austrian dancer Henriette Hiebl, alias "La Jana." Many dance sequences borrowed from a codified lexicon of the erotic, as did La Jana's comi-magic striptease to bring a knight in armor to life in *Es leuchten die Sterne* and Marika Rökk's Oriental belly dance as "bad" sister Kora in an Algerian hotel in *Kora Terry* (Ufa, 1940), sequences that merit further study for a larger understanding of the deployment of female sexuality in the Nazi period.

If the militarization of the sexual in the staged revue and the revue film ran the risk of reducing pleasure, the sexualization of the military ran the risk of trivializing politics.[65] Did the overdetermination of the political in the cultural realm reinforce or reduce its import? In other words, how did mass culture connect to mass politics? On the surface, the production of revue girls in ornamental patterns looks very much like the political pageantry of Hitler Youth and SA men at Nazi rallies and mass marches. In his later work, Kracauer makes a direct connection between the cultural and political mass ornament, referring to the "living ornaments" and "tableaux vivants" of Nazi spectacle.[66] The parades of bonded male soldiers produced a sexually laden homosocial paradigm, as the homoerotic bathing scenes in the prologue to Riefenstahl's *Fest der Schönheit* suggest. Embodying what Peter Reichel has called "der schöne Schein des Dritten Reiches" [the beautiful appearance of the Third Reich], the SS in particular has provided material for erotic fantasy.[67] In "Fascinating Fascism," Susan Sontag claims that theatricality stands behind any sadomasochistic

---

[65] Indeed, as Peter Jelavich points out, the Reich Theater Chamber banned explicit "military" dance performances in July 1940 due to the state of actual war (254–55). The absurdity of putting cabaret performance into the service of the state can be seen most clearly in Mel Brook's parodic send-up in *The Producers* (1967) in which kicklines of chorus girls form a swastika to the refrain "Springtime for Hitler."

[66] Siegfried Kracauer, *From Caligari to Hitler* (Princeton, 1947), 301.

[67] See Peter Reichel, "Ästhetisierung des Außergewöhnlichen: Die SS," in *Der schöne Schein des Dritten Reiches: Faszination und Gewalt des Faschismus* (Frankfurt am Main, 1993), 222–31.

fantasy provoked by the SS, whose appeal derives from a visual emanation of the dual forces of supreme beauty and supreme violence.[68] In its visible projection of force, Nazi spectacle reverses the power of what has come to be understood as the "male gaze." Power resides in the object, as opposed to the subject, operating as a sort of kinetic force that seeks to draw the spectator into its field of influence. It is in the deployment of power that the fundamental difference between the representation of male troops and female troupes lies. While both are objects of the gaze, the former embodies state power in an aesthetic globalization of space that threatens to eclipse the spectator, while the latter remains a devalued object whose sexuality is contained in a nonthreatening, linear form. While mass politics cannot be reduced to mass culture, culture here appears to map onto politics, providing both a welcome escape and a subliminal support.

AUSDRUCKSTANZ: A SECULAR RELIGION?

Je donnerais tout Baudelaire pour une nageuse olympique
[I would give all of Baudelaire for an Olympic swimmer].

—L.-F. Céline

If the aesthetic of the revue was informed by the machine, *Ausdruckstanz* drew its inspiration from nature. Influenced by the avant-garde art movements of Dada, expressionism, and *Neue Sachlichkeit* (new objectivity), *Ausdruckstanz* shared with expressionism a rejection of objective representational modes and the quest for an outward expression of inner subjectivity.[69] With its emphasis on improvisation and subjective expression, *Ausdruckstanz* would provide an important legacy for later American modern dance movements.[70] Anti-Enlightenment and antimodern in its orientation, expressionist dance promised a return to the body and a return to the earth.[71] As such, *Ausdruckstanz* was deeply informed by the *Körperkultur* movement, which began in the early nineteenth century in Germany and found its extreme manifestation in the fascist cult of the

[68]Sontag, 99.
[69]See Dianne S. Howe, *Individuality and Expression: The Aesthetics of the New German Dance, 1908–1936* (New York, 1996), 13, 31. For a discussion of the relationship between the body and the body politic in Nazi Germany, see Howe, "Ausdruckstanz and Politics," in ibid., 34–40; Manning, "Body Politic," in *Ecstasy and the Demon*, 167–220; and Elaine Martin, ed., *Gender, Patriarchy and Fascism in the Third Reich* (Detroit, 1983).
[70]For a discussion of the influence of *Ausdruckstanz* on American modern dance, see Manning, "Mary Wigman and American Dance," in *Ecstasy and the Demon*, 255–85.
[71]The modern dance movements championed by Isadora Duncan and Ruth St. Denis in the United States and Rudolf von Laban and Mary Wigman in Germany have the curious status of being both "modern" and "antimodern." They are modern in the sense that they radically break with the tradition of classical dance but "antimodern" in their orientation toward nature and myth.

body. In the early twentieth century, *Lebensreform* (life reform) philosophers promoted body culture as a means to recover the body from the
industrial machine and to restore a more natural mode of existence. Alongside the "decadence" of cabaret culture, a cult of the body flourished in
the Weimar period, promising to reenergize a war-weary population and
to forge a new connection to the body. The era was infused with a sense of
movement, as is illustrated by the cover of a 1931 issue of the Swiss magazine *Die neue Zeit* (The new era), which featured a young, naked couple
leaping in the air.[72] In 1925, Ufa produced a documentary film entitled
Wege zu Kraft und Schönheit (Ways to strength and beauty), which featured an array of beautiful bodies in motion, healthy young people engaged in group dance, sports, and rhythmic gymnastics in the serenity of
the great outdoors.

The *Körperkultur* movement dates back to the beginning of the nineteenth century, when Friedrich Ludwig Jahn, known as "Turnvater Jahn,"
founded the first gymnastics club (*Turnverein*). The movement came into
full flower at the turn of the century with the development of a number of
life reform sects and youth organizations, such as the Wandervogel movement, a mixed gender youth group that would be subsumed in 1933 by
the Hitler Youth. The schools of the anthroposophist Rudolf Steiner and
the Swiss composer and pedagogue Emile Jaques-Dalcroze were based
upon the vision of a healthy life in tune with natural rhythms. At his artist's
colony in Hellerau, Jaques-Dalcroze developed the practice of "rhythmic
gymnastics," an attempt to harness cosmic rhythms through body rhythms.
Associated with nudism, vegetarianism, life reformism, and countercul-
ture, the body culture movement was embraced by movements that crossed
the political spectrum, from anarchists to Social Democrats to nationalists, including German nationalists, the Czech Sokol body culture movement, and Zionist organizations.[73]

While the *Körperkultur* movement's emphasis on communal living, life
reformism, and environmentalism aligned it with artistic and cultural movements on the Left, its mystical and nationalistic overtones lent it a particular
appeal for the Right. Nationalism was deeply embedded in the *Körperkultur*
movement. Beginning with Turnvater Jahn, physical vitality was seen as a

[72]For a reproduction of this image, see Gabriele Klein, *FrauenKörperTanz: Eine Zivilisationsgeschichte des Tanzes* (Berlin, 1992), 132.
[73]Mark M. Anderson, *Kafka's Clothes: Ornament and Aestheticism in the Habsburg Fin de Siècle* (Oxford, 1992), 76. According to George Mosse, the aestheticization of politics under National Socialism drew force from the organizing principles of the *Körperkultur* movement. Jahn's gymnastics movement, in particular, provided a foundation for the shap-ing of the mass in accordance with classical ideas of beauty and a national consciousness. However, as Mosse points out, the *Körperkultur* movement also appealed to other national groups, such as the Czech Sokol movement and Zionist organizations. See Mosse, *The Nationalization of the Masses: Political Symbolism and Mass Movements in Germany from the Napoleonic Wars through the Third Reich* (Ithaca, 1975), 127–60.

crucial component in the restoration of national health and the maintenance
of racial hygiene. *Lebensreform* philosophers envisioned the individual body
as an integral part of the social body, whose national vitalism was dependent
upon the health of its members. In an article entitled "Physical Fitness—A
National Necessity" (1926), Ernst Preiss wrote, "That the German people
have suffered a significant decline in their vital energies over the last two
decades has been proven repeatedly. . . . In the face of this threat to our
national body, adequate social-hygienic measures must be implemented to
reinvigorate our endangered common vitality."[74] Jahn's gymnastics movement, which he characterized as "love of fatherland through gymnastics,"
was originally inspired by military aims to create a disciplined and united
Germanic youth corps to prevail against the invading Napoleonic armies.[75]
Hans Surén's *Der Mensch und die Sonne* (Man and sunlight), originally published in 1925 and reprinted in 1936 with the subtitle *Arisch-olympischer
Geist* (Aryan-Olympian spirit), provided a written articulation of the vitalist
philosophies that run through the *Körperkultur* movement. Championing
natural living, the work was based upon the central thesis that a nation's
health is contingent upon the physical vitality of its population. The work
was so popular that it went through sixty-eight editions in its first year of
publication, a success that Surén attributed to "how aptly it reflects the aspi-
rations of the true German race."[76]

Much of the nationalistic philosophy of *Ausdruckstanz*, particularly in
the Nazi period, drew upon the notions of social and racial hygiene already embedded in the *Lebensreform* movements. For Jaques-Dalcroze,
rhythmic gymnastics provided the means to establish physical and moral
hygiene, which he considered the necessary foundation for the "new society."[77] *Ausdruckstanz* founder Rudolf von Laban conceived of his movement as a "new dance cult" that was "racially bound through and
through."[78] In the program of the 1934 German Dance Festival, Laban

[74]Ernst Preiss, "Die Körperausbildung—eine Volksnotwendigkeit," in *Neue Wege der
Körperkultur* (Stuttgart, 1926), translation in Kaes, 683.

[75]Quoted in Mosse, 128.

[76]Hans Surén, *Der Mensch und die Sonne* (Stuttgart, 1925), preface to the 61st ed.,
translation in Kaes, 678. The 67th edition appeared in English as *Man and Sunlight*, trans.
David Arthur Jones (Slough, England, 1927). In the preface to the first edition, Surén
writes, "If physical strength is allowed to decay, even the highest achievements of the spirit
and the most profound scientific knowledge will not avert national decline and death. Using every means possible with unflagging energy, a nation should be united in the will to
promote the strength of its people" (translation in Kaes, 678).

[77]Jaques-Dalcroze states, "I want to elevate rhythm to the level of a social institution
and to create a new style, one that grows naturally and thus bears genuine witness to the
souls of all the participants. . . . It is a sort of physical and moral hygiene, which should
provide the basis of the new society" (quoted in Müller and Stöckemann, 12).

[78]Laban writes in the *Nordische Rundschau* on July 29, 1936, of his group movement
that "strives to be a new dance cult which is racially bound through and through" (quoted
in Karina and Kant, 51).

envisioned Germany as the cradle of modern dance through whose force alone the beauty of the physical world could be rendered and human beings spiritually moved. "Germany is the country in which this ideal took root first and most profoundly," Laban wrote. "That is why people from all nations . . . call this dance 'German dance.'"[79] In the program for the 1935 dance festival, Laban's protégée Mary Wigman also linked dance to the earth: "The dance conveys man's deeply rooted love for all that binds him to the earth and to his homeland."[80] Like Laban, she considered Germany the heart of modern dance, whose aesthetic expression served as a living embodiment of the essence of the people.[81] As Susan Manning has illustrated, whereas Wigman's earlier philosophy had conceived of *Ausdruckstanz* in terms of universal expression, her later writings viewed it as an expression of the people.[82] In *Deutsche Tanzkunst* (German dance art, 1935), Wigman envisioned expressionist dance as a supranatural force that reached into the soul of the nation: "We German artists today are more aware of the fate of the *Volk* than ever before. And for all of us this time is a trial of strength, a measuring of oneself against standards that are greater than the individual is able to fathom. The call of the blood, which has involved us all, goes deep and engages the essential."[83]

Despite their openly stated nationalist sentiment, both Laban and Wigman fell out of favor with the Nazi regime at the time of the 1936 Berlin Olympic Games. In preparation for the opening night spectacle of the Olympic Games, Laban created a choreographed work entitled "Vom Tauwind und der neuen Freude" (Of the warm wind and the new joy). A "choric consecration play" that put Nietzsche to music, the piece was a massive production performed by a lay movement choir of one thousand dancers.[84] As Dianne Howe points out, the lay choir, which Laban called "the new folk dance movement of the white race," was particularly appealing to

---

[79]Rudolf von Laban, "Die deutsche Tanzbühne," in *Deutsche Tanzfestspiele 1934*, ed. Rudolf von Laban (Dresden, 1934), 3.

[80]Wigman goes on to elaborate the specific dances that convey this attachment to the earth and homeland: "Thus the various parts refer to exaltation (*Paean*), to painful burdens (*Road of the Suppliant*), to dark threats (*Song of Fate*), to elemental rhythm (*Fire Dance*), to the experience of nature (*Moon Song*), and to unending devotion (*Dance of Homage*)" (quoted in translation in Manning, 185).

[81]In a 1929 article, Wigman wrote, for example, "Since Germany is the cradle of modern dance, so its living expression will reflect the essence of the German people" ("Das 'Land ohne Tanz,'" *Tanzgemeinschaft* 1, no. 2 [April 1929]: 12, quoted in translation in Manning, 192).

[82]See Manning: "In contrast to her earlier writings, which had linked the Germanness of *Ausdruckstanz* to universal human experiences, her 1935 essay linked Germanness to the *Volk*" (ibid.).

[83]Mary Wigman, *Deutsche Tanzkunst* (Dresden, 1935), 11–12, quoted in translation in ibid.

[84]Karl Toepfer, *Empire of Ecstasy: Nudity and Movement in German Body Culture 1910–1935* (Berkeley, 1997), 315.

National Socialist ideologues because of its communal nature and *völkisch* echoes.[85] Laban's assistant for lay movement pedagogy stressed the link between the communal nature of the movement choirs and the fascist state: "We have grown out of the I-and-You era into the We era—but not so that we are merely 'masses': we are a people's community [*Volksgemeinschaft*], led by the *Führer*, and our lay dance is education in this sense: to lead and become led."[86] However, at the final dress rehearsal, the work was abruptly dismissed by Goebbels, who claimed in a diary entry that the work was "too intellectual": "Dietrich-Eckart Bühne dance festival rehearsal: loosely based on Nietzsche, a shoddy and artificial thing. . . . It is all so intellectual. I don't like it. We go there all dressed up, and it has absolutely nothing to do with us."[87] Wigman, on the other hand, made a significant contribution to the Olympic Games, collaborating on *Olympische Jugend* (Olympic youth), the elaborate opening night ceremony that celebrated youth, peace, and the fatherland.[88] Reminiscent of Wigman's 1930 *Totenmal* (Call of the dead), a choric commemoration of World War I heroes that Susan Manning considers her only protofascist work, Wigman's Olympic contribution celebrated the fallen German soldier. The fourth scene of the evening, the piece entitled "Heldenkampf und Totenklage" (Heroic struggle and death lament), cast a tragic pall over the spectacle. Following the sacrificial deaths of sixty soldiers in a sequence choreographed by Harald Kreutzberg, Wigman's composition featured eighty women engaged in a dance of lamentation. Despite the nationalist overtones of the piece, this was the last commission Wigman was to receive from the Cultural Ministry. While Laban left for England the following year, Wigman stayed in Germany through the duration of the war, holding her work to be "apolitical."

Why did the Nazi regime incorporate the form of *Ausdruckstanz* into its aesthetic productions while excluding its two figureheads? Why did the regime retain the dance while rejecting the foremost dancers? In *Tanz unterm Hakenkreuz* (Dance under the swastika), Lilian Karina puts forth the compelling idea that the dance movements of Laban and Wigman are fundamentally mystical in nature, representing alternative and threatening sects to the Germanic, Nordic cult of National Socialism.[89] The *Körperkultur* movement of the early twentieth century was already imbued with mystical overtones. In *Der Mensch und die Sonne*, for example, Surén wrote, "We experience a marvelous revelation in the beauty and strength of the naked body, transfigured by godlike purity shining from

[85]Hedwig Müller, ed., "3. Deutscher Tänzerkongress: Deutsche Tänzerwoche München 1930," *Tanzdrama* 13, no. 4 (1990): 19, quoted in translation in Howe, 36.

[86]Quoted in translation in Toepfer, 315.

[87]Goebbels, *Die Tagebücher*, June 21, 1936.

[88]For a description of the choreography of the *Olympische Jugend* ceremony, see Müller and Stöckemann, 171–84. See also Manning, 194–202; Toepfer, 314–17.

[89]See Karina and Kant, 54.

the clear and open eye that mirrors the entire depth of a noble and quest-
ing soul. Placed in the bright frame of exalted nature, the human body
finds its most ideal manifestation."[90] The mystical aspects that inform
Surén's discourse—the revelatory nature of the body, the exaltation of
nature, the godlike purity of the body and soul—found their echo in
Ausdruckstanz beliefs and practices. Through its creation of a spiritual
community, through the ritualistic aspects of the dance, and through its
hypnotic effects, the new dance, which Peter Adam calls "a messianic happening," constituted a sort of spiritual cult.[91] As such, it stood as a threat
to the "mystical positivity" that Julia Kristeva attributes to fascist ideology
in her discussion of Céline in *Pouvoirs de l'horreur* (Powers of horror).[92] In
an article entitled "Tanz in dieser Zeit" (Dance in this time) Max Merz
considers the dances of Elizabeth Duncan (Isadora Duncan's sister) the
expression of a "natural religiousness": "In Elizabeth Duncan's aesthetic
creed a strong ethos and a natural religiousness expresses itself. Life and
art are identical."[93]

   This "natural religiousness" found its strongest manifestation in the
dance productions choreographed by Laban and Wigman. Laban in particular, who saw himself as a "begnadeten Führer" (gifted leader), took on
the status of a cultlike figure.[94] When he assumed the position of ballet
director of the Staatsoper, an article in *Der Tanz* (The dance) exclaimed,

[90]Surén, *Der Mensch und die Sonne*, translation in Kaes, 679.

[91]Adam, 38. For a discussion of the mystical aspects of *Ausdruckstanz*, see Karina and
Kant, 52–54, 138–44. Dance historian Marion Kant suggests that the movements of Laban
and Wigman were part of a larger current in art tending toward an anti-Enlightenment,
secular religiousness. The notion of a "secular religion" refers to a set of religious attitudes,
beliefs, or practices that are worldly and temporal in nature. "Mysticism" refers to the belief
that direct knowledge of God, spiritual truth, or ultimate reality can be attained through
subjective experience. In its devotional worship of nature, the leader, and the artistic movement, *Ausdruckstanz* (particularly Laban's variety) constitutes more of a mystical cult than
a secular religion.

[92]See Julia Kristeva, *Pouvoirs de l'horreur: Essai sur l'abjection* (Paris, 1980), 209–10. In
The Nationalization of the Masses, George Mosse advances the thesis that National Socialism was fundamentally religious in nature, its mystical quality manifesting itself in liturgical
rituals and cult worship: "The worship of the people . . . became the worship of the nation,
and the new politics sought to express this unity through the creation of a political style
which became, in reality, a secularized religion" (2). Concerning the growth of this "secular religion," Mosse writes, "As in any religion, the theology expressed itself through a
liturgy: festivals, rites, and symbols which remained constant in an ever-changing world"
(16). Mosse does not draw a sharp distinction between a "secular religion" and mysticism
in his discussion here, the National Socialists holding a temporal religious belief system (a
worship of the nation, or themselves) that manifested itself in cultic rituals and mystical
rites. As an alternative sect within this secular religion, *Ausdruckstanz* posed a threat to the
national belief system expounded by the National Socialists.

[93]Max Merz, in *Tanz in dieser Zeit*, ed. Stefan Paul (Vienna, 1926), quoted in Karina
and Kant, 49–50.

[94]Quoted in ibid., 99.

"Habemus Papam" [We have a pope].[95] Mary Wigman called him the "Magiker, [den] Priester einer unbekannten Religion" [magician, the priest of an unknown religion].[96] In accordance with the Greek practice of open-air performance, Laban envisioned the creation of performance spaces in what he called "dance temples," cathedral-like amphitheaters covered by cupolas. Wigman articulated the unifying aspects of the "festival": "The Greeks had a theater that was inseparable from religion and the state, that embodied their being as *Volk*, nation, family, and individual. A theater that belonged to all, that served God and humanity, that became a festival [*Fest*] in the highest sense."[97] The sacred aspect of Laban's dramaturgy applied to his teaching as well. In his commune in Ascona, Laban projected an almost magical aura, creating a cultlike atmosphere of devoted disciples bound to him by artistic and erotic ties. According to Karl Toepfer, Laban's "harem of devoted women" demonstrated that "*Ausdruckstanz* involved the construction of a mysterious personality with an almost hypnotic control over the dynamic, liberated body."[98] A "gifted leader," a "priest," a "pope," Laban stood as a *Führer* substitute, a magnetic leader with a powerful hold over the group.

While Wigman did not project the same erotic mystique as Laban, she considered herself a spiritual messenger, an apostle of the new dance. In a diary entry, she wrote, "I am the dance / And am the priestess of the dance."[99] Wigman's dance cycles drew on the natural cycle of life, incorporating death into life in a way that rendered her alternatively ecstatic, demonic, and Dionysian. Her spiritual scope was extensive, ranging from the occult to the sacred. While some dances, such as *Tanztrance* (Dance trance) and *Hexentanz* (Witch dance), were mystical in nature, others, such as *Totentanz* (Dance of death) and *Seraphisches Lied* (Seraphic song), exuded a more sacred quality, incorporating religious symbolism in the form of the cross or hands clasped in prayer.[100] Wigman's costumes, which included long capes, dark hooded shawls, somber masks, and Oriental gowns, also shrouded her in a mystical aura.[101] According to Howe, Wigman's preference for cosmic powers over human forces rendered her threatening to the National Socialist state: "Her philosophy was considered dangerous by the Reich; she gave the highest importance to a superhuman power, and more

[95]Josef Lewitan, "Laban an der Spitze des Staatsopernballetts!" *Der Tanz* 3, no. 5 (May 1930), quoted in ibid., 81.

[96]Cited in Rudolf von Laban and F. C. Lawrence, *Effort: Economy in Body Movement*, 2nd ed. (London, 1974), 10, quoted in ibid., 52.

[97]Wigman, *Deutsche Tanzkunst*, 69, quoted in translation in Manning, 193–94.

[98]Toepfer, 99.

[99]Quoted in Hedwig Müller, *Mary Wigman: Leben und Werk der großen Tänzerin* (Berlin, 1986), 58, quoted in translation in Howe, 101.

[100]Ibid., 121. For a description of the spiritual quality in Wigman's dances, see ibid., 118–25; Manning, 59–73.

[101]For an elaboration of Wigman's costumes, see Toepfer, 113.

importance to fate and the cosmos than the state, the party, and the *Führer*."[102]

The Propaganda Ministry's response to the two central proponents of *Ausdruckstanz* underscores the importance of mysticism to National Socialism as well as its privileging of the totality over the individual. In a lecture given in 1990, dance historian and Wigman biographer Hedwig Müller emphasized the shift that *Ausdruckstanz* underwent under National Socialism from a dance serving individual expression to a functional dance in the service of the state:

> The central concept of *Ausdruckstanz* is individualism. . . . Self-realization got a new orientation [under National Socialism]. It would no longer support uncontrolled, free personality development, rather functionally oriented self-fulfillment. The dance no longer serves the individual exploration of its own personality and its relation to the outer world, rather there was a goal-orientation added to this individual exploration: the experience of individuality became part of the integration into an overall structure.[103]

The expressionist dance sequences in Leni Riefenstahl's *Olympia* provide an exemplary instance of "functionally oriented self-fulfillment" and the experience of individuality as an "integration into an overall structure." Like Laban and Wigman, Riefenstahl effected a return to nature, drawing upon the mystical aspects of *Lebensreform* and the sacred qualities of the human body in her choreography. However, Riefenstahl's role behind the scenes in the *Olympia* film allowed for the body to emerge as a signifying metaphor for the social body, one that effectively subsumed the individual body. Two sets of images in particular exemplify this process: the expressionist dance sequences in the prologue to "Fest der Völker" (Festival of the nation), the first part of Riefenstahl's documentary, and the mass gymnastics display in the "Fest der Schönheit" (Festival of beauty), the second part of the film. Taken together, these two sequences illustrate the way in which aesthetic representations of the female form may serve to privilege the dance over the dancer.

Riefenstahl's *Olympia* premiered on April 20, 1938, to much critical acclaim. The German premiere was held in Berlin at the Ufa-Palast am Zoo, which was draped with banners of the swastika and the five Olympic rings.[104] The event drew important representatives of the film industry and the main figureheads of the National Socialist regime. In the six months following its release, the film was screened with pomp and ceremony in almost every

---

[102]Howe, 109.
[103]Quoted in translation in ibid., 38.
[104]Taylor Downing, *Olympia* (London, 1992), 86.

European capital, including Vienna, Athens, Brussels, Belgrade, Paris, Copenhagen, Stockholm, Helsinki, and Rome.[105] *Olympia* was awarded the German Film Prize of 1937–38 and the Coppa Mussolini at the International Film Festival in Venice in September 1938. With its release to the general public, the film became a box-office hit, bringing in between 7 and 8 million RM in its European run.[106] The film found a much less receptive audience in the United States, where a boycott was carried out against the documentary and its director. On a trip to the United States in 1938, Riefenstahl was shunned by the American film industry, deemed by an American columnist "as pretty as a swastika" and later a "Nazi pin-up girl."[107] The political import of the film is a subject of ongoing controversy. It has been considered both "a paean of praise to physical culture and to the glory of victory on the fields of sport"[108] and a model of fascist art, which, in Susan Sontag's words, "glorifies surrender," "exalts mindlessness," and "glamorizes death."[109]

As a medium for total expression, the art of dance was a particularly resonant form for Riefenstahl. Riefenstahl herself was a dancer. She trained at the schools of Jutta Klamt in Berlin and Mary Wigman in Dresden and performed in cities in Germany and central Europe, only to turn to a career in film after an accident on stage. The staging of the female form in Riefenstahl's *Olympia* bears the mark of her mentors. As Susan Manning has pointed out, both Mary Wigman and Isadora Duncan, the American pioneer of modern dance who opened a dance school in Berlin in 1904, understood dance in gendered and nationalistic terms. In "The Dance of the Future," an essay written in 1903, Duncan conceived of dance as the means for the development of an ideal female race. The art of the new dance, she maintained, is "a question of race": "It is not only a question of true art, it is a question of race, of the development of the female sex to beauty and health, of the return to the original strength and to natural movements of woman's body. It is a question of the development of perfect mothers and the birth of healthy and beautiful children. The dancing school of the future is to develop and to show the ideal form of woman."[110] As opposed to sexually "frivolous" modern dance forms such as the fox-trot

[105]Cooper C. Graham, *Leni Riefenstahl and Olympia* (Metuchen, 1986), 195–209.
[106]Ibid., 200–201.
[107]Riefenstahl was considered "as pretty as a swastika" in a column by Walter Winchell ("Walter Winchell on Broadway") that appeared in the *Daily Mirror* on November 9, 1938 (ibid., 213). The second appellation comes from an article by Budd Schulberg entitled "Nazi Pin-Up Girl" that appeared in the *Saturday Evening Post* on March 30, 1946 (Erik Barnouw, *Documentary: A History of the Non-Fiction Film* [New York, 1974], 110).
[108]Anthony Slide, editor's foreword in Graham.
[109]Sontag, 91.
[110]Isadora Duncan, "The Dance of the Future," in *The Art of the Dance*, ed. Sheldon Cheney (New York, 1969), 61, quoted in Manning, 38.

and the Black-Bottom,[111] Duncan envisioned what she called a "Greek dance" of the future: "Long-legged strong boys and girls will dance to this music—not the tottering, ape-like convulsions of the Charleston, but a striking upward tremendous mounting, powerful mounting above the pyramids of Egypt, beyond the Parthenon of Greece, an expression of Beauty and Strength such as no civilization has ever known."[112]

Fulfilling Isadora Duncan's vision of a dance of Beauty and Strength transcending the wonders of the ancient world, Riefenstahl's prologue to the "Fest der Völker" transports the viewer back to classical times. Set in the ruins of ancient Greece, the prologue is a sustained hymn to the body beautiful. From the ancient acropolis, the camera travels in slow motion across the ruins, focusing on Doric columns and the remains of Apollonian statues. The mood is misty and oneiric, an effect achieved through the use of soft focus and smoke powder.[113] A Pygmalion dream come true, Myron's statue of a discus thrower comes to life, to segue into a montage of male forms in motion. As the heavy beats of Herbert Windt's score soften to the whimsical sounds of high woodwinds and strings, the lyrical movements of the shot-putter dissolve slowly into the feminine arms of four naked dancers, one of them perhaps played by Riefenstahl herself.[114]

The dance sequence in the prologue, choreographed by Riefenstahl and shot by Willy Zielke, is organized around elementary symbolism (fig. 2). Filmed in the Baltic sand dunes of the Valley of Silence in Lithuania, the sequence roots the dancers in an atemporal space of organic nature. Archetypal female forms, the dancers represent "ancient Greek temple dancers, the keepers of the sacred flame."[115] In keeping with the mythopoeic symbolism, the dance combines primary forms and fundamental elements. A backlit, shadowy sky casts a mystical light upon the naked forms, and a series of cross-dissolves sustains the dreamlike mood of the prologue: the shadowy arms of the four dancers blend into two hands playing catch in

---

[111]Duncan viewed the cabaret dance as a caricature of sexuality: "I say it is of utmost importance to a nation to train children to the understanding and execution of movements of great heroic and spiritual beauty, to raise their many bans on the realisation of sex, which is a fine thing in itself, and to put the same prohibitions on the frivolous caricature and symbols of sex which are found in such dances as foxtrot and Black-Bottom" (quoted in Sewell Stokes, *Isadora Duncan* [London: Brentano's, 1928], 172).

[112]Duncan, "I See America Dancing," in *The Art of the Dance*, 49, quoted in Manning, 39. Greek classicism was a tremendous influence on Isadora Duncan's expressive dance. In her solo dances, she danced barefoot on stage, draped in Greek-styled tunics and colored scarves, the whole an attempt to infuse modern dance with the spirit of ancient Greek drama.

[113]Downing, 41.

[114]According to Gordon Hitchens, Riefenstahl told him that she had played one of the nude dancers in the prologue, a claim supported by Riefenstahl cameraman Henry Jaworsky. See "Henry Jaworsky, cameraman for Leni Riefenstahl, interviewed by Gordon Hitchens, Kirk Bond, and John Hanhardt," in *Film Culture* 56–57 (spring 1973): 123–24.

[115]David B. Hinton, *The Films of Leni Riefenstahl*, 2nd ed. (Metuchen, 1991), 68.

Figure 2. Nude dancers in the prologue to the "Fest der Völker," the first part of Leni Riefenstahl's 1937–38 film *Olympia*. Photo courtesy of the Film Museum Berlin, Deutsche Kinemathek.

slow motion, into two legs slowly skipping. One dancer sways gently with an oversized hoop against a field of waving wheat; another moves against the silent rhythms of the sea. Finally, the three Greek temple dancers are united. Silhouetted against the gray sky, the dancers join hands and kneel to the ground. The sacred ritual comes to an imminent, ecstatic climax as the female forms dissolve into fire, a fire that envelops the entire screen. It is this flame that serves to kindle the Olympic torch. A series of male runners cross the map, taking the flame from the ancient Greek acropolis to the modern German Olympic stadium, where the prologue reaches its culmination in a fanfare of ringing bells, roaring crowds, and waving flags. Eric Barnouw writes, "The sequence seems to tell us that the torch of civilization has been carried from its ancient center, Greece, to modern Germany, watched over by a pantheon at whose apex is Hitler."[116]

As the bearers of the sacred flame and the physical embodiment of the Olympic torch, the dancers are the primary symbol of the Olympic Games, a symbolism recalled in the closing ceremonies of the Olympics in which human ornaments describe the Olympic hoops and a dome of light envisioned by Albert Speer settles over the Olympic stadium. The sacred flame was not only a symbol of the international games but also an important

[116]Barnouw, 109.

symbol of the Third Reich. As George Mosse has pointed out, the sacred flame was a potent emblem of the harmony and purity of the Germanic people. The symbolism of fire, which is rooted in Christian and pagan traditions, was used for nationalistic purposes in the Romantic period.[117] The "holy flame" brought together religion and nation, symbolizing the "sacred light" of Germanic unity and salvation. Of the "sacred light" that was rekindled in the Third Reich, Mosse writes, "The flame as it stood symbolized light over darkness, the sun as against the night. It reflected the mystical forces of the life-bringing sun which gave men strength and vitality. To the Nazis it meant 'purification,' symbolized brotherly community, and served to remind party members of the 'eternal life process.'"[118]

At the heart of the symbolism of the sacred flame in the film is ancient Greece. As Peter Adam has pointed out in his study of art in the Third Reich, the notion of a "Nordic" aesthetic in art and architecture was not limited to northern Europe but included the temples of ancient Greece, the coliseums of the Roman Empire, and the pyramids of Egypt.[119] Nazi aesthetics drew upon the classical Greek ideals of beauty and the monumentality of Roman architecture, the fusion of which is exemplified in the hypertropic sculptures of Arno Breker and Josef Wackerle that adorned the Olympic stadium.[120] Greek cultural norms were deeply ingrained in the body culture movement, from the ideal of the sculpted, athletic male body in Jahn's gymnastics clubs to Duncan's vision of a "Greek dance" of the future to Laban's open-air "dance temples." The influence of classical norms is particularly evident in the 1925 *Körperkultur* film *Wege zu Kraft und Schönheit*, in which Riefenstahl herself performed. In the program notes to the film, Felix Hollaender pointed to the classical roots in the modern forces of gymnastics, dance, and sports, which drew on the "pedagogical principles of Greek gymnastics" and the "sophisticated body culture of the Romans." In the ritualistic language common to *Lebensreform* philosophies, Hollaender understood body culture as a means for the "regeneration" of the individual body and with it the national body:

[117]Mosse points to the first-anniversary celebration of the victory over Napoleon in 1815, in which "pillars of flames" were constructed on hilltops and in the altars of public squares (40–41). An 1815 work on German fire and temple worship intones: "Let the holy flame of German unity cast its sacred light" (Karl Hoffmann, *Des teutschen Volkes feuriger Dank- und Ehrentempel* [Offenbach, 1815], 93, quoted in ibid., 40–41).

[118]Ibid., 42. Embedded quotes from Georg Sammler, "Mittsommerfeuer," *Der Schulungsbrief* 3 (June 1936): 211, 212.

[119]Adam, 23.

[120]For a larger discussion of Nazi aesthetics, see Mosse, 21–46; Adam, 175–205. On the influence of Greek ideals in German aesthetics, Mosse writes, "It served to define the 'ideal German man' from the time of the Greek statues which Winckelmann admired to the figures by Arno Breker which watched over the entrance to Hitler's new Reichs Chancellery. Beauty was expressed through a stereotype which would remain operative from the eighteenth century and eventually melt into the 'Aryan type' the Nazis and their predecessors praised so highly" (27).

What was created was meant to be a hymn to endeavors aimed equally at awakening the sense of beauty and contributing to recovering the nation's health. It sought to show with what vigor our maligned era has seized upon and developed the issue of body culture—the extent to which it has been able to approximate the Greek ideal of beauty . . . . This film seems to indicate the kind of forces now at work that would make a rebirth of the body in the spirit of antiquity possible.[121]

It is precisely the rebirth of the body in the spirit of antiquity that is realized in Riefenstahl's *Olympia*. The classical proportions of the nude dancers in the prologue accord with Greek standards of beauty, while their physical movements integrate the open-air physical culture of Greek life. Riefenstahl's Greek temple dancers fulfill not only a classical ideal but also a "feminine" one. In their strength and proportion, the dancers realize the beauty, health, and wholeness integral to Duncan's vision of the ideal woman and perfect mother. Through the associations drawn between the dancers and the primary elements of water, air, and fire and the fluid, circular gestures of the dancers' movements, the dance sequence establishes a mythical, organic community that echoes both the neoclassicism and Romanticism essential to German nationalism. The trajectory covered from Greece to Germany is thus a movement not only from the ancient world to its modern apotheosis but also from the heart of the earth to the full flowering of civilization. The mother remains as the core of the fatherland, its mystical and magical support.

The mass gymnastics sequence in the "Fest der Schönheit" partakes of the same mystical quality that characterizes the prologue to the "Fest der Völker" (fig. 3). The scene opens with a shot of a serene, golden-haired woman swaying rhythmically in a grassy field. The gentle cadences of the woodwinds recall the dance sequence in the prologue. Four or five women become visible, all performing "eurhythmics"—slow, waving movements of the limbs. A series of wide, low-angle shots reveals groups of dancers set against the vast sky, reinforcing the wholesome quality of the open-air movements. The camera focuses in on a smiling, blond woman with a Nordic air. The lilting melody emphasizes the mellifluous motions of the dancers, while the triple meter characteristic of a polonaise or Austrian *ländler* lends a folksy quality to the sequence. A wide-angle shot reveals long, diagonal lines of dancers, all swinging batons in uniform, curving arcs. As the camera angles widen, more and more women are revealed until ten thousand women in row upon vertical row fill the screen, becoming what Kracauer has called the mass ornament, the representation of the masses in highly rational, abstract patterns. The final aerial view of the patterned mass marks the climax of the sequence, which is punctuated by sweeping strings and a triumphant brass fanfare.

[121]Felix Hollaender, Program, "Wege zur Kraft und Schönheit" (1924), 5–10, translation in Kaes, 677.

Figure 3. Mass gymnastics display in the "Fest der Schönheit," the second part of Riefenstahl's *Olympia*. Photo courtesy of the Film Museum Berlin, Deutsche Kinemathek.

As in the visual parades of soldiers in Riefenstahl's 1934 Nazi Party Congress film *Triumph of the Will*, the composition of the gymnastics display in *Olympia* fills the frame, enfolding the spectator into the image itself. In the movement from the dance sequence in the "Fest der Völker" to the gymnastics display in the "Fest der Schönheit," the mystical, mythopoeic dancer becomes a rational abstraction and the individual dancer a living part of the social organism. Unlike the cabaret revue, in which the viewer has critical distance from the image, here the spectator is implicated, one of the docile and instrumental bodies of the body politic.[122] The image is a seductive one, inviting the viewer to join in the cult of the body and take part in the organic wholeness of the social sphere. Through the use of cross-dissolves, slow motion, and wide-angle tracking shots, the dance sequences in Riefenstahl's *Olympia* possess a certain hypnotic power. What was mechanical reproduction in the revue becomes mesmerizing repetition in the mass ornament. What was a linear ordering of space becomes an architectonic filling of the sensory screen. What evoked the technological calls forth the grandeur of sublime nature. An appeal to the senses becomes an appeal to the will.

[122]For a longer discussion of the mass gymnastics sequence in *Olympia*, see Ramsay Burt, "Totalitarianism and the Mass Ornament," in *Alien Bodies: Representations of Modernity, "Race" and Nation in Early Modern Dance* (London, 1998), 112–17. Burt argues

CONCLUSION

Despite the radical differences in the dance idioms, important similarities can be found in Anton's *Wir tanzen um die Welt* and Riefenstahl's *Olympia*. Both films draw on classical roots, and both rechannel female sexuality in politically productive ways. While *Wir Tanzen um die Welt* constructs the female body as a quasi-military corps that demands sacrifice, unity, and discipline in the service of a greater good, *Olympia* establishes the female body as an organic part of the whole. The linear revue in *Wir tanzen um die Welt* deploys female sexuality in a particularly contained form, sustaining a heterosexual norm and mediating potential fears of an uncontrolled female sexuality. The *Ausdruckstanz* sequences in *Olympia*, on the other hand, construct an image of essential femaleness, reinforcing the "natural" role of woman while also producing a homosocial paradigm usually reserved in Nazi aesthetics to the erotic "homophilic attachments" created through male bonding.[123]

Eric Rentschler's designation of three key elements in Nazi film aesthetics—the elemental, the ornamental, and the instrumental—is particularly useful for understanding Riefenstahl's orchestration of space in *Olympia*. Rentschler has pointed to a triadic paradigm at work in Riefenstahl's 1932 mountain film, *Das blaue Licht* (The blue light), one that can be found in much of "Nazi fantasy production": the establishment of a mythic community (the elemental), the restructuring of this community in new shapes and patterns (ornamentalization), and the realization of this process in accordance with a larger instrumental rationality (instrumentalization) whose function usually remains hidden.[124] If we take the two expressionist dance sequences in the *Olympia* film as a narrative unit, we find a striking example of the ornamentalization of the elemental to an instrumental end. In the first sequence, the female body is anchored in the roots of civilization and the earth, the feminine established as an

similarly that Riefenstahl's ornamentalization of the masses imbues the abstract patterns of the mass ornament with deeper meaning, suggesting a community of happy, docile bodies. According to Burt, through Riefenstahl's editing, the film "conveys what Kracauer would have described as regressive, organic meanings. . . . [T]he image of the mass gymnastics spectacle in Riefenstahl's *Olympia* suggests an imaginary community that is well co-ordinated, happy and healthy. . . . What images like those of the mass gymnastic display show are women happily internalising power over their bodies, power that has manipulated their desire to be part of a community. Through the pursuit of an elusive ideal, their bodies have become what Foucault has called docile bodies" (114–16).

[123]As Eric Rentschler has pointed out, eroticism in Nazi cinematic productions usually issued from "homophilic attachments" between male members bound together in duty to the state as opposed to heterosexual bonds between individuals. See Rentschler, "The Elemental, the Ornamental, the Instrumental: *The Blue Light* and Nazi Film Aesthetics," in *The Other Perspective in Gender and Culture: Rewriting Women and the Symbolic*, ed. Juliet Flower MacCannell (New York, 1990), 179.

[124]Ibid., 177–78.

essential element of nature. In the second sequence, this organic woman becomes part of a coordinated whole whose ornamental function is laid bare by the aerial patterns of the camera but whose instrumental value as a symbolic member of the larger social community remains hidden. In the movement from the theatrical mass ornament exemplified by the Hiller Girls to the massive, ornamentalized patterns in *Olympia*, the rational ordering of space achieves an irrational effect, a mystifying process by which the product is imbued with a magical power of its own. While the viewer maintains distance and objectivity in the case of the linear revue, he or she is integrated into the mass of ordered and cohesive bodies that form the political mass ornament. In the end, Riefenstahl's vision of the female form is a more seductive one than that found in *Wir tanzen um die Welt*, as the nudity of the female figures in the film is "natural," and their powers of seduction are hidden.

The dance sequences in *Wir tanzen um die Welt* and the *Olympia* film are emblematic of the larger dance movements of the period in that they harness both the "modern" and "antimodern" aspects of modern dance, the former drawing on the formal machine aesthetic of the revue and the latter on the neoclassicism, life reformism, and nationalism embedded in the expressionist dance movement. However, the question of the political value of the revue and *Ausdruckstanz* under the Third Reich remains a complicated one. While the militarized kickline harnesses the "excesses" of female sexuality by creating a masculinized body whose libidinal energy is often deployed in the service of the state, the prevalence of erotic dance sequences in filmed and staged performances and the continued popularity of individual, "exotic," non-German performers such as Zarah Leander and Marika Rökk open up further questions concerning the value of popular entertainment in the Third Reich. Furthermore, whereas *Ausdruckstanz* forms such as the lay choir proved popular in state-supported events, the Propaganda Ministry's lack of interest in the movement's two figureheads suggests that *Ausdruckstanz* performances may have projected an appeal to the self and to mystical forces that exceeded the boundaries of the state. In broaching the complexity of the issue of desire in Nazi Germany, this study has pointed to a number of specific instances in which female performance figured in fascist politics. In rendering the female body a vehicle for the projection of a seductive state, *Wir tanzen um die Welt* and *Olympia* politicized the erotic and eroticized the political, infusing the body politic with a libidinal charge. Like much of the iconographic material of the period, the imagery in these films has a subliminal appeal, one that could be as powerful a magnetic force for the state as explicit political measures and incentives.

Forbidden Company: Romantic Relationships between Germans and Foreigners, 1939 to 1945

BIRTHE KUNDRUS

Carl von Ossietzky University, Oldenburg

BY AUGUST 1944, over 7 million foreigners were living in the "Greater German Reich." The majority, which included 1.9 million prisoners of war and 5.7 million forced laborers, had been brought to Germany against their will. Among these foreigners were 1.3 million French citizens, 2.8 million Soviet citizens, and 1.7 million Poles. Women made up half of the Polish and Soviet citizenry in the Reich and roughly one third of the foreign laborers overall. On average, these women were under twenty years of age. Though no statistics exist regarding the age of male foreigners in the Reich, the majority of male prisoners of war and foreign laborers were probably between thirty and forty years of age. Though the Nazi regime had "imported" the foreign laborers to work in the agricultural economy and the war industries, their "deployment" was deemed to constitute a serious danger to the "preservation of the German *Volk*'s purity of blood."[1] Consequently, in 1940, the Office of Racial Policy (Rassenpolitsches Amt) warned:

> There can be little doubt that racial policy considerations demand that we combat with all available means the extraordinary threat of contamination and pollution this concentration of foreign workers

I would like to thank Katharina Hoffmann, who kindly provided me with the material from Oldenburg, as well as Patricia Szobar, Dagmar Herzog, and this journal's referees for their inspiring and challenging comments.

[1]See Heinz Boberach, ed., *Meldungen aus dem Reich 1938–1945: Die geheimen Lageberichte des Sicherheitsdienstes der SS*, vols. 1–17 (Herrsching, 1984), report of January 22, 1942, 3200–3201; see also Boberach, reports of May 8, 1940, 1358, and June 10, 1943, 5337–41; Bundesarchiv Koblenz (BA), R 22, no. 3361, 40, report of the president of the Regional Superior Court in Darmstadt of May 10, 1941, report of July 17, 1941, 48, and report of the head state's attorney in Düsseldorf of July 29, 1940, no. 3363, 75; Staatsarchiv Hamburg (StAHH), SBI, VG 30.69, report of the Oberfürsorgerin der

poses . . . to our Germanic lineage. This alien population was until recently our most bitter enemy, and inwardly remains so today, and we can and may not stand idly by while they invade the vital essence of our *Volk*, impregnate women of German blood, and corrupt our youth.[2]

The ever-increasing number of foreign laborers in Germany made lasting changes in the composition of civil society. In many regions, casual contacts, friendships, and romantic relationships developed between the German population and prisoners of war or foreign laborers. In response, the Nazi regime issued a series of complex regulations and directives governing the living and working conditions of the various classes of foreigners. Soviet prisoners of war, for example, were supposed to be kept under constant military supervision and remain in camps when not at work. French and Belgian military internees, in contrast, benefited from such special privileges as greater freedom of movement, since the German authorities deemed them to constitute a lesser security risk. However, maintaining this "racial" regulatory hierarchy was not always practicable; for example, prisoner-of-war camps were frequently short of military guards, and local authorities often failed to keep pace with the regime's "regulatory frenzy."[3] The regulations themselves were often vague and open to interpretation. On a few occasions, those governing certain classes of foreigners were reversed entirely, as happened in the case of Ukrainians and Italians dur-

---

Kreisdienststelle 8 of October 31, 1940. For other studies of romantic and sexual relationships between Germans and foreigners with diverse local foci, see Bernd Boll, "'. . . das gesunde Volksempfinden auf das Gröbste verletzt': Die offenburger Strafjustiz und der 'verbotene Umgang mit Kriegsgefangenen' während des 2. Weltkriegs," *Die Ortenau* 71 (1991): 645–78; Andreas Heusler, "'Straftatbestand' Liebe: Verbotene Kontakte zwischen Münchnerinnen und ausländischen Kriegsgefangenen," in Sybille Krafft, ed., *Münchner Frauen in Krieg und Frieden 1900–1950* (Munich, 1995), 324–41; Birthe Kundrus, "'Die unmoral deutscher Soldatenfrauen': Diskurs, Alltagsverhalten und Ahndungspraxis 1939–1945," in Kirsten Heinsohn, Barbara Vogel, and Ulrike Weckel, eds., *Zwischen Karriere und Verfolgung: Handlungsräume von Frauen im nationalsozialistischen Deutschland* (Frankfurt, 1997), 96–110; Christiane Rothmaler, "Fall 29," in *"Von Gewohnheitsverbrechern, Volksschädlingen und Asozialen": Hamburger Justizurteile im Nationalsozialismus,* ed. Justizbehörde Hamburg (Hamburg, 1995), 364–79; Gerd Steffens, "Die praktische Widerlegung des Rassismus: Verbotene Liebe und ihre Verfolgung," in *"Ich war immer gut zu meiner Russin": Zur Struktur und Praxis des Zwangsarbeitersystems im Zweiten Weltkrieg in der Region Südhessen,* ed. Fred Dorn and Klaus Heuer (Pfaffenweiler, 1991), 185–200; Antje Zühl, "Zum Verhältnis der deutschen Landbevölkerung gegenüber Zwangsarbeitern und Kriegsgefangenen," in *Faschismus und Rassismus, Kontroversen um Ideologie und Opfer,* ed. Werner Röhr, Dietrich Eichholtz, Gerhart Hass, and Wolfgang Wippermann (Berlin, 1992), 342–52. In addition, see Rolf Hochhuth, *Eine Liebe in Deutschland* (Reinbek, 1978). In his novel, Hochhuth depicts a romantic relationship between a German woman and a Polish man.

[2]Head of the local Rassenpolitisches Amt, Schäringer, of August 3, 1940, cited in Annegret Hansch-Singh, *Rassismus und Fremdarbeitereinsatz im Zweiten Weltkrieg* (Berlin, 1991), 138.

[3]Boberach, report of April 29, 1940, 51,978; see also Rothmaler, 370.

ing the course of the war.[4] Such situations served to confirm the misgivings of the organization in charge of National Socialist racial policy, the Head Security Office of the Reich (Reichssicherheitshauptamt, RSHA). In 1942 the Security Service (Sicherheitsdienst, SD) of the SS complained that "the conscription of many millions of men into military service, the lack of a universal prohibition against sexual relations for foreigners, and the incorporation of additional foreign workers, all have increased the threat of infiltration of the blood of the German *Volk*."[5]

The regime's prohibition of contacts between German men and women and forced laborers and prisoners of war must first be sited within the context of National Socialist racial policy, an aspect correctly emphasized by Ulrich Herbert's path-breaking work and, more recently, by a series of local studies.[6] As these studies have made clear, the Nazi regime's treatment of foreign laborers was shaped by ideological factors as well as economic considerations. The daily lives of the various categories of foreigners were governed by a harsh and meticulously detailed set of regulations that differentiated by nationality and race. In the hierarchy of these categories, the forced laborers from Eastern Europe occupied the lowest rung. This racist mode of thought, enshrined in national policy in 1933, has been cited by historians as one of the very few ideological constants of National Socialist rule and the driving force behind the regime's policies.[7] Within this worldview, "maintaining the purity" of the "Aryan race" was the prerequisite for survival and the basis for all claims of "racial" superiority. For this reason, sexual contacts with "alien peoples" struck at the core of National Socialist racial proscriptions.

The problem of associations between Germans and foreigners must also be analyzed against the background of National Socialist gender policies, which studies have shown were integrally linked to the regime's racial proscriptions. As Gisela Bock's study of forced sterilization, Gabriele Czarnowski's work on Nazi marriage and sexual policy, and Atina

---

[4]See the account in Klaus Heuer, "Die Region: Definitionsversuche, Aufgabenstellungen, Beispiele, Erfahrungen," in Heuer and Dorn, eds., 30–36.

[5]Boberach, report of January 22, 1942, 3200–3201; see also reports of May 8, 1940, 1358; June 10, 1943, 5337–41; BA, R 22, no. 3361, 40, report of the president of the Regional Superior Court in Darmstadt of May 10, 1941, and of July 17, 1941, 48; report of the head state's attorney in Düsseldorf of July 29, 1940, no. 3363, 75; StAHH, SBI, VG 30.69, report of the head social worker at the district office 8 of October 31, 1940.

[6]Ulrich Herbert, *Fremdarbeiter: Politik und Praxis des "Ausländereinsatzes" in der Kriegswirtschaft des Dritten Reiches* (Berlin, 1985). See also the works listed in Michael Ruck, *Bibliographie zum Nationalsozialismus* (Munich, 2000).

[7]See, for example, the new synthetic accounts by Ludolf Herbst, *Das nationalsozialistische Deutschland 1933–1945: Die Entfesselung der Gewalt: Rassismus und Krieg* (Frankfurt am Main, 1996); and Bernd Jürgen Wendt, *Deutschland 1933–1945: Das Dritte Reich— Handbuch zur Geschichte* (Hannover, 1995).

Grossmann's study of the German sex-reform movement have shown, National Socialist racism was never gender-neutral; rather, debates surrounding an individual's "racial value" were molded by assumptions about the "nature" of sexual categories and distinctions. Moreover, the primacy of racism accorded men and women different roles, limitations, and opportunities within the Nazi state.[8] The first historian to assess the importance of gender in the "deployment of foreigners" was Jill Stephenson, whose work also examined the regime's treatment of romantic associations between Germans and non-Germans.[9] Among her conclusions, for example, is that the regime regarded the problem of illegal associations primarily as an issue involving "German" women and "racially foreign" men, a perception that cannot be entirely accounted for by the prevailing sexual double standard and the increasing numerical imbalance between men and women on the home front.[10] Rather, this belief was also informed by the notions of population policy in which the female body figured centrally to symbolize the "body of the *Volk*" and nation.

For most nations during the Second World War, the victorious power's sexual "occupation" of the "body" of another nation symbolized both the military defeat of the enemy nation and the humiliation of its male population.[11] Thus, under prevailing gender logic, any (sexual) advance made toward a male enemy national by a German woman was deemed a dishonor

---

[8]Gisela Bock, *Zwangssterilisation im Nationalsozialismus: Studien zur Rassenpolitik und Frauenpolitik* (Opladen, 1986), and "Antinatalism, Maternity and Paternity in National Socialist Racism," in *Maternity and Gender Policies: Women and the Rise of the European Welfare States, 1880s–1950s*, ed. Gisela Bock and Pat Thane (London, 1991), 233–55; Gabriele Czarnowski, *Das kontrollierte Paar: Ehe- und Sexualpolitik im Nationalsozialismus* (Weinheim, 1991), and "Die Ehe als 'Angriffspunkt der Eugenik': Zur geschlechterpolitischen Bedeutung nationalsozialistischer Ehepolitik," in *Rationale Beziehungen? Geschlechterverhältnisse im Rationalisierungsprozeß*, ed. Dagmar Reese, Eve Rosenhaft, Carola Sachse, and Tilla Siegel (Frankfurt am Main, 1993), 251–69; Atina Grossmann, *Reforming Sex: The German Movement for Birth Control and Abortion Reform 1920–1950* (New York, 1995).

[9]Jill Stephenson, "Triangle: Foreign Workers, German Civilians, and the Nazi Regime: War and Society in Württemberg, 1939–45," *German Studies Review* 15 (1992): 339–58; Jill Stephenson, "'Emancipation' and Its Problems: War and Society in Württemberg 1939–45," *European History Quarterly* 17, no. 3 (1987): 345–65.

[10]For another discussion of the supposed "femininity" of the home front, see Elizabeth D. Heineman, "Whose Mothers? Generational Differences, War, and the Nazi Cult of Motherhood," *Journal of Women's History* 12, no. 4 (2000): 138–63, esp. 141.

[11]See Christiane Eifler, "Nachkrieg und weibliche Verletzbarkeit: Zur Rolle von Kriegen für die Konstruktion von Geschlecht," in *Soziale Konstruktionen—Militär und Geschlechterverhältnis*, ed. Christiane Eifler and Ruth Seifert (Münster, 1999), 155–86, esp. 155–60; on the connection between the rape of women and German national identity, particularly after 1945, see Elizabeth Heineman, "The Hour of the Woman: Memories of Germany's 'Crisis Years' and West German National Identity," *American Historical Review* 101, no. 2 (1996): 354–95; and also Birgit Beck, "Vergewaltigung von Frauen als Kriegsstrategie im Zweiten Weltkrieg?" in *Gewalt im Krieg: Ausübung, Erfahrung und Verweigerung von Gewalt in Kriegen des 20. Jahrhunderts*, ed. Andreas Gestrich (Münster, 1995), 34–50.

to the German nation and *Volk* community. The Reich Ministry of Justice's guidelines regarding prohibited contact with prisoners of war, issued on January 14, 1943, thus stated: "German women who engage in sexual relations with prisoners of war have betrayed the front, done gross injury to their nation's honor, and damaged the reputation of German womanhood abroad."[12]

Finally, the regime's racial, gender, and nationalist concerns about illegal associations were further complicated by the wartime labor shortage as well as by the fact that the reality of daily regulatory practice often ignored official decrees. Such inconsistencies, as Herbert has shown, shaped the entire course of the regime's "deployment of foreigners" and by extension its treatment of "illegal associations." Thus, a variety of factors affected the evolving and often inconsistent manner in which the National Socialist regime pursued the problem of forbidden contacts with foreigners.

With this historiography as my point of departure, in this essay I shall examine how racial, gender, and nationalist precepts were reflected in the persecution of associations between Germans and foreigners during the Second World War. I shall first explore whether it is possible to uncover a coherent hierarchy among the three categories of race, gender, and nation—a "primacy of race," for example—or whether their configuration varied according to the situation at hand. The examination of the complex fashion in which these three categories were intertwined, particularly within racial and nationalist discourses and policies, will help to systematize the patterns that current research has highlighted as variable and inconsistent in the regime's treatment of contacts between Germans and foreigners.

To this end, I will examine daily practices of persecution and punishment at the local level, since it is here that tensions between National Socialist policy and social reality, between the aims and pronouncements of the Nazi leadership and the patterns and effects of daily enforcement, are most clearly evident.[13] As historical scholarship has shown, the administration of power in the Third Reich was not wholly a top-down affair. Rather, regional authorities possessed a limited form of autonomy, creating therewith a new dynamic and scope for action and interpretation "from below." Thus, regional authorities at times anticipated, adopted, or reformulated what were often conflicting directives from above, thereby contributing to the functioning of the dictatorship.[14] In keeping with this focus, records from northern Germany and the area surrounding Oldenburg form the basis of my account. While important sources such as the files of the Oldenburg Special Court (Sondergericht) were destroyed shortly before the end of the war, Gestapo files and judicial records from other courts survive. In structuring my argument as a local case study, my aim is to expand our understanding

[12]Cited in Rothmaler, 372.
[13]Heuer, 13–68, esp. 13–20.
[14]Herbert, 346–58.

of the workings of the National Socialist dictatorship and help expose the complex and paradoxical impact that National Socialist regulations, such as the policies on "foreigners," had on individuals at the time. Throughout, however, it is crucial to keep in mind that the experiences and fates of the foreign laborers and the prisoners of war can be reconstructed only to a very limited extent, as the surviving primary sources largely re-create the perspective of the oppressors.

THE "PROBLEM" OF FOREIGNERS IN THE THIRD REICH

To keep its leadership informed about the popularity of its policies, the Nazi regime instituted a system of reports that detailed popular opinion and morale. During the war years, in particular, morale reports were produced at nearly all levels of administration, from the family-allowance bureau, which oversaw support to families of drafted soldiers, to welfare workers and court officers, to agents in the SD's own "political early warning system." Nearly all the officials and agencies reporting confirmed that from the time of the foreigners' first arrival on German soil, sexual relationships began to develop between German girls and women and forced laborers and prisoners of war. In its report, the Rassenpolitsches Amt thus warned:

> Regrettably, it has come to our attention that there are many German women and girls who, unmindful of their duty to the *Volk*, are not ashamed to strike up a friendship or even intimate relations with these men of an alien *Volk*. They allow themselves to be plied with drinks quite openly in the pubs and then disappear with these men, who don't even speak German, into parks, adjacent woodlands, and meadows. . . . The foreign agricultural worker . . . on the farmstead always will try to instigate relations with the German farm-girl and farmer's wife, notwithstanding that her husband is off at the front. . . . For as long as he remains on our soil, the foreign laborer will exploit the woman of German blood to satisfy his sexual cravings, father children with her, and later . . . simply abandon the woman along with her half-breed children.[15]

As the number of foreign laborers imported into the Reich increased, such complaints by party offices, the security services, welfare agencies, and other authorities also increased.[16] Foreigners and Germans worked in close proximity on farms and in factories, making it inevitable that contacts would develop. As the SD noted with displeasure in 1943, such associations were not limited to any one social class or category. Moreover, as the SD report emphasized, it was by no means the case that all such relationships were

---

[15]Head of the local Rassenpolitsches Amt, Schäringer, cited in Hansch-Singh, 137–38.
[16]See, for example, Boberach, report of July 8, 1940; report of January 22, 1942; report of June 10, 1943.

initiated by the foreign men; German women were also playing an active role. The number of women involved in such relationships, the SD noted,

> was limited only by accident and opportunity. The women who be-
> come involved in relationships with prisoners of war came into daily
> contact with these men in their work on the farm and factory. Not all
> are women of loose morals, though this may well be true for the
> majority. The accused women include innocent farm girls of good
> reputation and family background, and also soldier's wives, some hap-
> pily married for many years, some the mothers of several children. In
> cases where French men are employed in higher positions, then the
> accused include also stenographers, housekeepers, estate secretaries,
> and women from the intelligentsia.[17]

The figure of the woman who had succumbed to sensation seeking after wartime conditions had deprived her of a father's or husband's control was a trope that had emerged in Germany as well as in other nations during the First World War.[18] In 1944 the SD wrote a report on the "immoral conduct of German women." Though their "waywardness" had not yet approached the level of the First World War, "a significant proportion of women and girls" were inclined to "exploit the situation sexually." This was particularly alarming in the case of "war wives," whom authorities and party officials deemed worthy of special mention: "The effect of war wives' marital infidelity on their husbands at the front must be regarded as especially serious. These men are very troubled by neighbors' reports of their wives' behavior. Many blame Germany's leadership for being unable to maintain order in the family while they fight at the front."[19] The drafting of millions of men into military service during the Second World War often entailed many years of separation for married couples. The regime regarded such separations as a threat to its "*Volk* and military power," as the head state's attorney of Frankfurt wrote in 1943.[20] Women's extramarital relationships were believed to endanger the stability of the

---

[17]Boberach, report of December 13, 1943, 6142.

[18]Birthe Kundrus, *Kriegerfrauen: Familienpolitik und Geschlechterverhältnisse im ersten und Zweiten Weltkrieg* (Hamburg, 1995), 212–20; on Great Britain, see, for example, Christine Gledhill and Gillian Swanson, eds., *Nationalising Femininity: Culture, Sexuality and British Cinema in the Second World War* (Manchester, 1996).

[19]Boberach, report of April 13, 1944, 6485; see also Marlies Steinert, *Hitlers Krieg und die Deutschen: Stimmung und Haltung der deutschen Bevölkerung im Zweiten Weltkrieg* (Düsseldorf, 1970), 425–28.

[20]Stadtarchiv Frankfurt (StadtAF), Chronik S 5/187, report of the head state's attorney of January 29, 1943. See also Brandenburgisches Landeshauptarchiv (BLHA), Rep. 2 A I, Pol, no. 1256, 236, letter from Gestapo Potsdam of October 1, 1944: "For some time, the inhabitants of the town of Kyritz have noticed that German women are attending pubs and the cinema with French prisoners of war on leave, . . . bringing them to family events and . . . spending the night with them in their bedrooms. The women in question are those whose husbands died in the war or are missing in action, or who are still serving at the front."

family and thus pose a threat to peace and order at home as well as on the war front. Furthermore, women's increased sexual independence undermined military morale since soldiers were preoccupied with their wives' fidelity, blamed the state for the decline of traditional marriage and family values, and worried that their male prerogatives and authority were being undermined. Such "manifestations of waywardness" in women also promoted male promiscuity, since men now assumed "women today are all available for the asking." Furthermore, the "dissolute" lifestyle of mothers had a detrimental effect on their children. Finally, this pleasure-seeking lifestyle ran counter to Nazi racial precepts, in which sexuality first and foremost was to be an act between a "racially pure" couple in service to the "*Volk* community." For all these reasons, then, sexual relations between Germans and foreigners remained a highly fraught issue for the Nazi regime.

FORBIDDEN CONTACT WITH PRISONERS OF WAR

Authorities had not fully grappled with the problem of undesirable associations between Germans and foreigners at the time when war broke out in the fall of 1939; however, soon thereafter the National Socialist authorities agreed that contacts between Germans and foreigners, especially between German women and foreign prisoners of war, were in need of regulation. They issued the first decrees regarding contact with prisoners of war in November 1939.[21] The justifications for these regulations were largely shaped by considerations of military security; such associations, it was claimed, constituted a grave threat of espionage, sabotage, and the undermining of morale. An Oldenburg police edict issued in March 1940 summarized the new regulations in especially succinct form: "All association with prisoners of war on the part of the civilian population is prohibited. Personal contacts are understood to include: 1. sharing a home or meals with prisoners of war; 2. inviting prisoners of war to pubs and other places of entertainment; 3. serving prisoners of war in pubs; 4. attending religious services together and organizing joint church events."[22] The "Verordnung über den Umgang mit Kriegsgefangenen" (Decree on associations with prisoners of war), issued on May 11, 1940, forbade all contact with prisoners of war "beyond the strictly necessary."[23] This vague formulation meant that a simple handshake or a friendly good-bye, the use of familiar forms of address, gifts of food, or an invitation to the cinema could serve to instigate a Gestapo investigation. A December 13, 1943, SD report included a warning regarding the ease with which it was

[21]See RGBl. (Reich law gazette) I 1939, decree on the expansion of penal action to protect the military power of the German *Volk* of November 25, 1939.

[22]Oldenburg law gazette, police decree of March 19, 1940, 205–6.

[23]RGBl. I 1940, decree on the association with prisoners of war of May 11, 1940.

possible to overstep the boundaries and commit a serious offense: "Often what first appear to be harmless pleasantries develop into romantic relationships. . . . Even more frequent are cases in which German women have provided 'their' prisoner of war with civilian clothing, money, foodstuffs, and maps to aid in an escape."[24]

In order to obtain evidence of forbidden contacts, the Gestapo and the Wehrmacht carried out raids on prisoner-of-war camps. An atmosphere of denunciation and gossip also flourished, since block leaders, air-raid wardens, party nurses, and other party members were called on to monitor the daily activities and political reliability of their fellow citizens. However, most denouncers were probably ordinary citizens, not party members, who acted out of such "baser motives" as envy, jealousy, or revenge. In many cases, the denouncers were women—female neighbors and work colleagues—who hoped to settle ordinary quarrels with a phone call or a note to the Gestapo. While the regime's system of administration and persecution relied on such denunciations, false denunciations could quickly lead to popular unrest. The authorities were particularly concerned that false accusations against war wives would result in unrest among Wehrmacht soldiers.[25] For this reason, local conditions largely determined whether prohibitions against contact with prisoners of war and the Polish and "Eastern" laborers were enforced. When rural solidarity prevailed and a village "kept mum," prohibited contacts went unpunished.[26]

German women involved in forbidden associations were faced with high court costs and the loss of their civic rights. The regime, for example, withheld the state pension for war widows for as long as their loss of civic rights remained in effect. Women were subject to humiliating public exposure in the local press, where quite often their names were published. The *Oldenburger Nachrichten*, for example, reported one case of forbidden contact under the headline "Vier Jahre Zuchthaus für eine Ehrvergessene" (Four years penitentiary for her dishonor).[27] After the start of the war, German women discovered in relationships with Polish prisoners of war had their head shaved and were paraded before the public. Although local party and government officials initially believed that such

[24]Boberach, report of December 13, 1943, 6142.

[25]On the issue of denunciation, see Gisela Diewald-Kermann, *Politische Denunziation im NS-Regime oder die kleine Macht der "Volksgemeinschaft"* (Bonn, 1995); Katrin Dördelmann, *"Die Macht der Worte": Denunziationen im nationalsozialistischen Köln* (Cologne, 1997); Robert Gellately, *The Gestapo and German Society: Enforcing Racial Policy 1933–1945* (Oxford, 1990), 130–58; Eric A. Johnson, *Nazi Terror: The Gestapo, Jews, and Ordinary Germans* (London, 2000), 353–79; Ingo Marßolek, *Die Denunziantin: Helene Schwärzel 1944–1947* (Bremen, 1993).

[26]See also, for example, the account by Marie-Luise K. in Walter Kempowski, *Das Echolot: Ein kollektives Tagebuch Januar und Februar 1943* (Munich, 1993), 519–20.

[27]*Oldenburger Nachrichten*, October 9, 1942. See also the reports dated October 3, 1941, and February 6, 1942.

public punishments would have a deterrent effect, in fact, they often elicited popular pity and sympathy for the accused. At times, female observers were more repelled by the sexual double standard in evidence than by the forbidden relationship itself. In early 1941 in the town of Ebern, for example, a crowd watched while a woman whose hair had been shaven off was paraded through the streets alongside a sign that read: "I sullied the honor of German womanhood." A number of women in the crowd "let it be known that they disapproved of this action. A few women also ventured to ask whether the same would be done to a man who had an affair with a French woman while in France."[28] On October 31, 1941, in part as a concession to opinion abroad, Hitler issued a directive prohibiting all public punishments.[29]

Women who were accused of forbidden associations continued to be subjected to humiliating and voyeuristic interrogations and trials by the Gestapo and the courts. Male interrogators expressed great interest in determining whether and how often a "completed act of sexual intercourse" had taken place, since this determined the severity of the case and whether a penitentiary sentence was in order.[30] The state's attorney was authorized to decide whether a trial should be conducted as a summary proceeding before the district court or whether it should be held before the Special Court to accommodate the seriousness of the case or a perceived need for "public instruction." Defendants who had close personal contacts or who had assisted in escape attempts were almost always tried before the Special Court and usually received a penitentiary sentence. Thus, whether the accused couple was successful in downplaying the extent and intensity of their "forbidden contact" was crucial in determining their fate.

In the case of the "dishonorable" woman reported by the *Oldenburger Nachrichten*, the defendants clearly failed in their attempt to downplay their relationship. Bertha B., who lived in a village near Rastede, was married to a farmer serving at the front. When she became pregnant in the course of an affair with S., a Serbian prisoner of war, fear of punishment led her to denounce S. for rape, "against her better judgment."[31] Her case was regarded as especially serious because she was the mother of three children and because she had shown herself to be "unfavorably disposed

---

[28]SD branch office Ebern, report of March 14, 1941, cited in Hochhuth, 63; see also Gellatelly, 232–44; and Herbert, 79–80.

[29]See Bormanns's directive of October 13, 1941, reprinted in Beatrice und Helmut Heiber, eds., *Die Rückseite des Hakenkreuzes: Absonderliches aus den Akten des Dritten Reiches* (Munich, 1993), 234–35.

[30]See OLG 9000–9479, 20, Reich Ministry of Justice to the presidents of the regional Superior Courts, January 14, 1943; Steffens, 194–95.

[31]StAOl, 140-4, no. 106, head state's attorney letter to the Reich Ministry of Justice regarding the defense petition for a commutation of the sentence of October 23, 1944.

toward National Socialist rule in Germany."[32] Thus, she received a comparatively harsh sentence of four years' penal servitude. In a similar case, Erna B., a thirty-one-year-old widow, was convicted in February 1945 of a relationship with S., a Belgian prisoner of war. Though Erna B. claimed that S. had promised to become a German citizen and marry her, it is clear that her argument failed to win the sympathy of the Oldenburg Special Court. As its head magistrate, a District Court judge named Baldamus, argued, "Her husband's heroic death imposed upon her an obligation that should have prevented her from entering into a relationship with a foreigner. The defendant was well aware of this fact. There are enough German men around if she needed someone to provide and care for her and her children."[33] A mitigating factor, according to the judge, was that her husband's death had presumably shaken her moral grounding. This fact, along with what was determined to be a mild mental deficiency, led the judge to impose a sentence of eighteen months' penal servitude.

It is nearly impossible to assess how the number of arrests and convictions and the pattern of sentencing changed over the course of Nazi rule. First, any attempt to assess arrest and conviction rates would need to take into account not only the official statistics on offenses against Paragraph 4 of the "Wehrkraftschutzverordnung" (Decree for the preservation of military power) but the statistics on Gestapo arrests as well. Neither the Gestapo nor the military maintained separate statistics on the number of cases involving sexual relations with a foreigner, further complicating any attempt to arrive at reliable figures.[34] In his investigation of Offenburg, Bernard Boll came to the conclusion that the number of convictions for forbidden associations with prisoners of war rose drastically until 1943 and that more German women than German men were convicted for sexual contact with foreigners.[35] Along the same lines, in 1944 the head state's attorney of Berlin stated that "the number of cases involving forbidden association with prisoners of war . . . has not noticeably decreased."[36]

---

[32]StAOl, 140-4, no. 106. In a few similar cases, the farming couples attempted to obtain a lesser sentence by arguing that the farm would go to ruin should they be incarcerated. See Beatrix Herlemann, *"Der Bauer klebt am Hergebrachten": Bäuerliche Verhaltensweisen unter dem Nationalsozialismus auf dem Gebiet des heutigen Landes Niedersachsen* (Hannover, 1993), 281.

[33]StAOl, 140-5 Acc 13/67, no. 7, 8, verdict of February 15, 1945.

[34]Herbert cites a figure of 1,240 Gestapo arrests for "forbidden contact" in the year 1942 (123). Bock claims that each year up to ten thousand German women were arrested for forbidden associations with "foreign" men (*Zwangssterilisation*, 439). More research would be necessary in order to arrive at an accurate assessment of these figures.

[35]Boll, 650–51, 663. Rothmaler also argues that the year 1943 was the peak year for such cases (378).

[36]Report of the head state's attorney at the Superior Court of Berlin of May 31, 1944, cited in Hans Dieter Schäfer, *Berlin im Zweiten Weltkrieg: Der Untergang der Reichshauptstadt in Augenzeugenberichten* (Munich, 1985), 196.

At first, the sentences imposed by the courts were subject to a great deal of variability, as the SD noted with disapproval. In 1941, for example, the Speyer regional court sentenced a woman to four months in jail for her relationship with a Frenchman. At roughly the same time, the Leithmeritz Special Court imposed a sentence of five years' penal servitude for a similar offense.[37] The Reich Ministry of Justice was also displeased with sentencing standards and expressed its concern that insufficiently rigorous verdicts would cause the "members of the *Volk*" to lose faith in Germany's leadership:

> Repeatedly, women who out of pity gave a piece of bread to a prisoner of war have received . . . inordinately long prison sentences. Unmarried women who have become pregnant as a result of their sexual relations with prisoners of war have been sentenced to lengthy penitentiary terms, while women who became pregnant in the course of a relationship with civilian workers from the former enemy nations have applied for and received permission to marry. Given the similarity in their circumstances, such discrepancies often result in confusion.[38]

The SD also reported that many Germans failed to understand the purpose of the regulations and remained hostile to them. This was true not only in the case of Czechs and Ukrainians but also for the French. If the Frenchman was a prisoner of war, his female partner was always punished, but if he was a foreign laborer, the couple was sometimes permitted to marry.[39]

Though the SD demanded in 1943 that all cases of forbidden contact between German women and prisoners of war be punished with three years' penal servitude, it is unclear whether this uniformity of sentencing was achieved.[40] Rather, it seems more likely that sentencing patterns continued to depend on a variety of factors, particularly, the court's assessment of the accused woman's character, which in turn relied upon stereotypes of femininity. A seeming lack of shame, a loose sexual lifestyle, and a failure to conform politically could all serve as exacerbating factors. The defendant's age and, especially, her maturity and experience in life seem also to have

---

[37]Boberach, report of December 13, 1943.

[38]OLG 9000–9479, 13, Reich Ministry of Justice letter of October 10, 1942.

[39]Boberach, report of December 13, 1943, 6141 and 6146; see also Elizabeth D. Heineman, *What Difference Does a Husband Make? Women and Marital Status in Nazi and Postwar Germany* (Berkeley, 1999), 57; Heusler, 325–27. In only a few instances were civilian workers from France as well as Belgium, Spain, and Bulgaria convicted for "undesirable sexual intercourse with a German." See Hansch-Singh, 139; Hans-Henning Krämer and Inge Plettenberg, *Feind schafft mit . . . Ausländische Arbeitskräfte im Saarland während des Zweiten Weltkrieges* (Ottweiler, 1992), 134–35; and Steffens, 190. See also, for example, BLHA, Rep. 2 A I, Pol, no. 1256, 287, Schutzpolizei report of September 29, 1944.

[40]Boberach, report of December 13, 1943, 6144–45. According to Heusler, the sentences imposed by the Munich courts declined over the course of the war (336).

played a role.[41] However, the most important factor was whether sexual intercourse had actually taken place. Married women, particularly if they were mothers, war wives, or war widows, typically received harsher sentences than did single women.[42] In the June 1943 issue of *Richterbriefe* (Judicial letters), Otto Georg Thierack, the Reich Minister of Justice, commented on the problem of war wives' affairs with foreigners.[43] According to Thierack, a woman's duty to "manage the home and the farm in [her husband's] stead" and preserve "his will to battle by her faithfulness" had a racial basis in ancient Germanic custom. The war wife "who fails to uphold and defend her honor" disgraced both her husband and the community and "should not expect to benefit from their protection." Thierack's comments suggested that war wives' "marital fidelity" was not a moral issue but, rather, a racial imperative and in wartime a national obligation in service of the "*Volk* community."[44] The publication of these decrees and commentaries signaled to war wives that their offences would be subject to harsher judgment. However, in cases where the husband had submitted a petition for pardon, stating that he had forgiven his wife and wished to continue the marriage, the sentence could be commuted from penitentiary to prison and the convicted wife's civic rights restored.[45]

British and French prisoners of war who engaged in intimate relations with German women were sentenced by the military courts to prison sentences of three years in normal situations or six years in especially serious cases, in accordance with Paragraph 92 of the military penal code, which covered cases of military insubordination.[46] In the case of Polish and Soviet prisoners of war and "civilian workers," the Wehrmacht turned its jurisdiction over to the Gestapo, with the result that Polish and Soviet citizens were taken into protective custody, convicted by a Gestapo summary court, and either transferred to a concentration camp or hanged.[47]

[41]Heusler, 337.

[42]Boll, 668–71; Heineman, *What Difference*, 59.

[43]The *Richterbriefe* were distributed by the Reich Ministry of Justice to regional and local courts beginning in October 1942 with the aim of instructing local jurists on the National Socialist system of justice. See Heinz Boberach, ed., *Richterbriefe: Dokumente zur Beeinflußung der deutschen Rechtsprechung 1942–1944* (Boppard, 1975).

[44]"*Verfügungen, Anordnungen, Bekanntgaben*, hg. von der Parteikanzlei." Vol. 4 (Munich, 1942–1944).

[45]Boberach, report of December 13, 1943, 6145.

[46]See Boll, 661; Herbert, 79, 125; see also BA, R 43 II, no. 1544a, 70, confidential Reich Ministry of Justice guidelines regarding the adultery of war wives and related crimes of November 1942.

[47]See Earl R. Beck, *Under the Bombs: The German Home Front 1942–1945* (Lexington, 1986), 25; Hans Peter Bleuel, *Das saubere Reich, Theorie und Praxis des sittlichen Lebens im Dritten Reich* (Bern, 1972), 265–75; Dieter Galinski and Wolf Schmidt, eds., *Die Kriegsjahre in Deutschland 1939 bis 1945: Ergebnisse und Anregungen aus dem Schülerwettbewerb deutsche Geschichte um den Preis des Bundespräsidenten 1982/1983* (Hamburg, 1985), 81–94, 121–34; Herbert, 122–29; William L. Shirer, *Berliner Tagebuch: Aufzeichnungen 1934–1941*

FORBIDDEN CONTACT WITH FOREIGN LABORERS

The "Polen-Erlasse" (Polish decrees) issued in March 1940 were a series of racially motivated special regulations that governed associations with Polish forced laborers. These decrees, which later served as a model for ordinances designed to deal with Soviet "Eastern workers," regulated contacts between Germans and Polish forced laborers in exhaustive detail. They subjected Polish men and women to a comprehensive system of restriction and repression, forbade all association with the German population, and emphatically warned against all "racially" inappropriate conduct. In the spring of 1940 the Oldenburg Regional Propaganda Office (Gaupropagandaamt) issued a leaflet entitled *Wie verhalten wir uns gegenüber den Polen?* (How do we behave toward the Poles?) that exhorted the German population: "Maintain the purity of German blood! This applies to both men and women! Just as engaging in relations with a Jew is a matter of ultimate dishonor, it is equally sinful for any German to engage in intimate relations with a Polish man or woman."[48] Placards and pamphlets commanding restraint in associations with "foreign peoples" were distributed and posted in all public venues and on factory floors.[49] German women were threatened with prison sentences and, after 1941, with transfer to a concentration camp. This was the fate of Elisabeth W., from the town of Dammen, who was arrested by the Gestapo for her relationship with a Polish man. Initially incarcerated in the Oldenburg prison from July 1940 to August 1941, Elisabeth W. was later transferred to the Ravensbruck concentration camp.[50] By contrast, German men charged with rape (as opposed to a romantic relationship) received prison sentences of at most a few months.[51] In the case of Polish laborers, however, a pamphlet issued by the regime stated in no uncertain terms, "Anyone who enters into a sexual relationship with or makes an indecent advance toward a German woman or a German man will be sentenced to death."[52] After June 1940, Poles accused of *GV-Verbrechen* (sex crimes) were hanged, often publicly,[53] though on rare occasions the death penalty was deferred. In May 1942, for example, the Oldenburg Special Court sentenced N., a Polish forced laborer, to death for having allegedly clasped both

---

(Leipzig, 1991), 435, 482; on convictions for "prohibited associations with prisoners of war," see Bernd Schimmler, *Recht ohne Gerechtigkeit: Zur Tätigkeit der berliner Sondergerichte im Nationalsozialismus* (Berlin, 1984), 85–91.

[48]Cited in Herlemann, 277.

[49]See Boll, 649; Herbert, 126.

[50]StAOl, 145-1, Acc 9/84 no. 24.

[51]Herbert, 128. According to Herbert, the German man was to be turned over to a concentration camp for a three-month sentence. Herlemann discusses the case of a farmer who died while incarcerated in a concentration camp for relations with his Polish farmworker (284).

[52]Cited in Jürgen Bombach, *". . . zu niedriger Arbeit geboren . . .": Zwangsarbeit im Landkreis Stade 1939–1945* (Stade, 1995), 5.

[53]See Herbert, 127–28; Johnson, 59, 358.

his arms around a German woman in an attempt to rape her; subsequently, the Reich Ministry of Justice commuted N.'s sentence to five years' penal servitude.[54] In late 1942 the increasing labor shortage seems to have resulted in the issuance of a directive that foreign offenders be transferred to a concentration camp.[55] Beginning at roughly the same time, a Polish man could be spared hanging if a medical officer issued a favorable racial certificate that enabled the Pole's "Germanization."[56] Thus, a racial hygienic logic and a system of "selection," already in place for the "*Volk* community," was transferred and reformulated to apply to the "Slavic race." Instead of "wasting" individuals who were similar in custom and "racial" appearance, these were now to be incorporated into the "body of the German *Volk*." In such instances, the men were incarcerated only briefly in a concentration camp and in some cases were even permitted to escape punishment entirely and marry their German partner.[57]

Two years earlier, in September 1940, Himmler had announced a change in the penalties for Polish women:

> as recent reports have shown, intimate relations with Polish women are almost always instigated by the German man. Quite often the Polish woman is in a relation of dependence with the German man. In many cases it is the farmer's son or the work supervisor, sometimes even the employer himself, who induces the Polish women into sexual intercourse. It is particularly those Polish women who desire to fulfill their work obligations and keep their jobs who are most inclined to submit to their employer's or overseer's demands.[58]

[54]For information on these two cases, see Jens Luge, *Die Rechtsstaatlichkeit der Strafrechtspflege im oldenburger Land, 1939–1945* (Hannover, 1993), 146–47.

[55]See Matthias Hamann, "Erwünscht und unerwünscht: Die rassenpsychologische Selektion der Ausländer," *Beiträge zur nationalsozialistischen Gesundheits- und Sozialpolitik,* Band 3: *Herrenmenschen und Arbeitsvölker: Ausländische Arbeiter und Deutsche 1939–1945* (Berlin, 1986), 143–80, esp. 163.

[56]See Hamann; Gabriele Czarnowski, "Zwischen Germanisierung und Vernichtung: Verbotene polnisch-deutsche Liebesbeziehungen und die Re-Konstruktion des Volkskörpers im Zweiten Weltkrieg," in *Die Gegenwart der NS-Vergangenheit,* ed. Helgard Kramer (Berlin, 2000), 295–303; Heineman, *What Difference,* 58–59. Heineman argues that the "racial classification" of the Pole was not what was at stake here, since it was actually the figure of the German woman who was the focus of the majority of the attention. If the woman was a prostitute or married, no examination was deemed to be necessary. However, it should be kept in mind that racial constructions always entail a transfer of biological categories into the realm of the social. Thus a Pole who entered into a relationship with a prostitute or who committed adultery would by this very fact have already demonstrated that he could not be successfully "Germanized." Such actions in themselves would be taken as proof of the Pole's "lesser value."

[57]Herbert, 74–82.

[58]Letter from Himmler to the Staatspolizei (State Police) on September 3, 1940, cited in Hansch-Singh, 150–51.

The driving force behind this change in policy was that the SS, for economic reasons, wanted to preserve the "labor deployment" of Polish women who were willing to work. In cases of rape, Polish and Soviet women were no longer to be sentenced to death but confined for three weeks in protective custody.[59]

An illustrative example is the case of Genowefa W., a fourteen-year-old Polish girl who had been assigned to a Sedelsberg peat works in the summer of 1940. In September 1940 Genowefa W.'s overseer, Hermann B., attempted to "forcibly abuse her sexually; in addition . . . on December 15, 1941 [he also maltreated] her with a horsewhip . . . and then forced himself on her sexually . . . which resulted in the Polish girl experiencing pain in her lower abdomen."[60] News of these incidents circulated on the factory floor. Genowefa W. also wrote her father, who lived near Posnan, who in turn reported the incidents to the police. As is implied by the judge's comments in his verdict, this "publicity" likely contributed to the decision to prosecute the case: "On the other hand, no mitigating circumstances speak in favor of the accused, in spite of the fact that he has no criminal record; by his actions he has done grave harm to the image of the German *Volk*. Knowledge of his actions is widespread in Polish circles."[61] Moreover, Genowefa W. had made a favorable impression on the Gestapo officials during her interrogation, which might partly have been due to the fact that her parents were of "Germanic extraction." The Gestapo's final report thus stated, "W. made a highly favorable impression during her interrogation. From her responses, it was clear that she is a young girl with no experience in sexual matters. . . . It is incomprehensible that he [B.] could have committed such an assault on W., who is nothing more than a child, as her appearance makes perfectly clear."[62]

Since, by abusing his position of authority, B. had tarnished the nation's reputation, and because Genowefa W.'s youth and "racial" descent spoke in her favor, the court sentenced B. to four years' penal servitude, a relatively harsh verdict compared to similar cases involving German men and Polish women. Despite the fact that this was a case of forbidden Polish-German relations, the court seems to have based its sentence on Paragraph 177 of the penal code, in which rape was punishable by a penitentiary term of up to fifteen years.

The Reich SD would have preferred to prohibit all sexual relations between foreigners and Germans, male and female alike, to provide German

---

[59]In all other cases, they were turned over to a concentration camp for an indefinite period of incarceration. See Herbert, 127–29.

[60]Staatsarchiv Oldenburg (StAOl), 140-5 Acc 14/76, no. 71, 26, District Court of Oldenburg on February 23, 1942.

[61]StAOl, 140-5 Acc 14/76, no. 71, 68, verdict of July 17, 1942.

[62]StAOl, 140-5 Acc 14/76, no. 71, 20, final report of the Gestapo on February 12, 1941.

soldiers with "the assurance that the wives they had left behind would come to no harm."[63] However, worries about the reaction abroad made the regime reluctant to undertake such a far-reaching measure.[64] Racial prejudice thus had to take a back seat to considerations of foreign policy and relations with allied nations such as Italy, Croatia, Romania, Spain, Hungary, and Yugoslavia. Nonetheless, the Gestapo attempted to quash such personal contacts "in view of our racial beliefs."[65] Such differences of opinion among the highest authorities led to the issuance of contradictory rulings "from above," which in turn resulted in confusion and uncertainty at lower levels of administration. One issue in dispute, for example, appears to have been the matter of sexual relations between German and Czech citizens. In November 1942 the Dresden Gestapo office issued a statement that "sexual intercourse between individuals from the Protectorate and Germans . . . is prohibited, unless the district governor has granted them permission to marry."[66] What led to such a vacillating directive is unclear, but couples who were subject to the directive faced an impossible dilemma. Though their association was forbidden, it was nonetheless possible that their relationship might yet be legalized; but by bringing their relationship to official attention, the couple risked forced separation and even punishment. This dilemma led to the arrest of Edith K., a German woman employed in Nordenham, who was detained "for having repeatedly engaged in sexual intercourse with Vaclav S., a Czech, despite the fact that her application for permission to marry had been turned down by the Nordenham Public Health Office in March 1941."[67]

[63]Bundesarchiv (BA), R 16, no. 162, record of the meeting of the working group on foreigners of the RSHA on August 8, 1941. Beginning in 1941, brothels for foreign laborers were established as an additional measure to ensure the "maintenance of the purity of German blood." The brothels were established to "protect German womanhood" by ensuring that foreign women satisfied the sexual urges of foreign men, whose libido was deemed to be "untamed" in accordance with highly traditional notions of masculinity. However, this policy was not pursued very energetically, as can be seen by the fact that the number of brothels remained low; by 1943, approximately sixty brothels with approximately six hundred women had been established to accommodate a population of several million prisoners of war. However, unauthorized prostitution also flourished in the camps and, according to Herbert, was so widespread that it overshadowed the state-run institutions (203). On this issue, see also Christa Paul, *Zwangsprostitution: Staatlich errichtete Bordelle im Nationalsozialismus* (Berlin, 1994), 117–30.

[64]See R 43 II, no. 1544a, 57, letter of Bormanns to Lammers of November 13, 1942.

[65]See, for example, the letter from the Weimar Gestapo to the Thuringian Ministry of the Interior of September 12, 1941, reprinted in "Dokumentation: Ausgrenzung—Deutsche, Behörden und Ausländer," *Beiträge zur nationalsozialistischen Gesundheits- und Sozialpolitik,* Band 3: *Herrenmenschen und Arbeitsvölker,* 131–41, quote on 132; Gestapo Darmstadt written notice of April 1, 1943, cited in Heuer, 31–32.

[66]Gestapo Dresden, November 16, 1942, cited in "Dokumentation," 138.

[67]StAOl, 289, no. 187, 730. Daily report by the Gestapo Wilhelmshaven head office, no. 3, March 1942. An Oldenburg man and a Czech woman had already been arrested in

This gray zone in the ideology and practice of enforcement was of little practical advantage to its victims, as the story of Hanny Olga J. from the town of Elsfleth makes clear. A confluence of circumstances makes this case a particularly tragic one. In 1941 the twenty-year-old Hanny Olga J. fell in love with Mikola G., a Ukrainian who worked as a forced laborer at the Rüttgers shipyard and lived in Hanny Olga's parents' home. The couple was engaged in August 1942. According to the parents' testimony, a number of agencies, including Oldenburg's Public Health Office (Gesundheitsamt) and the Rassenpolitsches Amt, had given the couple to understand that nothing stood in the way of their marriage. However, policies on Ukrainians had been a matter of controversy among the Nazi leadership for several years. While the Ministry of Foreign Affairs and other agencies did not want to sabotage the possibility of friendly relations with the Ukrainian population, the RSHA regarded the Ukrainians as "Russians" subject to the "Ostarbeiter-Erlasse" (Decrees on eastern workers).[68] It is likely that this lack of unanimity contributed to the local Elsfleth authorities' initial tolerance of Hanny Olga J.'s relationship. In November 1942, however, the district party head intervened. J. and G. were issued a summons to appear at the Public Health Office, where the physician in charge determined that Hanny Olga J. was pregnant. G. was arrested later that day and transferred to a work camp near Trier shortly thereafter. J.'s father was ordered to appear before the Wesermarch regional headquarters, located in the town of Brake, where he was informed that should he ever "venture to pursue the matter of [his daughter's] marriage to the Ukrainian G.," then his family would be subject to "police" action.[69] Refusing to accept this warning, Hanny Olga J. wrote to the regional headquarters, arguing: "I was never aware that relations with Ukrainians were prohibited. The newspapers never reported this either. I did read about Jews and Poles, but nothing ever was mentioned about Ukrainians. . . . Ukrainians were free, and had the same rights as Germans."[70] Her letter met with no response. When Hanny Olga J. later gave birth to a son, G. acknowledged his paternity. Nearly two years later, on December 1, 1944, Hanny Olga J. was imprisoned in the Nordenham jail and later was transferred to the Ravensbrück concentration camp, where it appears she died. The records make no mention of the cause for her arrest. G. survived the war and remained in Germany after the fall of the Third Reich.

November 1941 for having repeatedly engaged in sexual intercourse. See StAOl, Best. 136, no. 2886, 606, daily report of the Gestapo Wilhelmshaven head office, no. 7, November 1941.

[68]Herbert, 154–57. See also Ralf Dünhoft, *Fremdarbeiter in Delmenhorst während des Zweiten Weltkrieges* (Oldenburg, 1995), 66–72.

[69]StAOl, 140-5 Acc 1/62 no. 256, 6, minutes of the interview of the father on December 5, 1942.

[70]StAOl, 140-5 Acc 1/62 no. 256, 7, letter of December 5, 1942. On this case, see also "Ist denn da was gewesen?" in *Frauen in der Wesermarsch im Nationalsozialismus*, ed. Landkreis Wesermarsch—Frauenbüro (Oldenburg, 1996), 134–44.

Hanny Olga J.'s reputation had already been tarnished by bearing a child out of wedlock. Her parents were Jehovah's Witnesses, and she herself openly disagreed with National Socialist racial policies and rejected the regime's prohibitions on associations with foreigners. What is more significant, however, is that Hanny Olga J. refused to believe she had committed a crime, particularly since she had obeyed all of the regulations known to her. Hanny Olga J. also did not regard the Ukrainians with whom she had personal associations as members of an alien, "less valuable" race. Clearly, what on one day was legal could become illegal the next, and the law provided little by way of reliable standards or security, even for "members of the *Volk*." The reality that the rule of law was little more than an empty phrase in the terrorizing regime of the Third Reich was very difficult for Germans to accept, particularly when they believed themselves innocent of any crime.

Contemporary Interpretations

In 1944 the SD attempted to explain the supposed sexual permissiveness of so many war wives and other "women of the *Volk*." The central reason given was the "long duration of the war," which had brought with it a number of changes. Women's increased mobility, initially due to employment and later to the evacuations, had uprooted them from their normal existence and led to a "weakening of moral fiber" among some. Standards for marital fidelity had declined overall, and women living alone often succumbed to loneliness. Neighbors and acquaintances introduced women to previously unfamiliar lifestyles. In pubs, women met soldiers and foreign men who wished to strike up new female acquaintances but preferred a casual love affair to a more permanent alliance. When bombardments made danger a daily affair, many reacted by seizing whatever enjoyment they could from "earthly pleasures." Films, magazines, and popular music had excessively eroticized public life. Elites set a poor example: more and more public figures divorced, and affairs with artists and secretaries had become the order of the day. Some women were motivated by a desire for scarce and coveted goods, such as coffee, chocolate, alcohol, and stockings, that soldiers brought back with them from the occupied territories. Similar impulses spurred women's desire for contact with foreigners. While some claimed they wanted to brush up on their language skills by associating with foreigners, particularly with French men, others were clearly "sexual sensation seeking."[71] The head of social services in Hamburg's welfare bureau, Käthe Petersen, who was responsible for "mentally fragile women," also blamed soldiers' sexually undisciplined lifestyle for their wives' infidelity: "These women have begun to hold the view that anything a

---

[71]Boberach, report of April 14, 1944, 6481–88, and report of July 2, 1942, 3902; see also Stephenson, "Triangle," 344.

man does should be permitted to them as well."[72] Even if an individual "lapse" was understandable, the SD and Käthe Petersen argued, it was necessary to combat such "excesses."

In the debate surrounding the supposed promiscuity of German youth, the central concern was the moral decline of an entire generation that was to have served as the "biological" future of Germany. A key focus of official attention was thus the danger of sexually transmitted disease. The reasons given for the proliferation of promiscuity among German youth put forth by the courts, welfare agencies, and the SD were very similar to those proffered on behalf of adult women. In addition, officials suspected that adolescent boys believed foreign women were an easier sexual conquest than German girls or, especially, German women.[73]

It is difficult to assess whether such fears and accusations had any basis in reality or whether they were based on grossly exaggerated suspicions fueled by erotic fantasy, sexual jealousy, and voyeurism. Even more difficult are generalizations about the frequency, extent, and circumstances of such cases of "forbidden contact." Clearly, not every rendezvous would have resulted in an intimate relationship, and not every relationship was discovered by the authorities. What can safely be said, however, is that Germans always had more sexual options and freedom of action than did the "foreign workers." Prisoners of war and foreign laborers, whether male or female, presumably hoped that any gestures of friendship and affection might distract from the oppressive conditions of daily life. Soviet and Polish men and women may even have hoped to receive gifts of food or assistance in escape. Some relationships involved the explicit use of coercion by the man, most often the German man; others involved manipulation or exploitation by a woman. But however exaggerated their claims might be, it is likely that the motives cited by the SD did account for much of the behavior of those Germans involved in illegal encounters.

Any nuanced assessment of the conduct of German women and youth in this era would need to evaluate carefully the regime's steady charges of immorality. It does seem clear that the war and the presence of millions of foreigners allowed some Germans to engage in new behaviors and experience different forms of heterosexuality as well as homosexuality. Nonetheless, the presence of foreigners elicited a broad range of responses among the German population, which included not only the desire to explore forbidden territory but also a wish to uphold traditional norms.[74]

[72]StAHH, SBI, EF 70.24, letter by Petersen of February 17, 1943; see also StadtAF, Chronik S5/187, report of January 29, 1943.

[73]See Robert Waite, "Teenage Sexuality in Nazi Germany," *Journal of the History of Sexuality* 8, no. 3 (1998): 434–76; Stephenson, "Triangle," 344, 349.

[74]On England, see Penny Summerfield and Nicole Crocket, "'You Weren't Taught That with the Welding': Lessons in Sexuality in the Second World War," *Women's History Review* 1, no. 3 (1992): 435–54.

Despite unceasing propaganda and severe prosecution by the police and the courts, the Nazi regime remained unable to quash the proliferation of associations between Germans and foreigners during the war. This was especially the case with regard to the "workers from the West" (i.e., France and Belgium). The German population remained unconvinced by slogans urging them to "protect German blood," since such proscriptions "found no echo in existing popular prejudice," as Ulrich Herbert has noted.[75] But it was sometimes the case with respect to the "Eastern workers." Prohibitions against associations with Polish and Soviet prisoners of war were undermined, though more slowly, whenever a personal relationship gave the lie to the prejudicial image of the "subhuman Slav"—that negative stereotype that exploited fears of the faceless, anonymous, and undifferentiated horde.

CONCLUSION

In the late 1930s, prompted by the sudden incorporation of millions of foreigners into the Reich, the Nazi regime introduced a complex set of regulations governing relationships between German citizens and various categories of foreigners—forced laborers and prisoners of war, Eastern and Western Europeans, males and females. These regulations were based upon Nazi racist ideologies that simultaneously celebrated the superiority of German blood and expressed fear for its pollution. They were enforced differentially, depending upon whether the relationship involved coercion (rape) or romance. They were applied differentially to foreigners based upon their position in a racial hierarchy: the Poles and Russians, for example, fared much worse than did the Belgians and French. When a relationship involving a German and an Eastern European displayed signs of emotional intimacy, the convicted foreign female was usually sent to a concentration camp, the foreign male hanged.

Against German offenders, the regulations were also applied differentially but according to gender. In conformance with the traditional sexual double standard, the purity of German blood necessitated women's chaste behavior more than it did men's. The relationship of a German man with a foreign woman, though illicit, could be considered another form of "conquest." Consequently, the German man who violated the regime's racial proscriptions was half-heartedly punished for exercising his male sexual prerogatives. But the "sexual surrender" of a German woman to a foreign worker or, worse yet, to a foreign soldier was a humiliation for the entire *Volk*. Variations in sentencing, then, had their basis in a confluence of ideologies of racism, militarism, and masculinity. When considerations of

[75]Herbert, 126. See also, for example, "Unsere Verantwortung in der Fremdarbeiterfrage," *NS-Frauenwarte* 10, no. 3 (1941): 38.

gender and nationalism conflicted with those of race and economic efficiency, however, the equation was resolved in favor of the latter.

Although these regulations remained in effect throughout the war, enforcement of them varied over time and from place to place, depending upon circumstances. Fears of subterfuge and concerns about national security helped justify and sustain the prohibitions against associating with prisoners of war, the "enemy within." But the regime's economic dependency upon foreign laborers (which had impelled their immigration in the first place) sometimes mitigated strict enforcement of the regulations, as did the need for cordial relations with a number of foreign powers. At times, German public sentiment was also a deterrent. Throughout the war, many Germans remained skeptical about the need for such prohibitions. This was especially so with respect to Western Europeans, who had not been stigmatized in this way before and continued to enjoy many liberties. And it was occasionally so with regard to Eastern Europeans—at least when individual Germans had occasion to know them. However, none of these mitigating factors was sufficiently effective to prevent the regulations that prohibited relationships between Germans and foreigners from devastating the lives of thousands of otherwise innocent people.

Translated by Patricia Szobar

Sex with a Purpose: Prostitution, Venereal Disease, and Militarized Masculinity in the Third Reich

ANNETTE F. TIMM

Trinity College, University of Toronto

SEX IN THE THIRD REICH was for too long a virtual terra incognita for historians of Germany. There was an understandable desire to avoid providing titillating details about so murderous a regime. Still, the paucity of research on the subject meant that a rather one-sided understanding of Nazi attempts to harness the sexual energies of German citizens emerged, and that initial interpretation has only recently begun to be replaced with more complex analyses. This essay contributes to the effort by exploring how Nazi attitudes toward sexuality and masculinity were expressed in policies on prostitution and the control of venereal disease. This specific vantage point requires us to go beyond a simple argument that Nazism was sexually repressive. The totalitarian impulse to make even the most private of human activities serve national goals meant that Nazi leaders sought not only to define acceptable sexual behavior but to redefine sexual acts as acts with public—not simply private—significance. Sex and reproduction were crucial elements of population policy, indispensable in the formation of a strong state. This followed from the fear that a declining birth rate and the spread of congenital and endemic disease would weaken the nation, a fear compounded by Nazi racial ideology and German expansionist dreams.

On the surface, most National Socialist propaganda that bore any relationship to sexuality concerned itself with issues of reproduction. The advertised goal of health and welfare policy was to promote large Aryan families to ensure the survival of the racial state that the Nazis wished to create. However, while extolling the virtues of the chaste Aryan family, Nazi leaders simultaneously provided support (both verbal and financial) for various kinds of extramarital sex. Three examples come immediately to mind. First, sexual crimes were committed under military authority and in the concentration camps during the war.[1] Second, in his October 1939 order, Himmler argued that truly patriotic and racially valuable Germans should produce illegitimate children to strengthen and replenish the warring nation. These two examples lie mostly outside the scope of this essay, which will focus instead on the third form of nonmarital sex condoned by the Nazi regime: prostitution. Having branded prostitutes as asocial, sending tens of thousands of them to concentration camps in the early 1930s for "conspicuously . . . inciting immoral acts,"[2] the regime eventually came to treat prostitution as a necessary sexual outlet for productive male citizens. Primarily under Himmler's influence, the regime came to accept prostitution as necessary for satisfying male sexual drives, which, if left unsatisfied, would lead men into homosexuality, dampen their fighting spirit, or diminish their labor productivity. This logic led to the construction of brothels for soldiers and "ordinary" Germans and, by 1942, for slave laborers and concentration camp inmates. The regime's sponsorship of prostitution greatly complicates the idealized imagery of Nazism's support for a nation of chaste families.

This essay will discuss the apparently contradictory stances toward sexuality in the Third Reich by examining the regime's policies on prostitution and venereal disease control and by presenting examples from a local case study of Berlin. A study of prostitution encourages a reconsideration of some common assumptions about National Socialist attitudes toward sexuality. On the surface, support for prostitution seems to conflict with the findings of voluminous historical research on Nazi propaganda about sanitizing family life and promoting policies designed to encourage German citizens to limit sexual activity to the production of as many "racially fit" children as possible.[3] The regime's public support for chastity, however, masked the intentions of several party leaders to put the sexual urges of the population to work for the national cause. One might argue that this contradiction simply reflects well-known tendencies within the Nazi Party of in-fighting and fiefdom building by well-placed individuals. Many of

[1] See Birgit Beck, "Vergewaltigung von Frauen als Kriegsstrategie im Zweiten Weltkrieg," in *Gewalt im Krieg: Ausübung, Erfahrung und Verweigerung von Gewalt in Kriegen des 20. Jahrhunderts*, ed. Andreas Gestrich (Münster, 1996), 34–51; and Freya Klier, *Die Kaninchen von Ravensbrück: Medizinische Versuche an Frauen in der NS-Zeit* (Munich, 1994).

[2] See the Decree for the Protection of the *Volk* and State (issued on February 28, 1933) and May 1933 revisions to the VD law and Clause 361 of the criminal code.

[3] The collection of literature on this subject is vast. Recent works include Irmgard Weyrather, *Muttertag und Mutterkreuz: Der Kult um die "deutsche Mutter" im Nationalsozialismus* (Frankfurt am Main, 1993); and Lisa Pine, *Nazi Family Policy, 1933–1945* (New York, 1997). My own dissertation also contributes to the line of argument that focuses attention on attempts to confine sexuality to marriage. See Annette F. Timm, "The Politics of Fertility: Bevölkerungspolitik and Health Care in Berlin, 1919–1972," Ph.D. diss., University of Chicago, 1999. The present essay revises my initial arguments and is an attempt to take the attitude toward sexuality more seriously as an active force in the construction of reproductive health care policies.

the efforts to promote sex in the Third Reich were pet projects of the Reichsführer SS, Heinrich Himmler. The Lebensborn maternity homes for pregnant girlfriends and wives of SS soldiers and other "Aryans" provide one example of how Himmler sought to gain prominence in the field of population policy.[4] But the assault on "bourgeois prudery" launched by Himmler and other Nazi leaders cannot be seen as a strange sideshow. As Dagmar Herzog has demonstrated, it is inaccurate to think of the Third Reich solely in terms of sexual repression. That view of the Nazi regime, she argues, is a creation of the 1960s and 1970s and owes much to the post–World War Two generation's misunderstanding of their parents' experience under Nazism and to the influence of Wilhelm Reich on progressive students in the 1960s and 1970s.[5] Nevertheless, it would also be a simplification to argue that the Nazis were trying to cover all of the public opinion bases—playing to conservative, Christian opinion in their family policy while appealing to the less wholesome sexual cravings of the population with their support for prostitution.

The contradiction in official Nazi statements about sexuality was not simply a matter of pragmatism. It is possible to make sense of the seemingly contradictory positions if one recognizes the underlying consistency of policies that were all directed toward the same goal: the creation of a racially sanitized state with the power to rule Europe and beyond. Sexuality, in other words, was viewed as a means to an end. It was to be deployed within racially "desirable" families to produce future soldiers for the war machine and by individual men to strengthen their productive capacities and their fighting spirit. The goal was purposeful sexuality (sexual activity with a national purpose), not sex for the sake of individual pleasure.

Very much like the Victorians in Foucault's *The History of Sexuality, Volume 1*, Nazi leaders did something other than simply repress sex. The Nazis fostered a system of policing sex and "regulating sex through useful public discourses" that included a preoccupation with perversity and fecundity.[6] Although this essay will not attempt the analysis necessary to reconcile Foucault's theory with the empirical case in question, the very

---

[4]Himmler was quick to warn others away from interfering in what he saw as his domain. He reacted angrily, for instance, when Leonardo Conti, the Reich director of health, wrote about "Raising the Birth-Rate by Marital Introduction, Marriage Guidance and Fostering." See Hans Peter Bleuel, *Sex and Society in Nazi Germany*, ed. Heinrich Fraenkel, trans. J. Maxwell Brownjohn (Philadelphia, 1973), 170–71. The most authoritative book on the Lebensborn is Georg Lilienthal, *Der "Lebensborn e. V.": Ein Instrument nationalsozialistischer Rassenpolitik* (Stuttgart, 1985).

[5]She points out that the SS newspaper *Das schwarze Korps* was full of explicit rejections of bourgeois prudery. See Dagmar Herzog, "Sexuelle Revolution und Vergangenheitsbewältigung," *Zeitschrift für Sexualforschung* 13, no. 2 (2000): 87–103.

[6]Although Foucault alludes to race and tentatively ventures into the twentieth century, he does not deal with Nazism per se. See Michel Foucault, *History of Sexuality, Volume 1: An Introduction*, trans. Robert Hurley (New York, 1978), quote from 25.

terms of the present argument will resonate loudly enough with his work that it is worth recapping some of his main points in *The History of Sexuality*. Significantly, I consciously avoid applying to the subject at hand one of Foucault's key insights—that power mechanisms and discourses on sex do not simply repress but also create pleasures, since the persecution and discrimination associated with prostitution in the Third Reich would make this an ethically problematic task. Nevertheless, an engagement with Foucault's categories of modern sexuality informs my analysis. I make two key revisions to the Foucaultian model. First, I attempt to account (as Foucault does not, despite his allusions to twentieth-century racism) for the impact of twentieth-century militarism.[7] Second, I add men to the list of iconic figures that populate Foucault's account of the creation of modern sexuality. To "the hysterical woman, the masturbating child, the Malthusian couple, and the perverse adult"[8] I add the sexually satisfied male—or, perhaps more accurately, the presumed to be sexually satisfied male, since we must assume that at least some of the men pressured into visiting military brothels were less than enamored of the experience.[9] As will become clear, one cannot understand constructions of sexuality in twentieth-century Germany (or anywhere else, for that matter) if one assumes masculinity to be unchanging, unconstructed, and easily normative. It is necessary to move outside Foucault's categories to understand the full salience of militarized masculinity in Nazi Germany.[10]

Nazi leaders believed that the state needed to intervene directly in the private sexual sphere to make sure that "valuable" male citizens (and other men temporarily useful as laborers) were sexually satisfied. To some degree, sex was a reward to be doled out to supporters of the regime, and the male's sexual gratification was deemed to take precedence over the female's.

---

[7]On the place of racism in Foucault's thought, see Ann Laura Stoler, *Race and the Education of Desire: Foucault's* History of Sexuality *and the Colonial Order of Things* (Durham, 1995).

[8]Foucault, 105.

[9]Of course, the sexually satisfied male did not produce "targets and anchorage points of the venture of knowledge" to the same degree that Foucault's four "objects of knowledge" did (quotes from ibid.). In this sense, Ann Laura Stoler's plea for adding the colonized subject to Foucault's list is perhaps more defensible than what I argue here, since the types of technologies and regimes of power associated with the colonial were more equivalent to Foucault's use of his four "targets." But just as Foucault's four figures could not exist "without a racially erotic counterpoint, without reference to the libidinal energies of the savage, the primitive, the colonized" (Stoler, 6–7), they could also not exist without the anchor of normalized heterosexual male sexuality and male sexual dominance.

[10]I arrived at the formulation "the militarization of masculinity" before having read Eleanor Hancock's article on Ernst Röhm (see "'Only the Real, the True, the Masculine Held Its Value': Ernst Röhm, Masculinity, and Male Homosexuality," *Journal of the History of Sexuality* 8, no. 4 [1998]: 616–41). Our two articles have much different starting points: I begin with heterosexual relationships and issues of fertility, while she writes about Röhm's

The view that male sexual urges were basically uncontrollable had long been a feature of anti-VD policies in Germany,[11] but National Socialism took this belief one step further, equating sexual gratification with masculine power to a degree unprecedented in Germany (though not unknown in Italy).[12] Soldiers, it was thought, drew strength from their sexual encounters with prostitutes that enabled them to fight with increased vigor. Himmler was convinced that the best soldiers—those most likely to require prostitutes for sexual relief because of their strong masculine energies— would also be the most prolific citizens once they returned to their wives. Even slave laborers would produce more material goods for the Reich if given sexual rewards. Masculine vitality was thus viewed as highly dependent upon sexual gratification. However, gratification in and of itself was not the goal. Himmler and other leading Nazis did not speak about sexual pleasure but about the power of sexual activity to rejuvenate the nation and achieve racial superiority. Masculine sexual drives, like feminine maternal instincts, were to be channeled into the purpose of achieving the racial state.[13] The regulation of prostitution and the glorification of motherhood were both intended to strengthen military prowess, the former by offering sexual rewards to soldiers and war workers, the latter by creating a "fitter" and more numerous population from which to draw a fighting force. It is not enough, then, to set up dichotomies such as masculinity versus femininity or marriage versus promiscuity and then to explore the contradictions in National Socialist rhetoric and policy. Beneath the seeming contradictions was an underlying consistency of purpose.

One of the reasons why National Socialist attitudes toward sexuality seem contradictory is that the regime was always highly sensitive to the impact of its policies on public opinion. The promotion of sexuality was thus countered with active attempts to remove it from public view so as not to offend bourgeois sensibilities. In the first years of the regime, indi-

---

homosexuality and the complete absence—even the negation—of a feminine and reproductive aspect to his life. It is instructive, I think, that we wound up making similar arguments.

[11]Timm, "The Politics of Fertility," 106–17. The German word that I have translated as "urges" is *Geschlechtstrieb*, which one might more accurately (but less eloquently) translate as "sexual drive." Elsewhere I use the words "desire," "sexual need," "pleasures," "gratification," and so on. While my terminology would not satisfy the stricter categorizations of today's *Sexualwissenschaft*, I have tried to remain stylistically faithful to the colorful language used by Nazi politicians, who consciously rejected the inheritance of Weimar sexology. Sometimes, it must be noted, male sexual gratification was simply assumed or alluded to without giving it an explicit name or description.

[12]In the 1920s Italian eugenicists began to "depict Italian racial superiority in terms of innate sexual prowess, libidinousness and prolificity," a claim later wholeheartedly endorsed by Mussolini. See Maria Sophia Quine, *Population Politics in Twentieth-Century Europe* (London, 1996), 27.

[13]The term "racial state" is from Michael Burleigh and Wolfgang Wippermann, *The Racial State: Germany, 1933–1945* (Cambridge, 1991).

viduals who were considered "sexually deviant," including prostitutes, were confined to concentration camps, and leaders paid much lip service and attention to the "purification of the streetscape" [Säuberung des Straßenbildes].[14] Before the war, this attempt to remove sexuality from the public sphere was particularly evident in the intensification of VD raids and controls on prostitutes during the 1936 Olympics. In subsequent years, particularly during the war, police and health authorities redoubled their efforts to eradicate streetwalking and confine prostitution to state-sanctioned brothels.

The development of prostitution policy was by no means internally consistent or uniform throughout the Reich. Nevertheless, it is useful to distinguish three elements within Nazi policy: (1) public endorsement of chastity while cracking down on asocial sexual behavior and defining prostitutes as legally marginal; (2) toleration of extramarital sex, particularly prostitution, as long as it did not offend "public sensibilities"; and (3) subordination of all policies on sexuality and prostitution to the war effort. Only the last of these represented a clear policy shift. During the course of the war, Nazi policy decisively turned its back on decades of officially sanctioned social hygienic practice, forsaking health concerns for the strategic goals of higher productivity and improved fighting spirit. After the autumn of 1939, venereal disease control in Germany became almost entirely an effort to regulate and control prostitution in the interests of providing soldiers and war workers with a "safe" outlet for their sexual energies.

THE APPEARANCE OF CHASTITY

In the first years of the Third Reich, the Nazi leadership cultivated the appearance of chastity, seeking to depict the new social system as one entirely devoted to the foundation and maintenance of healthy, racially fit families. The stated goal was to strengthen the German family as a bulwark against racial degeneration and miscegenation. Nazi marriage policy and most of the leaders' official pronouncements about sexuality were meant to project an aura of respectability. George Mosse argues that after the violence and virtual anarchy of the early years of the National Socialist movement, its leaders recognized that bourgeois sensibilities would have to be addressed if the regime was to stabilize its position. This meant insisting on the absolute sanctity of marriage and vilifying deviations from the marital, heterosexual norm.[15]

[14]The term is from "Die Prostitutionsfrage," *Arbeitsgemeinschaft für Volksgesundung e.V.—Mitteilungen*, February 14, 1934, 1. The obsession with cleansing the streets of visible signs of prostitution was, however, very widespread. See also "Die Prostitution unter dem Geschlechtskrankengesetz," *Deutsches Ärzteblatt* 62 (1933): 100; and Adolf Sellmann, *Der Kampf gegen die Prostitution und das Gesetz zur Bekämpfung der Geschlechtskrankheiten* (Schwelm, 1935), where the author writes of "Reinhaltung des Straßenbildes" (26).

[15]George L. Mosse, *Nationalism and Sexuality: Middle-Class Morality and Sexual Norms in Modern Europe* (New York, 1985), 158–59.

Publicly extolling the virtues of the pure and chaste German family, Nazi leaders misled many commentators into believing that the regime would repress overt displays of sexuality. In the early years of National Socialism, experts in public health and welfare who supported the regime reacted positively to the rhetoric endorsing chastity and decrying sexual license, and they expressed confidence that the "National Socialist spiritual direction," with its emphasis on the family and its very strict definition of healthy sexuality, would be much more successful at combating prostitution and other sexual excesses than previous strategies.[16] Articles in medical journals, newspapers, and educational literature stressed the positive benefits of eugenic controls (which, it was said, would eventually weed out "inferior" social elements like prostitutes) and organized youth activities, sponsored by organizations like the Hitler Youth, the League of German Girls (Bund deutscher Mädel), and the labor organization Strength through Joy (Kraft durch Freude). Channeling youthful energies into sports and outdoor activities, according to Johannes Breger, the Berlin head of the German Society for Combating Venereal Disease, would prevent exposure to deviant sexual behavior.[17] The author of an article in the principal journal for female doctors wrote that males in particular could benefit from an education that stressed physical health and de-eroticized women. Femininity would then be appreciated for its link with motherhood rather than sex.[18] This, at least, was the ideal. The classic image so common in Nazi propaganda depicted the dutiful German *Hausfrau*, a guardian of home and hearth, an attentive mother devoid of all erotic characteristics.

Experts in VD control contributed to this valorization of marriage. The director of the German Society for Combating Venereal Disease, Bodo Spiethoff, argued that sexual self-control served the interests of the state. He laid these views down in the creed of his organization, which read:

> The Family is the nucleus of the state and of the state-conscious *Volk*.
> The essence of the family is a marriage founded on loyalty and faith.
> The wife has a particular duty in marriage to be the protector and educator of the young generation.
> The wife can only fulfill her duty if the husband is conscious of her calling and if the wife is supported by the respect of the husband.
> The husband should not only respect the woman [*Weib*], the mother of his children, he should also view every woman as the bearer of *völkischer* duties and stand before her chivalrously and protectively.

[16]Asta v. Mallinckrodt-Haupt, "Die Prostitution und ihre Bekämpfung," *Die Ärztin* 14, no. 9 (September 1938): 250.

[17]Johannes Breger, *Die Geschlechtskrankheiten und ihre Gefahren für das Volk*, 2nd ed. (Berlin, 1937 [1926]), 23, 99–101. For similar arguments, see Mosse's summary of Himmler's Bad Tölz speech to the SS on sexuality (167) and his discussion of sport-inspired Nazi sculpture (170 ff.); Mallinckrodt-Haupt, 250; and Hermann Roeschmann, *Die Bedeutung der Geschlechtskrankheiten für Jünglinge und Männer* (Berlin, [1934]), 14.

[18]Mallinckrodt-Haupt, 250.

The behavior of the grown man should always and under all conditions be exemplary for male youth.

If the woman displays the demeanor worthy of her duty, then she will be a model for future mothers and will command the respect of the man.

The woman shall never allow herself to be demeaned or to be estranged from her duty by the man.

If the man dishonors the woman, he dishonors himself, since he disgraces the meaning of the family as an integral part of a healthy *Volk* with a secure future.

Young man and young girl, do not succumb to your urges, rather, command them. Know: your youth is not a time for carrying on but, rather, a time to slowly gather strength for your life's duties.

For this reason, chastity is the uppermost ethical command.

Fight to remain victor in the battle for this highest command.[19]

The fact that such a detailed stance on the ethics of marriage was issued by an organization dedicated to the control of venereal diseases should come as no surprise. The battle against VD, according to experts, was a battle against unhealthy, unethical sexual practices.

The commentators mentioned above were all prominent figures in the anti-VD campaigns of the Weimar Republic. Possibly their praise for the new ethical direction of the National Socialist movement was an attempt to ingratiate themselves with a regime that they thought would take a sexually repressive line in public policy. Perhaps Breger, Spiethoff, and others truly believed or hoped that the Nazis would bring about the reforms that they had long been working to achieve. Given their desire to maintain their standing in the new regime, it was in their interest to believe that these early pronouncements on prostitution were indicative of the Nazis' general attitude on sexuality and that the Third Reich would continue to uphold conventional norms of bourgeois respectability. The period's literature on VD control resolutely avoids any mention of the arguments against bourgeois sexual norms made by Joseph Goebbels and Ernst Röhm.[20] Medical experts and religious groups that endorsed the regime instead focused on policies and rhetoric that supported sexual purity.

[19]Quoted in Breger, *Die Geschlechtskrankheiten*, 27.

[20]In January 1934 Goebbels railed against *Bettschnüffelei* in *Der Angriff* (the press organ of his Berlin *Gau*) and again, later that year, in the pages of the *Völkischer Beobachter*. He claimed to be a "champion of progressive sexual morality." See Bleuel, 75. (*Bettschnüffelei* can best be translated as "bed snooping," in other words, sniffing out the sexual histories/practices of others.) Ernst Röhm openly rejected bourgeois sexuality and its hypocrisies in his 1928 autobiography, *Die Geschichte eines Hochverräters* (Munich, 1928). But, as Eleanor Hancock has argued, this position was always an uncomfortable one in the Nazi Party and "came into conflict with the more usual National Socialist view of sexuality, which saw its main purpose as reproduction" (623–24).

Soon after seizing power in 1933, the Nazis took steps to enshrine the principle that sexuality, reproduction, and marriage were virtually synonymous concepts under law. The Sterilization Law (Erbgesundheitsgesetz) of 1933 and the Marital Health Law (Ehegesundheitsgesetz) and Blood Protection Law (Blutschutzgesetz), both of 1935, were all aimed at this goal. A logical corollary of these policies was the beginning of discussions about making birth control illegal, a policy supported by Adolf Hitler himself.[21] Opponents of birth control voiced concern about the continued distribution of prophylactics for VD prevention, since most of them, particularly condoms, could also be used as contraceptives. Vending machines selling condoms continued to be in use after 1933, and police did not charge vendors with "offending public morality and decency" as would have been possible under the 1927 VD law.[22] The dilemma posed by anti-VD prophylactics was the subject of intense debate. Despite concerns about promiscuity, experts insisted that condoms had to remain available to fight VD, and they were successful in insuring public access to condoms throughout the Nazi era.[23] However, all creams, salves, tablets, and other medications or objects meant to prevent VD or pregnancy were considered medically dangerous (they might, for example, lead to damage of the male sperm [*Keimzelle*] or female reproductive capacities, which would cause congenital defects).[24] Consequently, on January 21, 1941, other forms of birth control except condoms were criminalized by Himmler.

[21]Minutes of meeting of Sachverständigen Beirat für Bevölkerungs und Rassenpolitik, August 3, 1933, in Bundesarchiv Berlin, hereafter BArch(B), R43 II/720a, 120ff.

[22]The situation is summarized in J[ohannes] Breger, "Die Auswirkung des Reichsgesetzes zur Bekämpfung der Geschlechtskrankheiten vom gesundheitspolitischen Standpunkt," *Deutsches Ärzteblatt*, May 11, 1933, 210.

[23]Gabrielle Czarnowski writes that condoms were openly available for the duration of the Third Reich. "One medical officer noted that, especially after weekends, large numbers of them could be seen in the drains of the municipal sewage facilities." See her article "Hereditary and Racial Welfare (*Erb- und Rassenpflege*): The Politics of Sexuality and Reproduction in Nazi Germany," *Social Politics* 4 (1997): 129. Her source is Dr. Wollenweber, "Das Gesundheitsamt im Kampfe gegen den Geburtenschwand," *Der öffentliche Gesundheitdienst* 5 (1939–40): 447–59. Similar evidence for the widespread availability of condoms can be found in Pieter Lagrou, *The Legacy of Nazi Occupation: Patriotic Memory and National Recovery in Western Europe, 1945–1965* (Cambridge, 2000). Lagrou cites a report on conditions for French and Belgian workers in Nazi Germany, one of whom complains that the "abundance of contraceptive devices, available to all (there are vending machines on Metro and railway platforms, in public toilets), . . . creat[es] a climate of sexual excess, which surprises even many French workers" (145).

[24]The idea that acquired deficiencies could be passed on was not unique to the field of venereal disease. See the discussion of *Keimschädigung* in Alfred Kühn, Martin Staemmler, and Friedrich Burgdörfer, *Erbkunde, Rassenpflege, Bevölkerungspolitik: Schicksalsfragen des deutschen Volkes* (Leipzig, 1935), 102–7. Among other things, the authors cite a study by A. (Agnes) Bluhm that claimed to demonstrate the genetic transmission of physical damage caused by the consumption of alcohol in mice. By 1935, however, the idea that VD could cause a *Keimschädigung* had been discounted. See Bodo Spiethoff, *Die Geschlechtskrankheiten im Lichte der Bevölkerungspolitik, Erbgesundheits- und Rassenpflege* (Berlin, [1934]), 13.

Although nonprophylactic birth-control materials continued to be widely available at least until Himmler's order,[25] there was an attempt to remove these items and behaviors associated with their use from public view. In 1933 new policies decreed that birth control and prophylactics other than condoms could only be sold in pharmacies and that—in the interests of protecting youth—no decorative packaging or advertising could be displayed.[26] These laws, and particularly the 1941 total ban on birth control, understandably led contemporary commentators to assume that the Nazis were attempting to discourage all extramarital and nonreproductive sexual intercourse. This impression was reinforced by the Nazi persecution of homosexuals and prostitutes.

The persecution of homosexuals is one of the few aspects of sexuality in the Third Reich that has received attention from historians and other scholars; even a brief analysis of this literature would take us very far beyond the bounds of this essay. But a quick summary of the legal position of homosexuality in the Third Reich and some mention of the reaction of religious groups to these laws is instructive here. A revision to Paragraph 175 of the criminal code, which prohibited male homosexual relations (and bestiality), seemed to indicate that the Nazi state would not tolerate extramarital, nonreproductive sex. In its original wording, Paragraph 175 called for punishment of sexual relations between men when violence, seduction of a minor, or "intercourse-like behavior" was involved.[27] However, the

[25]Historians have not yet achieved consensus on the availability of birth control in the Third Reich. This is perhaps a problem of definition. The fact that condoms were excluded from laws outlawing birth control in the Third Reich meant that they were officially classified as prophylactics against venereal disease, despite the fact that they could also be used for birth control. Historians (not to mention their historical sources) have not always been specific enough about what they mean when they write about birth control. It is thus hard to know exactly how to evaluate statements like that of a British observer, writing just after the war, who argued that the Nazi laws had succeeded in decreasing knowledge about the use of birth control. See Vera Houghton, "Birth Control in Germany," *Eugenics Review* 43, no. 4 (1951): 185. It seems unlikely that she could have been referring to condom use. See also Atina Grossmann, *Reforming Sex: The German Movement for Birth Control and Abortion Reform, 1920–1950* (Oxford, 1995), 151. Robert G. Waite, in contrast, has found evidence in local police files that even teenagers were "well acquainted with contraceptives" in the early 1940s and that teenage girls in Lüneburg, for instance, were using birth control regularly. What kind of contraceptives and what kind of birth control, one wonders. See Robert G. Waite, "Teenage Sexuality in Nazi Germany," *Journal of the History of Sexuality* 8, no. 3 (1998): 434–76. It is necessary, in other words, to distinguish between prophylactic birth control (condoms), nonprophylactic birth control (which can include, of course, various forms of continence and "natural" methods), and nonprophylactic contraceptive devices.

[26]Minutes of meeting of Sachverständigen Beirat für Bevölkerungs und Rassenpolitik, August 3, 1933.

[27]For a brief discussion of the history of Paragraph 175 from 1871 into the postwar period, see Robert G. Moeller, "'The Homosexual Man Is a "Man," the Homosexual Woman Is a "Woman"': Sex, Society, and the Law in Postwar West Germany," *Journal of the History of Sexuality* 4, no. 3 (January 1994): 398.

wording of the law and policies for enforcement ensured that only denunciation or being caught in flagrante delicto was likely to lead to prosecution.[28] In 1935, a year after the Gestapo removed the embarrassment of having prominent homosexuals within the Nazi leadership by murdering SA leader Ernst Röhm and many of his associates in the Night of the Long Knives, June 30, 1934,[29] the National Socialist state revised Paragraph 175 and substantially strengthened both the criteria for and the consequences of arrest. As the ordinance stated:

> A man who fornicates with another man or who allows himself to be abused for the purposes of fornication will be punished with a prison sentence.
> If a participant has not yet reached the age of twenty-one at the time of the act, the court can refrain from imposing a sentence in particularly trifling cases.[30]

The new law also added subsections outlining prison (*Zuchthaus*) sentences for men who used violence or a position of superiority to coerce another man into having sexual relations, for older men who seduced boys under twenty-one, and for male prostitutes. According to the Working Group for Promoting the Health of the *Volk*, a voluntary group closely associated with the Protestant churches, these provisions were conceived as part of a program to punish "offenses against marriage" and "attacks on marriage. . . . The goal of the law-makers . . . [was] the protection of sexual morality and the promotion of healthy sexual intercourse."[31] Clearly, Christian commentators believed that the attack on homosexuality was part of a larger strategy of purifying sexual behavior in the new regime, confining it, in other words, to marriage. This perception, however, was misguided.

As with homosexuality, the regime's initial policy statements on prostitution seemed to suggest an intention to eradicate all forms of extramarital sex. In keeping with the general outward appearance of promoting chastity, prostitutes experienced an intense phase of legal marginalization.

[28]Moeller cites the description of the law and its implementation from Jürgen Baumann, *Paragraph 175: Über die Möglichkeit die einfache, nichtjugendgefährdende und nicht öffentliche Homosexualität unter Erwachsenen straffrei zu lassen* (Berlin, 1968), 40–46.

[29]Moeller describes the antihomosexuality context of this event in some detail; see ibid., 400–401. See also Robert Gellately, *The Gestapo and German Society: Enforcing Racial Policy 1933–1945* (Don Mills, Ontario, 1990), 201–3.

[30]Cited in Moeller.

[31]"Strafverschärfung der Unzucht zwischen Männern," *Arbeitsgemeinschaft für Volksgesundung e.V.—Mitteilungen*, August 8, 1935, 1–2. Jurists claimed that procreative power was completely destroyed in male homosexual relations (they could become "psychologically impotent"), but women were "always sexually prepared" and remained available for future motherhood duties (cited in Moeller, 403). Although much better off than the men, female homosexuals also faced persecution in the Third Reich. See Claudia Schoppmann, *Days of Masquerade: Life Stories of Lesbians during the Third Reich*, trans. Allison Brown (New York, 1996).

In 1933 tens of thousands of them were rounded up and sent to work-houses and concentration camps.[32] These measures occurred under the authority of the Decree for the Protection of the *Volk* and State (issued on February 28, 1933) and the May 1933 revisions to the VD law and Clause 361 of the criminal code. Modifications to the law included provisions for punishing anyone "who publicly and conspicuously or in a manner *likely* to annoy the public incites immoral acts or offers immoral services."[33] In 1935 the Racial Purity Law further delineated categories of acceptable sexual behavior by banning marriages and nonmarital sex between Jews and Gentiles. This created the legal category of "race defilement"—sexual contact that might lead to miscegenation.[34] Within two years of coming to power, then, the Nazis used the authority of law to label prostitution and "interracial" sexual activities as "asocial." Female promiscuity too came within the purview of the law. "Asocial" behavior for women (though not for men) included such vague categories as becoming too easily sexually aroused ("sexuelle Erregbarkeit") or creating a "strongly erotic impression."[35] "Oversexed" women, along with those who infected soldiers with venereal disease, were immediately placed in one or more of three categories: promiscuous individual, prostitute, or sterilization candidate.[36]

---

[32]Gisela Bock, *Zwangssterilisation im Nationalsozialismus: Studien zur Rassenpolitik und Frauenpolitik* (Opladen, 1986), 417. Although I have taken issue with many of Bock's arguments elsewhere (see Timm, "The Politics of Fertility," 59, 322), I see no reason to doubt her statistical information.

[33]The emphasis on *likely* is my own. (The German text, difficult to translate accurately, reads: "wer öffentlich in auffälliger Weise oder in einer Weise, die geeignet ist, Einzelne oder die Allgemeinheit zu belästigen, zur Unzucht auffordert oder sich dazu anbietet.") One should note that this is a major change from previous laws, which made it necessary to prove that someone had actually been annoyed.

[34]Patricia Szobar is currently writing a dissertation on this subject, forthcoming from Rutgers University.

[35]Christa Paul, *Zwangsprostitution: Staatlich errichtete Bordelle im Nationalsozialismus* (Berlin, 1995), 18. She cites Bock, 401 ff.

[36]The most detailed account of forced sterilization in the Third Reich is still Gisela Bock's *Zwangssterilisation im Nationalsozialismus*, though the arguments in this book have come under fire, particularly from historians in the United States. For summaries of these trans-Atlantic debates, see Atina Grossmann, "Feminist Debates about Women and National Socialism," *Gender & History* 3, no. 3 (1991): 350–58, and Adelheid von Saldern, "Victims or Perpetrators? Controversies about the Role of Women in the Nazi State," in *Nazism and German Society, 1933–1945*, ed. David F. Crew (London, 1994), 141–65. Bock's arguments that the main thrust of reproductive health care policies in the Third Reich were antinatalist and that these policies were both directed primarily toward and suffered by women are not very helpful for the kind of more nuanced gender analysis required of these subjects. Nonetheless, the book provides a useful presentation of historical research on the subject. For a local case study, see Monika Daum and Hans-Ulrich Deppe, *Zwangssterilisation in Frankfurt am Main 1933–1945* (Frankfurt, 1991); and for a bibliography of further sources, see Christoph Beck, *Sozialdarwinismus—Rassenhygiene—Zwangssterilisation und Vernichtung "lebensunwerten" Lebens: Eine Bibliographie zum Umgang mit behinderten Menschen im "Dritten Reich"—und Heute* (Bonn, 1992).

The regime did not launch any concerted propaganda or educational campaigns aimed at the general population. Evidence of propaganda against VD and promiscuity in the Third Reich is very sparse. The few official educational materials available, such as the Ufa film *Geißel der Menschheit* (Scourge of humanity), were wholly concerned with medical descriptions of the disease. The Reich Working Group for Combating Venereal Disease in the Reich Subcommittee for the People's Health Service did organize lectures for students and Hitler Youth doctors. The Working Group for Injury Prevention in the Reich Ministry for Public Enlightenment and Propaganda also funded anti-VD efforts, such as short plays with titles like *German Woman, Protect Yourself from Contact with Foreign Workers* and *SOS Shipwreck of Life*.[37] But these pale in comparison to the anti-VD campaigns of the Weimar and postwar periods. Despite the attempts to establish respectability and Hitler's early pronouncements in *Mein Kampf* against the scourge of prostitution,[38] the Third Reich launched no concerted campaign against promiscuity. In general, the transition from the Weimar Republic to the Third Reich brought about a significant decrease in the amount of attention paid to VD in the medical and welfare literature.[39] The marginalization, persecution, deportation, and murder of large numbers of Socialist and Jewish doctors, sex reformers, and welfare workers was in part responsible for this.[40] But in 1935, the German Society for Combating Venereal Disease (Deutsche Gesellschaft zur Bekämpfung der Geschlechtskrankheiten, DGBG) had already reoriented its activities away from "mass public events for the unchanging audience of large cities" toward more concentrated efforts among "the smallest cells of the organizations, in the work camps, for the troops, etc."[41]

[37]See BArch(B) R58/149, 135; BArch(B) R55/1221, 139–40.

[38]For allusions to Hitler's pronouncements on prostitution, see "Die Prostitutionsfrage," 6; "Stellungnahme zur Prostitutionsfrage," *Christliche Arbeitsgemeinschaft für Volksgesundung e.V.—Mitteilungen*, September 1, 1937, 1–3, which cites an article by Spiethoff quoting Hitler's call for a "battle against the spiritual [*seelischen*] preconditions for prostitution."

[39]This is a somewhat subjective assessment formed in the course of my research on both periods, but it is confirmed by a simple statistical analysis of journal articles cited in the IBZ; for the Nazi years, this is F[elix] Dietrich et al., eds., *Bibliographie der deutschen Zeitschriftenliteratur: Mit Einschluß von Sammelwerken* (Osnabrück, 1897–1964). While the late 1920s saw a proliferation of articles in medical, welfare, and other journals on venereal diseases, reaching a peak of just over 140 a year in 1927 and 1928, the Nazi years witnessed a dramatic decline, with only 20–50 articles in the years 1933–38. A slight increase is evident at the beginning of the war (62 articles in 1940), though many of these are official pronouncements on the apparent lack of an increase in VD cases during the war. It is also significant that a large percentage of articles written on the subject in the Third Reich were authored by a small number of officially sanctioned experts, such as Bodo Spiethoff and Hans Gottschalk of the DGBG.

[40]See Grossmann, 136–47.

[41]Florian Werr, "Professor Spiethoff—60 Jahre," *Dermatologische Wochenschrift*, nos. 5–6 (November 1935): 3.

Perhaps the most public effort to educate the population about the dangers of VD was the attempt to sanitize the streets of Berlin in preparation for the 1936 Olympics. The prospect of the arrival of thousands of international visitors for this event encouraged city and federal governments to contemplate the best ways of projecting a favorable image of the Nazi state. Aside from the more obvious and well-known attempts to glorify Aryan racial superiority in the games themselves, such as Leni Riefenstahl's officially commissioned propaganda film, *Olympia*, the Nazis made more mundane efforts to cleanse the streets of images that might disturb visitors. Anti-Semitic propaganda and racial segregation signs over park benches and public washrooms were temporarily removed, and Jewish residents generally experienced a brief respite from coercive measures. These measures have received attention in numerous historical accounts.

Less well known are the measures to purify the streets of asocial and deviant sexual behavior that might offend tourists or reveal the prevalence of VD in Berlin. Police conducted a round-up of "work-shy" and asocial residents, including the indigent, of Berlin and other German cities and sent them to the Dachau concentration camp.[42] A special health committee for the Olympics within the Main Health Office was put in charge of making certain that the streets were free of VD-infected persons. This office ordered the hours in the central forced examination center (*Zwangsvorführungsstelle*) to be extended; between the end of July and the middle of September 1936 it was open from 7:30 A.M. to 9:00 P.M., seven days a week. Supervisors ordered the employees to work extra shifts.[43] Beginning in the middle of July, the Main Health Office required welfare workers in the VD clinics to assist the criminal police in conducting intensified surveillance to find as many infected individuals as possible.[44] The raids were intended to pick up any individuals who might provoke even the slightest suspicion that they carried a venereal disease. But the health authorities were also careful to establish procedures that would prompt as little public outcry as possible. A special quick examination center (*Schnelluntersuchungsstelle*) was set up in Charlottenburg to handle these extra cases, and an "expedited examination procedure" was established. Individuals whose VD tests came up negative were to be released immediately, "so that they do not suffer harm that would be difficult to redress as a consequence of extended detention."[45] "A needlessly heartless procedure to the detriment of the apprehended individual is not called for," warned the Main Health Office directive. Welfare workers were given a large degree of discretion in making their

---

[42]Jeremy Noakes, "Social Outcasts in the Third Reich," in *Life in the Third Reich*, ed. Richard Bessel (New York, 1987), 93.

[43]Hauptgesundheitsamt, hereafter HGA, to specialists, July 25, 1936, and August 22, 1936, in Landesarchiv Berlin, Ost, hereafter LAB East, Rep. 03-03/3, no. 36.

[44]HGA (Spiewok) to specialists and VD clinics, July 10, 1936, in ibid.

[45]HGA internal memo, July 9, 1936, in ibid.

decisions about who would be detained and forced into treatment. Nevertheless, the tone of the Main Health Office directive suggests that health authorities were planning to cast a very wide net in their pre-Olympics raids; consequently, they felt much more obligated than usual to warn their workers to make sure that innocent individuals would not be needlessly shamed or harmed. Patients were even given the opportunity to speak with a welfare worker "to express any suggestions and wishes that she [the implication being that most patients would be female] finds appropriate to limit the effects of the forced measures to that degree of harm that is unavoidable."[46]

The extreme sensitivity to public perceptions of these measures was a common feature of Nazi policy on sexuality. Although health officials were keen to erase the specter of VD from the image of the Nazi Olympics, they were also careful to conduct the intensified VD controls in a manner that denied any impression that the Third Reich condoned promiscuity. Clearly, policy makers feared that any hint of venereal disease lurking in the Third Reich's capital city would seriously damage the regime's international reputation. The *appearance* of sexual purity was uppermost in the minds of health authorities and their political superiors. The main concern of VD policies during the Olympics was to clean the streets of unsavory individuals likely to tarnish the image of the city and the Reich while keeping the crimes of the regime hidden from the international public.[47] Image, needless to say, had little to do with reality, and a pragmatic tolerance for prostitution as a practice always hid behind the public demonization and legal marginalization of prostitutes as individuals.

TOLERATING SEXUAL VICE

The effort to clean up the streets should not be confused with an attempt to eradicate prostitution. It is necessary to distinguish controls aimed at the streetwalker from those directed toward the prostitute working in a brothel. Streetwalkers were subject to very harsh penalties, particularly if they refused to comply with strict health guidelines and restrictions on their movements. A much more ambivalent policy developed toward brothels. Although the National Socialists did not repeal Paragraph 17 of the 1927 Law for Combating Venereal Diseases, which banned locked brothels and police-regulated prostitution, many city administrations took the Nazi

---

[46]Ibid.

[47]The very superficial and virtually undocumented book by Duff Hart-Davis, *Hitler's Games: The 1936 Olympics* (London, 1986), contains a passage (139) citing the importation of *extra* prostitutes into the city of Berlin to service international guests. This point is not footnoted, and I have found nothing in the files of the Berlin health administration to support it. Confirmation or definitive refutation awaits further research in the police files.

crackdown on street prostitution as support for reinstituting brothels and red light districts. Government officials rejected arguments from VD and welfare experts, who argued that confining prostitutes to locked brothels increased the risk of spreading VD.[48] In fact, they insisted that brothels were necessary to *protect* public health.[49] As Wolfgang Ayass has argued, the 1927 compromise between police regulation of prostitution and full legalization was overthrown in the Nazi era—the pendulum swung decisively back toward regulation.[50] In some cities, particularly in Essen, Hamburg, and Lübeck, confinement of prostitutes to brothels and red light districts occurred long before any legal basis for it had been enacted.[51]

The state-sponsored brothel system was solidified in February 1936, when the Supreme Command of the Wehrmacht declared the construction of military brothels to be "an urgent necessity" and insisted that health authorities should restrain themselves from arresting prostitutes who might be used for this purpose.[52] In a speech to SS commanders in 1937, Himmler explicitly announced his intention to continue tolerating prostitution: "In this area [prostitution] we will be as tolerant as we can possibly be, since one cannot on the one hand wish to prevent the entire male youth from deviating into homosexuality and on the other hand leave them no alternative."[53] The legal and social marginalization of prostitutes in civilian society contrasted, then, with their official toleration—even promotion—in military circles.

While praising the government's cleansing of the streets, religious organizations and VD experts immediately voiced strong objections to official pronouncements expressing the need for more brothels or for the

[48]Arguments against regulating prostitution dominated the discussion of the issue in the Weimar Republic. The most well known expert on prostitution in the Weimar Republic was Alfred Blaschko. His antiregulationist stance is outlined in detail in Alfred Blaschko, *Hygiene der Geschlechtskrankheiten*, 2nd ed. (Leipzig, 1920).

[49]In response to individual petitions from members of the public complaining about the presence of brothels in their area, the Reichsministerium für Volksaufklärung und Propaganda argued that brothels were necessary to protect the public from venereal disease. See BArch(B) R55/1221, 123–24.

[50]Wolfgang Ayass, *"Asoziale" im Nationalsozialismus* (Stuttgart, 1995), 185–86. I am grateful to the anonymous "Reader 2" of this essay for reminding me that control of prostitution in Berlin was by no means typical.

[51]Ibid., 186. A detailed summary of the policies in Essen can be found in Sellmann. Authorities in Essen felt justified in establishing a red light district, because the Nazis had abolished Articles 114 and 115 of the constitution, which safeguarded "freedom of the person" and the inviolability of an individual's residence from unjustified incursions. See also E. Müller, "Die Kasernierung der Dirnen in Essen," *Die Polizei* 30, no. 19 (October 1933): 440–43.

[52]Paul, 12. Cited from "Niederschrift der Sitzung des Wohlfahrtsausschusses des deutschen Gemeindetages zum Thema 'Bewahrungsgesetz,'" February 27, 1936, in Detlev J. K. Peukert, *Grenzen der Sozialdisziplinierung: Aufstieg und Krise der deutschen Jugendfürsorge von 1878 bis 1932* (Cologne, 1986), 281.

[53]Quoted in Paul, 12.

regulation of prostitution.[54] Drawing on decades of experience in the field of VD control and alluding to the concerns of religion-based welfare organizations that saw their task as the rehabilitation of prostitutes, VD expert Bodo Spiethoff argued that ethical considerations must take precedence over "purely organizational-technical" priorities.

> The state cannot recognize a justification for extramarital intercourse or a right to extramarital intercourse if it wants to avoid infringing upon the foundations of the family. For this reason, it cannot be the duty of the state to create possibilities for extramarital sexual intercourse through the construction of brothels or to foster the practice of extramarital sexual intercourse through the granting of any type of concession or designation.
>
> It is the duty of the state to call a halt to the appearance of prostitution in all its forms and particularly to protect children and youth from coming into contact with prostitution.
>
> State-licensed brothels and red light districts are politically and ethically unbearable, but they are also to be rejected from another viewpoint, because the number of prostitutes housed in this way is never more than a small fraction of the prostitutes in a city, and this small fraction would not influence the city landscape in any way, so that no advantages can overcome the ethical, health, and economic disadvantages connected to any brothel-related business.[55]

Spiethoff's arguments were cited in an internal communication of the Department for the Protection of Endangered Girls (Gefährdetenfürsorge), part of the Inner Mission, a welfare organization of the Protestant church, and they were reprinted in the journal of the Working Group for Promoting the Health of the *Volk*, a union of close to three hundred social welfare agencies, women's groups, religious welfare organizations, and prominent social hygienists that had been active in Berlin since the early years of the Weimar Republic.[56] Both groups heartily applauded Spiethoff's assessment

[54]For a pamphlet-length example written from the Protestant perspective, see Sellmann.
[55]Quoted in "Bekenntnis zur Sittlichkeit als Grundlage des Kampfes gegen die Geschlechtskrankheiten," *Arbeitsgemeinschaft für Volksgesundung e.V.—Mitteilungen*, June 15, 1935, 2.
[56]The Arbeitsgemeinschaft für Volksgesundung was one of the only organizations concerned with issues of eugenics and sexuality to have escaped the process of *Gleichschaltung*. All other such organizations, many of which had large representations of Socialist and Jewish members, were either disbanded or absorbed into national organs once the Nazis came to power. See, for example, Atina Grossmann's account of the destruction of the sex reform movement in *Reforming Sex*. The close connection of the Arbeitsgemeinschaft to the Protestant Inner Mission, which maintained a close working relationship to Nazi welfare organs throughout the Third Reich, and the charismatic leadership of Hans Harmsen (himself a member of the Inner Mission) may explain its staying power. On the Inner Mission in the Nazi years, see Sabine Schleiermacher, "Die Innere Mission und ihr bevölkerungspolitisches

of the dangers of the Nazi policy on prostitution.[57] The Working Group published several articles on the subject in 1934 and 1937, in which anonymous authors rejected state involvement in organized prostitution. Although the Working Group acknowledged the much "cleaner street picture" that the National Socialist clampdown on prostitutes had achieved, they insisted that the conscientious implementation of the 1927 VD law, without the reconstruction of brothels, would have achieved the same result.[58] Nevertheless, the Working Group supported the existence of discrete brothels, run by madams instead of police and situated in the less-populated financial districts of the city. This pragmatic willingness to accept the existence of prostitution, they argued, was preferable to having the state implicitly sanction extramarital intercourse by becoming involved in the actual administration of prostitution, and it would also achieve the apparent goal of the National Socialist state to remove this activity from public view.[59] Brothels and walled-off red light districts, they argued, actually encouraged and incited deviant sexual behavior: they were sites of curiosity for the young, who would often peek past the walls and ape the behavior they spied;[60] they encouraged deviant sexual acts through their effects on the mass psychology of their visitors;[61] and they provided an incentive for the slave trade in women and children.[62] On the basis of these arguments, the Working Group complained bitterly when the Nazi state expanded its support for brothels after 1934. In 1937 they repeated their arguments that registration of prostitutes only increased the spread of venereal disease and gave men the false impression that state-run brothels would protect them from VD.[63]

The views expressed by the Working Group for Promoting the Health of the *Volk* were echoed in a report from the Group for the Protection of

Programm," in *Der Griff nach der Bevölkerung: Aktualität und Kontinuität nazistischer Bevölkerungspolitik*, ed. Heidrun Kaupen-Haas (Nördlingen, 1986), 73–89.

[57] See "Aus dem Jahresbericht 1935 über die Arbeit der evangelischen Konferenz für Gefährdetenfürsorge," January 29–31, 1935, in Archiv des diakonischen Werkes (hereafter ADW), CA Gf/St 10; and "Stellungnahme des Central-Ausschusses für die Innere Mission der deutschen evangelischen Kirche zur Prostitutionsfrage," in ADW, BP 1857.

[58] This view is also expressed in "Die Prostitution unter dem Geschlechtskrankengesetz," 100.

[59] "Die Prostitutionsfrage," 7–8.

[60] "Ist die zunehmende Kasernierung der Prostitution eine Massnahme der Jugendschutzes?" *Arbeitsgemeinschaft für Volksgesundung e.V.—Mitteilungen*, no. 16 (1934): 4.

[61] "Stellungnahme zur Prostitutionsfrage," 3. "Just as the masses can, through leadership, be made capable of greatness, so too can the consciousness of their numbers encourage them to feel justified in the satisfaction of their most base desires and to free themselves of countervailing inhibitions."

[62] "Die Prostitution als internationale Frage," *Arbeitsgemeinschaft für Volksgesundung e.V.—Mitteilungen*, June 14, 1934, 1–5.

[63] See "Kasernierung und Bordellierung," *Christliche Arbeitsgemeinschaft für Volksgesundung e.V.—Mitteilungen*, January 20, 1937, 1–5; "Stellungnahme zur Prostitutionsfrage," 1–3.

Endangered Girls in the Association of Female Welfare Workers. The welfare workers argued that regulated brothels and the forced registration and confinement of prostitutes worsened rather than improved the conditions for combating VD. Regulating prostitutes only forced more of them to avoid all forms of health care and surveillance, making them even more dangerous to the public. Men who visited brothels were likely to assume that the services provided included an implicit guarantee of medical safety, when in fact confinement had no effect on rates of VD infection. But worst of all, the welfare workers argued, was the ethical message that state-run brothels sent to the general population:

> The National Socialist state, which has given itself the duty to protect and support the family, whose youth should be trained in self-control and ethical responsibility for the next generation, would endanger its own educational goals through the toleration, even legalization, of particular places for extramarital sexual intercourse. When the police themselves confine women to certain streets to perform acts of prostitution, when they regulate, and, for instance, provide individuals who wish to engage in prostitution with a particular instructional pamphlet or even identification for which they have to pay, they are granting a concession to prostitution.[64]

The welfare workers believed that existing laws, if properly applied and enforced with confinement in a work house, would be effective in controlling prostitution without resorting to police regulation of brothels. They expressed indignation that the state intended to remove prostitution from public view without attacking it at its roots. They accused the Nazi state of not putting its "strong impulse toward ethically renewing our *Volk*" into practice.[65]

These protests were attempts to use the Nazi regime's own rhetoric against it. Each of the protesting organizations described above had long operated under the assumption that prostitutes were thoroughly marginalized and that welfare measures must be directed toward them in the interests of both individual rehabilitation and the protection of the larger society. Weimar politicians and VD experts had accepted the inevitability of prostitution as an outlet for what they considered to be irrepressible male sexual urges (*Geschlechtstriebe*). But the impulse to protect the population from VD and an understanding of the limitations of medical diagnosis and treatment had combined to defeat any arguments about the relative safety of brothels.[66] Prostitutes had to be provided with incen-

[64]Fachgruppe Gefährdetenfürsorge in der Fachschaft der Wohlfahrtspflegerinnen (no recipient named), July 12, 1934, in ADW, CA Gf/St 4.
[65]Ibid.
[66]Annette Timm, "Uncontrollable Urges and Diseased Bodies: Prophylactics and the Politics of Fertility in Weimar Germany," paper presented at the German Studies Association,

tives to return to "normal" lifestyles. Under the Nazis, this option was increasingly closed off. Despite the rhetoric about the evils of prostitution and the "racial inferiority" of prostitutes, their position as outlets for male sexual energies was institutionalized. The military authority and the Ministry of the Interior argued that brothels served hygienic and military functions; brothels decreased the risk of venereal disease by controlling the otherwise dangerous activities of "asocial" prostitutes, and they provided rewards for hard-fighting soldiers and productive workers.[67] Prostitutes were henceforth available to any German man who found his way to a state-run brothel. Given the relative absence of further protests against brothels after 1937, it seems plausible to assume that a regime discomfited by the apparent contradictions and ambiguities of its own policies quietly put a stop to further discussions of the subject.

The tolerance of prostitution in the Third Reich required a new system of categorizing promiscuous sexual behavior and prompted the creation of an increasingly complex system of designation, which built upon categories inherited from the Weimar era. Since the 1920s, VD-control efforts in Germany had labeled promiscuous individuals hwGs (people with "häufig wechselnder Geschlechtsverkehr" [frequently changing sexual partners]), or habitually promiscuous individuals. The category of hwG was always ambiguous in that it sometimes was synonymous with prostitution but sometimes not. But National Socialist racial ideology and the regime's desire to tolerate promiscuity in certain circumstances led to a proliferation of categories for sexual behavior that simultaneously criminalized and legitimized promiscuity and ended up leaving even more room for interpretation on the part of individual welfare workers and police officers than had previously been the case.

The proliferation of categories began with the legal codification of the definition of "asocial" in a directive from the Reich and Prussian Ministry of the Interior on December 14, 1937.[68] Known as the Preventive Detention Decree, this directive called for indefinite protective police custody for individuals who, while perhaps not career or habitual criminals, were endangering society through their behavior. "Asocials" were defined as

September 27, 1997, Washington, D.C. An example of the Weimar view of male sexual drives can be seen in Hertha Riese, *Geschlechtsleben und Gesundheit, Gesittung und Gesetz* (Berlin, 1932), 4.

[67]For the Ministry of the Interior's position on prostitution, see Conti to Landesregierungen, etc., September 18, 1939, in LAB C Rep. 03-03/3, no. 36; and the "Begründung" to the 1940 changes to the VD law in BArch(B) R43 II/725, 50–51. On the military's attitude toward prostitution, see Peukert, 281. For a general summary of policy, see also Bleuel, 225–28.

[68]For a summary of policies on asocials, see Jeremy Noakes, "Social Outcasts in the Third Reich," in *Life in the Third Reich*, ed. Richard Bessel (New York, 1987), 83–96.

"people whose perpetration of trivial but constantly repeated infringe-ments of the law show their unwillingness to integrate themselves into a system of order that is intrinsic to a National Socialist state (e.g., beggars, tramps [Gypsies], whores, alcoholics, those with contagious diseases, par-ticularly people afflicted with venereal diseases, who remove themselves from the measures of health authorities)."[69] Escapees from institutions were candidates for protective custody, as were individuals whose asocial behavior had resulted in extraordinary hospital costs. According to a Ber-lin Main Health Office official, this measure particularly affected "healthy hwG individuals, who despite being repeatedly brought before the courts interrupt continued [medical] observation."[70] In other words, individuals who might already have been known to welfare authorities in the Weimar Republic and categorized as hwG were now also given the additional label "asocial," with its associated endangerment of their personal freedom. But the categorization could also work the other way around. Someone whose behavior was considered asocial, according to the standards of the Third Reich, could later also earn the label "hwG" or "prostitute" as a conve-nient way of justifying certain types of punishment. Gaby Zürn notes that married women in Hamburg who had illegitimate children while their husbands were off fighting the war were frequently labeled "hwG" or "prostitute" by welfare authorities in the Youth Office (Jugendamt) and were treated accordingly. Zürn astutely argues that this displays the de-gree to which "the designation 'hwG-individual' and particularly the cat-egory 'prostitute' were not simply job designations but were used by welfare workers to describe nonconforming social behavior."[71]

The attempt to specify which types of behavior would qualify as asocial left much room for interpretation, depending upon the particular balance of power between medical, police, and welfare authorities in each region. A complex relationship between federal laws and local interpretations

[69]HGA (Schwéers) to specialists in the Berlin health administration, September 22, 1938, LAB East, Rep. 03-03/3, no. 36. The word "Gypsies" appeared in parentheses in the original. The official title of the directive is "Polizeiliche Vorbeugungshaft für Personen, die sich den Maßnahmen der Gesundheitsbehörde entziehen," Pol.s.Kr.3 Nr. 1682/37-2098-Abs. A II. On forced treatment of asocials, see also Landes-Wohlfahrts- und Jugendamt, Berlin to HGA, October 31, 1938; HGA internal memo, October 11, 1941, in LAB East, Rep. 03-03/3, no. 36. This correspondence discusses the administrative details of confin-ing asocials who removed themselves from treatment in institutional custody.
[70]The quote is from Dr. O. Schwéers in LAB East, Rep. 03-03/3, no. 36. See also Paul Werner, "Die vorbeugende Verbrechensbekämpfung durch die Polizei," *Kriminalistik* 12 (1938): 60, cited in Paul, 13.
[71]Gaby Zürn, "'A. ist Prostituiertentyp': Zur Ausgrenzung und Vernichtung von Prostituierten und moralisch nicht-angepaßten Frauen im nationalsozialistischen Hamburg," in *Verachtet—verfolgt—vernichtet: Zu den "vergessenen" Opfern des NS-Regimes,* ed. Projektgruppe für die vergessenen Opfer des NS-Regimes in Hamburg e.V. (Hamburg, 1988), 147.

guaranteed a haphazard and inconsistent implementation. In the case of prostitution, it had always been the case that laws were interpreted very differently in different parts of the Reich.[72] But the law on asocials and other related policies increased the level of control ceded to individual doctors in determining how sexual behavior should be categorized.[73] Doctors were given a large degree of discretion in determining the course of treatment and in deciding the extent of surveillance under which an individual might be placed. In 1938, an Interior Ministry directive advised state and municipal health authorities that doctors should be directed to determine how regularly hwG individuals were to be examined on the basis of "personal cleanliness, their outward living conditions (age, degree of prostitution), and the frequency of sexual intercourse."[74]

This reliance on experts for subjective interpretations of individual behavior was evident in the increasingly specific categories for sexual deviance that Berlin health-care authorities used to guide decisions about the appropriate degree of surveillance. In the early years of the Nazi era, the very definitions of categories of promiscuity were disputed and ambiguously interpreted. In 1936 the Main Health Office in Berlin refused to provide its VD experts with an exact definition of the newly coined category of "alternating intercourse" ("wechselnder Geschlechtsverkehr," or wG) used to describe occasionally promiscuous individuals whose behavior verged on but did not constitute prostitution or hwG. "The determination of 'alternating intercourse' can only be determined on an individual basis through discussions between the welfare worker and the patient," a policy statement explained. The distinction between wG and hwG was crucial in determining the degree of surveillance imposed upon an individual. Nevertheless, government authorities left the exact definitions of these terms to local welfare workers, and the more designations available to health authorities, the more discretion they had in categorizing the exact degree of promiscuity. The effort to classify thus only succeeded in

---

[72]For accounts of prostitution policy in Imperial Germany (mostly concentrating on Hamburg), see Richard J. Evans, "Prostitution, State, and Society in Imperial Germany," *Past and Present* 70 (February 1976): 106–29, and Lynn Abrams, "Prostitutes in Imperial Germany, 1870–1918: Working Girls or Social Outcasts?" in *The German Underworld*, ed. Richard Evans (London, 1991), 189–209. Descriptions of how these policies continued into the Weimar and Nazi periods can be found in A. W., "Prostitution: Prostitutionshäuser in Hamburg-Altona," *Die neue Generation* 22 (1926): 341; see also "Ist die zunehmende Kasernierung der Prostitution eine Massnahme der Jugendschutzes?" *Arbeitsgemeinschaft für Volksgesundung e.V.—Mitteilungen*, no. 16 (1934): 1–4.

[73]In Berlin, for example, an agreement between the medical profession and city health authorities, which took effect in July 1936, guaranteed that as many VD patients as possible were referred to doctors in private practice. See "Vereinbarungen zwischen der Stadt und der kassenärztlichen Vereinigung Deutschlands," circa July 1936, in LAB East, Rep. 03-03/3, no. 36.

[74]Reichs und preus. Ministerium des Innern to Landesregierungen (in Prussia directly to state and communal health bureaus), January 27, 1938, in LAB East, Rep. 03-03/3, no. 36.

blurring the boundaries, since what constituted immoral behavior was increasingly left to the lowest level of bureaucrat and/or welfare worker to decide. The results for the individual patient would have been extremely unpredictable. Treatment was wholly dependent upon the subjective interpretation of the attending welfare worker. Under the circumstances of Nazi Berlin, appearance, education, gender, job status, and "race" were all likely to have had a major impact on these evaluations. The subjective decision making involved in such evaluations had been further enshrined in a 1935 supplement to the civil penal code that stated: "Anyone shall be punished who commits an act that the law declares to be punishable or that merits punishment in accordance with the underlying idea of a penal law and with wholesome popular sentiment. Should no specific penal law be directly applicable to the act in question, it shall be punished according to the law whose intention most closely applies thereto."[75] Moral and sexual offenses, Hans Peter Bleuel has argued, could thus be categorized in such a way as to warrant any level of punishment. This arbitrary system meant that the regime had moved one step closer to totalitarianism. In Bleuel's words:

> Here we encounter the magic touchstone known as "wholesome popular sentiment," which transcends all legal codes and provides all totalitarian systems with a superlative pretext for their arbitrary acts. There are few sentiments more inhuman than the righteous indignation of the frustrated petty bourgeois who gives free rein to his outraged and virtuous sense of propriety. On this plane, the so-called decent average citizen can unhesitatingly identify himself with any government measure, however draconian and illegal.[76]

The subjective judgments allowed in the system of classifying degrees of promiscuity were particularly influential in the Third Reich, since the emphasis was on segregating and punishing dangerous elements of society, not, as had been the case in the Weimar Republic, on rehabilitating and reintegrating "fallen" individuals.

Women were in more danger of falling victim to these arbitrary classifications than men. Nazi policies encouraged authorities in the Berlin Main Health Office to use a broad definition of what constituted dangerous sexual behavior on the part of women. They included "bar women, table women, and waitresses" in their surveillance efforts, and they interpreted the Ministry of the Interior directive to mean that "women were also to be monitored when hwG or wG is impossible to determine."[77] Authorities assumed that mere presence in a certain bar indicated suspicious behavior. Despite

---

[75]Quoted in Bleuel, 8.

[76]Ibid.

[77]HGA (Conti) to GSÄ in districts with VD clinics, December 3, 1937, in LAB East, Rep. 03-03/3, no. 36.

gender-neutral language, the health office reports suggest that surveillance efforts were primarily focused on women.[78] While promoting promiscuity with their support for brothels, Nazi leaders also punished women for any public displays of sexuality that were not directly linked either to the war effort or to the strengthening of families. The "sanitation of the street scene," as this removal of prostitutes to brothels was often called, was meant to preserve the public facade of idyllic family life, to allow men a private release for their more base sexual "needs," and to protect the image of woman as mother from the contradictory image of the public whore.

There thus emerged a contrast between acceptable and unacceptable sexual behavior for women—a contrast that contained an ambiguous and contradictory image of female sexuality but that in some sense also gave all women a similar role in Nazi society. True mothers of the *Volk* and members of the "national community," so Nazi propaganda taught, contained their sexual expression entirely within the private realm. Their sexuality was inextricably linked to motherhood, and their sole public function was to act as educator and spiritual guide to their families—to produce, in other words, new citizens and soldiers.[79] The prostitute represented both a contrast and a mirror. She was defined as having abnormal sexual instincts that demanded her exclusion from the society at large. But, like "respectable" women, she was also prevented from expressing sexuality in public; she was confined to a brothel. And, like "respectable" women, her sexual services were also subjected to the demands of the state. Female sexuality was functionalized to serve the needs of the nation.

MILITARIZATION

The most famous attempt to harness women's reproductive capacities, regardless of marital status, to the purpose of military victory was Himmler's speech of October 1939, which called upon all racially "valuable" and patriotic Germans to produce children, even illegitimate ones, to fill the nation's need for soldiers. This was a controversial stance, even within the party,[80] and its impact on actual practice has been vastly overblown, particularly by those who have used it to make the inaccurate claim that Himmler's Lebensborn maternity homes were "breeding farms" where SS soldiers impregnated fertile Aryan women.[81] A much more significant

[78]This is clear in the occasional mention of an individual case and in an effort in 1937 to add up the actual financial costs that certain "female" practitioners of hwG had brought upon Berlin's health care service. See Conti to health authorities, April 21, 1937, and similar requests to hospitals, same date, in ibid.
[79]On the Nazi glorification of motherhood, see Claudia Koonz, *Mothers in the Fatherland: Woman, the Family, and Nazi Politics* (New York, 1987); Weyrather.
[80]See Mosse, 166–67.
[81]Bleuel suggests that these rumors had some small basis in fact, at least to the degree that they reflected the fantasies of some Nazi leaders about policies that might be introduced in

event in terms of the number of people affected occurred a few weeks earlier, on September 9, 1939, eight days after the invasion of Poland, when a secret directive from the Reich Ministry of the Interior ordered the "reconstruction of brothels and barrack-like concentration of prostitutes." This order foreshadowed a new orientation in VD and prostitution control.[82] Originally, this directive applied only to the operational area of the German military; the goal was to provide prostitutes to German soldiers. Women who were considered prostitutes according to previously instituted definitions were registered and incarcerated in brothels. If they removed themselves from police or medical control, they were put into concentration camps. This group also included women who had committed "race defilement": those who had broken the provisions of the 1935 Racial Purity Law by having sexual relations with men whose citizenship had been revoked for racial reasons.[83] Prostitutes and other "asocials" were placed at the bottom of the social hierarchy in the camps. In March 1942 Himmler ordered the construction of brothels in the concentration camps as well in order to provide "productivity" incentives for male inmates. Women incarcerated in the camps as prostitutes were the first to be chosen for employment in the camp brothels (the first of which was constructed at Mauthausen in the summer of 1942), though others were also forced into service, and some chose this option as a way to prolong their lives.[84]

After the beginning of the war, brothels were constructed for foreign workers in Germany. The official justification for this policy was that providing foreign workers with prostitutes (particularly when the prostitutes were themselves foreigners or "Gypsies") would protect German women from sexual danger and defilement.[85] By 1942 the criminal police, working

---

the future. He also describes the policy of providing soldiers on leave with pleasant female company with a view both to increasing the men's support for the party and to creating social situations that might in the end have positive population political outcomes (169).

[82]Paul, 13; HGA (Braemer) to GSÄ and VD clinics, September 21, 1942, in LAB East, Rep. 03-03/3, no. 36.

[83]Paul, 14–18.

[84]It is important to note, as Paul informs us, that many of them would have welcomed this opportunity, since conditions in the brothels were slightly better than in the camps at large and since working in the brothels guaranteed them at least a temporary reprieve from the gas chambers. Other inmates often expressed jealousy at the prostitutes' privileged position (ibid., 134). According to Paul, Himmler first ordered the construction of a brothel in KZ-Mauthausen in June 1941, but various administrative problems delayed its construction. He then restated his demand for brothels, this time for all concentration camps, in March 1942. By the end of the war, Paul estimates, there were at least nine concentration-camp brothels (23, 131).

[85]Ibid., 117. See also the concerns expressed about dangerous foreigners by members of the department for *Gefährdetenfürsorge* in the Inner Mission: "Tätigkeitsbericht der Bezirksstelle der Inneren Mission Kreuzberg für das Jahr 1943," circa 1944, in ADW, BP 645.

under the authority of the secret directive, had created twenty-eight brothels in Berlin.[86] Any complaints about the effects of state-regulated prostitution on the ethical or physical health of the population were countered with
the argument that this system was put in place "to defend members of the
Wehrmacht and the civilian population from the threatening dangers of
prostitution."[87] Throughout the war years government officials argued that
men could be better protected from venereal disease if prostitution were
confined to state-run brothels.[88]

Aside from these "secret" initiatives (which clearly could not have remained secret for long if the prostitutes were actually to attract customers), the Reich Ministry of the Interior also made public pronouncements
on the direction of VD-control policies during the war. On September 18,
1939, the ministry circulated a directive stressing the likely impact of the
war on the spread of venereal diseases.[89] All health authorities were directed to become even more alert about VD: they were to research infectious sources in every case and to request the police to detain forcibly
anyone resisting VD controls. These measures represented only minor
shifts in policy, simply emphasizing strategies already in place. More noteworthy was the directive to be particularly vigilant of all "women who
frequent bars and similar facilities for the purpose of stimulating, entertaining, etc. (so-called table or entertainment women, dancers, etc.)." This
represented a drastic expansion of the category for police surveillance,
since it included women who did not sell sex and who did not necessarily
show signs of having VD. Additionally, hwG individuals who were considered likely to spread VD and did not comply with orders to appear for
examinations were henceforth placed under "protective custody." This
repeated what had previously been a secret policy sanctioned by the law
on asocials of December 14, 1937. The regime made public its intention
to treat all open displays of female sexuality as signs of asocial and health-
threatening behavior.[90]

After 1940 even stricter control of promiscuous individuals was instituted
through modifications to the 1927 Reich Law for Combating Venereal Diseases. These modifications, in combination with the law on asocials of 1937,

---

[86]VD experts in Berlin's Main Health Office had been put in charge of monitoring the
women installed in these brothels. HGA (Braemer) to GSÄ and VD clinics, September 21,
1942, in LAB East, Rep. 03-03/3, no. 36.

[87]See the response from the Reichsministerium für Volksaufklärung und Propaganda to
a lawyer from Heidelberg who complained about the increase in prostitution near military
barracks, September 18, 1944, in BArch(B) R55/1221, 122.

[88]See, for example, Oberbürgermeister der Reichshauptstadt Berlin, HGA (Schröder)
to Oberregierungsrat Dr. Gußmann, Reichsministerium für Volksaufklärung und Propaganda, September 6, 1944, in BArch(B) R55/1221, 123–24.

[89]RMI (Conti) to Landesregierungen, etc., September 18, 1939, in ibid.

[90]The directive was published in Der öffentliche Gesundheitsdienst, October 5, 1939,
342–43.

allowed the National Socialist state to formulate increasingly harsh punishments for all forms of "sexual deviance." In October 1940 Paragraph 17 of the VD law effectively legalized civilian brothels and cleared the way for what would become substantial state involvement in the business of prostitution. In comparison to this change, other amendments to the VD law instituted at this time that dealt with free treatment for the poor and with jurisdictional issues appear insignificant and were possibly intended to deflect attention from what the government knew to be a controversial policy.[91] Officials justified their decision by stating: "The former Paragraph 17 [Verbot der Kasernierung der Prostituierten] does not reflect present needs and practical circumstances and will thus no longer be in force, as is already the case in the Reichsgauen Ostmark and the Sudetenland."[92] This rather bland statement foreshadowed a significant transformation of policies toward prostitution. Streetwalkers, for instance, who had once been punished with only short stays in jail, now fell under extremely strict police control and were often sent immediately to concentration camps.[93]

The beginning of the war had a dramatic effect on VD-control and prostitution policies at the local level in the Third Reich. Given the social disruption of drafting young men into the army, incidences of extramarital intercourse multiplied, and paranoia about its effects escalated dramatically. Meanwhile, national policies that condoned and even organized prostitution complicated attempts to control VD at the local level, since it threw into question traditional methods of labeling promiscuity as asocial behavior. Particularly after the beginning of the war and the dramatic expansion of the civilian and military brothel system (which made it much more difficult for women to move in and out of the profession of prostitution), local officials in Berlin were at pains to make a distinction between the occasionally or the habitually promiscuous and the prostitute.[94] Implicit in the proliferation of categories for deviant sexual behavior was the realization that the consequences of being labeled a prostitute in the Third Reich had become much more serious and difficult to escape.

At a meeting on January 10, 1941, Berlin health authorities attempted to devise exact classifications for degrees of promiscuity. Dr. Paulstich, head of the Main Health Office, told his subordinates to be aware of a growing problem of promiscuity, particularly among domestic servants,

[91]Two other sections of the VD law were changed: Paragraph 2, which outlined free treatment for the poor, was reworded to be more general and all-inclusive; and Paragraph 18, which discussed the administrative responsibility of the individual states for carrying out the law, was supplemented with a statement about the Reich Ministry of the Interior's responsibility for enacting appropriate laws and policies to aid in the fight against VD.

[92]"Begründung," n.d., in BArch(B) R43 II/725, 50–51.

[93]Ayass, 72.

[94]The head of Berlin's Main Health Office (Dr. Paulstich of the Hauptgesundheitsamt) instructed his subordinates to make this distinction very clear. See Paulstich to specialists and counseling clinics for VD, April 30, 1941, in LAB East, Rep. 03-03/3, no. 36.

office workers, saleswomen, and female factory workers.[95] These groups were increasingly turning up in military VD reports as the sources of infection, and social workers noted a prevalence of women from these circles in dancing halls frequented by soldiers. More surveillance, Paulstich argued, was called for, as wGs (the occasionally promiscuous) were actually more dangerous in terms of spreading the disease than hwGs (the habitually promiscuous, presumed prostitutes, who by this time would have come under the direct surveillance of health and police authorities). This effort at more precise definition represents a break with previous practice. Asocial, deviant behavior required more specific delineation in a state that severely punished outsiders for nonconforming social behavior. Perhaps sensitive to this broader context, Paulstich insisted that the distinction between occasional and habitual promiscuity be strictly maintained. Not having descended to the depths of commercial sex, wGs still had some hope of returning to mainstream society.

As another official at the meeting put it, the main concern was the protection of society at large, because promiscuous individuals had too negative an impact on society to be ignored. "All of our experience has shown that this type of personal decline and incorrect choice of leisure activity very quickly leads to a neglect of employment duties, in particular work productivity. There can be no doubt that stubborn cases absolutely must be monitored."[96] Beyond simply posing a health danger, then, promiscuous persons were considered a threat to the productivity and social cohesiveness of the nation. Drastic measures, involving the cooperation of health, police, and welfare authorities, were necessary to prevent further degeneration. The discussions of promiscuity in this meeting also demonstrated that health officials accepted the danger of overzealously policing individuals who were not actually engaging in promiscuous behavior. They argued that during a "war like the present one," the possibility of an individual injustice was justified "to protect national strength . . . and prevent sexual epidemics from cropping up."[97] The very fact that Paulstich felt the need to encourage his subordinates to act more harshly, however, suggests that he was aware of their reticence to do so.

As the war progressed, various attempts to streamline and rationalize the process of finding and monitoring "dangerous" spreaders of VD were made. Anyone who admitted to changing sexual partners frequently was placed under the surveillance of health care authorities, forced to appear for weekly or more frequent health-care examinations, and provided with

[95] Ibid.
[96] Comment from St. I. Kördel in ibid.
[97] The last comment was provided by Stadtdirektor Dr. Breitenfeld (ibid.).

counseling from welfare workers.[98] In many cases, Paulstich claimed, individuals voluntarily submitted themselves to these measures. In other cases, the health authorities had to resort to more intense methods of social control, including calling upon the police to place the individual under protective custody.[99] This system, of course, relied on cooperation between the various district clinics, the Main Health Office, and the police, a triangular relationship that became increasingly complex and difficult during the war. Government agencies informed health officials that all efforts must be drastically stepped up to meet wartime demands, but the limited resources of the district health offices led to inconsistencies in implementation. Administrators tried to counter these problems with longer working hours for clinic staff and authoritarian pronouncements about how clients should be treated. "Those individuals requested to appear in *our* offices," Paulstich admonished, "will over time have to become accustomed to the fact that they cannot respond to orders from the authorities according to their own free will."[100] But as the war dragged on, the attempt to create a seamless organizational structure for the administration of VD-control efforts in Berlin faltered. By late 1942 the Main Health Office was receiving constant complaints about various clinics' and administrative offices' unwillingness to cooperate.[101]

Despite the philosophy of unifying and streamlining the health care system at all levels (enshrined in the Law for the Standardization of the Health Care System of July 3, 1934), local health care ran up against the classic problems of a bureaucracy mired in red tape and governed by arbitrary and subjective decision making. Whether an individual was classified as being in need of public-health surveillance depended upon chance circumstances and the degree of ideological devotion of the individual welfare worker. In a system that forcibly confined prostitutes to state-run brothels and sent them to concentration camps, these subjective decisions had ominous consequences.

The internal contradictions of Nazi attitudes on prostitution were obvious even to contemporary observers. Policies were directed at reducing the visibility of prostitutes rather than at reducing their numbers. While extolling health, the Nazis promoted a form of activity that had always been considered the prime source of venereal infection. The rhetoric about "purification" forced health authorities to downplay the statistical realities

---

[98]On October 18, 1937, the HGA reminded its subordinates not to undertake lengthy and complex investigations of a person's sexual behavior if he or she already admitted to hwG. See memo signed by Schwéers in LAB East, Rep. 03-03/3, no. 36.

[99]HGA (Paulstich) to specialists, January 17, 1940, in ibid.

[100]Ibid.

[101]HGA (Paulstich) to specialists, October 7, 1942, in ibid.

of VD control. Objective evaluations of the extent of VD in the population are noticeably scarce in local and federal documents. Leonardo Conti, who had been appointed Reichsgesundheitsführer in October 1944,[102] was forced to conduct his own unscientific survey of the chiefs of the district health offices in 1942. Seventy percent of those questioned admitted to having detected a slight increase in VD rates in the previous years. But further statistical evaluations were curtailed by the circumstances of war.[103] The lack of statistical evidence makes an assessment of the effect of National Socialist policies on VD rates virtually impossible. What is certain, however, is that the exigencies of war dramatically shifted priorities in VD control. The war focused health officials' preventive efforts on the "control" of prostitution. This represented a radical departure from Weimar attitudes. In the 1920s, VD control was conceived as a crucial component of population policy, since these afflictions threatened the fertility of future generations and posed a long-term threat to the birth rate. The ever-diminishing distinction between prostitution control and VD control in the Third Reich (evident in the relative lack of concern with statistical evaluations of VD in the population at large) demonstrates the degree to which hygienic and even political concerns were subsumed under the all-consuming interest in achieving short-term military goals. Prostitution was considered useful for the war effort. Recognizing that it was also the site of transmitting venereal infection, the Nazis implied that their comprehensive control of all prostitutes and brothels made any further discussion of the VD problem irrelevant.

An example from Berlin provides striking evidence that the National Socialist government sought to functionalize female and male sexuality for the purposes of war. In September 1944 an official in the Main Health Office, Schröder, wrote to the Reich Ministry for the Enlightenment of the *Volk* and Propaganda in response to a complaint about prostitutes in Berlin.[104] A Wehrmacht sergeant had expressed indignation at the price of Berlin prostitutes. Schröder agreed that the "extraordinarily high prices," particularly when charged to soldiers unfamiliar with the going rate in Berlin, were unconscionable. He informed his counterpart in the Propaganda Ministry that he had months ago expressed concern about this situation to the criminal police and instructed them to intervene. He suggested that women who charged extortionate rates for their services should be referred immediately to the Labor Ministry for employment assignment. To protect soldiers from these women, Schröder also instructed police to set up brothels near all the

---

[102]Conti had far-reaching powers over all aspects of civilian health care. On his appointment as Reichsgesundheitsführer, see Führerhauptquartier, Bormann to Goebbels, October 3, 1944, BArch(B) R55/1221, 288.

[103]Reichsgesundheitsführer to Goebbels, February 17, 1944, in BArch(B) R55/1222, 38–39.

[104]Ibid., Bl. 124.

large train stations to serve soldiers exclusively during their temporary stays in Berlin. This intervention into one of the oldest relationships of supply and demand displays the degree to which public health officials had subordinated concerns about venereal disease to the particular demands of wartime Germany. The state's explicit aim to make prostitutes available to soldiers was so influential that local officials went far beyond controlling prostitution simply from a health perspective; they intervened in the actual commercial transaction between prostitutes and their customers. In doing so, they functionalized male sexuality to preserve the precarious social power system in times of war.[105] If male sexual urges could be channeled and provided for, the logic went, then workers would be more productive, soldiers would not lose their fighting spirit, and respectable women and families would be protected from a public confrontation with sex in the streets. The regime reconciled the contradiction between its claim to preserve family purity and the reality of its sponsoring prostitution with the argument that brothels served to keep prostitution off the streets and away from the curious eyes of children. Despite the fact that they had to be somewhat visible to attract customers, brothels were perceived as a discrete outlet for excess sexual energies. They were sites of private vice that could be deployed to help preserve order and conformity.

After 1939 health concerns that had long dictated attitudes toward prostitution in Germany were subordinated to the more pressing need to stabilize the Nazi regime in a time of war. Given this philosophy, it comes as no surprise that the Nazis rejected the arguments of VD experts and welfare advocates against state-run brothels. Although a feeble attempt was made to argue that brothels could better protect the population from VD since prostitution was inevitable and brothel inmates could be forced to undergo regular medical examinations, this was simply a smokescreen for a much more pressing concern with subordinating human sexuality to the needs of an aggressive, racist state. Men, it was thought, could only become effective soldiers if they were provided with sexual satisfaction.

It is important to note, however, that male sexual satisfaction was not viewed by the Nazis as a goal in itself. The expression of male sexuality was not a matter of individual pleasure but of the nation's military strength. The degree to which Nazi leaders viewed human sexuality as firmly linked to military strength is evident in discussions about whether sterilized individuals were fit to serve as soldiers. This issue was discussed in a meeting of top Nazi administrators from the Ministry of Justice, the Führer's office, the army and navy, the Health and Racial Political Offices, and the welfare administration in spring 1936. A military doctor from the War Ministry insisted that allowing sterilized individuals to become soldiers during peacetime was inadvisable, because they were not fit for service. Although some cases might be exceptions to this rule, he argued, the

---

[105]I owe the formulation "functionalized male sexuality" to Paul, 135.

teasing that sterilized soldiers were sure to receive from their comrades would make service a torture for them. If war were to come, the doctor advised, these individuals could be designated fit for conscripted civilian work. These recommendations were accepted and later endorsed by the Führer himself.[106] At another meeting three days later, it was emphasized that although sterilization must not be considered discriminatory or "honor destroying," those who had undergone the procedure were not "suited to service with weapons" partly because the individual's medical situation was unlikely to remain secret and would be the source of much taunting.[107] Weeks before the invasion of Poland, a directive from the Führer stipulated that sterilized volunteers would be allowed to serve if they were found to be fit (*tauglich*). Others would be assigned civilian work duties.[108]

This discussion tells us several interesting things about the place of sexuality in the thinking of the Nazi leadership. To them, sexuality was inseparably linked to fertility, which was itself a core feature of personhood and, particularly, of masculine identity. It was assumed that anyone could recognize a sterilized individual on sight and that this would make that individual's performance in a military context next to impossible. The link between fertility and a particularly militarized understanding of masculine sexuality is apparent.

The militarization of masculine sexuality paralleled the glorification of chaste motherhood in civilian Nazi society. Women's sexuality had long been seen as intimately linked to their reproductive capacities. But with the coming of World War Two, the Nazis also functionalized male sexuality, consciously and actively attempting to control male sexual energies for the purposes of war. Although Nazi rhetoric still insisted that VD policies were aimed at limiting fertility-destroying diseases, wartime policy sacrificed a concern with fecundity to the war effort, deploying female sexual services (in terms of both motherhood and prostitution) and male sexual energies to increase the regime's military might. Sex was thus viewed as entirely purposeful. It was more than simply a reward for loyalty to the regime—though it was that too. It was the underlying fuel of the military machine.

Although seemingly contradictory, the simultaneous glorification of the family and the construction of brothels arose from the demands of the

---

[106]"Ressortsbesprechung am 26. April d.Js. im Reichsministerium des Innern über die Durchführung des Gesetzes zur Verhütung erbkranken Nachwuchses," minutes dated May 8, 1936, BArch(B) R43 II/721a, 78–85.

[107]It should be noted that some exceptions were made for party members. In cases where "particularly reliable party members" had been recommended for sterilization, Hitler reserved the right to reverse the decision (ibid., 81, 83).

[108]Reichsamtsleiter to Martin Bormann, August 10, 1939, in ibid., 97–98.

Nazis' particular brand of population policy. While supporting increased fertility at home, the regime also pursued a relentlessly militaristic, expansionistic, and racist foreign policy that, combined with a particular understanding of male sexuality, justified both sexual violence on the front and the provision of sexual gratification as a reward for military service. The goal of both policies was the achievement of world domination on the basis of racial superiority. The contradiction of decrying promiscuity, on the one hand, and promoting sexual commerce, on the other, was justified with the argument that only the direct control of prostitution could stop the spread of venereal disease. National Socialist discussions of sexuality never escaped the strict confines of racial ideology and a highly masculinized militarism. Pleasure took on a very peculiar role in this worldview. In providing prostitutes for soldiers and workers, Himmler did not accept the human need for pleasure. Instead, he prioritized military victory, arguing, in effect, that male sexual drives needed to be satisfied to maximize military and industrial effectiveness.

The Denial of Homosexuality: Same-Sex Incidents in Himmler's SS and Police

GEOFFREY J. GILES

University of Florida

In public, Heinrich Himmler minimized the existence of same-sex sexuality within the elite Schutzstaffel (SS). "In the whole of the SS there occur about eight to ten cases per year," Himmler announced to his senior SS generals in February 1937, clearly satisfied that the "problem" of homosexuality was almost solved. Soon he hoped to reduce the number further by sending miscreants to concentration camps and having them "shot while trying to escape." Their fate would serve as a dire warning.[1] Himmler's estimate of the prevalence of homosexuality in the ranks of the SS was hardly accurate. In the city of Leipzig alone, four SS men were arrested for homosexual offenses in 1937 and 1938.[2] Burkhard Jellonnek's calculation that 57 percent of those arrested in Düsseldorf on such charges during the Third Reich belonged to one or another Nazi organization makes it likely that there were SS men among them, too.[3] In 1940, sixteen cases of homosexuality were brought before the internal SS courts, and in

The writing of this essay was made possible by the generous support of the Shapiro Senior Scholar-in-Residence Fellowship at the Center for Advanced Holocaust Studies, United States Holocaust Memorial Museum, Washington, D.C. Research for it also benefited from earlier fellowships from the Alexander von Humboldt Foundation, the German Marshall Fund of the United States, and the Division of Sponsored Research at the University of Florida.

[1] Günter Grau, ed., *Homosexualität in der NS-Zeit: Dokumente einer Diskriminierung und Verfolgung* (Frankfurt, 1993), 246.

[2] Ibid., 184.

[3] If we project onto Düsseldorf Jellonnek's finding of 4.8 percent SS members among Nazis charged in the rural Palatinate district of Speyer, we would arrive at a total of only six SS men for Düsseldorf for the whole period. Yet homosexual circles were more active in the city, as were the police entrapment schemes, so the numbers were probably higher. Jellonnek does not offer details of Nazi affiliation, however. See Burkhard Jellonnek, *Homosexuelle unter dem Hakenkreuz: Die Verfolgung von Homosexuellen im Dritten Reich* (Paderborn, 1990), 212, 318. See also the recent criticism by Frank Sparing of the very limited nature of Jellonnek's sample in *". . . wegen Vergehen nach §175 verhaftet": Die Verfolgung der*

the first quarter alone of 1943, no fewer than twenty-two convictions were recorded.[4] Richard Plant's proposition, that from the time of the Röhm Purge, "no halfway intelligent gay was likely to join the homophobic SS," seems to stand confounded.[5]

While these figures are modest when compared to the thousands of ordinary Germans convicted every year by Nazi courts for homosexual offenses, it is nonetheless instructive to focus on the incidence of such "crimes" in the SS and police. The SS was the organization meant to embody the highest National Socialist values, and it played a central role in the most public homosexual scandal of the entire regime, the murder of the chief of staff of Hitler's Sturmabteilung (SA), Ernst Röhm. As the leader of the SS and the police, Himmler himself deserves special attention. His speeches and writings dealt more obsessively with homosexuality than did those of any other Nazi leader, and his comments were broadly consistent in their sharp condemnation of homosexuality. On several documented occasions between 1934 and 1943, Himmler spoke or wrote of the acceptability, even the desirability, of killing homosexuals. However, the actual disciplining of suspected homosexuals in the SS and other organizations under Himmler's control was far from uniform or consistent. Since punishment for those convicted of homosexuality did not become increasingly severe, even after the legal enactment in November of 1941 of capital punishment for such offenses among the SS and police, the model of "cumulative radicalization" does not accurately describe Nazi policy on homosexuals. The precise nature of the offense was no predictor of the outcome of a trial. SS courts did not usually make snap judgments but weighed the evidence quite carefully and sometimes approached the evidence with a little common sense. When the death penalty was prescribed, appeals against the sentence were occasionally successful. Even Himmler's own position vacillated: while he was all for summary justice in 1943, he showed at least partial lenience in the winter of 1945 by sending convicted men to the front to prove themselves instead of ordering their executions. This essay suggests why he made such decisions at particular moments and examines them in the broader context of wartime policy and cultural fears.

Düsseldorfer Homosexuellen während des Nationalsozialismus (Düsseldorf, 1997), 10, which should not be allowed to negate Jellonnek's overall assessment, however.

[4]Himmler carefully highlighted the cases of homosexuality in the monthly SS crime statistics with the familiar green pencil that only he was permitted to use. See Burkhard Jellonnek, "Himmlers Sturmstaffel [*sic*] (SS) als Beispiel nationalsozialistischer Homosexuellenverfolgung" (unpublished paper, 1988), 14–15.

[5]Richard Plant, *The Pink Triangle: The Nazi War against Homosexuals* (Edinburgh, 1987), 143.

In a recent article, Peter von Rönn posits an orderly, logical, and consistent development of Himmler's responses to same-sex sexuality. His argument parallels the intentionalist thesis of Hans-Georg Stümke, who saw the central reason for the Nazi persecution of homosexuals as the regime's obsession with boosting population growth. However, I contend that this explanation is only partial.[6] Von Rönn sees a decisive shift to a political problematization of homosexuality and interprets Himmler's efforts as part of his attempt to extend his power. Von Rönn claims that the "central document" marking the shift to treating homosexuality as a purely political problem was the article "Das sind Staatsfeinde!" (These are enemies of the state!) published in the SS newspaper in March 1937.[7] Yet the decisive moment had surely come almost three years earlier with the Röhm Purge.[8] There is no question that after June 30, 1934, Himmler's political stock soared decisively and that his immediate subordinates worked shrewdly in the coming years to consolidate the SS and police empire. Von Rönn also oversimplifies the situation by asserting that after 1937 the etiology of homosexuality was a question of only subsidiary interest.[9]

[6]Hans-Georg Stümke, *Homosexuelle in Deutschland: Eine politische Geschichte* (Munich, 1989), 92–95. Curiously, von Rönn does not address Stümke's work directly.

[7]Peter von Rönn, "Politische und psychiatrische Homosexualitätskonstruktion im NS-Staat," *Zeitschrift für Sexualforschung* (June/September 1998): 99–129, 220–60, quote from 119–20. The article in question was one of several in the SS mouthpiece: "Das sind Staatsfeinde!" *Das schwarze Korps*, March 4, 1937, and its position as "das zentrale Dokument zur Neuformulierung des nationalsozialistischen Homosexuellenbildes" is debatable, to say the least.

[8]In a chapter in my forthcoming book on homosexuality and the Nazis, I have looked at the rhetoric that accompanied the Röhm Purge and concluded that it was Goebbels, not Himmler or Hitler, who brought suggestions of a homosexual orgy into the picture. The propaganda minister's comments that the scene was literally nauseating to a normal person like him were meant to titillate the reader into imagining that some incredibly perverse sex acts were going on. "Spare me," said Goebbels in his radio speech on the evening of July 1, 1934, "from describing the disgusting scenes that almost made us throw up." Hitler himself was generally more restrained about the sexual aspect (though he strongly and quite mendaciously suggested that Röhm had a predilection for teenage Hitler Youths) and reserved his real explosion of anger for his (also mendacious) accusations of Röhm's treason and disloyalty. See "Das Reich steht—und über uns der Führer. Rede des Reichsministers Dr. Goebbels in Düsseldorf," *Völkischer Beobachter*, Ausgabe A, July 3, 1934.

[9]Von Rönn (220–49) devotes rather more time to the psychiatrist, Professor Hans Bürger-Prinz, than he perhaps merits, seeing him as one of the principal spokesmen on homosexuality in the Third Reich. The professor was certainly an aggressively ambitious self-promoter who cultivated the support of the Nazi Party leadership in Hamburg. His intentional twisting of data to suit his Nazi masters is thus plausible. But his standing in the profession is another matter; his colleagues on the University of Hamburg medical faculty found him so impossible that they voted unanimously to have him removed as dean in the final months of the war. See Beschwerde der medizinischen Fakultät gegen Professor Bürger-Prinz, Staatsarchiv Hamburg, University of Hamburg Archives D.110.20.32/3. Von Rönn assigns other scholars in the vigorous debate over the nature of homosexuality to a subsidiary position, and he considers their work simply in its relationship to that of Bürger-Prinz, but see also Geoffrey J. Giles, "'The Most Unkindest Cut of All': Castration, Homosexuality, and Nazi Justice," *Journal of Contemporary History* (January 1992): 41–61.

The record of Nazi persecution of men accused of being homosexuals is complex. To the very end of the war, Himmler's police "experts" on homosexuality expended an enormous amount of energy on etiological questions, conducting ludicrously detailed investigations into the personal and medical backgrounds of prisoners' childhoods. Himmler himself was deeply interested in the medical-biological questions surrounding homosexuality and showed a keen interest in Dr. Carl Vaernet's appalling medical experiments on homosexual inmates at Buchenwald.[10] For Himmler, homosexuality was a multifaceted problem, one that was not, in his eyes, a straightforward racial issue. This standpoint occasionally allowed for his flexible treatment of suspected homosexuals, such as scaling back police intervention during the 1936 Berlin Olympics and prohibiting unauthorized arrests of actors and artists in 1937.[11] Antihomosexual policy, which in broad terms was embraced by the majority of the population, was a less rigid ideological tenet than the regime's unyielding opposition toward the Jews. While no Jews were officially tolerated in the army or even in German society, for practical and sometimes necessary reasons men under suspicion of being homosexuals were accepted and retained in the ranks of the armed forces. In my research, I have found no evidence of a programmatic decision to institute a "gay Holocaust."

THE ROOTS OF PROBLEMATIZATION

Some commentators have suggested that homosexuality flourished within the ranks of the SS, but that is an exaggeration. Such sensationalist accounts reflect a long-lived topos of German exile literature, in which writers (Bertolt Brecht among them) attempted to vilify the Nazi movement by painting it as riddled with homosexuals.[12] The present essay is not so much concerned with counting the frequency of offenses as with understanding their implications. The number of SS members apprehended on charges of homosexuality is small, especially given the constantly burgeoning size of Himmler's private army. Yet the cases are significant, since the way they were treated can help us to understand how the Nazi leadership perceived and dealt with sexuality. There was an inherent contradiction

[10]"Dr. Vaernet bitte ich absolut großzügig zu behandeln," ordered Himmler in November 1943, and the doctor continued his hormonal implants, often with fatal results, until he fled from Buchenwald early in 1945 to save his own life, eventually settling in Argentina. See the documents in Grau, ed., *Homosexualität*, 347–58.

[11]Ibid., 88, 179–80.

[12]See the studies by Jörn Meve, *"Homosexuelle Nazis": Ein Stereotyp in Politik und Literatur des Exils* (Hamburg, 1990); and Alexander Zinn, *Die soziale Konstruktion des homosexuellen Nationalsozialisten: Zu Genese und Etablierung eines Stereotyps* (Frankfurt am Main, 1997). See also James W. Jones, "'Gegenwartsbewältigung': The Male Homosexual Character in Selected Works about the Fascist Experience," in *Der Zweite Weltkrieg und die Exilanten: Eine literarische Antwort*, ed. Helmut F. Pfanner (Berlin, 1991), 303–10.

within the ideology of the Nazi movement, especially as applied to its elite branch, the SS. On the one hand, the leadership wanted to replicate within its own ranks the close male intimacy of the trenches of the First World War, something that only the shared dangers of front-line warfare could ever bring about. On the other hand, it shunned the soft, emotional, "feminine" underside of such relationships.

The party's first public statement specifically condemning homosexuality, issued in 1928, emphasized the fear of womanish emotionalism running wild among men and embedded the scenario within a background of crude social Darwinism: "[The German *Volk*] can only live if it fights, because to live is to fight. And it can only fight if it keeps itself manly. It can only remain manly if it practices discipline, above all in love. . . . Everything that unmans our *Volk* makes it into the plaything of our enemies."[13] It is not clear who composed this statement, although it is more in the style of party philosopher Alfred Rosenberg than of Hitler or Himmler. Nonetheless, it can be said to represent a general fear in the Nazi movement. While men were the authority figures, they needed to maintain the respect they were accorded by acting in a disciplined fashion, which meant not falling out of the role assigned to them. The Nazi movement, its supporters claimed, was unlike other all-male organizations of the early twentieth century, especially youth groups, whose close bonding was based on "friendship," which was subject to unpredictable and inconstant emotions; instead, the Nazi movement was based on the altogether more soldierly and manly concept of "comradeship." Yet the male bonding that the Nazis vigorously encouraged in the name of comradeship was not easily distinguishable from the Wandervogel movement, and there must have been millions of young German men who did not have a clear idea of the difference.

Whether comrade or friend, many Nazis developed relationships with other men that were laden with emotion and eroticism and often ran too close to the edge of sexuality to be pulled back. It was this confusion that made the control of homosexual feelings (as much as activity) a high priority for the Nazi leadership. Emotions in a private situation were virtually impossible to regulate, which is why the regime tried to eliminate the private sphere (while paradoxically celebrating it in the form of the traditional and "normal" family). At the same time the whole thrust of the rhetoric of party and state worked toward promoting a highly emotional adulation of leaders and fellow party members. The Nazis celebrated bonds with members of their own sex as more noble than relationships with

[13]There is a significant double entendre here, because the word for discipline, *Zucht*, also has the connotation of decency. This is clearer in its opposite, *Unzucht*, which was the legal term used for homosexuality (*widernatürliche Unzucht*, "unnatural indecency"). The statement of May 14, 1928, came in response to a survey of political parties carried out by the homerotic magazine, *Der Eigene*, and it is quoted in Jellonnek, *Homosexuelle*, 53–54.

women, but they were too embarrassed to admit that there was an emotional and therefore labile and not easily controllable side to them.

The young Himmler portrayed in Bradley F. Smith's careful study was rather prudish about sex and sought to cover his embarrassment and ignorance by seeking out texts that might rationalize his advocacy of sexual abstinence. Still, his lack of confidence around members of the opposite sex (more pronounced than that of his peers) brought with it no suggestion of homosexual attractions.[14] When he encountered the subject of homosexuality in his reading, Himmler was confused rather than titillated. His reaction on reading Hans Blüher's *Die Rolle der Erotik in der männlichen Gesellschaft* (The role of eroticism in male society) as a student is well known.[15] He instinctively wanted to reject Blüher's endorsement of homoeroticism but could not immediately come up with persuasive counterarguments. In the annotation in his reading list, Himmler twisted and turned uncomfortably:

> The man has certainly penetrated colossally deep into the male erotic, and has grasped it psychologically and philosophically [?]. Still he uses too much vague philosophy in order for it to convince me, even though much of it is wrapped up in learned language. That there must be male societies is clear. If one can call them erotic, I doubt. In any case the pure physical homosexuality is an error of degenerate individualism that is contrary to nature.

Bradley Smith observes that "to some observers such comments may betoken latent homosexuality," but he sees them as confusion about an unfamiliar topic.[16] While I would agree with that assessment, I am not so quick to set these remarks aside. They reflect a central dilemma for the Nazi movement that Himmler never resolved. Individuals in an organization that placed such a high premium on male bonding were bound to stray into homoeroticism on occasion, even if it was an embarrassment to call it that.[17]

[14]As a student in 1920, Himmler was much taken by Hans Wegener's *Wir jungen Männer: Das sexuelle Problem des gebildeten jungen Mannes vor der Ehe* (Königstein/Taunus, 1912), which put the case for sexual abstinence in terms of the physical and mental damage caused by promiscuity. Himmler found it "rich and surely right. Certainly the most beautiful book I have read on this question." By 1922, as Bradley F. Smith notes, "the frequency with which he discussed sex and sexual problems with his close male friends suggests that he was having trouble with his defenses" (*Heinrich Himmler: A Nazi in the Making, 1900–1926* [Stanford, 1971], 85–86, 114–15).

[15]Some impassioned letters from grateful readers, brought back from the brink of despair by his sanctioning, even welcoming, of homoerotic relations, are included in later editions of another of Blüher's books. See Hans Blüher, *Die deutsche Wandervogelbewegung als erotisches Phänomen: Ein Beitrag zur Erkenntnis der sexuellen Inversion*, 3rd ed. (Charlottenburg, 1918), 182–90.

[16]Smith, 115. Question mark in the original quotation, denoting Smith's uncertainty over the legibility of Himmler's shorthand.

[17]Detlev Peukert talks of Himmler's personality needing "an external armouring of authority and obedience to serve as protection for the softness concealed within" (*Inside Nazi*

It is not known when Himmler first learned of Ernst Röhm's sexual proclivities, but initially their relations were cordial. He noted in January 1922 that Röhm was "very friendly" to the twenty-one-year-old Himmler when they met at the latter's regimental club; if there had been the slightest whiff of sexual interest at this date, Himmler would surely have beaten a hasty retreat and reached for his pen to record the affront in his diary.[18] By the following year, very special, almost sacred, ties would bind them together as comrades-in-arms at the same barricade during the Beer Hall Putsch.[19] It is safe to assume that Himmler acquired most of his understanding of the "homosexual problem," like so many of his other ideas, from Hitler, although some of his own reading in the 1920s touched on the question.[20] For Hitler and Himmler the forced closure of gay bars in 1933 was an important gesture in the Nazi program to "clean up" Germany, yet neither showed much interest in cleansing the party ranks of individual homosexuals. The Röhm purge of June 1934 marked the decisive watershed for ending toleration within the Nazi movement. Hitler outlined his fundamental position in his ranting speech to the Reichstag a fortnight after the purge, and Himmler echoed it repeatedly: homosexuals formed cliques, cliques that would go on to hatch treasonable conspiracies against the state.[21] Two images associated with homosexuality ran through the mixed metaphors of Hitler's speech: it was both a coldly rational political conspiracy with a single-minded aim and a poisonous disease spreading inexorably but haphazardly.[22]

Germany: Conformity, Opposition, and Racism in Everyday Life [New Haven, Conn., 1987], 204). Reinhard Greve ignores the erotic element and sees only the cultic and pseudohistorical aspects ("Die SS als Männerbund," in *Männerbande, Männerbünde: Zur Rolle des Mannes im Kulturvergleich*, ed. Gisela Völger and Karin von Welck [Cologne, 1990], 107–12). See also Klaus Theweleit, *Männerphantasien*, vol. 2: *Männerkörper: Zur Psychoanalyse des weissen Terrors* (Basel/Frankfurt am Main, 1986), 390–91.

[18]Smith, 126. In fact it seems that Röhm may not have been homosexually active at this date. In a letter to Karl-Günther Heimsoth in 1929, Röhm noted: "I pride myself on being homosexual but first really 'discovered' this in 1924." See Eleanor Hancock, "'Only the Real, the True, the Masculine Held Its Value': Ernst Röhm, Masculinity, and Male Homosexuality," *Journal of the History of Sexuality* (April 1998): 616–41, quote from 625.

[19]For the iconographical significance of the famous picture of Himmler at the barricades with Röhm in November 1923, from which the latter was edited out after his murder, see Geoffrey J. Giles, "Die erzieherische Rolle von Sammelbildern in politischen Umbruchszeiten," in *Deutsche Umbrüche im 20. Jahrhundert*, ed. Dietrich Papenfuß and Wolfgang Schieder (Cologne, 2000), 260–61.

[20]Herwig Hartner, *Erotik und Rasse: Eine Untersuchung über gesellschaftliche, sittliche und geschlechtliche Fragen* (Munich, 1925), included a section about the homosexual problem, and Himmler recorded his approval of the book among the annotations to his reading list. Library of Congress (LC) Himmler File, Container 418.

[21]"Der Wortlaut der Führerrede vor dem Reichstag," *Völkischer Beobachter*, Ausgabe A, July 15–16, 1934, Beiblatt p. 1.

[22]The infection metaphor had entered Himmler's thinking by the fall of 1927, when he read Hartner's book, which explained homosexuality in these alarmist terms. Himmler

Several commentators have seen a turning point in Himmler's own policy in the article by SS legal expert Professor Karl August Eckhardt, published in the SS newspaper in the spring of 1935, one year after the Röhm purge. If one looks beyond the title, "Widernatürliche Unzucht ist todeswürdig" (Unnatural indecency deserves death), the article is in fact not so much a plea for capital punishment as an historical treatise, purporting to describe the traditional treatments of homosexuals. In ancient Germanic times, Eckhardt wrote, the accused might be thrown into a bog, burnt, or buried alive; in the modern period, he was subject to the "more lenient" punishment of beheading. Eckhardt endorsed the death penalty for homosexual offenses only in the very last paragraph, where he called for a return to the "Nordic principle of the eradication of the degenerate" because the future of Germany depended on the nation's purity. In 1935 this rhetorical flourish was not to be taken too literally.[23] In a long speech about homosexuality in 1937, Himmler himself waxed nostalgic about those good old Germanic customs of throwing the weighted homosexual into a muddy bog to drown. For the present day, added Himmler, "I must say: unfortunately," that was no longer possible. Nevertheless, in September 1938 the Reichsführer-SS suggested that within a year SS members would routinely be punished with a death sentence for homosexual offenses.[24] While the actual promulgation of the decree came later, Himmler's 1938 statement showed that the idea had already been planted in his mind.

Homosexual Behavior within the SS

Given Himmler's personal distaste for homosexual acts, one would think that he would have managed to keep his immediate surroundings free of any taint. Yet SS headquarters was sometimes the setting for scandalous goings-on. In March 1941 one SS man on Sunday duty invited his lover,

---

frequently borrowed books from other Nazi leaders, including Hitler (the copy of Hartner's *Erotik und Rasse* was on loan from party court chairman Walter Buch). It is likely that, since both of them had pretensions to intellectuality, they discussed books together. The notion of homosexuality as dangerously infectious was not new or exclusive to Hartner's book, but this happens to be one book covering the issue for which we have positive evidence of Himmler's study and endorsement. "If it [homosexuality] prevails," warned Hartner, "it will surely dig our graves," reasoning that an increase in homosexuals would mean a free fall in the birth rate and the eventual implosion of the German race (41–44). Parallel sentiments pervaded the eugenics movement at the end of the nineteenth century.

[23]SS-Untersturmführer Professor Eckhardt, "Widernatürliche Unzucht ist todeswürdig," *Das schwarze Korps*, May 22, 1935, 13. Jellonnek deplores the frequent misinterpretation of this article by "gay Holocaust" proponents and others who suggest that homosexuals were quite commonly given death sentences at this time (*Homosexuelle*, 31–33).

[24]Bradley F. Smith and Agnes Peterson, eds., *Heinrich Himmler: Geheimreden 1933–1945 und andere Ansprachen* (Frankfurt am Main, 1974), 93–104.

not an SS member, to join him. They slipped into the elevator, stopped it deliberately between the floors in order to be undisturbed, and had sex.[25] Nor was this the only such case. The previous year a seventeen-year-old male telephonist at the SS head office had also entertained a boyfriend there on several occasions, though the Gestapo only found out about the meetings two years later.[26]

Even Hitler's personal bodyguard, the SS Leibstandarte Adolf Hitler, did not entirely shun gay sex. What makes the following high-profile case, involving the former rector of Munich University, particularly puzzling is that the young SS man involved was not even reprimanded. Hans P. joined the Hitler Youth in October 1930, well over two years before Hitler became chancellor, and was transferred directly into the SS bodyguard in November 1933, when he was eighteen. By 1938 he had been promoted to SS-Scharführer (sergeant) and was serving with a unit in Munich when Professor Leopold K. met him at a café. P. was invited to visit the professor's institute at the university, which was doubtless flattering for someone who had never been to college, and he did so several times. On one such occasion, K. embraced and kissed him. When P. was transferred to Berlin at the end of 1938, he agreed to let K. visit him. During that meeting they masturbated together, apparently for the first time. Shortly afterward the two of them met for a weekend together in Frankfurt, where they shared a room and had sex again.[27]

Inexplicably, nothing happened to Hans P. in the way of a criminal charge. In February 1939, at the time of a Gestapo investigation into the professor's relationships with at least ten young men, P. left the SS. He was not publicly expelled, as one would expect, but departed "following a severe sports accident," as he testified. I can only conclude that he must have had an influential protector behind the scenes in the SS. After spending a year as a bookkeeper with a private wholesale firm, he was taken back into the SS reserve and continued to serve as a bookkeeper. Nine months later he advanced to the position of paymaster of the Waffen-SS military hospital at Hohenlychen. He evidently did well, because he was promoted to Hauptscharführer at the beginning of December 1942, just four days before he got married. This promotion would have been unthinkable for anyone found guilty of homosexual offenses by a court.[28] Clearly, SS men

[25]Following a denunciation, this escapade cost the SS man a seven-year penitentiary sentence, while his friend was sent to an ordinary prison for four years. See Andreas Pretzel and Gabriele Roßbach, eds., *"Wegen der zu erwartenden hohen Strafe . . .": Homosexuellenverfolgung in Berlin 1933–1945* (Berlin, 2000), 38.

[26]Gestapo mugshots of the SS telephonist Alfred W. in ibid., 48.

[27]I discuss the K. case more fully in my forthcoming book on homosexuality and the Nazis. The documents referred to here were kindly provided in photocopy from the Munich University archive by Professor Laetitia Boehm as well as from National Archives II College Park (NARA) BDC PK Leopold K. and SSO Hans P.

[28]Details from BDC personal records in NARA BDC RuSHA file Hans P.

like P. were not taking to heart either Himmler's warnings or the tirades against homosexuality printed in *Das schwarze Korps*.

The harsh treatment of homosexuals by courts in Nazi Germany might indicate that judges themselves were eager to set an example in such cases, all the more so if the accused were members of the SS. Surprisingly, however, in a Bavarian case at the beginning of 1940, the SS court actually rejected the need even for a full investigation. The case centered on two young SS recruits who had been discovered in bed together in their barracks room, one of them completely naked. This was incriminating enough, in Nazi eyes, to warrant corrective punishment. The two SS men were rather young (Hans V. was eighteen, Georg W. only seventeen), but that made it more likely that severe action would be taken to curb any budding homosexual tendencies. The testimony by other barracks roommates that the former had often "touched them indecently" against their protests should have sealed V.'s fate. Yet the SS court dropped the case. The police were unable to dig up any damaging material about the young men's pasts, and the court accepted the assertions of the pair that they were just talking together and had gotten into bed with each other so as not to disturb the rest of the men. In a remarkable ruling, the court noted that "lying side by side in a bed does not in itself constitute an indecent act in the sense of the criminal code." This statement was only formally accurate, because the elasticity of the post-1935 revision of Paragraph 175 allowed more harmless manifestations of desire than this to send men to prison. Yet in this case the court followed the letter of the law, explaining that "in order for the factual provisions of §175 to be fulfilled, the accused must have had a lascivious intent or, rather, must have committed indecent acts mutually or with the toleration of one party." Why did the court show a lenient face here? Perhaps it was reluctant to deplete the ranks of the SS at this early stage of war; perhaps it realized that soldiers in wartime do sometimes sleep together, simply for warmth or companionship.[29]

The Introduction of the Death Penalty

The official edict prescribing the death sentence for SS and police members found guilty of homosexuality came on November 15, 1941. No single case or surge in offenses had provoked it. Issued in Hitler's name, the edict suspended the jurisdiction of the regular law courts over SS and police members in cases of homosexuality, ruling that such cases would be dealt with secretly by the SS's own special courts. Although "less serious cases" might result in a prison or penitentiary sentence, the most ominous change lay in the principal section of the decree: "A member of the SS or

---

[29]Verfügung Eberstein und Knote, Ablehnung Einleitung eines Ermittlungsverfahrens, January 18, 1940, BAL NS7/1021.

police who commits indecency with another man or allows himself to be abused in an indecent manner will be punished with death." How drastic was this change? Günter Grau gives the impression that the introduction of the death penalty for homosexual offenses in the SS and police meant that such punishments subsequently became the norm, and therefore Himmler succeeded in "cleansing" the SS.[30] George Mosse goes to the other extreme and states erroneously that "no executions actually took place; suspected homosexuals were expelled or retired from the SS instead."[31] In fact, death sentences were carried out, but the new ruling was applied rarely and inconsistently.[32]

Hitler's decree represents such a fundamental policy change that it is surprising that no commentator has explored its immediate origins. Himmler did not move closer toward implementation of a death penalty in the late 1930s, despite his occasional inflammatory comments, though he certainly endorsed ever harsher treatment of homosexuals and encouraged the Ministry of Justice (Reichsjustizministerium) in March 1937 to change the sentence for homosexuality from prison to penitentiary terms. By the time the ministry had completed a draft for a new penal code, the Second World War had broken out, and Hitler, concerned about national morale, judged this an inopportune moment to introduce more heavily punitive measures. In November 1940 he rejected the initial draft decree to introduce the death sentence or life imprisonment for homosexuality between adult men.[33]

The catalyst for making homosexuality a capital offense was probably one of Hitler's rare private pronouncements on homosexuality, made on the evening of August 18, 1941, and it warrants closer examination. Goebbels had unintentionally provoked Hitler to discuss the topic by bringing up the German entertainment world. He recalled the conversation in his diary:

> [W]e came to speak of the State Theater in Berlin. The Führer doesn't like Gustav Gründgens. He is too unmanly for him. In his view, one should not tolerate homosexuality in public life under any circumstances. Above all, however, the Wehrmacht and the party must be kept free of it. The homosexual also tends to undertake the selection of men according to criminal or at least sick criteria but not their suitability. If you let him have his way, the whole state would become an organization of homosexuality in the long run,

---

[30]Grau, ed., *Homosexualität*, 242–51.

[31]George L. Mosse, *The Image of Man: The Creation of Modern Masculinity* (New York, 1996), 175.

[32]Of sixteen convictions for homosexuality in the SS and police in 1940, only one resulted in a death sentence. For the first quarter of 1943 (i.e., after the November 1941 decree came into effect), there were twenty-two convictions, not one of which was given the death sentence (Jellonnek, "Sturmstaffel," 15).

[33]Jellonnek, *Homosexuelle*, 115–19.

and not an organization of manly excellence. A real man will always put up resistance to such an attempt, if only for the reason that he sees in it an attack on his own possibilities for advancement.

There is much in the Catholic Church that can only be explained by the homosexual principle on which it at least in many respects rests. The National Socialist state must be a manly state. It is built upon the firm foundations of a natural selection that repeats itself in a constant cycle.[34]

This is fairly old hat: the condemnation of effeminacy, the fear of conspiratorial cliques,[35] the putative homosexual nature of the Catholic Church. Goebbels had heard it all before and did not bother, after dictating another seventeen pages of comments on his discussions with Hitler earlier that day, to go into much detail about the conversation on homosexuality. He certainly did not sense a change of policy here. The need to keep the party free of homosexuals had been on the table since the Röhm purge.

Other scholars have not noticed Goebbels's diary entry and have instead reacted to another memorandum about this same monologue of Hitler's, which Günter Grau claims was the trigger for the November decree.[36] Again it warrants our full attention:

Last night the Führer talked for a long time about the plague of homosexuality. We have to go after this with ruthless severity, he said, because there is a certain time in youth when the sexual feelings of a boy can easily be influenced in the wrong direction; it is precisely boys in this age group whom homosexuals seduce. And a homosexual will generally seduce a whole host of boys, so that homosexuality really is as infectious and dangerous as the plague. But our youth must not be ruined for us; on the contrary, they must be brought up in the proper manner. Therefore, wherever manifestations of homosexuality appear among our youth, we must pounce on them with barbaric severity.

Our state and our order above all can and should only be built on the principle of achievement. Any system of favorites must be rejected; we don't want the offshoots of nepotism and that sort of thing.

[34]Elke Fröhlich, ed., *Die Tagebücher von Joseph Goebbels. Teil II: Diktate 1941–1945* (Munich, 1996), Band 1, p. 272.

[35]This is where Steven Katz's analysis does not work for the Third Reich. He claims in his chapter, "The Persecution of Homosexuals" (specifically about the medieval period but with the broader implications that the book's title suggests), that the homosexual was "merely a sinner." Since the homosexual, unlike the Jew, was not regarded as having power, "one might loathe the homosexual but one need not live in dread of him." See Steven T. Katz, *The Holocaust in Historical Context*, vol. 1 (New York, 1994), 527. The fictitious yet nonetheless powerful dread in Nazi Germany derived from Hitler's mendacious analysis of the Röhm Putsch, reinforced by Himmler and passed on down the ranks of the Nazi movement.

[36]Unfortunately, Grau does not identify the office from which this *Aktenvermerk aus dem Führerhauptquartier vom 19. August 1941* came (Grau, ed., *Homosexualität*, 213–14, 242). Jeremy Noakes accepts the importance of the document and includes an English translation

The homosexual, on the other hand, does *not* assess other men according to their achievement; he rejects the most competent men if or even because they are not homosexual and gives preference to homosexuals. We've experienced it unfortunately in the case of Röhm, as well as other cases, that a homosexual will fill all crucial positions with other homosexuals.

Especially the party with its branch organizations and the Wehrmacht must proceed with ruthless severity against every case of homosexuality that appears in their ranks. If this happens, then the machinery of the state will remain clean, and it must remain clean.

But in *one* organization every case of homosexuality must be punished with death, namely, in the Hitler Youth. If that is one day going to represent the pick of the nation, then no other verdict must ever be passed within its ranks.

The account above and Goebbels's recollection overlap, notably in mentioning the potential for a homosexual conspiracy to take over the state (with an explicit reference to Ernst Röhm), the alleged predilections of homosexuals for young boys, the infectious disease metaphor, and the need to keep the Wehrmacht and party unsullied. The striking difference between the two records is in the last paragraph, which calls for the death penalty in cases involving the Hitler Youth. There is no evidence that Baldur von Schirach, the head of the Hitler Youth, felt moved to introduce the death penalty for illicit sexual relations among the nation's teenage boys in his charge, and Hitler did not call for the death penalty against perpetrators in the SS or police at this time.[37] Rather, it must derive from an initiative of Himmler that goes beyond "working toward the Führer" and represents what I would describe as "subordinate escalation." Himmler, who had undoubtedly heard about Hitler's pronouncements, wanted to outdo or perhaps preempt any possible move by Schirach. After all, the SS, the elite of the nation, could not remain without such a purifying regulation if the Hitler Youth put one in place. A note from Himmler to Hans-Heinrich Lammers, head of the Reich chancellery, casts some doubt on the likelihood that Hitler initiated the measure personally and suggests that agency lay elsewhere. Himmler thanked Lammers "for the efforts you have made to bring this decree to fruition."[38]

---

of it in his small selection of basic documents on Nazi policy against homosexuals (Jeremy Noakes, ed., *Nazism 1919–1945*, vol. 4: *The German Home Front in World War II* [Exeter, 1998], 392–93). The translation here is mine, differing somewhat from that of Noakes.

[37]However, the death penalty had been introduced generally for certain sex crimes, incuding assaults on children, on 4 September 1941. Jellonek documents four such death sentences carried out in 1943 in Vienna for same-sex offenses against 10–14 year-old boys but also notes that not one of them involved a violent attack. Rather, the accused adults had been involved in long-term relationships with the minors, in some cases for several years (*Homosexuelle*, 118–19).

[38]Grau, ed., *Homosexualität*, 245.

Whoever the initiator was, Hitler promptly and decisively sabotaged the full thrust of the ordinance at the moment he signed it on November 15, 1941. He told Lammers that it should on no account be made public in the *Reichsgesetzblatt*, in any official publication, or in the press, because its release would give the whole world the impression that homosexual offenses were so prevalent in the SS and police that "such draconian measures" were positively required to bring the problem under control. Lammers very sensibly pointed out that potential offenders needed to know in advance that the death penalty awaited them. Why would they desist from a crime if they did not know that the law now treated it as a capital offense? Hitler's response was that this was Himmler's problem. He could figure out how to get the message across to all current and future members of the SS and police "in an appropriate fashion."[39] Although the decree was to be kept secret, Lammers decided he had to let the Führer's chancellery know, albeit in the strictest confidence, because that was the office through which appeals to Hitler to commute death sentences would pass. And Bormann, as head of the party chancellery, had better be told, too, because appeals from party members passed through his office.[40]

It was not until March 7, 1942, almost four months later, that Himmler got around to issuing a confidential memo that outlined the procedures for disseminating the new policy. In it he stressed again that such offenses occurred "only *very rarely*" (emphasis in original) in the SS and police, but they nevertheless needed to be treated "with ruthless severity" because this was a "dangerous and infectious plague" from which the Führer wanted to keep these organizations "unconditionally clean." The decree was therefore to be communicated verbally "to *all* members of the SS and police." They would be told not to reveal the threat of the death sentence to any outsider. They were presumably to take only private satisfaction in being the "vanguards in the fight for the extermination of homosexuality among the German people."[41]

IMPLEMENTATION OF THE NEW POLICY

The November 1941 decree ought to have had a deterrent effect. SS members were now required to sign a declaration confirming that this entire question had been explained adequately to them and that they would not engage in any such acts. The form, which would be kept in their personnel

[39]Aktenvermerk Lammers, November 15, 1941, in Helmut Heiber, *Der ganz normale Wahnsinn unterm Hakenkreuz: Triviales und Absonderliches aus den Akten des Dritten Reiches* (Munich, 1996), 163–64.

[40]Aktenvermerk Reichskanzlei, January 23, 1942, with drafts of letters to the other two chancelleries, in Institut für Zeitgeschichte, ed., *Akten der Partei-Kanzlei der NSDAP: Rekonstruktion eines verlorengegangenen Bestandes* (Munich, 1983), microflches 101 20265-69.

[41]Upon being notifled, Bormann wrote to Himmler, saying he thought the party hierarchy—several dozen Gauleiter and Reichsleiter—should be told too and requesting Himmler

file, affirmed: "I have been instructed that the Führer has decreed in his order of November 15, 1941, in order to keep the SS and police clean of all vermin of a homosexual nature, that a member of the SS or police who commits an indecent act with another man or allows himself to be indecently abused by him will be put to death without consideration of his age." Furthermore, the 1941 decree itself was to be read out in full to the SS man at the time of signing. He was also ordered to report any "immoral approach" even if it involved a superior officer to whom he had otherwise sworn absolute obedience. In keeping with Hitler's concerns, he had to swear not to breathe a word to a soul outside the SS or police about this whole policy.[42]

Yet the existence of so few of these forms in personnel files suggests that these procedures were followed only sporadically. Several SS men in the incidents discussed below claimed never to have heard of the Führer's order. SS leaders themselves may have felt awkward about such sex education sessions (there is certainly clear evidence of such awkwardness in the Hitler Youth),[43] and the wartime shortage of paper may have meant that the forms were never readily available. Besides, SS men had to sign all kinds of forms, which they doubtless did not commit to memory. Those serving in the Czech area, for example, were obliged to sign an eighteen-line statement about the sexual prohibitions they were to observe; the form suggested that SS men check the passport or ID card of a prospective sexual partner in order to verify her racial credentials.[44] The fact was that for many soldiers, especially those serving on the eastern front, there were simply no "racially acceptable" women around. What were highly sexed young men to do? The record suggests that frequently they chose masturbation with each other as the most available solution. Many did not regard this behavior as especially reprehensible or anything more than mildly indecent and certainly not evidence that they were homosexuals.

---

to obtain Hitler's permission for this. The Reichsführer-SS responded that he thought it far better for *Bormann* to ask Hitler (despite the fact that Himmler had dinner with Hitler the very same day). Bormann to Himmler, January 29, 1942; Himmler to Bormann, February 4, 1942; Vertrauliches Rundschreiben Himmler, March 7, 1942, microflches 102 01280-84.

[42] A reproduction of the form, signed in Litzmannstadt in September 1942, in shown in Pretzel and Roßbach, eds., 39.

[43] Geoffrey J. Giles, "Straight Talk for Nazi Youth: The Attempt to Transmit Heterosexual Norms," in *Education and Cultural Transmission: Historical Studies of Continuity and Change in Families, Schooling, and Youth Cultures*, ed. Johan Sturm et al. (Ghent, 1996), 305–18.

[44] See an example of such a form, signed in Brno in February 1942, in NARA BDC SSM Walter Sprenger: "I have been instructed that I may not associate with any Czech person, and in particular may not have sexual intercourse with Czech women. I know that intercourse with women of foreign blood is severely punished. Contact is only permitted with Germans or ethnic Germans."

Despite the balanced work of Burkhard Jellonnek, the view is still current that a death sentence for homosexuality in the SS and police was the norm during the war.[45] Once the SS court handed down such a sentence and Himmler confirmed it, it was carried out. Nonetheless, expert medical opinion sometimes intervened to mitigate punishment. In three instances in 1943, Himmler signed death sentences for SS officers and policemen, but the medical expert in Professor Matthias Göring's Institute for Psychotherapy (Deutsches Institut für psychologische Forschung und Psychotherapie) who was assigned to evaluate the guilty parties dismissed each case as a "false verdict."[46] In the first case, an associate of Göring and regular SS medical expert, SS-Standartenführer Dr. Martin Brustmann, rationalized the homosexual acts of a policeman by explaining that he possessed "an abnormally large sex organ," which meant that not every woman was capable of accommodating him in sexual intercourse. Brustmann felt that the man was otherwise perfectly normal and had been led astray by this freak of his anatomy. A course of treatment at the Göring Institute offered every probability that he would not deviate in the future.

The second case dealt with a police corporal who had been condemned to death for sodomizing chickens, an offense that also fell under Paragraph 175 of the criminal code. Since Himmler, a former chicken farmer, could not believe that someone could be so perverse, he ordered an inquiry to see whether alcohol was to blame. In this instance, Dr. Brustmann diagnosed the corporal as being not responsible for his actions as a result of a swelling of the brain. In the third case, Brustmann declared that a Waffen-SS man condemned to death for homosexual offenses in October 1942 was both mentally and physically underdeveloped, and a second opinion went even further, stamping him as "feeble-minded." In 1939 that diagnosis would have been grounds enough for an institutionalized mental patient innocent of any crime to be euthanized, but, in a bizarre twist, the non compos mentis evaluation transformed the SS-Kanonier's execution into a five-year penitentiary sentence.[47] Himmler penned a very sharp letter to Brustmann, declaring that he had no need of the doctor's misguided lessons on the question of homosexuality and forbidding him from contradicting the verdicts of the SS court in the future.

---

[45]Heiber reinforces this impression with his selection of four documents, recording the rejection of successive appeals in a 1943 case, involving five instances of nonpenetrative sex with three youths (189-90).

[46]For more information on this institute, see Geoffrey Cocks, *Psychotherapy in the Third Reich: The Göring Institute*, 2nd ed. (New Brunswick, N.J., 1997).

[47]Kaltenbrunner to Himmler, July 20, 1943, Bundesarchiv Lichterfelde (BAL) NS19/2957. As other research of mine indicates, confession of complete inebriation was also used, albeit with relatively infrequent success, during the Third Reich as part of a plea that someone was not responsible for his criminal actions.

Himmler's letters contain crucial policy statements about the future handling of such cases in the SS and police. Himmler claimed to be perfectly comfortable with the idea of "reeducating" in special camps those who had gone astray through having been seduced. Nonetheless, he did not have high hopes for success. Experts could not "educate" someone who had become "abnormal." In any case, such experiments were out of the question until the successful conclusion of the war. For the moment he wanted to continue the most severe punishment of such offenses: "Leniency can only apply in those cases in which it really is a question of the seduction of an unambiguously normal youth." To Brustmann, Himmler explained his policy as a matter of military expediency. Germany was now in the fourth year of a world war and fighting for its very existence. Homosexuals in the ranks, he claimed with a familiar trope, would damage military effectiveness. The execution of these criminals was no great loss: "The war is taking away hundreds and thousands of normal people [still] in their youth. But that makes it a duty for us not to shy away from the extermination of abnormal people who are admittedly the victims of seduction but are damaging the troops [*Vernichtung anormaler, zwar Verführter, die Truppe aber schädigender Menschen*]."[48] While the November 1941 order instituting the death sentence for SS and police personnel found guilty of homosexuality was formal and secret, on this rare occasion Himmler openly advocated and justified the physical extermination of homosexuals as standard policy.[49]

It may be no coincidence that during this very same month, July 1943, the Reich Ministry of Justice began extensive discussions with military, government, and party agencies on the introduction of compulsory castration for homosexual offenders. The instigator of this initiative was none other than Himmler's deputy, Ernst Kaltenbrunner, eager to make his own mark on policy toward homosexuals outside the SS and police ranks.[50] Was this an example of the "cumulative radicalization" that has been said to characterize the war years? Again I suggest that the term "subordinate escalation" is a more accurate description. Kaltenbrunner's démarche was not part of a series of policy initiatives regarding homosexuals; rather, it was an isolated intrusion that tightened the screws in a way that he thought

[48]Himmler to Kaltenbrunner, June 23, 1943, and Himmler to Brustmann, June 23, 1943, in ibid. See also Jellonnek, *Homosexuelle*, 174–75.

[49]Von Rönn errs in claiming as a dramatic conclusion to the first part of his article that the document signals that Himmler had now abandoned all experiments with the educability of offenders (128–29). As my examples indicate, Himmler remained inconsistent, or "flexible," to the very end of the war.

[50]Reichsjustizministerium to RMdI, OKW, RPropM, Partei-Kanzlei, and Chef der Sipo u. des SD, July 7, 1943, Bundesarchiv-Militärarchiv Freiburg (BAMA) H20/479. See also Giles, "Castration," 55; and Geoffrey J. Giles, "The Institutionalization of Homosexual Panic in the Third Reich," in *Social Outsiders in Nazi Germany*, ed. Robert Gellately and Nathan Stoltzfus (Princeton, N.J., 2001), 249.

would earn him points with his superior. The Third Reich functioned in large part through subordinates' guessing at the proper interpretation of their superiors' general policy statements and implementing this interpretation in a manner most likely to win them applause and favor.[51] Although the phenomenon has been studied at the lowest levels of Nazi institutions, it is important to note that even the top deputies engaged in the practice.

Despite the radical outbursts that punctuated the Third Reich, it is important to stress the unevenness of implementation of disciplinary regulations and the law and to record the periodic exercise of a little humanity, even within the fearsome confines of the SS court. The following case deserves a close reading, for it offers an insight into the obsessive, investigatory zeal of Himmler's police and (from the multiple testimonies that have survived in the court records) the way that men thought and talked about homosexuality. What they did not say is as important as what they did say. There is no mention, for example, in this or any similar case about *emotional* deviancy. None of the soldiers accused their NCO of whispering sweet nothings to them when they had sex. He did not apparently say that he "loved" any of his men while fondling them, though one testimony below comes close to suggesting that there was more than straightforward, earthy, sexual physicality at play. I would suggest that the reason for this was in part a broad perception that sex without deep emotion was viewed as not especially reprehensible. Equally, one might say that emotion without sex was quite acceptable between men, insofar as very close male bonding was indeed a goal within the SS, whose motto stressed the members' unswerving "loyalty" to each other. Trouble arose, in the popular perception, when emotion and sex were brought together, for that meant that a man "loved" men and was therefore a homosexual.

SEXUAL FRUSTRATION AMONG FRONT-LINE SOLDIERS

The case in question concerned twenty-four-year-old Hans G., an SS-Hauptscharführer (sergeant major) with the Eleventh SS Volunteer Panzer Grenadier Division Nordland. G. had served with distinction and had been wounded in action in 1942, but in the fall of 1944 he was apprehended on charges of homosexual assault. The interrogations and testimonies reveal a sexually frustrated, perhaps lonely, soldier at the front with strong homoerotic leanings. G. admitted to mutual masturbation with two of his men while having no idea whether it was one of them who had turned him in. His men certainly found some of his actions strange but were offended only by direct sexual assault.

---

[51] Ian Kershaw terms this process as "working towards the Führer," a phrase drawn from a routine but interesting speech by an official in the Prussian Agriculture Ministry. See Ian Kershaw, *Hitler 1889–1936: Hubris* (London, 1998), 527–31, where he also refers to Hans Mommsen's use of the term "cumulative radicalization."

Sturmmann (lance corporal) D. described his mutual masturbation with G. and admitted that he was himself sexually excited and had reciprocated for about ten minutes. They were both drunk. Subsequently, D. was rather embarrassed, stating: "The incident didn't particularly concern me, I just really wanted to forget about it. I know that it's a bit unusual. I have never heard of the Führer's decree, and I didn't know that this sort of thing was punishable." Unfortunately, the impression of unsullied innocence created by this account of an isolated occurrence was damaged by D.'s initial interrogation, in which he admitted to two further incidents with G. while the two were out on patrol. Even more damaging, they had kissed on those occasions, and G. had thrust his penis between D.'s thighs. Such intercrural intercourse was an indictable homosexual offense even under the Weimar Republic, because it closely replicated the standard heterosexual act. The police fired off a telegram to the station in D.'s home town of Stettin, requesting details of his criminal record and instructing the officers to investigate for any hereditary disorders in his family. Within a week the Stettin police reported back that D.'s father, a conductor on the local trams, and the whole family of eleven children seemed perfectly normal, healthy, and crime-free.[52]

G.'s advances to other men were often quite public. When sharing sleeping quarters with his platoon in a barn, for example, he would have one of them pull off his boots and help him to undress, even giving attention to his underwear. He would then sometimes have one of his men remain beside him, holding his hand; G. attempted to shrug off the criticism that this was not typical soldierly behavior. "It's true that I often had O. D. hold my hand in the evening. But I did this without any kind of sexual intent. It was no big deal for me." His excuse to his men was that it helped him sleep better.[53]

The young man in question, nineteen-year-old signalman Otto D., certainly found it rather improper that, three weeks after being assigned to this unit, he was sitting holding hands with his sergeant major. But their contact went further. G. made sure that O. D. slept beside him, and one night, the latter awoke to find the sergeant major masturbating him. The younger man allowed his NCO to proceed, not resisting at all ("I remained completely passive"). G. then climbed on top of him and made paracoital movements with his hips until finally he rolled back, "moaning and gasping." The next day, however, the younger man felt sufficiently disturbed by these advances to turn to a fellow soldier for advice. They decided they could take no action in the absence of witnesses. Still, since the men were all sleeping together in a barn, it was easy to find witnesses. G. clearly thought that he had found a willing partner for sex, but two nights later, when G. tried again, O. D.

[52]Vernehmung Sturmmann D., September 29, 1944; Schupo Stettin to Reichszentrale zur Bekämpfung der Homosexualität, October 7, 1944; Protokoll Hauptverhandlung, October 10, 1944; BAL NS7/1137.
[53]Vernehmung SS-Hauptscharführer Hans G., October 1, 1944, ibid.

rebuffed him. Several of the other soldiers were not yet asleep this time and heard the whispered exchange between them:

G.: Just take mine, and I will play with yours.
O. D.: No, Ser'nt Major, I won't do it, it's disgusting.
G.: If we just play around a bit, we can sleep better afterward. You're crazy! Why don't you want to? We already did it once.

O. D. replied that he had been caught unawares while sleeping the first time and firmly took hold of both of G.'s hands to prevent matters from going any further. G. did not force himself on O. D. after this.[54]

But now a private matter had become public, and one of the men (probably O. D.) reported G., initiating an intrusive, if brief, investigation into the intimate lives of the men of this unit. The depositions provide an unusual view of the kind of intimacy perhaps not so uncommon among soldiers at the front. Significantly, in the testimony of all of the parties concerned, no soldier thought of himself or accused the other of being a homosexual.

It is interesting to analyze the use of ideas of manliness or femininity in the testimony of witnesses, the statements of the defendant, and the judgment of the court. Take Sturmmann Franz B., just turned twenty-one. He was aware that he was a favorite of his NCO, but he did not feel repulsed by G.'s attentions. His evidence of assault was important to the prosecution, although the perceived effeminacy of his mannerisms might tend to discredit him as being homosexual himself and thus an unreliable witness. Most unusually, the chairman of the SS court added a personal comment about him as an addendum to his interrogation: "Outwardly B. gives a soft and girlish impression, yet he is described by his company commander as an exemplary soldier and irreproachable. I myself had the impression that he was telling the truth, and he left behind the very best impression of himself. In his external appearance he is without doubt a type that homosexuals fall for." The judge's statement conveyed the common prejudice that gay men are attracted to effeminate partners, but his reasoning was unusual: the homosexual *appearance* of the witness proved the *actual* homosexuality of the accused!

B.'s testimony about G.'s behavior revealed a similar conflation of sex and gender roles. While fondling B., the sergeant major "looked like a girl in love and moaned strangely all the while." This gender role reversal followed a direct sexual advance. The two men were alone together in a bunker, lying on some straw. G. began stroking the other's hair and then chest, and without undue resistance on B.'s part he gradually reached for the other man's genitals. At this point B. stopped him and moved his

---

[54]Vernehmung Otto Ernst D., September 29, 1944, ibid. The whispered exchange is my composite rendering, drawn also from the corroborating testimony of two other soldiers, Vernehmung Konrad G., September 29, 1944, and Vernehmung Otto R., September 29, 1944, ibid.

hand away but otherwise did not appear to have taken exception to the caressing: "[G.] often took me into his arms and pressed my head against his breast. However, I never had the feeling that this was an abnormal gesture, I didn't give it a second thought." The testimony encapsulates the Nazi Party's general problem with homosexuality: the party wished to promote the very closest male friendship and trust but without allowing relationships to cross over a certain line of intimacy that not everyone viewed as a taboo.[55] In this case, that line between comradeship and physicality seemed to have been crossed, though the men involved did not see it that way. Their protestations of innocence and normality should not be seen as a clever manipulation of Nazi discourse in their favor; in fact, their comments tended to incriminate them. Perhaps B. was trying to instrumentalize commonplace notions of masculinity through his reference to G.'s girlishness in order to underline his own "normality." However, his candid admission to being the passive and regular recipient of G.'s embraces seriously undermined that defense strategy. His remarks are so natural in tone that it is likely they were recorded as spoken. And I would contend that the interrogators (through whose pen the statements are handed down) were not necessarily trying to entrap the witnesses; rather, the latter were simply naive. Himmler, had he read the full details of the case, would doubtless have been astonished to learn that his SS men at the fighting front could spend their evenings holding hands or caressing one another without any feelings of guilt or concern.

Hans G. himself strenuously denied being a homosexual. His defense was a common one among front-line soldiers in such cases: "My behavior can simply be attributed to the fact that I have had no leave for a long time and thus have had no opportunity for normal sexual intercourse." That was true, because the troops were strictly forbidden to have any intimate contact with the native women in the occupied territories. Less plausibly, he claimed to be completely innocent about homosexuality. G. had volunteered for the Waffen-SS while still only sixteen years old and had been assigned to the SS Death's Head Division (Division Totenkopf) for training at Dachau by the time he reached eighteen, the normal age for entry. He was later transferred to Mauthausen and Flossenbürg, concentration camps with noteworthy concentrations of pink triangle inmates. Let us examine G.'s comments in this regard:

> I did not experience anything like that [intimacy among the men] in the [SS] Viking Division [Division Wiking]. I had my first sexual intercourse [with a woman] when I was eighteen. Before that I knew nothing about [gay sex], I didn't even masturbate. The first urges came to me in July 1944. I heard about such things in the concentration camp, but I didn't know anything about it. Paragraph 175 didn't

[55]Vernehmung SS-Sturmmann Franz B., October 3, 1944, ibid.

mean anything to me. I don't know the Führer's decree either. It was never read out to me.

This testimony suggests that G. probably subscribed to the common perception that participation in anal intercourse defined a homosexual; in some concentration camps, for example, the Paragraph 175ers were made to wear a badge with the letter "A" to denote "ass fucker" (*Arschficker*). It is entirely plausible that such was the talk of the common guards. Furthermore, his statement provides further evidence of the timidity of the SS leadership in giving warnings about infractions in this area that were explicit enough to be of any use.[56]

G. also tried to "prove" that he was not a homosexual by insisting that he had turned in someone who had reached for his private parts in a public toilet in Brno, where his SS unit had been stationed in 1939. G. claimed to have boxed him on the ears and gone straight to the Gestapo office to report him. When it came to substantiating his claim, the story became rather fuzzy. G. asserted that he attended the court hearing to listen to the trial of the man but was never called as a witness. "He got two and a half years' penitentiary and a punishment beating every day, as I later heard." If that was meant to suggest that G. thought this an appropriate punishment for a "real" homosexual, it was not a particularly prudent remark, because this alleged assault was little different from his own unwanted advances against the men in his unit.[57]

The SS judges did not believe him and annotated their copy of his testimony with exclamations of doubt. They underlined the fact that he had spent two years at a Catholic monastery school, since that was an immediate indicator of possible homosexuality. They scrawled a large question mark in the margin next to his account of his lively relations with women, at least fifteen in all. G. asserted that as his wartime duties had grown more strenuous, he had become deeply involved with one woman, Lotti Kortum. He spent his last leave with her and had sex with her. Could he provide her current address? No, she had recently moved, and, since his unit was constantly on the move, he had thrown away all her letters. It sounded very much like a fiction. The judges knew that he had already misled their inquiry by admitting to just two instances of mutual masturbation. "These are the only incidents," he stated categorically on September 28, 1944. "A lie!" wrote one of the judges on the transcript later. What probably clinched the case for the court was the fact that, despite a minimal difference in ages, about five years, the assaults were carried out by a superior against junior NCOs in his charge. Such an abuse of rank was always treated in an especially stern manner. On October 10,

[56]Vernehmung G., October 1, 1944, and Hauptverhandlung, October 10, 1944, ibid.
[57]Vernehmung G., October 7, 1944, ibid.

1944, the SS court pronounced the death sentence on Hans G. for five completed and two attempted homosexual acts.[58]

THE APPEALS PROCESS

Initially, G.'s case seems to be a clear example of the enforcement of Hitler's November 1941 edict. Yet immediately, the tide began to turn for Hans G. Within one week, the commanding officer of the Third SS-Panzer Corps, General Steiner, wrote a strong plea for clemency, arguing that "the condemned displayed for years a magnificent fighting spirit and won for himself in these long war years every medal that he possibly could" and that "he was a particularly competent junior officer who enjoyed general respect." His reasons suggest that the pragmatic needs created by the worsening war situation overrode the ideological imperatives of homophobia. The general's final justification for his plea for leniency showed that he agreed with G.'s own excuse that the conditions of war were to blame:

> I do not believe his action can be judged to be the consequence of a sick or depraved disposition, because he has never before come under suspicion of similar offenses or a similar disposition. Rather, this really does seem to be an example of sexual deprivation. . . . In my opinion we have here a strong psychic and erotic aberration that has been formed by the conditions of war. The accused is certainly no national parasite [*Volksschädling*], since he has continuously been in action of the most dangerous kind for his country.[59]

Unfortunately, the outcome of the case is not clear, since the chaotic conditions of the war's end prevented the preservation of a paper trail. The files were sent to the head office of the SS courts for a decision on the clemency appeal, and it appears that the case was then handed over for a further opinion to the civilian criminal police authorities in the Reichszentrale zur Bekämpfung der Homosexualität (Reich Central Office for Combating Homosexuality). With Berlin already largely in ruins in early 1945, this office continued its laborious investigations, wanting in the first place to know why at the age of twelve G. had suddenly left the Catholic school attached to the Fürstenstein monastery. G. claimed to have been expelled for reading the Nazi newspaper, the *Völkische Beobachter*. No incriminating evidence was found; the gendarmerie post in the small town responded that G.'s version was entirely plausible. The local policeman had known G. personally since 1930 and could testify that even as a twelve year old the latter had shown an unusual interest in politics, which doubtless derived from his father's early support for the Nazis before their

---

[58]Vernehmung G., September 28 and October 7, 1944; Feldurteil, October 10, 1944, ibid.

[59]Verfügung Steiner, October 17, 1944, ibid.

seizure of power. Neither was there "the slightest suspicion of a homosexual disposition." G.'s relations with women had been entirely normal during his youth. He had had a number of girlfriends over the years and had contemplated marrying several of them. In fact, during his last home leave he had made more concrete moves in this direction with one woman, only to have the plans blocked by his widowed mother.[60]

There is something grotesque in the fact that in the winter of 1945, with Germany close to collapse, the police office on homosexuality was still going to these extraordinary lengths to pry into the private life of an individual in order to see whether he might be cured of his homosexual tendencies or else be put to death. As late as February 1945, the police were still pursuing G. He was brought from the Schöneberg prison, to which he had been transferred, for an interrogation in the central office in the bombed-out heart of Berlin, which disproves the view that the employees of this office did little more than shuffle index cards.[61] Agent Dornhöfer wanted precise details about G.'s relations with women. When he was stationed at Dachau in the mid-1930s, G. asserted that he "had sexual intercourse with a girl at least once a fortnight." Evidently, these young men in SS uniforms had their pick of the local women and made the most of it in the local dance halls. He could not recall any of their names, because these had been merely fleeting acquaintances.

Making no progress here, Dornhöfer pressed G. more closely about his homosexual acts: "Did you find pleasure in these activities?" G. was smart enough to offer a very circumspect answer: "I had the desire to find sexual satisfaction under any circumstances." Eliciting from the prisoner the admission that mutual masturbation between men was not normal behavior for well-balanced heterosexuals, Dornhöfer tried to trip him up by asking him why, if he realized that this was wrong, he had come to repeat the offenses. G. replied that his will was weakened by heavy drinking—an admission that appears to have been partly true, according to earlier testimony, and was in any case an argument that sometimes worked in favor of a defendant. We do not know whether it worked for Hans G., because the file breaks off with this February 1945 interrogation, and additional documents did not survive the end of the war.[62]

While the historical record is incomplete, the case repays careful study because it demonstrates the difficulties of sexuality for both the average soldier and the legal system. There is little doubt that Hans G., former concentration camp guard in some of Nazi Germany's most notorious

[60]Gendarmerieposten Werberg to Reichszentrale, January 22, 1945, ibid.

[61]Günter Grau, "Final Solution of the Homosexual Question? The Antihomosexual Policies of the Nazis and the Social Consequences for Homosexual Men," in *The Holocaust and History: The Known, the Unknown, the Disputed and the Reexamined*, ed. Michael Berenbaum and Abraham J. Peck (Bloomington, 1998), 338–44, quote from 342.

[62]Vernehmung G. im Reichskriminalpolizeiamt Berlin, February 2, 1945, BAL NS7/1137.

camps, was a pretty unsavory character. Yet his SS record is not at issue here. What is important is the treatment of homosexual acts. Men in closed societies (such as prisons or armies) do become sexually frustrated and seek a release. In part, the German generals sought to address that need for front-line soldiers through the provision of brothels; yet brothels could not be set up everywhere, especially in the more isolated areas. Once a complaint concerning sexual abuse or assault by a superior had been lodged, it had to be taken seriously. This case could not be shrugged off as an isolated incident, since a total of seven incidents came to light, revealing a pattern of homosexual activity. Consequently, it became important to establish the exact nature of the offenses. There had not been just manual stimulation but also paracoital movements of the hips and even kissing. This simulation of heterosexual intercourse was the most damning factor. This and the abuse of rank pointed toward the death sentence. Yet some empathy seems to have prevailed in the SS judiciary in its acknowledgment that the harsh privations of front-line duty created special circumstances that would try the willpower of even the most upright of characters. Those charged with enforcing Himmler's homophobic policies did not respond simply with a knee-jerk reaction. They leavened ideology with pragmatism, even in this sensitive area.

Most records of the head office of the SS courts were destroyed at the end of the war, apart from a few cases that came from courts in the occupied territories (like the one discussed above) and a batch of 186 cases, mostly with incomplete documentation, that ended up in the Berlin Document Center. An examination of these 186 files reveals that only four are concerned with homosexual offenses. While these four cases cannot be regarded as representative, for they are simply chance survivals among the records, they are nonetheless acutely interesting in terms of their verdicts. One would expect increasingly harsh punishments, but that is not what we find.

DANGEROUS TALK ON THE WESTERN FRONT

Although even in the final weeks of the war German men convicted as homosexuals faced the threat of execution, the following case contains a strange twist. Werner S., the only son of a foreman in a metalworks factory in Düsseldorf, joined the junior branch of the Hitler Youth as soon as he could but never held rank in that organization, concentrating instead on music and advancing to the district Hitler Youth orchestra. He was a fairly good student, attending the local, nonclassical high school. He intended to go to college to study the humanities and physiology but was still rather vague, listing astrology and graphology (!) as possible areas of study. Three months before he was due to graduate and a couple of weeks after his twentieth birthday in June 1942, he was called up for army service. Passing his basic training with flying colors, he was assigned to an anti-aircraft unit on the eastern front, where he was soon singled out as officer candidate material. He completed officer training with the rank of lieutenant in August 1944. The report card noted his "particularly decent character" as well as his diligence and sense of duty. His superiors judged that he would make a good "political officer" because he could communicate National Socialist ideas to others convincingly. A subsequent report claimed that he positively "embod[ied] solid soldierly and National Socialist ideals."

Immediately after officer training, Werner S. was sent back to combat, this time to the western front, as an officer in charge of a gun battery unit. Now he was on his own, with real responsibility for the lives of his soldiers. He was still quite young himself, but his men were slightly younger. On the night of September 13, 1944, he lay down with his nineteen-year-old orderly, private Engelbert Sch. The latter was already dozing when S. suddenly pulled him over and asked if Sch. had ever "screwed" a girl. When Sch. said that he had not, S. kissed him, evidently with some passion, explaining that this was a French kiss. A couple of nights later, S. found a place with three beds in different rooms for the six of them. Having retired, he and his roommate stripped down to their shirts and climbed into bed. Werner then embraced and kissed the other soldier, the eighteen-year-old gunner K., several times and suggested that they masturbate each other. K. subsequently asserted to the military court that he had initially refused, but when Werner continued to badger him, he succumbed just so he could shut him up and get some sleep. He was not an entirely unwilling partner, because K. admitted that both had ejaculated. K. allowed himself to be kissed several more times before they fell asleep. But that was that—when Werner asked K. a week later to sleep with him, K. refused, saying he had no interest in doing it again. There are two significant points here: first, the initial sexual encounter was not a particularly big deal for K.; second, although he agreed to participate, K. was able to tell S. in a nonconfrontational way that he did not care for a repeat performance.

Two nights after this incident, S. shared a tent with another soldier and kissed him, too. Nothing further happened. Two nights later he entered the tent of lance corporal G., lay down beside him, and cuddled up to him. The corporal thought nothing of this, assuming that the lieutenant was simply cold, until the latter began to kiss him. Getting nowhere, S. left the tent. Two nights later, he asked his men twice for a volunteer to sleep with him, but none came forward. There is no evidence that they had compared notes yet, although perhaps S. had made advances to all of them by now. At any rate, a new man had just joined the unit, twenty-two-year-old corporal A., and S. simply told A. that he would share with him. After awhile, A. noticed S. pulling him closer. Since A. was cold and assumed that S. was too, he simply moved closer himself and was surprised when S. kissed him. Werner asked if he would like "to do it with him." "Do what?" replied A. and, receiving only a laugh for an answer, rolled over and went back to sleep. Let us step back and take note of the situation again. The corporal thought nothing of snuggling up to his lieutenant in a rather intimate way in order to keep warm. Thousands of other soldiers must have done so at the front. Nonsexual snuggling seems to have been unexceptional.

The following day the unit again changed position. Werner S. appointed nineteen-year-old private T. as his new orderly and had him set up a bivouac for the two of them. It was another cold night, and T. was planning to go to sleep with his greatcoat on. S. told him to remove it, which he did, and he lay down with his back to his lieutenant. Soon S. asked him to turn round, and when T. did so, S. pulled T. toward himself, kissing him. Sensing no resistance, he then unbuttoned T.'s trousers and grasped his penis. Still finding no objection, S. took T.'s hand and placed it on his own erection, allowing T. to masturbate him to the point of ejaculation.[63] The next morning, while T. was still sleeping, S. took him in his arms again and kissed him. Probably this kissing offended the other man most directly, since it was an unmistakable display of affection that overturned sex roles far more disturbingly than mutual masturbation, which could be dismissed as two men releasing their sexual tension in the absence of any women. At any rate, when S. asked T. to sleep with him the following night, T. refused, saying that he had had enough the previous night. S. admitted that maybe he had gone too far but added that perhaps he was not the only one to blame. In none of these incidents did Werner S. force his men to be intimate with him. S. was not a violent sex criminal.

All this happened within the space of ten days. Inevitably, the men in this small unit talked to one another about their officer. Corporal A. spoke to G. about his experience and then to T., and they all realized they had been kissed by their lieutenant. It suddenly became clear that the young lieutenant was experimenting with everyone who bunked with him. A. promptly reported the matter to the battery officer, and the whole business of a formal investigation ensued. Things moved very swiftly; within a mere fortnight the court-martial sentenced Werner S. to death.

Yet the story had an additional twist. While the interrogations of the men in his unit were proceeding, Werner S. asked T. if he had had to give the officers any details. When T. admitted that he had, S. declared he had only two courses of action remaining: he could shoot himself or find some other way out. The nature of the second solution became clearer when he asked another soldier how well the Americans treated German deserters.

---

[63]This must have been an unusual case for this military court, for the verdict could not quite manage to get the terminology correct. The record states that "the accused for his part did not carry out self-abuse [*Selbstbefriedigung*] on T." Feldurteil, October 7, 1944, NARA BDC SS-Gericht, Werner S.

He had a similar conversation at battery headquarters, asking the sergeant major directly if he thought he should desert, since he had no intention of shooting himself. Soon thereafter he was placed under arrest.

Perhaps the most intriguing aspect of this case is that the death sentence was not given for Werner S.'s homosexual offenses but for his planned desertion (which of course was prompted by his fears about the severe punishment that homosexual offenders could expect). *Talking* about his plans with other soldiers was deemed to be an act of sabotage. Since S. was not a regular member of the SS or police, execution was not the prescribed penalty for homosexuality; such offenses merited five years in a penitentiary, according to the verdict. The court judged that S. was not a "real" homosexual and was merely guilty of an aberration, explainable by his youth and inexperience. That, the judges felt, coupled with his excellent military record, should be counted in his favor. Yet S. had not erred on only one occasion but had systematically made advances to virtually every soldier in his unit; if he had succeeded in "committing a punishable offense" with another soldier on merely two occasions, it was not for want of trying. This, too, is an interesting comment, because the court recognized only the masturbation as a punishable offense and not the kissing, despite the leeway allowed by the revised Paragraph 175, on which the court based its opinion. But if it was lenient in this interpretation, it was harsh in its terms of punishment: a single instance of masturbation merited three years in a penitentiary (and the two proven cases combined merited five) because they were aggravated by S.'s abuse of his authority over his subordinates. Even though there was no significant difference in age between S. and his men, the abuse of rank was a serious matter.

All this tortuous weighing of mitigating and aggravating circumstances surrounding the sexual offenses was purely academic, because there was never any intention to allow Werner S. to serve out his penitentiary sentence. The death sentence took precedence. There was, of course, an appeal, and Heinrich Himmler was the judge of last resort, because S. happened to belong to a Volksgrenadier division now under Himmler's command. In preparing a summary of the case for Himmler's decision at the end of October, the SS court itself did not push for a confirmation of the sentence. Its memo to Himmler stressed that S. was "very young and immature," that this was "doubtless" the first time that he had carried on like this, and that he only realized the seriousness of the offenses after the event. Indeed, it did not even count both instances of masturbation but reported that there were "serious indecent acts" on only one occasion. The SS officer preparing the memo apparently endorsed the court-martial's observation that the two soldiers had "quickly succumbed" to S.'s advances and that T. in particular "gave the impression of being not inexperienced in sexual matters." He also emphasized the fact that there had been no adverse effects to morale among the other soldiers and repeated the defense counsel's assertion that the talk

284 Geoffrey J. Giles

of desertion only came up because the accused had had no opportunity to talk with superior officers about his situation.[64] It was several weeks before Himmler managed to attend to this matter, but on December 3, 1944, he rejected the appeal without comment. Even the SS judge on Himmler's staff sounded surprised in reporting this decision to the SS court's head office, finding it necessary to explain that Himmler did not view S. as "worthy of clemency—despite the extenuating factors about his person that doubtless speak in his favor." On February 9, 1945, at Trier, a few weeks before the city fell to the Allies, Werner S. was executed. He was twenty-two years old.[65]

COUNTEREXAMPLES TO CUMULATIVE RADICALIZATION

The three other cases of homosexual offenses in Germany that remain among the files of the SS court deserve a brief commentary. In June 1944 a sergeant in an SS anti-aircraft unit was apparently supervising some men in the Reich Labor Service. These would have been youths not of age for military service, probably engaged in bomb clearance or other manual labor. One of the youths brought charges that he had been forced to masturbate in front of Sergeant O. on the latter's explicit orders. O. was immediately suspended but not brought before the SS court. For reasons that are not entirely clear, SS-Standartenführer Bender, the chief judge of the SS court, wrote to the Reich Labor Leader, leaving it to him to have O. arrested. The probable explanation is that, since the accuser was not under the formal jurisdiction of the SS, the Labor Service was the responsible authority. Nonetheless, O. was a member of the Waffen-SS. Although there was no physical contact, the incident was still a serious abuse of rank by an NCO. The SS court gave the appearance of wanting to follow this up but waited for the outcome of the criminal proceedings in the regular courts. After a trial, a verdict was handed down on November 8, 1944, sentencing O. to two years in a penitentiary. Since no notification was sent to SS headquarters, Bender's office queried the Labor Service and learned the result of the trial only in late January 1945. A copy of the verdict was not included, and nothing further could be done without it, so the case was left hanging.[66]

The two other cases are more interesting because Himmler made a decision about both of them on the same day in February 1945. The first involved a first lieutenant of the Replacement Army (Ersatzheer), Hans-

[64]Vorlage für Himmler, "Offizierssache, Todesurteil, Heeressache," October 24, 1944, ibid.

[65]Verfügung Himmler, December 3, 1944; SS-Richter beim RFSS to Hauptamt SS-Gericht, December 13, 1944; telegram Oberstabsrichter Dyckmans to Heeresfeldjustizabteilung OKH, March 3, 1945, ibid.

[66]Telex draft Bender to Reichsarbeitsführer, June 2, 1944; Reichsarbeitsführer to SS-Richter beim RFSS, January 15, 1945, ibid.; NARA BDC Hauptamt SS-Gericht Feldmeister O.

Robert W. The exact nature of his offense is unknown, because the files that were forwarded to the police Central Office for Combating Homosexuality, with instructions to establish whether or not the accused was a genuine homosexual, were lost or destroyed at the end of the war. The remaining documentation suggests that only minor homosexual acts were committed on two separate occasions. This looks very much like another case of sexual frustration at the front lines. Hans-Robert W., also not a member of the SS or police, was sentenced by a military court to three years in a penitentiary on October 4, 1944. There is no indication that W. himself made an appeal against this sentence, but his family did send letters to Himmler personally. W.'s father took great exception to the court's assumption that his son was a "compulsive offender" (*Hangtäter*) and a "biological failure." Hans-Robert had proven, wrote his father, that he was the "bearer of top-quality genes" by producing four splendid children, and he sent along a photograph of the wife and children to emphasize his point. This was a smart move, whether the father knew it or not, given Himmler's predilection for making snap judgments about racial soundness based on physical appearance. The father's reminder that he had been a financial supporter of the SS since 1933 probably counted for less.[67] A second letter had even sounder credentials, coming from the father's brother-in-law, Walther Sonntag, a colonel. He assured Himmler that he totally agreed with the policy of delivering the harshest of punishments to compulsive homosexuals so that they could do no further harm, because they did indeed "represent a danger for their fellow men and fail to contribute to the procreation of racially valuable offspring." Of course, Hans-Robert was not one of those. He was a National Socialist, a farmer, a soldier, and, not least, a husband and father, wrote the colonel, as though that settled the matter. Furthermore, Sonntag insisted that Hans-Robert was a "man without the slightest hint of femininity." Sonntag could not imagine that anyone could be a "real" homosexual unless they acted effeminately.[68] Himmler granted a measure of clemency, despite the fact that the police antihomosexual office had apparently uncovered a third incident. He allowed Hans-Robert W. to "prove himself" through front-line military service.[69]

Wolfgang G., a sergeant of the Replacement Army, lacked powerful protectors. He himself wrote to Himmler from Spandau jail, and his wife wrote

[67]Rittmeister d. Res. a.D. Robert W. to Himmler, October 30, 1944, ibid.; Oberlt. d. Res. Landwirt Hans-Robert W., NARA BDC Hauptamt SS-Gericht, Hans-Robert W.

[68]Sonntag had worked in the SS-Oberabschnitt Northwest headquarters in 1934 and 1935 under Friedrich Jeckeln (one of the central actors in the Holocaust as a police chief in the occupied Soviet Union). Shamelessly dropping the names of other SS generals whom he knew, such as Hausser, Heißmeyer (Curt Wittje's successor at the SS head office), Hennicke, and the Freiherr von Eberstein, Sonntag could not resist mentioning that he was actually a cousin of SS Obergruppenführer Ulrich Greifelt (Himmler's deputy in the resettlement and Germanization program). Sonntag to Himmler, November 4, 1944, ibid.

[69]Forch to Bender, November 22, 1944; Wehser to Robert W., February 4, 1945, ibid.

independently. Here was another case of things getting a little out of hand following one of those alcoholic, aptly named "comradeship evenings." Wolfgang, very much in his cups, had made sexual advances to a lance corporal, for which he was sentenced to two years in a penitentiary. He was forty-seven years old and had served in the First World War with distinction, been wounded, and been awarded the Iron Cross First Class. During the Second World War, G. had participated in both the French and the Russian campaigns. He had been a willing soldier and told Himmler he wanted to get back to active service. Never before had he done "this sort of thing"; on the contrary, he had been happily married for twelve years and had always viewed homosexual acts as "directly nauseating." His wife filled in further extenuating details: her husband had at the time been suffering from a concussion, and the party was held by a group of convalescent soldiers. No one had warned her husband of the dangerously heightened effect that alcohol might have on him. Husband and wife did not coordinate their requests but asked Himmler for two different things. G. asked to be transferred from the penitentiary to an ordinary prison, while his wife begged that he be allowed to atone for his misdeed at the front. Himmler chose the latter, with an important difference from the other case on which he ruled that day. Wolfgang G. was ordered to prove himself in the ranks of the Dirlewanger Brigade, composed largely of hardened criminals and concentration camp inmates. This was one of the main units that was employed in the destruction of the city of Warsaw in September 1944 and that subsequently fought in the most dangerous places of all on the front line. Assignment to the Dirlewanger Brigade was thus virtually a death sentence, though G. and his wife would not have known that, and doubtless Himmler felt he was being generous. There is no record if G. survived.[70]

If the theory of cumulative radicalization of Nazi policy toward homosexuals were correct, why would Himmler approve a death sentence in fall 1944 but not in the winter of 1945? The fact that none of these men was covered by the November 1941 decree, specifying the death sentence for SS and police members, is relevant but not crucial. After all, there was no regulation that permitted the SS deliberately to kill homosexuals in concentration camps, but it regularly happened. Since the cases described above were dealt with by the SS court, it would have been easy for Himmler to extend his prerogative over all the men serving under his command and modify the sentence as he saw fit. In 1943 he had moved swiftly to block further commutations of death sentences by the Göring Institute's Dr. Brustmann, whom he saw as too soft on homosexuals, and in December 1944 he was deaf to appeals to commute the death sentence of Werner S.

[70]Wolfgang G. to RFSS, November 22, 1944; Franka G. to RFSS, December 19, 1945; Wehser to Frau Franka G., February 4, 1945, NARA BDC Hauptamt SS-Gericht, Wolfgang G.

Was Himmler simply inconsistent here? It certainly looks like that, but let us look at the context a little more closely. In 1944, Himmler was the second most powerful man in Germany. Following the failed July Plot to kill Hitler, he added to his already enormous SS and police empire by accepting the command of the Replacement Army. We know that he entertained doubts about Hitler's ability to win the war and by October was making secret overtures to the British for an alliance against the Soviet Union. Himmler was by this stage so divorced from reality that he saw himself as the future chancellor of Germany. When he confirmed the death sentence for Werner S. on December 3, he knew about the planned Ardennes Offensive, which would commence two weeks later. That might turn the tide and lead to a victory for Germany after all, in which case he could go ahead with plans to create a racially pure state in which there was no room for homosexuals. Of course, at this particular moment there was no room for deserters, either. It is probable that this military necessity swayed Himmler to set an example by having Werner S. executed.

What had changed between December 1944 and February 1945, when Himmler ruled on the other two cases? On January 26, 1945, the SS blew up the last remaining crematorium at Auschwitz-Birkenau, and the following day Soviet troops liberated the death camp. While the outcome of the war was by now certain, Hitler was still making desperate attempts to salvage the situation. On January 25, 1945, he appointed Himmler as commander of Army Group Vistula (Heeresgruppe Weichsel), whose mission was to block the Soviet advance into Pomerania. As an active military commander Himmler proved to be a disaster, a fact that became abundantly clear within a couple of weeks. But during that short space of time, Himmler, always happy to wear several hats at once, took time out to rule on the two cases that were pending at the SS court. The timing explains his decision to send the two men to the front: they would be part of his effort to become a brilliant general. Himmler needed men who would give their all in order to redeem their good names. In both cases, using the same phraseology, he warned that only "iron fulfillment of duty and total engagement" would win their redemption.[71]

CONCLUSION

If Himmler himself was now fully focused on the war effort, the same cannot be said for his police antihomosexual office. The prurient thoroughness of their investigations up to the final weeks of the war in an evident attempt to uphold the death penalty for essentially trivial, minor sexual assaults provides a sharp reminder of how serious this issue remained for some Nazi officials.

---

[71]Wehser to Robert W., February 4, 1945; Wehser to Frau Franka G., February 4, 1945, NARA BDC Hauptamt SS-Gericht, Hans-Robert W. and Wolfgang G.

The central office for combating homosexuality continued business as usual, even when the country was collapsing. Devoting every possible resource to the final defense of Berlin seemed less pressing to the criminal police than establishing whether an SS man of proven courage had masturbated twelve years earlier with other adolescent boys at school. This surely gives the lie to the claim that the persecution of homosexuals was driven principally by rational concerns.[72] Admittedly, the circumstances of spring 1945 were unusual, and we may interpret the everyday activity of the police antihomosexual office as a desperate attempt to cling to some form of warped normality in the face of the imminent total collapse of the Reich.

This brings us back to the situation in the nineteenth century, less drastic to be sure, when the debate about sexual normality took shape. Then, too, the world seemed to some middle-class Germans to be collapsing. The cause was not war but the shifting social boundaries and cultural values of the time, exacerbated by the rise of Socialism. Out of the hopes that change was indeed possible grew a greater (or certainly more assertive) role for women in public life. These shifting gender roles in a previously male-dominated society led to the formation of new definitions of respectability and sexual normality in an effort to shore up traditional family life.[73] Beginning in the 1880s, a whole host of associations sprang up to quash sexual deviancy, aimed notably at curbing prostitution. But as John Fout puts it, "The moral purity movement reflected considerable gender and sexual anxiety; and the fear of homosexuality was rampant in that society as a whole—homophobia was the norm."[74] We must not think that an almost hysterical opposition to homosexuality was peculiar to the Nazi era. It is common enough in other conservative regimes, where "sexual variants and fluid sexual differences disturb a homogeneity that forms the image of society, and guarantees authoritarianism in government and the economy." In the words of Taeger and Lautmann, "Politics and sexuality perhaps never stood in such an intimate interrelationship."[75]

[72]Stümke, 92–95. See also Michael Burleigh's assessment that "the primary reason for the assault on homosexuals was because the latter were self-evidently failing in their duty to contribute to the demographic expansion of the 'Aryan-Germanic race,' at a time when millions of young men had perished in the First World War" (*Ethics and Extermination: Reflections on Nazi Genocide* [Cambridge, 1997], 162).

[73]George Mosse's study of this topic is exemplary. See George L. Mosse, *Nationalism and Sexuality: Respectability and Abnormal Sexuality in Modern Europe* (New York: Howard Fertig, 1985).

[74]John C. Fout, "Sexual Politics in Wilhelmine Germany: The Male Gender Crisis, Moral Purity, and Homophobia," in *Forbidden History: The State, Society, and the Regulation of Sexuality in Modern Europe: Essays from the Journal of the History of Sexuality*, ed. John C. Fout (Chicago, 1992), 259–92, quote from 290.

[75]Angela Taeger and Rüdiger Lautmann, "Sittlichkeit und Politik: §175 im Deutschen Kaiserreich (1871–1919)," in *Männerliebe im alten Deutschland: Sozialgeschichtliche Abhandlungen*, ed. Rüdiger Lautmann and Angela Taeger, Sozialwissenschaftliche Studien zur Homosexualität (Berlin, 1992), 239–68, quote from 268.

Yet those pre–World War One upheavals were small compared to the gendered battleground of the 1920s, when women obtained the vote for the first time and homosexuals felt confident enough to be more open in public than ever before. Indeed, Berlin became the homosexual capital of Europe. The German right wing raged against such developments, and the Nazi Party depended upon their support to consolidate power, even after Hitler's appointment as chancellor in January 1933. The immediate bans on obscene literature, on nudist clubs, and on gay bars were in part gestures toward the conservative Right. But these were more than political moves. In this respect I disagree with Ian Kershaw's assessment that the Röhm Purge simply reflected the opportunism of the SS in a bid to expand its power.[76] Himmler was not just acting cynically here; he, as well as Hitler and many Nazis, genuinely wanted to be thought of as respectable, hence their delight when influential parts of the foreign press, such as the *Times* of London, interpreted the purge as a return to civility. As Detlev Peukert has noted for the Third Reich generally: "Majority public approval was certainly accorded to the terror which the National Socialists directed at . . . homosexuals."[77]

If the Nazi movement in general aspired to be respectable, the SS, as its elite arm, especially sought to be respected. Despite monumental violations of basic humanity against the victims of the Holocaust and others, the SS enjoyed some success in this regard. But even within the confines of traditional bourgeois ideals, the Black Corps remained as "flawed" as any cross-section of society. Homosexuals stood within SS ranks as much as outside them. Like the majority of men in German or any other society, most SS men had little taste for homosexual adventures, and same-sex sexuality was not particularly prevalent.[78] That made the excessively homophobic response toward homosexual infractions all the more irrational.

Beyond a doubt, Nazi ideology and policies were hostile to homosexuality. Still, the record reveals a much more complex set of responses to homosexuality than the inflammatory rhetoric of Nazi leaders would indicate. Implementation of policies against homosexuals was neither consistent nor unfailingly rigorous. Several factors account for varying degrees of severity of punishment, including an uncertainty about the etiology of homosexuality—whether it was "curable" or not and whether it was brought on by the

---

[76]During his remarks at the United States Holocaust Memorial Museum during "An Evening with Ian Kershaw," January 11, 2001, subsequently also broadcast on C-SPAN.

[77]Peukert, 219.

[78]Thomas Nipperdey's comment on the pre-Nazi Youth Movement seems apposite here: "It is clear that in the Youth Movement, initially an organization purely for boys, male bonding [*männerbündische*], homoerotic tendencies found their expression; nudity, for example, was a 'temple of manliness.' . . . Yet the ideal of the community of comradeship and friendship, and the mechanisms of neutralization, kept such sexual tendencies sufficiently in check; beyond literary reflection, they did not in actuality play a large role" (*Deutsche Geschichte 1866–1918*, vol. 1: *Arbeitswelt und Bürgergeist* [Munich, 1990], 112).

lack of other forms of sexual release. Fear that an all-out attack on homosexuality might bring greater recognition that there were homosexuals throughout Germany, including within the SS and police, also subverted the open promulgation of antihomosexual measures. Furthermore, countervailing pressures sometimes mitigated the full penalty demanded by the law; it seemed more difficult to apply the harshest measures against men who had fought valiantly for their country or who could mobilize family connections. Even Himmler, the most homophobic of the Nazi leaders, could sometimes be swayed by a carefully worded appeal from family members or military superiors of accused homosexuals. Finally, the successful waging of the war took priority over a consistent application of the laws aimed at homosexuals. For all of these reasons, Nazi enforcement of measures against homosexuality did not become a holocaust.

While not a holocaust, Nazi treatment of homosexuals was horrific, and it might have become even more so if the Nazis had been more successful in World War II and not had to compromise their ideology on this matter. Homophobia unquestionably lay embedded among the German public in 1933. The embers needed to be fanned, and the agent of that escalation was not Hitler, who considered the topic only occasionally. Rather, it was the head of the German police, Heinrich Himmler, who by his consistently harsh official pronouncements on the subject kept reinforcing the perception that the death of a homosexual was no great loss for Germany. Although he did commute some death sentences in 1945, it is virtually certain that his support for clemency would have evaporated following a German victory in World War II. Although a reliable definition of a homosexual would prove infinitely more elusive than the definition of a Jew, especially in light of the mystifying incidence of homosexuality in the racially elite SS, in victory the temptation to turn to a sweeping "final solution" for homosexuals would grow all the stronger. At that point, attitudes that already allowed minor homosexual assaults to be treated as a capital offense could be expanded seamlessly into a decisive radicalization of judicial and penal practice. Appeals would fall on deaf ears.

Victims, Villains, and Survivors: Gendered Perceptions and Self-Perceptions of Jewish Displaced Persons in Occupied Postwar Germany

ATINA GROSSMANN

Cooper Union

As WE WRITE the history of the post-1945 years, we are only now redis-covering what was amply obvious to contemporaries: that in the immedi-ate postwar period occupied Germany was the unlikely, unloved, and re-luctant host to hundreds of thousands of its former victims, housed in refugee camps in the U.S. and British zones and in the American sector of Berlin. Of course, at war's end, millions of people, including ethnic Ger-mans expelled from Eastern Europe as well as former soldiers, forced la-borers, and survivors of death and work camps, were on the move. The available statistics, both those collected at the time and those calculated by historians, are highly variable and surely inaccurate, itself a sign of the chaos that accompanied peace and the speed with which conditions changed. Some twenty million people clogged the roads, straggling from East to West and West to East. Astonishingly, between May and Septem-ber 1945, the victors had managed to repatriate about six million of the seven million persons defined as "displaced" and eligible for return to

Versions of this work have been presented in many venues; some portions overlap with material published in *Archiv für Sozialgeschichte* 38 (October 1998): 230–54. I am grateful for suggestions and criticisms received from colleagues at the Rutgers Center for Historical Analysis (October 1999); Clark University Center for Holocaust Studies (November 1999); Ravensbrück Conference on Gender and Memory (October 1999); Schloss Elmau (July 2000); Bar Ilan University, Tel Aviv (January 2001); and the workshop on "Birth of a Refugee Nation: Displaced Persons in Postwar Europe 1945–1951," Remarque Institute, New York University (April 2001). I am also indebted to my co-organizer for the NYU workshop, Daniel Cohen, the two anonymous reviewers for this journal, Dagmar Herzog for her suggestions and encouragement, and, as always, the German Women's History Study Group in New York.

their homelands, hence not including the Germans expelled from occupied areas. A significant number of those who remained uprooted and on western Allied territory as displaced persons (DPs) were Jewish survivors of Nazi genocide and involuntary migration, primarily from Poland to the Soviet Union; precisely the people that both the Allies and the Germans had least expected to have to deal with in the aftermath of National Socialism's genocidal war.[1]

The existence of displaced persons and the "DP problem" in postwar Europe are certainly not new topics for historians. Yet it has been particularly difficult for historians to chronicle or understand adequately the Jewish DP experience. For both scholars and survivors, the transitional years of the displaced persons have generally been bracketed and overshadowed by the preceding tragedy of war and holocaust and the subsequent establishment of new communities and the state of Israel. The problem is certainly not one of available sources. Yet, despite the very recent proliferation of publications, conferences, films, and exhibitions, spurred in large part by the efforts of the "second generation" born in DP camps or communities, the social history of Jewish DPs remains a topic for which there are many more contemporary sources than good current work that mines them.[2] Moreover, some of the most important studies have been written either for

---

[1]The wide range of figures cited depends on who is counting whom and when and how they were defined: Zorach Wahrhaftig, *Uprooted: Jewish Refugees and Displaced Persons after Liberation, from War to Peace*, No. 5, Institute of Jewish Affairs for the American Jewish Congress and World Jewish Congress, New York, November 1946, estimated that the Allied Armies had to cope with over seven million DPs in occupied territories, plus some twelve million ethnic German expellees. Robert G. Moeller, in *Protecting Motherhood: Women and the Family in the Politics of Postwar West Germany* (Berkeley, 1993), 21, refers to ten million ethnic German expellees plus "another eight to ten million 'displaced persons'—foreigners forced to come to Germany as workers during the war and others removed from their homelands by the Nazis for racial, religious, or political reasons, including survivors of concentration camps." Donald L. Niewyk, *Fresh Wounds: Early Narratives of Holocaust Survival* (Chapel Hill, 1998), 21, notes that in 1945 Jews were "less than one percent of the fourteen million refugees from Hitler's War, although by 1947, they made up a far larger proportion—perhaps as much as one third—of the approximately 700,000 unrepatriated displaced persons in Europe." It should be noted that, especially in the case of liberated Soviet prisoners of war, some of these repatriations were forced.

[2]See the archives of the United Nations Relief and Rehabilitation Administration (UNRRA), the American Joint Distribution Committee (AJDC) relief organization, and the East European Jewish Historical Archive (YIVO) in New York City, the United States Holocaust Memorial Museum in Washington, D.C., and Yad Vashem and the Central Zionist Archives in Jerusalem (to name just a few of the most prominent), Allied government and military reports, American Jewish organizational records, local German records, the DP press and institutional papers, memoirs and diaries, and oral history collections. Recent popular and historical interest in the Jewish DP experience is reflected in several exhibitions, conferences, and publications. A conference in Munich in 1995, convened in part by scholars and writers who had been born or raised in Föhrenwald or other DP camps near

a German-speaking audience interested in the postwar history of Jews in Germany[3] or as part of an Israeli historiography focused on the history of Zionism and the role of Holocaust survivors in the founding of the state.[4]

Munich, launched the German exhibit *Ein Leben aufs Neu—Jüdische "Displaced Persons" auf deutschem Boden 1945–1948*. See also *Rebirth after the Holocaust: The Bergen-Belsen Displaced Persons Camp, 1945–1950*, exhibit at the B'nai B'rith Klutnick National Jewish Museum, Washington, D.C., 2000. On a larger scale, see *Life Reborn: Jewish Displaced Persons 1945–1951. Conference Proceedings*, ed. Menachem Z. Rosensaft (Washington, D.C., 2000), which accompanied the exhibit *Life Reborn: Jewish Displaced Persons 1945–1951* at the United States Holocaust Memorial Museum, and the museum's 2001 calendar with photographs and text from that exhibit, as well as the documentary film *The Long Journey Home*, Simon Wiesenthal Center, Los Angeles, 1997. Basic political histories include Yehudah Bauer, *Out of the Ashes* (New York, 1989); Michael Marrus, *The Unwanted* (New York, 1985); Abram L. Sachar, *Redemption of the Unwanted* (New York, 1983); and Mark Wyman, *DPs: Europe's Displaced Persons, 1945–1951* (Ithaca, 1998).

[3]Among a recent flood of German-language publications, after Wolfgang Jacobmeyer's pioneering article "Jüdische Überlebende als 'Displaced Persons': Untersuchungen zur Besatzungspolitik in den deutschen Westzonen und zur Zuwanderung osteuropäischer Juden 1945–1946," *Geschichte und Gesellschaft* 9 (1983): 421–52, see Susanne Dietrich and Julia Schulze-Wessel, *Zwischen Selbstorganisation und Stigmatisierung: Die Lebenswirklichkeit jüdischer Displaced Persons und die neue Gestalt des Antisemitismus in der deutschen Nachkriegsgesellschaft* (Stuttgart, 1998); Angelika Eder, *Flüchtige Heimat: Jüdische Displaced Persons in Landsberg am Lech, 1945 bis 1950* (Munich, 1998); Angelica Koenigseder, *Flucht nach Berlin: Jüdische Displaced Persons 1945–1948* (Berlin, 1998); Angelica Koenigseder and Juliane Wetzel, *Lebensmut im Wartesaal: Die jüdischen DPs (Displaced Persons) in Nachkriegsdeutschland* (Frankfurt am Main, 1994); and Juliane Wetzel, *Jüdisches Leben in München, 1945–1951: Durchgangsstation oder Wiederaufbau?* (Munich, 1987). Two excellent unpublished German theses are Nicholas Yantian, "Studien zum Selbstständnis der jüdischen 'Displaced Persons' in Deutschland nach dem Zweiten Weltkrieg," master's thesis, Technical University Berlin, 1994; and Jacqueline Dewell Giere, "Wir sind unterwegs, aber nicht in der Wüste: Erziehung und Kultur in den jüdischen Displaced Persons-Lagern der amerikanischen Zone im Nachkriegsdeutschland, 1945–1949," Ph.D. diss., Goethe Universität, Frankfurt, 1993.

[4]Indeed, the liveliest (and most controversial) discussions about Jewish DPs have been conducted in the context of Israeli debates about the treatment of Holocaust survivors in Palestine and Israel and the general revision of the Zionist historiographical narrative. Much of this material is only slowly being translated from Hebrew (which I do not read). See the review essay by Yfaat Weiss, "Die Wiederkehr des Verdrängten: Das jüdische Siedlungsgebiet in Palästina (Jischuw) und die Holocaustüberlebenden in der israelischen Historiographie," *Babylon: Beiträge zur jüdischen Gegenwart* 18 (1998): 139–47; also Anita Shapira, "Politics and Collective Memory: The Debate over the 'New Historians' in Israel," *History and Memory* 7, no. 1 (spring/summer 1995): 9–40. In Hebrew, see, for example, Yosef Grodzinsky, *Chomer enoshi tov* (English translation, *Human Material of Good Quality—Jews versus Zionists in the DP Camps, Germany, 1945–1951*) (Tel Aviv, 1988); Arieh Kochavi, *Displaced Persons and International Politics* (Tel Aviv, 1992); David Engel, *Between Liberation and Flight: Holocaust Survivors in Poland and the Struggle for Leadership, 1944–1946* (Tel Aviv, 1996); Irit Keynan, *Holocaust Survivors and the Emissaries from Eretz-Israel: Germany 1945–1948* (Tel Aviv, 1996); and Tuvia Friling, *Arrow in the Dark: David Ben Gurion, the Yishuv Leadership and Rescue Attempts during the Holocaust* (Kiryat Sedeh-Boker, 1998). In English, see Yisrael Gutman and Avital Saf, eds., *She'erit Hapletah, 1944–1948: Rehabilitation and Political Struggle*, Proceedings of the 6th Yad Vashem International

To add to the confusion, the history of the Jewish DPs, perhaps like that of any community that had endured overwhelming losses and lived in transit, is not only their own but that of many other interested (and more or less powerful) parties. It involves Allied occupation policy, which evolved from unconditional surrender and de-Nazification to Cold War anti-Communism and cooperative reconstruction in western Germany; the British policy toward Palestine; the U.S. policy on immigration in general and American Jewish pressures in particular; the Zionist demands and actions to deliver Jews to Palestine for the establishment of a Jewish state; the politics of the Soviet Union and the newly Communist Eastern European nations from which many of the survivors came; the emerging mandates of the United Nations and the international relief organizations; and finally the varied experiences of the by no means monolithic Jewish survivor community itself. In my previous work, I have juxtaposed German and Jewish postwar history, insisting (as I would still, despite some highly skeptical responses) that the story of the Jewish DPs (and other survivors) needs to be firmly inserted into our ever more sophisticated narrative of postwar German history.[5]

In this essay, however, I want to jettison for the moment the relative safety net of a more familiar German history approach and focus upon a few aspects of the specifically Jewish experience. In particular, I want to discuss three linked points: first, the contradictory and ambivalent perceptions and self-perceptions of Jewish DPs as survivors, victims, and, indeed, villains (or, at least, disturbers of the new, fragile peace) and, more cursorily, how those perceptions changed over time and entered into our present debates about trauma, memory, and memorialization; second, the remarkable baby boom among Jewish survivors, which, while duly noted, has until very recently escaped the serious attention of current researchers;[6] and third, some ways of thinking about notions of revenge and memory in relation to sexuality and reproduction.

Historical Conference (Jerusalem, 1990); Tom Segev, *The Seventh Million: Israel Confronts the Holocaust* (New York, 1993); Shabtai Teveth, *Ben Gurion and the Holocaust* (New York, 1996); Idit Zertal, *From Catastrophe to Power: Holocaust Survivors and the Emergence of Israel* (Berkeley, 1998); Aviva Halamish, *The Exodus Affair: Holocaust Survivors and the Struggle for Palestine* (Syracuse, 1998); and Hanna Yablonka, *Survivors of the Holocaust: Israel after the War* (Basingstoke, 1999). A translation of Ze'ev Mankowitz's important study *Between Memory and Hope: Survivors of the Holocaust in Occupied Germany 1945–1946* is forthcoming from Cambridge University Press. See his English language articles, "The Formation of *She'erit Hapleita*: November 1944–July 1945," *Yad Vashem Studies* 20 (1990): 337–70 and "The Affirmation of Life in *She'erit Hapleita*," *Holocaust and Genocide Studies* 5 (1990): 13–21.

[5]See Atina Grossmann, "Trauma, Memory, and Motherhood: Germans and Jewish Displaced Persons in Post-Nazi Germany, 1945–1949," *Archiv für Sozialgeschichte* 38 (1998): 215–39.

[6]The two outstanding exceptions are Judith Tydor Baumel, "DPs, Mothers and Pioneers: Women in the *She'erit Hapleita*," *Jewish History* 11, no. 2 (1997), and Margarete L.

PERCEPTIONS: "MIR SZEINEN DOH"

As difficult as it was to comprehend that European Jewry had been subjected to systematic extermination and that the "Final Solution" had indeed been put into operation, at times it was almost more difficult to
grasp that there were in fact survivors—several hundred thousand—who
required recognition and care. American officer Saul Padover's early description of the "veritable *Völkerwanderung*" of refugees is telling in its
assumption that the Jews had all been murdered: "Thousands, tens of
thousands, finally millions of liberated slaves were coming out of the farms
and the factories and the mines and pouring onto the highways. . . . They
were all there, all except the Jews. The Jews, six million of them, the
children and the women and the old men, were ashes in the incinerators
and bones in the charnel houses."[7] But, in fact, not all European Jews had
turned to ashes. Between 1945 and 1948, the U.S. and British zones of
occupied Germany became a temporary home for approximately—and
again, the numbers are rough and constantly changing—a quarter of a
million Jewish survivors (some recent estimates are higher, up to 330,000).[8]
Some were German Jews who had emerged from hiding or returned from
exile or the camps; most were Eastern European survivors who had been
liberated by the Allies on German soil (some 90,000 were liberated alive,
but many died within three weeks, leaving about 60,000 or 70,000). Their
ranks were soon swelled by tens of thousands of Jews who poured in from
Eastern Europe. These mostly Polish Jews comprised three distinct groups:
concentration and labor camp and death march survivors who had been
freed in Germany but initially returned to their hometowns hoping, generally in vain, to find lost family members or repossess property; Jews who
had survived among the partisans or in hiding; and, beginning in spring
1946, a large cohort of over 100,000 Jews who had been repatriated to
Poland from their difficult but life-saving refuge in the Soviet Union and

---

Myers [Feinstein], "Jewish Displaced Persons: Reconstructing Individual and Community
in the U.S. Zone of Occupied Germany," *Leo Baeck Institute Yearbook* 42 (1997). See also
Baumel, *Double Jeopardy: Gender and the Holocaust* (London, 1998), and Myers Feinstein,
"Domestic Life in Transit: Jewish DPs," paper presented at the workshop "Birth of a Refu-
gee Nation: Displaced Persons in Postwar Europe 1945–1951," Remarque Institute, New
York University, April 2001.

[7]Saul K. Padover, *Experiment in Germany: The Story of an American Intelligence Officer*
(New York, 1946), 343. Many survivors recount their problems in convincing Soviet soldiers
that they were Jews and not Germans; "Ivrey [Jews] kaputt," they were frequently told.

[8]Statistical data are inexact and bewildering, largely because of change over time, inconsistencies in categorizations among those collecting data, and the difficulties of counting a
highly mobile and sometimes illegal population. Giere, 102, cites Joint Distribution Committee figures of 145,735 Jewish DPs officially registered in the U.S. zone (alone) in November 1946, with 101,614 in DP camps, 35,950 "free livers" in German towns and cities,
4,313 in children's homes, and 3,858 in *Hachschara* (agricultural kibbutzim). Yosef

who then fled again, this time in a western direction, when postwar anti-Semitism convinced them there was no future for Jews in Communist-occupied Eastern Europe. This last group, which had escaped the Holocaust, included virtually the only Eastern European Jews to enter the DP camps in family groups that included young children.[9]

In August 1945 Earl G. Harrison, dean of the University of Pennsylvania Law School and a former U.S. immigration commissioner, submitted to President Truman a report on his fact-finding tour of the DP camps in the U.S. zone. It declared: "We appear to be treating the Jews as the Nazis treated them except that we do not exterminate them. They are in concentration camps in large numbers under military guard, instead of the SS troops. One is led to wonder whether the German people, seeing this, are not supposing that we are following or at least condoning Nazi policy."[10] The passionate outrage of this highly publicized report was hyperbolic and unfair to the substantial efforts that had been made by the U.S. military, but

---

Grodzinsky lists figures that now seem to be commonly accepted: an estimated 70,000 in late summer 1945, 220,000–260,000 Jewish DPs altogether at the height of Jewish flight west in late 1946, and 245,000 in the summer of 1947. However, by looking at migration patterns to target countries (rather than trying to establish figures in Europe), he comes to a remarkably high total of 330,000 Jewish DPs altogether between 1945 and 1951. The higher figures for 1946 and 1947 include the influx into the American zone of Jews who had been repatriated from the Soviet Union. Given the conflicts with British authorities over immigration to Palestine and recognition of Jews as a special separate group, those "infiltrees" were steered or themselves migrated to the U.S. zone.

[9]It should be stressed that these tens of thousands of mostly Polish Jews who had fled from the Nazi occupation to the Soviet Union, often ending up in Soviet Central Asia, constituted a distinct, numerically large group among the DPs. Although the postwar situation in Poland is well covered, there is to my knowledge remarkably little published material on the Soviet period, at least in English. See Yosef Litvak, "Polish-Jewish Refugees Repatriated from the Soviet Union to Poland at the End of the Second World War and Afterwards," in *Jews in Eastern Poland and the U.S.S.R., 1939–46*, ed. Norman Davies and Antony Polansky (New York, 1991), 227–39; L. Dobroszycki, "Restoring Jewish Life in Post-war Poland," *Soviet Jewish Affairs* 3, no. 2 (1973): 58–72; the Dr. Jerzy Glicksman Collection at YIVO archives in New York; and (in Hebrew) Benjamin Pinkus, *Yahadut Mizrah Eropah ben Sho'ah li-tekumah, 1944–1948* (Eastern European Jewry from Holocaust to redemption, 1944–1948) (Kiryat Sedeh-Boker, 1987). One compelling unpublished memoir is Regina Kesler, M.D., *A Pediatrician's Odyssey from Suwalki to Harvard*, ed. Irving Letiner and Michael Kesler. Joseph Berger, *Displaced Persons: Growing up American after the Holocaust* (New York, 2001), conveys very well how murky this history still is; see especially the vivid segments from his mother, Rachel Berger's account of her experiences in the Soviet Union, postwar Poland, and German DP camps (276–312).

[10]Among many sources, see Michael Brenner, *Nach dem Holocaust: Juden in Deutschland 1945–1950* (Munich, 1995), 18; also in English, *After the Holocaust: Rebuilding Jewish Lives in Postwar Germany* (Princeton, 1997). For an excellent analysis of the Harrison Report and the international politics of the DP issue, see Dan Diner, "Jewish DPs in Historical Context," paper presented at the workshop "Birth of a Refugee Nation: Displaced Persons in Postwar Europe 1945–1951," Remarque Institute, New York University, April 2001. The full text of the report and Truman's response are available online at <www.ushmm.org/dp/politic6.htm>.

it did push military authorities and especially General Eisenhower to appoint an advisor on Jewish affairs and meet Jewish demands for separate camps with improved conditions and rations and some internal autonomy. As a result, by 1946 American-controlled DP camps in Germany, Austria, and Italy became magnets for Jewish survivors fleeing renewed persecution in the homelands to which they had briefly returned and for Zionist organizers seeking to prepare them for *Aliyah* to Palestine, especially after the pogrom in Kielce, Poland, on July 4, 1946.[11]

It seemed, to both Germans and the Allied Military Government, that Jews in Germany were more present than ever before, increasing in number and demands daily. The Military Government and local German officials as well as overwhelmed American Jewish and United Nations Relief and Rehabilitation Administration (UNRRA) relief workers in the camps, Zionist Palestinian emissaries, and DP teachers and leaders themselves often saw the DPs as "beaten spiritually and physically," hopeless, depressed, afflicted with "inertia" and "an air of resignation," unsuited to any kind of normal life. Both sympathetic and hostile witnesses regularly and graphically bemoaned the "uncivilized" state of the survivors. They seemed oblivious to the most elementary rules of hygiene, uninhibited in regard to the opposite sex, unwilling to work or take any sort of active initiative. At the same time, they were labeled "jittery, excitable, anxiety prone."[12] All these reports cited symptoms that today are clearly associated with posttraumatic stress disorders. Already in 1946, social workers and psychiatrists were defining pathologies that the psychiatrist William Niederland, himself a refugee from

---

[11]On the Kielce pogrom, in which a charge of ritual murder led to the massacre of at least forty Jews who had tried to return to their hometown, see Abraham J. Peck, "Jewish Survivors of the Holocaust in Germany: Revolutionary Vanguard or Remnants of a Destroyed People?" *Tel Aviver Jahrbuch für deutsche Geschichte* 19 (1990): 35. On the Bricha network, which transported Jews into the American zone of Germany and Italy for eventual *Aliyah* to Palestine, see, especially, Yehudah Bauer, *Flight and Rescue: Bricha* (New York, 1970), and Zertal. In May 1947 the American zone housed 60 assembly centers, 14 children's centers, 38 *Hachscharot*, 17 hospitals, 1 convalescent home, 3 rest centers, 3 sanitoria, 1 transit camp, 1 staging area, and 139 recognized groups of "free-living" DPs in German communities. Additionally, there were two assembly centers in the American sector of Berlin and eighteen camps in the U.S. zone of Austria. By comparison, there were only two assembly centers and two children's centers in the British zone and one children's center in the French sector of Berlin. See Abraham S. Hyman, *The Undefeated* (Jersualem, 1993), 146–47. There were also camps and *Hachscharot* in Italy. Jacobmeyer counts sixteen small sites for Jewish DPs in the French zone and notes that German Jews were concentrated in communities in the north of the zone. On the British zone, see, for example, Jo Reilly et al., eds., *Belsen in History and Memory* (London, 1997).

[12]Quoted in Alex Grobman, *Rekindling the Flame: American Jewish Chaplains and the Survivors of European Jewry, 1944–1948* (Detroit, 1993), 57. See also Leonard Dinnerstein, *America and the Survivors of the Holocaust* (New York, 1982). For examples of such basically sympathetic but highly unsentimental and critical views of survivors, see the remarkable letters home to wives in the United States by two American Jewish officials, one military and the other from the American Joint Distribution Committee: Jacob Rader Marcus and

Nazi Germany, would later explain as a particular "survivor syndrome"—
which, painfully, would become both a stigmatizing label for people who,
in most ways, eventually became ultrafunctional citizens of their new homelands and a necessary diagnosis for claiming restitution from the future
West German government.[13]

Given our own inflationary romance with the language and theory of
trauma and memory and its corollary valorization, one might even say sacralization, of Holocaust survivors, it is salutary to recall how very unroman-
tic, unappealing, and alien the DP survivors appeared, even to those who
meant to aid them.[14] In his autobiographical novel, Hanoch Bartov recalled
the reaction of tough Jewish Brigade soldiers from Palestine who entered
Germany determined to "hate the butchers of your people—unto all generations!" and fulfill their mission of "the rescue of the Jews, immigration
to a free homeland," with "dedication, loyalty and love for the remnants of
the sword and the camps." But despite these "commandments for a Hebrew soldier on German soil," the Brigade men were not prepared for what
they found once they actually encountered the remnants they had pledged
to avenge and rescue: "I kept telling myself that these were the people we
had spoken of for so many years—But I was so far removed from them that
electric wire might have separated us."[15]

The Israeli historian Idith Zertal has characterized the painful, shock-
ing encounter of the Yishuv with the survivors, "between the Jews of Europe and the 'reborn Israel,'" as a kind of "return of the repressed" that
provoked the fear and anxiety Freud diagnosed when something that had
once been *heimlich*, familiar and homelike, becomes *unheimlich*, frighten-
ing and inexplicable.[16] Today, immersed in our highly politicized memorial cultures, we have mostly repressed the powerful contemporary
consensus among Allies, Germans, Zionists, and Jewish observers that the
survivors were "human debris," at best to be rehabilitated and resocialized

---

Abraham J. Peck, eds., *Among the Survivors of the Holocaust 1945: The Landsberg DP Camp
Letters of Major Irving Heymont*, Monographs of the American Jewish Archives, vol. 10
(Cincinnati, 1982), and Oscar A. Mintzer, *"In Defense of the Survivors": The Letters and
Documents of Oscar A. Mintzer, AJDC Legal Advisor, Germany, 1945–46*, ed. Alex Grobman
(Berkeley, 1999).

[13]See William G. Niederland, *Folgen der Verfolgung: Das Überlebens-Syndrom Seelenmord*
(Frankfurt am Main, 1980), based on his pioneering article in *Hillside Hospital Journal*
(1961). On the trauma and trauma diagnoses of Jewish survivors, see, among many other
sources, Aaron Haas, *The Aftermath: Living with the Holocaust* (Cambridge, 1995); and
Israel W. Charny, *Holding on to Humanity: The Message of Holocaust Survivors: The Shamai
Davidson Papers* (New York, 1992).

[14]For a smart critique, see Michael André Bernstein, "Homage to the Extreme: The
Shoah and the Rhetoric of Catastrophe," *Times Literary Supplement*, March 6, 1998, 6–8.

[15]Hanoch Bartov, *The Brigade*, trans. David S. Segal (New York, 1968; originally published in Hebrew, 1965), 56, 148.

[16]Zertal, 8–9.

into good citizens (and soldiers) of a future Jewish state, at worst to be marked as "asocial" and beyond human redemption.[17] I. F. Stone, the American Jewish leftist journalist who covered as a "participant observer" the underground route to Palestine, noted briskly about his first impression of the DPs in the camps, "They were an unattractive lot."[18] As one survivor ruefully stated, "The concentration camp experience is nothing that endears you to people."[19]

Paradoxically, however, the reverse side to the stigmatization of Jewish DPs as both incorrigible and pathetic was a kind of romantic vision, heavily influenced by the Zionist ethos that dominated DP life, of the tough survivor who had emerged like a phoenix from unimaginable devastation. Kathryn Hulme, an adventurous young American wartime welder turned UNRRA worker, described her reaction to the Jewish DPs assigned to her camp. They were hardly the "ashes of a people" announced by so many reporters; on the contrary, they were indeed survivors, "charged with the intensest life force I had ever experienced." They were—at least their toughened leaders—entirely unlike either the docile, well-behaved defeated Germans or the "professional" non-Jewish Polish and Baltic DPs with whom she had previously worked; rather, they were "contrary, critical, and demanding." Resorting to nonetheless admiring stereotypes, she described "their wiry bodies . . . smoldering eyes . . . voices unmusical and hoarse . . . their hands moved continuously." In fact, she concluded, "They didn't seem like DPs at all."[20]

Hulme vividly recorded the indignities of the "strange half world of the DP camps," "a small planet adrift from earth like a raft in space" where the war's uprooted lived, "bracketed between the two liberations," first from the Nazis in 1945 and then finally from the DP camps after 1947 and into the 1950s. She worried that DPs had nothing else "to do than sit around and produce babies at such a frightful pace that soon the per capita birth rate of DP land would exceed that of any other country except possibly China." Jews, she explained, were less than one fifth of the U.S. zone's DP population, but "they were such an articulate minority that if you only read the newspapers to learn about occupation affairs, you gained the impression that they were the whole of the DP problem." Jews made headlines with arrests for black market activities and not infrequent violent confrontations with local Germans and American GIs; they staged angry demonstrations and

---

[17]Phrases such as "human debris" or "living corpses" were ubiquitous in contemporary reports (indeed, there is a remarkably consistent and repetitive language in most documents describing Jewish DPs). For one example, see the accounts in Karen Gershon, *Postscript: A Collective Account of the Lives of Jews in West Germany since the Second World War* (London, 1969).

[18]I. F. Stone, *Underground to Palestine and Reflections Thirty Years Later* (New York, 1978), 24. In general, see Bauer, *Out of the Ashes* and *Flight and Rescue*.

[19]Haas, 18.

[20]Kathryn Hulme, *The Wild Place* (Boston, 1953), 71, 212–13.

dramatic hunger strikes denouncing anti-Semitic acts by occupation authorities and Germans and demanding emigration to Palestine. They were inspected by U.S. officials and journalists on high-level inspection tours who, Hulme thought, handled them with "kid gloves."[21]

Eleanor Roosevelt dramatized her efforts to draft an International Declaration of Human Rights with her 1945 tour of Zeilsheim camp near Frankfurt. In September 1946, at a ceremony conducted in the War Room of the U.S. headquarters in the I. G. Farben Building in Frankfurt, General McNarney extended full recognition to the Central Committee of Liberated Jews as official representatives—at least on matters of social welfare and self-governance—of Jewish DPs. Indeed, while survivors who had expected to be treated as allies by the occupiers bitterly protested the lack of attention to their plight (especially the devastating fact that their German victimizers were running around free in their own country while Jews sat in camps waiting for emigration permits), it was also true that "the Jewish DPs were on exhibit to visitors from the moment of their liberation." Moreover, the DP leadership knew very well how to manipulate these displays and stage their calls for better treatment and entry to Eretz Yisrael.[22] To their sullen and resentful German neighbors, the DP camps appeared as a kind of Schlaraffenland of "sugar and spam, margarine and jam, plus cigarettes and vitamized chocolate bars," as well as centers of black market activity fed by privileged access to the cigarette and food supplies of the occupiers. As Hulme conceded, "They sounded like the prima donnas of the DP world, but I thought that perhaps they deserved the rating."[23]

Despite the overcrowding, the unappetizing rations, the lack of privacy, the smells, the sheer hopelessness of idle waiting, the sometimes humiliating and uncomprehending treatment by military and relief workers who "looked down on us . . . as if we were some kind of vermin or pests,"[24] the DP camps and the new families they housed provided a make-shift therapeutic community for survivors who had "been liberated from death" but not yet "been freed for life."[25] The Americans, in cooperation with the UNRRA, had indeed made the commitment that "reasonable care be taken of these unfortunate people."[26] But they did so with great reluctance and resentment; as Irving Heymont, the American (and, as he later revealed, Jewish) commander of Landsberg DP camp, confessed in his memoir, "When I raised my right hand and took the oath as an officer, I never dreamed that there were jobs of this sort."[27] In the characteristic

[21]Ibid., 124.
[22]Hyman, 250ff.
[23]Hulme, 211–12.
[24]Jacob Biber, *Risen from the Ashes* (San Bernardino, 1990), 14.
[25]Wahrhaftig, *Uprooted*, 86.
[26]Lt. Col. Mercer (U.S. Army), February 5, 1946, OMGUS 4/20–1/10. See also Wahrhaftig, *Uprooted*, 39.
[27] Marcus and Peck, eds., 38.

rapid turnaround of sentiment in the postwar years, it was the victims of Nazism, still displaced and unruly, who soon came to be seen, even by the victors, as the disreputable villains, while the Germans, with their "clean German homes and pretty, accommodating German girls," came to be viewed as victims, pathetic but appealing, and later, with the Airlift in Berlin, even heroic.[28] As the impact of the Harrison Report faded into Cold War politics, it seemed to many that "the guilt of the Germans was forgotten," and that, as a depressed Jewish observer, Zorach Wahrhaftig, put it: "Eighteen months after liberation . . . the war is not yet over for European Jewry. They are impossible to repatriate and almost as difficult to resettle. No one wants them now just as no one wanted them before and during the war."[29] When it came to the Jewish DPs, disgust and fear were mingled with, and often outweighed, admiration and sheer awe at the fact of their survival. Moreover, support for the Jewish DPs, sympathy for their Zionist vision, and outrage at their treatment were often linked to left-wing sentiments, anger at weakening de-Nazification, and the re-jection of the politics of vengeance and justice in favor of reconciliation with the former enemy in the service of the Cold War, a process daily reinforced by the omnipresent fraternization with German *Fräuleins*.[30] Only a day before the moving ceremony at the I. G. Farben headquarters, Secretary of State Byrne's conciliatory speech in Stuttgart on September 6, 1946, signaled these shifts in policy and the upcoming end of the brief relative "golden age" for the Jewish DPs under U.S. occupation.

By 1948 DP leader Samuel Gringauz stated sourly in the American-Jew-ish journal *Commentary* that "Jewish survivors in German DP camps are an obstacle to Cold War reconciliation with Germany. . . . They are still in acute conflict with the nation which Allied occupation policy wants to make into an ally."[31] For antifascists involved in postwar reconstruction and relief efforts, such as Bartley Crum of the Anglo-American Committee of In-quiry on Palestine, which investigated conditions in the DP camps, and Ira Hirschmann, Fiorello La Guardia's personal UNRRA representative, who

[28]Samuel Gringauz, "Our New German Policy and the DPs: Why Immediate Resettle-ment Is Imperative," *Commentary* 5 (1948): 510. In general, see also Dinnerstein.

[29]Zorach Wahrhaftig, "Life in Camps 6 Months after Liberation," November 27, 1945, in *Archives of the Holocaust*, 9:134; Wahrhaftig, *Uprooted*, 39. For case studies of relations between Jewish DPs and the local German population in Landsberg, see Angelika Eder, "Jüdische Displaced Persons im deutschen Alltag: Eine Regionalstudie 1945–1950," *Fritz Bauer Jahrbuch* (1997), 163–87; and D. Kohlmannslehner, "Das Verhältnis von deutschen und jüdischen Displaced Persons in Lager Lampertheim 1945–1949," paper, Fritz Bauer Institut Archives, Frankfurt am Main.

[30]Contemporary critics regularly blamed American GI and officer contact with German women for the conciliatory policies and antipathy toward Jewish DPs. This is a complicated theme that deserves much more analysis; German women did exercise real influence in the early postwar years not only through their sexual relationships with the occupiers but also in their positions as translators and clerical workers.

[31]Gringauz, 508–14, esp. 508. He sees the period from the fall of 1945 until the sum-mer of 1947 as a "golden age" (509).

distrusted the Germans and mourned the demise of the alliance with the Soviet Union, the poor treatment of the DPs and denial of emigration to Palestine and elsewhere were just another aspect of a dangerous policy that coddled the Germans and corrupted the occupiers. Especially liberal and leftist Americans, including a significant number of former German-Jews now stationed in Germany, saw the turn toward reconciliation and recovery for Germany as a source of future fascism. The new agenda of "business before democracy" persecuted former resisters and punished the victims by keeping them locked away in DP camps rather than supporting their desire to begin a new life in Palestine, which many officials had discovered on official tours to be a "miracle of orange groves and olive trees."[32] Outrage at the treatment of Jewish DPs and pro-Zionism were thus frequently linked to bitterness over the Cold War and the sacrifice of de-Nazification and real democracy in the name of anti-Communism and rebuilding Germany.

Clearly also, these perceptions shifted over time, from the initial sympathetic shock of liberation, to frantic irritation at the mass influx in 1946 combined with enthusiastic or reluctant admiration, especially for Zionist commitments (which, not incidentally, relieved the Americans of having to worry about large-scale Jewish immigration) in 1947–48, and finally, the well-known disdain for the "hard core" of DPs who had either integrated into German economic life (generally via the black or gray market) or were simply too sick or exhausted to move and therefore remained in Germany after 1948. In any case, at least between 1945 and 1949, Jewish DP life in occupied Germany, which was centered around the large camps near Munich and Frankfurt, had generated a unique transitory society: simultaneously, a final efflorescence of a destroyed Eastern European Jewish culture, a preparation for an imagined future in Eretz Yisrael, and a "waiting room" in which new lives were indeed—against all odds—begun.

Maschiachskinder: THE BABY BOOM

In some kind of supreme historical irony, Jewish DPs in occupied Germany, after the war and the *Shoah*, produced a record number of babies. In 1946 occupied Germany, far from being *judenrein*, counted the highest Jewish (some, pointing to the unusually skewed young and fertile population of survivors, say the highest overall) birth rate in the world.[33] The "steady rush of weddings"[34] in the DP camps united, sometimes within days, neighbors in the next barrack or distant kin or friends from what had

---

[32]Ira A. Hirschmann, La Guardia's inspector general for the UNRRA, in his passionate book, *The Embers Still Burn: An Eye-Witness View of the Postwar Ferment in Europe and the Middle East and Our Disastrous Get Soft with Germany Policy* (New York, 1949), 149, 45.

[33]See, among numerous sources, Peck, 38; Brenner, *Nach dem Holocaust*, 36; Myers, 306–8.

[34]Biber, 49.

once been home who did not necessarily know each other very well or love each other very much. There were, as a young woman survivor recalled, "so many marriages, sometimes really strange marriages that never would have happened before the war."[35] Certainly they did not, could not, produce "normal" domestic life. The young mothers in the DP camps were in many ways utterly unsuited for motherhood and domesticity (in any case, limited in the camps). They had come into Nazi ghettos and death camps, or joined partisan groups, or gone into hiding, or fled their homelands as teenagers and had been given no time in which to grow up. Their own mothers were generally dead (often killed or selected for death before the survivors' eyes). Some of the women had once had children, now lost and murdered, sometimes hidden with Christians and very hard to repossess.[36] Reading postwar accounts, it seems that so many young survivors told their interviewers, "The hardest moment was when they took my mama away."[37] As a shocked U.S. Army rabbi reported back to Jewish agencies in New York: "Almost without exception each is the last remaining member of his entire family. . . . Their stories are like terrible nightmares which makes one's brain reel and one's heart bleed."[38] No one knew how to respond to people who had survived the unimaginable. When Saul Padover finally encountered the Jewish survivors he had thought no longer existed, he wrote, "I never knew what to say to these people. What sense did words make?"[39]

The veritable baby boom of 1946–47 was, however, a phenomenon much more complicated and remarkable than the "manic defense" against

[35]Edith Horowitz in Brana Gurewitsch, *Mothers, Sisters, Resisters: Oral Histories of Women Who Survived the Holocaust* (Tuscaloosa, 1998), 73.

[36]See Deborah Dwork on the contest over hidden children in postwar Netherlands in Peter Hayes, ed., *Lessons and Legacies: The Meaning of the Holocaust in a Changing World* (Evanston, 1998), and the paper by Marion P. Pritchard on Jewish DP children for the conference "Lessons and Legacies: The Meaning of the Holocaust in a Changing World," Dartmouth College, 1994, revised, 1997 (I am grateful to Marion Pritchard for sending me a copy of her paper). In a fascinating article based on numerous memoirs by women survivors, Fionnuala Ni Aolain, a law professor at the Hebrew University, has attempted to identify the specific gender-based harm caused to women by forcible separation from their children as experiences that are "sex-based" even if they are not categorizable within what we generally understand as sexual violence. See Fionnuala Ni Aolain, "Sex-Based Violence and the Holocaust—A Reevaluation of Harms and Rights in International Law," *Yale Journal of Law and Feminism* 12, no. 1 (2000): 53.

[37]Edith Z. in Niewyk, 171.

[38]Letter to Stephen S. Wise, June 22, 1945, in Abraham J. Peck, ed., *The Papers of the World Jewish Congress 1945–1950: Liberation and the Saving Remnant, Archives of the Holocaust,* American Jewish Archives, Cincinnati (New York, 1990), 9:30. On the important role of U.S. military rabbis in dealing with Jewish DPs, see Grobman; and Louis Barish, *Rabbis in Uniform: The Story of the American Jewish Military Chaplain* (New York, 1962). Note again that Jewish DPs who had been in the Soviet Union and did not begin to arrive in the U.S. zone in large numbers until the second half of 1946 were more likely to have survived in intact families.

[39]Padover, 359.

catastrophic experience and overwhelming loss diagnosed by contemporary psychoanalytically oriented psychiatrists and social workers.[40] And the
perceptions of this drive for marriage and children, among both DPs and
those who dealt with them, were multilayered, strongly felt, and contradictory. "In the midst of the depressed desert life" of the DP camps (the
recurring Exodus metaphors were of course not accidental), one male survivor wrote in a memoir titled *Risen from the Ashes*, "a noticeable change
occurred: people who had survived singly in all age groups were struck
with a strong desire to be married."[41] The American Jewish journalist Meyer
Levin also sensed that, for all the Jews' immediate preoccupation with the
barest necessities of survival, their primary need was "to seek some link on
earth. . . . This came before food and shelter."[42]

The rapid appearance of babies and baby carriages in the dusty streets
of DP camps throughout the American and British zones served as a conscious and highly ideologized reminder that "mir szeinen doh" (Yiddish
for "we are here"). Despite everything, women who only weeks or months
earlier had been emaciated, amenorrheic "living corpses" became pregnant and bore children.[43] A *She'erit Hapleitah* (surviving remnant, or, more
literally, leftover remnant of a remnant) had survived the Nazis' genocide
and seemed determined to replace the dead at an astonishingly rapid rate.[44]
Attempting to dramatize survivors' desperate determination to emigrate
to Palestine, Bartley Crum of the Anglo-American Committee claimed,
"In many camps I was told that Jewish women had deliberately suffered
abortions rather than bear a child on German soil."[45] Remarkably, however, the opposite was more common. Survivors were not deterred even

[40]For a fine analysis of this literature, see Isidor J. Kaminer, "'On razor's edge'—Vom
Weiterleben nach dem Überleben," *Fritz Bauer Institut Jahrbuch 1996*, 146–47, 157.

[41]Biber, 37.

[42]Meyer Levin, *In Search: An Autobiography* (New York, 1950), 183–84.

[43]See Zalman Grinberg, "We Are Living Corpses," in *Aufbau*, August 24, 1945. For a
strong argument against the view of survivors as "living corpses" and for the agency, and
what Peck has called "the revolutionary ideology," of the She'erit Hapleita (which focuses
on political organization rather than reproduction), see Ze'ev Mankowitz, "The Formation
of She'erit Hapleita: November 1944–July 1945," *Yad Vashem Studies* 20 (1990): 337–70,
and "The Affirmation of Life in She'erith Hapleita," *Holocaust and Genocide Studies* 5, no.
1 (1990): 13–21.

[44]See Juliane Wetzel, "Mir szeinen doh: München und Umgebung als Zuflucht von
Überlebenden des Holocaust 1945–1948," in Martin Broszat, ed., *Von Stalingrad zur
Währungsreform: Zur Sozialgeschichte des Umbruchs in Deutschland* (Munich, 1988). See
also Koenigseder and Wetzel, 104–5, 187; Peck, 35–38. The term She'erit Hapleitah derives from reworkings of biblical references to the survivors of the Assyrian conquest.

[45]Bartley C. Crum, *Behind the Silken Curtain: A Personal Account of Anglo-American
Diplomacy in Palestine and the Middle East* (Jerusalem, 1996; originally published, New
York, 1947), 90. There is, not surprisingly, little information on the number and experience
of Jewish women DPs who considered, sought, and/or underwent abortions at a time
when they were widespread among German women. This is a topic for which careful research with memoirs and oral histories is particularly important.

by the knowledge that for purposes of *Aliyah* to Palestine and emigration elsewhere, pregnancy and young children were only an obstacle.[46] David P. Boder, the American psychologist whose interviews with survivors conducted shortly after liberation have recently been edited and published by Donald L. Niewyk, described a young woman who had lost her entire family. Now, "recently married and visibly pregnant, she eagerly awaited her turn to emigrate to Palestine" and "was perhaps the most cheerful and open of the survivors."[47] The dominant U.S. relief agency, the American Joint Distribution Committee, found itself having to scramble to build Jewish ritual baths for brides (*Mikveh*) and to produce gold wedding rings as well as wigs for Orthodox wives.[48] Major Heymont noticed in Landsberg that "the use of contraceptives is highly frowned upon by the camp people. They believe it is everyone's duty to have as many children as possible in order to increase the numbers of the Jewish community."[49] Whatever the surely highly variable nature of individual experiences, there is no doubt that for the DPs themselves and for those who managed and observed them, the rash of marriages, pregnancies, and babies collectively represented a conscious affirmation of Jewish life. This was true for both men and women. But women especially were determined to claim domestic reproductive roles that they had once been promised in some long ago and now fantastic past. Women survivors of the death camps, sometimes of medical experiments, were anxious to reassure themselves of their fertility, as well as to prove male potency (which, it was widely rumored, had been subjected to emasculating potions and experiments in the camps). Pregnancy and childbirth served as definitive material evidence that they had indeed survived.[50]

[46]Levin notes, "And the urge to arrive in time for the birth of the child in *Eretz* was real on every vessel that left for Palestine with its host of pregnant women, some of whom were smuggled onto the ships in their ninth month despite the *Haganah* regulation making the seventh month the limit." See also Wahrhaftig, *Uprooted*, 52–54.

[47]Niewyk, 94.

[48]Baumel, "DPs, Mothers and Pioneers," 103. See also her *Kibbutz Buchenwald: Survivors and Pioneers* (New Brunswick, 1997).

[49] Marcus and Peck, eds., 44.

[50]An American relief worker reported that a Belsen survivor describing medical experiments "believes that well over the majority of Jews alive—certainly 90% of those the Nazis could get at, will not have children—including himself and his wife." Mintzer, letter to his wife dated February 17, 1946 (166). It is worth noting how many "Holocaust memoirs" actually include (or conclude with) time in the DP camps and experiences of marriage, pregnancy, and childbearing. See, among many memoirs, Sonja Milner, *Survival in War and Peace* (New York, 1984); and Sala Pawlowicz with Kevin Klose, *I Will Survive* (London, 1947). In general, see Lenore Weitzman and Dalia Ofer, eds., *Women in the Holocaust* (New Haven, 1998); also Sybil Milton, "Gender and Holocaust—Ein offenes Forschungsfeld," Sara R. Horowitz, "Geschlechtsspezifische Erinnerungen an den Holocaust," and Atina Grossmann, "Zwei Erfahrungen im Kontext des Themas 'Gender und Holocaust,'" in Sigrid Jacobeit and Grit Philipp, eds., *Forschungsschwerpunkt Ravensbrück: Beiträge zur Geschichte des Frauen-Konzentrationslagers* (Berlin, 1997), 124–46.

Observers were shocked by a kind of "hypersexuality" among the mostly youthful inhabitants of the DP camps who had been denied the usual processes of adolescent sexual and romantic experimentation. They noted with a certain astonishment, both impressed and appalled, that "the appearance of numbers of new-born babies has become a novel feature of the Jewish DP camps."[51] Abraham S. Hyman, a legal affairs officer attached to the U.S. Jewish Adviser's Office, observed unsentimentally, as did virtually everyone, that "the overpowering desire to end the loneliness and to establish or reestablish family life led to marriages of men and women who patently had nothing else in common and were acknowledged as 'marriages of desperation' by the people themselves." He cited an explanation by a DP in Zeilsheim camp near Frankfurt to a member of the Anglo-American Committee of Inquiry: "I was lonely; she was lonely. Perhaps together we will be half as lonely." At the same time, however, Hyman—again, like virtually everyone who came into contact with the DP survivors—was moved and impressed by their "amazing recuperative powers" and apparently irrepressible "zest for life."[52] As many survivors have articulated, they were young and finally freed from constant fear; they wanted to taste the pleasures of youth long denied: "Our young bodies and souls yearned to live."[53] Yet sexual longing was mixed with a painful sense of inexperience, of having missed out on some crucial youthful socialization and pleasures. The quick marriages— "Hitler married us," DPs wryly noted[54]—promised some sense of comfort and stability to people who possessed neither but were often also cause for more anxiety and insecurity. Buried deeply were stories of rape and sexual assault at the hands of Soviet liberators and other protectors as well as Germans and local fascists (and also in the forest partisan encampments, where women were subject to sexual coercion and assault by both Red Army soldiers and Jewish partisans).[55] It is worth noting in this context that the experience of liberation (and the prospect of future heterosexual relations) may have been profoundly different for women and men precisely because so many

---

[51]Wahrhaftig, *Uprooted*, 54. Occupation and relief officials, as well as Germans, were often caught between disbelief at the horror and magnitude of the extermination and incomprehension of the fact that there remained, after all, hundreds of thousands of survivors who resisted repatriation and for whom there had to be found not just "relief" but a new life (what was still called a "final solution") outside of Europe. See Wahrhaftig, "Life in Camps," 130.

[52]Hyman, 246, 270, 17.

[53]Biber, 46.

[54]Berger, 291.

[55]See especially Nechama Tec's treatment in *Defiance: The Bielski Partisans: The Story of the Largest Armed Rescue of Jews by Jews during World War II* (New York, 1993), 126–70, and her forthcoming book *Resistance and Courage: Jewish Women during the Holocaust* (New Haven, 2002).

women found themselves having to fear or, indeed, undergo renewed attack, this time from those whom they had welcomed as liberators.[56]

Nonetheless, over and over again, relief workers and interviewers heard the same message: "All I wanted right away was a baby. This was the only hope for me."[57] By the winter of 1946, reports claimed that "a thousand [Jewish] babies were born each month" in the American zone.[58] A 1946 American Joint Distribution Committee survey recorded 750 babies born every month just in the official U.S. zone DP camps and perhaps even more dramatically that "nearly one third of the Jewish women in the zone between 18 and 45 were either expectant mothers or had new-born babies."[59] The recorded Jewish birth rate in Germany for 1948, right before the proclamation of the state of Israel on May 16, 1948, and the easing of U.S. immigration regulations eventually reduced the Jewish DP "problem" to small but highly visible proportions, was a whopping 35.8 per 1,000.[60] All of these striking demographic markers can, of course, be related to empirical data such as the youthful age cohort and 3:2 (or even 2:1) male/female sex ratio among Jewish survivors,[61] as well as the higher rations (up to 2,500 calories a day) and guaranteed (if primitive) housing granted Jews by the American occupiers. Having sex and making babies

[56]Haas, 98–99. I am indebted to Michael Brenner for formulating this point about the particular experience of female survivors based on his mother, Henny Brenner's unpublished memoirs. In fact, if one rereads Holocaust memoirs with this issue in mind, the fear of rape by Red Army liberators comes up frequently. Brana Gurewitsch notes in her introduction: "After liberation, when chaos reigned and all women were considered fair game by Soviet liberators, women survivors took extraordinary measures to avoid rape" (xviii).

[57]Haas, 102. See also the numerous examples in the testimonies collected by the American psychologist David P. Boder right after war's end in Niewyk.

[58]Grobman, 17. This baby boom is well portrayed in the American documentary film *The Long Journey Home*, Simon Wiesenthal Center, Los Angeles, 1997.

[59]Cited in Hyman, 247. In January 1946 the AJDC counted 120 children between the ages of one and five; in December 1946, 4,431. Not all these babies had been conceived in the DP camps; the high birth and young child numbers also reflected the many new arrivals from Poland who had survived with their families in the Soviet Union. In some cases, children who had been born in the Soviet Union were registered, for political or bureaucratic reasons, as having been born in Poland or in DP camps. See Joseph Berger's story (276–81). (Given the current revival of historiographical debate about [neo]totalitarianism, it may be not incidental to point out that this too was a major difference between Nazism and Stalinism; Jews survived in Stalin's Soviet Union, albeit under difficult conditions.)

[60]See Brenner, *Nach dem Shoah*, 36. For 1946 figures in Bavaria (29/1,000 for Jews, 7.35/1,000 for Germans), see Jacobmeyer, 437. For comparative purposes, the German birth rate in 1933 stood at 14.7 (9.9 in Berlin); in the aftermath of the First World War it had reached 25.9 in 1920. Some two thirds of Jewish DPs eventually ended up in Israel; altogether about 100,000 went to the United States and 250,000 to Israel. For differing views of the reaction in Israel, see Segev; Yablonka.

[61]Wahrhaftig, *Uprooted*, 54 (and in numerous other sources). By comparison, in Berlin at war's end, approximately the opposite (over 60 percent female) ratio applied.

was also a way to deal with the frustration and loneliness of leading a waiting life ("auf dem Weg") in the transit camps and the disappointment at the reality of the long-yearned-for liberation.

Still, the high birth statistics require attention. For Jewish survivors, fertility and maternity worked as a mode of reidentifying and reconstructing. It provided a means both of claiming personal agency and an intact individual body and of constructing a viable new community after extraordinary trauma and even in transit. Let me be clear: the baby boom among the *She'erit Hapleitah* could not offer any redemptive meaning to the catastrophe (*Churban*) that had been experienced.[62] But it did offer a possible means to "redeem the future"[63] or at least to begin the regenerative work of making and imagining one. We can draw here on Dominick La Capra's insistence that "one be attentive as well to the efforts of victims to rebuild a life and to make use of counterforces that enable them to be other than victims, that is, to survive and to engage in social and political practices related to the renewal of interest in life (for example, having children)."[64] Having babies—the most normal of human activities under normal circumstances and indeed precisely what would have been expected by Eastern European Jewish religious and social tradition—now became both miraculous and an entry into "normal" humanity, even if it often seemed to offer only a kind of make-believe normality, a "parallel life" to the memories of the preceding trauma. New babies and families provided a means of bridging the "radical discontinuity" of the life cycle that the survivors had endured. If, as many psychologists and psychiatrists have now argued, Holocaust survivors' loss of "basic trust" had fundamentally and permanently damaged their faith in themselves and the outside world, caring for an infant could perhaps initially offer the most direct and primal means of reaffirming the self.[65]

REVENGE AND MEMORY

In that sense, the quick construction of new families could also be interpreted as a kind of genealogical and biological revenge in a situation where the possibilities (and, indeed, the motivation) for direct vengeance were

[62]The most insistent critic of any attempts to lend "meaning" to the Holocaust has been Lawrence L. Langer. See his most recent book, *Admitting the Holocaust: Collected Essays* (New York, 1995). On this theme also there is a huge literature, ranging from the theological to the psychoanalytic and political.

[63]Mankowitz, "The Formation of She'erit Hapleita," 351.

[64]Dominick La Capra, *History and Memory after Auschwitz* (Ithaca, 1998), 204–5.

[65]On the problem of destroyed trust and the influence of psychiatric work done with Holocaust survivors on later treatment of refugee trauma, see the essays in *Mistrusting Refugees*, ed. E. Valentine Daniel and John Chr. Knudsen (Berkeley, 1995), especially the introduction (4). On the relationship between survivors and their children, see, among many studies, *Generations of the Holocaust*, ed. Martin S. Bergmann and Milton E. Jucovy (New York, 1982), and the pioneering work of Judith Kestenberg and Henry Krystal.

very limited.[66] Jewish infants, born on territory that had been declared *judenrein* to women who had been slated for extermination, were literally dubbed *Maschiachskinder* (children of the Messiah).[67] Marriage, pregnancy, and childbirth clearly represented a possible reconstruction of collective or national as well as individual identity for the Jewish DPs. The baby boom was the counterpart, indeed, was closely linked, although in ambivalent ways, to the passionate political Zionism that gripped (in one form or another) virtually all survivors. It offered a means of establishing a new order and a symbolic sense of "home," even and especially in the refugee camps.[68]

It is also crucial to keep in mind that this Jewish baby boom did not simply go on behind the gates of the DP camps, unnoticed by Germans. Jewish interaction with Germans was certainly not limited to the oft-cited arenas of black marketeering or bar ownership. Jews gave birth in German hospitals where they were treated by German physicians and nurses; Jews hired German women as housekeepers and nannies; they sometimes, especially given the surplus of men, dated, had sex with, and even (in a much stigmatized minority of cases) married German women (by 1950, one thousand such marriages had been registered, and surely there were many more relationships).[69] DP mothers crisscrossed the streets of German towns with their baby carriages; the many Jewish marriages and births in the DP camps were registered in the German *Standesämter* (marriage bureaus).[70]

Indeed, the much photographed parades of baby carriages proudly steered by DP parents were intended as conscious displays of self-assertion, for themselves and also for others. They clearly communicated the politics of "we are here" to politicians debating Palestine and immigration policy, relief organizers adjudicating rations and housing, and German citizens confronted with their discomfiting former victims. Just as historians have expanded their definitions of resistance during the war and Holocaust to encompass actions that did not rely on weapons, perhaps we

---

[66]We might consider this gendered view of "revenge" in light of current discussions about the relative lack of vengeful actions by survivors and a newer focus on a few dramatic actions (such as the scheme to poison German wells recently portrayed in a German documentary). See John Sack, *An Eye for an Eye* (New York, 1993), among other texts. For an interesting analysis of discussions about revenge among German-Jewish survivors, see Jael Geiss, *Übrig sein-Leben "danach": Juden deutscher Herkunft in der britischen und amerikanischen Zone Deutschlands 1945–1949* (Berlin, 2000), 207–38.

[67]I am grateful to Samuel Kassow of the History Department at Trinity College for this reference.

[68]Comparative anthropological literature is useful in this context. See especially Lisa Malkii's analysis of the ways in which refugee camp settings encourage "construction and reconstruction of [their] history 'as a people'" and the importance of children in that process in *Purity and Exile: Violence, Memory, and National Cosmology among Hutu Refugees in Tanzania* (Chicago, 1995), 3.

[69]Figure from Yantian, 43.

[70]See Eder, "Jüdische Displaced Persons."

too should think about broadening our notions of "revenge" when analyzing the DP experience. Jewish survivors in Germany, it should be stressed, saw their presence on that "cursed soil" not only as a perverse historical "irony" but also as a kind of justice and "payback." The Germans, Jews contended, owed them their space, their former barracks and estates, their rations, and their services. There was a kind of "in your face" quality to Jewish mothers brandishing their babies, just as there was to the banners flying from former German official buildings or the posters carried in processions and parades through German towns; a pleasure in rousing a village baker and insisting that he bake *challah* for Shabbes or ordering a grocer to supply pounds of herring for a holiday feast.[71]

Significantly, there is very little record of what might be construed as the most obvious form of bodily "revenge," namely, rape or sexual possession of German women by Jewish survivors or soldiers. The Red Army had engaged in mass rape as it fought its way west into Nazi Germany; the Soviet Jewish writer Ilya Ehrenburg was widely believed to have incited Red Army soldiers to "take the flaxen-haired women, they are your prey," an accusation never proven and that he vigorously denied.[72] Those assaults had been interpreted—and anticipated—as acts of revenge, but they had, in fact, been relatively indiscriminate. Jewish survivors relate multiple stories of having to flee rape by their Soviet liberators, even as others (or sometimes the same women) talk of the Russians' kindness.[73] Certainly, Germans complained about rapes and pillage by DPs, but the villains are generally identified as non-Jewish Eastern European former slave laborers. In the early Yiddish edition of his memoir, Elie Wiesel referred to nights of rape and plunder by liberated Buchenwald survivors: "Early the next day Jewish boys ran off to Weimar to steal clothing and potatoes. And to rape German girls" [un tsu fargvaldikn daytshe shikses], but the passage is not central to his account and is revised and then expurgated in

[71]Interestingly, Theodor W. Adorno makes a point in his *Soziologische Schriften II* (Suhrkamp, 1975), 258–60, of discussing the *Rachesucht* (lust for revenge) attributed to DPs and Jews by Germans after their defeat (*Zusammenbruch*).

[72]Ilya Ehrenburg, in his memoir *The War: 1914–1945*, vol. 5 of *Men, Years—Life*, trans. Tatiana Shebunina in collaboration with Yvonne Kapp (Cleveland, 1964), 32, explicitly denied longstanding accusations that he, a Soviet Jew in the Red Army, had been "urging the Asiatic peoples to drink the blood of German women. Ilya Ehrenburg insists that Asiatics should enjoy our women. 'Take the flaxen-haired women, they are your prey.'" Ehrenburg insisted, however, that despite "isolated cases of excesses committed in East Prussian towns that had aroused our general indignation . . . the Soviet soldier will not molest a German woman. . . . It is not for booty, not for loot, not for women that he has come to Germany" (175).

[73]See, for example, the accounts by women survivors in Gurewitsch, ed. On the rape of German women by Red Army soldiers, see Atina Grossmann, "A Question of Silence: The Rape of German Women by Occupation Soldiers," in Robert G. Moeller, ed., *West Germany under Construction: Politics, Society and Culture in the Adenauer Era* (Ann Arbor, 1997), 33–52; and Norman Naimark, *The Russians in Germany: A History of the Soviet Zone of Occupation, 1945–1949* (Cambridge, Mass., 1995), 69–140.

later editions.[74] Hanoch Bartov's autobiographical novel contains a riveting description of his Palestine Brigade unit's efforts to contain and come to terms with the rapacious actions of some of their comrades while also insisting on understanding and protecting the violators. The protagonist recognizes that even the "unwritten law of the Red Army," granting a twenty-four-hour free zone for acts of vengeance, could not "help my sick heart. I could not shed innocent blood, I would never know peace."[75] The American Jewish journalist Meyer Levin included in his account of his journeys across devastated liberated Europe a tormented analysis of his own fantasies about raping "blond German" women and how they wilted in the face of the women's abject surrender. He and a buddy steered their U.S. Army jeep, imagining their revenge: "The only thing to do was to throw them down, tear them apart" on "a wooded stretch of road" with "little traffic, and a lone girl on foot or on a bicycle." But when they finally encountered the perfect victim, alone on a bike, "young, good looking and sullen . . . her presence was a definitive challenge," they finally realized that while her fear was "exciting," "it wasn't in us."[76] There was little sympathy to be found among survivors for the women victimized by the Red Army but also little appetite for joining in. Larry Orbach, a young Jewish survivor, recalled with bitter satisfaction his trip home to Berlin from Auschwitz and Buchenwald after a three-week quarantine for typhus:

> I wore the dark blue Eisenhower jacket the Americans had given me on which I had sewn my number, B.9761, and my yellow prison triangle on the lapel pocket so that any Nazis I might meet could appreciate the dramatic reversal in our relationship. The other travelers tried to avert their eyes from me, but they could not. Beyond the trauma, they were now compelled to confront the living reminder of the monstrous horror they had so long ignored, or from which they had at least managed to blind themselves. . . . As the train chugged on under the night sky, a drunken Russian soldier raped a young German girl in full view of everyone. No one raised a hand to help her; there was no sound but her screams. So much for the Master Race, who, in Auschwitz, I had watched slam the head of a Jewish baby into the wall of a shower room. The baby had died instantly, his brain protruding and his blood spurting; they had laughed, full of triumph and swagger. Now they were too meek even to protect one of their own children. Nor did I intervene; these were people who had set me apart, told me I could not be one of them.[77]

[74]See Naomi Seidman's careful study of Wiesel and the various versions of *Night* in "Elie Wiesel and the Scandal of Jewish Rage," *Jewish Social Studies* 3, no. 1 (fall 1996): 1–19, esp. 6.
[75]Bartov, 117, 245; see also 46–47, 224–29.
[76]Levin, 278–80.
[77]Larry Orbach and Vivien Orbach-Smith, *Soaring Underground: A Young Fugitive's Life in Nazi Berlin* (Washington, D.C., 1996), 330–31.

Revenge took other forms. One of the most striking features of the DPs' presence was the calculated appropriation of former Nazi "shrines" and German terrain for their own symbolic purposes. Representatives from the first DP conference at St. Ottilien in July 1945 chose to announce their demand for open emigration to Palestine in the Munich Brau Keller, from which Adolf Hitler had once launched his 1923 attempted putsch. When the Central Committee of Liberated Jews of Bavaria moved into a "bombed out floor" of the Deutsches Museum in Munich, Abraham Hyman of the U.S. Theater Judge Advocates Office pointed out with a certain amount of glee that "Hitler once prophesied that the time would come when a person would have to go to a museum to find a Jew." In January 1946 the Congress of the Central Committee of Liberated Jews met in the Munich City Hall, center of the former *Hauptstadt der Bewegung* (capital of the Nazi movement), festooned for the occasion with a banner that read, "So long as a Jewish heart beats in the world, it beats for the Land of Israel." The Council of the Central Committee convened its September 12, 1946, meeting in Berchtesgarten, right near Hitler's Eagle's Nest redoubt, already richly adorned with the autographs of many GIs and survivors. Examples of such resignifying abound; perhaps the most famous was the Streicherhof, a socialist Zionist kibbutz on the former estate of the notorious Bavarian *Gauleiter* (Nazi regional leader). It "became a prime attraction for journalists and others," where "all the visitors were treated to the experience of seeing the dogs on the farm respond to Hebrew names that the trainees had taught them, as their salute to Streicher."[78]

Historians who have recognized such public actions as "symbolic revenge" have generally not problematized the "baby boom" in those terms, situating it, rather, as a "personal" response on an individual or familial level, naturally linked to the effort to restore a sort of normality to traumatized disrupted lives.[79] I would suggest however, that Jews—very clearly in the published record and in political representations —perceived pregnancy and maternity as another form of this resignifying, indeed, of a certain kind of revenge, marking that they were more than just "victims" and precisely did not dwell obsessively on the traumatic past. DP culture did place a premium on collecting personal histories, on bearing witness for the future. Almost immediately after liberation, the first memorials were raised, and a day of remembrance was proposed; the latter was set for the anniversary of liberation as a deliberate representation of the inescapable link between mourning the catastrophe and hope for renewal.

[78]Hyman, 35, 393.
[79]For example, Ze'ev Mankowitz, author of *Between Memory and Hope: Survivors of the Holocaust in Occupied Germany 1945–46* (forthcoming in English). Personal conversation, Jerusalem, Israel, January 2001.

The DPs quickly set up their own Central Historical Commission, head-quartered in Munich, and charged it with collecting eyewitness accounts of persecution as well as any cultural artifacts such as art and songs that could be recuperated from camp and partisan life. In fact, the very first DP Congress in St. Ottilien, Bavaria, in July 1945 had called on survivors to collect the names of all the exterminated. At the same time, with the help of the legendary rogue U.S. Army chaplain Abraham Klausner, lists of survivors were quickly published. By summer 1945 five volumes with over 25,000 names had already been published; in December the army printed the sixth volume of this *She'erit Hapleitah*. Theater, music, cabaret, and press in the refugee camps directly addressed the horrors of the war years, so much so that Jewish relief workers were both shocked by the matter-of-fact treatment of extreme horror in DP culture and irritated by what they deemed obsessive remembering. The DP orchestra in the U.S. zone per-formed its premiere in striped pajamas with a piece of "barbed wire fence" marking the stage.[80] Koppel S. Pinson, the educational director of the Joint Distribution Committee in Germany, complained: "The DP is pre-occupied almost to a point of morbidity with his past. His historical inter-est has become enormously heightened and intensified. He is always ready to account in minutest detail the events of his past or the past of his rela-tives."[81] But in its preoccupation with the mundane everydayness of camp life and political association, with all its customary factionalism and bick-ering, daily life in the DP camps also fostered a kind of productive forget-ting. Especially the young Zionist survivors were too consumed with planning their future to spend time recording a painful past. As Israel Kaplan, the Riga historian who headed the Commission, noted with some chagrin, "In such a period of instability and living out of suitcases, and given the background of dramatic events, it is possible to make history, but not to write history."[82] In another example of the paradoxical expecta-tions and images attached to Jewish survivors, they were simultaneously berated for remembering too much and not enough.

[80]Hyman, 252. Hyman offers marvelous examples of Jewish occupation of German space and is especially eloquent about interpreting memorialization as a "step into the land of the living."

[81]Koppel S. Pinson, "Jewish Life in Liberated Germany," *Jewish Social Studies* 9, no. 2 (January 1947): 108, cited in Yantian, 29. Similarly, the British were highly irritated by the insistence of Jewish DPs in their zone on still calling their DP camp in Hohne, near Bergen Belsen concentration camp, Bergen Belsen—a conscious maneuver by their leader, Josef Rosensaft. See Hyman, 78.

[82]For a fine analysis of the debates about remembering, see Yantian, 27–42. Interest-ingly, the DP proposed Day of Remembrance, on the date of liberation, the 14th day of the Hebrew month of Ijar, was never accepted either in the Diaspora or in Palestine. The state of Israel declared Yom HaShoah for the 27th Nissan because it fell right between the re-membrance of the Warsaw Ghetto uprising and the establishment of the state of Israel, thus safely bracketing Holocaust remembrance between two markers of resistance and rebirth.

Let me interject at this point that, along with noticing how our perceptions of survivors have radically changed, it is also useful to note how much our current obsession with memorializing is a product of our own late-twentieth-century and turn-of-the-millennium preoccupations. It is perhaps our own panic about the loss of individual and collective memory that shapes our conviction that memory is crucial for recovery and reconstruction.[83] Directly after the war, both for survivors and those who worked with them (albeit in different ways), remembering was not necessarily considered the optimal way to deal with trauma. Indeed, one of the most powerful forces driving the quick marriages among survivors was surely the need to be with someone who required no explanation or rehearsal of the traumatic recent past, who recognized the many references that were invoked, and who understood, at least on some level, the lack of words or the inadequate words that were available.

At the same time, it is clear that the conventional impression of "silence," of the inability to speak, that constitutes the very essence of trauma, as formulated by current psychoanalytic and literary theory, has to be relativized. Memorialization and commemoration commenced, as we have seen, virtually immediately. Survivors, buffeted between their assigned roles as fonts of moral authority, bearers of new life, and asocial self-pitying wrecks, were keenly aware of their role as guardians of memory and eyewitnesses to the indescribable as well as their obligation, often repeated, to "find revenge in existence." In a sermon on September 17, 1945, the first Yom Kippur after liberation, DP leader Samuel Gringauz exhorted the young, "the carriers of our revenge": "You must show the world that we live. You must create and build, dance and sing, be happy and live, live and work."[84]

The most powerful metaphor for "life reborn" was the dream of a new Jewish state, physically and emotionally cut off from the traumatic history of European Jewry. In the powerful DP film *Lang ist der Weg*, filmed in the camps in 1946, the young heroine tries to tell her handsome partisan veteran lover about how damaged she is; he cuts her off, telling her that he doesn't want to know, she must not remember. He pledges to spirit her away to Eretz Yisrael because she will not be able to forget as long as she remains on bloodied and cursed German soil. In the final scene of the

[83]The literature on trauma and memory is, by now, enormous. Among many examples, see LaCapra; Cathy Caruth, ed., *Trauma: Explorations in Memory* (Baltimore, 1995). On the relationship between our memory panic and memory boom, see Andreas Huyssen, *Twilight Memories: Marking Time in a Culture of Amnesia* (New York, 1995); on the "fetishizing" of memory, see Marita Sturken, "The Remembering of Forgetting," *Social Text* 16, no. 4 (winter 1998): 102–25; for a critique of our fascination with (and confusion of) individual and collective trauma, see Pamela Ballinger, "The Culture of Survivors: Post-Traumatic Stress Disorder and Traumatic Memory," *History and Memory* 10, no. 1 (spring 1988): 99–131.

[84]Dr. Samuel Gringauz in his Yom Kippur sermon at Landsberg DP camp on September 17, 1945. Cited in Hyman, 16–17.

film, the young couple have resolved the problem: while they have not yet
reached Palestine, they are lounging on the grass of a kibbutz (*Hachschara*,
agricultural settlement) in Bavaria, preparing for their *Aliyah* and playing
with a newborn child—the most eloquent statement of survival and the
ability to start anew.[85]

Bearing children worked to mediate the continuous tension between remembering and forgetting. Babies, in their names and in their features, bore
the traces of the past, of those who were dead and lost. Indeed, in some
significant ways, the bearing of new life was not only a signal of survival and
hope but also an acknowledgment of the losses that had gone before. Jewish
DPs were continually accused of manically "acting out" rather than "working through" their mourning. Since the Jewish religion (in Ashkenazi practice) prohibits naming children after the living, survivors did, in their
naming practices, recognize the death of loved ones, whom they had, for the
most part, not been able to bury or even to confirm as dead. Certainly,
however, imaginatively and in their ever-present demandingness, children
also represented futurity. As the first issue of the DP newsletter *Unzre
Hoffnung* stated, employing the language of health and hygiene that remained dominant after the war: "We must turn to today and prepare a better
tomorrow, a beautiful and a healthy tomorrow."[86]

Jewish women survivors, living in a kind of extraterritoriality on both
German and Allied soil, were prefiguring on their pregnant bodies a kind of
imaginary nation which they hoped—at least that was the public message—
to realize in Palestine/Eretz Yisrael. Their babies had "red hot" political
valence not only for the Allies but also for the Zionists, who dominated
political and cultural life in the DP camps. The DP press and political actions demanding open emigration from Germany to Palestine invariably
foregrounded images of babies and baby carriages.[87] The DP camp newslet-
ters drove their message home with pages of marriage and birth announcements, always juxtaposed to ads searching for lost relatives or details on
their death, business and death announcements, and immigration notices.

---

[85] *Lang ist der Weg*, German/Polish coproduction, 1947. Available from the National
Jewish Film Center, Brandeis University. For a critical analysis, see Cilly Kugelmann, "Lang
ist der Weg: Eine jüdische-deutsche Film-Kooperation," *Fritz Bauer Institut Jahrbuch 1996*,
353–70.

[86] Dieter E. Kesper, *Unsere Hoffnung: Die Zeitung Überlebender des Holocaust im Eschweger
Lager 1946* (Eschwege, 1996). The newspaper of the UNRRA camp in Eschwege, no. 1,
June 4, 1946, discovered in Heimatarchiv. The published German text is a translation of
the original Yiddish.

[87] Maj. John J. Maginnis referred to the DP influx in Berlin as a "red hot" political crisis
in his *Military Government Journal: Normandy to Berlin* (Amherst, 1971), 326. For the
ubiquitous babies and baby carriages, see, for example, the extraordinary photo collection
in *Ein Leben aufs Neu: Das Robinson Album. DP- Lager: Juden auf deutschen Boden 1945–
1948* (Vienna, 1995). See also the photographs in the 2001 calendar of the United States
Holocaust Memorial Museum, culled from the recent exhibition *Life Reborn: Jewish Displaced Persons 1945–1951*.

In sharp contrast to women's often prominent (and heroized) roles in the anti-Nazi resistance, women did not fill important public positions in the DP camps and were not part of the DP leadership. Indeed, when David Ben Gurion attended the first Congress of Jewish DPs, convened at the Munich Rathaus in January 1946, he asked with some bewilderment and genuine "censure" why there were no women delegates. Contrasting this glaring absence with the resistance heroines celebrated in Palestine, he demanded (according to at least one observer): "Don't the women . . . who endured so much and showed so much courage have anything to say here? In Palestine I met women who fought in the ghettos. They are our greatest pride. Isn't it sad enough that you lack children? Must you in addition artificially eliminate the women and create a population of men only?"[88] Ben Gurion's early admonition about the lack of children contained, of course, at least part of the answer to his own question about women's apparent nonparticipation in the active and often rancorous political life of the DP camps; very soon most women survivors would be preoccupied with the bearing and raising of new families.[89] That activity in turn was desperately overdetermined because it occurred in the aftermath of a Nazi Final Solution that had specifically targeted pregnant women and those with young children for immediate and automatic extermination. Problematizing and not merely noting the privileged place of motherhood in DP women's lives, on the one hand, and in DP politics in general, on the other, is all the more crucial, because for Jewish women during the Holocaust, motherhood was, in Judith Baumel's words, literally "lethal."[90] Afterward, so many felt—as so many memoirs attest—"an eagerness to get our lives under way, . . . to create new families and bring Jewish children into the world."[91]

CONCLUSION

For the Jewish DPs, then, the personal and the political aspects of survival were linked: in the birthing of babies and the social glue of fervent Zionism. Current critical, especially Israeli, historiography has decried the cynical instrumentalization of Jewish survivors (the "seventh million," in Segev's terms) by the Yishuv, the contempt that Zionist leaders felt, more or less openly, for the many traumatized survivors, the manipulation of media and officials to create the impression that every Jew was desperate to go to

---

[88]Quoted by Leo W. Schwarz in *The Redeemers: A Saga of the Years 1945–1952* (New York, 1953), 87.

[89]On the image of women in the Resistance and their valorization in Palestine and early Israeli society as well as their simultaneously central and marginal roles in the DP camps, see Baumel's essays in *Double Jeopardy*. Baumel writes of a "biological deterrent towards female organizational activism" (24). On women in the DP camps, and especially the drudgery of makeshift housework in the camps, see Myers and Myers Feinstein.

[90]Baumel, *Double Jeopardy*, ix.

[91]Berger, quoting his mother, 306.

Palestine, and the harsh determination with which the "reservoir" of "human material" in the DP camps was recruited by Zionists to populate the land and man its military.[92] Still, it seems to me that the dream and the passionate commitment were genuine and intense. Especially young people who had lost their entire families (the majority, except for families who had survived in Soviet Central Asia) found self-affirmation and community in the Zionist peer culture and, perhaps, the utopian vision that sustained survival.[93] As one impressed American-Jewish Zionist GI noted admiringly about the young survivors he encountered at Kibbutz Buchenwald, "the recuperative powers of the average human being, physical and mental, are remarkable, provided only that there is something to recuperate for."[94]

And so, to continue the theme of paradoxical perceptions: the same observers who were horrified by the depressing culture of a remnant community-in-waiting and angered by its "villains," the idle and the criminal, the "bedraggled" and "abject," caught in "a continuation of the war—not the destructive war of mortars, but the despairing war of morale"—were also deeply impressed by its dynamism and stubborn survival. As Ira Hirschmann, La Guardia's personal representative to UNRRA, reported, DPs' dignity was continually assaulted by the "insufficient tasteless food, . . . broken-sized shoes and clothing, their self-respect crushed, with no prospect of a normal life ahead of them." Wondering that they did not "tear them limb from limb," he was both impressed and aghast at the "incredible self-restraint" Jews observed toward German POWs in a nearby camp and the surrounding placid German farmers who were better treated by the American victors. Clearly, revenge is an important theme to follow, and it took multiple forms. But despite some dramatic stories, actual plans and actions of violence were few. The evidence is quite contradictory: on the one hand, many Jews did not even want to engage with Germans enough to violate them; on the other hand, Military Government officials groused that "they love getting into fights with Germans."[95] Revenge operated on complicated (surely also gendered) levels in everyday interactions with Germans and, most importantly, internally. It meant proving that there was a future, expressed both in terms of Zionism and the establishment of a Jewish state where Jews would no longer be a vulnerable minority and in the birth of babies and the formation of new families. Indeed, "revenge" may very well be an insufficiently pliant term to convey Jewish DPs' excruciatingly complicated mix

[92]See, for example, Segev; Zertal; Grodzinsky.

[93]It is important to keep in mind that many of the Zionist groups in the DP camps had arrived together via the Bricha and traced their origins back to the ghettos, partisan groups, and camps. In fact, much of the early DP leadership in Bavaria came from the same workcamp, Dachau Kauffering, which had received many Jews as they arrived on death marches from the East.

[94]Kieve Skiddel, unpublished letter, Ober Peissen, June 21, 1945.

[95]Mintzer, 301.

of overwhelming loss, satisfaction at surviving against all odds, urgent desire to reclaim "normality," and finally determination to demonstrate—to
Germans, Allies, and other Jews—that "we are here." Angered at the denial
of free immigration to Palestine and the United States, Hirschmann suggested that the Jewish DPs should properly be called not DPs but BPs,
"Betrayed Persons." Nonetheless, he insisted, "These people who had
cheated the death chambers had emerged physically scarred and beaten,
but spiritually triumphant."[96] Today, we might argue differently, understanding the baby boom and DP culture as expressions of a parallel life, a
living on when one had, in a sense, as the philosopher Susan Brison has put
it, outlived oneself; surviving in a life that did not replace or displace the
horrors that had been experienced but existed alongside and with it in a
highly vibrant form.[97]

   DP experience suggests important questions about the intersection of the
personal and the political and definitions of mourning, trauma, and revenge.
It poses questions about the place of sexuality, pregnancy, childbirth, and
motherhood in defining survival and victimization as well as furnishing possible reconstructions of ethnic or national identity in the wake of Nazism
and World War II (or other violent trauma, either individual or collective).
Precisely because, as legal scholar Fionnuala Ni Aolain has pointed out, during the Holocaust, "established conventions of motherhood are deliberately
ravaged and assaulted," the emphasis in DP culture and politics on "life
reborn" raises issues about how to recognize the centrality of maternity
without reproducing in our analysis conventional gender assignments.[98] We
are confronted with the "stubborn question" of how, as Denise Riley has
memorably put it, to "assert a category without becoming trapped within
it."[99] The baby boom in particular challenges us to conceptualize historically
the entangled levels of individual and personal, familial and cultural, and
collective and national experience and representation of the body, gender,
and sexuality. It points finally to the simultaneous human "normality" of the
survivors—even as they were categorized by others as victims, villains, or
survivors—and to the tragic mystery that still shadows and blocks our understanding of what they endured and how they continued to live.

[96]Hirschmann, 72, 75, 81, 101.
[97]See Susan Brison, "Outliving Oneself: Trauma, Memory, and Personal Identity," in
Feminists Rethink the Self, ed. Diana T. Meyers (Boulder, 1997), 12–39.
[98]Ni Aolain, 52. The article takes this question very seriously from the point of view of
feminist and legal theory. On "the fantasy of maternal love" as a force in feminist theory
and women's activism, see, most recently, Joan W. Scott, "Fantasy Echo: History and the
Construction of Identity," *Critical Inquiry* (winter 2001): 284–304, esp. 303–4.
[99]Denise Riley, "Some Peculiarities of Social Policy concerning Women in Wartime and
Postwar Britain," in *Behind the Lines: Gender and the Two World Wars,* ed. Margaret Higonnet
et al. (New Haven, 1987), 269. See also her *Am I That Name? Feminism and the Category
of Women in History* (Minneapolis, 1989).

The Pink Triangle and Political Consciousness: Gays, Lesbians, and the Memory of Nazi Persecution

ERIK N. JENSEN

University of Wisconsin—Madison

Wʜᴇɴ, ɪɴ ᴛʜᴇ ᴡɪɴᴛᴇʀ ᴏғ 1993, the gay magazine *10 Percent* criticized the use of the pink triangle as an emblem of gay identity, it touched a nerve.[1] "As a symbol of shared victimization, it is indefensible," wrote Sara Hart, a senior editor of the magazine. "To equate the discrimination and harassment of the present with the savagery inflicted upon the lesbians and gay men of the Holocaust trivializes their suffering."[2] Readers disagreed, however, and the letters in the following two issues underscored the relevance of the pink triangle to the gay and lesbian community. One reader stated, "You editorialize about how the wearing of this symbol 'trivializes' the suffering of concentration camp victims. . . . Are the deaths of tens of thousands of people (as a result of the Reagan administration's inaction on AIDS) trivial?"[3] Another argued that the pink triangle raised the political consciousness of gays and lesbians and "compels us to take action against homophobic trends, such as current attempts to pass antigay initiatives throughout the country."[4] A third reader, even though she deplored the

---

[1]Here, I use "gay" to designate both gay and lesbian, as I do throughout this essay for stylistic reasons. When I refer to gay men only, I state so specifically. When I refer primarily, but not exclusively, to gay men, it should be clear from the context.

I extend my heartfelt thanks to the following people for taking the time to read drafts of this essay, for answering my questions, and for offering their comments, criticisms, and support: Jim Steakley, Dagmar Herzog, Rudy Koshar, Suzanne Desan, David Ciarlo, Ralf Dose, Claudia Schoppmann, Gayle Rubin, Lisa Heineman, Jeffrey Merrick, Hans-Georg Stümke, Rick Landman, Catherine Odette, the two anonymous readers for the *Journal of the History of Sexuality*, and David J. Zelman, who allowed me to screen his underground film *Nazi Barbie*, in which Barbie pins a pink triangle on a Ken doll.

[2]Sara Hart, "A Dark Past Brought to Light," *10 Percent* (winter 1993): 74.

[3]Michael Lehman, *10 Percent* (January–February 1994): 8.

[4]Sharon Matthies, *10 Percent* (March–April 1994): 6.

319

commercialization of the pink triangle, still supported its display "on somber occasions, such as in remembrance of victims of queer-bashings."[5]

Each of these reactions illustrates the continued resonance of the pink triangle, the insignia that identified homosexual inmates in the Nazi concentration camps. The readers attributed their political consciousness as gay men and women, at least in part, to a particular collective memory of the Nazi persecution of homosexuals. This historical memory, refracted in the symbol of the pink triangle, has mobilized vigilance against contemporary oppression, from queer bashings to antigay initiatives. The letters also show that gays and lesbians perceived this oppression as part of a long historical pattern that extended from the Nazi era to the present. Sara Hart concluded her article with the admonition, "Before we can wear the button or carry the banner that reads 'Never Again,' we must first remember."[6] The letters to the magazine indicate, though, that the gay and lesbian community already has remembered the Nazi persecution of homosexuals, albeit in very particular political, social, and national contexts and quite often independently of historical research on the subject.

In the following essay I shall trace the evolution over the past thirty years of collective memories in both the American and German gay communities in order to show what these communities have remembered and why.[7] I acknowledge from the outset the problems associated with speaking of a single gay and lesbian community, even within a national border; and I recognize that a single gay memory of Nazi persecution does not exist. In fact, this essay shows how cleavages in the communities have fostered alternate memories and how the American and German memories reflect different national experiences. Furthermore, many gays and lesbians remain altogether unaware of the historical significance of the pink triangle. Nevertheless, a larger memory has emerged that, despite differences, does contain shared symbols, narratives, and referents and has significantly influenced the consciousness of the broader gay and lesbian community.[8]

[5]Miriam Imblum, *10 Percent* (January–February 1994): 8.

[6]Hart, 74.

[7]A huge body of scholarship on the concept of collective memory now exists. For one of the seminal texts, see Maurice Halbwachs, *On Collective Memory*, ed. and trans. Lewis Coser (Chicago, 1992). For a useful and concise introduction to the distinction between history and memory, see Pierre Nora, "Between Memory and History: *Les Lieux de Mémoire*," in *Representations* 26 (spring 1989): 7–25. See also John R. Gillis, "Memory and Identity: The History of a Relationship," in *Commemorations: The Politics of National Identity*, ed. John R. Gillis (Princeton, 1994), 3–24.

[8]Steven Epstein has noted the relative homogeneity of the mainstream gay and lesbian movement in the United States (primarily white and middle class), which contrasts with the diverse gay and lesbian population that it purports to represent. See Steven Epstein, "Gay and Lesbian Movements in the United States: Dilemmas of Identity, Diversity, and Political Strategy," in *The Global Emergence of Gay and Lesbian Politics: National Imprints of a Worldwide Movement*, ed. Barry D. Adam, Jan Willem Duyvendak, and André Krouwel (Philadelphia, 1999), 43.

Collective memory, which Iwona Irwin-Zarecka has defined as "a set of ideas, images, feelings about the past," often eludes attempts to locate its sites and delineate its contours. Irwin-Zarecka has argued that one should look for it "not in the minds of individuals, but in the resources they share."[9] For the memory of the Nazi persecution of gays the shared resources include the gay press, which has discussed issues important to gay identity and gay rights over the last three decades; literary works and films; protest demonstrations and memorial actions conducted by gay and lesbian organizations; and, finally, the appropriation of the pink triangle.

A shared memory of the Nazi persecution of homosexuals emerged in the 1970s in the politicized context of gay liberation. It first appeared several decades after the defeat of the Nazi regime, rather than immediately thereafter, for a number of reasons. First of all, immediately after the war, neither an unrestricted gay and lesbian press nor a large, organized gay and lesbian community that might memorialize its persecution existed in either West Germany or the United States. The homophile groups that did exist were too small and too hidden from the public to foster a collective memory.[10] Not until the late 1960s, in the wake of civil rights protests, antiwar demonstrations, and the second wave of feminism, did gays and lesbians begin to organize on a broad basis and push for radical changes in their legal and social status.

A second reason is the absence of testimony, of personal memories, from the victims themselves. Almost all of the survivors lived in either East or West Germany or in Austria; and in all three countries the penal codes continued to criminalize homosexual acts after the war, and police regularly harassed and arrested gay men throughout the 1950s and 1960s. Because the legal and social stigma attached to homosexuality remained, homosexual survivors were understandably wary of telling their stories of persecution, let alone demanding public acknowledgment. The mayor of the village of Dachau, Hans Zauner, typified the hostile climate that these survivors faced when he, with apparent disgust, told an interviewer in 1960: "You must remember that many criminals and homosexuals were in Dachau. Do you want a memorial for such people?"[11]

A third reason for the relatively late emergence of the collective memory, as Burkhardt Riechers points out, is that many gay men and women in immediate postwar Germany wished to forget the Nazi period altogether.

[9]Iwona Irwin-Zarecka, *Frames of Remembrance: The Dynamics of Collective Memory* (New Brunswick, 1994), 4.

[10]Burkhardt Riechers, for example, has argued that homosexuals in West Germany in the 1950s formed at best "a fictional community" ("Freundschaft und Anständigkeit: Leitbilder im Selbstverständnis männlicher Homosexueller in der frühen Bundesrepublik," *Invertito—Jahrbuch für die Geschichte der Homosexualitäten* 1 [1999]: 44).

[11]Hans Zauner, interview by Llew Gardner, *Sunday Express*, 1960, quoted in Albert Knoll, "Totgeschlagen—totgeschwiegen: Die homosexuellen Häftlinge im KZ Dachau," *Dachauer Hefte* 14 (November 1998): 101.

After struggling through the lean years of the 1940s, most gay men and women sought sanctuary in the economic boom of the 1950s; along with other West Germans, they avoided reminders of a painful past during which some had sympathized with the regime, even as others had faced persecution.[12] Elmar Drost, a West German gay activist, recalled only one time prior to the 1970s when an older acquaintance of his referred obliquely to the Nazi persecution; otherwise, as Drost flatly stated, "I never heard of it."[13] Not until the student protest movements of the late 1960s, which also helped to usher in West Germany's gay liberation, did that society begin to examine its Nazi past in earnest and did gays begin to focus, in particular, on the fate of homosexuals under National Socialism.

This focus on the Nazi past formed part of a larger search for the existence of homosexuals throughout history and an examination of the ways in which societies treated them. Gay activists sought to reclaim the "erased histories and historical invisibility" that Wendy Brown has described as "integral elements of the pain inscribed in most subjugated identities."[14] Drost, for example, remembered the 1950s and 1960s as "dark years, years without history," because the absence of a known past had denied homosexual men and women knowledge of earlier emancipation movements and strategies.[15] Beginning in the 1970s, gays and lesbians in both West Germany and the United States established archives, research projects, and oral history collections. The titles of many of the resulting books, such as *Becoming Visible* and *Hidden from History*, suggest the sense of both liberation and permanence that came from having a past.[16] In addition, this newfound history provided historic analogies to contemporary injustices as well as examples of past strategies for homosexual emancipation. It also helped to unite a potentially disparate gay and lesbian community around a shared history and to galvanize this nascent community into political action.

Gays and lesbians not only met silence in the postwar period regarding the Nazi persecution of homosexuals, but they also faced the pernicious myth that homosexuals themselves had formed the backbone of the Nazi movement. As early as the 1930s, Socialists and Communists had linked

[12]Riechers, 42.

[13]Elmar Drost, "Mit dem Schwanz gedacht: Meine Geschichte fängt da an, wo schwule Geschichte aufgehört hat," in *Schwule Regungen—Schwule Bewegungen*, ed. Willi Frieling (Berlin, 1985), 13.

[14]Wendy Brown, "Wounded Attachments: Late Modern Oppositional Political Formations," in *The Identity in Question*, ed. John Rajchman (New York, 1995), 220.

[15]See Drost, 10.

[16]Kevin Jennings, ed., *Becoming Visible: A Reader in Gay and Lesbian History for High School and College Students* (Boston, 1994); Martin Duberman, Martha Vicinus, and George Chauncey Jr., eds., *Hidden from History: Reclaiming the Gay and Lesbian Past* (New York, 1989). Not coincidentally, the titles of gay and lesbian histories have occasionally mirrored those of earlier histories of women. See, for example, Renate Bridenthal and Claudia Koonz, eds., *Becoming Visible: Women in European History* (Boston, 1977).

homosexuality to fascism in order to exploit this purported linkage for political gain.[17] After the war, Samuel Igra seized upon this trope by explicitly connecting homosexuality to the atrocities committed by the Germans during the Second World War, and William Shirer reinforced it by highlighting a handful of gay Nazis in his best-selling book, *The Rise and Fall of the Third Reich*.[18] Although serious scholarship on Nazism has long since dispelled this myth, it persists to this day.[19] Gays and lesbians adopted the pink triangle in the 1970s in part, as the historian Jonathan Ned Katz has noted, to refute "the vicious, influential myth created by antifascists that Nazis were themselves, in some basic way, homosexual."[20]

A very few individuals had written in the immediate postwar period about the Nazi persecution of homosexuals, but their work had little impact on the consciousness of homosexuals or of the wider public.[21] In 1946 the pioneering East German homosexual-rights advocate Rudolf Klimmer petitioned the Organization of Those Persecuted by the Nazi Regime (Vereinigung der Verfolgten des Naziregimes) to recognize homosexual victims, and he later sought compensation for these victims from the East German government.

---

[17]For a contemporary's criticism of this tendency, see Klaus Mann, *Homosexualität und Faschismus* (1934; reprint, Kiel, 1990). For a more recent analysis of this phenomenon, see Harry Oosterhuis, "The 'Jews' of the Antifascist Left: Homosexuality and Socialist Resistance to Nazism," in *Gay Men and the Sexual History of the Political Left*, ed. Gert Hekma, Harry Oosterhuis, and James Steakley (New York, 1995), 227–57.

[18]Samuel Igra, *Germany's National Vice* (London, 1945); William Shirer, *The Rise and Fall of the Third Reich* (New York, 1960). Similarly, a series of Italian films, including Luchino Visconti's *The Damned* (1969), Bernardo Bertolucci's *The Conformist* (1971), and Pier Paolo Pasolini's *Salo, or the 120 Days of Sodom* (1975), portrayed National Socialism as rooted in same-sex attraction.

[19]On November 24, 1987, for instance, the Left-oriented German newspaper, *die tageszeitung*, published an article that attributed much of the Nazi movement's early formation to the "dynamic of male-bonding homosexuality." Quoted in Hans-Georg Stümke, *Homosexuelle in Deutschland: Eine politische Geschichte* (Munich, 1989), 100. On the political Right, the 1995 book, *The Pink Swastika*, made a concerted effort to resurrect this myth in the aftermath of an Oregon measure to repeal gay rights. See Scott Lively and Kevin Abrams, *The Pink Swastika: Homosexuality in the Nazi Party* (Keizer, 1995). Some postwar academics have also interpreted the writings of Theodor Adorno as suggesting a connection between totalitarianism and homosexuality. See Randall Halle, "Between Marxism and Psychoanalysis: Antifascism and Antihomosexuality in the Frankfurt School," in Hekma, Oosterhuis, and Steakley, eds., 295–317. On this point, see also Andrew Hewitt, *Political Inversions: Homosexuality, Fascism, and the Modernist Imaginary* (Stanford, 1996).

[20]Jonathan Ned Katz, "Signs of the Times: The Making of Liberation Logos," *Advocate*, October 10, 1989, 49.

[21]L. D. Classen von Neudegg, for example, published a serialized account in the West German homophile journal *Humanitas* in the mid-1950s. See "Schicksale," *Humanitas* (February 1954, March 1954, May 1954, July 1954, December 1954, February 1955). Another homophile journal, *die runde*, published an account of a concentration camp survivor in the fall of 1958. See Karl-Heinz Steinle, *Die Geschichte der Kameradschaft die runde 1950 bis 1969*, Heft 1 der Reihe, Hefte des Schwulen Museums (Berlin, 1998), 12–13. Eugen Kogon discussed the persecution of homosexuals in his 1947 book, *Der SS-Staat* (Stockholm, 1947), translated as *The Theory and Practice of Hell: The German Concentration Camps and the*

Both initiatives failed.[22] Not until the late 1960s did works appear that focused exclusively on the nature and extent of the persecution.[23] In May 1969 the West German news magazine *Der Spiegel* called wide attention to the Nazi persecution of homosexuals as part of its cover story on the reform of Paragraph 175 of the criminal code, a legislative measure that decriminalized homosexual acts for men over the age of twenty-one.[24] With this partial decriminalization, gay magazines began to appear on newsstands, and a few gay student groups were formed, notably, those at Bochum and Münster.

The 1971 release of Rosa von Praunheim's film *Nicht der Homosexuelle ist pervers, sondern die Situation, in der er lebt* (The homosexual isn't perverse but, rather, the situation in which he lives), with its concluding slogan ("Out of the closets, into the streets!"), signaled the complete emergence of a vocal and activist gay liberation movement in West Germany.[25] The film's July premiere in West Berlin inspired a number of men to found the radical gay liberation organization Homosexuelle Aktion Westberlin (HAW) the following month, initiating a larger trend across West Germany. Members of the older generation of homophiles, who had advanced politically moderate demands, now felt overtaken by a new generation of leftist gay activists who had emerged from the radical movements of the late 1960s and sought a complete transformation of society.

System Behind Them, trans. Heinz Norden (New York, 1950). Other texts and documents, including the testimony of Auschwitz commandant Rudolf Höss at his postwar trial, also referred to the persecution of homosexuals.

[22]See Karl-Heinz Steinle, "Homophiles Deutschland—West und Ost," in *Goodbye to Berlin? 100 Jahre Schwulenbewegung*, Eine Ausstellung des Schwulen Museums und der Akademie der Künste (Berlin, 1997), 200. See also Rainer Herrn, *100 Years of the Gay Rights Movement in Germany*, exhibition catalog (New York, 1997), 28–33. In 1953, to give a West German example, the Hamburg homophile organization, Gesellschaft für Menschenrechte, pushed unsuccessfully for the official recognition of homosexual concentration camp inmates (ibid., 33).

[23]Wolfgang Harthauser published an early foray into this field with his article, "Der Massenmord an Homosexuellen im Dritten Reich," in *Das große Tabu: Zeugnisse und Dokumente zum Problem der Homosexualität*, ed. Willhart Schlegel (Munich, 1967), 7–37. Harry Wilde followed this up two years later with his full-length book, *Das Schicksal der Verfemten: Die Verfolgung der Homosexuellen im 'Dritten Reich' und ihre Stellung in der heutigen Gesellschaft* (Tübingen, 1969).

[24]"Paragraph 175: Das Gesetz fällt—Bleibt die Ächtung?" *Der Spiegel*, May 12, 1969, 55–76. The reform also repealed those changes to Paragraph 175 that the Nazi regime had imposed in 1935, changes that enabled the escalated persecution of homosexuals. East Germany had already repealed these changes to Paragraph 175 in the 1950s, but because of its authoritarian government, this did not lead to an open and active homophile movement. See *Die Geschichte des §175: Strafrecht gegen Homosexuelle*, ed. Freunde eines Schwulen Museums, e.V. (Berlin, 1990).

[25]The German phrase "raus aus den Toiletten, rein in die Straßen" literally means "out of the men's rooms, into the streets." In the context of the film, it conveyed the dual message of coming out of the closet and also of leaving behind the furtive cruising areas of the past and becoming both more visible and more politically engaged.

Initially, these activists paid scant attention to the history of Nazi persecution. Not only did very little information exist on the subject, but, as Michael Holy has argued, gay liberationists regarded the older generation as stiflingly conservative, perhaps even cryptofascist, and felt that its history and experiences had little to teach them.[26] This attitude began to change in 1972, when Heinz Heger published *Die Männer mit dem rosa Winkel* (*The Men with the Pink Triangle*), the memoir of a gay concentration camp survivor. This was the first and is still one of very few firsthand accounts of the persecution of homosexuals under the Nazi regime.[27] This individual memory provided the framework for a larger collective memory. The following spring brought another important change, when the West German Parliament reformed Paragraph 175 a second time by lowering the age of consent for homosexuals to eighteen. Holy argues that the ensuing explosion of bars, clubs, and bathhouses prompted many to spurn the gay liberation movement and immerse themselves in the burgeoning subculture: "Essentially, the gay movement had no answer to the question of many gays in the scene: 'What do you want now? We're already free!'"[28]

The HAW responded in the fall of 1973 with its "Feministenpapier," which debated the fundamental question of whether the gay liberation movement should focus on overturning patriarchy or on collaborating with the Socialist revolution. In addition, though, the "Feministenpapier" urged gays for the first time to wear the pink triangle and declared that, by doing so, "everyone would, as a gay man, be recognized, discovered, discriminated against, and oppressed!"[29] Only then would these liberated gays truly realize the homophobia that surrounded them. Andreas, an HAW activist, recalled in 1975 how often he had easily avoided difficult situations by remaining in the closet. He then compared wearing the pink triangle in public to wearing drag, something that would force him to "stand up for myself and not deny who I am."[30]

Holy interprets this as the search for an *Opferidentität* (victim identity), a strategy to raise awareness within the community of oppression,

[26]See Michael Holy, "Der entliehene rosa Winkel," in *Der Frankfurter Engel, Mahnmal Homosexuellenverfolgung: Ein Lesebuch*, ed. Initiative Mahnmal Homosexuellenverfolgung (Frankfurt am Main, 1997), 74–87. Ulf Preuß-Lausitz saw the leftist movement as crucial to his own coming out and to the foundation of a radical gay rights movement, since gays necessarily lived contrary to the "ruling norm" and were thus inherently revolutionary. See "Der Linke und der schwule Mann," *Ästhetik und Kommunikation* 11, nos. 40–41 (September 1980): 30.
[27]Heinz Heger, *Die Männer mit dem Rosa Winkel* (Hamburg, 1972), translated as *The Men with the Pink Triangle*, trans. David Fernbach (Boston, 1980), republished in 1994 with an introduction by Klaus Müller.
[28]Holy, 82.
[29]Quoted in ibid., 83.
[30]Andreas, "Meine persönliche H.A.W. Geschichte," in *Schwule sich emanzipieren lernen*, material for the exhibition *Da will ich hin, da muss ich sein*, ed. Peter Hedenström (West Berlin, 1976), 43.

and even to provoke it, in order to goad that community to political action.[31] Whereas Holy sees victim identity as aimed primarily inward, at the gay community itself, Wendy Brown sees it as a strategy aimed outward. She focuses on how communities have publicized their own victimization in order to gain sympathy and support from those outside it.[32] Holy's emphasis on the internal importance of a victim identity is a useful corrective to Brown's exclusive focus on outward motivations. However, he overlooks the fact that the HAW promoted the pink triangle partly to establish its credibility vis-à-vis other radical, antifascist political movements of the time by presenting gays as fellow victims of Nazi persecution.[33] Holy also downplays the fact that many gay and lesbian activists in West Germany experienced discrimination in their own lives, discrimination that had already prompted them to organize without having to look to the Nazi past. Lesbians, for instance, faced particularly virulent hostility in 1973 and 1974, when the boulevard press maliciously targeted them during a sensational murder trial involving a lesbian couple. Martina Weiland, an early activist, saw the ensuing protest marches and public information campaigns by lesbian activists as key moments in the politicization of the nascent West German lesbian movement.[34]

The pink triangle also symbolized a continuum of legal persecution from the Nazi era to the postreform 1970s, a comparison of the Nazi and postwar governments that Holy rightly portrays as strained. Nevertheless, it reminded activists to be wary of governmental power, and it reaffirmed their determined opposition to the capitalist state. The so-called Radikalenerlass of 1972, which ratified the dismissal of civil servants who had joined radical political organizations, simply confirmed suspicions of the fascist nature of the Bonn government, which already had the power to dismiss openly gay people from the military and civil service. Activists, therefore, turned increasingly to the pink triangle as an historical analogy and a dire warning.

In March 1975 *Emanzipation* and *H.A.W.-Info*, two West German gay magazines, published cover articles on the Nazi persecution of homosexuals. The article in *H.A.W.-Info* encouraged gays to make themselves visible by wearing the pink triangle, which it promoted as a symbol of ongoing as well as past persecution. It declared at its conclusion, "SHOW WHAT HAPPENED TO GAYS UNDER FASCISM! DISCRIMINATION IS

---

[31] Holy, 82. Holy also refers to the pink triangle as an "ersatz stigma" (81).

[32] Brown, 216.

[33] This information on the strategy and politics of HAW comes from James Steakley, an activist in HAW in the early 1970s (personal conversation with the author, July 14, 2001).

[34] See Martina Weiland, "'Und wir nehmen uns unser Recht!' Kurzgefaßte Lesbenbewegungsgeschichte(n) der 70er, 80er, 90er Jahre in West-Berlin, nicht nur für Berlinerinnen," in *Lesbenjahrbuch 1: Rücksichten auf 20 Jahre Lesbenbewegung*, ed. Anke Schäfer and Kathrin Lahusen (Wiesbaden, 1995), 33–35.

STILL GOING ON! WEAR THE PINK TRIANGLE!"[35] Similarly, the 1976 film *Rosa Winkel? Das ist doch schon lange vorbei . . .* (Pink triangle? That was such a long time ago . . .) traced a direct line from the Nazi concentration camps through the repression of the Adenauer era to the situation of gays in West Germany in the 1970s and argued that the same societal prejudices that had allowed the earlier Nazi persecution to take place still existed.[36] Similarly, a 1977 report in *Emanzipation* sought to commemorate homosexual victims of National Socialism and to encourage readers to "reflect on the causes of gay oppression and on the earlier strategies for emancipation that failed."[37]

Though the legislative reforms of 1969 and 1973 granted greater freedom to West German gays, the subsequent incidents of governmental repression triggered concern about a backward slide that might parallel the Nazis' destruction of the German homosexual emancipation movement in the 1930s. During the so-called hot autumn of 1977, the Bonn government's heavy-handed crackdown on terrorism conjured images of a renascent fascist state; fears intensified, for example, when the police stepped up their monitoring of left-wing organizations, including gay and lesbian ones.[38] In describing this situation, one HAW activist hoped that the knowledge of past persecution would jostle gay men out of their complacency: "Most gay people think homosexuality has nothing to do with politics. This is a ridiculous attitude. Paragraph 175, for example, has always been used as an instrument to discipline political opponents. Gay people must be aware of this."[39]

Gay activists sought to heighten community vigilance by underscoring the parallels between the Nazi past and contemporary forms of state repression. In February 1980 the gay journal *Rosa Flieder* announced: "The pink triangle . . . is not only a remembrance of the past extermination of gays. There is oppression of and discrimination against gays even in this day and age. It must be precisely established whether this gay oppression is once again marching in the direction of a general police state."[40] The article raised the specter of a Gestapo-like apparatus emerging from the government's increasing infringements of individual liberties. The very

---

[35]Ina and Funny, "Die Männer mit dem Rosa Winkel," *H.A.W.-Info*, no. 18 (March 1975): 8.

[36]The film was written and directed by Peter Recht, Detlef Stoffel, and Christiane Schmerl. For an analysis of the film, see "Rosa Winkel? Das ist doch schon lange vorbei . . . ," *Emanzipation* (January–February 1977): 11–13.

[37]"Rosa Winkel . . . ," *Emanzipation* (March–April 1977): 25.

[38]Martina Weiland mentioned the "criminalization of the entire Left and with it the women's and lesbian centers, too" (37).

[39]Hans, "In Neo-Nazi Germany," interview by Barry Mehler, *Christopher Street* 3, no. 11 (June 1979): 65.

[40]Announcement for the Antifaschistischer Bundeskongreß (held April 4–6, 1980, in Frankfurt am Main), *Rosa Flieder*, no. 14 (February 1980): 55.

fact that Paragraph 175 still remained on the books, despite the second liberalization in 1973, heightened concern over the exercise of state power. The Nazi regime, after all, had extended the scope of the law, which originally dated to nineteenth-century Prussia, and used it to justify the regime's internment of homosexual men. The campaign in the 1970s and 1980s to repeal the paragraph altogether emphasized this association with National Socialism. On Gay Action Day in 1981, for instance, a Nuremberg gay organization set up a street display that presented the contemporary legal status of West German gays as a direct legacy of the Nazi regime.[41] The discovery that police in various parts of the country had long compiled lists of gay men understandably prompted further comparisons to the Nazi era. A 1982 protest statement in *Rosa Flieder* concluded, "Under fascism, such lists became the basis by which 50,000 homosexuals were murdered in the concentration camps."[42]

The American gay press in the 1970s also fostered a memory of Nazi persecution that served as a locus for gay identity and political mobilization. As early as 1973 the San Francisco journal *Gay Sunshine* reported that homosexuals had died in the Nazi concentration camps, and the author advocated displaying the pink triangle as a sign of remembrance.[43] In February 1974 the *Body Politic*, a gay journal based in Toronto, gave the subject much greater exposure by featuring a full-sized pink triangle on its cover. James Steakley wrote the accompanying article, in which he summarized the most recent West German accounts of the victimization of homosexuals under National Socialism, including that of Heinz Heger.[44] In August of that same year, activists in New York wore the pink triangle during a demonstration against the city's Orthodox Jewish groups, which had opposed a gay rights bill before the city council. As David Thorstad, a protest organizer, recalled, "Picketers wore pink triangle armbands in an effort to demonstrate that homosexual men had been fellow victims with Jews (and others) in the Nazi concentration camps."[45]

In September 1975 Ira Glasser, the executive director of the New York Civil Liberties Union, published an editorial in the *New York Times* on the eve of a city council vote to ban discrimination against homosexuals in employment, housing, and public accommodations. He emphasized the

[41]"Kampagne gegen Paragraph 175," *Rosa Flieder*, no. 24 (January 1982): 32.

[42]"Protesterklärung: An den Innensenator und den Polizeipräsidenten in Berlin," *Rosa Flieder*, no. 26 (May 1982): 41. Regarding the compilation of such lists, see Hans-Georg Stümke and Rudi Finkler, *Rosa Winkel, Rosa Listen: Homosexuelle und 'Gesundes Volksempfinden' von Auschwitz bis heute* (Reinbek bei Hamburg, 1981), 373–74.

[43]This article came from the British gay journal *Come Together* and relied entirely on Kogon's *The Theory and Practice of Hell* for its information ("Gays and Nazi Oppression," *Gay Sunshine*, no. 18 [June–July 1973]: 11).

[44]James Steakley, "Homosexuals and the Third Reich," *Body Politic* (February 1974): 1.

[45]E-mail message posted to AOL Gay and Lesbian Community Forum on March 13, 1996, by David Thorstad, president of the Gay Activists Alliance, 1975–76.

persecution of gays under the Nazi regime and argued that broader awareness of this fact would lead to greater social tolerance: "Many know about
the yellow star, but the pink triangle still lies buried as a virtual historical
secret. As a result, there is tolerance among good people of discrimination
against homosexuals."[46] Glasser then encouraged all readers to wear the
pink triangle as a sign of support for the ordinance, lest gays and lesbians
in New York City suffer a fate similar to those in Nazi Germany. As these
particular examples show, activists in the United States, more so than in
West Germany, tended to direct the memory of Nazi persecution outward
in order to secure the support of the broader society. Whereas a certain
segment of West German gays enjoyed the relative tolerance of the post-
1973 liberalization and may have needed a reminder of past victimhood,
American gays, in general, never doubted the omnipresent hostility of the
society in which they lived.

As the American gay rights movement faced growing signs of conservative backlash in the mid-1970s, it drew ever more direct analogies to Nazi
persecution as a means of galvanizing political support inside the community and outside of it. In February 1977 the gay journal *Christopher Street*
published a feature story on the persecution of gay men in Nazi Germany.
The accompanying cover photo, in which a disembodied arm sheathed in
a Nazi swastika violently grabs the collar of a young man, suggested a
menacing parallel to the back-alley fag bashings in 1970s New York.[47]
During the 1977 campaign to repeal a gay rights ordinance in Dade County,
Florida, gay organizations placed advertisements in the *Miami Herald*
that featured the text of an antihomosexual decree by Heinrich Himmler.[48]
The *Body Politic* reinforced this parallel when it entitled its review of a
book by Anita Bryant, the leader of the repeal campaign, "Taking Another Crack at the Final Solution."[49] On June 26, 1977, two weeks after
Dade County voters repealed the ordinance, marchers in San Francisco's
annual Gay Freedom Day parade carried protest signs with pictures of
both Bryant and Adolf Hitler.[50] As the *San Francisco Sentinel* warned that
same year, "We must all be ever aware that mass murders similar to Nazi
Germany's could occur in this country."[51]

Harvey Milk, an openly gay San Francisco politician, similarly invoked
the memory of Nazi persecution during the 1978 campaign in California
against the Briggs Initiative, which would have prevented gays and lesbians

---

[46]Ira Glasser, "The Yellow Star and the Pink Triangle," *New York Times*, September 10,
1975, 45.

[47]Richard Plant, "The Men with the Pink Triangle," *Christopher Street* 1, no. 8 (February 1977): 4–10.

[48]Reprinted in *Christopher Street* 2, no. 2 (August 1977): 26.

[49]Michael Riordan, "Taking Another Crack at the Final Solution," review of *At Any
Cost* by Anita Bryant, *Body Politic*, no. 53 (June 1979): 30.

[50]For a photograph of the parade, see *Christopher Street* 2, no. 2 (August 1977): 18–19.

[51]*San Francisco Sentinel*, February 24, 1977, 5.

from teaching in the state's public schools. In a speech on Gay Freedom Day that year, Milk declared, "We are not going to sit back in silence as 300,000 of our gay brothers and sisters did in Nazi Germany. We are not going to allow our rights to be taken away and then march with bowed heads into the gas chambers."[52] Milk employed this Holocaust metaphor to illustrate the high political stakes involved in the proposed referendum, and in so doing he conflated the Nazi persecution of Jews, which involved the systematic gassing of human beings, with that of homosexuals during the same period.[53] Milk thus gave voice to a growing trend in the American gay community of using the Jewish Holocaust as a model for conveying an understanding of the Nazi persecution of homosexuals.

Martin Sherman's play *Bent*, which opened on Broadway in January 1980 and received its German debut four months later, made similarly overwrought comparisons between the Nazi persecution of Jews and that of homosexuals. The play focuses on the experiences of Max and Horst, two homosexual inmates in a German concentration camp. In the most controversial scene of the play, Max exchanges his pink triangle for a yellow star, the insignia of Jewish inmates, in order to avoid the worst treatment. The *Village Voice*'s Richard Goldstein criticized this scene in particular for its historical inaccuracy, and *Spectator* chided it for coming "dangerously close to enlisting the unspeakable horrors of Dachau in the propaganda services of Gay Lib."[54] The gay press, however, praised *Bent* and highlighted the play's message that gays had suffered the worst fate of any of the persecuted groups.[55] *Bent* reminded one reviewer of a police raid on a Toronto bathhouse three months earlier: "Viewers will inevitably draw comparisons between the play's general subject—the Nazi persecution of homosexual men starting in 1934—and the degenerate treatment of homosexuals by the Metro Toronto Police."[56] Sherman himself compared the contemporary gay community's political apathy to that of his play's characters: "What I see happening in New York did happen in

[52]Harvey Milk, speech on June 25, 1978, quoted in Randy Shilts, *The Mayor of Castro Street: The Life and Times of Harvey Milk* (New York, 1982), 364.

[53]In some cases the SS did systematically murder homosexual inmates in the concentration camps, as, for example, in Sachsenhausen during July and August 1942, when they killed eighty-nine pink triangle prisoners. See Andreas Sternweiler, "Chronologischer Versuch zur Situation der Homosexuellen im KZ Sachsenhausen," in *Homosexuelle Männer im KZ Sachsenhausen*, ed. Joachim Müller and Andreas Sternweiler (Berlin, 2000), 46. In general, however, homosexuals died in the concentration camps of starvation, disease, forced labor, and physical torture, not in the gas chambers.

[54]Richard Goldstein, "Whose Holocaust?" review of *Bent* by Martin Sherman, *Village Voice*, December 10, 1979, 46; Peter Jenkins, "Profane Propaganda," review of *Bent* by Martin Sherman, *Spectator*, May 12, 1979, 25.

[55]See, for example, Charles Ortleb, "Sharing the Holocaust," *Christopher Street* 4, no. 5 (January 1980): 10–13; "Bent: Rosa Winkel," *Homosexuelle Emanzipation* (July–August 1980): 34–37. Both articles reprinted scenes directly from the play.

[56]Michael Lynch, "Bent under Hitler, Bent under Ackroyd," *Body Politic* (April 1981): 28.

pre-holocaust Germany. . . . Everyone in Europe is always talking about how liberated gays in America are . . . but that [political mobilization] didn't happen when they were trying to pass the bill in the City Council year after year."[57]

The notion that gays had suffered most among the victims of the Nazis fit well with the political strategy that had emerged in the United States by the late 1970s. A 1984 prescription for securing gay rights expressed this bluntly: "In any campaign to win over the public, gays must be cast as victims in need of protection so that straights will be inclined by reflex to assume the role of protector."[58] *Bent*'s message continued to shape the American gay community's collective memory of past suffering well beyond the 1980s. Sara Hart's 1993 article in *10 Percent* quoted dialog from *Bent*, including Horst's statement, "Pink's the lowest," even as it criticized contemporary use of the pink triangle as inappropriate.[59] Even the United States Holocaust Memorial Museum (USHMM) tapped into this memory in a 1996 fundraising letter aimed at gay and lesbian donors: "[Homosexual inmates] wore pink triangles on their pockets . . . and in the cruel hierarchy of the concentration camps, they were the lowest of the low."[60]

In 1981, a year after *Bent* opened on Broadway, the first reports of AIDS began to circulate. As the number of AIDS-related deaths among North American and European gay men skyrocketed, writers and activists increasingly turned to the Holocaust as a metaphor for the contemporary epidemic and to the pink triangle as the most appropriate symbol of current suffering. Larry Kramer entitled his AIDS memoir *Reports from the Holocaust*, and Tony Kushner compared the U.S. government's response to the AIDS crisis to Nazism.[61] The AIDS organization ACT-UP reappropriated the pink triangle as its identifying symbol. ACT-UP members, however, wore the concentration camp insignia defiantly turned upsidedown to signal their determination to survive.[62] The suggestion by some religious conservatives that the U.S. government incarcerate those who

[57]Martin Sherman, interview by Charles Ortleb, *Christopher Street* 4, no. 5 (January 1980): 11.

[58]Marshall Kirk and Erastes Pill, "Waging Peace," *Christopher Street* 8, no. 11 (December 1984): 38.

[59]Hart, 36–37.

[60]Letter from Roberta Bennett, chairperson of the Gay and Lesbian Campaign of the USHMM, on USHMM letterhead stationery (n.d., 1996).

[61]Larry Kramer, *Reports from the Holocaust: The Making of an AIDS Activist* (New York, 1989); Patrick Pacheco, "Tony Kushner speaks out on AIDS, Angels, Activism and Sex in the Nineties," *Body Positive*, an online magazine (September 1993) <http://gopher.hivnet.org:70/0/magazines/pos/posi002.txt>.

[62]Stuart Marshall astutely observes that ACT-UP's use of the pink triangle over the slogan "SILENCE = DEATH" would have been reversed for gays and lesbians in Nazi Germany to read "SILENCE = SURVIVAL." Stuart Marshall, "The Contemporary Political Use of Gay History: The Third Reich," in *How Do I Look? Queer Film and Video*, ed. Bad Object-Choices (Seattle, 1991), 69–70.

tested HIV-positive understandably heightened anxiety within the gay community of the return of Nazi-style persecution.

Some German gays also suspected an approaching internment in latter-day Dachaus after Peter Gauweiler, Bavaria's State Secretary for the Interior, advocated in 1987 the detention of HIV-positive people accused of spreading the virus.[63] Dieter Schiefelbein has noted that many West German AIDS activists recognized the political utility of comparing AIDS to Nazi persecution in order to thwart proposals such as Gauweiler's: "in this situation, reminders of the other catastrophe of homosexuals in twentieth-century Germany—their persecution in the 'Third Reich'—could be politically astute and morally useful in order to check the zealots who, 'under the sign of AIDS,' cry out for the registration, tagging, quarantine, and internment of those infected."[64]

Schiefelbein's reference to the AIDS epidemic and the Nazi persecution as the central catastrophes to befall gay men in the twentieth century reflected the viewpoint of most gays in both West Germany and the United States. José Arroyo, an American activist, underscored this linkage when he wrote that the pink triangle put gays "in touch with the present situation of AIDS as another kind of risk." He also noted that "the risk of wearing it, the terror of wearing it in a non-gay place, also had a powerful effect."[65] Arroyo's remark echoed earlier claims that the pink triangle would remind gays of social intolerance, but it also suggested that this intolerance now stemmed not just from homophobia but also from the fear and prejudice that surround AIDS.

Despite the growing AIDS epidemic and the relatively hostile policies of the Reagan administration, other activists in the United States also felt the need to remind gay men of past persecution and of the intersection between politics and private life. A 1986 article in the *Advocate* emphasized that pre-Nazi Germany had a large, well-organized gay scene and warned: "Those of us who say that a developed, public gay scene cannot be crushed should look again."[66] In a 1987 book review, Michael Denneny also pointed to the lesson of Nazi Germany: "Although paying lip service to the concept of gay oppression, many gay people do not experience it in the day-to-day reality of their lives. . . . In these circumstances it is useful to turn to history, to what has happened, for once anything has been actualized we know it is a real possibility."[67]

[63] *Rosa Flieder*, no. 52 (April–May 1987): 11.
[64] Dieter Schiefelbein, "Auftakt," in Initiative Mahnmal Homosexuellenverfolgung, ed., 12. Schiefelbein apparently took the phrase "im Zeichen von Aids" [under the sign of AIDS] from Martin Dannecker's book, *Der homosexuelle Mann im Zeichen von Aids* (Hamburg, 1991).
[65] José Arroyo, quoted in Marshall, 97.
[66] Peter Cummings, "Gays and Nazi Death Camps: After 40 Years, Still a Sad, Sordid Chapter in the History Books," *Advocate*, January 21, 1986, 37.
[67] Michael Denneny, "Paragraph 175," review of *The Pink Triangle: The Nazi War against Homosexuals* by Richard Plant, *Christopher Street* 9, no. 11 (January 1987): 54.

For most gays, however, the memory of Nazi persecution only helped to frame the intolerance that they experienced in their own lives in the 1980s and 1990s. The upsurge in neo-Nazi violence in Germany that followed reunification in 1990, for instance, evoked images of earlier attacks against marginalized groups in the Nazi period. In the aftermath of a xenophobic attack on a hostel for asylum seekers in Rostock in August 1992, one gay publication printed a placard with a large pink triangle and the words: "Yesterday Dachau, Today Rostock, Tomorrow?"[68] In the United States, a 1992 cover of the *Advocate* compared the Nazi persecution of gays to the pending antigay referenda in Oregon and Colorado. It featured a giant swastika and an article entitled "The Rise of Fascism in America." Similarly, Oregon governor Barbara Roberts described the 1992 ballot measure as "literally, almost like Nazi Germany."[69]

As gay men increasingly invoked the pink triangle in the face of the AIDS epidemic, some lesbians began to seek their own memory of Nazi oppression. During much of the 1970s, lesbians shared the pink triangle and its memory of persecution with gay men, and lesbian activists played a role in promoting it. Increasingly, however, lesbians felt overlooked or consciously ignored by gay men in the movement. "Lesbians are constantly assigned to the gay men—when not simply as their 'wives,' then at least as little sisters," wrote Jutta Oesterle-Schwerin, the first openly lesbian member of the German parliament.[70] The women's movement contributed to this consciousness, as feminists pointed to patriarchy in all aspects of society, including gay politics and the writing of history. When feminist historians created the field of women's history, some began researching the lesbian past. In many ways, the lesbian community's search for a distinctive memory of its experience under Nazi rule mirrored the earlier search by the predominantly male gay community for its memory in the early 1970s. Just as gay men had to counter the stereotype of the homosexual Nazi, lesbians confronted the pervasive image of the butch, sadistic, female concentration camp guard.[71]

The lesbian community, even more than the gay male community, faced a dearth of information about the fate of lesbians under National Socialism. Consequently, throughout the 1980s lesbian journals issued pleas for further research into the subject.[72] A 1982 article in the West German

---

[68] *Rosige Zeiten: Magazin aus Oldenburg für Lesben und Schwule*, no. 23 (December 1992–January 1993): 12.

[69] *Advocate*, November 3, 1992, 36–43. "Roberts Ties Measure 9 to Persecution by Nazis," *Oregonian*, August 26, 1992, A1.

[70] Jutta Oesterle-Schwerin, "Lesben sind keine Homos," in Schäfer and Lahusen, eds., 79.

[71] See Sabine Schrader, "Formen der Erinnerung an lesbische Frauen im Nationalsozialismus," in *"Das sind Volksfeinde!": Die Verfolgung von Homosexuellen an Rhein und Ruhr 1933–1945*, ed. Centrum Schwule Geschichte (Cologne, 1998), 33–43.

[72] The sociologist Ilse Kokula produced some initial research in the 1980s, including interviews with older lesbians. See Ilse Kokula, *Jahre des Glücks, Jahre des Leids: Gespräche*

334 ERIK N. JENSEN

lesbian journal *Unsere kleine Zeitung* (*UkZ*) stated, "We are beginning to reflect upon what was done to lesbians in the concentration camps. We are searching for the few bits of evidence."[73] Seven years later, the information gap had scarcely narrowed, and *UkZ* reissued its plea: "Since so little about the persecution of lesbians under National Socialism is known and documented, it seems to us especially important to conduct investigations so that this injustice is not forgotten."[74] Given the lack of information, some lesbians adopted the model of the Nazi persecution of homosexual men, just as gay men had earlier appropriated the model of the Nazi persecution of Jews. In a 1985 article Gerda Bierwagen criticized the gay community's exclusive focus on men. Her description of the Nazi persecution of lesbians, however, mirrored that of gay men: "As lesbians, they (like homosexual men) were marked with the pink triangle and held under arrest and often sent to the concentration camps without prior judicial process."[75]

While Bierwagen claimed the pink triangle for lesbians, other activists argued that the Nazis had marked lesbians with a black triangle, the concentration camp insignia that designated "asocials," and they promoted this as the symbol of a specifically lesbian memory of Nazi persecution. In a 1987 speech at Dachau, a lesbian organization declared that the Nazis had marked homosexual women with a black triangle and that, just like male homosexuals, these women belonged at "the bottom of the scale" in the concentration camps. The speech continued: "To the silenced victims of that era, just as today, belong lesbian women, even when, or precisely because, lesbian women were made so invisible that they weren't included as a [separate] prisoner category, even though they were systematically persecuted."[76] The reference to the "silenced victims" referred both to lesbians living under the Nazi regime and to contemporary lesbian activists who felt silenced by the post-1971 gay movement in West Germany, especially with regard to commemorating Nazism's victims. A 1999 letter

---

mit älteren lesbischen Frauen: Dokumente (Kiel, 1986). Claudia Schoppmann has written the only dissertation on lesbians under National Socialism, published as *Nationalsozialistische Sexualpolitik und weibliche Homosexualität* (Pfaffenweiler, 1991). She has since written several other important books on the subject, including *Zeit der Maskierung: Lebensgeschichten lesbischer Frauen im "Dritten Reich"* (Berlin, 1993), translated as *Days of Masquerade: Life Stories of Lesbians during the Third Reich* (New York, 1996), and *Verbotene Verhältnisse: Frauenliebe 1938–1945* (Berlin, 1999).

[73] *UkZ* (November 1982): 26. I have relied heavily on *UkZ* for my reconstruction of lesbian memory in West Germany and postunification Germany both because it has covered the issue extensively over the last two decades and because I had access to an almost complete run of the magazine at my research library. Other lesbian journals in pre- and postunification Germany also covered the issue.

[74] "Verfolgung lesbischer Frauen im Nationalsozialismus," *UkZ* (January 1989): 3.

[75] Gerda Bierwagen, "Lesben im Nationalsozialismus," *UkZ* (May 1985): 10.

[76] "Eine Rede des Lesbenrings zur Gedenk- und Protestveranstaltung für vergessene KZ-Opfergruppen am 11.01.87 in Dachau," *UkZ* (February 1987): 44.

to the feminist magazine *Emma* expressed concern that even other women were ignoring the persecution of lesbians. An outraged reader criticized the editors for overlooking lesbian victims in an earlier article on the Nazi period and asked, "Where are the lesbians who were murdered in the concentration camps of the German fascists?"[77]

A number of American activists took their cue from these earlier West German initiatives and began promoting a memory of the black triangle in the United States.[78] In a 1990 *Washington Blade* article, Professor Magda Mueller criticized historians for overlooking the persecution of lesbians: "The writers of these reports [on women in concentration camps] do not question *what* the asociality of the women who had to carry the black triangle was. They never asked, 'why were they labeled asocials?'"[79] The following year, in the lesbian journal *Off Our Backs*, Terri Couch recalled her first gay pride march in Minneapolis in 1973 and what an impression the symbol of the pink triangle had made on her at the time. She then described her subsequent conviction that lesbians wore the black triangle and concluded with a call to reclaim this as a symbol of lesbian identity and a marker of Nazi persecution: "Black triangles could be sold for donations in bookstores and places where women gather. The truth about Lesbian Herstory could be spread."[80] In a 1996 article R. Amy Elman not only argued that the pink triangle rendered lesbian victims invisible but also suggested that the color black better represented lesbian identity anyway: "It is unseemly that girls and women long taunted by forced pink, feminine identifiers are now, as lesbians, to believe that a pink triangle signifies gendered rebellion."[81]

The black triangle, though, never established itself to the same degree as the pink triangle, and many lesbians continued to wear the latter throughout the 1980s and 1990s. This stemmed partly from the fact that gay women had attached so many different meanings to the black triangle that it no longer served as a conduit for the memory of Nazi persecution. In 1991, the same year that Terri Couch promoted the black triangle as a specific memory catalyst, the *Lesbian Herstory Archives Newsletter* published an article that explored the myriad ways in which lesbians already

[77]Monika Golla, *Emma*, no. 2 (March–April 1999): 110.

[78]The documentary film *Desire* contributed to the memory of lesbian persecution in English-speaking countries. See *Desire*, directed by Stuart Marshall (Water Bearer Films, Inc., for Channel 4 Television, Great Britain, 1989), videocassette.

[79]Quoted in Naina Ayya, "Scholars Disagree Who Were Marked by Black Triangles," *Washington Blade*, March 9, 1990, 7.

[80]Terri Couch, "An American in West Germany or . . . Did Lesbians Wear Pink Triangles?" *Off Our Backs* (March 1991): 23. The fact that Couch remembers seeing the pink triangle in the United States as early as 1973 points again to the fact that we do not know exactly when the gay movement first appropriated it as a symbol of gay identity.

[81]R. Amy Elman, "Triangles and Tribulations: The Politics of Nazi Symbols," *Journal of Homosexuality* 30, no. 3 (1996): 2.

interpreted the symbol and proposed that the Nazis probably never persecuted lesbians specifically on account of their homosexuality.[82] Nonetheless, the black triangle has maintained some currency. The web site
BLKTrianGurl, a link for lesbians of color, for example, currently uses the
black triangle and explains its symbolic significance.[83]

In addition to the emergence of an independent lesbian memory, the
1980s also witnessed a growing memorial culture within the American and
West German gay communities that represented a response both to the
trauma of the AIDS epidemic and to the larger trend toward Holocaust
memorialization in both countries.[84] As early as the 1970s, gay and lesbian
associations in West Germany, and later in East Germany, organized guer-
rilla wreath-laying ceremonies at various concentration camps.[85] These ceremonies often coincided with gay pride celebrations in June, illustrating the
role that this collective memory played in the German gay community.
President Richard von Weizsäcker signaled an era of official commemoration
in West Germany when, in an address to the Bundestag in May 1985, he
acknowledged the persecution of homosexuals. Prior to this, the only official
recognition had come from the former concentration camp Mauthausen, in
Austria, which allowed a gay organization to place a plaque specifically memorializing the homosexual victims of Nazism—a pink triangle with the inscription "Totgeschlagen—Totgeschwiegen" [Beaten to death—Silenced to
death]. In the years following Weizsäcker's speech, several former camps on
West German soil unveiled memorials to the homosexual victims, and the
Sachsenhausen concentration camp dedicated its official 1999 remembrance
to its former homosexual inmates.[86]

Several cities erected memorials to the homosexual victims of Nazism,
and these, in particular, have served a political as well as a commemorative
function. The sculpture of an angel with a partially severed head, unveiled
in a gay district of Frankfurt am Main in 1994, for example, faced in the

---

[82]Lucinda Zoe, "The Black Triangle," *Lesbian Herstory Archives Newsletter*, no. 12 (June
1991): 7.

[83]<www.geocities.com/WestHollywood/Park/7200/mission.htm>.

[84]For a good discussion of Holocaust memorialization, see James E. Young, *The Texture
of Memory: Holocaust Memorials and Meanings* (New Haven, 1993).

[85]Beginning in 1975, Munich's Verein für sexuelle Gleichberechtigung laid a wreath for
the homosexual victims of Nazi persecution at the Dachau concentration camp, and beginning in 1983, representatives of gay organizations in East Germany laid a wreath at the
Buchenwald concentration camp (Herrn, 46, 51). The first reported commemoration by a
lesbian group in East Germany took place on April 20, 1985, when eleven women attempted to lay a wreath on the fortieth anniversary of Ravensbrück's liberation. The police
prevented that action from taking place. Denis M. Sweet, "The Church, the Stasi, and
Socialist Integration: Three Stages of Lesbian and Gay Emancipation in the Former German Democratic Republic," in Hekma, Oosterhuis, and Steakley, eds., 356–58.

[86]The following former concentration camps in Germany have placed a memorial marker
to the homosexual victims of the Nazi regime: Neuengamme (1985), Dachau (1987), and
Sachsenhausen (1992). The Dachau memorial, in particular, provoked ongoing opposition

direction of the nearby courthouse in order to underscore the terrible consequences of judicial decisions rendered against homosexuals in the postwar years as well as during the Nazi period itself.[87] The inscription reinforced the memorial's concern with the present as much as the past by reminding viewers that "men who love men and women who love women can always be persecuted again."[88] Furthermore, the decision to locate the memorial in Frankfurt's gay center suggested that its initiators wished to direct the memorial's message inward, toward the gay community itself, in order to remind this urban enclave of the perils of political apathy.

The debate over the location of a proposed memorial in Berlin, on the other hand, indicates an outward focus aimed at eliciting political support from beyond the gay community. Because of the memorial's "special function," some have advocated its placement in the Tiergarten, near the federal parliament, where "it should become, in its proximity to the government district, the irrepressible marker and visible remembrance of gay men in German society."[89] Frank Wagner, a member of the memorial initiative, has argued that the memorial should not be oriented to gays, most of whom know of the Nazi persecution of homosexuals, but, rather, to the larger public "as a measure of its [society's] democracy and liberalness."[90]

Both the completed memorial in Frankfurt and the proposed one in Berlin reveal the latent tensions in the gay and lesbian community over whom to commemorate, whom the Nazis persecuted. In the case of the

from the administration of the camp site. See Thomas Rahe, "Formen des Gedenkens an die Verfolgung Homosexueller in den deutschen KZ-Gedenkstätten," in *Homosexuelle in Konzentrationslagern*, ed. Olaf Mußmann (Bad Münstereifel, 2000), 151. For a critique of the various memorials to the Nazi persecution of homosexuals, see Frank Wagner, "Der Engel unterm Rosa Winkel: Kritische Würdigung bestehender Denkmäler und Denkmalsentwürfe zur NS-Verfolgung von Schwulen und Lesben," in Initiative Schwulendenkmal, *Der homosexuellen NS-Opfer gedenken: Denkschrift* (Berlin, 1995), 69–85.

[87]For a detailed discussion of the planning and design of the Frankfurt memorial, see Initiative Mahnmal Homosexuellenverfolgung, ed. Among the postwar injustices against homosexuals that the Frankfurt Angel commemorates, the trials of 1950–51 rank at the top of the list. After a male prostitute, Otto Blankenstein, divulged the identities of his clients to police, they arrested one hundred people. Several served prison sentences; seven of those arrested later killed themselves; many emigrated; and even more lost their jobs because of the revelations. See Dieter Schiefelbein, "Wiederbeginn der juristischen Verfolgung homosexueller Männer in der Bundesrepublik Deutschland: Die Homosexuellen-Prozesse in Frankfurt am Main 1950/51," *Zeitschrift für Sexualforschung* 5, no. 1 (1992): 59–73.

[88]Schiefelbein, "Auftakt," 33. Dieter Schiefelbein, who played an important role in establishing the memorial, also noted, however, that the organizing committee had mixed feelings about memorializing both past and present injustices and that some committee members argued vehemently against it (31–32).

[89]Initiative Schwulendenkmal, 15.

[90]Wagner, 73. The effort to secure a memorial to homosexual victims received a big boost on May 3, 2001, when the initiators presented a public appeal signed by, among others, Paul Spiegel, the leader of Germany's Jewish community, and Lea Rosh, the initiator of the recently approved central memorial to the Jewish victims of the Nazi regime.

Frankfurt angel, the initiative originally sought a memorial to homosexual men; however, in 1990 it decided to commemorate the suffering of both men and women, albeit under the guidance of a steering committee that had shrunk to just six men. Although the inscription on the memorial expressed inclusiveness by remembering homosexual men and women, the dedication ceremony mentioned only men. In response, two women wrote an inflamed letter to the newspaper *Frankfurter Rundschau*: "We are sad and extremely outraged that the speeches did not remember the situation of homosexual women and the specific form of their persecution under National Socialism with a single word. The event is scandalous."[91]

The proposed Berlin memorial has exposed similar internal tensions. In 1996 the planning group decided to include lesbians in the memorial along with homosexual men, and it changed its name from "Initiative Schwulendenkmal" (Initiative for a memorial to gay men) to "Initiative HomoMonument." Shortly thereafter, Joachim Müller, an early proponent of the initiative, quit the organization. He protested in a letter that "under the banner of apparent political correctness the ideologically grounded myth of a National Socialist persecution of lesbians is to be written in stone."[92] The initiators have struggled for a balance between appeasing the demands of the contemporary gay and lesbian community for inclusiveness, on the one hand, and demands for historical accuracy, on the other, by presenting "a differentiated consideration of the victim groups."[93]

The gay community in the United States has placed less emphasis on memorializing than has the German community and, when it has acted, it has usually done so as part of a larger commemoration of Holocaust victims. As early as 1975, a gay organization in West Hartford, Connecticut, lobbied for the inclusion of homosexual victims in the city's Holocaust memorial.[94] In a much more prominent example, gays lobbied early on for the inclusion of homosexual victims in the United States Holocaust Memorial Museum, viewing the outcome of this lobbying effort as a barometer of the acceptance of gays and lesbians in the United States. When a 1979 report on the proposed museum failed to mention homosexual victims, the *Gay Community News* protested this exclusion by asking, "If we are refused acknowledgement of our darkest hour, how can we possibly feel safe and secure in our contemporary, emerging-into-sunshine exhilaration?"[95] In January 1980 the Gay and Lesbian Alliance urged President

[91]Gabriele Dietrich and Eva Heldmann, *Frankfurter Rundschau*, December 30, 1994, reprinted in *Die Schwule Presseschau* 14, no. 1 (January 1995): 9.

[92]Joachim Müller, open letter to the Initiative HomoMonument, October 19, 1996, reprinted in Initiative Schwulendenkmal, 119.

[93]Initiative HomoMonument, "HomoMonument: Eine Replik auf eine selbstgestellte Frage," in Initiative Schwulendenkmal, 13.

[94]The city finally rejected the proposal three years later. Tony Domenick, "Memorial to Holocaust Will 'Ignore' Gays," *Gay Community News*, July 15, 1978, 1.

[95]John Mehring, "Gays and the Holocaust," *Gay Community News*, November 24, 1979, 5.

Carter to include lesbians and gays on the museum's advisory panel and to ensure that part of the museum's educational mission include "anti-gay genocide."[96]

In response to these efforts by the gay community, the museum ultimately dedicated part of its permanent exhibition to the Nazi persecution of homosexuals. Auspiciously, the museum's dedication in April 1993 coincided with a nationwide gay pride march in Washington, D.C. At a memorial ceremony held at the museum, one gay leader pointed to the political implications of this coincidence and emphasized that gays need to consider the past as they demand a better future.[97] Other grass-roots initiatives have sprung up in the last decade. Rick Landman, for instance, spearheads an effort to unveil a granite memorial marker for homosexual victims in the Sheepshead Bay Holocaust Memorial Park in Brooklyn, New York, an effort that the borough president has repeatedly thwarted.[98]

As the preceding examination of the gay community's collective memory of Nazi persecution has shown, over the last three decades the initiatives of activists, researchers, and writers in West Germany and the United States have mutually influenced one another. Films, plays, historical studies, and commemorative strategies produced in one country have often found a receptive audience in the other. This sharing has both reflected and contributed to the transnational quality of the gay and lesbian community's collective memory, one in which the national setting of an historical event assumed secondary importance to the central fact that it involved gay men and women. In West Germany gays and lesbians in many major cities have long celebrated the annual Christopher Street Day in recognition of a specifically American historical event, the 1969 Stonewall Riots in New York City. German gays have borrowed a prominent aspect of their memory from American history, just as American gays have adopted their memory of the Nazi persecution of homosexuals from German history.

Despite similarities and mutual influence, however, the collective memories in the German and American gay communities differ in significant ways. The gay community in the United States has made more direct references to the Holocaust and more overt comparisons between the situations of gays and Jews than has the German community. This stems primarily from the fact that most Americans, to the extent that they knew of Nazi persecution at all, knew of the persecution of Jews rather than that of other groups. Furthermore, many of the promoters of a memory of the

[96]Quoted in Edward T. Linenthal, *Preserving Memory: The Struggle to Create America's Holocaust Museum* (New York, 1995), 305.

[97]Barrett Brick, executive director of the World Federation of Gay and Lesbian Jewish Organizations, quoted in Aras van Hertum, "Ceremony Honors Gay Holocaust Victims," *Washington Blade*, April 30, 1993, 5.

[98]For a discussion of the controversy in Brooklyn, see "Sheepshead Bay Holocaust Memorial Park," <www.infotrue.com>.

Nazi persecution of homosexuals were themselves Jewish. As American Jews devoted greater energy to researching and commemorating the Holocaust in the 1970s and 1980s, many Jewish gays began to explore the particular experiences of homosexuals under National Socialism through the familiar prism of the Jewish Holocaust.[99]

Martin Sherman, in response to criticism of *Bent*'s comparison of Jewish and homosexual suffering in the concentration camps, insisted, "I wrote the play every bit as much as a Jew as a gay." Sherman noted that people ignored the persecution of gays just as they overlooked many aspects of Jewish history, and he credited his sensitivity to this fact as a motivation for writing the play.[100] Rick Landman has also discussed how his Jewish identity heightened his interest in the Nazi persecution of homosexuals: "As a Jewish son of two Holocaust survivors, I grew up with a constant reminder of the Holocaust. I developed a vigilance against right wing politics, and a special sensitivity to those who are being persecuted."[101] Significantly, the Congregation Beth Simchat Torah, a gay synagogue in New York City, houses perhaps the only memorial in the United States to the homosexual victims of Nazi persecution.[102]

Jewish gay writers have regularly emphasized the parallels between the Jewish community and the gay community—stereotypes, ghettoization, persecution. Seymour Kleinberg argued in a 1983 article, "The Homosexual as Jew," that gays and Jews had suffered a common history and that when one group faced persecution, the other group invariably did as well.[103] In the conclusion to his book on the Nazi persecution of homosexuals, Richard Plant traced a larger pattern of targeting Jews and homosexuals together, one that the historian George Mosse has also underscored.[104] Similarly, a 1987 article in *Gay Community News* presented anti-Semitism and homophobia as two sides of the same ideological coin, concluding, "Both lead to Auschwitz and the Gulag."[105] This tendency to see parallel histories for Jews and homosexuals convinced many gays and lesbians that the Holocaust of the former necessitated a holocaust of the latter.

[99]For an analysis of the interest of American Jews in the Holocaust, see Peter Novick, *The Holocaust in American Life* (New York, 1999).

[100]Sherman, interview by Ortleb, 11.

[101]"Homophobia and the Holocaust," under the heading, "Holocaust Articles of Interest," <www.infotrue.com>.

[102]It is a mural by the artist Noreen Dean Dresser, unveiled on May 6, 1999. See "World-Wide Memorials and Monuments" under the heading "Dr. Magnus Hirschfeld," <www.infotrue.com>.

[103]Seymour Kleinberg, "The Homosexual as Jew," *Christopher Street* 7, no. 1 (February 1983): 35–41.

[104]Richard Plant, *The Pink Triangle: The Nazi War against Homosexuals* (New York, 1986), 185; George L. Mosse, *The Image of Man: The Creation of Modern Masculinity* (New York, 1996), especially chap. 4, "The Countertype."

[105]Bill Percy, "Anti-Semitism and Homophobia Linked in Discussion of Holocaust Victims Memorial," *Gay Community News*, March 8, 1987, 8–9.

Lev Raphael, a child of Holocaust survivors, explored the coexistence of gay and Jewish identities and the issue of pink triangle identity in his 1990 short story, "Abominations." It centers on Nat and Brenda, a gay Orthodox Jew and his sister, before and after an arson attack on Nat's dorm room in an antigay hate crime. After the incident, Brenda recalls an earlier argument that she had over the appropriation of the pink triangle as a symbol of gay identity: "Don't you hate that they use something from the camps? You never see Jews wearing yellow stars in a parade!"[106] By the story's conclusion, though, Brenda comes to realize the importance of the gay community's memory of Nazi persecution. In the final scene, she remembers "how the King of Denmark had worn a yellow star when the occupying Nazis started persecuting Danish Jews," and she pins a pink triangle button to her dress.[107] The story not only suggests parallels between the Nazi persecutions of Jews and homosexuals but examines the occasionally tense coexistence of the two collective memories—one Jewish, the other gay—as reflected in Brenda's conflicted feelings about the contemporary appropriation of the pink triangle. Raphael discussed in another essay some Jews' discomfort over the historic linking of the two groups: "To speak of Jews and homosexuals as victims of Nazis . . . does not in any way decrease the significance of the catastrophe for Jews. Yet too many Jews recoil in disgust and horror."[108]

Indeed, the emergence of a memory that has often explicitly appropriated the imagery of the Holocaust has created occasional tension between the gay and Jewish communities in the United States. One of the first appearances of the pink triangle, after all, was at a protest in 1974 against Orthodox Jewish groups that opposed a New York gay rights ordinance. That same year, a Jewish lesbian described her dismay at a Holocaust conference's silence regarding homosexual victims: "Not even now can most heterosexual Jews feel any kinship with gays the Nazis killed in the concentration camps."[109] The decision to include homosexual victims in the United States Holocaust Memorial Museum has also sparked some opposition during the last two decades, including a threatened boycott of the museum by two groups of Orthodox rabbis in 1997.[110]

Opposition has come not only from Orthodox Jews. A 1979 letter by a Jewish group to *Lesbian Tide* supported gay rights but nonetheless protested the gay community's indiscriminate comparisons to the Holocaust:

[106]Lev Raphael, "Abominations," *Christopher Street* 13, no. 6 (August 1990): 41–42.
[107]Ibid., 42.
[108]Lev Raphael, "Judaism's Moral Strength," in *Journeys and Arrivals: On Being Gay and Jewish* (Boston, 1996), 135.
[109]Janet Cooper, "A Jewish Gay's Reflection on Auschwitz," *Gay Community News,* May 10, 1975, 10.
[110]Debra Nussbaum Cohen and Leslie Katz, "Rabbis Attack Gay Inclusion in Shoah Museum," *Jewish Bulletin of Northern California,* March 14, 1997, <www.jewishsf.com/bk970314/1arabbi.htm>.

"As Jews we feel that more caution and sensitivity needs to be used when talking and generalizing about the Holocaust. . . . This means that we cannot go out and . . . use the Holocaust opportunistically."[111] Lev Raphael has also criticized the overuse of the Holocaust "as a handy club with which to beat your opponent."[112] Nancy Ordover sought common ground in a 1995 article in which she recounted instances of insensitivity on both sides and pleaded for a collective memory that could bring the gay and Jewish communities closer together.[113] The two communities have, in many respects, already found this common ground, particularly in their cooperation on the United States Holocaust Memorial Museum.

While the American gay community often employed the Jewish Holocaust as a template for understanding the persecution of homosexuals, the German gay community generally avoided this comparison. Instead, as the historian and activist Ralf Dose has pointed out, many gay activists in West Germany saw closer parallels in the Nazis' persecution of Communists and Socialists.[114] Public comparisons of the persecution of homosexuals to that of the political Left had the added benefit of solidifying the West German gay movement in the 1970s and early 1980s as an equal partner in the larger movement of radical politics at the time. Furthermore, gay activists and the radical Left in West Germany shared a deep distrust of the state and its ability to exercise power judiciously. While activists in the United States invoked the memory of the pink triangle to *solicit* governmental intervention on behalf of gays and lesbians, those in Germany did so to *protest* such intervention—to oppose, for example, the compilation of lists of homosexuals by the police and the continued existence until 1994 of Paragraph 175.

When they reflected on the Nazi persecution of homosexuals, German gays also had to wrestle with their dual and often competing identities as

---

[111]Jews against Briggs, "Jews Say 'Gay Holocaust' Insensitive," *Lesbian Tide* 8, no. 4 (January–February 1979): 23.

[112]Lev Raphael, "Deciphering the Gay Holocaust," *Harvard Gay and Lesbian Review* 2, no. 3 (summer 1995): 20. Similarly, gay activists often invoke the epithet "Nazi" to label their opponents. Kevin Ivers, a member of the gay organization Log Cabin Republicans, for instance, has recently remarked, "I get all kinds of e-mails telling me I'm working with the Nazis." Quoted in "Gays See Bush with Wariness and Optimism," *New York Times*, January 26, 2001, A1.

[113]Nancy Ordover, "Visibility, Alliance, and the Practice of Memory," *Socialist Review* 25, no. 1 (1995): 119–34.

[114]Ralf Dose offered this interpretation in an e-mail exchange with the author, February 22 and February 23, 2001. See also *Schwule und Faschismus*, ed. Heinz-Dieter Schilling (West Berlin, 1983). Nonetheless, German gays also drew inspiration for the commemoration of homosexual victims from similar efforts on behalf of the Jewish victims. Frankfurt's gay community, for example, first lobbied for a memorial after witnessing the Jewish community's initiative in 1987 to commemorate the persecution of Frankfurt's Jews. See Schiefelbein, "Auftakt," 14–15. Similarly, the initiative to establish a central memorial in Berlin to the Nazi persecution of homosexuals reflected a response to the establishment of such a memorial to the persecution of Jews.

both German and gay—as both *Täter* (perpetrator) and *Opfer* (victim). During a 1989 visit to Auschwitz made by several gay men from West Germany, one participant expressed a mixture of indignation and guilt: "I thought, I come here as a member of the victimized group from that period. But I am also German. I also belong to those people who were the former perpetrators. How should I handle this schizophrenia?"[115] In 1992 another German revealed a different but related tension between his national and sexual identities after watching an American production of a play about gay concentration camp inmates. During the postperformance discussion, he bristled at American audience members' generalizations about the German national character and what he saw as their arrogant refusal to examine their country's own troubled past. He commented, "I was proud as a German to sit in on this discussion. Would the Americans deal with the problem of the Ku-Klux-Klan in exactly the same way as they command us Germans in our dealings with the Nazis?"[116] In this particular situation, the man clearly, and resentfully, identified first as a German, whose Nazi legacy the Americans apparently painted with a broad brush, rather than as a gay man, with whose victimized legacy the Americans seemed to sympathize.

Gay journals in West Germany began expressing this double identity as early as 1975, when *H.A.W.-Info* cautioned against a one-sided portrayal of homosexuals as victims, arguing that some had certainly supported the National Socialists.[117] By calling for a balanced interpretation of the gay experience under National Socialism, the magazine raised the issue of how gays and lesbians living in contemporary Germany should reconcile two potentially conflicting memories. *Siegessäule* raised it again in 1999, when it declared: "The view of gays and lesbians as victims is also too one-sided. Their history in the ranks of the perpetrators has not yet been fully examined."[118] Manfred Herzer, for one, seemed to have resolved this conflict for himself when, in 1985, he argued that gays had a responsibility to accept the burden of their German identity first and foremost: "In silence one sidesteps the obvious fact that only an extremely small minority of gays were among the victims of the Nazi regime, held imprisoned in the concentration camps and marked with the pink triangle. Rather, the large majority, due to their extremely effective disguise, among other things, belonged to the willing subjects and beneficiaries of the Nazi state just like other German men and

---

[115]Quoted in Lutz van Dick and Christoph Kranich, "Zeugnisse des Schreckens: Schwule besuchen die KZ-Gedenkstätte in Auschwitz," *Magnus*, no. 1 (October 1989): 50.

[116]Holger, "Amerikanische Kultur einmal anders: Homosexuellenverfolgung bei den Nazis," *Rosige Zeiten: Magazin aus Oldenburg für Lesben und Schwule*, no. 23 (December–January 1992–93): 23.

[117]Ina and Funny, 5–6.

[118]*Siegessäule* (January 1999): 15.

women."[119] Instead of commemorating the fortieth anniversary of the end of the Nazi regime by laying wreaths at the memorials to victims, Herzer proposed that the gay community should examine more fully its own history of collusion during the Nazi period.

Other historians have also criticized certain omissions and exaggerations in the ways in which gays and lesbians have remembered the Nazi persecution. Over the past three decades, the gay community, especially in the United States, has reported widely varying estimates of the number of homosexuals killed by the Nazis.[120] With regard to overestimates, the historian Klaus Müller has asked, "Who do we remember? Up to 1 million dead gays and lesbians as claimed by some gay groups and researchers? . . . Although big numbers create big emotions, here they only document a disturbing attitude in our community."[121] The most recent research estimates that no more than 10,000 homosexuals died as a result of Nazi persecution.[122]

The gay press has also perpetuated the notion that homosexual inmates faced the worst treatment of any of the persecuted groups, a trope that originated with Heinz Heger's memoir and gained broader currency with the production of *Bent*.[123] In 1975, for example, Alfred Heinlein wrote in *Emanzipation* that the pink triangle signified "that its wearer belonged to the lowest stratum in the camp hierarchy."[124] In 1993 the gay journal *Bay*

[119]Manfred Herzer, "Das dritte Geschlecht und das Dritte Reich," *Siegessäule* (May 1985): 31.

[120]In 1975, for example, an article in *Gay Sunshine* estimated that the Nazis killed 430,000 gays and lesbians in the death camps. See W. I. Scobie, "Death Camps: Remembering the Victims," *Gay Sunshine*, no. 25 (summer 1975): 28. In 1985, the *Advocate* estimated the number of gays that the Nazis killed at 250,000 (June 11, 1985, 25). Robert Reinhart's novelized account of the Holocaust, *Walk the Night*, stated that "tens of thousands of gays" died in the concentration camps (*Walk the Night: A Novel of Gays in the Holocaust* [Boston, 1994], 6). Some of the most egregious exaggerations have come from the *Wisconsin Light*, a Milwaukee-based gay newspaper. In a 1995 article it claimed that the Nazis exterminated between 150,000 and 3 million homosexuals by the end of the war. "Fiftieth Anniversary of the Liberation of the Nazi Camps Is Time to Recall the Horrors," *Wisconsin Light*, March 16–29, 1995, 16.

[121]Klaus Müller, "The Holocaust Does Not Equal AIDS," *Advocate*, May 4, 1993, 5.

[122]In 1977 Rüdiger Lautmann produced the first solid research on the number of homosexuals killed during the Nazi persecution, which he estimated at between 5,000 and 15,000 ("Der rosa Winkel in den nationalsozialistischen Konzentrationslagern," in *Seminar: Gesellschaft und Homosexualität* [Frankfurt am Main, 1977], 333). Richard Plant made these figures available to an English-speaking audience in 1986 (185). Subsequent research has begun to revise these numbers slightly downward. Rainer Hoffschildt, for example, has recently estimated that perhaps 7,000 homosexuals died in the Nazi concentration camps ("Projekt zur namentlichen Erfassung verfolgter Homosexueller im Naziregime [Entwurf]," in Initiative Schwulendenkmal, 107).

[123]Dieter Schiefelbein points out that Heger had very little information about the persecution of homosexuals to assist him in writing his book and so utilized what he knew of the persecution of Jews as a model ("'. . . so wie die Juden . . .': Versuch ein Mißverständnis zu verstehen," in "Auftakt," 35–73).

[124]Alfred Heinlein, "Massenmord an Homos bis heute unaufgeklärt," *Emanzipation* (March 1975): 2.

Area Reporter also claimed, "Gays and lesbians were among the first to be exterminated and had the least chance of survival."[125] By propagating this idea, writers and activists have, at the very least, fueled a crass game of competitive victimhood. More significantly, they have blurred the fact that the Nazis singled out Socialists and Communists as their first targets upon seizing power and that the Nazis' relentless persecution of Jews and Roma and Sinti meant that these latter groups had the least chance of survival.

The gay press has also exaggerated the extent to which the Nazis persecuted lesbians, an exaggeration that stems from the dearth of research on the subject. In the 1970s most activists and writers simply subsumed lesbians within the pink triangle memory of gay men. Some lesbians began to claim a separate memory in the 1980s, but it was one in which the persecution of lesbians paralleled that of homosexual men in both form and intensity. However, in the last decade the pioneering research of Claudia Schoppmann has called into question this memory: she has concluded "that there was no systematic prosecution of lesbian women comparable to that of male homosexuals."[126] The social scientist Christa Schikorra has corroborated this finding. After examining the files of two thousand female black triangle prisoners from the Ravensbrück concentration camp, she found only four that mentioned lesbianism, and then only as a secondary notation.[127] Lesbians certainly faced hardships under the Nazi regime, including economic discrimination, ideological pressure to marry and have children, and the destruction of their institutions and social networks, but they did not experience the direct and systematic persecution implied by the memory of the black triangle.

Historians, however, do not sit as the final arbiters of collective memory. Collective memory has influenced historical debates just as much as the debates have influenced memory. One of the most contentious debates has centered on the comparability of the Nazi persecution of homosexuals to that of Jews. In a 1991 essay, Hans-Georg Stümke criticized one study for downplaying the intensity of Nazi policy toward homosexuals. Stümke, who insisted on the need to view this policy through the lens of Nazism's obsession with racial cleansing, argued that the Nazis viewed homosexuality as a disease, as much a threat to "Aryan racial hygiene" as Jewishness

[125]Jeff Fast, "Holocaust Museum Opens in Washington," *Bay Area Reporter*, April 29, 1993, 21.

[126]Claudia Schoppmann, "The Position of Lesbian Women in the Nazi Period," in *Hidden Holocaust? Gay and Lesbian Persecution in Germany, 1933–45*, ed. Günter Grau, trans. Patrick Camiller (London, 1995), 15.

[127]According to Christa Schikorra's research, 25 percent of those prisoners who wore the black triangle were prostitutes or heterosexual women who changed partners often and thus, in the eyes of the regime, spread venereal disease. Among the others were homeless, unemployed, beggars, Africans, Roma and Sinti, immigrants, women who married non-Aryans, and those who didn't fulfill service duties ("'Statt nach Hause kam ich ins Lager': Die Verfolgung 'asozialer' Frauen während des Nationalsozialismus," paper presented at Galerie Olga Benario, Berlin, April 19, 1998).

and for which they also sought a "final solution."[128] Rüdiger Lautmann, on the other hand, has argued that the Nazis' persecution of homosexuals is more comparable to that of political and religious dissidents—"those groups whom the Nazis deemed inimical but not racially undesirable."[129] Günter Grau has also emphasized the qualitative differences between the persecution of homosexuals and that of Jews. He argues that the Nazis sought not the physical elimination of all homosexuals but, rather, the elimination of homosexuality through a variety of policies, including brutally hard labor, castration, dangerous and experimental hormone treatments, and "reeducation."[130]

This debate has both shaped and reflected a larger tension in the gay community over what to remember and how to remember it. As the 1993 debate in the pages of *10 Percent* showed, gay men and women in the United States continued to identify with the pink triangle and the memory of persecution that it signified, an attachment also felt by many German gays. During a 1996 debate over the design of the pending memorial in Berlin to homosexual victims, one man defended proposals to incorporate the pink triangle by asking, "Isn't the pink triangle the proudest symbol that homosexuals can put forward?"[131] To those invested in the memory of persecution, the pink triangle has served multiple functions: it has united a diverse population of gay men and women, mobilized political action, and provided an interpretive framework for contemporary experiences.

The pink triangle has also served to project the memory outward as well as inward, to nongays as well as gays. Its display has prompted questions from those outside the community, which could have the positive effect of eliciting support and protection from the larger society. Law professor Kenji Yoshino has noted the relevance of Nazi persecution to contemporary legal battles on behalf of gay rights in the United States: "One of the things you consider in equal protection cases is whether there is a history of discrimination. How far can you get into the history of discrimination against gays without encountering the pink triangle, the absolute symbol of that discrimination?"[132] In Germany this question has played a central role in ongoing legal efforts to secure official recognition

[128]Hans-Georg Stümke, "'Endlösung' oder 'Umerziehung,'" review of *Homosexuelle unter dem Hakenkreuz* by Burkhard Jellonnek, *Die Zeit*, March 29, 1991, 42.

[129]Rüdiger Lautmann, "Gay Prisoners in Concentration Camps as Compared with Jehovah's Witnesses and Political Prisoners," in *A Mosaic of Victims: Non-Jews Persecuted and Murdered by the Nazis*, ed. Michael Berenbaum (New York, 1990), 201.

[130]Günter Grau, "Persecution, 'Re-education' or 'Eradication' of Male Homosexuals between 1933 and 1945: Consequences of the Eugenic Concept of Assured Reproduction," in Grau, ed., 1–7.

[131]Hans Scherer, "Rosa Winkel: Eine Berliner Diskussion über das Homosexuellen-Mahnmal," *Frankfurter Allgemeine Zeitung*, December 12, 1996, reprinted in Initiative Schwulendenkmal, 123.

[132]Kenji Yoshino, quoted in Kristin Eliasberg, "Making a Case for the Right to Be Different," *New York Times*, June 16, 2001, A17.

from the federal government of pink triangle prisoners as victims of unjust Nazi persecution. This decades-old quest for the legal rehabilitation and compensation of prosecuted homosexuals unfortunately has yet to achieve its goal.

The pink triangle, though, has also had the negative effect of burdening its wearer with a sense of perpetual victimhood. The German activist Werner Hinzpeter recently published a book-length criticism of what he perceived as a fixation on oppression among German gay organizations. "Ultimately," he wrote, "one lives a good life in the role of the victim, in which blame for personal dissatisfaction can simply be shifted to the allegedly terrible society."[133] A younger generation of gay men and women has increasingly begun to question this focus on victimization, a reflection, perhaps, of the emergence of queer identity in the 1990s and a rejection of the historical consciousness associated with an earlier generation. Professor Henry Abelove observed the shift in the 1990s: "What I think they [his students] suspect is that we older historians need the trope of marginalization, project it onto everything, use it obsessively; and that this trope is somehow weak, even when it produces a story of struggle."[134] Instead, Abelove's students favored a history that focused on subversion and resistance rather than victimization. They might very well agree with Sasha, the gay hairdresser in Mel Brooks's 1983 film, *To Be or Not to Be*, who says of the pink triangle, "I hate it. It clashes with everything."

The 1991 book on gay life in Cologne under the Nazi regime, *"Verführte" Männer*, has complicated our understanding of the experience of homosexuals in Nazi Germany by including memories of cruising, survival, and the resilience of an underground scene in addition to the horrifying accounts of arrest, imprisonment, torture, and killing. While the bulk of the book centers on the victimization of homosexuals, the concluding testimonials of four men who lived during that period present a more differentiated picture. The men speak of the fear, the police raids, and the disappearance of friends, but they emphasize the ongoing quest for sexual contact, the formation and dissolution of relationships, and the resistance and acquiescence to the new regime that enabled them to make it through alive. In the introduction to these testimonials, the editors wrote, "Everyone had justifiable fear. Nonetheless, no one went without his gay life."[135]

In 2000 the former concentration camp at Sachsenhausen and the Gay Museum in Berlin jointly organized the largest exhibition to date on the Nazi persecution of homosexuals. The final chapter in one of the exhibit's

[133]Werner Hinzpeter, *Schöne schwule Welt: Der Schlußverkauf einer Bewegung* (Berlin, 1997), 18.
[134]Henry Abelove, "The Queering of Lesbian/Gay History," *Radical History Review*, no. 62 (spring 1995): 49.
[135]Nina Oxenius et al., "Lebensbilder: Zeitzeugen berichten," in *"Verführte" Männer: Das Leben der kölner Homosexuellen im Dritten Reich*, ed. Cornelia Limpricht, Jürgen Müller, and Nina Oxenius (Cologne, 1991), 129.

348 E R I K N. J E N S E N

two accompanying books examines the persistence of a homosexual sub-culture in Berlin throughout the Nazi years and includes lists of bars, swim-ming pools, and public parks where men met one another. The editors introduced this section with a statement almost identical to that in the Cologne book: "And nonetheless: despite all of the persecution and pun-ishment, gay life in Berlin was possible. There were meeting places to form friendships and begin affairs, places for flirting, tenderness, and sex."[136] Those who lived through the Nazi period have often recalled moments of surprising freedom. One woman, during a 1985 public forum on lesbians under National Socialism, happily remembered that she had once again been able to wear pants during the war, since the scarcity of cloth eased National Socialist pressure to conform to prescribed gender roles. Ilse Kokula, who moderated the forum, also noted the greater autonomy that women achieved during the war years, which lent the home front the atmosphere of a "clandestine matriarchy."[137]

These tentative gestures toward a history of homosexual life in Ger-many between 1933 and 1945, along with resistance from a younger gen-eration to a memory simply of victimization, call into question the future role of collective memory for gays and lesbians.[138] The initiators of the Berlin memorial have asked, "Does the fourth generation of gay men since the concentration camps need this memory in order to work through the suppression of their own, also painful, history of oppression—in order to recognize that not everything is sweetness and light?"[139] They wonder whether the memorial might serve to maintain the victim identity of a gay community that, if one believes Hinzpeter, already has it pretty good.

These discussions about the function of the Berlin memorial show that the collective memory of Nazi persecution must be directed not only in-ward but also outward to the larger society. Those advocating the memo-rial see its mission as partly, if not primarily, that of reminding nongays, especially the politicians in the nearby parliament, of the persecution of homosexuals. In a similar initiative in the United States, the Pink Triangle

---

[136]"Schicksale," in *Wegen der zu erwartenden hohen Strafe . . . Homosexuellenverfolgung in Berlin 1933–1945*, ed. Andreas Pretzel and Gabriele Roßbach (Berlin, 2000), 186. For the chapter on the persistence of a gay scene in Berlin during the Nazi period, see Carola Gerlach, "Außerdem habe ich dort mit meinem Freund getanzt," 305–32.

[137]Ilse Kokula, "Lesbische Frauen in der NS-Zeit," report on a public forum held in Berlin on October 31, 1985, *UkZ* (March 1986): 6–8.

[138]The exploration of the everyday experiences of homosexual men and women in the Nazi period poses special challenges since the sources consist primarily of either criminal records, which provide discussions of gay life only as they relate to the proceedings at hand, or oral testimonies, which many older men and women are reluctant to give. Regarding the use of criminal records, see Gerlach, 310.

[139]Initiative HomoMonument, 18.

Coalition recently received a grant of over $500,000 from the federal government to promote awareness and remembrance of the Nazi persecution of homosexuals in both the gay community and the general public.[140]

The answer to the question of whether the gay community still needs a memory of Nazi persecution is clear: it does. However, gays and lesbians must temper the memory of persecution with an awareness of the resistance, subversion, survival, and even complicity of homosexual men and women under National Socialism. This suggests, perhaps, the need for a bifurcated memory, with one strand oriented toward the gay community that challenges the tropes and exaggerations that have circulated during the past thirty years, and another strand oriented toward nongays that reminds the public of the historical consequences of intolerance toward sexual minorities.

The documentary film *Paragraph 175*, which premiered in January 2000, suggests how such a bifurcated memory might coexist within the same project. To the gay community, the film offered a necessary corrective to some of the exaggerations about the Nazis' persecution of homosexuals, and especially to the spurious comparisons to the persecution of Jews. As the codirector Jeffrey Friedman stated in explaining his motives for making the film, "There was no gay Holocaust. There was persecution of gay people. But there was no systematic annihilation."[141] To those outside the gay community, however, the film's relatively broad distribution communicated the important fact that the Nazis harassed, incarcerated, and killed thousands of homosexuals; that they destroyed the most developed homosexual emancipation movement the world had yet seen; and that discrimination against gay men and women continues to this day.

---

[140]See Will O'Bryan, "U.S. Funds Gay Holocaust Survivor Projects," *Washington Blade*, June 8, 2001, 22.

[141]Jeffrey Friedman, "When Life Was No 'Cabaret,'" interview by Michael Sragow, *Salon*, September 7, 2000, <www.salon.com>. The film was codirected by Rob Epstein.

Notes on Contributors

GEOFFREY J. GILES is Associate Professor of history at the University of Florida. His article on "The Institutionalization of Homosexual Panic in the Third Reich" recently appeared in *Social Outsiders in Nazi Germany*, edited by Robert Gellately and Nathan Stoltzfus (Princeton: Princeton University Press, 2001). He spent the academic year 2000–2001 as senior scholar-in-residence at the United States Holocaust Memorial Museum in Washington, D.C., under the J. B. and Maurice C. Shapiro Fellowship at its Center for Advanced Holocaust Studies. He is currently completing a book about homosexuality within the Nazi movement.

TERRI J. GORDON teaches in the French Department at Barnard College of Columbia University. Her scholarly interests lie in the areas of ethics, aesthetics, and gender studies. She has published on Josephine Baker and the cabaret and is currently at work on a book-length study of projections of femininity in the Third Reich.

ATINA GROSSMANN is Associate Professor of history at the Cooper Union in New York City, where she teaches modern European history and gender studies. Her publications include *Reforming Sex: The German Movement for Birth Control and Abortion Reform, 1920–1950* (New York: Oxford University Press, 1995); "A Question of Silence: The Rape of German Women by Occupation Soldiers," *October* (1995); "Trauma, Memory, and Motherhood: Germans and Jewish Displaced Persons in Post-Nazi Germany, 1945–1949," *Archiv für Sozialgeschichte* (1998); and *Crimes of War: Guilt and Denial in the Twentieth Century*, which she is coediting with Omer Bartov and Mary Nolan (forthcoming in 2002). She is working on *Victims, Victors, and Survivors: Germans, Allies, and Jews in Occupied Postwar Germany, 1945–1950* (forthcoming from Princeton University Press in 2003).

ELIZABETH D. HEINEMAN is Associate Professor of history at the University of Iowa. She is the author of *What Difference Does a Husband Make? Women and Marital Status in Nazi and Postwar Germany* (Berkeley: University of California Press, 1999) as well as numerous articles on women, sexuality, memory, and public policy in twentieth-century Germany. She is currently researching sexual consumer culture through an examination of Beate Uhse, who transformed a black-market business in condoms and contraceptive information in the late 1940s into Germany's largest erotica firm today.

DAGMAR HERZOG is Associate Professor of history at Michigan State University. She is the author of *Intimacy and Exclusion: Religious Politics in Pre-Revolutionary Baden* (Princeton: Princeton University Press, 1996), and is currently writing a book on sexual moralities in post-Nazi Germany.

ERIK N. JENSEN is completing his Ph.D. in modern European history at the University of Wisconsin, Madison. His dissertation explores sport, gender, and the emergence of the modern body in Weimar Germany.

BIRTHE KUNDRUS is Assistant Professor of German history at the Carl von Ossietzky University, Oldenburg. She is the author of *Kriegerfrauen: Familienpolitik und Geschlechtsverhältnisse im Ersten und Zweiten Weltkrieg* (Hamburg: Christians, 1995). She has been granted a fellowship from the Deutsche Forschungsgemeinschaft to complete her Habilitation on colonial visions in the Kaiserreich. Recent publications include "Nur die halbe Geschichte: Frauen in der Wehrmacht zwischen 1939 und 1945—Ein Forschungsbericht," in *Die Wehrmacht: Mythos und Realität*, edited by Rolf-Dieter Mueller and Hans-Erich Volkmann (Munich: Oldenbourg, 1999); and "Gender-Wars: The First World War and the Interpretation of Gender Relations in the Weimar Republic," in *Gender-Wars: The Military, War, and Gender in 20th-Century Central Europe*, edited by Karen Hagemann and Stefanie Schüler-Springorum (Oxford: Oxford University Press, 2001).

STEFAN MICHELER is writing his dissertation at the University of Hamburg on the subject of identities and the persecution of same-sex-desiring men in Weimar and Nazi Germany. He is an editor of the queer history journal *Invertito* and has published numerous essays on sexuality in the history of the 1968 student rebellions and on gay and lesbian cultures and organizations in Weimar and Nazi Germany.

JULIA ROOS received her Ph.D. in history from Carnegie Mellon University and is currently an Affiliated Scholar at the Center for Advanced

Feminist Studies at the University of Minnesota, Twin Cities. In the academic year 2002–3, she will be a Visiting Fellow in the History Department at Princeton University. Her research interests focus on the history of gender relations and sexuality in twentieth-century Germany.

PATRICIA SZOBAR is a translator and doctoral candidate in history at Rutgers University. Her dissertation, entitled "Gender and the Legal Enforcement of Nazi Racial Policy," is a larger study of the race-defilement trials in the Third Reich.

ANNETTE F. TIMM is Lupina Research Associate in the Comparative Program on Health and Society at the Munk Centre for International Studies at Trinity College, University of Toronto. She did her graduate work at the University of Chicago, completing a dissertation entitled "The Politics of Fertility: Population Politics and Health Care in Berlin, 1919–1972" in 1999, which focused on the history of marriage counseling and venereal disease control. Her research and teaching interests include the history of population policy in Germany and Europe, gender history, and the social impact of the violence of the two world wars on twentieth-century Europe.